Time Out

Paris Guide

Penguin Books

PENGUIN BOOKS

Published by the Penguin Group
Penguin Books Ltd, 27 Wrights Lane, London W8 5TZ, England
Penguin Books USA Inc., 375 Hudson Street, New York, New York 10014, USA
Penguin Books Australia Ltd, Ringwood, Victoria, Australia
Penguin Books Canada Ltd, 10 Alcorn Avenue, Toronto, Ontario, Canada M4V 3B2
Penguin Books (NZ) Ltd, 182-190 Wairau Road, Auckland 10, New Zealand

Penguin Books Ltd, Registered Offices: Harmondsworth, Middlesex, England

First published 1990
Second edition 1992
Third edition 1994
Fourth edition 1995
10 9 8 7 6 5 4 3 2 1

Colour reprographics by Precise Litho, 34-35 Great Sutton Street, London EC1
Mono reprographics, printed and bound by William Clowes Ltd, Beccles, Suffolk NR34 9QE

Edited and designed by
Time Out Magazine Limited
Universal House
251 Tottenham Court Road
London W1P 0AB
Tel: 0171 813 3000
Fax: 0171 813 6001

Editorial
Managing Editor
Peter Fiennes
Editor
Nick Rider
Consultant Editor
Natasha Edwards
Copy Editor
Jackie Holmes
Researcher
Harriet Jerram

Design
Art Director
Warren Beeby
Art Editor
John Oakey
Designers
Paul Tansley, James Pretty
Picture Editor
Catherine Hardcastle

Advertising
Group Advertisement Director
Lesley Gill
Sales Director
Mark Phillips
Sales Manager (Paris)
Christopher Seth
Sales Executives
Matthew Tembe, Philippe Thareaut

Administration
Publisher
Tony Elliott
Managing Director
Mike Hardwick
Financial Director
Kevin Ellis
Managing Director, Paris
Karen Albrecht
Marketing Director
Gillian Auld
Production Manager
Mark Lamond

Features in this Guide were written and researched by:
Introduction Nick Rider, Natasha Edwards. **Essential Information** Nick Rider. **Getting Around** Nick Rider.
Accommodation Gregory Economou. **Paris by Season** Tim Baker. **Sightseeing** Natasha Edwards, Ian
Phillips. **History** Nick Rider. **Paris Today** Andrew Bell. **Architecture** Natasha Edwards. **Paris by Area** Andrew
Gumbel, Ian Phillips. **Restaurants** Alexander Lobrano. **Cafés & Bars** Alexander Lobrano. **Nightlife** Toby Rose.
Fashion Mary Gallagher. **Specialist Shops** Mary Gallagher. **Food & Drink** Margaret Kemp. **Services** Gregory
Economou. **Museums** Fiona Dunlop, Natasha Edwards, Ian Phillips. **Art Galleries** Natasha Edwards. **Media** Ian
Phillips. **Dance** Marcelle Katz, Guillaume Bernardi. **Film** Toby Rose. **Music: Classical & Opera** Tim Baker.
Music: Rock, Roots & Jazz Tim Baker. **Sport & Fitness** Gregory Economou. **Theatre** Marcelle Katz,
Guillaume Bernardi. **Business** Rose Burke. **Children** Jane Marshall. **Gay & Lesbian** Gregory Economou, Harriet
Jerram. **Students** Harriet Jerram. **Women's Paris** Harriet Jerram, Sarah Long. **Trips Out of Town** Natasha
Edwards, Ian Phillips. **Survival** Natasha Edwards, Gregory Economou, Nick Rider.

The Editors would like to thank the following for help and information:
Gregory Economou, Nicholas Royle, Tonya Meli.

Photography by Jean-Louis Aubert, Brian Jackson and Jon Perugia except for:
pages 35, 269 **Allsport**; pages 75, 78 **Giraudon/Bridgeman Art Library, London**; page 80 **John Hay Whitney
Collection/Bridgeman Art Library**; page 218 **Louvre Paris/Bridgeman Art Library**; pages 220, 221 **Musée
d'Orsay, Paris/Bridgeman Art Library**; pages 63, 64, 66, 68, 69, 70, 73, 76, 79 **Mary Evans Picture Library**;
pages 62, 65, 83, 86, 324 **Hulton Deutsch**; pages 301, 306, 309, 310, 312 **Barrie Smith/French Picture Library**;
pictures on pages 15, 239, 245, 247, 272 were provided by the featured companies.

Contents

About the Guide

The fourth edition of the *Time Out Paris Guide* has been thoroughly revised and updated by resident Parisians. Our hard-working team has revisited familiar sights and explored new ones; travelled the main streets and obscure squares of the city; and dined, wined and drunk deep in Paris' incomparable restaurants, cafés and bars. No world-famous tourist trap or low-life club has been left unvisited; we hope you'll agree that it's been worth it.

PRACTICAL GUIDE

Above all, we've tried to make this book as useful as possible. Addresses, telephone numbers, transport details, opening times, admission prices and credit card details are all included in our listings. And, as far as possible, we've given details of facilities, services and events.

All the information in the guide was checked and correct when we went to press; but please bear in mind that owners and managers can change their arrangements at any time. We urge you to phone before you set out, and check opening times, the dates of exhibitions, admission prices and other important details. The same applies to information on disabled access, which we have tried to include where possible: it's always wise to phone first to check your needs can be met.

ADDRESSES

Paris is divided into 20 *arrondissements* or districts, which form a tight snail-shell spiral beginning at Notre Dame and finishing at the Porte de Montreuil on the eastern edge of the inner city limits. The addresses in our guide include the *arrondissement* in the postcode, which for Paris begins with the prefix 750. So, for example, an address in the 1st *arrondissement* would have the postcode 75001, and one in the 20th the postcode 75020.

PRICES

The prices listed throughout the guide should be used as guidelines. Fluctuating exchange-rates and inflation can cause prices, in shops and restaurants especially, to change rapidly. If prices vary greatly from those we've quoted, ask whether there's a good reason. If not, go elsewhere. Then, please let us know. We try to give the best and most up-to-date advice, so we always want to hear if you've been badly treated or overcharged.

CREDIT CARDS

Throughout the guide, the following abbreviations have been used for credit cards: **AmEx** American Express; **DC** Diners' Club; **EC** Eurocheques; **MC** Mastercard/Access; **TC** travellers' cheques in any currency; **£TC, $TC** travellers' cheques in US dollars or pounds sterling; **V** Visa/Barclaycard.

LET US KNOW

It should be stressed that the information we give is impartial. No organisation or enterprise has been included in this guide because its owner or manager has advertised in our publications. Their impartiality is one of the reasons our guides are so successful and well respected. We hope you enjoy the *Time Out Paris Guide* and that it makes your trip a more enjoyable one. However, if you disagree with any of our reviews, let us know; your views on places you have visited are always welcome. There's a reader's reply card in the book for your comments.

Phone Number Changes

From October 1996 all French telephone numbers will have ten digits. Numbers in Paris and the Ile-de-France will start with **01**, the rest of France will be divided into five zones (**02-06**). The old system of dialling 16 to the provinces will be abolished. International dialling codes will begin with **00**.

Introduction

Arriving in Paris can be a bewildering experience. This is a city about which we all know so much, both from the depths of our subconscious and from our daily intake of news and TV. We all know of the city of legendary monuments, of style and *haute couture*, of wonderful food, of any number of artistic avant-gardes, of Emperors, revolutions and literary giants of the past; equally, we may all have heard of it more recently as a city of self-conscious modernity, world music, racial tension, interminable passageways in métro stations and proverbially dismissive waiters. For centuries, people famous and obscure have praised it to the skies or condemned it as a pit of iniquity. When a place carries so much imagery, it can be difficult to take it in as a real, complex community, a habitable place occupied by an enormous variety of people.

And yet, despite gentrification and the invasion of office buildings, Paris is a very lived-in city. Real communities do exist: every quarter has its local food market, often an important meeting place, and its cafés. Visit one of these markets on a Sunday morning or watch the queues outside the best *boulangerie* and you will begin to understand how Paris works. Wander the side streets on the Fête de la Musique, not for the big crowd-pullers at place de la République but for the spontaneous jam sessions outside someone's house or the out-of-tune accordion sing-along in a nondescript brasserie, and you will discover a culture that is not organised by Ministry or *Mairie*.

However well you think you know Paris, there are always parts to discover. Even life-long residents will admit there are areas they do not know, *arrondissements* they have yet to explore. Paris is both a public city of ostentation and grand monuments and a private one, where gardens hide behind high walls and severe doors give way to tranquil courtyards.

May 1995 had a real feel of the end of an era, as the people of France drew a line under the 14-year Presidency of François Mitterrand. Perennially aloof and pharaonic, he had presided over the affairs of France for longer than anyone else since Napoleon III. He was identified with grand ambitions, both for France and, above all, for Paris, and a confidence in a particularly grand idea of modernity ideally fitted to the expansive eighties, as seen in his famous *grands projets*. Many of his new monuments were dramatic additions to the urban fabric; equally, this image of being a capital of dynamic modernity also appealed to Paris' incorrigible collective vanity.

The other major figure in the life of Paris at this time was Mitterrand's eventual successor, Jacques Chirac, as Mayor of Paris. Unable to compete with the President in giant building schemes, he worked to make Paris a showcase of a different sort, promoting the renovation of whole districts, sponsoring office developments, and transforming the street cleaning service to ensure the city would be as spotless as possible.

Despite the talk of social problems, Paris still has unique qualities that the developments of the past fifteen years have helped to enhance. Simply to see, Paris looks better than ever, its fantastic repertory of architecture better cared for than it has ever been. The public transport system remains ideal. And, despite rumours and dire reports to the contrary, bland fast-food outlets have failed to displace entirely the Parisian neighbourhood brasserie or bar. Modern Paris can be a hard city at times, but look along its sweeping boulevards, or across the Seine, and Paris is still the city that has held the world's attention for centuries. Millions are drawn to it every year, and each one finds their own object of fascination.

What's on this week in Paris?

Every week inside **Pariscope**
(3F at all Paris-area newsagents)
you'll find the English-language supplement
Time Out *Paris*.

From the editors of this guide,
Time Out *Paris* contains up-to-the-minute
listings of the city's essential arts
and entertainment events, plus
the hottest spots for going out.

Around Town • Art & Exhibitions • Entertainment
Film • Music : Classical & Opera • Music: Rock, Roots & Jazz
Nightlife • Restaurants • Bars, Cafés & Tea Rooms • Help

Time Out *Paris* - 100 Fbg St Antoine, 75012 Paris
Tel: 44.87.00.45 - Fax: 44.73.90.60

Essential Information

The basics you need to find your feet in the French capital – when to go, where to change money and how to tip.

For information on dealing with emergencies, or on how to set yourself up on a more long-term basis in Paris, *see chapter* **Survival**.

Visas & Customs

European Union nationals do not need a visa to enter France, nor do US, Canadian and New Zealand citizens for stays of up to three months. Nationals of other countries should enquire at the nearest French Consulate before they leave home. If you are travelling to France from one of the countries included in the Schengen agreement (most of the EU, but not Britain, Ireland, Italy or Greece), your visa from that country should be sufficient to enter France. British citizens on short-term visits can travel with a full passport or a British Excursion Document. EU and non-EU citizens who stay for over three months need to obtain a *carte de séjour* (resident's permit). For more information on residency, *see chapter* **Survival**.

Customs

There are no limits on the quantities of goods that you can take into France from another European Union country for your personal use, provided tax has been paid on them in the country of origin. However, Customs are still entitled to question whether large quantities of goods really are for your own use. Sporadic checks are also made for drugs. Quantities of tobacco and alcohol accepted as being for personal use are:
• up to 800 cigarettes, 400 small cigars, 200 cigars or 1kg of loose tobacco

• 10 litres of spirits (over 22% alcohol), 90 litres of wine (under 22% alcohol) and 110 litres of beer.
For goods brought from outside the EU the following limits apply:
• 200 cigarettes or 100 small cigars or 50 cigars or 250 grams (8.82 ounces) of loose tobacco
• 1 litre of spirits (over 22% alcohol) and 2 litres of wine and beer (under 22% alcohol)
• 50 grams (1.76 ounces) of perfume
Visitors can also carry with them up to 50,000F worth of currency without being obliged to declare it. Non-EU residents can also reclaim the Value-Added Tax (TVA) paid on some purchases when they leave France, under the **Détaxe** scheme. For details *see chapter* **Fashion**.

Insurance

EU nationals are entitled to make use of the French state health service provided they have form E111, available in Britain from post offices, Health Centres and Social Security offices. All other nationals should check whether their country has reciprocal arrangements with France.

The state system will cover you in emergencies, but given the many complexities of the French system the simplest solution for both European and non-European travellers on a short-term visit is to take out private travel insurance before departure. This should also cover you for stolen or lost cash, cameras, and other valuables, as well as medical expenses. For more information on all health services, *see chapter* **Survival: Health**.

Money

The currency in France is the French franc, usually abbreviated to 'F' or sometimes 'FF' after the amount. One franc is made up of 100 centimes, although the smallest coin in circulation is now for five centimes. There are coins for five-, ten-, 20- and 50-centimes, one, two and five francs, and the heavier ten- and 20-franc pieces, silver-centred coins with a copper rim. Notes begin with 20F and roughly increase in size according to their value (50F, 100F, 200F and 500F). When changing money in banks avoid being given 500F notes, as you may find it difficult to change them elsewhere.

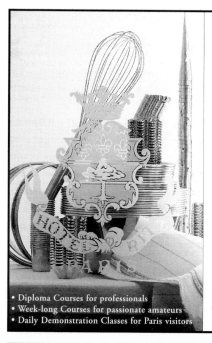

Banks & Foreign Exchange

Holders of major credit cards can obtain money from bank cash machines around the clock, and some bank branches also have automatic cash exchange machines that accept notes of a number of major currencies in good condition. Outside normal banking hours you can also change money at the main rail stations, and at private change offices, listed in full in the yellow pages (*Pages Jaunes*) under 'Change, Bureaux de'. For business banking services, *see chapter* **Business**.

On Arrival

If you expect to arrive in Paris late at night, you should make sure you have some French currency before you set out. The Bureaux de Change at **Roissy** and **Orly** airports are open from 6.30am to 11.30pm daily. At the main train stations, the change offices are open from roughly 7am or 8am to 7pm or 10.30pm (daily at **Gare de l'Est**, **Gare de Lyon**, **Gare Montparnasse** and **Gare du Nord**; closed Sunday at **Gare St-Lazare** and **Gare d'Austerlitz**). There are also cash machines at both airports and at the Gare du Nord that accept major credit cards (*see below*).

Banks & Banking Hours

French banks are usually open from 9am to 4.30pm Monday to Friday, and 9am to noon on Saturdays. Some also close at lunchtime (from 12.30 to 2.30pm). All are closed on public holidays, and from noon on the previous day (*see below* **Holidays**). Note that not all bank branches in Paris have foreign exchange counters. Commission rates also vary considerably between banks, and it's worth checking them before changing money. The state Banque de France usually offers good rates at its branches, and will change less common currencies that are not readily accepted elsewhere. Banks readily accept travellers' cheques (so long as you have your passport with you), but may be reluctant to accept personal cheques with the Eurocheque guarantee card, which is not widely used in France.

Credit Cards & Cash Machines

Major international credit cards such as MasterCard or Visa are used a great deal in France, although Visa (the French *Carte Bleue*) is the most widely accepted. There is often a 100F minimum charge for card transactions. Note that French-issued credit and debit cards now have a special security system, with a microchip in each card. The card is slotted into a card reader, and the holder then keys in his or her PIN number to authorise the transaction. The reader may reject foreign cards without a chip, which can cause embarrassment in shops or restaurants where the staff are unaware of the difference. This rarely happens in Paris, but in such cases you should ask that your card is read or imprinted in the conventional way. Credit card companies can provide holders with a note confirming the validity of their cards.

Withdrawals in francs can be made from bank and post office automatic cash machines with both French and non-French cards. You must of course know your PIN number. The specific cards accepted are marked on each machine, and most give instructions in English as well as French. Credit card companies charge a fee for cash advances, but exchange rates are often better than bank rates. Banks will also advance cash against a credit card over the counter.

Credit card emergencies

Call the following 24-hour lines to report credit card loss or theft. All have English-speaking staff.
American Express *(47.77.72.00)*.
Diners Club *(47.62.75.75)*.
MasterCard/Access/Eurocard *(45.67.84.84)*.
Visa *(42.77.11.90)*.

American Express

11 rue Scribe, 75009 (47.77.77.07). Métro Opéra. **Open** *all transactions* 9am-6.30pm Mon-Fri; 9am-5.30pm Sat; *bureau de change only* 8.30am-6.30pm Mon-Fri; 9am-5.30pm Sat; 10am-6pm Sun; 9am-5pm public holidays.
Bureau de change, poste restante, card replacement, a travellers' cheque refund service and a cash machine for AmEx card holders. Money can also be transferred there from any American Express office anywhere in the world.

Barclays

21 rue Lafitte, 75009 (44.79.79.79). Métro Richelieu-Drouot. **Open** 9am-4.30pm Mon-Fri.
Call the special Expat Service (44.79.48.33) for information on direct debits, international transfer of funds, and so on.

CCF

115-117 avenue des Champs-Elysées, 75008 (40.70.27.22). Métro George V. **Open** *bureau de change* 8.45am-8pm Mon-Sat.
Large bureaux de change with offices also at both airports, in Galeries Lafayette and at Carrefour de l'Odéon.

Chequepoint

150 avenue des Champs-Elysées, 75008 (49.53.02.51). Métro Charles de Gaulle-Etoile. **Open** 24 hours daily.
This is the only Paris Chequepoint office open 24 hours. The several other branches in the city are open 8.30am-9pm, Mon, Sat, and 10am-6pm Sun. No commission is charged.

Thomas Cook

52 avenue des Champs-Elysées, 75008 (42.89.80.32). Métro Franklin D. Roosevelt. **Open** 8.30am-midnight daily.
Thomas Cook has over 30 offices around Paris, including branches at boulevard St-Michel, Eiffel Tower and major train stations. They can also issue travellers' cheques.

Western Union Money Transfer

Banque Rivaud *4 rue du Cloître-Notre-Dame, 75004 (43.54.46.12). Métro Cité.* **Open** 9am-5.30pm daily.
Banque Rivaud is the sole agent for Western Union in Paris, with seven branches around the city. Except for the La Défense office they also open on public holidays. Money transfers sent from abroad should arrive within one hour. Charges are paid by the sender.

Tourist Information

The official tourist offices provide a wide range of basic information on attractions and events in and around Paris. For full information on what's on in the city at any time, though, the best sources are local listings magazines (*see chapter* **Media**). For details of recommended city maps and the public transport system, *see chapter* **Getting Around**.

If you intend to do some serious sightseeing and museum-visiting in Paris it will be worth your while to buy the **Paris Carte Musées et Monuments** museum pass, available from museums, some métro stations and tourist offices. For details, *see chapter* **Museums**.

Office de Tourisme de Paris

127 avenue des Champs-Elysées, 75008 (49.52.53.54/English-language information line 49.52.53.56/fax 49.52.53.00). Métro Charles de Gaulle-Etoile. **Open** *information & ticket office* 9am-8pm, *hotel reservations & bureau de change* 9am-7.30pm, daily. Closed 1 May.

Brochures, guidebooks and information on sights and events in Paris, the suburbs, and the rest of France, although they do not provide free maps. It has a souvenir and book shop, and also sells phonecards, museum cards and travel tickets (*see chapter* **Getting Around**). There is also a ticket desk for tickets to museums, theatres, tours and many other attractions, a bureau de change, and a hotel reservation service (for which a fee is charged). All the staff are multi-lingual. The branch offices have more limited facilities.
Branch offices:
Eiffel Tower *Champ de Mars, 75007 (45.51.22.15). Métro Bir-Hakeim.* **Open** *May-Sept* 11am-6pm daily.
Gare d'Austerlitz *Arrival Hall, 75011 (45.84.91.70). Métro Gare d'Austerlitz.* **Open** 8am-3pm Mon-Fri; 8am-1pm Sat.
Gare de l'Est *Arrival Hall, 75010 (46.07.17.73). Métro Gare de l'Est.* **Open** *April-Oct* 8am-9pm, *Nov-Mar* 8am-8pm, Mon-Sat.
Gare de Lyon *Exit Grandes Lignes, 75012 (43.43.33.24). Métro Gare de Lyon.* **Open** *May-Oct* 8am-9pm, *Nov-April* 8am-8pm, Mon-Sat.
Gare Montparnasse *Near Platform 18, 75014 (43.22.19.19). Métro Montparnasse-Bienvenüe.* **Open** *May-Oct* 8am-9pm, *Nov-April* 8am-8pm, Mon-Sat.
Gare du Nord *Near International Arrivals, 75010 (45.26.94.82). Métro Gare du Nord.* **Open** *June-Oct* 8am-9pm, *Nov-May* 8am-8pm, Mon-Sat.

The Seasons

Spring: Paris in the spring is proverbially magical, but also crowded. The weather is usually fine, if a bit rainy.
Summer: A great time to visit so long as you don't expect to find too much going on. Parisians flee the city in July and August, and those who are left are less stressed. The absence of business travellers means that it's surprisingly easy to find a hotel room, traffic is relatively smooth, and parking possible. Unfortunately, cultural programmes are thin on the ground, and many shops are closed. It can get pretty hot and muggy by day, but evenings are just right, and it stays light late.
Autumn: The weather is usually good; September and October are peak months for tourism and business visitors – finding a hotel can be difficult.
Winter: In spite of the cold (temperatures sometimes below freezing point) and the rain (especially in February and March), there are more cultural events during the winter than in any other season.

Average Temperatures

January 7.5°C (45.5°F); **February** 7.1°C (44.8°F); **March** 10.2°C (50.4°F); **April** 15.7°C (60.3°F); **May** 16.6°C (61.9°F); **June** 23.4°C (74.1°F); **July** 25.1°C (77.2°F); **August** 25.6°C (78.1°F); **September** 20.9°C (69.6°F); **October** 16.5°C (61.7°F); **November** 11.7°C (53.1°F); **December** 7.8°C (46°F).

Savoir-Faire

Holidays

On *jours feriés* (public holidays) many bus routes do not run and all banks, some museums and most shops are shut, but the métro, cinemas and other entertainments and many restaurants keep going. Some holidays are more important than others – New Year, May Day, Bastille Day and Christmas are the most fully observed – and on other holidays you may find that many places stay open..
New Year's Day (Jour de l'An) 1 January; **Easter Monday (Lundi de Pâques)**; **Fête du Travail (May Day)** 1 May; **VE Day (Victoire 1945)** 8 May; **Ascension Day (Jour de l'Ascension)**; **Whit Monday (Pentecôte)**; **Bastille Day (Quatorze**

Juillet) 14 July; **Feast of the Assumption (Jour de l'Assomption)** 15 August; **All Saints' Day (Toussaint)** 1 November; **Remembrance Day (L'Armistice 1918)** 11 November; **Christmas Day (Noël)** 25 December.

Opening Hours & Rush Hours

Standard opening hours for shops are from 9am or 10am to 7pm or 8pm, Mondays to Saturdays. Some shops also close on Mondays. Shops and businesses often close for lunch for at least an hour, sometimes more, usually between 12.30pm and 2pm. Many shops are closed for all or part of August.
Busiest times on public transport are 7.30-9am and 5-8pm, Mondays to Fridays. Road traffic stays heavy until after 9pm most evenings (especially Fridays), and incoming traffic is very dense on Sunday evenings. Traffic can also be totally impenetrable in central, nightlife areas around midnight on Saturdays.

Smoking

Earnest official health campaigns have made only a slight dent in French lighting-up habits, and in most public places a great many people still smoke. Under a 1991 law restaurants and cafés are obliged to provide a non-smoking area for clients. However, if you ask to be sat in the *non fumeurs* space you will very likely find yourself given the worst table in the house, tucked away next to the toilets or the stairs, and unless you're seriously allergic to tobacco you'll probably find it more pleasant to sit amid the smoke with the rest.
Smoking is banned in most theatres and cinemas, and the ban is generally observed. It is also officially banned on buses and throughout the métro, although people tend to think this applies to the trains only and not to the métro station platforms. Many still smoke in the stations, and then stub their cigarettes out as the train arrives.

Street Crime

Paris is like any other large European city: generally pretty safe, although as one might expect it's advisable to be careful walking round at night after most of the bars and brasseries have closed (ie., after 2am). Parts of the 18th, 19th and 20th *arrondissements* are generally the areas where it's most necessary to proceed with a little care, and the Bois de Boulogne and Bois de Vincennes are also best avoided at night. Places to be on your guard for pickpockets are the main rail stations, particularly the Gare du Nord, and among the milling crowds outside the Centre Pompidou. For details of what to do if you are a victim of crime, *see chapter* **Survival: Police & Security**.

Time

France is one hour ahead of Greenwich Mean Time (GMT), except between the end of September and the end of October (when it's the same). Hence, when it's 6pm in Paris, it's usually 5pm in London and noon in New York.
In France 'am' and 'pm' are not commonly used. Instead, times are often given using the 24-hour system. Thus, 8am is 8 *heures*, noon is *12 heures (midi)*, 8pm is *20 heures* and midnight is *0 (zéro) heure (minuit)*.

Tipping

Restaurants and cafés: By law, a 15% service charge is added to your bill automatically. However, this amount is taxed, which is why restaurant staff often hope to be given an additional cash tip as well. This can cause irate reactions among foreign visitors, who assume that they've paid all they need to for service already. This extra tip is more a courtesy or a bonus for good service than an obligation, and 1F-2F in a café and 5F-15F in a restaurant (or more for a very fancy meal) are sufficient amounts to leave.
Hotels: there is no real need for tipping in a hotel, except in grand ones, where a note to the porter will ensure good service.
Taxis: Round the fare up to the nearest 5F or 10F.

Essential Vocabulary

In French, as in other Latin languages, the second person singular (you) has two forms. Phrases here are given in the more polite *vous* form. The *tu* form is used with family, friends and young children, and you should be careful not to use it with people you do not know sufficiently well. You will also find that courtesies such as *monsieur*, *madame* and *mademoiselle* are used much more than their English equivalents. *See also chapters* **Students** for information on language courses and **Restaurants: A la carte** for help in deciphering menus.

General Expressions

good morning/good afternoon, hello *bonjour*
good evening *bonsoir;* **goodbye** *au revoir*
hi (familiar) *salut;* **OK** *d'accord;* **yes** *oui;* **no** *non*
Do you speak English? *Parlez-vous anglais?*
How are you? *Comment allez vous?/vous allez bien?*
How's it going? *Comment ça va?/ça va?* (familiar)
Sir/Mr *monsieur (M);* **Madam/Mrs** *madame (Mme)*
Miss *mademoiselle (Mlle)*
please *s'il vous plaît;* **thank you** *merci;* **thank you very much** *merci beaucoup*
sorry/excuse me *pardon/excusez-moi;* **excuse me** (before a question) *pardon monsieur/madame/mlle*
Do you speak English? *parlez-vous anglais?*
I don't understand *Je ne comprends pas*
Speak more slowly, please *parlez plus lentement, s'il vous plaît*
Leave me alone *Laissez-moi tranquille*
how much?/how many? *combien?*
Have you got change? *Avez-vous de la monnaie?*
I would like.... *je voudrais....*
good *bon/bonne;* **bad** *mauvais/mauvaise*
small *petit/petite;* **big** *grand/grande*
beautiful *beau/belle;* **well/badly** *bien/mal*
expensive/cheap *cher/pas cher*
It's too expensive *C'est trop cher*
very *très;* **with** *avec*
and *et;* **or** *ou;* **because** *parce que*
who? *qui?;* **when?** *quand?;* **what?** *quoi?;* **which?** *quel?;* **where?** *où?;* **why?** *pourquoi?;* **how?** *comment?*
at what time/when? *à quelle heure?*
forbidden *interdit/défendu*
out of order *hors service/en panne*

On the Phone

hello (telephone) *allô;* **who's calling?** *C'est de la part de qui?/C'est qui à l'appareil? (familiar)*
Hold the line *Ne quittez pas/patientez s'il vous plaît*

Getting Around

Where is the (nearest) métro? *Où est le métro (le plus proche)?;* **When is the next train for... ?** *C'est quand le prochain train pour... ?*
ticket *un billet;* **station** *la gare;* **platform** *le quai*
entrance *entrée;* **exit** *sortie*
left *gauche;* **right** *droite*
straight on *tout droit;* **far** *loin;* **near** *pas loin/près d'ici*
street *la rue;* **street map** *le plan;* **road map** *la carte*
Is there a bank near here? *Est-ce qu'il y a une banque près d'ici?*
bank *la banque;* **Post Office** *La Poste*
tobacco shop *un tabac;* **a stamp** *une timbre*

Sightseeing

museum *le musée;* **church** *une église*
exhibition *une exposition*
ticket (for theatre, concert) *une place*
open *ouvert;* **closed** *fermé*
free *gratuit;* **reduced price** *un tarif réduit*
except Sundays *sauf le dimanches*

Accommodation

Do you have a room (for this evening/ for two people)? *Avez-vous une chambre (pour ce soir/ pour deux personnes)?*
full *complet;* **room** *une chambre*
bed *un lit;* **double bed** *un grand lit;*
(a room with) twin beds *une chambre à deux lits*
with bath(room)/shower *avec (salle de) bain/douche*
breakfast *le petit déjeuner;* **included** *compris*
lift *un ascenseur;* **with air-conditioning** *climatisé*

At the Café or Restaurant

I'd like to book a table (for three/at 8pm) *Je voudrais réserver une table (pour trois personnes/à vingt heures)*
lunch *le déjeuner;* **dinner** *le dîner*
coffee (espresso) *un café;* **white coffee** *un café au lait/café crème;* **tea** *le thé;* **wine** *le vin;* **beer** *la bière*
mineral water *eau minérale;* **fizzy/still** *gazeuse/plat*
tap water *eau normale/une carafe d'eau*
the bill, please *l'addition, s'il vous plaît*

Behind the Wheel

give way *ceder le passage*
it's not your right of way *vous n'avez pas la priorité;* **no parking** *stationnement interdit/stationnement gênant;* **deliveries** *livraison*
toll *péage;* **speed limit 40** *rappel 40*
petrol *essence;* **unleaded** *sans plomb*
traffic jam *embouteillage/bouchon*
traffic moving freely *traffic fluide*
dangerous bends *attention virages*

Numbers

0 *zéro;* **1** *un, une;* **2** *deux;* **3** *trois;* **4** *quatre;* **5** *cinq;* **6** *six;* **7** *sept;* **8** *huit;* **9** *neuf;* **10** *dix;* **11** *onze;* **12** *douze;* **13** *treize;* **14** *quatorze;* **15** *quinze;* **16** *seize;* **17** *dix-sept;* **18** *dix-huit;* **19** *dix-neuf;* **20** *vingt;* **21** *vingt-et-un;* **22** *vingt-deux;* **30** *trente;* **40** *quarante;* **50** *cinquante;* **60** *soixante;* **70** *soixante-dix;* **80** *quatre-vingts;* **90** *quatre-vingt-dix;* **100** *cent;* **1000** *mille;* **1,000,000** *un million.*

Days, Months & Seasons

Monday *lundi;* **Tuesday** *mardi;* **Wednesday** *mercredi;* **Thursday** *jeudi;* **Friday** *vendredi;* **Saturday** *samedi;* **Sunday** *dimanche.* **January** *janvier;* **February** *février;* **March** *mars;* **April** *avril;* **May** *mai;* **June** *juin;* **July** *juillet;* **August** *août;* **September** *septembre;* **October** *octobre;* **November** *novembre;* **December** *décembre.* **Spring** *printemps;* **Summer** *été;* **Autumn** *automne;* **Winter** *hiver.*

Time Out City Guides

World Series

Amsterdam Berlin Madrid New York Prague Rome

New editions in September 1995

London & Paris

New titles in February 1996

Budapest & San Francisco

Getting Around

All you need to know to get from the Butte to the boulevards like a true Parisian.

Outsiders can look at a map and see Paris as a massive, sprawling city of nearly nine million people, straddling across northern France. To its inhabitants, however – and officially – Paris is not this conurbation but rather a compact city that's rarely more than 10km (6 miles) across at any given point, has little more than two million inhabitants and is still confined within boundaries that have scarcely expanded since 1859. It is oval in shape and cut across the middle by the River Seine, which separates the *rive droite* (Right Bank) from the *rive gauche* (Left Bank). Today the city is also neatly delimited by a giant ring road, the boulevard Périphérique. Everywhere beyond this multi-lane highway is in the *banlieue* (suburbs), and of less interest to the true Parisian than Samarkand or Madagascar. Most visitors, too, rarely make more than brief excursions into the urban sprawl beyond the Périphérique.

Because Paris proper is so concentrated and compact it's relatively easy to explore on foot. It's advisable to be careful walking at night in some areas, such as the two *Bois* and parts of the 18th and 19th *arrondissements*, and wherever you are you'll soon be aware that Parisian drivers have very little respect for pedestrians. Overall, though, Paris remains a wonderfully 'walkable' city.

When it's too far to walk, a well-organised public transport system is at your disposal. Whichever way you move around, it's useful to become familiar with the division of Paris into 20 *arrondissements* (districts), numbered 1er (1st) to 20ème (20th) and spiralling out in a snail-like pattern from the Ile de la Cité. Parisians continually refer to them to orientate themselves – geographically and socially –, and they are also written as part of a postcode (thus 75001 signifies the 1st *arrondissement*). This is the way they are indicated in every address in this Guide. Street name signs also indicate which *arrondissement* you are in.

If you come to Paris by car you are probably best advised to leave it outside the Périphérique, in the outer *arrondissements* or in a hotel car park, as atrocious traffic and expensive parking make driving rarely the most convenient means of moving around the city centre. Cycling in Paris is also a death-defying feat most of the time, although Parisians have been lobbying for more special cycle lanes. A car or bike is of course much more useful for excursions into the surrounding towns

and countryside (*see chapter* **Trips Out of Town**). For more on roads, driving conditions and parking, *see chapter* **Survival: Driving in Paris**. For information on bike and car hire, and travel agencies, *see chapter* **Services**. For boat services on the Seine and the Paris canals, and other organised tours and walks, *see chapter* **Sightseeing**.

Crossing the road: essential tips

Crossing Paris' multi-lane boulevards has certain peculiarities, which can make them lethal for the uninitiated. By law drivers are only fully obliged to stop when they have a red light. Where there is a crossing, whether it has a flashing amber light or a sign saying *Priorité aux Piétons*, most drivers will simply just ignore pedestrians and keep going even if you're already standing in the middle of the road. If you make eye contact this will usually cause a driver to stop, but if one car stops that doesn't mean the rest will.

Maps

Free maps of the métro, bus and RER systems are available at airports and all métro stations. The Paris transport authority RATP also offers other free brochures, available from métro stations: *Paris Visite – Le Guide* has details of transport tickets and a small map; the *Grand Plan de Paris* is a fold-out map that also indicates the *Noctambus* night bus lines (*see below* **Buses**). Plans of the métro and RER and general street maps are also included at the back of this Guide.

If you're staying more than a few days it'll be worth buying a map book covering the city in detail. The Michelin *Paris-Plan*, *Paris par Arrondissement* (Editions l'Indispensable), the small paperback *Plan de Paris* (Editions Leconte) and the slightly larger *Collection Plan Net* (Ponchet Plan Net) are all available from kiosks and bookshops.

From Charles de Gaulle Airport

Most international flights arrive at Roissy-Charles de Gaulle airport, 30km (19 miles) north-east of Paris. Its two main terminals are some way apart, and it's important to check which is the right one for your flight, above all when leaving. All Air France flights and some others use Terminal 2; most international flights on other airlines use Terminal 1, while a few charters use the small Terminal T9. A free shuttle bus runs every five minutes between all the terminals.

The airport has a 24-hour information service, with English-speaking staff, on 48.62.22.80.

By train (RER)

The suburban rail line the RER is the quickest and most reliable way into Paris. There are two stations at Roissy, on the same line. One gives direct access to Terminal 2; from Terminal 1 free shuttle buses run to the main Roissy station. RER line B runs from Roissy direct to central Paris, with trains every 15 to 20 minutes between 4.56am and 11.56pm daily. Trains from Châtelet and other city-centre stations to Roissy run from 5am-midnight daily. Tickets, bought inside the station, cost about 40F one-way, and the trip takes about 45 minutes. The RER line can also be used for connections to Orly (*see below*).

By bus

There are two main bus services between Roissy and Paris. The RATP-run **Roissybus** leaves every 15 minutes, calling at all three terminals, from 6am-11pm daily, and terminates in Paris at the corner of rue Scribe and rue Auber, very centrally located next to the Opéra métro station. Tickets can be bought from automatic machines or on the coach itself. The bus costs 35F each way, and journey time is about 50 minutes, depending on the traffic. Buses from Paris run 5.45am-11pm daily. **Air France** buses run every 20 minutes from 6am-11.30pm daily, between both airport terminals and stops at Porte Maillot and Charles de Gaulle-Etoile (5.40am-11pm, Etoile-Roissy). From 7.30am-7.30pm daily an Air France bus service also runs between Roissy and the Gare Montparnasse, with one bus an hour on the hour, in each direction (7am-9pm, Montparnasse-Roissy; tickets 64F).

By taxi

The most expensive and least reliable means of transport between Charles de Gaulle and Paris. Cabs can take as little as 40 minutes, but will need at least another half hour in rush hours. If there are no taxis in sight outside the Arrivals area, press the button at the front of the taxi rank to call one up from the car park. Expect to pay around 150F-230F, plus 6F for each item of luggage over 5kg, if you're travelling to the centre of town. There are also limousine services that operate from the airport, which are a good deal more expensive. **Do not** use a taxi to the airport if you're in a hurry – the

highest-risk times are evening rush hours, above all on Fridays. What you gain in comfort, you lose in anxiety when you're trapped in traffic on the Périphérique.

From Orly Airport

French domestic and several international flights use Orly airport, south of the city. It also has two terminals, Orly-Sud and Orly-Ouest, although all transports stop at both. It is closer to Paris (18km/11 miles) than Roissy, and so travelling into the city by taxi or bus poses fewer problems.

Orly information (English-speaking) is on 49.75.15.15, and open 6am-11.45pm daily.

By train

The **Orlyval** shuttle train runs every 5-8 minutes between the Orly terminals and Antony station on the RER line B (6am-10.30pm Mon-Sat; 7am-10.55pm Sun). The full trip from Orly to central Paris takes about 30 minutes, and single tickets cost 50F (25F, 4-10s). Line B can be used for connections to Roissy (*see above*). There is also a free shuttle bus, **Orlyrail**, between the airport and Pont de Rungis station on RER line C, from 6am to 11pm daily. Buses run every 15 minutes at peak times (30 min, off-peak) and journey time to central Paris is about 50 minutes. The fare is 27F.

By bus

Air France buses leave from both terminals every 15 minutes from 5.50am-11pm daily. Tickets are available on board or from the AF Terminus, and cost 35F one-way. Buses stop at Porte d'Orléans, Les Invalides and Gare Montparnasse, and journey time is about 30 minutes. The RATP **Orlybus** costs 30F and runs every 15 minutes between Orly and Denfert-Rochereau RER/métro station, 6.30am-11.30pm daily (6am-11pm, Paris-Orly). Bus tickets are available from machines in the airport lobby, and the trip takes about 40 minutes. There is also a **Jetbus** service which runs every 12 minutes from 6am-10.15pm, daily, between Orly and Villejuif-Louis Aragon station at the end of métro line 7.

By taxi

A taxi from Orly into Paris should take 30 to 40 minutes and cost about 120F, plus 6F for each item of luggage over 5kg. Again, expect another half-hour or more during rush hours.

Arriving by Bus

International coach services to Paris arrive at the **Gare Routière International Paris-Gallieni** on avenue Général de Gaulle in the suburb of Bagnolet, just outside the Périphérique at Porte de Bagnolet. Next to it is the Gallieni métro station, at the end of line 3. For information or reservations call Eurolines on 49.72.51.51. The line is open 6am to 11.30pm daily, and has English-speaking staff.

Arriving by Train

There are six main rail termini in Paris. All are on the métro network, and some also connect with suburban RER lines. The central number for SNCF information is 45.82.50.50. For more information on all rail services, *see chapter* **Trips Out of Town: Travelling beyond Paris**.
Gare St-Lazare *Métro lines 3, 12, 13.* Trains from Normandy and from Britain via Dieppe and the Normandy ports.
Gare du Nord *Métro lines 4, 5/RER lines B, D.* Trains from north-east France, Belgium, the Netherlands and from Britain via Calais, Boulogne, Dunkirk and the Channel Tunnel (*see p14* **Tunnel Visions**).
Gare de l'Est *Métro lines 4, 5, 7.* Trains from eastern France, Alsace and Germany.
Gare de Lyon *Métro line 1/RER line A.* Trains from Burgundy, south-east France, the Mediterranean coast, Switzerland, Italy and eastern Spain.

Gare d'Austerlitz *Métro lines 5, 10/RER line C.* Trains from south-western France and most of Spain.
Gare Montparnasse *Métro lines 4, 6, 12, 13.* Trains from western France, Brittany and Bordeaux.

Left Luggage

Luggage can be checked in at Roissy (25F per item per day) and at Orly airports (20F). At Paris-Galliéni bus station left luggage costs 10F-30F per item per day, depending on the size of the article. There are also both automatic left-luggage lockers and staffed counters at all rail stations.

Public Transport

The Parisian public transport system, made up of the **métro** (underground/subway), **bus** routes and the **RER** suburban railway, is comparatively easy to understand. All three services are run by the local transport authority, the **RATP**. Paris and its suburbs are divided into five main fare zones; most visitors only travel in zone 1 (Paris within the Périphérique) or zone 2 (the inner suburbs); beyond are zones 3, 4 and 5 and the airports. A different system of zones, with more, smaller *sections*, applies on buses (*see below* **Buses**). The RATP also runs tours and day trips; for information, call 40.06.71.45. For information on transport services outside Paris, *see chapter* **Trips Out of Town**.

RATP Offices

53 bis quai des Grands Augustins, 75006 (40.46.44.50). Métro St-Michel. **Open** 8.30am-noon, 1-4.30pm, Mon-Fri; 8.30am-noon, 2-4.30pm, Sat.
Kiosk near Marché aux Fleurs, place de la Madeleine, 75008 Paris (40.06.71.45). Métro Madeleine. **Open** *May-Sept* 8.30am-noon, 1-4.30pm, Mon-Fri; 8.30am-noon, 2-4.30pm, Sat.

RATP Information Phoneline

(43.46.14.14). **Open** 24 hours daily.
Recorded information, in French only. There is a staffed line (36.68.77.14) open 6am-9pm daily, for more direct attention.

Tickets & Travel Passes

RATP tickets are valid on the métro, on buses, on central Paris RER trains and on the Montmartre funicular (*see chapter* **Sightseeing**). They can be bought at RATP offices, tourist offices, the airports and at all métro stations. Single tickets and carnets can also be bought at tobacco shops (*tabacs*). One ticket will take you anywhere on the métro and on the RER network within city limits. On RER trains there are first and second class carriages; a standard ticket is valid for second class travel. Keep the ticket on you at all times, as you will need it to exit RER stations, and official *contrôleurs* also carry out spot-checks on the métro and buses. Children under ten travel for half the regular fares (ID may be required), and under-4s travel free.

If you expect to make more than a few journeys it may be worthwhile buying one of the various travel passes:

Individual tickets Buying tickets one at a time is expensive and time-consuming. They cost 7F each, and a better idea is to buy *un carnet*, or block of ten.
Carnet Ten individual tickets for 41F – good value if you're only staying in Paris for a few days.
Carte Orange The main local travel pass, which offers unlimited travel on all services in the relevant zones for a week or a month. Both consist of a ticket (the *coupon*), same size as the basic métro ticket, and an identification pass (passport photo needed). At métro stations you put the coupon through the automatic barrier as you would a single ticket. Note that each weekly card is valid from Monday to Sunday, and the monthly card for a specific calendar month, irrespective of which day in the week or month you buy them – hence, if your visit does not coincide with the period of the card but runs over two weeks or months they may not actually save you money. Monthly cards are available from the 20th of the preceding month. A weekly pass (*Coupon Hebdomadaire*) for zones 1-2 costs 63F; the monthly *Coupon Mensuel* for the same zones costs 219F.
Formule 1 Unlimited travel on all systems for one day. A card for zones 1-2 only costs 28F; the card for zones 1-5, which includes both airports, is 95F.
Paris Visite A special tourist travel card that gives unlimited travel on city transport and SNCF trains within the relevant zones. They are valid for three or five consecutive days from the day of purchase. A pass for zones 1-3 costs 95F for three days and 150F for five, while passes valid for all five zones, both airports and Disneyland Paris cost 210F and 285F. The card also gives you discounts at some attractions, including the Grande Arche de la Défense, the Cité des Sciences, the Parc Astérix and some river and canal trips (*see chapters* **Sightseeing** *and* **Children**). However, within the city centre you'll often find that the *carnet* or a *Carte Orange* offers better value.

Métro

The Paris métro, first opened in 1900, now has 15 lines, running through 199km (123 miles) of tunnels. It is at most times the quickest, cheapest and most convenient means of travelling around central Paris. Stations are plentiful and rarely far apart within Paris proper, but most lines end at one of the *Portes* on the Périphérique or extend only a few stops into the neighbouring suburbs. Currently under construction is the new high-speed *Météor* line from the new Bibliothèque de France at Tolbiac to the Madeleine via the Gare de Lyon, due to open at some time in 1996.

Finding your line

Trains run about every two to nine minutes on all lines from 5.30am to 12.30am daily. When entering the métro you should insert your ticket (or *coupon*, if you have a travel pass) in the slots in the automatic ticket barriers, remembering to reclaim it from the second slot before you go through the gate. The doors on métro trains do not open unless the metal door handles are pushed upwards, on the older trains, or a button is pushed, on the newer models. A single tone sounds when the door is about to close. The morning rush hour on the métro is between 7.30am and 9.30am; the evening busy period lasts longer, from 5pm till 8pm.

Each line is marked with a different colour on métro maps, but on platforms and at station interchanges lines in any direction are indicated only by the line number and the name of the station at the end of the line. So, Line 4 running north is signposted *Direction Porte de Clignancourt*, while Line 4 south will be shown as *Direction Porte d'Orléans*. It is important to know the names of the final stations on the lines you are using, above all when changing lines. At line interchanges the connecting passages (*correspondances*, signposted in orange) can be very long, and as stations are commonly short distances apart you'll often find it quicker to get off and walk rather than change lines for just one stop. At the larger stations push-button illuminated maps can show you which changes you need to make in any particular journey. You'll find that many métro and RER journeys will involve passing through Châtelet-Les Halles, which, with nearly 2km of passageways, is Europe's busiest underground railway station.

Enjoy a Sightseeing Tour of Paris with PARIS Bus

Paris at your Leisure

The complete tour lasts approximately 2h15, with frequent daily departures. **Nine stops** are scheduled. Commentaries are in **French** and **English**. Some tours also have commentary in **Spanish**, **Italian** or **German**. Your ticket is **valid for 2 days** and can be bought on the bus. You may **take the bus or break your tour(s)** at any PARISBUS stop and continue later.

Price: adult 125F, child 60F.

Timetable:

Stops \ Tours	1	2	3	4	5	6	7	8	9
TROCADERO corner av. Paul Doumer	9.30	10.20	11.15	12.00	12.50	13.40	14.30	15.20	16.20
EIFFEL TOWER quai Branly, opposite Pont d'Iéna	9.55	10.45	11.40	12.25	13.15	14.15	14.55	15.45	16.55
MUSÉE DU LOUVRE near Pont des Arts	10.20	11.10	12.05	12.50	13.40	14.40	15.20	16.10	17.20
NOTRE DAME opposite 21 rue d'Arcole	10.35	11.25	12.20	13.05	13.55	14.55	15.35	16.25	17.35
OPÉRA - GALERIES LAFAYETTE opposite 15 rue Scribe	11.05	11.55	12.50	13.35	14.25	15.25	15.55	16.55	18.05
CHAMPS ELYSÉES-ETOILE opposite 156 av. des Champs-Elysées	11.35	12.25	13.20	14.05	14.55	15.55	16.20	17.25	18.35

RER

Opened in 1969, the *Réseau Express Régional* is a high-speed suburban railway that interconnects with the métro at major stations. Métro tickets are valid on the RER within Paris; for journeys to outlying districts and airports there is a range of fares, and you must buy a separate ticket unless you hold a travel pass that covers the airport zones.

RER lines

The four RER lines (A, B, C, D) run across Paris and into the Ile-de-France commuter land. Each line has several branches. Line C2 goes to Orly, Line C5 to Versailles and Line B3 to Roissy-Charles de Gaulle airport. Line A4 runs eastwards to Disneyland Paris at Marne-la-Vallée-Chessy. Within Paris, the RER is useful for making faster journeys – Châtelet-Les Halles to Charles de Gaulle-Etoile is, for example, only two stops on the RER compared to eight on métro Line 1, and Line C provides a quick and hassle-free way of getting along the Left Bank. Services operate 5.30am-12.30am daily, with trains every 15 minutes (more in the centre).

Buses

Unless you have a travel pass buses are more expensive than the métro for journeys across Paris, and get very crowded at peak times. However, they can be more convenient for shorter trips, or those between places with no obvious métro connection. Also, travelling by bus can be a fun way of getting to know Paris, particularly on the rare remaining buses that still have open platforms at the back.

Times, tickets & fares

City buses run on all routes every four to 15 minutes, depending on the time of day, 6am-8.30pm daily, and a reduced service is also available on some routes until 12.30am. Several routes do not run at all on Sundays and public holidays. At bus shelters and on buses there are maps outlining the routes and the bus fare *sections*, which are different from and smaller than the métro/RER zones. On buses you can use either single bus tickets, bought from the driver (7F) or métro tickets. One ticket is sufficient for one to two *sections*; three to five *sections*, two tickets; and six to eight *sections*, three tickets. If in doubt, ask the driver. The tickets must be punched in the machine next to the driver or in the centre of the bus. If you have a travel pass **do not** put your *coupon* into this machine; just show your pass to the driver. When you want to get off, press the red request button near the exit; there is also a separate green button on many buses that you must press actually to open the door.

Useful routes

As well as the standard routes a special scenic **Balabus** service runs on Sundays and holidays during the summer (*see chapter* **Sightseeing**). The following normal routes also pass interesting places and, unless stated, run on Sundays:
29 Gare St-Lazare, past Opéra Garnier, boulevard Haussmann, Centre Pompidou and through the Marais to the Bastille and the Gare de Lyon (no service Sunday).
38 Centre Pompidou to place de Châtelet, past the Palais de Justice and the Saint Chapelle in one direction, Notre Dame in the other, up boulevard St-Michel past the Musée de Cluny, the Sorbonne and the Jardins de Luxembourg and down to the catacombs at Denfert-Rochereau.
48 Montparnasse, St-Germain-des-Près, Louvre, Palais Royal, Richelieu-Drouot (no service Sunday).
67 From sleazy Pigalle via the Louvre to Porte d'Italie, taking in the Jardin des Plantes and the Mosque.
68 From Place de Clichy via Opéra, the Palais Royal and the Louvre to Musée d'Orsay, then up boulevard Raspail to Montparnasse, the Catacombs and Porte d'Orléans.
69 From Père Lachaise in the north east, via Bastille, the Hôtel de Ville and Châtelet along the quais of the Seine to the monuments of the 7th *arrondissement*, the Musée d'Orsay, Invalides, Champ de Mars (no service Sunday).
72 From the 16th *arrondissement* to the Hôtel de Ville along the Seine in one direction and the rue de Rivoli in the other.
73 From La Défense past the Arc de Triomphe and along the Champs-Elysées to place de la Concorde and across the river to Musée d'Orsay (no service Sunday).
82 Smart residential districts of Neuilly to the Jardins du Luxembourg via the Eiffel Tower and Invalides.
84 From chic Parc Monceau in the 17th *arrondissement* to the Grands Boulevards, the Madeleine, St-Germain-des-Près and St Sulpice, to finish at the Panthéon (no service Sunday).
95 One arty hill to another: Montparnasse to Montmartre.
PC (or *Petite Ceinture*, the small belt) goes all the way around the outer boulevards, just within the Périphérique.
Montmartrobus A minibus service that runs on a circular route through the winding streets of Montmartre between place Pigalle and the *Mairie* of the 18th, via the Butte Montmartre and the Sacré Coeur.

Night Buses

After the métro and normal bus services stop running at about 12.30am the only form of public transport available – apart from taxis – are the **Noctambus** night bus routes. The ten routes are identified by letters A to J (missing out I) and also, strangely, R. All run from Châtelet, where the stops are on avenue Victoria and rue St-Martin, out into the suburbs. There is one bus on each route every hour from 1.30am to 5am daily. Travel passes are valid on *Noctambuses*; otherwise, three bus tickets are required for each journey (four if you transfer to another route).

Stops are marked with the *Noctambus* logo – an owl, in black against a yellow circle. Night bus maps are available from métro stations. The routes A to J fan out in a clockwise circle, beginning with A, along the Champs-Elysées past Etoile to La Défense and Neuilly, and ending at J, past St-Michel and Denfert-Rochereau to Porte d'Orléans. Route R is between H and J and runs past Place d'Italie to Rungis. The Right Bank is much better served by the *Noctambus* than the Left, which has only the R and J routes. In particular, there is no night bus service to south-west Paris, the 7th, 15th and 16th *arrondissements*.

Taxis

Paris does not have enough taxis, and at peak times finding an empty one is a challenge. Rather than try to hail one in the street it's generally best to make for a taxi rank, found at most major road junctions and indicated by a blue sign with *Taxis* in white. Ranks also take precedence, as taxis in the street are theoretically not allowed to stop for a fare within 50m (165ft) of a rank.

When a taxi is free the white light on the roof of the cab is lit up. A glowing orange light beneath the main light means the cab is occupied, and if the white light is covered or off the taxi is off duty.

Fares

The minimum fare in Paris taxis is 12F, and fares for journeys within central Paris average between 35F and 60F. Fare rates vary according to **zone** and **time**. Which of the three tariffs (A, B and C) applies at any point is shown on the taxi meter and on lights beneath the main light on the cab roof.

Tunnel Visions

It's been a long time coming, construction costs long ago parted company with the initial budget, and various international banks may be wondering whether it's all been worth it. The inauguration of the Channel Tunnel passenger train service has also not been without its technical hitches, both in the trains themselves and in the over-rigid computer reservations system – all of them gleefully picked up by a determinedly negative British press. Nevertheless, with Eurostar trains every hour between London Waterloo and the Gare du Nord from September 1995, the tunnel rail link does bring London and Paris closer together than ever before.

Journey time is three hours, with little of the time wasting and hassle involved in getting to and checking in at airports, and on arrival you are of course right in the centre of each city. Those who have taken the train without a hitch would never want to travel any other way. From early 1996, too, direct services will operate from Glasgow (9¼ hours to Paris), Manchester (5¾ hours), Birmingham (5 hours) and other destinations in the UK, with sleeper services from some cities.

Eurostar

In London *(Information & reservations 01233 61 75 75).* **Open** 7am-8pm Mon-Sat; 9am-5pm Sun.
In Paris *(Information & reservations 05.12.21.22/Minitel 3615 SNCF).* **Open** 7am-8pm Mon-Sat; 9am-5pm Sun.
From September 1995 trains will run once an hour from 7am-10pm Mon-Sat in both directions between London and Paris, with a more limited service on Sundays. At time of writing the standard return fare is £155 (£195 first class), but APEX returns of £95 (£84 at weekends) are available if you book 14 days in advance. Reduced fares are also available for children under 11, under-26s, over-60s and holders of Eurrail and other rail passes. All trains are accessible to wheelchair users. For information on *Le Shuttle* tunnel service for cars, call 0990 353535 in the UK.

A The cheapest tariff, it applies in Paris within the Périphérique 7am-7pm, Mon-Sat.
B 7pm-7am Mon-Sat, 24-hours Sun and public holidays, within the Périphérique; 7am-7pm daily, inner suburban zone and airports.
C 7pm-7am daily, inner suburban zones and airports; 24 hours daily, journeys outside inner suburban zone.
A reduced rate applies for trips outside central Paris if the passenger returns to Paris in the same cab.

There are also supplements of 6F for each item of luggage, for a fourth passenger (8F) and for animals (3F). It is normal to tip cab drivers by rounding up the fare to the nearest 5F or 10F, especially for the handling of heavy or awkward packages. A 5F surcharge also applies on fares from the ranks at main rail stations, at the Invalides and in the avenue Carnot.

Receipts & Complaints

Taxi drivers provide receipts on request. Ask for *un reçu, s'il vous plaît*. If you wish to make a complaint about charging or any other matter involving a cab, insist that you be given a receipt in full, double check the cab number and write to *Service des Taxis, Préfecture de Police, 36, rue des Morillons, 75732 Paris Cedex 15 (45.31.14.80).*

Phone Cabs

The following taxi firms accept telephone bookings 24 hours daily. Operators may sometimes speak English. Phone cabs will start the meter from the moment the call is answered.
Alpha *(45.85.85.85).* **No credit cards.**
Artaxi *(42.41.50.50).* **Credit** MC, V.
G7 *(47.39.47.39).* **Credit** AmEx, DC, JCB, MC, V.
Taxis Bleus *(49.36.10.10).* **No credit cards.**
Taxi Etoile *(42.70.41.41).* **No credit cards.**

Disabled Travellers

Neither the métro nor city buses are suitable for wheelchair users, although the buses do have some seats reserved for people with mobility problems. However, some stations on **RER** lines **A** and **B** are accessible to wheelchairs, via lifts (among them Châtelet-Les Halles, Gare de Lyon, Gare du Nord, Roissy airport and Marne-la Vallée-Chessy, the station for Disneyland Paris). You must ask station staff (and sometimes insist) if you want to use them. If travelling on **SNCF** trains, check with the information desk at the relevant terminus, as some trains are equipped for wheelchairs.

All Paris **taxis** are officially obliged to take passengers in wheelchairs, but the willingness of drivers to do so varies greatly. For specific trips it can be a better idea to book transport with one of the specialised hire services, some of which are listed below. For more information on access and facilities in Paris for the disabled, *see chapter* **Survival**.

Aihrop

4 passage Saint-Antoine, 92504 Rueil-Malmaison (40.24.34.76). **Open** 10am-3pm Mon-Fri.

GiHP

98 rue de la Porte Jaune, 92210 St Cloud (47.71.74.90). **Open** 8.30am-noon, 2-6pm, Mon-Thur; 8.30am-noon, 2-5pm, Fri.

Le Kangourou

92500 Rueil-Malmaison (47.08.93.50). **Open** 9am-6pm Mon-Fri; answering machine at other times.
All these agencies have taxi/minibus vehicles that are fully adapted for wheelchairs, which should be booked at least 24 hours in advance. Aihrop specialises in trips to and from the airports, charges for which are comparable to those in standard taxis; the others are more geared to hire in and around Paris. Costs are higher than for standard cabs, particularly since the companies are all based around the city outskirts.

Accommodation

Palatial luxury, a comfortable pied-à-terre, or that elusive good cheap room – our pick of the best.

Paris boasts more hotels than any other European capital, often within minutes of the city's most famous sights and museums. What's more, many have been imaginatively converted from old private residences, located in charming neighbourhoods. So finding a nice place to stay is relatively easy – unless of course you are travelling to Paris in high season.

To the uninitiated, the months that constitute high season in Paris can make little sense. The city's hotels are swamped during such times as the fashion weeks (January and early July for couture, March and October for _prêt-à-porter_) and trade fairs, which are similarly most common in spring and autumn. Easter and June are also very busy. At these times it's best to book a room before setting off. Note that most hotels ask for a deposit (_arrhes_) when you reserve a room in advance.

At other times of the year you may find some hotels so quiet that they're prepared to offer rooms at less than the quoted price. This is especially true during late July and August, the low season for

French visitors, when smaller, family-run hotels may even close for their own holidays.

Same-day reservations can be made by drop-in callers (not by phone) at all branches of the **Office de Tourisme de Paris** (_see chapter_ **Essential Information**). A small fee is charged (8F-50F), depending on the category of the hotel.

STAR RATINGS

The French hotel classification system, while reliable at the top end, is imprecise, and can often produce surprises – sometimes pleasant ones – at the one- and two-star level. Stars are given on the basis of a range of set factors such as room size, the presence of a lift, guest services and so on. This means that oddly enough room prices are independent of classification, so it is not necessarily cheaper to move down a star when choosing a hotel.

Starting at the top, the four-star de luxe (L****) establishments are justly called 'Palace Hotels', with 24-hour hot and cold running service and concierges who will open almost any Parisian door you wish to enter. Regular four-star hotels have a

The jury's still out on whether heaven can be as good as the Paris **Ritz**_. See page 19._

*T*here are places that take your fancy at first glance. Hotel Novanox is one : simplicity linked with refined detail create a welcoming yet very Parisian atmosphere. At Hotel Novanox you will find attentive hosts. Bertrand Plasmans, who spent four years at The Crillon, and his team offer a traditional welcome and service combined with contemporary comfort and style.

Highlights:

A patio sheltered by trees, personalized hospitality and service; easy access to airports and trade fairs.

155 BD. DU MONTPARNASSE, 75006 PARIS
TEL: (1) 46 33 63 60 FAX: (1) 43 26 61 72

slightly less glamorous aura, although they're still very luxurious, and offer a slew of services for the business traveller.

Three- and two-star hotels offer good accommodation at lower rates. In recent years many mid-range hotels have undergone substantial renovation, without necessarily being re-classified, so that most two- and three-star hotels now have lifts, and private bathrooms and TV in each room.

At the bottom of the scale are the one-star and no-star hotels, where bathroom facilities are sometimes shared, and the staff probably won't speak much English. Many do not accept credit cards (or travellers' cheques), and some will not have night porters, so you must check with the staff before heading out for a late night. They may issue you with a key, but others still lock up tight for the night at around 1am.

The prices quoted below for a double room are for two people. Since 1994, all hotels are also required to add on room tax (*taxe de séjour*), levied per person, per night. Depending on the category of the hotel, it ranges from 1F to 7F. Also, since hotel rates go up, and renovations can cause a hotel to change grade, it's always worth ringing ahead to check prices before arrival.

Palace Hotels

Le Bristol

112 rue du Faubourg St-Honoré, 75008 (42.66.91.45/fax 42.66.68.68). Métro Champs-Elysées-Clémenceau. **Rates** *single* 2,500-2,950F; *double* 3,100-4,400F; *suite* 4,400-15,600F; *breakfast* 155F. **Credit** AmEx, DC, EC, MC, TC, V.

Built in 1924, the Bristol, along with La Résidence, the wing added in 1975, is discreet and very, very smart. All the 195 rooms overlook gardens, and both the summer and winter restaurants – the latter an oak-panelled, eighteenth-century oval room – are stunning. Rooms in the Bristol proper are furnished traditionally; rooms in La Résidence are contemporary, with Italian marble bathrooms. There's also a dramatic indoor swimming pool on the rooftop.

Hotel services *Air-conditioning. Bar. Business services. Car park. Fitness centre. Hairdresser. Laundry/dry-cleaning. Restaurant. Swimming pool. Ticket agency.* **Room services** *Minibar. Room service (24-hour). Telephone. TV (Satellite).*

Hôtel de Crillon

10 place de la Concorde, 75008 (44.71.15.00/fax 44.71.15.02). Métro Concorde. **Rates** *single* 2,500-2,800F; *double* 3,100-4,000F; *breakfast* 150F. **Credit** AmEx, DC, EC, JCB, MC, TC, V.

The title of grandest hotel in Paris is most closely disputed between the Crillon and the Ritz (*see below*). Opinions differ, but the Crillon is hard to match for the sheer magnificence of its location, in a palace built in 1752-70 by Jacques-Ange Gabriel as part of the place de la Concorde, and correspondingly spectacular views. The high-profile clientèle is eclectic

The Hôtel Meurice

The end of the Napoleonic Wars made Paris safe again for the British, who returned to the former imperial capital in droves, thus reviving one of the city's oldest traditions – tourism. The opportunity this presented was not wasted on Calais post-master Augustin Meurice, already in the business of transporting passengers to Paris, safely and in no less than 36 hours.

In 1817 he opened a hotel on the rue St-Honoré to welcome his coach, and founded what was to become the English nobility's home away from home for generations. At times derisively referred to by locals as the *ménagerie anglaise*, the Hôtel Meurice was a rare address in Paris where British aristocrats could count on their port being perfectly served.

The hotel moved to its present site in 1835. This elegant address opposite the Tuileries together with its reputation for luxurious accommodation would guarantee the hotel a glittering clientèle throughout the nineteenth century. Guests, however, would have to hold out until 1890 before the hotel installed its first individual modern bathrooms. In 1906 the Meurice acquired the adjacent Hôtel Métropole, and expanded the property as far as the rue Castiglione. The main entrance was moved to the rue du Mont Thabor, infinitely more discreet than the rue de Rivoli for the comings and goings of the hotel's guests, among them kings, queens and sundry lesser rulers, deposed or not.

During the German occupation, while the Gestapo set up residence at the Lutétia, General von Choltitz, the Commandant of Paris credited with having saved the city by disobeying Hitler's orders to blow it up in 1944, chose the Meurice as his headquarters. More recently, the hotel has welcomed many artists such as Salvador Dali, soprano Kathleen Battle and Kirk Douglas, but one gets the impression that Meurice is happy to see showbiz stars stay at the Ritz, preferring royalty more in keeping with its 'Hotel of Kings' image.

On the one hand there is opulence at every turn – the *Salon Pompadour* is the closest you'll get to Versailles without leaving Paris, and the rooms above are adorned with art and antiques that anywhere else would be heirlooms. And yet, a sense of extreme discretion permeates the place. Such a combination of luxury and privacy comes dear, but it's hard to imagine the Queen of Thailand or the Arab sheikhs who regularly take entire floors quibbling over the bill. For details, *see page 19.*

– both showbiz celebs and politicians – but the hotel itself continues to stand on gilt-edged tradition. The neo-classical façade, the butterscotch marble lobby, the blue-draped *Jardin d'Hiver* salon de thé, and the magnificent presidential suites that overlook the *place* all ooze prestige, echoed in all of its 123 rooms and 40 suites.
Hotel services *Air-conditioning. Babysitting. Bar. Boutique. Business services. Conference services. Restaurants. Ticket agency. Wheelchair access.* **Room services** *Hairdryer. Minibar. Room service (24-hour). Safe. Telephone. TV (Cable).*

Hôtel George V

31 avenue George V, 75008 (47.23.54.00/fax 47.20.40.00). Métro George V. **Rates** *single* 1,800-2,300F; *double* 2,500-3,900F. **Credit** AmEx, DC, EC, JCB, MC, F£$TC, V.
The ornate and exclusive George V – part of the Forte chain – continues to dazzle its guests with its opulence and the high standards of service in its 298 rooms. The trappings could scarcely be more lavish – the hotel is stuffed with antiques, and in the *Salon Louis XIII* there is even a Renaissance fireplace from a Loire Valley château and a seventeenth-century Aubusson tapestry.
Hotel services *Air-conditioning. Babysitting. Bar. Boutiques. Bureau de change. Business services. Car rental. Hairdresser. Laundry/dry-cleaning. Limousine service. Restaurants. Ticket agency.* **Room services** *Minibar. Room service (24-hour). Telephone. TV.*

Hôtel Meurice

228 rue de Rivoli, 75001 (44.58.10.10/fax 44.58.10.15). Métro Tuileries. **Rates** *single* 2,250-2,550F; *double* 2,550-3,650F; *suite* 5,000-8,000F; *breakfast* 140-190F. **Credit** AmEx, DC, EC, JCB, MC, F£$TC, V.
The dowager palace hotel, with 180 rooms. *See p17* **The Hôtel Meurice**.
Hotel services *Air-conditioning. Bar. Babysitting. Business services. Car park. Conference services. Hairdresser. Jet rental. Laundry service. Lift. Restaurant. Ticket agency.* **Room services** *Hairdryer. Minibar. Radio. Room service (24-hour). Telephone. TV (Satellite).*

Hôtel Plaza Athénée

25 avenue Montaigne, 75008 (47.23.78.33/fax 47.20.20.70). Métro Alma-Marceau. **Rates** *High season (May, June, September, October): single* 2,400-2,850F; *double* 3,150-4,950F; *suite* 6,690-9,820F. *Low season: single* 2,300-2,740F; *double* 3,310-4,750F; *suite* 6,430-9,440F; *extra bed* 380; *breakfast* 150-230F. **Credit** AmEx, DC, EC, JCB, MC, F£$TC, V.
A location amid the couture houses on avenue Montaigne has made this sumptuous 211-room, Forte-owned hotel a favourite with the fashion world. With a staff of 400 and lavish silk-and-satin décor in each room, it certainly pampers its guests. The restaurant and bars offer ample star-spotting opportunities, and in summer the *Cour Jardin* becomes a six-storey cascade of ivy, a perfect place for afternoon tea.
Hotel services *Air-conditioning. Babysitting. Bars. Boutiques. Business services. Car park. Hairdresser. Laundry/dry-cleaning. Restaurant. Ticket agencies.* **Room services** *Minibar. Radio. Room service (24-hour). Telephone. TV (Satellite).*

Hôtel Ritz

15 place Vendôme, 75001 (43.16.30.30/fax 43.16.36.69). Métro Tuileries. **Rates** *single* 2,600-3,200F; *double* 3,200-4,570F. **Credit** AmEx, DC, EC, JCB, MC, F£$TC, V.
Coco Chanel, the Duke of Windsor and Marcel Proust all lived here, as did Ernest Hemingway, who reputedly said that he hoped heaven would be as good as the Ritz. Hopefully heaven is a bit less exclusive. There isn't even a lobby (no loitering for paparazzi) and the windows overlooking the place Vendôme are sound- and bullet-proof. The health club looks like a pre-Vesuvius Pompeii, and there's a gorgeous,

tiled swimming pool. The restaurant is superb, and guests in the 142 rooms and 45 suites are even entitled to attend classes at the *Ecole Gastronomique Française Ritz-Escoffier*.
Hotel services *Air-conditioning. Bars. Babysitting. Business services. Conference services. Cookery school. Hairdresser. Health spa. Nightclub. Restaurant. Swimming pool. Ticket agency.* **Room services** *Hairdryer. Jacuzzi. Minibar. Room service (24-hour). Stereo. Telephone. TV (Satellite). Video.*

Le Raphaël

17 avenue Kléber, 75016 (44.28.00.28/fax 45.01.21.50). Métro Kléber. **Rates** *single or double* 1,970-3,520F; *suite* 4,020-7,040; *breakfast* 115-160F. **Credit** AmEx, DC, EC, JCB, MC, F£$TC, V.
The Raphaël, opened in 1925, is an echo of a more civilised age. Although only a few steps away from the crowds at the Arc de Triomphe and the Champs-Elysées, it remains a haven of peace, with rug-strewn floors, carved wooden panelling and club-like English bar as well as 87 elegant, antique-stuffed rooms. There's even a Turner in the lobby.
Hotel services *Air-conditioning. Babysitting. Bar. Business services. Conference services. Laundry/dry-cleaning service. Restaurant. Ticket agency.* **Room services** *Hairdryer. Minibar. Room service (24-hour). Telephone. TV (Satellite).*

Royal Monceau

37 avenue Hoche, 75008 (45.61.98.00/fax 45.63.28.93). Métro Charles de Gaulle-Etoile. **Rates** *single* 2,100-2,600F; *double* 2,600-3,900F; *suite* 4,500-13,000F; *extra bed* 450F; *breakfast* 135-185F. **Credit** AmEx, DC, EC, JCB, MC, F£$TC, V.
A temple to twenties opulence, with marble floors, crystal chandeliers and Gobelins tapestries in the lobby. The 219 rooms and suites are more restrained, but still impressively decorated in luscious materials. The hotel boasts one of the city's best Italian restaurants, Il Carpaccio, and a superb health club, Les Thermes, where one can luxuriate the day away in a setting that may recall the splendours of ancient Rome. It's also very well equipped for business travellers.
Hotel services *Air-conditioning. Babysitting. Bar. Business services. Conference rooms. Hairdresser. Health club/gym. Restaurants. Swimming pool. Ticket agency.* **Room services** *Hairdryer. Minibar. Room service (24-hour). Telephone. TV (Satellite). Video.*

De Luxe/Expensive

L'Hôtel

13 rue des Beaux-Arts, 75006 (43.25.27.22/fax 43.25.64.81). Métro Mabillon. **Rates** *single or double* 950-2,300F; *suite* 2,800-3,800F; *breakfast* 90F. **Credit** AmEx, DC, EC, MC, F£$TC, V.
The small hotel – 27 rooms – where Oscar Wilde lived and died in 1900, when it was the rather shabby Hotel d'Alsace. It was acquired in 1968 by Guy-Louis Duboucheron, who refurbished it from top to bottom. Wilde's room has been restored, as has the art deco furniture installed here by the music hall star Mistinguett, and the whole place is decorated in an ornate, kitsch style which seems to go down well with the show- and fashion-biz clientèle.
Hotel services *Air-conditioning. Babysitting. Laundry service. Lift. Massage. Piano bar. Restaurant. Ticket agency.* **Room services** *Air-conditioning. Hairdryer. Minibar. Radio. Room service (24-hour). Safe. Telephone. TV (Satellite).*

Hôtel de l'Abbaye

10 rue Cassette, 75006 (45.44.38.11/fax 45.48.07.86). Métro St-Sulpice. **Rates** *single or double* 900-1,400F; *suite* 1,800F; *extra bed* 150F; *breakfast* included. **Credit** AmEx, EC, MC, F£$TC, V.

A complete renovation in 1994 has turned this eighteenth-century residence into an oasis of quiet luxury. Wood panelling, well-stuffed sofas and an open fireplace add provincial charm to three intimate lounges, which open onto a large, verdant garden where breakfast is served in warmer months. The 46 rooms vary from small to grand, but each is an exercise in good taste and promises a relaxing stay.
Hotel services *Air-conditioning. Babysitting. Bar. Garden. Laundry service. Lift. Safe. Ticket agency.* **Room services** *Hairdryer. Radio. Telephone. TV (Satellite).*

Hôtel Buci Latin

34 rue de Buci, 75006 (43.29.07.20/fax 43.29.67.44). Métro St-Germain-des-Prés. **Rates** *single or double* 1,100F; *duplex* 1,500F; *suite* 1,600F; *breakfast included.* **Credit** AmEx, DC, EC, MC, F£$TC, V.
Designed with the help of stylist Alain Perrier, the Buci Latin is a mixture of the classical and the very modern. There are bold colours, clean lines and classical bathtubs, and young artists have painted a different picture on the door of each of the 27 rooms (you recognise yours by the matching picture on the key-ring). Room 140 is a duplex, with bathroom on the top floor, and suite 162 comes with an Olympic-size jacuzzi. The hotel is on the narrow, bustling rue de Buci, above a lively market.
Hotel services *Air-conditioning. Bar. Coffee shop. Lift. Safe.* **Room services** *Hairdryer. Minibar. Radio. Room service. Telephone. TV (Cable).*

Hôtel du Jeu de Paume

54 rue St-Louis-en-l'Ile, 75004 (43.26.14.18/fax 40.46.02.76). Métro Pont-Marie. **Rates** *single or double* 795-1,340F; *suite* 2,300-2,400F; *extra bed* 150F; *breakfast* 75F. **Credit** AmEx, DC, EC, MC, V.
In 1634, when the Marais and the Ile St-Louis were being built up as a fashionable home for the aristocracy, Louis XIII ordered the construction of the city's first *Jeu de Paume* or royal tennis court here on the island. Since enclosed and restored, the court now contains a secluded 32-room hotel in a very romantic setting, with a serene secret garden.
Hotel services *Bar. Conference facilities. Laundry service. Lift. Safe.* **Room services** *Hairdryer. Minibar. Telephone. TV (Satellite).*

Hôtel Lutétia

45 boulevard Raspail, 75007 (49.54.46.46/fax 49.54.46.00). Métro Sèvres-Babylone. **Rates** *single or double* 950-1,650F; *suite* 1,950-3,000F; *extra bed* 350F; *breakfast* 65F-125F. **Credit** AmEx, DC, EC, JCB, MC, F£$TC, V.
Opened in 1910 to serve provincial shoppers coming to the Bon Marché, the Lutétia is a masterpiece of art nouveau and early art deco architecture, the grandest hotel on the Left Bank. It has long been popular with literary and political figures, and was also seized by the Gestapo during the German occupation. Most recently, the 271 rooms have been luxuriously revamped by Sybille de Margerie maintaining an elegant thirties feel with shades of purple, gold and pearl grey.
Hotel services *Air-conditioning. Babysitting. Bar. Car park. Conference services. Laundry service. Lift. Restaurants.* **Room services** *Hairdryer. Minibar. Radio. Room service (24 hour). Safe. Telephone. TV (Cable).*

Left Bank Hôtel

9 rue de l'Ancienne Comédie, 75006 (43.54.01.70/fax 43.26.17.14). Métro Odéon. **Rates** *single* 895F; *double* 990F; *suite* 1,400F; *extra bed* 100F; *breakfast* 30F. **Credit** AmEx, DC, EC, MC, TC, V.
Antique furniture, a wood-panelled lobby and a perfect location near the Flore, the Deux Magots and the St-Germain shops are the main attractions of this three-star, 31 room hotel. It was opened in 1989, in a seventeenth-century building next to Paris's oldest café, the Procope. The area is lively at night, but the hotel's street-side windows are sound-proof.

Hotel services *Air-conditioning. Laundry service. Lift. No smoking rooms.* **Room services** *Hairdryer. Minibar. Safe. Telephone. TV (Cable).*

Relais Saint-Germain

9 carrefour de l'Odéon 75006 (43.29.12.05/fax 46.33.45.30). Métro Odéon. **Rates** *single* 1,260F; *double* 1,500-1,650F; *suite* 1900F; *breakfast included.* **Credit** AmEx, DC, EC, JCB, MC, F£$TC.
Down the street from the Odéon Theatre in the heart of the Left Bank, this three-star hotel is smart yet very inviting, and has established a very high reputation. The 22 generously-sized rooms are splendidly decorated, combining antique furnishings, sumptuous fabrics and entirely modern fittings. All deliver creature comforts in great style.
Hotel services *Air-conditioning. Laundry service. Lift. Safe. Ticket agency.* **Room services** *Hairdryer. Minibar. Room service (7-11pm). Safe, Telephone. TV (Cable).*

La Villa

29 rue Jacob, 75006 (43.26.60.00/fax 46.34.63.63). Métro St-Germain-des-Prés. **Rates** *single or double* 800-1,600F; *suite* 1,950F; *breakfast* 80F. **Credit** AmEx, DC, EC, JCB, MC, TC (F,$,£), V.
La Villa sports the latest in post-modern chic. The 32 rooms are bold and bright, furnished in leather, burnished metals and sanded glass. All have flashy marble, chrome and glass bathrooms, the perfect place for your Philippe Starck toothbrush. 'Le Bar' on the ground floor is suitably done out in shades of purple and orange. This is St-Germain jazzland, and the Villa also boasts one of the best jazz clubs in Paris (*see chapter* **Music: Rock, Roots & Jazz**).
Hotel services *Air-conditioning. Bar. Jazz club. Laundry service. Lift.* **Room services** *Hairdryer. Minibar. Radio. Safe. Telephone. TV (Satellite).*

Villa Maillot

143 avenue de Malakoff, 75016 (45.01.25.22/fax 45.00.60.61). Métro Porte Maillot. **Rates** *single* 1,500F; *double* 1,700F; *suite* 2,300-2,500F; *breakfast* 100F. **Credit** AmEx, DC, EC, MC, F£$TC, V.
Minutes away from the Arc de Triomphe is this splendid art deco hotel, once an Embassy. Its 39 rooms and suites – the latter named after Picasso, Chagall and Modigliani – were transformed in 1988 with bleached wood, polished pink marble and thirties' fixtures. For anyone needing to be near the Palais des Congrès convention centre, this is a blissful alternative to the tower hotels that blot the Porte Maillot district.
Hotel services *Air-conditioning. Bar. Conference services. Laundry service. Lift. Safe. Ticket agency.* **Room services** *Hairdryer. Minibar. Room service (7-11pm). Telephone. Trouser press. TV (Satellite).*

Moderate

Axial Beaubourg Hôtel

11 rue du Temple, 75004 (42.72.72.22/fax 42.72.03.53). Métro Hôtel-de-Ville. **Rates** *single* 440-520F; *double* 550-580F; *triple* 650F; *extra bed* 100F; *breakfast* 35F. **Credit** AmEx, DC, EC, MC, FTC, V.
Fully renovated in 1991, the Axial Beaubourg provides comfort and taste in a very central location close to the Pompidou Centre. Exposed beams in some of the 39 rooms and a breakfast room that's an excavated, sixteenth-century cellar add a touch of charm to this modernised hotel, whose staff offer a warm welcome. It's very popular, so book in advance.
Hotel services *Laundry service. Lift.* **Room services** *Double glazing. Hairdryer. Safe. Telephone. TV (Satellite).*

Bac St-Germain

66 rue du Bac, 75007 (42.22.20.03/fax 45.48.52.30). Métro Rue du Bac. **Rates** *single* 490F; *double* from 590F; *breakfast* 59F. **Credit** AmEx, DC, EC, MC, F£$TC, V.

Centrally located in the heart of St-Germain, the Bac is a modern and comfortable 21-room hotel. Breakfast is served on a lovely roof-top terrace which has a sweeping view of the city, to which the management intends to add a grand fountain.
Hotel services *Laundry service. Lift.* **Room services** *Double glazing. Hairdryer. Radio/alarm. Safe. Telephone. TV (Satellite).*

Bastille Spéria

1 rue de la Bastille, 75004 (42.72.04.01/fax 42.72.56.38). Métro Bastille. **Rates** *single* 510-544F; *double* 544-610F; *triple* 740F; *breakfast* 40F. **Credit** AmEx, DC, EC, JCB, MC, FTC, V.
Rather bland and businesslike in appearance, but nonetheless comfortable and tastefully decorated, the 42 room Spéria has an ideal Bastille location, a few steps from the Opéra, the place des Vosges and the rue de Lappe nightspots.
Hotel services *Laundry service. Lift.* **Room services** *Double glazing. Hairdryer. Minibar. Safe. Telephone. TV (Satellite).*

Le Brittanique

20 avenue Victoria, 75001 (42.33.74.59/fax 42.33.82.65). Métro Châtelet-Les Halles. **Rates** *single* 600F; *double* 720-830F; *extra bed* 90F; *breakfast* 49F.
Credit AmEx, DC, EC, JCB, MC, FTC, V.
An understated 40-room hotel in a central location off the place du Châtelet, the Brittanique served as a Quaker mission in World War I. The lobby was smartly redecorated in 1994 with antique-style furniture and floral print sofas, but its curious, if impressive model galleons remain.
Hotel services *Laundry service. Lift.* **Room services** *Double glazing. Hairdryer. Safe. Minibar. Telephone. TV (Satellite).*

Grand Hôtel de Besançon

56 rue Montorgueil, 75002 (42.36.41.08/fax 45.08.08.79). Métro Etienne-Marcel. **Rates** *single* 420-490F; *double* 520-550F; *extra bed* 150F; *breakfast* 40F.
Credit MC, FTC, V.
Re-opened in 1995 after a complete makeover, the Besançon boasts quaint but tasteful rooms with new bathrooms and a calm first floor lobby. It's just off the bustling and colourful Montorgueil street market, right by Les Halles. Although all the 20 rooms have double-glazed windows, late risers might prefer the rooms facing the back in warmer months.
Hotel services *First floor lift. Safe.* **Room services** *Double glazing. Hairdryer. Radio. Telephone. TV (Cable).*

Grand Hôtel Malher

5 rue Malher, 75004 (42.72.60.92/fax 42.72.25.37). Métro St-Paul. **Rates** *single* 470-620F; *double* 570-720F; *breakfast* 45F. **Credit** AmEx, EC, MC, F£$TC, V.
Thoroughly renovated to appeal to business travellers, the Malher is also ideally situated for sightseeing. The place des Vosges, the Pompidou centre and the Ile St-Louis are all within walking distance of this 31-room Marais hotel. Breakfast is served in the seventeenth-century vaulted wine cellar.
Hotel services *Lift. No smoking rooms. Safe. Small conference room.* **Room services** *Double glazing. Hairdryer. Minibar. Telephone. TV (Cable).*

Hôtel Belle Epoque

66 rue de Charenton, 75012 (43.44.06.66/fax 43.44.10.25). Métro Ledru-Rollin. **Rates** *low season (11 Jan-31 Mar, July-Aug): single* 500-620F; *double* 580-850F; *triple* 820-900F. *High season: single* 530-700F; *double* 630-950F; *triple* 900-1000F; *breakfast* included. **Credit** AmEx, EC, MC, FTC, V.
A modern hotel behind an old façade which pays hommage to art deco style. The 29 rooms are furnished with reproductions of original designs by Printz and Ruhlmann, and come with marbled bathrooms. It's also well situated for Bastille nightlife and the Gare de Lyon.

Hotel services *Bar. Conference services. Garden. Laundry service. Lift. Restaurant. Safe.* **Room services** *Double glazing. Minibar. Telephone. TV.*

Hôtel Bonaparte

61 rue Bonaparte, 75006 (43.26.97.37/fax 46.33.57.67). Métro St-Sulpice. **Rates** *single* 430F; *double* 550-665F; *triple* 740F; *breakfast* included. **Credit** EC, MC, FTC, V.
A small, friendly hotel around the corner from St-Sulpice and next to an art gallery, with plenty of fresh flowers in the newly-renovated, neo-classical lobby. The 29 rooms are large and nicely furnished – most have antique style armoires, and room 13 has a mantle with a gilt mirror. The bathrooms have also been redone recently, with rose-coloured marble.
Hotel services *Lift.* **Room services** *Double glazing. Hairdryer. Minibar. Safe. Telephone. TV.*

Hôtel Brighton

218 rue de Rivoli, 75001 (42.60.30.03/fax 42.60.41.78). Métro Tuileries. **Rates** *single* 530-870F; *double* 560-900F; *breakfast* included. **Credit** AmEx, DC, EC, MC, FTC, V.
This 70-room place has got slightly left behind by its luxurious neighbours, which means you can obtain rue de Rivoli status at reasonable prices. Plenty of old-fashioned charm – uniformed porters, a salon de thé with marble columns and a view over the Tuileries from the rooms at the front.
Hotel services *Laundry service. Lift. Safe. Salon de Thé.* **Room services** *Double glazing. Hairdryer. Minibar. Room service (24-hour). Telephone. TV.*

Hôtel Caron de Beaumarchais

12 rue Vieille-du-Temple, 75004 (42.72.34.12/fax 42.72.34.63). Métro Hôtel de Ville. **Rates** *single or double* 620F-690F; *breakfast* 48F. **Credit** AmEx, DC, EC, JCB, MC, F£$TC, V.
A delightful 19-room hotel in the heart of the Marais, re-opened in June 1993 after complete renovation. Fresh flowers, antique furniture and a Louis XVI fireplace grace the lounge. The wood-beamed rooms are rather small but beautifully appointed, and hung with pages from first editions of *The Marriage of Figaro*. Breakfast includes freshly squeezed juice, home-made jams and excellent teas and coffee.
Hotel services *Air-conditioning. Laundry service. Lift. Safe.* **Room services** *Double glazing. Hairdryer. Minibar. Telephone. TV (Satellite).*

Hôtel du Lion

1 avenue du Général Leclerc, 75014 (40.47.04.00/fax 43.20.38.18). Métro/RER Denfert-Rochereau. **Rates** *single* 370-470F; *double* 470-570F; *extra bed* 120F; *breakfast* 40F. **Credit** AmEx, EC, MC, FTC, V.
A fierce wooden lion startles guests at the top of the stairs leading to the first floor reception but the courteous, friendly staff quickly put you at ease, offering service above the norm for a two-star hotel. It has 33 rooms, all recently modernised. The rooms on the sixth and seventh floors all have balconies, and excellent views of the Eiffel Tower, Tour Montparnasse and Montmartre. Though not very central the location has excellent metro, RER and airport connections.
Hotel services *Lift. Limited parking. No smoking floor.* **Room services** *Double glazing. Hairdryer. Safe. Telephone. Trouser press. TV (Satellite).*

Hôtel Novanox

155 boulevard du Montparnasse, 75006 (46.33.63.60/fax 43.26.61.72). RER Port-Royal. **Rates** *single or double* 680F; *breakfast* 50F. **Credit** AmEx, DC, MC, F£$TC, V.
A bit of fifties' Paris upgraded with nineties' comfort. With 27 rooms, the Novanox has brightly-coloured, fifties-style décor in bedrooms and bathrooms and a pretty, plant-lined terrace, where breakfast is served when weather allows.
Hotel services *Bar. Laundry service. Lift.* **Room services** *Double glazing. Minibar. Radio. Telephone. TV.*

*The leafy heart of the **Select Hotel**.*

Hôtel de Saint Germain

*50 rue du Four, 75006 (45.48.91.64/fax 45.48.46.22).
Métro St-Sulpice.* **Rates** *High season (1 Apr-30 Jun, 1
Sep-18 Nov): single 585F; double 695F. Low season: single
415F; double 520F; breakfast 50F; extra bed 120F.* **Credit**
AmEx, DC, EC, JCB, MC, F£TC, V.
Recent renovation has given the public areas of this well-run
hotel a clean, modern look, while the 30 comfortable rooms
have English pine furniture and matching Laura Ashley-
style prints, making for a cosy stay. The busy street is excel-
lently located for St-Germain shopping territory.
Hotel services *Laundry service. Lift.* **Room services**
*Double glazing. Hairdryer. Minibar. Radio. Safe.
Telephone. TV (Cable).*

Hôtel Saint-Merry

*78 rue de la Verrerie, 75004 (42.78.14.15/fax
40.29.06.82). Métro Hôtel-de-Ville.* **Rates** *single or
double 400F-1,200F; breakfast 45F.* **No credit cards.**
A tiny, 11-room hotel with a great history and fascinating
décor, located on a lively – and noisy – pedestrian street close
to the Pompidou Centre. Incorporated into a seventeenth-century presbytery adjoining the sixteenth-century church of
St-Merri, it was once a brothel. Now all the rooms are filled
with high-Gothic woodwork, painstakingly commissioned
by the owner Christian Crabbe, while room 9 is built into the
church buttresses. The lack of such things as a lift or TV in
the rooms is all part of its character. Book well in advance,
as it has a devoted following.
Hotel services *Safe.* **Room services** *Double glazing.
Hairdryer. Telephone.*

Hôtel des Trois Collèges

*16 rue Cujas, 75005 (43.54.67.30/fax 46.34.02.99).
Métro Cluny-La-Sorbonne/RER Luxembourg.* **Rates**
*single 360-600F; double 450-600F; triple 750F; breakfast
40F.* **Credit** AmEx, DC, EC, MC, FTC, V.

Just down the street from the Sorbonne, among a cluster of
rather ordinary and similarly-priced hotels, the Trois
Collèges stands out with its ultra-modern lobby and appealing tea lounge, both done in cool marble with contemporary
wooden furniture. The 44 rooms are small and more conventional, but the young staff are friendly and professional.
Hotel services *Laundry service. Lift. Safe. Salon de
Thé.* **Room services** *Double glazing. Hairdryer.
Telephone. TV.*

Hôtel du Vieux Marais

*8 rue du Plâtre, 75004 (42.78.47.22/fax 42.78.34.32).
Métro Hôtel-de-Ville.* **Rates** *single 380-500F; double 500-
540F; triple 650F; extra bed 100F; breakfast 35F.* **Credit**
EC, MC, FTC, V. Closed Aug.
In contrast to the nicely redone public rooms, the 44 guest
rooms here could use a facelift, but they're so clean and well-
kept that one can well ignore the late-seventies floral decor.
The excellent location on a calm Marais street and an aim-
to-please staff also ensure popularity, so book in advance.
Hotel services *Lift.* **Room services** *Double glazing.
Telephone. TV.*

Select Hotel

*1 place de la Sorbonne, 75005
(46.34.14.80/fax 46.34.51.79). RER Luxembourg.*
Rates *single 530F; double 650-780F; triple from 890F;
suite 1250F; extra bed 30F; breakfast 30F.* **Credit**
AmEx, DC, JCB, MC, F£$TC, V.
Next to the busy café pavements of place de la Sorbonne, the
Select greets guests with gleaming granite floors and pillars,
a flower- and palm tree-filled interior, and an inner garden
complete with waterfall. The 68 stylishly renovated rooms
are thoroughly modern and make clever use of limited space.
In a central location on the Left Bank, it's a couple of minutes' walk from the Jardins du Luxembourg.
Hotel services *Air-conditioning. Bar. Laundry service.
Lift. Safe. Wheelchair access.* **Room services** *Double
glazing. Hairdryer. Minibar. Telephone. TV (Cable).*

Inexpensive

ALHotel Vertus

*5 rue des Vertus, 75003 (44.61.89.50/fax 48.04.33.72).
Métro Arts-et-Métiers.* **Rates** *single 370F; double 470F;
suite 590F; extra bed 100F; breakfast 35F.* **Credit** AmEx,
EC, MC, F£$TC, V.
This small new hotel is in a renovated seventeenth-century
building, and all nine rooms combine original architectural
features with modern conveniences including air-conditioning. It's centrally based in the north of the Marais, where costume jewellers and Chinese wholesalers have yet to give way
to gentrification. When booking, it's worth mentioning that
you are a *Time Out* reader.
Hotel services *Air-conditioning. Laundry service. Lift.
Safe.* **Room services** *Double glazing. Hairdryer. Radio.
Telephone. TV.*

Familia Hotel

*11 rue des Ecoles, 75005 (43.54.55.27/fax 43.29.61.77).
Métro Maubert-Mutualité.* **Rates** *single or double 370-
480F; extra bed 100F; breakfast 30F.* **Credit** AmEx, DC,
EC, JCB, MC, F£$TC,V.
Aptly named, this newly-renovated hotel near the Sorbonne
offers a homely atmosphere yet with an extremely high level
of service. The more expensive rooms feature newly-added
monochrome murals of Parisian scenes. Several of the 30
rooms have balconies, and the double glazing has been
renewed and is very efficient. The hotel offers a very friendly welcome to readers of *Time Out*.
Hotel services *Laundry service. Lift. Safe.* **Room
services** *Double glazing. Hairdryer. Minibar. Radio.
Telephone. TV (Cable).*

Grand Hôtel Jeanne d'Arc
3 rue de Jarente, 75004 (48.87.62.11/fax 48.87.37.31).
Métro St-Paul. **Rates** *single* 295-380F; *double* 295-450F;
triple 500F; *extra bed* 75F; *breakfast* 35F. **Credit** EC, MC,
FTC, V.
There has been a hotel on this quiet Marais street, near the
place des Vosges and the rue de Turenne, since the seventeenth century. This history, its location, and reasonable
rates all make it very popular. In 1994 new management
removed its floral wallpaper and redid the public areas, but
left the Gaudi-esque mirror in the reception. Most of the 36
rooms have also been nicely renovated, and all have private
bathrooms.
Hotel services *Lift. Safe.* **Room services** *Telephone.*
TV (Cable).

Hôtel Apollo
11 rue de Dunkerque, 75010 (48.78.04.98/fax
42.85.08.78). Métro Gare du Nord. **Rates** *single* 300-
325F; *double* 360-415F; *breakfast* 30F. **Credit** AmEx, DC,
EC, JCB, MC, F£$TC, V.
A great find in an area that's packed with doubtful inexpensive hotels, directly opposite the Gare du Nord and near
the Gare de l'Est. The 45-room hotel is immaculately clean
and has true old world charm, its rooms decorated country-
style,with large armoires and florid wallpaper. Book well in
advance for the handful of cheaper rooms without facilities.
Hotel services *Lift. Safe.* **Room services** *Double*
glazing. Minibar. Telephone. TV.

Hôtel des Arts
7 Cité Bergère, 75009 (42.46.73.30/fax 48.00.94.42).
Métro Rue Montmartre. **Rates** *single* 325-345F; *double*
350-380F; *triple* 500F; *breakfast* 28F. **Credit** AmEx, DC,
EC, MC, F£$TC, V.
One of many hotels in a celebrated passageway-courtyard
in a late-night part of town, the 26-room Hôtel des Arts has
reams of theatre and museum posters plastered about the
halls, and larger than average rooms. There's a chatty par-
rot in the reception area, and the owners also have four free
parking spaces for residents – even more of a rarity.
Hotel services *Car park. Lift. Safe.* **Room services**
Double glazing. Hairdryer. Radio. Telephone. TV.

Hôtel Chopin
46 passage Jouffroy, 75009 (47.70.58.10/fax
42.47.00.70). Métro Rue Montmartre. **Rates** *single* 355-
435F; *double* 450-490F; *triple* 565F; *breakfast* 36F. **Credit**
DC, EC, MC, FTC, V.
Tucked away in a picturesque covered *passage*, this hotel
has lashings of character. Chesterfields and billowing curtains give the entrance hall a turn-of-the-century feel, and the
36 renovated rooms provide more of the same, with wooden
armoires and tables, and pretty printed curtains. In the surrounding area there are several good late-night haunts.
Hotel services *Lift. Safe.* **Room services** *Double*
glazing. Hairdryer. Telephone. TV (Cable).

Hôtel Ermitage
24 rue Lamarck, 75018 (42.64.79.22). Métro Lamarck
Caulaincourt. **Rates** *single or double* 440F; *breakfast*
included. **Credit** FTC.
It's a stiff climb to the top of Montmartre – this family-run
hotel is in the shadow of Sacré-Coeur – but it's worth every
step. All 12 rooms are large, endearingly over-decorated and
come with private bathroom. The ground-floor rooms give
onto a garden, while all those on upper-floors have exceptional views of the city. Breakfast is served in your room.
Hotel services *Safe.* **Room services** *Double glazing.*
Hairdryer. Telephone.

Hôtel Esmeralda
4 rue St-Julien-le-Pauvre, 75005 (43.54.19.20/fax
40.51.00.68). Métro St-Michel or Maubert-Mutualité.

Plush décor at the **Hôtel Ermitage.**

Rates *single* 160F; *double* 320F-490F; *triple* 550F; *shower*
10F; *breakfast* 40F. **Credit** EC, F£$TC.
Basic but characterful, the Esmeralda charms with its views
of Notre Dame, ancient wooden staircase, cosy lobby and resident cat. It also has an excellent location right in the heart
of the most humming part of the Latin Quarter and only 19
rooms, so it's best to book well in advance.
Hotel services *Safe.* **Room services** *Hairdryer.*
Telephone.

Hôtel Keppler
12 rue Keppler, 75016 (47.20.65.05/fax 47.23.02.29).
Métro Charles de Gaulle-Etoile. **Rates** *single or double*
450F; *triple* 520F; *breakfast* 30F. **Credit** AmEx, EC, MC,
F£$TC, V.
The 49-room Keppler is tucked away on an elegant, quiet
street behind the chic avenue Marceau, and everything about
it whispers 16th *arrondissement*. A vintage, wonderfully
ornate nineteenth-century lift and well-sized, tastefully furnished rooms are to be expected in this neighbourhood – but
not often at these prices.
Hotel services *Bar. Lift.* **Room services** *Double*
glazing. Hairdryer. Radio. Safe. Telephone. TV.

Hôtel du Lys
23 rue Serpente, 75006 (43.26.97.57/fax 44.07.34.90).
Métro Odéon or St-Michel. **Rates** *single* 380-430F; *double*
460F; *triple* 560F; *breakfast* included. **Credit** EC, FTC.
A seventeenth-century building near the place St-Michel, just
oozing with charm. Each of the 22 rooms is tastefully decorated *à l'ancienne* and sprinkled with antiques, and comes
with private bathroom. If you can brave the stairs, room 19
on the top floor has a lovely terrace with plants, at no extra
charge. A faithful following makes reservations a must.
Hotel services *Safe.* **Room services** *Double glazing.*
Hairdryer. Telephone. TV (Cable).

The dignified **Hôtel Keppler**. *See page 25.*

Hôtel Montpensier

12 rue de Richelieu, 75001 (42.96.28.50/fax 42.86.02.70). Métro Palais-Royal. **Rates** *single* 240-285F; *double* 370-430F; *triple* 500F; *breakfast* 32F. **Credit** AmEx, EC, JCB, MC, F£$TC, V.
Once the *hôtel particulier* of the capricious Mademoiselle de Montpensier, cousin of Louis XIV, this hotel now offers an eclectic mix in its 43 rooms, from large, high-ceilinged first floor doubles to small singles with no shower or bath. Some have been renovated, while others, like room 36 with its historic painted wood panelling and wall sconces, should really remain untouched forever. The friendly staff are happy to let you have a look first, and don't miss the ancient lift.
Hotel services *Safe.* **Room services** *Double glazing. Hairdryer. Telephone. TV (Satellite).*

Hôtel de Nevers

83 rue du Bac, 75007 (45.44.61.30/fax 42.22.29.47). Métro Rue du Bac. **Rates** *single* 380F; *double* 410-440F; *breakfast* 30F. **Credit** EC, FTC.
In an expensive neighbourhood, this small seventeenth-century house offers unpretentious charm. The entire place has been renovated, and though the nine rooms are tiny, they are bright and spotless. Each has a private bathroom.
Hotel services *Safe.* **Room services** *Telephone.*

Hôtel Place des Vosges

12 rue de Birague, 75004 (42.72.60.46/fax 42.72.02.64). Métro St-Paul. **Rates** *single* 300-410F; *double* 410-430F; *breakfast* 40F. **Credit** EC, JCB, MC, FTC, V.
Once a stables, this hotel just off the place des Vosges has been nicely renovated, with the beamed ceilings carefully preserved. Although the 16 rooms tend to be small, they are tastefully decorated and the view from room 60 is particularly picturesque. It's just a short walk from the Bastille.
Hotel services *Lift. Safe.* **Room services** *Telephone. TV (Satellite).*

Hôtel St-André-des-Arts

66 rue St-André-des-Arts, 75006 (43.26.96.16/fax 43.29.73.34). Métro Odéon. **Rates** *single* 230-330F; *double* 330-450F; *triple* 520F; *shower* free; *breakfast* included. **Credit** AmEx, EC, FTC, MC, V.
Housed in a building occupied by the king's musketeers in the seventeenth century, on one of the most bustling streets of St-Germain, this is a hotel with a lot of character and a laid-back, sociable atmosphere. It has oak beams and an impressive, winding, half-timbered staircase, and the gregarious owner provides a steady stream of recorded jazz in the tiny lobby that doubles as a breakfast room. The only drawback might be the thinness of some of the bedroom walls. Most of the 33 rooms have private bathrooms.
Hotel services *Safe.* **Room services** *Telephone.*

Hôtel Sansonnet

48 rue de la Verrerie, 75004 (48.87.96.14/fax 48.87.30.46). Métro Hôtel-de-Ville **Rates** *single* 240-360F; *double* 345-370F; *extra bed* 20F; *shower* 20F; *breakfast* 32F. **Credit** EC, JCB, MC, FTC, V.
In a historic Marais building, this small hotel is very centrally located. The interior boasts an early wrought-iron staircase, and the high ceilings of the lobby appear even higher thanks to the daring vertically-striped wall paper. The 25 immaculate rooms are less striking – most singles are without toilet or bathroom, but the doubles are all en suite. The couple who've managed the hotel for 25 years offer a seasoned, patient welcome.
Hotel services *Safe.* **Room services** *Double glazing. Hairdryer. Telephone. TV (Satellite).*

Hôtel de Turenne

20 avenue de Tourville, 75007 (47.05.99.92/fax 45.56.06.04). Métro Ecole-Militaire. **Rates** *single* 300F; *double* 360-410F; *triple* 500F; *extra bed* 60F; *breakfast* 35F. **Credit** AmEx, DC, EC, MC, F£$TC, V.
Inexpensive rooms are thin on the ground in this well-heeled neighbourhood. However, the Turenne, down the street from Napoleon's tomb, manages to keep up appearances at very reasonable rates. All 43 rooms are clean and comfortable, with private bathrooms.
Hotel services *Laundry service. Lift. Safe.* **Room services** *Double glazing. Hairdryer. Telephone. TV (Satellite).*

Prima Lepic

29 rue Lepic, 75018 (46.06.44.64/fax 46.06.66.11). Métro Abbesses or Blanche. **Rates** *single* 350F; *double* 380-400F; *triple* 450-500F;*breakfast* 40F. **Credit** MC, FTC, V.
A five-minute walk from Sacré-Coeur, on a winding street, lined with good food shops, that leads up to the top of the Butte Montmartre, the Prima Lepic is bohemian Montmartre *par excellence.* There are potted plants and flowers in the foyers and florid wallpaper in the 38 rooms, all of which have en suite bathrooms, phones and TV.
Hotel services *Lift. Safe.* **Room services** *Double glazing. Hairdryer. Telephone. TV.*

Résidence du Pré

15 rue Pierre-Sémard, 75009 (48.78.26.72/fax 42.80.64.83). Métro Cadet. **Rates** *single* 390F; *double* 450-475F; *triple* 600F; *extra bed* 100F; *breakfast* 50F. **Credit** AmEx, DC, EC, JCB, MC, F£$TC, V.
On a street of nineteenth-century buildings festooned with ornate wrought iron balconies, the recently renovated, 40-room Résidence du Pré is the least expensive of three Hôtels des Pré, and benefits from the group's efficient management. The interior is modern, clean and with a tasteful but innocuous décor done in ochre tones. It's not far from the Gare du Nord and has good access to the RER.
Hotel services *Bar. Lift. No smoking rooms. Safe.* **Room services** *Double glazing. Hairdryer. Telephone. TV.*

Budget

Confort Hotel

*3 et 5 rue de Trévise, 75009 (42.46.12.06/fax
48.01.09.82). Métro Montmartre.* **Rates** *single* 255-295F;
double 270-415F; *triple* 510F; *breakfast* 26F. **Credit**
AmEx, JCB, MC, FTC, V.
Well located for the rue Montmartre club scene, the 45-room
Confort is a bit different from the other hotels nearby.
Beyond the lobby with its plastic plants are white stuccoed
halls lit by electric candle wall sconces, stained wood doors
and large rooms with painted brass beds, thick tasselled curtains and big bathrooms. It's popular with groups.
Hotel services *Lift. Safe.* **Room services** *Double
glazing. Telephone. TV.*

Grand Hôtel Lévêque

*29 rue Cler, 75007 (47.05.49.15/fax 45.50.49.36). Métro
Ecole-Militaire.* **Rates** *single* 195F; *double* 225-360F; *triple*
425F; *shower* free; *breakfast* 25F. **Credit** MC, FTC, V.
If you want to mix with the locals, a stay at the Lévêque is
a good bet. It's located on a popular pedestrian market street
in a residential part of town near the Eiffel Tower, a short
walk from the Musée d'Orsay. The halls could use a fresh
lick of paint and the 50 rooms are simple, but many have
been nicely redone in the last few years, and most have
private bathrooms.
Hotel services *Safe.* **Room services** *Double glazing.
Telephone.*

Hôtel des Académies

*15 rue de la Grande-Chaumière, 75006 (43.26.66.44).
Métro Vavin.* **Rates** *single* 180F; *double* 245-295F;
breakfast 28F. **Credit** EC, FTC.
Near the cafés, brasseries and cinemas of the boulevard
Montparnasse and a short walk from the Luxembourg gardens, the no-frills family-run Hôtel des Académies may look
a bit worn nowadays, but its 21 rooms are clean and the rates
are attractively low.
Room services *Double glazing.*

Hôtel Castex

*5 rue Castex, 75004 (42.72.31.52/fax 42.72.57.91).
Métro Bastille.* **Rates** *single* 215-265F; *double* 280-340F;
triple 440F; *breakfast* 25F. **Credit** EC, MC, FTC, V.
Young, enthusiastic Blaise Bouchand will bend over backwards for his guests, in a hotel which has been in his family for four generations. The rooms are regularly spruced up
and larger than average for this price range, so that even the
singles give you enough space to walk around an open suitcase. All 27 rooms have a shower or bath, and most have
their own toilet. It's also central, between the Bastille and the
Ile St-Louis.
Hotel services *Safe. TV.* **Room services** *Telephone.*

Hôtel de la Herse d'Or

20 rue St-Antoine, 75004 (43.54.62.41). Métro Bastille.
Rates *single or double* 150-250F; *shower* 10F; *breakfast*
25F. **No credit cards.**
The stone corridor leading to the reception is infinitely
grander than the rest of the hotel, but the 35 rooms are perfectly clean and acceptable for the price. Choose between
light but noisy rooms at the front, or quiet but dark ones at
the back. On a busy street near the Bastille, with excellent
food shops.

Hôtel de Lille

*8 rue du Pélican, 75001 (42.33.33.42). Métro Palais-
Royal-Louvre.* **Rates** *single* 180F; *double* 210-260F;
shower 30F. **Credit** EC, FTC.
With the Louvre just a minute away, this hotel makes up in
convenience what it may lack in comfort. The 13 rooms share
toilet facilities, but all have sinks, and the six most expensive rooms have showers. Extremely basic but very clean.

Hôtel de Nesle

*7 rue de Nesle, 75006 (43.54.62.41). Métro St-Michel or
Odéon.* **Rates** *single* 160F; *double* 210-300F; *shower* 25F;
breakfast 25F. **No credit cards.**
Mme Renée charms young backpackers at her basic but
relaxed 20-room hotel, in a central location. Each room is decorated with kitsch, naive paintings based on historical
themes. If your French is up to it, ask about the Nesle (pronounced 'nell') and she'll entertain you with tales and photos from back when the place looked (even) more like an
opium den. She doesn't take reservations, so be sure to arrive
early and don't be surprised if she suggests loners share a
room. There is also a large garden at the back complete with
two feisty ducks, Donald and MacDonald.

Hôtel Pratic

9 rue d'Ormesson, 75004 (48.87.80.87). Métro St-Paul.
Rates *single* 150F; *double* 230-340F; *shower* free;
breakfast 25F. **Credit** EC, FTC.
Off the restaurant-lined Place du Marché Ste-Cathérine, this
hotel is simple but friendly and impeccably clean. A recent
renovation has created a breakfast room, freshened up the
halls and added new if mismatched touches to the rooms,
but left the remarkable egg-shaped loo between the first and
second floors intact. All 23 rooms are equipped with sinks.
Those at the front are more expensive with private toilet,
bath and a view of the lively square.
Room services *Double glazing. Telephone.*

Hôtel Résidence Orsay

*93 rue de Lille, 75007 (47.05.05.27/fax 47.05.29.48).
Métro Solférino.* **Rates** *single or double* 290-450F;
breakfast 30F. **Credit** EC, MC, F£$TC, V.
It's only coincidence that this 32-room place, around the corner from the Socialist Party headquarters, looks like a French
version of Soviet planning. But it's a cheap sleep in a pricey
neighbourhood, a stone's throw from the Musée d'Orsay. The
friendly but quirky staff give the place a Jim Jarmusch touch.
Hotel services *Lift. Safe.* **Room services** *Telephone.
TV.*

Hôtel Saint-Michel

*17 rue Gît-le-Coeur, 75006 (43.26.98.70). Métro St-
Michel.* **Rates** *single or double* 180-320F; *triple* 400-445F;
shower 12F; *breakfast* 25F. **Credit** FTC.
On a rare quiet street off the perpetually agitated heart of
boulevard St-Michel, this modest 25-room hotel offers excellent value, especially for two willing to share a double bed
and not much else. The higher-priced rooms come with twin
beds and private bathrooms. Handy for the lively rue St-
André-des-Arts and Left Bank night life.
Hotel services *Safe.* **Room services** *Double glazing.
Telephone.*

Hôtel Tolbiac

*122 rue de Tolbiac, 75013 (44.24.25.54/fax
45.85.43.47). Métro Tolbiac.* **Rates** *single* 110-145F;
double 150-190F; *shower* free; *breakfast* 15, 25F. **Credit**
EC, F£$TC.
In the heart of Chinatown, the seven-storey Tolbiac may not
be the most convenient but is certainly the least expensive,
and among the nicest, of the budget hotels. Renovated at the
beginning of 1995, the 47 bright rooms have hardwood
floors, mercifully plain walls and cheery bedspreads. All are
perfectly clean and have sinks, while many also offer a
shower and TV. The corridors serve as an art gallery for the
owner's three, thankfully talented, young daughters.
Room services *Double glazing. TV.*

Résidence Magenta

*35 rue Yves Toudic, 75010 (42.40.17.72/fax
42.02.59.66). Métro Jacques Bonsergent.* **Rates** *single*
285-325F; *double* 360-380F; *triple* 435F; *quad* 540F;
breakfast 35F. **Credit** AmEx, DC, MC, FTC, V.

Like some strange George Segal sculpture fantasy, plaster sheets drape the reception of this otherwise sane hotel on a quiet street near place de la République. Genial staff welcome young travellers who can double, triple or even quadruple up in large, spotless rooms. All 32 have bathrooms, and those on the ground floor are accessed directly from the courtyard, where breakfast is served in warmer months. **Hotel services** *Laundry service. Lift. Safe.* **Room services** *Telephone. TV (Satellite).*

Chain Hotels

Hôtel Ibis
15 rue Bréguet, 75011 (43.38.65.65/fax 43.38.09.33).
Métro Bréguet-Sabin. **Rates** *from 450F; breakfast 35F.*
Credit AmEx, EC, V.
This mid-price French chain has six massive establishments in Paris, as well as nine smaller hotels.
Hotel services *Bar. Car park. Conference services. Lift. Restaurant. Wheelchair access.* **Room services** *Telephone. TV (Cable).*
Branches include: 77 rue de Bercy, 75012 (43.42.91.91).

Novotel
8 place Marguerite de Navarre, 75001 (42.21.31.31/fax 40.26.05.79). Métro Châtelet-Les Halles. **Rates** *single 860F; double 915F; suite 1,200-1,500F.* **Credit** AmEx, V.
A major French chain, with three ultra-modern Paris hotels.
Hotel services *Air-conditioning. Conference services. Bar. Lifts. Restaurant. Wheelchair access.* **Room services** *Double glazing. Hairdryer. Minibar. Telephone. TV (Satellite)*
Branches: 2/8 rue Hector Malot, 75012 (44.67.60.00); 85 rue de Bercy, 75012 (43.42.30.00).

Quality Inn Paris Rive Gauche
92 rue de Vaugirard, 75006 (42.22.00.56/fax 42.22.05.39). Métro St-Placide. **Rates** *single 840F; double 920F; breakfast 68F.* **Credit** AmEx, DC, EC, JCB, MC, V.
Another dependable chain, with good facilities.
Hotel services *Air-conditioning. Car park. Conference services. Lift. Piano bar. Wheelchair access.* **Room Services** *Hairdryer. Minibar. Safe. TV (Satellite).*

Timhotel
Central reservations 44.15.81.15/fax 40.20.96.98. **Rates** *single 345-440F; double 430-540F; triple 560-680F; breakfast 49F.* **Credit** AmEx, EC, MC, V.
A bit different from the hotel chain norm, Timhotels are usually quite small, individually decorated and well located. There are fourteen around Paris: phone the central number for details. All offer amenities superior to those available at most similarly-priced Paris hotels.
Hotel services *Conference services. Wheelchair access.* **Room services** *Radio. Telephone. TV (Cable). Video.*

Bed & Breakfast

Café Couette et Châteaux
8 rue d'Isly, 75008 (42.94.92.00/fax 42.94.93.12). Métro Gare St-Lazare or Havre-Caumartin. **Rates** *(including breakfast, 2 night minimum) single 220-370F per night; double 280-520F per night.* **Open** 10am-6pm Mon-Sat.
Credit AmEx, MC, V, Money orders.
B&B is not a likely option in this hotel-packed capital, as Parisians tend to be a little reserved about inviting strangers into their home. Nonetheless, Café Couette has 80 participating hosts in Paris (and 420 more throughout France), with varying levels of privacy and luxury as indicated by their coffee-pot rating system. B&B's with three or four cafetières have private bath and toilet, those with two involve sharing. Reservations must be made at least 24 hours in advance.

Short-term Rentals
Residence Hotels

Studios and one- or two-bedroom flats with kitchenettes, generally let by the week. Towels, sheets and kitchenware are provided, and there is maid service once a week or every three days. A refundable deposit (1,000F-3,500F) is payable on arrival.

Le Claridge
74 avenue des Champs-Elysées, 75008 (44.13.33.00/fax 42.25.04.88). Métro Franklin D Roosevelt. **Rates** *studios from 1,080F per night; two-bed flats 1,700F; three-bed flats 2,700F.* **Credit** AmEx, DC, JCB, MC, FTC, V.
Two hundred clean-cut, rather standard apartments above the Claridge mall, in what was once one of the grandest mansions on the Champs-Elysées. Discounts for longer stays.
Hotel services *Air-conditioning. Conference services. Fax. Minitel. Laundry. Lift.* **Room service** *Room service (breakfast only). Safe. Telephone. TV (Satellite).*

Hall'Studios Résidence Hôtel
4 rue des Halles, 75001 (44.76.81.23/fax 44.76.81.22). Métro Châtelet-Les Halles. **Rates** *studios: 1-2 persons 550-680F per night; 3-5 persons 1,090F.*
Credit AmEx, DC, MC, V.
Eleven rooms for rent by the day, week or month. Lower rates for stays of one week or longer.
Hotel services *Conference services. Fax. Laundry . Lift. Minitel.* **Room services** *Room service (24-hour). Minibar. Safe. Telephone. TV (Cable).*

Home Plazza
74 rue Amelot, 75011 (40.21.20.00/fax 47.00.82.40). Métro St Sébastien Froissart. **Rates** *studios 1-2 persons 880F per night; 3 persons 1,180F; 4 persons 1,480F; 5 persons 1,780F.* **Credit** AmEx, DC, EC, MC, F$£TC, V.
Rooms are available by the day, week or month in this 289-unit residence, opened in 1989. Standard rooms are bright and attractive; the suites are more suited to the business traveller. Discounts for longer-stay residents.
Hotel services *Bar. Babysitting. Business services. Conference services. Health spa. Garden. Restaurant.* **Room services** *Hairdryer. Telephone. TV (Satellite).*

Pierre et Vacances Montmartre
10 place Charles Dullin, 75018 (42.57.14.55/ fax 42.54.48.87). Métro Anvers. **Rates** *studios 490-600F; 3-room flats 1,050F-1,250F.* **Credit** AmEx, DC, EC, MC, FTC, V.
A 76-unit residence, close to Sacré-Coeur, with apartments that sleep from one to six people. Discounts for longer stays.
Room services *TV (Cable).*
Branch: Pierre et Vacances Porte de Versailles
20 rue Oradour-sur-Glane, 75015 (45.54.97.43/fax 45.57.28.42). 188 units.

First Résidences International – Résidence Kennedy
100 avenue du Président Kennedy, 75016 (45.25.95.01/fax 42.88.29.91). Métro Passy. **Rates** *studio 1,000F per night; 2-bedroom flat 2,000-3,000F.* **Credit** DC, EC, MC, F£$TC, V.
Forty apartments, near the Trocadéro. Long-stay discounts.
Hotel services *Business services. Car park. Fitness centre. Hairdresser. Pool.* **Room services** *TV (Cable).*
Branch: Résidence Kennedy 2 79 quai André Citroën, 75015 (40.60.70.15/fax 42.88.29.91). 27 units.

Not the average youth hostel, the **MIJE Maubuisson.** *See page 30.*

Rental Agencies

Several agencies specialise in short-term rentals of furnished flats for foreign temporary residents.

Allô Logement Temporaire

64 rue du Temple, 75003 (42.72.00.06/fax 42.72.03.11).
Métro Rambuteau. **Open** noon-8pm Mon-Fri.
A non-profitmaking organisation which helps families, students and business people find furnished apartments. Annual membership is 300F, although other fees may apply as well. Phone for details.

Apalachee Bay

56 rue Galilée, 75008 (40.21.39.67/fax 48.07.14.34).
Métro George V. **Open** 9am-7pm Mon-Fri; 10am-4pm Sat. **Credit** AmEx, DC, EC, MC, V.
Run by two young Englishmen, this agency has flats available for long- or short-term rental. Lists and photos of flats can also be provided via the Internet. Phone for details.

De Circourt Associates

170 rue de Grenelle, 75007 (47.53.86.38/fax 45.51.75.77). *Métro Latour-Maubourg.* **Open** 9.30am-7pm Mon-Fri. **Credit** MC, FTC, V.
A professional organisation catering to corporate clients as well as individuals, with over 5,000 furnished long- and short-term flats at various price levels. Clients are billed only after accommodation has been secured.

Paris Appartements Services

8 boulevard Poissonnière, 75009 (48.24.19.98/fax 48.01.04.70). *Métro Bonne-Nouvelle.* **Open** *by appointment only* 9am-6pm Mon-Fri. **Credit** AmEx, EC, MC, F£$TC, V.
Thirty furnished (IKEA-style) studios and flats in the 1st to the 4th *arrondissements.* Studios from 3,150F per week, one-room flats from 4,550F per week, with maid service.

RothRay

10 rue Nicolas-Flamel, 75004 (48.87.13.37/fax 40.26.34.33). *Métro Châtelet Les Halles.* **Open** 8am-6pm Mon-Fri; 8am-1pm Sat. **Credit** EC, F£$TC.
Fully-furnished apartments for lease by the week or longer. All are centrally located – in the Marais, Châtelet or Ile St-Louis. Studios from 9,000F per month.

Youth Accommodation

Paris has a range of hostels for youth and students, usually with shared accommodation. The **AJF** youth information centre (*see chapter* **Students**) has a booking service for youth hostels and other budget accommodation for travellers aged 18-30, at all of its branches. There is a 10F fee. They're always busy, so turn up rather than phone.

Association des Etudiants Protestants de Paris

46 rue de Vaugirard, 75006 (46.33.23.30/fax 46.34.27.09). *Métro Mabillon or St-Sulpice.* **Open** *office* 8.45am-noon, 5-7pm, Mon-Fri; 8.45am-noon, 6-8pm, Sat; 10am-noon Sun. *hostel* 24 hours daily. **Rates** (incl breakfast) *Jan-15 Sept* 75F; *16 Sept-Dec* 68F per person per night. **No credit cards.**
In a good location just by the Luxembourg, the AEPP offers accommodation mainly in dormitories for 18-26s. No reservations are accepted, and membership is 10F, payable upon arrival plus a 100F deposit. There are also some singles and doubles, at a slightly higher fee. The maximum stay is five weeks, and there are cooking facilities and a café.

Auberges de Jeunesse

Le D'Artagnan *80 rue Vitruve, 75020 (40.32.34.56/fax 40.32.34.55). Métro Porte de Bagnolet.* **Open** *office* 8am-1am, *hostel* 24 hours, daily.
Rates (incl breakfast) *dormitory* 109F; *double* 256F. **Credit** MC, FTC, V.
The four official youth hostels in and around Paris are part of the International Youth Hostel Federation booking network, which allows members of affiliated organisations in other countries to book from home (up to six consecutive nights) and pay in advance in their local currency. For details contact your local IYHF association. The Jules Ferry, near place de la République, is the only one with a location that is fairly central.
Branches: Jules Ferry 8 boulevard Jules Ferry, 75011 (43.57.55.60/fax 40.21.79.92); **Cité des Sciences** 24 rue des Sept-Arpents, 93310 Le Pré St-Gervais (48.43.24.11/fax 48.43.26.82); **Léo Lagrange** 107 rue Martre, 92100 Clichy (42.70.03.22/fax 42.70.52.63).

BVJ

Les Halles *5 rue du Pélican, 75001 (40.26.92.45/42.33.40.53). Métro Louvre.* **Open** *Mar-Sept only* 6am-2am daily. **Credit** FTC.
All the BVJ hostels offer single or shared rooms (for up to eight people) for 120F per night, including breakfast. Some branches may be open all year round, but it's advisable to check in advance.
Branches: Quartier Latin 44 rue des Bernardins, 75005 (43.29.34.80); **Opéra** 11 rue Thérèse, 75001 (42.60.77.23); **Paris/Louvre** 20 rue J-J Rousseau, 75001 (42.36.88.18/40.26.66.43/42.33.82.10).

MIJE

Maubuisson *2 rue des Barres, 75004 (42.72.72.09). Métro Hôtel de Ville.* **Open** *reservations* 7am-9pm daily; *hostels* 6am-1am daily. **Rates** (incl breakfast) 118F per person per night. **No credit cards.**
Three pretty converted historic mansions in the Marais, with friendly management, that are probably the best hostels in Paris. Their rooms sleep from three to eight people, and all have a shower and washbasin. There's a dining hall at Le Fourcy, open to guests at all three MIJE hostels. They are understandably popular, so book ahead.
Branches: Le Fauconnier 11 rue du Fauconnier, 75004 (42.74.23.45); **Le Fourcy** 6 rue de Fourcy, 75004 (42.74.23.45).

Résidence Bastille

151 avenue Ledru-Rollin, 75011 (43.79.53.86/fax 43.79.35.63). Métro Ledru-Rollin/Voltaire. **Open** 7am-12.30pm, 2pm-1am, daily. **Rates** (incl breakfast) 115F per person per night. **Credit** FTC.
This hostel has 167 beds to dormitory-style rooms, for people aged from 18 to 35.

Camping

Camping du Bois de Boulogne/Ile de France

allée du Bord de l'Eau, Bois de Boulogne, 75016 (45.24.30.00). Métro Porte Maillot (free shuttle-bus to campsite during summer) or bus 43. **Open** 24 hours daily. **No credit cards.**
The only major campsite in the Paris area, on the western side of the Bois de Boulogne, operates a no-reservations policy: there is no demand in the winter, and huge queues every day in summer. A one- to two-person plot with electricity and water for either a tent or caravan costs 112F per night, or 81F per night for a pitch without electricity. Add 22F for each additional person regardless of type of accommodation. Reservations are sometimes accepted for large groups.

Paris by Season

Manic fireworks, Baroque fountains and music fests – the events that mark out the calendar in Paris.

Paris has something to offer in every season. The overcast months from late autumn to early spring are when major art retrospectives are launched, and the best musicians come through town. As soon as the sun breaks out, café tables appear in city squares, and strollers crowd the streets of the Latin Quarter and the Marais. May to September is the time to celebrate the external beauty of the city: its gardens, parks, squares and riverside *quais*, and its distinctive neighbourhoods.

For additional dance, film and sporting events, *see chapters* **Dance**, **Film** *and* **Sport & Fitness**.

Information

Office de Tourisme de Paris

127 avenue des Champs-Elysees, 75008 (49.52.53.54/English language information line 49.52.53.56/fax 49.52.53.00)0. Metro Charles de Gaulle-Etoile. **Open** *information & ticket office* 9am-8pm, *hotel reservations & bureau de change* 9am-7.30pm, daily. Closed 1 Jan, 1 May, 25 Dec.

The tourist office publishes a free multi-lingual monthly guide to events in Paris, *Paris Sélection*, and also has many leaflets and brochures on concerts and other events. The not-overly helpful staff should also have additional information on the events below closer to the date. The shop also sells the *Calendrier des Foires et Salons* (120F), which lists all of the major trade fairs in Paris each year. For a list of tourist office branches, *see chapter* **Essential Information**.

Spring

Spring weather in Paris is notoriously unreliable, yet there are certain things you can depend on. The streets will be full of Travellers selling bright bunches of jonquils at the end of March, lilacs in April and *muguet* (lily of the valley, the traditional harbinger of spring) on 1 May. Hotels and restaurants will be packed during the *prêt-à-porter* collections in March, and, as the song promises, April in Paris sees the chestnuts in blossom.

Salon de l'Agriculture

Parc des Expositions de Paris, Porte de Versailles, 75015 (49.09.60.00). Métro Porte de Versailles. **Dates** last week Feb, first week Mar. **Open** 9am-7pm. **Admission** 50F.

Rural France comes to town to create the largest farm in the world. Farmers inspect perfectly-groomed animals and sub-sidy-hungry machinery, then repair to the food and drink hall to sample regional produce. If there's any kind of election on the horizon politicians will be out in force there too.

Salon de Mars

Espace Eiffel Branly, 29-55 quai Branly, 75007. Métro Bir-Hakeim/RER Champs de Mars-Tour Eiffel. **Dates** late Mar. **Admission** 50F. **Information** Medi-Art (44.94.86.80).

An international antiques fair currently held in a large temporary exhibition space near the Eiffel Tower. Antiques and seventeenth-, eighteenth- and nineteenth-century paintings predominate, but you can also find quality examples of tribal and contemporary art.

Foire du Trône

Pélouse de Reuilly, Bois de Vincennes, 75012. (46.27.52.29). Metro Porte Dorée. **Dates** end Mar-end May. **Open** 2pm-midnight Mon-Thur, Sun; 2pm-1am Fri, Sat, eve of public holidays. **Admission** free; rides 10F-35F.

Noisy, smelly, colourful, and the largest funfair in France, with a huge Ferris wheel, roller coasters, chocolate waffles, candy floss (cotton candy) and other sickly treats.

La Passion à Ménilmontant

Théâtre de Ménilmontant, 15 rue du Retrait, 75020 (46.36.98.60). Métro Gambetta. **Dates** Mar-Apr. **Admission** 40F-80F.

This Easter-time Passion Play has been acted by a mixture of local residents and professional actors since 1932.

Le Chemin de la Croix

square Willette, 75018. Métro Anvers, Abbesses. **Information** *(44.92.70.21).* **Date** 12.30pm Good Friday.

A large crowd follows the Archbishop of Paris, Cardinal Lustiger, from the bottom of the hill of Montmartre at the square Willette up the steps to the Sacré Coeur, as he performs the 14 traditional stations of the cross.

Banlieues Bleues

Seine St-Denis and area. **Information** (43.85.66.00). **Dates** end Mar-early Apr. **Admission** 70F-150F.

Held in the more down-at-heel Paris suburbs, mainly to the north, this two-week festival draws some of the greatest names in jazz, blues, r'n'b, soul and funk. Venues are not always easy to get to, but shows are cheaper than you'd find in Paris. Regulars include BB King and Ornette Coleman.

April Fool's Day

All over France. **Date** 1 Apr.

Known to the French as *Poisson d'Avril*, the fish of April. The big idea is to try to stick a paper fish to some unsuspecting sucker's back. French journalists also pride themselves on putting April Fool's tricks over on the public.

Paris Marathon

Starts around 9am avenue des Champs-Elysées, first runners finish about 11am avenue Foch. **Information** *AMSP, 17 rue de Sévigné, 75004 (53.17.03.10).* **Date** one Sun, mid-late Apr.

One of the world's biggest marathons, with a route that takes in some of the city's most famous sites. Huge crowds encourage the runners. *See also chapter* **Sport & Fitness**.

Foire de Paris

Parc des Expositions de Paris, Porte de Versailles, 75015.
Métro Porte de Versailles. **Information** *(49.09.60.00).*
Dates end Apr-early May. **Admission** about 40F.
A giant fair that's traditionally a bargain hunter's delight,
with a solid emphasis on food and wine. Anyone interested
in shipping home cases of wine and gourmet delicacies can
get a good deal if they're prepared to buy in bulk.

May Day

All over France. **Date** 1 May.
The French Communist Party isn't what it used to be, but
this is still the one day each year when rubbish isn't collected in Paris. All museums and monuments, except for the
Eiffel Tower, are closed too. The unions and various leftist
groups stage a colourful, friendly march through working-
class eastern Paris. The Bastille is a popular place to watch.

La Mairie de Paris
Vous Invite au Théâtre

Theatres all over Paris. **Information** *(42.78.44.72).*
Dates three days at end Apr-early May.
A theatrical treat laid on by the City Hall. The subtitle of the
event is *Prenez une Place, Venez à Deux*: anyone buying a
theatre ticket receives another one free. A good opportunity
to brush up your French or catch a visiting foreign troupe.

TBB Jazz Festival

Théâtre de Boulogne-Billancourt, 60 rue de la Belle-
Feuille, 92 Boulogne Billancourt (46.03.60.44).
Métro Marcel Sembat. **Dates** early-mid May.
Tickets 110F-160F.
Started in 1984, a laid-back jazz festival in a garden suburb
of Paris with a knack for harmoniously mixing seemingly
unusual acts. Past stars have included Henry Threadgill and
the Giuffre-Bley-Swallow Trio.

Festival Exit

Maison des Arts et de la Culture de Créteil, place
Salvador Allende, 94000 Créteil (45.13.19.19). Métro
Créteil-Préfecture. **Dates** early May.
A festival of avant-garde dance, theatre and performance
held in the cultural centre in the suburb of Créteil (*see chapter* **Dance**). Launched in 1994, the event has made an immediate impact with its radical multi-national programming.

Vintage Car Rally, Montmartre

Departure 10am rue Lepic. arrive place du Tertre,
75018. Métro Abbesses or Anvers. **Information**
(46.06.79.56). **Date** Sun closest to 15 May.
Begun in 1924, when cars weren't even that old, this is one
of the oldest annual vintage car races in the world. Crowds
line the streets to cheer beautiful old vehicles which labour
– or sometimes zoom – up the steep streets of Montmartre.

Marching on **May Day.**

Les Cinq Jours Extraordinaires

rues du Bac, de Lille, de Beaune, des Sts-Pères, de
l'Universite and quai Voltaire, 75007. Metro Rue du Bac
or St-Germain-des-Prés. **Information** *(42.61.31.45).*
Dates third week of May. **Admission** free.
The antique dealers clustered in the chic *Carré Rive Gauche*
quadrangle on the Left Bank each showcase one extraordinary item, all chosen around a theme, such as 'the five continents'. Participating shops are all decorated with flowers,
and red carpets down the pavements mark out the relevant
streets. There are also special evening and Sunday openings.

D'Anvers aux Abbesses

Information *Syndicat d'Initiative du Vieux Montmartre,*
21 place du Tertre, 75018 (42.52.79.78). Métro Abbesses
or Anvers. **Dates** third weekend in May. **Admission** free.
Artists in historic Montmartre open their studios to the public for three days. A nice way to investigate some of the more
out-of-the-way sidestreets of the 'village' and to meet, and
maybe collect, some of the artists who live and work there.

Summer

Orson Welles once said that 'in August invaders
could take Paris by telephone.. if they could find
someone to answer it'. In early summer the city is
still bustling, but late July and August is the quiet-
est time to be in the city. Parisians who remain
behind swear this is the best time to be here.

Grandes Eaux Musicales
& Grandes Fêtes de Nuit de Versailles

Parc du Château de Versailles. RER line C to Versailles
Rive Gauche. **Information** *(39.50.36.22).*
Grandes Eaux Musicales *Performances* 11.15-
11.35am, 3.30-5pm, every Sunday mid May-early Oct,
also 25 May, 15 Aug. **Admission** 21F, free under-10s.
Grandes Fêtes *Performances* 10.30pm, two Saturdays
in July; 10pm, two Saturdays in Sept. **Admission** 70F-185F.
In the *Grandes Eaux Musicales* the magnificent gardens of
Versailles come alive as the fountains built in 1663-1685 for
Louis XIV glide into action to the strains of Baroque music.
Still more unforgettable are the *Grandes Fêtes*, a combination of *son et lumière*, fireworks and masque in the style of
the Sun King, presented just four times a year. For further
details on Versailles, *see chapter* **Trips Out of Town.**

French Tennis Open

Stade Roland Garros, 2 avenue Gordon Bennett, 75016
(47.43.48.00). Métro Porte d'Auteuil. **Dates** last week in
May-first week in June.
The international tennis circus descends on Paris in what is
also one of the glitziest events on the social calendar. For full
details, *see chapter* **Sport & Fitness.**

Fireworks at La Villette

Parc de la Villette, 75019. Métro Porte de la Villette or
Porte de Pantin. **Information** *(40.03.75.03).*
Dates mid June. **Admission** free.
An impressive fireworks display on the banks of the Canal
de l'Ourcq, which runs through the park. Each year a leading designer or architect designs the display, working with
a team of pyrotechnic wizards.

Festival Chopin à Paris

Orangerie de Bagatelle, parc de Bagatelle, Bois de
Boulogne, 75016. Métro Porte Maillot, then bus 244.
Information *(45.00.22.19).* **Dates** mid June-mid July,
8.45pm Mon-Fri; 4.30pm, 8.45pm Sat, Sun.
Admission 100F-150F plus 10F entry to park.
An annual treat for piano lovers, staged in the Orangerie of
the Bagatelle gardens. Evening concerts are candlelit.

Fête de la Musique

All over Paris. **Information** *(40.03.94.70).* **Date** 21 June.
On the longest day of the year, thousands of musicians, professional and amateur, perform all over the city. Most events are free. Traditionally there is a big name free rock concert at place de la République, newer indie rock bands at place Denfert-Rochereau and a top-class classical orchestra in the courtyard of the Palais-Royal. Smaller events include traditional dancing in the place Catherine in the Marais and a gay riverside disco at the Quai de Montebello, while every *arrondissement* has a live band outside its town hall, and lots of more anarchic gigs are put on in local cafés or bars.

Gay Pride March

Information *(47.70.01.50).* **Date** Sat in June.
The annual parade by gays and lesbians (not always on the same date) has normally gone from République via the Marais to Beaubourg, but in future may begin in Montparnasse. *See also chapter* **Gay & Lesbian Paris**.

Feux de la Saint-Jean

Quai St-Bernard, 75005. Métro Gare d'Austerlitz. **Date** 24 June, 11pm.
Once celebrated atop Montmartre, this fireworks display for the feast of Saint John the Baptist now takes place along the banks of the Seine, casting fierce shadows across the river.

La Course des Garçons de Café

Starts and finishes Hôtel de Ville, place de l'Hôtel de Ville, 75004. Métro Hôtel de Ville. **Information** *(46.33.89.89).* **Date** a Sunday in late June-early July.
Over 500 café waiters and waitresses – in uniform, complete with bow-ties, aprons and high-heel shoes – race around the city holding trays laden with a small bottle and glasses. Any breakage during the 8km (5 mile) race disqualifies the participant. If you've ever waited hours to be served, you may be surprised to see just how fast a *garçon* can move.

Fête du Cinéma

All over Paris. **Dates** 3 days, beginning last Sun in June.
To try to get Parisians out of the sunshine and into the flickering darkness of a cinema, movie-goers get a passport which allows them to see as many films as they like for 10F each time, after paying normal entry for the first film.

New Morning All-Stars Festival

7-9 rue des Petites Ecuries, 75010 (45.23.51.41/bookings 42.31.31.31). Métro Château d'Eau.
Dates all July, 8.30pm. **Admission** 110F-130F.
The famed Paris club New Morning (*see chapter* **Music: Rock, Roots & Jazz**) hosts a month-long festival of jazz, blues, funk and salsa, featuring top of the line talent such as Betty Carter, Ray Barretto and the Brecker Brothers.

La Goutte d'Or en Fête

9 rue St-Bruno, 75018. Metro Barbès-Rochechouart. **Information** *(42.62.11.13).*
Dates usually first week of July. **Admission** free.
This music festival was initiated to restore pride to the poor, largely Arab and African Goutte d'Or district (*see chapter* **Paris by Area: The Right Bank**), and has been so successful that external promoters have begun to move in on it. *Rai*, rap and reggae, with young local performers playing alongside established names on the world music scene.

Halle that Jazz

Grande Halle de la Villette, 211 avenue Jean-Jaurès, 75019 (40.03.75.75). Metro Porte de Pantin.
Dates end June-early July. **Admission** 160F; 120F unemployed, students.
A ten-day jazz feast held in Paris' former abattoirs in La Villette. Names such as Joe Henderson, Wynton Marsalis and Herbie Hancock perform in the main hall, while other gigs go down in several smaller venues inside the complex.

Bastille Day (Le Quatorze Juillet)

All over France. **Information** *(49.52.53.54).* **Dates** 13 July (evening), all day 14 July.
Parisians dance in the streets on the eve of France's *fête nationale*. Celebrations start on the evening of 13 July. The scene at the Bastille once again resembles a war zone, as revellers fire skyrockets and toss bangers at each other with indiscriminate abandon. Similar fun goes on in other parts of the city, particularly the Trocadéro-Champ-de-Mars area. Less dangerous partying takes place at the firemen's balls organised in local *casernes de pompiers*, where the dancing usually goes on until dawn. The fire stations of rue de Sévigné near the Bastille, rue du Vieux-Colombier near St-Sulpice, rue Blanche near Pigalle and boulevard de Port-Royal near the Luxembourg are renowned for throwing a mean *bal*. The Communist Party also hosts an evening bash, usually on Ile St-Louis.
At 10am on the 14th crowds line the Champs-Elysees to watch the President, surrounded by the horses of the *Garde Républicaine*, lead a military parade. A variety of clattering tanks and other military machinery tear up the asphalt, although perhaps the biggest round of applause is reserved for the sleepless firemen bringing up the rear. Overhead jets tear across the sky, pluming red, white and blue smoke. Unless you arrive hours ahead of the parade, bring a footstool or light step ladder, or you'll see nothing except the backs of crowds eight-deep. In the evening there's a slightly portentous *son et lumière* show at Trocadéro, rescued by spectacular and inventive fireworks. Thousands gather at the Champs de Mar for the best view.

Paris, Quartier d'Eté

Various venues around Paris. **Information** *L'Eté Parisien, 43 rue de Rivoli, 75001 (40.28.40.33).* **Dates** 14 July-15 Aug. **Admission** to some events free.
A festival designed for those left in Paris after Bastille Day. Most venues are outdoors – the parvis of La Défense, the place de la Sorbonne, the Luxembourg – and there's a strong emphasis on music and dance. Major international companies take part, and one of the most popular events is *Le Bal Moderne*, an introduction to contemporary dance, with audience participation, held at the Théâtre National de Chaillot. Film features include Cinéma en Plein Air, an outdoor film season at La Villette, and the *Etrange* festival of bizarre films at the Passage du Nord-Ouest (*see chapter* **Film**).

Tour de France

Finishing point on the Champs-Elysées. **Information** *(49.35.69.00).* **Date** third or fourth Sun in July.
As much a fixture of French life as the *képi* and the *quatorze juillet*, the cyclists enter Paris by different routes each year, but the race always finishes on the Champs-Elysées. A huge throng gathers to catch a glimpse of the winners. *See also chapter* **Sport & Fitness**.

Fete de l'Assomption

Notre Dame, place Notre Dame, 75004. (43.34.56.10). Metro Cité. **Date** 15 Aug. **Admission** free.
Banners are unfurled from the towers of Notre Dame to celebrate the Feast of the Assumption. You don't know what crowded is until you've tried to enter the cathedral and catch a glimpse of the religious ceremonies.

Autumn

The time when Parisians resume social obligations after the long summer break. The weather can still be glorious, yet shortening days and new arts seasons combine to send everyone back indoors. It's also the time of the great salons, such as the **FIAC** art fair and the autumn *prêt-à-porter* shows.

Fête de L'Humanité

Parc de la Courneuve, La Courneuve, 93000 Seine-St-Denis. RER line B to La Corneuve-Aubervilliers, then free festival bus. **Information** *(49.22.72.72).* **Dates** second weekend of Sept. **Admission** 40F; free under-12s.

The French Communist Party has been in steady decline ever since 1989, and so too has its newspaper *L'Humanité*, and so this vast three-day celebration of music, dance and street theatre combined with political rhetoric is not what it used to be. Gone are the Cold War-era posters, and gone too probably is Johnny Halliday as a regular attraction after his recent support for Chirac. International environmentally-sound groups like Midnight Oil have stepped into the breach to augment a mainly French line up.

Journées Portes Ouvertes

Various venues in Paris and the Ile-de-France. **Information** *(44.61.20.00).* **Date** weekend closest to 15 Sept.

It doesn't sound like much of an event to visit a government office or ministry, but when you take a look at the sumptuous palaces the French usually locate them in, you begin to understand the extraordinary popularity of this annual two days of 'Open Doors'. Thousands of Parisians patiently wait up to five hours for the right to enter the President's or Prime Minister's official quarters, driven by curiosity and the democratic need to step on their leaders' carpet. This is the only opportunity to see many churches, military establishments and private mansions normally off-limits to the public, and also famous monuments such as the **Arc de Triomphe** and the **Panthéon** are free. A list and map of all the buildings affected is available from tourist offices (*see above*).

Festival d'Automne

Various venues. **Information** *56 rue de Rivoli, 75001 (42.96.96.94).* **Dates** 15 Sept-31 Dec. **Admission** 100F-250F.

A cultural feast par excellence with world-class performers presenting innovative theatre, music and contemporary dance productions at such prestige venues as the Théâtre de la Ville, the Odéon-Théâtre de l'Europe and the big public theatres in the suburbs (*see chapter* **Theatre**). It regularly features leading international directors such as Bob Wilson, Peter Sellars, Peter Brook and Werner Herzog. Programmes are available by mail.

Salon d'Art Contemporain de Montrouge

Mairie de Montrouge, 43 rue Emile Boutroug, 92000 Montrouge (46.12.75.73). Métro Porte d'Orleans, then bus 68, 126 or 128. **Dates** Sept-Oct (perhaps May-June in 1996). **Admission** free.

Contemporary art exhibition for new artists held in a working-class suburb. Some 2,000 painters, sculptors and photographers submit work, but only a few end up on show.

Fêtes des Vendanges à Montmartre

All over Montmartre and in the Mairie of the 18th arrondissement, 1 place Jules-Joffrin, 75018. Métro Abbesses, Lamarck-Caulaincourt or Jules-Joffrin. **Information** *Syndicat d'Initiative, place du Tertre, 75018 (42.62.21.21).* **Date** first or second Sat in Oct.

A celebration of the grape harvest at the last remaining vineyard of the many that once covered the hill of Montmartre. Local residents dress in nineteenth-century clothes, bands parade and speeches are declaimed. The allegedly undrinkable wine (called Clos Montmartre) is auctioned off at exorbitant prices in the name of charity.

Prix de l'Arc de Triomphe

Hippodrome de Longchamp, Bois de Boulogne, 75016 (45.53.76.76). **Date** early Oct.

France's première horse race, when *le tout-Paris* take their best frocks and champagne coolers out for a canter. *See also chapter* **Sport & Fitness**.

FIAC (Foire Internationale d'Art Contemporain)

Espace Eiffel Branly, 29-55 quai Branly, 75007. Métro Bir-Hakeim/RER Champs de Mars-Tour Eiffel. **Dates** early Oct. **Admission** 50F.

Since it opened in 1975 FIAC has become one of the main events on the international contemporary art calendar. With over 150 galleries represented, around half of them foreign, it's a perfect opportunity to catch up on current trends in contemporary art. The inclusion of photography for the first time in 1994 has helped open up an increasingly staid event. Like several other major fairs it has moved to the temporary Espace Eiffel-Branly while repairs are carried out on the **Grand Palais**, to which it will probably return in future.

Le Génie de la Bastille

Artists' studios and galleries in the Bastille area. Métro Bastille. **Information** *20 rue St-Nicolas, 75012 (43.42.52.22).* **Dates** four days mid-Oct. **Admission** free.

During the 1970s and 1980s artists moved into many of the old furniture workshops of the Bastille district. Commercial development since the 1989 opening of the new Opera has put many of them under threat, and to draw attention to their plight local artists began to hold a collective open-house that has became a popular point on the cultural calendar. For four days in October, you can wander through over 100 studios, galleries and private homes, chatting with the artists, buying their work or checking out their record collections. Many studios are located in ancient and atmospheric courtyards.

Armistice Day

Arc de Triomphe, 75008. Métro Charles de Gaulle-Etoile. **Date** 11 Nov.

There is no military parade at the remembrance ceremony for the dead of both world wars. Wreaths are laid by the President and others at the Tomb of the Unknown Soldier under the Arc de Triomphe.

Beaujolais Nouveau

All over France. **Date** third Thur in Nov.

The first day of the arrival of each year's Beaujolais Nouveau is no longer the event it was a few years ago, but a dozen or so of the best-known wine bars still attract the crowds. The rowdiest scenes are outside Le Rubis on rue du Marché-St-Honoré (*see chapter* **Cafés & Bars**), where hundreds gather to assess the new vintage and trample broken glass.

Winter

In early December major avenues acquire their Christmas illuminations, street markets begin to glisten with festive lights and shellfish heaped on ice, and roast chestnuts perfume street corners. Christmas itself is a family affair, with a dinner on Christmas Eve that traditionally includes foie gras, goose or capon and a rich yule log (*bûche de Noël*) of chocolate, sponge and/or ice cream. Immediately afterwards begins the sales season, as Parisians storm the stores for discounts of up to 50 per cent.

La Crèche sur le Parvis

place de l'Hôtel de Ville, 75004 (42.76.40.40). Métro Hôtel de Ville. **Dates** early Dec-early Jan. **Admission** 30F.

Every year the City Hall of Paris invites a foreign city to install a large crèche with all the trimmings under a tent at the place de l'Hotel de Ville. If you like life-size Nativity scenes, this is your big chance. Proceeds go to charity.

Christmas Mass at Notre Dame

Notre Dame, place de Notre Dame, 75004 (42.34.56.10). Metro Cité. **Date** 24 Dec.

June means tennis fans converge on Roland Garros for the **French Open**. *See page 32.*

Christmas Eve is when the nominally Catholic French return to their religion, and in Paris the cathedral is packed. Candles flicker in the chill air, organ pipes rumble and a rare sense of solidarity is achieved. Arrive by 11pm to get a seat, and be prepared to walk home, as taxis will be very scarce.

New Year's Eve
Avenue des Champs-Elysées and all over Paris.
Date 31 Dec.
Mainly tourists and teenagers crowd the avenue des Champs-Elysées, the former dodging bangers and insistent demands for a kiss that come from the latter.

La Grande Parade de Montmartre
Departs place Pigalle, 75018, Métro Pigalle.
Arrives 3pm place Jules-Joffrin, Métro Jules Joffrin.
Information *SIVM, 21 place du Tertre, 75018 (42.62.21.21).* **Date** 1 Jan, 2pm.
With bands, floats, and marching girls from all over the world, this parade does its best to rouse Paris out of its post-New Year's Eve hangover.

Epiphany (Fête des Rois)
All over France. **Date** 6 Jan.
On the Feast of the Three Kings pâtisseries sell thousands of *galettes des rois*, a pastry cake with an almond filling in which a tiny charm is hidden. Whoever finds the charm dons a cardboard crown (sold with each *galette*), becomes king or queen for a day, and chooses a consort.

La Mairie de Paris
Vous Invite au Concert
Concert halls and jazz clubs around Paris.
Information *(42.78.44.72.).* **Dates** mid-Jan.

Like the mid-May theatre event (*see above* **Spring**), this two-week promotion by the City Hall runs on the *Prenez une Place, Venez à Deux* principle: for every concert ticket bought, you get a second one free. Needless to say, it's extremely popular. Most of Paris' classical and jazz venues participate.

Commemorative Mass for Louis XVI
Chapelle Expiatoire, 29 rue Pasquier, 75008 (42.65.35.80). Métro St-Augustin.
Date Sun closest to 21 Jan.
Members of France's aristocracy gather with die-hard royalists and assorted other far-right crackpots to mourn the beheading of Louis XVI on 21 January 1793. Bring your camera or friends won't believe you. Firm republicans, on the other hand, are supposed to mark the day by eating *tête de veau*.

Chinese New Year Festival
Around avenue d'Ivry and avenue Choisy, 75013.
Métro Porte de Choisy or Porte d'Ivry. **Information**
Association Culturelle Franco-Chinoise (45.20.74.09).
Date in Jan or Feb.
The 13th *arrondissement* Chinatown comes alive to the sound of fireworks and the clash of cymbals, as dragon dancers snake through the streets. The right-bank Chinese area in Belleville is quiet by comparison.

18 Heures 18 Francs
Cinemas all over Paris. **Date** usually second week of Feb.
For one week, from a Monday, all movie sessions starting closest to 6pm (18 heures) cost only 18F. Check the press for precise dates. Very popular on the weekend, so arrive early to avoid disappointment.

Sightseeing

The best of the sights and sites, from the Louvre to skeletons underground

Notre Dame de Paris. *See page 39.*

In a much-photographed city like Paris, most people's top ten must-sees are familiar from television, books or films. But this doesn't diminish the power of the real thing, and discovering the city for yourself is a fairly simple matter since many sights are within walking distance, close to the Seine.

If you are touring the sights it's possible to make things even easier with the **Paris Carte Musées et Monuments** museum pass, which enables you to cut costs and circumvent the queues. For details, *see chapter* **Museums**.

Hearts of the City

Arc de Triomphe
place Charles de Gaulle (access via underground passage), 75008 (43.80.31.31). Métro Charles de Gaulle-Etoile.
Open *Oct-Mar* 10am-5.30pm (last tickets 5pm) daily.
Apr-Sept 9am-6.30pm (last tickets at 6pm) Mon-Thur, Sat, Sun; 9.30am-9.30pm (last tickets at 9pm) Fri. Closed

public holidays. **Admission** 32F; 21F 18-25s; 10F 12-17s; free under-12s. **Credit** (shop only) AmEx, MC, V.
At the western end of the Champs-Elysées, the Arc de Triomphe forms the centrepiece of Paris' grand east-west axis from the **Louvre**, through the Arc du Carrousel and the **place de la Concorde** on the one side, and away up to **La Défense** on the other. A potent symbol of military might, the Arc was commissioned by Napoleon in 1806 as a homage to (his own) military victories. A modest 50m (164ft) tall, 45m (148ft) wide and decorated with a giant frieze, the arch was only finished in 1836. In 1920 the Tomb of the Unknown Soldier was laid here, and an eternal flame burns to commemorate the dead of both World Wars. The manic drivers zooming around the arch turn the place Charles de Gaulle into a race track, but fortunately there's a subway. Via lift or steps you can reach the top of the arch, from where you can appreciate the masterful geometry of Haussmann's great redesign of Paris, with its uniform façades and twelve radiating avenues, which include some of the smartest residential streets in the city. Queues build up at the foot of the Arch, so try to arrive early.

Avenue des Champs-Elysées
75008. Métro Concorde, Champs Elysées-Clemenceau, Franklin D Roosevelt, George V, Charles de Gaulle-Etoile.
Perhaps the most famous street in Paris, the Champs-Elysées (the 'Elysian Fields') can be a disappointment on first tourist-filled sight. Nonetheless, despite the proliferation of burger bars, over-priced cafés, car showrooms and shopping malls, vestiges of the street's grandeur remain, whether in the vivacity of its night life, the queues outside the cinemas, the pomp and ceremony of the 14 July parade, the excitement of the final stage of the Tour de France, or quite simply the impressive vista at night stretching from the floodlit **place de la Concorde** at one end to the **Arc de Triomphe** at the other. One of Jacques Chirac's worthier efforts as mayor was a major facelift for the avenue, with new underground car parks and smart granite paving. As anywhere in Paris, you have to accept the traffic congestion as part of the landscape – on Friday nights, it's an especially popular runway for suburban bikers out on the town. Despite some early landscaping in the seventeenth century, the Champs-Elysées long remained pretty rural, and shortly before the Revolution the local guard worried that the area's dark corners offered 'to libertines and people of bad intentions a refuge that they can abuse'. Real development took place during the Second Empire, which is when the Champs-Elysées really took off as a focus of fashionable society and the backbone of Parisian life. The Prussian army in 1871 and Hitler's troops in 1940 both made their point by marching down it, amid a silently hostile reception, but loud celebrations accompanied the victory march along the avenue in 1944. The English Gardens by place de la Concorde, the **Grand Palais**, the Petit Palais, the Arc de Triomphe and the elegant houses at the Rond-Point are some of the area's major highlights. Better still, just amble around, ignore the hustlers, and explore the many squares and parks which flank the lower half of the avenue, towards place de la Concorde.

Napoleon's folly, the **Arc de Triomphe**.

Louis XIII rides out in the **Place des Vosges.** *See page 39.*

Cathédrale de Notre Dame de Paris

place du Parvis-Notre-Dame, 75004 (42.34.56.10). Métro Cité. **Open** 8am-6.45pm Mon-Sat; 8am–7.45pm Sun. **Admission** free.
Archaeological crypt (43.29.83.51). **Open** 10am-5.30pm daily. **Admission** 27F; 18F 18-25s, over-60s; 10F 12-17s; free under-12s.
Towers (43.29.50.40) entrance at foot of the northern tower. **Open** *Dec & Jan* 10am-4pm; *Feb, Mar & Nov* 10am-5pm; *1 Apr-14 Sept* 9.30am-6pm; *15 Sept-31 Oct* 9.30am-5.30pm. **Admission** 27F; 18F 18-25s; 10F 12-17s; free under-12s. **No credit cards.**
It's said that all the roads of Paris lead to the *Kilomètre Zéro* in the square in front of Notre Dame Cathedral on the Ile de la Cité. In the crypt, one can see part of the defensive wall and other relics of the original Roman city of Lutetia, discovered during the building of an underground car park. Above, Catholics and, equally devoutly, tourists from all over the world come to pay homage to the Gothic masterpiece of Notre Dame, which has been altered and renovated many times since the foundations were laid by Pope Alexander III in 1163. Completed in 1345, the cathedral straddles two architectural eras, echoing the great galleried churches of the twelfth century and looking forward to the buttressed cathedrals, such as Chartres, which were to follow. Among its most famous features are the three glorious rose windows. The evolution of this Gothic milestone was not without its setbacks. During the Revolution, the cathedral was turned into a temple of reason and a wine warehouse, and the statues of the kings were destroyed – those seen today are nineteenth-century replicas. Unexpectedly, several of the originals were discovered in 1979 and are now on show at the **Musée de Cluny**. The structure had fallen into such a state of delapidation by the early nineteenth century that artists, politicians and writers, among them Victor Hugo, petitioned the King, Louis Philippe, to restore the cathedral, which was done with great mastery by Viollet-Le-Duc. During the Nazi occupation, all the panes from the magnificent stained-glass windows were removed, numbered and replaced with sandbags to save them from destruction. A

dim staircase winds up through one of the bell towers, leading to a gallery adorned with gargoyles who peruse the surrounding view with weary malice. Walk around the back of the cathedral for the best view of its arched flying buttresses. *See also chapter* **Paris by Area: The Islands.**

Eiffel Tower

Champ de Mars, 75007 (44.11.23.45/recorded information 44.11.23.23). Métro Bir-Hakeim/RER Champ de Mars. **Open** *18 Sept-17 Mar* 9.30am-11pm; *18 Mar-30 June and 4 Sept-17 Sept* 9am–11pm; *1 July-3 Sept* 9am-midnight daily. **Admission** *by lift 1st storey* 20F/10F (4-11s); *2nd storey* 38F/19F (4-11s); *3rd storey* 55F/26F (4-11s); *free under-4s; by stairs 1st & 2nd storeys only* 12F. **No credit cards.**

*Paris' biggest wedding cake, the **Sacré Coeur**. See page 50.*

The symbol of Paris was the tallest building in the world at 300m (984ft) when it was built in 1889 for the Universal Exhibition on the centenary of the Revolution. Now, with the addition of an aerial, it reaches to 321m (1,053ft). The view of it from the Trocadéro across the river is monumental and much photographed, but the distorted view from its base most dramatically shows off the graceful ironwork of Gustave Eiffel. Be prepared for a long wait for a ride in the lifts, as the tower gets four million visitors a year, its present popularity contrasting with the spluttering indignation which greeted its construction. To save time and money you can stop at the first or second platform, but those who travel all the way to the top can view Gustave Eiffel's cosy *salon* and enjoy amazing panoramas: you can see for 67km (42 miles) on a good day. The queue is not so long at night, when the city lights twinkle in the Seine and the city lives up to its romantic image. There's a brasserie on the first level, and the smart Jules Verne restaurant – served by its own lift – on the second, as well as a post office and souvenir shops.

La Grande Arche de la Défense

Paris la Défense (49.07.27.57). Métro Grande Arche de la Défense. **Open** *April-Oct* 9am-8pm daily (roof-top closes one hour later). *Nov-Mar* 9am-6pm Mon-Sat; 9am-7pm Sun, public holidays (roof-top closes one hour later). **Admission** 40F; 30F under-18s, students, unemployed.
Planned to complete the axis of the Champs-Elysées and the Arc de Triomphe – and then skewed at a slight angle – the Grande Arche is simultaneously one of the most pointless and most successful of the *grands projets*, providing a landmark amid the previously featureless towers of Paris' modern business reservation in the western suburbs. It also catapulted the obscure Danish architect Johan Otto von Spreckelsen to fame, although he died before it was completed. British engineer Peter Rice finished the work and designed the canvas 'clouds' suspended in the arch's aperture. Only from close up do you realise quite how vast the structure is, as the arch's cuboid form disguises its immense height. A stomach-churning ride in high-speed glass lifts takes you up through the 'clouds' to the roof where there is

an exhibition space and a bird's eye view into Paris and out to the city's western reaches. See also chapter **Paris by Area: Beyond the Périphérique**.

Palais & Musée National du Louvre

entrance through Pyramid, Cour Napoléon, 75001 (40.20.50.50/recorded information 40.20.51.51). Métro Palais Royal-Musée du Louvre. **Open** *permanent collection* 9am-9.45pm Mon (only the *Aile Richelieu*) & Wed (last tickets 9.15pm); 9am-6pm Thur-Sun (last tickets 5.15pm); *temporary exhibitions* 10am-10pm Mon, Wed-Sun; *Medieval Louvre & Bookshop* 9am-9.45pm. Closed Tuesdays. **Admission** *permanent collection* 40F (until 15h)/20F (after 3pm & Sun); free under-18s; *temporary exhibitions* admission varies. **Credit** (bookshop only) AmEx, EC, MC, V.
Arguably the greatest art collection in the world. The Louvre's miles of galleries take in the sculptures of ancient

Featured above are clothes from: RICCI, MUGLER,
SAINT LAURENT, LACROIX, ALAIA, CHANEL
(except the model in salmon)

⪦ RECIPROQUE ⪧
Nicole Morel

Syria, Rome and Greece, and such cultural icons as the *Mona Lisa*, the *Venus de Milo*, Géricault's *Raft of the Medusa* and Delacroix's *Liberty Leading the People*. The palace itself is the largest in Europe, and was home to generations of French monarchs from the fourteenth century onwards. Although it can look very homogeneous, it was built over several centuries. Part of the original twelfth-century keep built by King Philip Augustus remains hidden within the later building, and one consequence of all the recent renovations of the Louvre has been that a section of its massive walls is now open to view in the underground complex that forms the new main entrance to the museum. In the 1540s, Francis I replaced the old medieval palace with a new building by Pierre Lescot, of which the finest part is the enclosed Cour Carrée, at the eastern end of the building, its walls etched with royal monograms – H interlaced with C and D for Henry II, his queen Catherine de Medici and favourite Diane de Poitiers; L and A for Louis XIII and Anne of Austria; and L and MT for Louis XIV and Marie-Thérèse. This was then added to by his successors. Napoleon built the galleries along the rue de Rivoli, complete with imperial figures (this wing now houses the **Musée des Arts Décoratifs**); his nephew Napoleon III then added the Cour Napoléon.

After the court left for Versailles under Louis XIV most of the Louvre was given over to offices and apartments for a multifarious variety of state servants. The museum collection was first opened to the public in 1793, but the last government department, the Ministry of Finance, remained in the palace until the eighties, when the Louvre's last great transformation, the *Grand Louvre* project, began. One major feature of it has been the extension of the museum into the former ministry, now the Louvre's Richelieu Wing; another, the best-known and most controversial, is the wonderful glass pyramid by IM Pei, opened in 1989 on the bicentenary of the Revolution, that now dominates the Cour Napoléon and provides the main entrance to the museum. West of the pyramid is the little **Arc de Triomphe du Carrousel**, with its rose-coloured marble columns, erected in 1805 to commemorate Napoleon's victories in 1805. It served as a gateway to the Tuileries Palace, burned down in 1871, and is linked visually to the greater Arc de Triomphe by the Champs-Elysées and the Tuileries. The arch now triumphs above an underground shopping and restaurant development, the **Carrousel du Louvre**, opened in 1993, the new venue for the fashion shows and another dramatic element in the *Grand Louvre* project. The **Aile Richelieu** was opened in 1993, and new sculpture courts created in October 1994, but work on the *Grand Louvre* will not be finally completed until 1997, causing the temporary closure of many areas. To avoid the queues enter through the Carrousel du Louvre, at 99 rue de Rivoli. *See also chapter* **Specialist Shops**.

Place de la Bastille

75011/75012/75004. Métro Bastille.
Nothing remains of the infamous Bastille prison which, on 14 July 1789, was stormed by the assembled forces of the plebeian revolt. Although by that time only a handful of prisoners were incarcerated there, the event provided the rebels with gunpowder, and gave the insurrection momentum. It remains the eternal symbol of the Revolution, which is still celebrated here with a particularly lively street *bal* every Bastille Day. The prison was quickly torn down, and most of its stones were used to build the Pont de la Concorde, although supposed bits and pieces of it could be bought from local entrepreneurs for months afterwards. In the Bastille métro station vestiges of the prison's foundations can be seen. Today the **Colonne de Juillet**, topped by a gilded statue of Liberty, stands in the middle of the square, commemorating the Parisians killed during the later revolutions of July 1830 and 1848. The *place* has traditionally been a boundary point between central Paris and the more proletarian districts to the east, but this is an area which has been undergoing enormous rejuvenation of late. This has been been sparked partly by the vast new **Opéra Bastille** and

other major renovations such as the creation of the **Port de l'Arsenal** marina to the south, but also by the Bastille's having gained momentum as one of the most buzzing and fashionable areas in town for hip cafés, nightlife and artists' workshops.

Place de la Concorde

75008. Métro Concorde.
Planned by Jacques-Ange Gabriel for Louis XV in 1753, the place de la Concorde is the largest square in Paris, a great hub of the city, with grand perspectives stretching east-west from the **Louvre** to the **Arc de Triomphe**, and north-south from the **Madeleine** to the **Assemblée Nationale**, on the other side of the Seine. The construction of this giant space required several years, and disaster marred the fireworks planned here to celebrate the marriage of the Dauphin to Marie Antoinette in 1770, when over a hundred people were crushed falling into a ditch in the unpaved *place*. Gabriel also designed the two grandiose colonnaded mansions on either side of rue Royale: the one on the west now houses the exclusive Crillon hotel (*see chapter* **Accommodation**), while the other is the Navy Ministry. The *place* was further embellished in the nineteenth century when the fountains, depicting river and maritime navigation, sturdy classical lamp-posts and the obelisk from Luxor were added. It's at its most beautiful at sunset or when lit up at night, the best view being from the terrace by the **Jeu de Paume** at the end of the **Jardin des Tuileries** (*see p48* **Paris Parks**). *See also chapter* **Paris by Area: The Right Bank**.

Place des Vosges

75004. Métro St-Paul.
The place des Vosges, earliest of Paris' *grandes places*, was built between 1605 and 1612 by Henry IV, and now rules at the heart of the narrow streets of the Marais. Originally called the place Royale, the king's beautifully harmonious square inspired the nobility to build lavishly in the surrounding district (*see chapter* **Paris by Area: The Right Bank**). Mme de Sévigné, the famous salon hostess and letter writer of the Marais' seventeenth-century heyday, was born here in 1626. With its regular red brick and stone arcaded façades and steeply pitched roofs, the square is intimate, and quite distinct from the more pompous grandeur of later Bourbon Paris. In Mme de Sévigné's time the garden reputedly saw duels and romantic trysts; it now attracts a mix of boules players and children.

The Islands

La Conciergerie

1 quai de l'Horloge, 75001 (43.54.30.06). Métro Cité.
Open *Apr-Sept* 9.30am-6.30pm (last tickets 6pm), *Oct-Mar* 10am-5.30pm (last tickets 5pm), daily. **Admission** 27F; 18F students; 10F 12-17s; free under-12s.
Credit (shop only) MC, V
Viewed from the Right Bank, the Conciergerie looks just like the forbidding medieval fortress and prison it once was. However, much of the gloomy façade was added by nineteenth-century neo-Gothic restorers, although the thirteenth-century Bonbec tower (furthest to the west) was part of the palace of the Capetian kings. Inside you can see the cell where Marie Antoinette was held during the Revolution. Her enemies Danton and Robespierre later ended up here too, following thousands of others who had passed through on their way to the guillotine under the Terror. The Chapelle des Girondins contains some grim souvenirs, such as Marie Antoinette's crucifix and a guillotine blade, ready to replace its blunted predecessor. A visit also takes you through the massive medieval kitchens and the Salle des Gens d'Armes, an impressive vaulted Gothic hall built for Philip the Fair at the beginning of the fourteenth century. On the outside, have a look at the Tour de l'Horloge. Built in 1370 and carefully restored, it was the first public clock in Paris.

Under the Bridges of Paris

Henry IV's **Pont Neuf** *sans amants.*

An artery running through the city, the Seine is itself one of the essential sights of Paris, crossed by magnificent bridges and lined with some of its most impressive monuments. In the sixteenth century a ban on constructing houses on bridges confirmed the river as an aesthetic as well as a functional asset, and many subsequent buildings were designed with an eye to enhancing the vista.

Even though to the west and east the river is now lined with expressways, between the Invalides and the Bastille the tree-lined, paved *quais* are still ideally walkable. Strolling here with a light breeze from the river and some of the best views in the world spread out before you can be a welcome relief after the crush of the busy boulevards. Between the Louvre and Notre-Dame, too, you can stop to browse through the second-hand books and old postcards sold by *bouquinistes* from bottle-green stands. In the summer, the *quais* turn into Paris Beach, full of aspiring tanners. For serious sunbathing hit the stretch near the **Pont du Carrousel** below the Louvre.

In the west of the city, the **Pont Mirabeau**, between the 15th and 16th *arrondissements*, inspired Apollinaire to write his famous poem of the same name, meditating on the passage of time. It also offers great views of the Eiffel Tower. Further east, beneath the **Pont de Grenelle**, is the Allée des Cygnes, a thin strip of an island where horses' bones and dead Protestants were dumped in the sixteenth century. Now the island is a delightful, tree-lined pathway with its own copy of the Statue of Liberty.

The bridges of **Iéna** and **Alma** both commemorate Napoleonic victories. Back towards the centre of Paris, the glittering decoration of the **Pont Alexandre III** comes into view, connecting the Invalides and the Grand Palais. All wrought-iron lamp-posts, gilded statues and precious putti, this has to be the city's most exuberant bridge, unveiled for the 1900 Exhibition. Lining the right bank just to the east are some house boats inhabited by a few artists and modern-day bohemians, overlooked by the stern façade of the Assemblée Nationale on the opposite side of the river.

Beneath the Louvre is the most romantic bridge in Paris, the wonderful 1803 iron footbridge the **Pont des Arts**, from which you can enjoy superb views over the Ile de la Cité. Easily recognisable with its turret-shaped recesses, the **Pont Neuf** at the tip of the island is in fact the oldest, and longest, bridge in Paris. When Henry IV opened it in 1605 it was the first crossing over the Seine without houses crowded along it, and the first with raised pavements. The views quickly made it popular for promenades, and street hawkers and sideshows also competed for space and attention. If you take a boat trip, you'll be able to see the grinning gargoyles carved on its arches, which supposedly portray members of Henry IV's court.

Continuing east, you'll glimpse the sleek lines of the **Institut du Monde Arabe** before drifting into the **Musée de Sculpture en Plein Air** (open air sculpture museum) on quai Saint Bernard, where modern works lurk sheepishly amongst kissing couples. Fans of modern architecture will find plenty to interest them just beyond the Pont de Bercy, where the turf-covered **Palais des Omnisports** squats across the river from the four glass towers of the new **Bibliothèque Nationale de France**.

Ideal for lingering, the **Pont des Arts**.

*Taking one's ease in the colonnades of the **Palais-Royal**. See page 47.*

Sainte-Chapelle & Palais de Justice

4 boulevard du Palais, 75001 (43.54.30.09). Métro Cité.
Open *Apr-Sept* 9.30am-6.30pm (last tickets 6pm), *Oct-Mar* 10am-5pm (last tickets 4.30pm), daily.
Admission 27F; 18F students; 10F 12-17s; free under-12s. **Credit** (bookshop only) MC, V.

Tucked away inside a courtyard of the Palais de Justice is the exquisite Sainte-Chapelle. France's devout King Louis IX (1226-70), later canonised as Saint Louis, was an enthusiastic collector of holy relics – some of them of very doubtful authenticity, as the king was the target for every conman in Europe. In the 1240s he ordered Pierre de Montreuil to design a suitable church in which to house them. Seemingly built almost entirely of stained glass, the two-level chapel is a monument to high Gothic style, with beautiful star-painted vaulted ceilings. Bring binoculars, and come on a sunny day to view the fine details of the stained glass, which depicts biblical scenes. The chapel is regularly used for concerts by early music ensembles. It is surrounded by the warren of buildings that form the Palais de Justice, the seat of authority from Roman times until 1358, although most of the present buildings date from the eighteenth and nineteenth centuries. It is still the focal point of justice in Paris – after going through the security system, you can walk through the marble corridors, full of black-gowned lawyers, and sit in on cases in both the civil and criminal courts.

Royal & Imperial Paris

La Madeleine

place de la Madeleine, 75008 (44.51.69.00). Métro Madeleine. **Open** 8am-7pm Mon-Sat; 9am-1pm, 3.30-7pm, Sun. **Admission** free

The building of a giant church on this site was first begun in 1764, but little had been completed by the time of the Revolution. In 1806 Napoleon decided to continue the project as a 'Temple of Glory' dedicated to his Grand Army, and commissioned Barthélemy Vignon to design a semi-

Athenian temple that is the epitome of the neo-classicism that fascinated Paris in the early nineteenth century. Following the Emperor's fall the building suffered from a severe lack of public support, but it was finally consecrated as a church in 1845. The colonnades of the façade, recently restored, closely mirror those of the **Assemblée Nationale** across the river, with the Concorde obelisk as midpoint. The unofficial parish church of Paris' showbiz community, the Madeleine hosts celebrity weddings and funerals, filling the surrounding place with weeping fans. A greater attraction though might be the luxury food shops that line the square.

Opéra Garnier

place de l'Opéra, 75009 (40.17.33.33/recorded information, reception 40.01.24.93). Métro Opéra.
Open *tours, museum, shop* 10am-5pm (last tickets 4.30pm) daily. **Admission** 30F, incl museum; 18F 10-16s; free under-10s. **Guided tours** 2.30pm daily, 60F, 45F, 25F. **No credit cards.**

The opulent Palais Garnier, with its sumptuous grand staircase, mass of sculptures and glittering chandeliers is a monument to the ostentation of the French haute bourgeoisie under the Second Empire. Designed by Charles Garnier in 1862, it has an immense stage and an auditorium that holds more than 2,000 people. It even had a ramp up the side of the building on rue Scribe for the Emperor to drive his carriage straight to the royal box. The façade is equally opulent, and in its time a source of controversy. The sculpture of a group of dancers by Carpeaux to the right of the entrance shocked Parisians with its frank sensuality, and in 1869 someone threw a bottle of ink over their marble thighs; the original is now safe in the Louvre. The surrounding streets and squares were laid out by the ubiquitous Baron Haussmann. It's normally possible to tour most sections of the building, but the auditorium is closed for renovation until March 1996. Since the construction of the Opéra Bastille, only dance had been performed here, but when it reopens the Garnier will again host occasional opera productions as well as ballet. Visitors will also be able to see once again the false ceiling, painted with lyrical scenes from opera and ballet by Chagall in 1964.

A Sense of Place

Paris' proliferation of squares provides an ideal counterpoint to its avenues and Haussmannian axes. There are squares to suit every taste. Henry IV's **place des Vosges**, the first planned square in Paris, offers intimate elegance, while the **place de la Concorde** stretches out with immense classical grandeur, but some of the less famous alternatives are also full of charm, or vitality, or both.

One of the earliest centres of Paris was the **place du Châtelet**, on the site of a twelfth-century fortress built to protect the Ile de la Cité. After a spell as a torture house and prison, it was demolished by Napoleon in 1802. In its place stand two theatres, the Théâtres de la Ville and du Châtelet, both built in the 1860s. There's also a fountain in the middle of the square, built in the Egyptian style made fashionable by Napoleon's campaigns. Another originally-medieval square is the **place de la Contrescarpe** in the Latin Quarter, famous as a meeting place since the 1530s, when writers Rabelais, Ronsard and Du Bellay frequented the cabaret de la Pomme de Pin at no. 1. Today, it's still popular with students, who flock into the bars and cheap restaurants of nearby rue Mouffetard.

As well as the place des Vosges, another square commissioned by Henry IV was the **place Dauphine** on the Ile de la Cité, of 1607. A leafy refuge amongst the surrounding grand buildings, home to several small art galleries and restaurants, it feels peculiarly insulated from the city, and was a great favourite of surrealist André Breton. André Malraux had a Freudian analysis of its appeal – 'the sight of its triangular formation with slightly curved lines, and of the slit which bisects its two wooded spaces. It is, without doubt, the sex of Paris which is outlined in this shade.'

Although overshadowed by the nearby place des Vosges, the pretty **place du Marché Ste-Catherine** in the Marais is also worth a detour. Built on the site of a former priory, it's now lined with restaurants. The remains of the priory can be seen in the cellars of one of the eateries.

Louis XIV introduced the grand Baroque square to Paris. First Parisian square built in his honour was the circular **place des Victoires** in the 1st, designed by Hardouin-Mansart in 1685 to set off an equestrian statue of the Sun King. The original disappeared during the Revolution, and the current statue dates from 1822. Today, the sweeping façades shelter some of the most prestigious names in fashion, such as Kenzo and

Thierry Mugler. Still more plush is another of the same architect's creations, the **place Vendôme**.

From the eighteenth century, and on the Left Bank in the 6th, is the semi-circular **place de l'Odéon**, dominated by the neo-classical theatre built in 1779. Revolutionary Camille Desmoulins was arrested in 1794 in a third-floor apartment at No. 2, and No. 1 used to be home to the Café Voltaire, frequented by the Romantic poets, Symbolists and the writers of the Lost Generation.

For a contrast, Paris also has some veritable village squares. A kind of rural simplicity characterises the tiny **place de Furstemberg**, not far from the Odéon, on the site of the courtyard of the abbey of St-Germain-des-Prés. There's not much more here than a few trees, a lamppost and a bench. Between 1857 and 1863 Delacroix lived and worked at No. 6, now the **Musée Delacroix**. Formerly a real village square and now one of the biggest tourist traps in Paris is the **place du Tertre** at the top of Montmartre, full of hustling quick-portrait sketchers and tacky restaurants. Instead of buying, make for the nearby **place du Calvaire**, which offers a magnificent view over the capital.

Palais-Royal

main entrance place du Palais-Royal, other entrances in rue de Montpensier, rue de Beaujolais, rue de Valois, 75001. Métro Palais-Royal. **Open** *gardens only* dawn-dusk daily. **Admission** free

The Palais-Royal has a rich and racy history. It was built for Cardinal Richelieu by Jacques Lemercier as his own private residence, and known as the Palais Cardinal. Richelieu left the palace to Louis XIII, whose widow moved in, preferring it to the vast halls of the Louvre and giving it its present name. Later, under the occupancy of Philippe II of Orléans, it became a notorious scene of debauchery. It was, however, in the 1780's, when his descendant the Duc d'Orléans known as *Philippe Egalité* enclosed the gardens within a three-storey peristyle, that the building's most remarkable era began. Housing cafés, theatres, sideshows and shops, its arcades came into their own as a popular society trysting place. Its cafés saw revolutionary plotting before the Revolution, and the Palais-Royal also became known once again for its depravity, as a hot-bed of gambling and prostitution. Of the old cafés, the Grand Véfour remains, now one of the best restaurants in town (*see chapter* **Restaurants**). Today the gardens offer a surprisingly tranquil spot in the heart of Paris, while many of the little shops in the arcades specialise in prints and antiques. The former palace houses the Conseil d'Etat and the Ministry of Culture, and is open to the public only during the **Journées Portes Ouvertes** (*see chapter* **Paris by Season**). The main courtyard, after years of ignominy as a car park, now contains Daniel Buren's controversial sculpture of 280 black and white striped columns of different heights. Some are hidden underground below grates; others are just the right height to sit on. *See also chapter* **Paris by Area: The Right Bank.**

Place Vendôme

75001. Métro Tuileries/Opéra.

The place Vendôme got its name from the *hôtel particulier* built by the Duc de Vendôme previously on this site. Inaugurated in 1699, the place was conceived by Hardouin-Mansart to show off an equestrian statue of the Sun King. This statue was torn down in 1792, and in 1806 a *Colonne de la Grande Armée*, modelled on Trajan's column in Rome and with a bronze frieze made out of 1,250 Russian and Austrian cannons captured at the battle of Austerlitz, was erected by Napoleon to celebrate his own martial triumphs. During the 1871 Commune this symbol of 'brute force and false glory' was pulled down by the revolutionaries, among them the painter Courbet. The present 44m-high column is a replica, put in place only three years later, with most of the original frieze. Today the square is now home to Paris' most exclusive jewellers, international banks, the Justice Ministry and the Ritz hotel, at no. 15. The composer Chopin died at no. 12, in 1849. The *place* was recently given a face-lift, and an underground car park has removed cars from its surface.

Beaubourg & the Marais

Centre Pompidou

Centre National d'Art et de Culture Georges Pompidou, rue Beaubourg, 75004 (Information 44.78.12.33). Métro Châtelet-les Halles, Rambuteau. **Open** noon-10pm Mon, Wed-Fri; 10am-10pm Sat, Sun, holidays, closed 1 May. **Admission** *Musée de l'Art Moderne permanent exhibitions* 35F, 24F under 24s, free under 18s. *Temporary exhibitions* 25-50F. *One day pass* - access to all exhibitions 60F, 40F students, under 24s. **Guided Tours** (phone for details) 35F; 24F 18-24s; free under 18s. **Credit** (bookshop/exhibitions 500F minimum) AmEx, MC, EC, V.

The primary colours and exposed pipes and air ducts make the Centre Pompidou one of the most instantly recognisable buildings of Paris. Commissioned in 1968 by President

Georges Pompidou, and opened in 1977, it was bravely slotted into a then run-down historic district, ironically called Beaubourg ('beautiful village'). The Italo-British architectural duo of Renzo Piano and Richard Rogers won the competition for its design with their notorious 'inside-out', boilerhouse approach, which put all the services such as air-conditioning, lifts and escalators on the outside, leaving a freely adaptable space for the galleries within. The Centre, often known simply as 'Beaubourg', was a pioneer in the concept of a multi-media space; it includes a vast public library and music library, the CCI specialising in industrial design and architecture, the **Salle Garance** cinema and the centre for research in contemporary music **IRCAM**, housed in the red-brick building across the place St-Merri. There's also the treasure-packed **Musée National d'Art Moderne**, which continues the history of twentieth-century art from where the Musée d'Orsay leaves off in 1914. The fifth floor exhibition area is used for blockbuster theme shows and retrospectives, while smaller contemporary art and design exhibitions are staged on the mezzanine levels and in the central forum space. The escalators also offer one of the best views in Paris, although they get very crowded and, despite continual cleaning, the synthetic glass is grubby. With eight million visitors each year, the building is in sore need of repair, and will undergo a major renovation programme from 1997 to 1999 which will involve closure of different parts of the Centre at different times. The vast plaza in front of the Centre is inhabited by street performers and hecklers, fire eating or singing for the queues. As a result, crowds of tourists and teenagers pack Beaubourg's front yard all year round, and a policy of free entry allows them to spread easily into the Centre's giant ground-floor lobby. *See also chapters* **Film**, **Music: Classical & Opera** *and* **Students**.

Fortified Wall of Philip Augustus

rue des Jardins-St-Paul, 75004 Paris. Métro Pont Marie or St-Paul

King Philip Augustus (1165-1223) was the first great builder Paris had known since Roman times. Not only did he order the major roads of his capital to be paved, he also enclosed the various *faubourgs* of Paris on the Left and Right banks of the Seine within a great defensive wall. The largest surviving section of this wall, complete with towers, extends along the rue des Jardins-Saint-Paul, between the rue Charlemagne and the rue l'Avé-Maria. Another chunk of the wall can still be seen at 3 rue Clovis in the Latin Quarter.

Hôtel de Sully

62, rue St-Antoine, 75004 (44.61.20.00/information 44.61.21.69). Métro Saint-Paul or Bastille. **Open** 10am-7pm daily. **Admission** 37F; 27F students, over-60s. **Guided tours** phone for details. **No credit cards.**

This perfectly restored Louis XIII-style *hôtel particulier* is one of the most distinguished town mansions still standing in the Marais. Designed by Jean Androuet du Cerceau in 1624, it was bought by Henry IV's former minister the Duc

Paris Parks

Haussmann's transformation of Paris aimed to open up green spaces to 'ventilate' the city, and the area devoted to gardens increased from 19 to 1,800 hectares. The Tuileries and the Luxembourg are typical formal French gardens, but wider and wilder spaces can be found in the Bois de Boulogne and Vincennes. And for unexpected character, try the smaller parks listed below. Most parks are open from early morning until early evening.

Bois de Boulogne

75016. Métro Porte-Dauphine.
Covering over 865 hectares, the Bois is a series of gardens within sometimes-scruffy woodland. Most pleasant is the Parc de Bagatelle, surrounding a château that was the scene of the romantic adventures of the Comte d'Artois, brother of Louis XVI and later King Charles X. Its walled garden is famous for its roses and water lilies. The Jardin d'Acclimatation is an amusement park for children, while scenes from the bard's famous works are performed in the Jardin du Shakespeare. The Bois also has two lakes, two racecourses (Longchamp and Auteuil), 140,000 trees and many tracks and paths to accommodate horse riders and cyclists (for more on its sports facilities, *see chapter* **Sport & Fitness**). During the day it's popular with dog walkers, picnickers and sports enthusiasts, but at night it's much more seedy, and despite clean-up attempts is still associated with kerb-crawling and prostitution.

Bois de Vincennes

75012. Métro Porte-Dorée.
East of the city is Paris' biggest park. Formerly the royal forest of the Valois, it was made into a park in 1860 by Napoleon III, and owes much to Haussmann's landscape architect Adolphe Alphand, who added the lake and cascades that are a major part of its charm. Boats can be hired on the lake, and there are various cycle paths, a Buddhist temple, a racetrack, baseball field and flower gardens (for more on sports facilities, *see chapter* **Sport & Fitness**). It also contains Paris' **Zoo**, and the Cartoucherie theatre centre (*see chapter* **Theatre**), while next to the park is the imposing **Château de Vincennes**, where Henry V of England died in 1422.

Jardin & Palais du Luxembourg

75006. Métro Odéon/RER Luxembourg.
A welcome breathing space on the Left Bank, and perhaps the most romantic of Parisian parks. The **Palais du Luxembourg**, which now houses the French Senate, was originally built for Henry IV's widow Marie de Medici in the 1620s. Its Italianate style was intended to resemble the Pitti Palace in her native Florence, although she did not enjoy it for long, as Richelieu had her banished from France. It remained a royal palace until the Revolution. The gardens were laid out at the same time as the palace, but much reworked by Chalgrin in the last century. To the right of the palace is the original 1624 Fontaine de Médicis, with a looming Cyclops. Artists, poets and writers have often strolled about the park, among them Balzac, George Sand and Gertrude Stein. Today, children can enjoy sandpits, slides and roundabouts, sail their boats on the large circular pond and watch a puppet show. There are also tennis courts, boules pitches, a basketball hoop and even an apiary where you can study the art of bee-keeping.

Jardin des Plantes

75005. Métro Gare d'Austerlitz.
The oldest of Paris' gardens, developed by Louis XIII's doctor Guy de La Brosse as the first royal medicinal plant garden in 1626. It was originally designed for the education of students in medicine and pharmacy, but was opened to the public in 1640. Today, there are more than 10,000 species of plants, winter and Alpine gardens, large greenhouses, the **Muséum National d'Histoire Naturelle** and a zoo.

Jardin des Tuileries

75001. Métro Tuileries or Concorde.
Stretching between the Louvre and the place de la Concorde, the gravelled alleyways here have been a fashionable promenading spot since the seventeenth century. They were laid out by André Le Nôtre, who began his illustrious career as royal gardener here in 1664. Today, Maillol sculptures line the avenues where the Tuileries palace stood until 1871. It still has a pleasure-garden feel, with pony rides, boules players and a big fun fair every summer. For some years a programme of replanting has been in operation, designed to restore trees damaged by pollution, and to recapture Le Nôtre's original layout.

Parc des Buttes Chaumont

rue Botzaris, 75020. Métro Buttes-Chaumont.
A fantasy wonderland designed by Alphand for Haussmann on the site of a gypsum quarry. A 50 metre-high rock rises from an artificial lake, above which hangs an impressive suspension bridge. Make sure to visit the famous waterfalls within a man-made cave and climb to the little classical gazebo at the top of the island, from where there's a great view of the Sacré-Coeur.

Parc Monceau

boulevard de Courcelles, 75005. Métro Monceau
Surrounded by grand *hôtels particuliers*, the Monceau is a favourite with well-dressed *BCBG* children and their nannies. It was laid out during the eighteenth century in the English style then fashionable, with a variety of follies – an Egyptian pyramid, a vast oval basin with a Corinthian colonnade, and a Renaissance arcade near the central alley.

Parc de Montsouris

boulevard Jourdan, 75014. Métro/RER Cité-Universitaire.
Another of Alphand's parks for Haussmann, on the southern edge of the city. Its gently sloping lawns descend towards a lake, with turtles and ducks, and the variety of its bushes and trees and beautiful flowerbeds make it the most colourful of all the capital's parks.

de Sully, who lavished money on decorating and extending it. The *hôtel* has been carefully restored, and it's possible to tour the Duke's apartments. Inside there are two beautifully proportioned courtyards, one with a pretty *orangerie*, which lead through into the place des Vosges. Today it's home to the **Caisse Nationale des Monuments Historiques**, which offers a vast array of guided tours (in French) of Paris.

Hôtel de Ville

place de l'Hôtel de Ville (main public entrance at 29 rue de Rivoli), 75004 (42.76.50.49). Métro Hôtel de Ville.
Guided tours 10.30am Mon. **Admission** free
The fanciful confection of the Hôtel de Ville, the city hall, symbolises the power of the City of Paris rather than state government. There has been a town hall here since 1260, but it's best remembered for the part it played in the Revolution. King Louis XVI was obliged to kiss the tricolour here in 1789, and three years later Danton, Marat and Robespierre made the Hôtel their seat of government. Revolutionaries again made it their base in 1871, when the Commune was proclaimed, but in May of that year the building was recaptured by the government and wrecked in savage fighting. It was rebuilt in 1873-82, and much enlarged in a faithfully neo-Renaissance style. Guided tours take visitors to view the seven different types of wood on the dining-room floor, the 24 lavish chandeliers throughout the building and the statue on the roof symbolising the city of Paris. Tours are sometimes cancelled, and it's wise to phone beforehand. The fountains and square in front are a popular meeting place.

Tour St-Jacques

Place du Châtelet, 75004 Paris.
Métro Châtelet-Les Halles or Hôtel de Ville.
Much-loved by the surrealists and complete with gargoyles, this solitary Flamboyant-Gothic bell-tower is all that remains of the church of St-Jacques-La-Boucherie, built for the powerful Butchers' Guild in 1523. Pascal carried out experiments into the weight of air here in the seventeenth century. A weather station now crowns the tower, 52 metres (172ft) high, which can only be admired from outside.

Les Halles to the *Passages*

Bibliothèque Nationale

58 rue de Richelieu, 75002 (47.03.81.26). Métro Bourse orPalais-Royal. **Open** 9am-8pm Mon-Fri, 9am-5.30pm Sat.
Admission *Galerie Mansart and Mazarine: both galleries* 35F, 24F students, over-60s, under-26s, *one gallery* 22F, 15F. *Galerie Colbert* free. *Cabinet des Médailles et des Antiques* 15F. **No credit cards.**
The genesis of the French National Library dates from the 1660s, when Louis XIV's finance minister Colbert brought together the manuscripts of the royal library in two town mansions which had belonged to Mazarin. By 1724, the institution had received so many new acquisitions that the neighbouring Hôtel de Nevers was added to it. The Bibliothèque Nationale was first opened to scholars in 1720. Some parts of the present building date from the seventeenth and eighteenth centuries, but most of it, including the grand reading room, was transformed in the 1860s. Architect Henri Labrouste's metal columns and vaulting and ceramic domes were very innovative in their time, and are still impressive. Most of the building is open only to researchers who have managed to get one of its elusive readers' passes. Pressure on space will be relieved when the 12 million books currently stored here will be transferred in late 1996 to the new library near Tolbiac (*see below* **Further Afield**). The library's priceless collection of engravings and photographs will remain in the old building. Currently, visitors can tour the courtyards, as well as the Cabinet des Médailles et des Antiques, to which all ancient coins discovered in France must be submitted. Many temporary exhibitions are also held in the Mansart, Mazarine and Colbert galleries.

Forum des Halles

75001. Métro/RER Châtelet-Les Halles
Punks, pickpockets and pleasure-seekers prowl around what was the site of the old central produce market of Paris, transferred to suburban Rungis in 1969. There had been markets here since 1181, and their heyday was in the last century, when Napoleon III commissioned Baltard to construct large pavilions of cast iron and steel to house them. What now stands in their place is the Forum des Halles, a giant underground shopping mall which incorporates numerous cinemas, the **Vidéothèque de Paris**, a swimming pool, a marine park and the **Musée de l'Holographie**. The first part of the centre was completed in 1979, and the second phase near the Bourse du Commerce added in 1986. Both are now severely shabby. Above ground, there is a garden covering five hectares, bordered by a plethora of shops, fast-food eateries and cafés.

Palais de la Bourse

place de la Bourse, 75002. Métro Bourse. **Guided tours** *mid Sept-June* every half hour, 11am-12.30pm Mon-Fri; *July-mid Sept* noon Mon-Fri. **Admission** 10F.
It was Napoleon who gave Paris its temple of business, also known as the Bourse des Valeurs, to differentiate it from the former corn exchange at Les Halles, the Bourse du Commerce (*see chapter* **Business**). After being housed at different times in the rue Vivienne, the Louvre and the Palais-Royal, the stock exchange moved to the building which Alexandre Brongniart conceived for it in 1808. Its grandiose columned frontage is typical of the neo-classical tastes of the First Empire; two new wings were added in 1902 to give the building the shape of a cross. The steps to the east and west are flanked by four allegorical statues representing Business, Justice, Agriculture and Industry.

St Eustache

rue du Jour, 75001 Paris (40.26.47.99). Métro Châtelet-Les Halles. **Open** *Nov-Apr* 8am-7pm, Mon-Sat; 8am-1pm, 3-8pm, Sun. *May-Oct* 8am-8pm Mon-Sat; 8am-1pm, 3-8pm, Sun. **Guided tours** 3pm daily, free. **Organ recitals** 5-5.30pm daily, free.
This ugly, cathedral-sized church dominates Les Halles. Its structure is essentially Gothic, but its decoration is just as distinctively Renaissance. During the Revolution it became the Temple of Agriculture, appropriately enough, given the proximity of the market. A favourite with musicians and music-lovers, it boasts a magnificent 8,000-pipe organ.

The Bastille & Eastern Paris

American Center

51 rue de Bercy, 75012 (44.73.77.77). Métro Bercy.
Open noon-8pm Wed-Sat; noon-6pm Sun.
Paris' American cultural centre reopened in its new, purpose-built space near the Bercy sports palace in 1994. It's worth taking a trip out to this unloved district simply to admire the architecture. In Californian architect Frank Gehry's sculptural new building a series of dramatic blocks and planes merge to create one of the most successful examples of contemporary architecture in Paris. Inside, a varied array of funnels and skylights in the foyer lead to an 18,000-square metre space that incorporates a large art gallery, a cinema and a theatre. The Center has already staged innovative film, theatre and dance programmes and contemporary art exhibitions. In front of the centre are geometric lawns – the first part of the Parc de Bercy gardens, begun in January 1993, which will eventually stretch along the banks of the Seine. Guided visits of the new park are given on some Sundays (for park information, phone 40.71.75.23).

Opéra Bastille

place de la Bastille, 75012 (40.01.19.70). Métro Bastille.
Open by tour only, usually 2-3 per week, lasting 75 mins,

The **Grand Palais** *has some of Paris' most impressive* Belle Epoque *ironmongery.*

tickets available 10 mins in advance, phone for details.
Admission 50F; 30F students, under-16s, over-60s.
No credit cards.
The megalithic Bastille Opera has been one of the most controversial of all François Mitterrand's *grands projets*, whether because of the cost of its upkeep, its scale, the quality of the architecture or the opera productions put on here. Some described it as a stroke of socialist genius to deliberately implant a high-culture edifice in a traditionally working-class district; others suggested it was a typical piece of Mitterrand skulduggery, an extravagant piece of diversionary propaganda. There's no doubt, however, that the curved, marble-faced structure has contributed to the renewal of the *quartier*. It has been called the world's largest public toilet; you'll have to make up your own mind.

Champs-Elysées & the West

Grand Palais

avenue Winston Churchill, avenue du Général Eisenhower, 75008 (recorded information 44.13.17.17/exhibition information 44.13.17.30). Métro Champs-Elysées-Clemenceau. **Open** *exhibitions* 10am-8pm Mon, Thur-Sun; 10am-10pm Wed, last tickets 45min before closing. **Admission** varies. **Credit** V.
The Grand Palais was built for the *Exposition Universelle* of 1900, and covers a wide tract of land between the Champs-Elysées and the Seine – it's impossible to miss its immense glass dome, and galloping bronze horses pulling chariots. Its three different façades were designed by three different architects, which explains the rather eclectic wealth of decoration. Today the Palais is divided into three main exhibition spaces. The entrances on avenue du Général Eisenhower lead into spaces for blockbuster art shows; the wing nearest to the Seine holds the **Palais de la Découverte** science museum. The avenue Winston Churchill wing has been used to house Paris' major art salons, book fairs and trade shows, but had to be closed for restoration in 1994 when bits started to fall off the dome, and is not due to reopen until 1998.

Facing the Grand Palais across avenue Winston Churchill is the smaller building that houses the **Musée du Petit-Palais**, also built for the Exhibition and now an art museum and exhibition space.

Trocadéro & Palais de Chaillot

place du Trocadéro, 75016. Métro Trocadéro.
Looming across the river from the Eiffel Tower, the Palais de Chaillot in the place du Trocadéro is home to a whole clutch of museums and cultural institutions, such as the **Musée de la Marine**, the **Musée de l'Homme**, the **Musée des Monuments Historiques**, the **Musée du Cinéma-Henri Langlois**, the **Cinémathèque** and the Théâtre National de Chaillot. It's an immense, intimidating, pseudo-classical building that was built for yet another international exhibition, in 1937, and is typical of the monumental neo-totalitarian architecture of the time. The Trocadéro gardens below it are a little dilapidated, but the impressive tiered terraces and pool with bronze and stone statues showered by powerful spraying fountains form a spectacular ensemble with the Eiffel Tower and Champ de Mars across the river. Watch out for roller-skaters coming towards you from all directions as you walk across the esplanade.

Montmartre

Sacré Coeur

35 rue Chevalier-de-la-Barre, 75018 (42.51.17.02). Métro Abbesses or Anvers. **Open** *crypt/dome* Oct-Mar 9.30am-6pm, *Apr-Sept* 9am-7pm, daily; *church* 6.45am-11pm daily. **Admission** *dome* 15F; 8F 6-25s; free under-6s; *crypt* 15F; 8F 6-25s; free under-6s; *dome & crypt* 25F; 13F 6-25s; free under-6s. **No credit cards.**
The icing sugar-white dome is one of the most visible landmarks in Paris. Take a walk up the many (very steep) steps to the basilica for a stunning view – or hop onto the funicular run by the métro system for a ride to the top. Building was started on the Sacré Coeur as an act of penance after the nation's defeat by the Prussians in 1870 (and the take-over

of Paris by the pagan Commune the following year). It wasn't finished until 1914, and another brush with the enemy to the east meant that it wouldn't be consecrated before 1919. The mock Romano-Byzantine edifice dominates Montmartre's Butte, and the pristine white towers can be seen from a great distance. A jumble of architects worked on the project, but its kitsch style is held in great affection by many. The lavishly adorned church, the crypt and the gallery in the dome, where the view is even better, are all open to visitors.

St-Germain to the Luxembourg

Ecole des Beaux-Arts

14 rue Bonaparte, 75006 (47.03.52.15). Métro St-Germain-des-Prés. **Open** 8.30am–8pm Mon-Fri.
Exhibitions entrance at *13 quai Malaquais, 75006.*
Admission 20F; 10F students, over-60s.
No credit cards.
One of Paris' most prestigious arts schools, installed in what remains of a seventeenth-century convent and the eighteenth-century Hôtel de Chimay. After the Revolution, the buildings were transformed into a museum of French monuments, and then into the Ecole in 1816. Today, it is often used as a venue for fashion shows and exhibitions, but at other times only the courtyard is open to visitors.

Institut de France

23 quai de Conti, 75006 (44.41.44.41). Métro St Germain-des-Prés. **Guided tours** 10am-3pm Sat, Sun, nominal charge.
The Classical building designed by Le Vau which houses the Institut de France dates from 1663-84. Dominated by its dome, it was originally founded by Mazarin as a school for provincial children. In 1805 the five academies of the institute were transferred here from the Louvre by Napoleon. Most prestigious is the Académie Française, renowned for outbursts against *Franglais*, whose 40 eminences work steadily away at their dictionary of the French language. Inside the building is Mazarin's tomb, as well as the Bibliothèque Mazarine, which holds 500,000 volumes.

St-Germain-des-Prés

place St-Germain-des-Prés, 75006 (43.25.41.71). Métro St-Germain-des-Prés. **Open** 8am–7.30pm daily. **Guided tours** *informal* 1-5pm Tues & Thur (except school holidays) *formal* 3pm the third Sunday of every month.
Admission free.
On the advice of Saint Germain, who would become bishop of Paris in 555, Childebert, son of Clovis, had a basilica and a monastery built towards 543. The oldest church in Paris, for many years it was known as *St-Germain-le-Doré* ('Saint-Germain the Golden') because of its copper roof. However, the original church was destroyed and pillaged by Normans, to be rebuilt around the year 1000 in Romanesque style. Much of this structure was in turn destroyed during the Revolution, when the abbey was burnt and a saltpetre refinery installed in the church. Today, the only remaining part of the original building is the tower, the top of which was, however, also altered during the clumsy restoration work undertaken in the last century, when a spire was also added. Other parts of the building, including the Gothic choir, which was inspired by the one at St-Denis, do date from the 12th century. The village-like charm of the outside of the church is not matched by the building's rather disparate interior, although it does contain some interesting tombs. Under the window in the second chapel you will find the funeral stone of the philosopher Descartes, whose ashes (bar those of his skull) have been in the church since 1819.

St-Sulpice

place St-Sulpice, 75006 (46.33.21.78). Métro St-Sulpice. **Open** 8.30am-7.30pm daily. **Guided tours** 3pm the second Sunday of every month. **Admission** free.

Work on this giant church started in 1646, but it was only completed 120 years later after six architects had worked on the building. The grandiose Italianate façade is the work of Jean-Baptiste Servandoni, from 1733-45, although the two towers remained unfinished at his death. The south one has never been completed, and is still five metres short of its neighbour. Servandoni had originally planned to construct a semi-circular *place* in front of the church, but this was never carried out and the present one was designed in the last century by Visconti, who also designed the fountain. The church's interior is famed for the three murals by Delacroix in the first chapel: on the left, *Jacob fights with the Angel*; to the right, *Heliodorus is chased out of the temple* and on the vault, *Saint Michael killing the Dragon*.

The Latin Quarter

Arènes de Lutèce

between rues Monge and Navarre, 75005. Métro Jussieu. **Open** *May-Sept* 10am-8.30pm, *Oct-April* 10am-5.30pm, daily.
This was once the Roman arena, where roaring beasts and wounded gladiators met their deaths. The site was only discovered in 1869, and if you enter via the passageway at 49 rue Monge you may feel you've stumbled on a secret. But so have the gangs of kids playing football and groups of drunks, so don't expect romantic seclusion.

Institut du Monde Arabe

1 rue des Fossés St-Bernard, 75005 (40.51.39.53/restaurant 46.33.47.70). Métro Jussieu. **Open** 10am-6pm Tue-Sun; *library* 1-8pm Tue-Sat; *café* noon-6.30pm Tue-Sat, noon-3pm Sun; *restaurant* noon-3.30pm, 8pm-midnight, Tue-Sat; noon-3.30pm Sun.
Admission *building, roof-top terrace, library* free; *exhibitions* 25F; 20F students, over-60s.
This wedge-shaped building was purpose-designed by French architect Jean Nouvel in 1980 as an Arab cultural centre. The distinctive windows were inspired by the screens of Moorish palaces – as originally designed they were programmed with photo-electric cells, so that they would adjust automatically always to admit the same amount of daylight. However, of late a mix of technical and financial problems has led to this gadget being shut down, possibly for good. It's still one of the finer buildings of eighties' Paris, and inside is a permanent collection of Middle Eastern art, temporary exhibition spaces that present work ranging from ancient civilisations to contemporary design and photography, a specialist library, and a restaurant and café. The view from the roof-top terrace is worth the ride up in the glass lift.

Musée de Cluny (Musée National du Moyen Age)

6 place Paul Painlevé, 75005 (43.25.62.00). Métro St-Michel or Cluny-La Sorbonne. **Open** 9.15am-5.45pm Mon, Wed-Sun. **Admission** 27F; 18F students, over 60s and all visitors Sun; free under-18s. **Guided tours** *medieval collections* 3.30pm Wed, Sat, Sun; *baths* 2pm Wed, Sat, Sun. 61F; 21F under 18s, in addition to entry charge.
Along with the Hôtel de Sens in the Marais this castellated building is one of only two remaining examples of important fifteenth-century secular architecture in Paris. It was built by Jacques d'Amboise between 1485 and 1498 at the request of the Abbé de Cluny, who wanted somewhere to put up priests passing through the capital, on top of an earlier Gallo-Roman baths complex dating from the second and third centuries. These are the most important Roman remains in Paris, and three large rooms are just visible – the *frigidarium, tepidarium* and *caldarium*. The building was devastated during the Revolution, and a printer, a laundry and coopers set up shop here in 1807, before it was turned into a museum in 1844. Today, it houses an exceptional collection of medieval art and artefacts (*see chapter* **Museums**). Some

*The Baroque temple of **Val de Grace**.*

of the Roman remains can be seen from the street; wander too into the main courtyard and admire the magnificent staircase, Gothic mullioned windows and balustrade lined with dramatic gargoyles.

Le Panthéon

place du Panthéon (entrance place du Panthéon), 75005 (43.54.34.51). RER Luxembourg. **Open** *1 April-30 Sept* 9.30am-6.30pm daily (last admissions at 5.45pm). *1 Oct-31 Mar* 10am-5.30pm daily (last admissions 4.45pm). **Admission** 32F; 21F 18-25s; 10F 12-17s; free under-12s. **No credit cards**.

Designed by Soufflot, who also planned the surrounding square, this neo-classical megastructure was the great architectural work of its day. A grateful Louis XV had it built to thank Ste Geneviève, patron saint of Paris, for helping him recover from an illness. But events caught up with its completion in 1790, and in post-Revolutionary spirit it was re-dedicated as a temple of reason and the resting place of the heroes of the nation. It was definitively secularised in 1885, in a neat reversal of the history of Rome's famed Pantheon, upon which it was modelled, which started as a pagan temple only to be turned into a Catholic church. Until recently, the church had been closed for restoration, and parts of it are still cordoned off. However, you can still admire the elegant Greek columns and numerous domes, which give the building an airy grandeur, as well as the murals by Puvis de Chavannes depicting the life of Ste-Geneviève. In the barrel-vaulted crypt the great figures of France repose, statesmen, politicians and thinkers, as well as Voltaire, Rousseau, Victor Hugo and Zola. New heroes are added extremely rarely, the most recent being Pierre and Marie Curie, whose remains were transferred here in early 1995, the latter being the first women to be interred in the Pantheon in her own right. The steep spiral stairs leading to the colonnade around the dome are worth the climb for the wonderful views over Paris.

St-Etienne-du-Mont

place Ste-Geneviève, 75005 (43.54.11.79). Métro Cardinal-Lemoine or RER Luxembourg. **Open** *Sept-June* 8am-noon, 2-7pm, Mon-Sat; 9am-noon, 2.30-7pm, Sun; *July, Aug* 10am-noon, 4-7pm, Tue-Sat; 9am-noon, 3-7pm, Sun. **Admission** free.

The shrine of Ste Geneviève is inside this church, to the right of the choir. The stained glass windows show scenes from her life, including her restoration of her mother's sight by washing her eyes with well water. The church that survives today was built – in a variety of different styles – between 1492 and 1626. It has a Gothic rose window and the only remaining Renaissance-style rood screen in Paris, a riot of fine carving. The Gothic **Tour de Clovis** opposite is one of the few remains of Saint Geneviève's Abbey. The Lycée Henri IV, which now occupies the site, doesn't allow visitors.

St Séverin

1 rue des Prêtres-Saint-Séverin, 75005 (43.25.96.63). Métro Cluny-La Sorbonne or St-Michel. **Open** 11am-7.45pm Mon-Fri; 11am-8pm Sat; 9am-9.30pm Sun. **Admission** free.

The Primitive and Flamboyant Gothic styles merge in this complex, composite little church, mostly built between the thirteenth and fifteenth centuries, although further alterations were carried out in the 1680s, paid for by Louis XIV's cousin the 'Grande Mademoiselle'. The ambulatory is renowned for its remarkable 'palm tree' vaulting.

La Sorbonne

47 rue des Ecoles, 75005 (40.46.20.15). Métro Cluny-La Sorbonne. **Open** 9am-11.30am, 2pm-4.30pm. **Admission** limited public access.

Founded in 1253 by the cleric Robert de Sorbon as one of several separate 'colleges' in this area (*see chapter* **Paris by Area: The Right Bank**), the University of the Sorbonne was at the centre of the Latin Quarter's intellectual activity from the Middle Ages until May 1968, when its premises were occupied by students and stormed by the CRS (riot police). The authorities subsequently splintered the University of Paris into less strategically threatening suburban outposts, but the Sorbonne remains home to the Faculté des Lettres. The building, mostly built in 1885-1900, includes a labyrinth of classrooms and quaint lecture theatres, as well as an observatory tower, still visible from the rue St-Jacques. The elegant dome of the seventeenth-century chapel dominates the place de la Sorbonne. The chapel is generally closed to the public except for occasional concerts; Cardinal Richelieu is buried in an ornate tomb inside. Members of the public who wish to visit the Sorbonne must make reservations one month in advance; phone 40.26.20.15, and confirm in writing to Mme Bolot, 47 rue des Ecoles, 75005.

Val-de-Grace

place Alphonse Laveran, 75005 (40.51.47.00). RER Port-Royal. **Open** 10am-noon, 2-5pm, daily.

This church and its surrounding Benedictine monastery – now a hospital and a small medical museum – were built by François Mansart and Jacques Lemercier, in fulfilment of Anne of Austria's vow to erect 'a magnificent temple' if God blessed her with a son. He promptly presented her with two. Extraordinarily expensive and built over several decades, the recently restored Val-de-Grâce is the most luxuriously Baroque of the city's seventeenth-century domed churches, closely influenced by the Redentore in Venice, with a few Bernini-esque touches like the *baldaquin* with spiral columns borrowed from St Peter's in Rome. Bernini himself, however, greatly admired Mignard's dome fresco, saying that it was 'the masterpiece of French art'. Its swirling colours and forms are meant to give the viewer a foretaste of heaven.

*A dramatic detail at **St Sulpice**. See page 51.*

The Impressionist's terminus, the **Musée d'Orsay**.

The Monumental 7th

Assemblée Nationale

*33 quai d'Orsay, 75007 (40.63.60.00). Métro Assemblée
Nationale.* **Open** *guided tours only* 10am, 2pm and 3pm
Sat when Chamber is not in session, ID required.
The Palais Bourbon has been home to the Assemblée
Nationale, the lower house of the French parliament, since
1827. It was also the seat of the German military administration during the Occupation of Paris in World War II.
Originally built in 1722 for Louis XIV's daughter, the
Duchess of Bourbon, the palace was later extended by the
Prince of Condé, who added on the Hôtel de Lassay, today
the official residence of the Assembly's president. The Greek-
style façade facing the Seine was simply stuck onto the building under Napoleon in 1806 to echo that of the **Madeleine**
on the other side of the river; the real entrance is via the place
du Palais Bourbon. Inside, the library is decorated with
Delacroix's *History of Civilisation*.

Les Invalides

*Esplanade des Invalides, 75007 (Information
44.42.30.11/Musée de l'Armée 44.42.37.67). Métro
Invalides.* **Open** *April-Sept* 10am-6pm (last tickets
5.30pm), *Oct-Mar* 10am-5pm (last tickets 4.30pm), daily.
Admission 35F; 25F students, over-60s.
Visible from miles away because of the gleaming golden
Eglise du Dôme (regilded for the 1989 bicentenary of the
Revolution), Les Invalides is actually a collection of buildings. The huge classical-style **Hôtel des Invalides**, constructed between 1671 and 1676 for Louis XIV, was first built
as a military hospital for the King's soldiers. It was also a
retirement home for wounded soldiers that at one time
housed up to 6,000 invalids, hence the name. Other buildings
on the site include the **Musée de l'Armée**, the **Musée de
l'Ordre de la Liberation** and the **Eglise St-Louis**. The
army museum has a staggering display of weapons, maps
and war-time paraphernalia from the *ancien régime* to the
two world wars. The church of the Dôme is a typical, highly-
decorated example of French architecture from Louis XIV's
time. Designed by Hardouin-Mansart, with a square ground
plan, it is one of the grandest Baroque churches in the city.
Since 1840 it has been dedicated to the worship of Napoleon,
whose body was brought here from the island of St Helena
19 years after he died there. It now lies beneath the coffered
Baroque dome, in a red porphyry sarcophagus in a hushed
circular crypt. The church of St-Louis is also known as the
Church of the Soldiers, decorated with captured flags, and
with a crypt filled with the remains of military men.

Musée d'Orsay

*1 rue de Bellechasse, 75007 (40.49.48.14/recorded
information 45.49.11.11). Métro Solférino.* **Open** 10am-
6pm Tue, Wed, Fri, Sat; 10am-9.45pm Thur; 9am-6pm
Sun. **Admission** 35F; 24F 18-25s, over-60s, all visitors
Sun; free under-18s. **Credit** (bookshop only)
AmEx, EC, MC, V.
Opened in 1986, the Musée d'Orsay was originally a train
station, designed by Victor Laloux as part of the enormous
works for the 1900 *Exposition Universelle*. You can still see
the names of towns it once served on the Seine-side façade.
Trains ceased to run there in the fifties as its platforms
proved too short, and for a long time it was threatened with
demolition, until in the late seventies President Giscard
bowed to public pressure and scrapped plans to demolish
the fine *Beaux-Arts* edifice with its distinctive twin clock
towers. It was decided instead to turn it into a museum of
the nineteenth century, housing the splendid Impressionist
canvases formerly crammed into the **Jeu de Paume**, plus
paintings and sculpture from the Louvre and other museums, in a boldly redesigned interior by Italian architect Gae
Aulenti. The never-ending crowds snaking their way into
the building attest to the project's success: a perfect fusion
of form and content. The collection spans the fertile period
from around 1830 to 1914, and the main attraction, besides
Manet's *Olympia* on the ground floor, is the skylit
Impressionist gallery on the upper floor, filled with masterpieces by Monet, Renoir, Pisarro and Van Gogh.

Pied-à-terre for Parisian parliamentarians, the **Assemblée Nationale**. *See page 55*

Further Afield

Bibliothèque Nationale de France

9 boulevard Vincent Auriol, quai de la Gare, 75013 (44.23.03.70). Métro Quai de la Gare. **Open** one-hour tours 10am-5pm Sun, public holidays. **Admission** free.
The new Bibliothèque Nationale de France (or TGB – *Très Grande Bibliothèque*) is not only the last of President Mitterrand's *grands projets*, but also the most expensive, and the most controversial. Heated debate has raged ever since the announcement of plans to build the biggest library in the world. Much of the criticism has been aimed at the design of architect Dominique Perrault, chosen directly by the former President himself, but condemned by most of the architectural profession. It has since had to be significantly modified. Perrault had the curious idea of storing books in four L-shaped glass towers rather than underground; when it was pointed out that keeping precious documents behind glass meant that sunlight could destroy them, wooden shutters had to be installed, at still more expense. Equally, again in contrast to the traditional logic of building a library in the form of a rectangle so that documents could be accessed as quickly as possible, Perrault's plans called for the centre to be left open and filled with a garden of 140 trees, which have been uprooted from Fontainebleau at a cost of 40 million francs. Arguments have also raged over the height of each tower, the layout of the reading rooms and the use of rare wood for the esplanade. Many are still horrified by the resulting structure, which was inaugurated by Mitterrand in one of his last acts in office in March 1995. It has now gone far beyond the stage where it could be cancelled, and the library is due to open to the public in 1996, with over ten million volumes, 420 kilometres of shelves and room for 3,000 readers.

La Villette

Cité des Sciences et d'Industrie, 30 avenue Corentin-Cariou 75019 Métro Porte de la Villette.
Cité de la Musique, Grande Halle, Zénith, Parc de la Villette 75019. Métro Porte de Pantin.

Reception (40.03.75.03), guided tours (40.03.75.05/75.64). **Guided tours** of the park 3pm Wed from the intersection of the Canal de l'Ourcq and the Canal St-Martin. 35F; 30F students, over-60s; 15F under 18s.
A post-modern park and giant arts and science complex running either side of the Canal de l'Ourcq in the north-east of Paris, La Villette has proved an enormously successful example of eighties' urban renewal. It was the site of Paris' principal cattle market and abattoir, and was originally going to be replaced by a high-tech slaughterhouse. Instead there's a fascinating ultra-modern Science Museum full of interactive exhibits, particularly in its special children's section, the **Cité des Enfants**; the shiny spherical Géode, an innovative cinema; the **Cité de la Musique** music complex, designed by Christian de Portzamparc; and Bernard Tschumi's bright red deconstructivist pavilions, or *folies*, dotted around the park on a grid plan, fulfilling a variety of functions from café to first-aid post. There are also 'prairies' to picnic on, and a variety of themed gardens. On the southern side of the canal is the aircraft-hangar-like Zénith, used for pop concerts. The **Grande Halle de la Villette** is the last remaining part of the old iron abattoir structure and is used for trade fairs and festivals. It is winged by the two parts of the Cité de la Musique, another *grand projet* – music school on one side, and concert hall, rehearsal rooms and music museum on the other. *See also chapters* **Museums, Film, Music: Classical & Opera, Music: Rock, Roots & Jazz** *and* **Children**.

Basilica of St-Denis

2 rue de Strasbourg, 93200 St-Denis (48.09.83.54). Métro St-Denis-Basilique. **Open** *Apr-Sept* 10am-6.30pm Mon-Sat; noon-8.30pm Sun. *Oct-Mar* 10am-4.30pm Mon-Sat; noon-4.30pm Sun. **Admission** *cathedral* free. *royal tombs* 27F; 18F 18-26s, 10F 12-17s; free under-12s.
Guided tours *cathedral* 3pm Mon-Fri, every half hour from 2.30-4.30pm Sat and Sun (phone for tour in English), nominal charge. *cathedral and abbey 15 Apr-15 Sept* 4pm Sat, Sun. 25F; 20F students, over-60s, under 18s.

Legend has it that when Saint Denis was beheaded, he rose to his feet, picked up his head and, accompanied by a choir of angels, walked to *Vicus Catulliacus* (now St-Denis), where he wished to be buried. In fact, he was sent to Gaul to preach the Gospel in the third century, under the Emperor Decius, and became the first bishop of Paris. The first church on this site was built over his tomb in around 475. However, the present edifice dates from the thirteenth century, and is commonly regarded as the first example of true Gothic architecture, as well as one of the finest. It stands today at the heart of the old town of St-Denis, now surrounded by one of Paris' most sprawling industrial suburbs (*see chapter* **Paris by Area: Beyond the Périphérique**). Much more impressive inside than the damaged façade suggests, the basilica was begun by Abbot Suger in the twelfth century, although it was only in the middle of the following century that the architect Pierre de Montreuil erected the spire and rebuilt the choir, nave and transept. This was the burial place for all monarchs of France between 996 and the end of the *ancien régime*, with the exception of three. However, during the Revolution the basilica was greatly damaged, in one giant explosion of popular anger in 1792 when the tombs weredesecrated and the royal remains thrown into a communal pit nearby. In 1805, Napoleon ordered the restoration of the building, which was completed by Viollet-le-Duc in 1875. Part of the fifth-century church can still be seen in the crypt, which is crammed with royal tombs, the greatest collection of funerary sculptures in France. On display are the tombs of Henry II, Catherine de Medici, Louis XVI, Marie-Antoinette and other monarchs. Beside the basilica is the former abbey, which is now a high school and is only open to the public by way of guided visits at the weekend.

Château de Malmaison

avenue du Château, 92500 Rueil-Malmaison. (41.29.05.55). RER La Défense, then bus 258. **Open** *April-Sept* 10am-noon, 1.30pm-5.30pm (last entry at 5pm) Mon, Wed-Sun. *Oct–March* 10am-noon, 1.30pm-5pm (last entry at 4.30pm) Mon, Wed-Sun. **Guided tours** Sat, Sun. **Admission** 27F; 18F 18–25s, over-60s, and all visitors Sun; free under 18s.
The château at Malmaison, today within Paris' smart western suburbs, owes its renown to its Napoleonic connections. Bought in 1799 by Josephine, it was the Emperor's favourite retreat during the Consulate (1800–03) and one of the few

places he could feel at ease. Most of the building dates from the seventeenth century, but the entrance was turned into the form of a military tent by the couple, who also enlarged and decorated the reception rooms in neo- Roman style and added an orangery, greenhouse, stables and theatre. After their divorce in 1809 Napoleon left the château to Josephine, who died there in 1814. Later, following his defeat at Waterloo, he stopped off at Malmaison on his way to exile. In 1896, the sadly-decayed château was bought by a banker who restored it and left it to the state in 1904 on condition that it be made a Napoleonic museum. Inside you can see portraits of Napoleon by Gros and David, as well as the *Salle du Conseil*, in which the Emperor took many of his most important decisions. Next to the house is Josephine's rose garden, and a cedar which she is supposed to have planted in celebration of victory at the Battle of Marengo. Napoleon's coach, seized by Marshal Blücher at Waterloo, is on display in the stables. There is an annex of the museum in the nearby Château de Bois Préau.

Tours

Coach Tours

All the tours listed below start in the centre of Paris and last about two hours. They either have a guide or pre-recorded commentaries, and pass the major sights, but do not stop at all of them.

Balabus

Hours *April-Sept 12.30-8pm, Sun and public holidays.* **Tickets** four RATP tickets or fewer depending on the length of the journey.
A 50-minute bus route, run by Paris' RATP city transport system, which takes in many tourist sites between La Défense in the west and Gare de Lyon in the east, including the Arc de Triomphe, Champs-Elysées, place de la Concorde, the Louvre, Notre Dame and the Latin Quarter.

Cityrama

Depart from Cityrama bus stop, 4 place des Pyramides, 75001 (44.55.61.00). Métro Palais Royal. **Trips** *Cityrama tour (pre-recorded) 2 hours* 9.30am, 10.30am,

Underground Paris

Those who've had enough of Parisian beauty can take a plunge into the bowels of the city for a sniff of something more macabre.

Les Catacombes

1 place Denfert-Rochereau, 75014 (43.22.47.63). Métro Denfert-Rochereau. **Open** 2-4pm Tue-Fri; 9-11am, 2-4pm, Sat, Sun. Closed public holidays. **Admission** 27F; 15F under-18s. **No credit cards**.
These dank, subterranean passages stretching for miles have existed since Roman times. Towards the end of the eighteenth century many of the old over-crowded Paris cemeteries were emptied out, and their contents transferred here. Stacks of bones are neatly arranged in patterns, interspersed with tidy rows of skulls, while mottoes and quotations inscribed on stone tablets add philosophical reflections on death. There are supposedly bits of some six million people down here, including many victims of the Revolutionary Terror. For more communing with the dead, *see page 59* **Gone but not Forgotten**.

Les Egouts de Paris (The Sewers)

Entrance by the Pont de l'Alma, opposite 93 quai d'Orsay, 75007 (47.05.10.29). RER Pont de l'Alma or Métro Alma-Marceau. **Open** 11am-5pm Sat-Wed. Closed three weeks in Jan. **Admission** 25F; 20F students, under 16s.
Truly the city's underbelly. Part of its sewers have been made into one of the smelliest museums in the world. One can no longer wander as far as one could some years ago, but it's still possible to take a tour through several tunnels, with huge metal pipes overhead and murky green water flowing rapidly beneath the grating underfoot. On display there are various pieces of equipment used in the purifying process, while a slide show and display recount the history of the Parisian water and sewer systems. You can find out that it was a certain M. Poubelle ('Mister Dustbin') who first initiated household waste collection, and that each Paris sewer is marked with a replica of the corresponding street sign above it, making the 2,100 kilometre system a real city beneath a city.

Viewpoints

From ground level, the most spectacular view in Paris is the one along the great axis stretching from the **Louvre** across the **Tuileries** and up the **Champs-Elysées** to the **Arc de Triomphe**, with the **Grande Arche de La Défense** looming in the background. But it is only from up high that you can really appreciate the layout of Paris as envisaged by Haussmann, with its network of wide boulevards and homogeneous façades.

The view from the top level of the **Eiffel Tower**, 274m high, can stretch to 67 kilometres on a clear day and takes in the whole of the city. It has a competitor in the **Tour Montparnasse**, the skyscraper built in 1974 on the site of the former Gare Montparnasse. At 209m high, it's lower than the Eiffel, but more central, and offers some excellent views of the Left Bank. A lift whisks you in just 40 seconds up to the 56th floor, where you'll find a display of aerial views of Paris some of which date back to 1858, allowing you to see how the city has changed over the past century. If you want to know more, a machine offers a description of the panorama in English for 10F. You can also make your way up three flights of stairs for an open-air view from the rooftop.

Of the classic viewpoints, the towers of **Notre-Dame** are only 70m high, but you can easily make out the spire of the Ste-Chapelle in the middle of the Palais de Justice, the place du Châtelet and the dome of the Institut de France across the river. The **Centre Pompidou** offers similar views. From the steps in front of the **Sacré Coeur** the whole of Paris stretches out before you, with the jumbled rooftops of Montmartre in the foreground, and you can climb to the top of the dome for an even better view.

Less well-known are the superb views from the top of the **Panthéon**, which reward energetic climbers. Lifts take the legwork out of things at the **Arc de Triomphe** and the **Grande Arche de La Défense**. One of the very best views of Paris can also be found on the roof terrace of the **Samaritaine** department store – take the lift to the ninth floor, and walk up (*see chapter* **Specialist Shops**).

Tour Maine-Montparnasse
33 avenue de Maine, 75015 (45.38.52.56) **Open** *Apr-Sept* 9.30am-11pm, *Oct-Mar* 9.30am-10pm, daily. **Admission** 42F; 36F over-60s; 26F under-14s; 18F students.

11.30am, 12.30pm, 1.30pm, 2.30pm, 3.30pm, 4.30pm daily. **Tickets** 150F; 75F 4-11s. *Artistic tour (in English)* 3 *hours, stops Notre-Dame, Louvre* 9.45am Wed-Mon. **Ticket** 260F; 130F 4-11s. *Panoramic tour (in English)* 4 *hours, via Seine, stops Invalides, Eiffel Tower* 2.15pm daily. **Ticket** 260F; 130F 4-11s. **Credit** AmEx, MC, V. Tours that take in all the classic sites of Paris. Customers are provided with individual cassettes with recorded commentary in various languages, and a hostess also accompanies each tour.

Parisbus
(42.30.55.50). First and last bus leave from Eiffel Tower, quai Branly, 75007; stops include Notre-Dame, Musée d'Orsay, Opéra, Arc de Triomphe, Grand Palais. **Trips** *Easter weekend to end July* 10am-5pm; *Aug-mid Oct* 9.45am-4.50pm; *mid Oct-Easter* 9.55am-2.55pm, daily. **Tickets** 125F; 100F students; 60F under-12s; free under-4s. **No credit cards.**
Red London doubledeckers do a two hour, 15-minute round trip with a pre-recorded commentary in French and English. The advantage is that you can get off and on at will, at any of nine stops, making your own itinerary. Tickets are valid for two days, which works out to be quite economical, and are purchased on the bus. Parisbus runs every 50 minutes.

Paris Vision
(42.60.31.25). Coaches depart from 214 rue de Rivoli, 75001. Métro Tuileries. **Trips** 9.30am, 10.30am, 11.30am, 12.30pm, 1.30pm, 2.30pm, 3.30pm daily. **Tickets** 150F; 72F 4-11s; free under-4s. **Credit** AmEx, DC, JCB, MC, EC, V.
Paris Vision coaches have pre-recorded commentaries. Tickets are available from 1 rue Auber, 75009 in advance, or from the departure point 15 minutes before the trip.

Walking Tours

Walking tours are a good idea if you prefer to see the city at first hand instead of from the restricted comfort of a bus. There are many individual guides who organise walks (in French), of which details are published weekly in *Pariscope*. Most simply specify a meeting place, and do not require pre-booking.

Caisse Nationale des Monuments Historiques et des Sites
Hôtel de Sully, 62 rue St-Antoine, 75004 (44.61.20.00). Métro Bastille or St-Paul. **Tours** phone for details or stop by for brochures.
Tours of monuments, museums and historic districts. English-speaking guides can be arranged.

Anne Hervé
(47.90.52.16). **Tickets** 40F, plus any admission prices.
Anne Hervé is a registered guide who does well-informed one-and-a-half hour tours in English of historic Paris *quartiers*, such as St-André-des-Arts, the Marais and Beaubourg, about twice weekly in summer and fortnightly in winter. She will also arrange tailor-made tours for groups.

Paris Walking Tours
Oriel and Peter Caine (48.09.21.40). **Tours** usually Tue, Thurs, Sat, Sun, phone for details. **Tickets** 60F; 40F students; free under 10s (except sewers visit)
An English couple who are registered Paris guides and organise a range of walks around the Marais, Père Lachaise and the other cemeteries, the sewers, some museums, literary Paris and other interesting parts of the city. Tours last around 90 minutes, and focus on the historical, architectural or anecdotal aspects of the area.

Paris Contacts

*Jill Daneels, 26 rue des Trois Frères, 75018
(42.51.08.40).* **Tours** *specialised* 2.30pm Mon-Fri,
otherwise phone for details of daily tours. **Tickets** 110F
specialised tours, 50-60F daily tours.
A variety of 'exclusive guided adventures' plus specialised
tours including wine production, and artists in Montmatre.
Personal guided tours also available.

Walking the Spirit

(42.29.60.12). **Tours** 9.30am Fri, Sat, Sun.
Tickets 100F.
Two different walks visiting places, mostly in the sixth and
ninth *arrondissements*, associated with African-Americans
in Paris.

Bike Tours

Paris-Vélo

*2 rue du Fer-à-Moulin, 75005 (43.37.59.22). Métro
Censier-Daubenton.* **Open** 10am-12.30pm, 2-7pm Mon-
Sat; 10am-2pm Sun. **Tickets** 150F; 120F under-26s; 150F
night-time tours; includes tour, bike rental, insurance.
Credit EC, MC, V.
Paris-Vélo propose gentle three-hour tours of such areas as
the Latin Quarter, the Marais or the Ile St-Louis. Tours are
accompanied by a bilingual guide, and you don't need to be
a cycling or fitness fanatic to enjoy the visits. A special *Paris
by Night* tour follows a surprise itinerary with stops for a
drink and photos. *See also chapter* **Services.**

Gone but not forgotten

If you're feeling exhausted by the whirl of the
capital, try a spot of contemplation in one of
Paris' fine and atmospheric cemeteries, or a gentle stroll to seek out the city's illustrious former
inhabitants.

Cimetière du Père Lachaise

*Main entrance boulevard de Ménilmontant, 75020
(43.70.70.33). Métro Père-Lachaise.* **Open** *mid-Mar-5
Nov* 8am-6pm Mon-Sat; 9am-6pm Sun, public holidays;
6 Nov-mid-Mar 8.30am-5pm Mon-Sat; 9am-6pm Sun,
public holidays.
With its thousands of tightly packed tombs arranged along
cobbled lanes and tree-lined avenues, this vast cemetery is
almost like a miniature city in itself. It is supposedly the
most visited cemetery in the world, with funerary memorials
and family vaults ranging from the plain and sombre to the
grandiose, and plots can still be leased. The many famous
inhabitants include the presumed remains of the medieval
lovers Abélard and Héloise, in a suitably pseudo-Gothic
tomb, Simone Signoret, Colette, Edith Piaf, Delacroix, Ingres,
Bizet, Balzac, Proust and Chopin (his empty tomb), to name
a few, as well as a host of lesser-known figures, many of
whom have contributed to Parisian history. Undoubtedly
the biggest draw is Jim Morrison, who was buried here in
1971. His grave still attracts a steady flow of worshippers;
the graffiti will show you the way. Also visit Oscar Wilde's
tomb, whose headstone was carved by Epstein. It's a
winged, naked, male angel which was considered so offen-
sive when first erected (the *mot juste*), that it was neutered
by the head keeper, who subsequently used the offending
part as a paper-weight. The cemetery wall, known as the
'Mur des Fédérés', got its name after 147 survivors of the
Paris Commune of 1871 were shot against it. Maps are available at the entrance for a small fee.

Cimetière de Montmartre

*20 avenue Rachel, access by stairs from rue
Caulaincourt, 75018 (43.87. 64.24). Métro Blanche.*
Open 8am-6pm Mon-Fri; 8.30am-5.30pm Sun.
A small, romantic spot on the slopes of the Butte
Montmartre, where you will find playwright-actor Sacha
Guitry, François Truffaut, Zola, Nijinsky, Berlioz, Dégas
and many other writers and artists, reflecting the the-
atrical and artistic past of the area. There's also *La
Goulue*, real name Louise Weber, first great star of the
Can-Can and model for Toulouse Lautrec, and the con-
sumptive heroine Alphonsine Plessis, inspiration for
Dumas' *La Dame aux Camélias* and Verdi's *La Traviata*.

Cimetière de Montparnasse

*3 boulevard Edgar-Quinet, 75014. Métro Edgar
Quinet (44.10.86.50).* **Open** *16 March-5 Nov* 8am-
6pm Mon-Fri; 8.30am-6pm Sat; 9am-6pm Sun, public
holidays. *6 Nov-15 Mar* closes at 5.30pm.
Pick up a free map at the *Conservation* near the entrance
(closed between 12am and 2pm, and all day Saturday and
Sunday), and pay homage to writers Jean-Paul Sartre and
Simone de Beauvoir, Baudelaire, Maupassant, composers
César Frank and Saint-Saëns, sculptors Rude and
Zadkine, the unfortunate Captain Alfred Dreyfus, André
Citroën of car fame, and the delightful M and Mme Pigeon
reposing in their double bed. More recent occupants of
this 44-acre cemetery include beloved comic Coluche and
provocateur Serge Gainsbourg. In the northeast corner is
one of Brancusi's best known sculptures, *Le Baiser*, adorning one of the tombs.

Seine Boat Trips

Taking a boat down the Seine may be corny, but it's also a perfect way to see the grand sights in just an hour, and to get your bearings in the city. On summer evenings an almost continuous stream of tour boats passes along the Seine. Tours leave from various points, but all do a one-hour circuit up and down the Right and Left Banks between the Eiffel Tower and the Ile-St-Louis. Most have commentaries in different languages.

Bateaux-Mouches

pont de l'Alma, right bank, 75008 (40.76.99.99 recorded info, 40.76.99.99/lunch or dinner booking 42.25.96.10). Métro Alma-Marceau. **Departs** every half hour from 10am-12.30pm, 1.30-11pm, daily, trip lasts one hour. **Tickets** 40F; 20F under-14s. Book ahead for lunch 1pm departure (300F, 150F under 12s Tue-Sat; 350F, 175F under12s Sun, holidays) and dinner 8.30pm departure (500F – smart dress required) cruises. **Credit** AmEx, DC, MC, V, JCB
These huge boats with open-air and covered decks carry around 800 people, with a recorded commentary in numerous languages, including English. It may be of interest that the owner of this company is a major financial supporter of M. Le Pen's National Front.

Bateaux Parisiens Tour Eiffel

port de la Bourdonnais, 75007 (44.11.33.55). Métro Bir-Hakeim or Trocadéro. **Departs** half-hourly 10am-10pm daily. **Tickets** 45F; 20F under-12s. **Credit** (for meal cruises only) MC, V.
Glass-topped boats for around 400 passengers, with a live English commentary. Phone for a schedule of lunch-time cruises that last from 12.30-2.45pm (300F). Evening dinner cruises (550F) are from 8.30-11pm daily, offering a three-course menu on a smarter boat.

Bateaux Vedettes de Paris

port de Suffren, near Eiffel Tower, 75007 (47.05.71.29) Métro Bir-Hakeim/RER Champ de Mars. **Departs** half hourly 9am-9pm daily. **Tickets** 45F; 20F 4-11s; free under-4s.
Live commentary in French and English.

Batobus

From Eiffel Tower (44.11.33.44). Métro Bir-Hakeim/RER Champ de Mars. Departs Apr-Sept half hourly 10am-7pm daily. Tickets per station 12F; day pass 60F.
A river bus service, with stops at the Musée d'Orsay, the Louvre, Notre Dame and the quai de l'Hôtel de Ville.

Les Vedettes du Pont Neuf

1 square du Vert-Galant, 75001 (46.33. 98.38). Métro Pont-Neuf. **Departs** every 30 mins 10am-noon, 1.30-6.30pm, daily; *floodlit evening trips* 9-10.30pm daily. **Tickets** 20F; 15F under 15s.
Boats carry between 100 and 350 people. They are smaller and more personal than the Bateaux-Mouches, and there is live commentary in French, English and German and a friendly atmosphere. Boats are open topped in summer.

Canal Trips

Canal trips give the chance to inspect the old canal system (*see chapter* **Paris by Area: The Right Bank**), with its quaint bridges and locks, and to see areas currently undergoing substantial transformation. It's advisable to book in advance.

Canauxrama

(42.39.15.00). **Departs** *Bassin de la Villette, 5 bis quai de la Loire, 75019, Métro Jaurès* 9.15am, 2.45pm daily, and *Porte de l'Arsenal, 75012, Métro Bastille* 9.30am, 2.45pm daily. **Tickets** 75F.
Trips last 2-3 hours. There's a live commentary in French, and in English as well if there are enough foreigners; otherwise a written text is available.

Navettes de la Villette

(42.39.15.00). Shuttle service between *Parc de la Villette, Métro Porte de Pantin* and *Rotonde de Ledoux, Métro Jaurès.* **Departs** weather permitting, every 30 mins 11am-6.30pm, *Apr-Sept* Wed, Sat, Sun, holidays; *Jul-Aug only* daily. **Tickets** 10F single; 15F return.
Small ferry boats that run through the Parc de la Villette and across the canal basin alongside it.

Paris Canal

(42.40.96.97). **Departs** *Musée d'Orsay, Métro Solférino* 9.30am, arrives *Parc de la Villette, Métro Porte de Pantin* 12.30pm, daily. **Departs** *5 Mar-11 Nov* Parc de la Villette 2.30pm, arrives Musée d'Orsay 5.30pm, daily. **Tickets** 95F; 70F 12-25s, over-60s (except afternoons on Sunday and Bank Holidays); 55F 4-11s; free under 4s. Commentary in French and English. Reservations required.

Unusual Trips

Funiculaire de Montmartre

Leaves from rue Tardieu, 75018. Métro Abbesses or Anvers. **Open** 6am-midnight daily.
Tickets one métro ticket.
A high-tech cable car which goes up the steep hill from rue Tardieu to the base of the Sacré Coeur.

Le Petit Train de Montmartre

Leaves from place Blanche, 75018 (42.62.24.00). Métro Blanche. **Open** *summer* 9.30am-2am daily; *winter* 10am-6.30pm daily. **Trips** trains leave every 40 minutes. **Ticket** 30F; 15F under-12s; groups 25F, 10F.
A miniature sightseeing train which takes a route full of hairpin bends around the crowded streets of Montmartre. You can get off at the place du Tertre to visit the artists' square, or at Sacré Coeur, and get another train back. Large groups are advised to book on 42.62.24.00.

Hélifrance

4 avenue de la Porte de Sèvres, 75015 (45.54.95.11/ 45.57.53.67). Métro Balard. **Open** 8am-8pm Mon-Fri; 9am-6pm Sat, Sun. **Price** 850F or 1,200F scenic tour. **Credit** AmEx, EC, MC, V.
A maximum of five passengers can take off for a helicopter trip over the St-Cloud forest near Versailles, touching down at the Abbaye des Vaux de Cernay for a light repast, then coasting back via the Chevreuse Valley. Total flight time is 30 minutes. Parisian skies are unfortunately off-limits, but the 1,200F 45-minute trip follows a more extended flight plan, including an aerial scan of the Périphérique and the Seine. Alternatively, throw caution to the winds and negotiate your own itinerary.

Armchair Viewing

Paristoric

11 bis rue Scribe, 75009 (42.93.93.46). Métro Opéra. **Open** shows hourly 9am-9pm daily. **Admission** 50F. **No credit cards**
A multivision extravaganza flashing through 2,000 years of Paris history, from Roman Lutetia to the Louvre Pyramid in just 45 minutes. Images are beamed from 26 projectors onto a huge screen, accompanied by music and the sounds of Dolby cannon fire. Headsets with English commentary.

History

Key Events

Roman Paris & the Dark Ages

c 250 BC *Lutetia* founded on the Ile de la Cité by a Celtic tribe, the Parisii
52 BC Paris conquered by the Romans
260 St Denis executed on Montmartre
361 Julian, Governor of Lutetia, becomes Roman Emperor
451 Attila the Hun nearly attacks Paris
508 Frankish king Clovis makes Paris his capital
635 first Fair of St-Denis
800 Charlemagne, first Holy Roman Emperor. Moves capital from Paris to Aix-la-Chapelle
840-880 Paris sacked by the Vikings
987 Hugh Capet, Count of Paris, first King of France

Middle Ages to Renaissance

1136 Abbot Suger begins Basilica of St-Denis
1163 Building of Notre Dame begun
1215 University of Paris recognised with Papal Charter
1340 Beginning of Hundred Years' War with England
1364 Charles V moves royal court to the Louvre.
1420-1436 Paris under English rule
1473 First printing press in Paris
1528 Francis I begins rebuilding of Louvre
1572 St Bartholomew's Day massacre of Protestants
1593 Henry IV becomes a Catholic, ending Wars of Religion

Ancien Régime

1605 Building of place des Vosges begun
1610 Henry IV assassinated
1634 Académie Française founded by Cardinal Richelieu
1648-1653 Paris occupied by the *Fronde* rebellion
1661 Louis XIV begins personal rule
1667 Paris given its first street lighting
1682 Louis XIV transfers Court to Versailles
1700 Beginning of War of the Spanish Succession
1715 Death of Louis XIV.
1720 John Law's bank scheme collapses
1751 First volume of Diderot's *Encyclopédie* published.
1753 Work begun on place de Louis XV, later place de la Concorde
1785 Tax Wall built around Paris
1789 First meeting of Estates-General called since 1614

Revolution & Empire

1789 14 July: Paris mob takes the Bastille. October: Louis XVI forced to leave Versailles for Paris. Population of Paris is then about 600,000
1791 20 June: Louis XVI attempts to escape from Paris
1792 22 September: Republic declared
1793-1794 The Terror in Paris
1794 July: Jacobins overthrown; Directory takes over the Republic
1799 Napoleon stages coup, and becomes First Consul
1804 Napoleon declares himself Emperor
1806 Napoleon orders building of the Arc de Triomphe
1814 Napoleon defeated; Russian army occupies Paris
1815 Napoleon regains power for the 'Hundred Days'

Artists & Rebellions

1815 Bourbons restored, with Louis XVIII
1828 Paris given its first horse buses
1830 July: Charles X overthrown: Louis-Philippe of Orléans becomes king
1837 First railway line in Paris, to St-Germain en Laye
1848 Louis Philippe overthrown: Second Republic. Louis-Napoléon Bonaparte is elected President
1851 Louis-Napoléon stages coup, and later declares himself Emperor Napoléon III
1853 Haussmann appointed Prefect of Paris
1863 Manet's *Déjeuner sur l'Herbe* first exhibited
1870 Prussian victory at Sedan. Napoleon III abdicates

The Third Republic

1871 Commune takes over Paris after the Prussian siege
1889 Paris Exhibition on centenary of Revolution: Eiffel Tower built
1900 Paris World Exhibition: population of Paris then two million
1904 Pablo Picasso moves to Paris
1914 As World War I begins, Germans beaten back from Paris at Battle of the Marne
1919 Peace conference held at Versailles
1936 France elects Popular Front government
1940 Germans occupy Paris
1942 Mass deportation of Paris Jews
1944 25 August: Paris liberated

De Gaulle to Chirac

1946 Fourth Republic established
1949 Simone de Beauvoir publishes *The Second Sex*
1955-1956 Revolt begins in Algeria
1958 De Gaulle President: Fifth Republic
1968 May: student riots and strikes in Paris and across France
1969 De Gaulle resigns; Les Halles market closes
1973 Boulevard Périphérique around Paris inaugurated
1977 Centre Pompidou opened
1981 François Mitterand elected President
1989 Bicentenary of the Revolution celebrated: Louvre pyramid and the Opéra Bastille both completed
1992 Disney theme park opens outside Paris
1995 May: Jacques Chirac, President of France

Roman Paris & the Dark Ages

After a first flourish under Rome, Paris was buffeted between miraculous saints and degenerate monarchs.

In about 250 BC a Celtic tribe called the Parisii first established a settlement on the Ile de la Cité. They probably did so because they had been driven from lands further east by the more powerful Belgae. Their new settlement, though, on a road linking Germany to Spain and at the confluence of three rivers, the Seine, the Marne and the Oise, was a natural crossroads. Rich in agricultural land and stone quarries, the community flourished. The Celts were canny traders, and grew wealthy: a collection of local gold coins from the first century BC – now in the **Musée des Antiquités Nationales** in St-Germain en Laye (*see chapter* **Paris by Area: Beyond the Périphérique**) – indicates the extent of the city's prosperity.

Its strategic position also made the city a prime military target, and by the first century BC the Romans had appeared in northern Gaul. Julius Caesar mentions 'the city of the Parisii, situated on an isle in the Seine', known as *Lutetia*, in his *Gallic Wars*. In 53 BC he launched his final confrontation with the Gauls, united against him under their chieftain Vercingétorix. In 52, his lieutenant Labienus crushed the Parisii, and took the city. Shortly afterwards Caesar defeated Vercingétorix at Alésia, and the conquest of Gaul was complete.

Lutetia, however, thrived under Roman rule. The town spread from the Cité to the Left Bank, fanning out towards the Montagne Ste-Geneviève, on either side of the *cardus* (main thoroughfare), the present-day rue St-Jacques. Many of its buildings were of masonry, brick and mortar, some embellished with carving, stucco and frescoes. As in every city in their empire, the Romans built baths and amphitheatres, where the Celts could be introduced to sophisticated pleasures and to savage and ferocious combats between gladiators and wild animals. The amphitheatre in Lutetia could hold a crowd of 10,000, making it the second-largest in Gaul. As well as an arena, it boasted a stage for more refined entertainment – mime shows, dances, plays and acrobatics. A model of the ancient city – along with architectural vestiges such as column capitals, fragments of murals and mosaics – is on view at the **Musée Carnavalet**.

It was during the golden age of Gallo-Roman architecture (from about AD 50 to AD 200) that Lutetia acquired its grandest public buildings. The remains have been uncovered of a forum (on rue Soufflot, between boulevard St-Michel and rue St-Jacques) and a trio of bathing establishments (rue des Écoles, rue Gay-Lussac and boulevard St-Michel). There was also a temple where Notre Dame now stands. Only the **Arènes de Lutèce** (the amphitheatre) and the baths at the **Musée du Cluny** reflect anything of their former glory today.

DENIS' REMARKABLE HEAD

Christianity made its first appearance in the city in the third century AD, when Saint Denis, first bishop of Lutetia, arrived from the south to evangelise its people. Legend has it that one day, he and two companions began to knock pagan statues off their pedestals. They were immediately arrested, and the Roman governor decreed that they should be decapitated on Mount Mercury, thereafter known as the Mount of Martyrs, or Montmartre. Headless and bleeding, the plucky Denis picked up

Emperor Julian, the Apostate.

his bonce and walked away, his lips chanting psalms. He finally fell at a seemingly predestined site north of Paris, where a pious Christian woman buried him. A sanctuary was later erected on the spot where this was believed to be, eventually to be replaced by the giant **Basilica of St-Denis**.

By the time of Denis, around 260, Roman power was weakening, and Lutetia was under increasing attack from barbarian invaders from the east. Many of its inhabitants retreated to their ancestral island in the Seine, and a wall was built around the Cité. Lutetia, however, would still be able briefly to become one of the capitals of the Roman Empire.

In 313 the Emperor Constantine effectively made Christianity the new religion of the Empire. In 357, however, a new governor arrived in Lutetia, a young Greek, Julian. He did a great deal to improve the city and its defences; he could also be said to be the first independent Parisian intellectual, seeking to return to Classical ideals in opposition to what he saw as the crudity and brutality of the new Christian emperors. In 361, following a series of victories against the barbarians, his army declared him Roman Emperor in Paris. For his renunciation of Christianity, he would be condemned for ever by Christian historians as 'Julian the Apostate'. But he could do little to turn back the new faith or the decline of Rome, for he was killed in battle in 363.

LONG-HAIRED DYNASTIES

Gradually, Christianity had taken root in Paris. By the beginning of the fifth century, however, Roman rule had effectively collapsed in northern Gaul, and its cities were left to fend for themselves. It was around this time that Lutetia began to be known by the name of its early Gallic settlers, as Paris.

In the chaos that followed the collapse of Rome, it was the exemplary life of Saint Genevieve – and the threat of war – that helped confirm many converts in the new faith. As the legend goes, in 451 Attila the Hun and his army were approaching Paris. Its people panicked, and prepared to flee. But Genevieve, a saintly Christian girl, urged them to stay put. She told them the Hun would spare their city so long as they repented of their sins and prayed with her. And miraculously, Attila did not attack but moved off to the south. Genevieve was acclaimed as the saviour of Paris.

Her powers of resistance were not limitless. In 464 another barbarian, the Frank Childeric, attacked Paris, and in 508 his son Clovis made it his capital, with the former Roman governor's palace on the Ile de la Cité as the seat of his realm. The now-aged Genevieve was, however, successful in converting the new king to Christianity. She died in about 512, and was buried on the hill that bears her name, Montagne Ste-Geneviève. She has been regarded as patron saint of Paris almost ever since, and there are relics of her in churches in the area such as **St-Etienne-du-Mont**.

The Emperor Charlemagne.

Clovis began the Merovingian dynasty, known as the 'Long-haired kings' because they never cut their hair. On the Left Bank he founded a basilica and abbey where he, his queen, and Genevieve could be buried side by side, Ste-Geneviève (where the **Panthéon** now stands) and his son Childeric founded the equally renowned abbey of **St-Germain-des-Prés**. This did not mean that the Merovingians were especially pious. Rather, they were extremely brutal, particularly to each other. Under their law an inheritance had to be divided equally among any heirs. This led to regular bloodletting and infanticide between royal princes, dowager queens and uncles, in fratricidal antics that would finally snuff out the line in 751. Most productive of the dynasty for Paris had been Dagobert (628-637), who in 635 established the Fair of St-Denis just outside the city. This annual event, which would grow throughout the middle ages, would play a major part in cementing Paris' position as the commercial – and cultural – hub of northern France.

The Merovingians were succeeded by the Carolingians, after Charles Martel, credited with having halted the spread of Islam by his victory over the Moors at Tours in 732. In 754 his son Pepin 'the Short' was crowned King of all the Franks at St-Denis. His heir was Charlemagne, who extended the Frankish kingdom and became first Holy Roman Emperor in 800. He also, though moved his capital to Aix-La-Chapelle (Aachen). Paris became something of a backwater, entrusted to a hereditary Count. In the next century, the city suffered from famine, floods and marauding Vikings, who sacked the city four times between 840 and 880.

After Charlemagne, the Carolingian empire gradually fell apart, as its predecessors had done. In the western part of the empire, the local aristocracy and clergy were ever more frustrated at the inability of their 'emperors' to help them against the Norsemen, and sought a leader of their own. As the first millennium drew to a close, many believed it heralded the end of the world as they knew it. But in 987, the Count of Paris, Hugh Capet, was elected King of France by his peers at Senlis, and made Paris his capital. It was clear that a new era was beginning.

Middle Ages to Renaissance

In the twelfth century, Paris first set out to be cultural capital of Europe.

The proclamation of the Capetian dynasty (from Hugh Capet) is the point from which 'France' can be said to exist. For a long time, however, the 'kingdom' consisted of little more than the Ile-de-France, and powerful local lords – in Normandy, Burgundy, the south, and in the possessions of the Kings of England – would defy the royal authority for centuries. France would largely be created through the gradual extension of Parisian power. Equally, the entire country's history is peculiarly inseparable from that of its capital city.

The early Capetians, though, made very slow progress, for they were mostly deeply unremarkable and quickly forgotten. Even so, Paris continued to grow in importance, thanks in good part to its many powerful abbeys, and to its fair and shrine in neighbouring St-Denis. In the twelfth-century, the city became the centre of a spectacular renaissance, as a boom in commerce and construction made Paris into a political, economic, religious, and cultural capital.

A major figure in this expansion was Suger, Abbot of St-Denis and minister to a series of weak monarchs. Abbot Suger did much to hold the state together and give it an administration; as a priest, in 1136 he commissioned the **Basilica of St-Denis**, since the old church had become totally inadequate to house the pilgrims who flocked to the saint's shrine. Considered the first true Gothic building, St-Denis had a prodigious influence across France and beyond, setting the style for church and secular building for the next four centuries. In Paris, Gothic spires began to soar above the skyline. In 1163, Bishop Sully of Paris began the construction of **Notre Dame**, the embodiment of the high Gothic aesthetic, which would perhaps reach its apogee in the following century with the building of the **Sainte-Chapelle**.

Simultaneously, Paris had also seen some development of a more intangible nature, and been the scene of one of its first and greatest romantic legends. Learning had been kept alive in the Parisian abbeys during the darkest hours of the preceding centuries, and in the eleventh century the Canon school of old Notre Dame was

The utterly dashing Francis I.

already widely admired for its scholarship. In about the year 1100, scholars also began to move out from the cathedral school and teach independently, around the Montagne Ste-Geneviève on the Left Bank (*see chapter* **Paris by Area: The Left Bank**). Their reputation spread, and Paris became a magnet for students and the learned from all across Europe.

One of the first independent teachers on the Left Bank was a brilliant logician and dialectician called Peter Abelard. In 1118, when he was

39, he was employed by Canon Fulbert of Notre Dame as tutor to his 17-year old niece Heloise. They began a very passionate affair, which was discovered by the Canon. Twice he enjoined them to remain celibate; twice they failed to obey him, until Fulbert, enraged, had Abelard castrated, while Heloise was consigned to a convent. During the rest of their lives, Abelard wrote some of the most refined works of medieval philosophy, while Heloise wrote the ardent, poetic letters to her lost lover that have ensured their story has never been forgotten.

Abelard's difficulties did not impede the expansion of the Paris schools. They became more formally organised, and in 1215 combined to form a 'university', under papal protection. The greatest and most influential medieval thinkers studied and taught in this 'New Athens'; the German theologian Albert the Great, the Italians Thomas Aquinas and Bonaventure, the Scots Duns Scotus and the Englishman William of Ockham. Most famous of its colleges was the **Sorbonne**, founded in 1253 by Robert de Sorbon, chaplain of King Louis IX (Saint Louis).

In the area of the Ile de la Cité that lies between the rue du Cloître Notre Dame, the rue d'Arcole and the Seine it's still possible to walk the same streets as medieval scholars. Students were boarded with cathedral canons in houses like those at Nos 22 and 24 rue Chanoinesse. On rue des Ursins, the courtyard of No. 19 – the Chapelle St-Aignan – once part of the Notre Dame cloister, can still be admired.

ROYAL POWER

As Paris grew in cultural prestige, so too did it expand its political power. The first great monarch of the Capetians was Philip Augustus (1180-1223), the great rival, and possibly lover, of Richard the Lionheart of England. As well as crusading, Philip greatly extended the power of the French crown. He was also the first great royal builder to leave his mark on Paris. Abandoning the city's old Roman defences, he built a new, stone city wall enclosing all the new *faubourgs*, parts of which can still be seen in the Marais and the Latin Quarter (*see chapter* **Sightseeing**). He also founded a new royal fortress on the Right Bank, the **Louvre**, although his main residence was still on the Ile de la Cité, where the **Conciergerie** now stands. In 1181, he established permanent covered markets, *Les Halles*, on the site that they would occupy until 1969; in addition, Philip Augustus sought to do something about the city's putrid mud and foul odours, ordering the first-ever paving of streets in post-Roman Paris, and closing its most pestilential cemeteries.

Trade flourished still more, and Paris' merchants and trade guilds were able to establish a position of power that they would retain for centuries. The

Heloise, pining for Abelard.

centre of city institutions (as opposed to the Court) was the place de Grève and the Châtelet, where the **Hôtel de Ville** stands today.

Philip's grandson Louis IX (1226-1270) was famed for his extreme piety, eventually being made Saint Louis and a virtual second patron saint of France, after Saint Denis. When not abroad on crusade, or scouring Europe for holy relics, he also put his stamp on Parisian architecture, commissioning the Sainte-Chapelle and convents, hospices and even student housing. The Saint wasn't above making a few improvements on his palace either, but it was his grandson, Philip the Fair (1285-1314) who converted the inelegant fortress on the Cité into a palace fit for a king. His monumental *Salle des Gens d'Armes* in the Conciergerie, built to receive petitioners to the king, was reputedly the most beautiful hall in the country. He also commissioned the building's magnificent Gothic façade, now heavily altered by later restoration.

The fourteenth century signalled the start of troubled times for the French crown. Philip the Fair died in 1314, the end of his reign marred by the debasement of the currency, insurrection in Paris and riotous debauchery at Court. In suspiciously quick succession, his three sons ascended the throne. They all perished within 15 years of their father's death; the last, Charles IV, died in 1328 leaving no male heir, bringing to an end the direct Capetian line.

All this proved irresistible to the English, who claimed the French crown for young Edward III, son of Philip the Fair's daughter. The French refused to recognise her claim, since the traditional Salic law of the Franks barred women from the throne. Philip of Valois, the late king's cousin, claimed the crown for himself, and thus began the Hundred Years' War.

Throughout this time, Paris was in turmoil. The Black Death arrived in Europe a few years later, in the 1340s, and outbreaks of the plague would alternate with battles, bourgeois revolts, popular insurrections and bloody vendettas between aristocratic factions and their bands of hired thugs. The conflicts between French and English were by no means the only ones that tore the country apart: in 1355, a rich Paris bourgeois named Etienne Marcel seized Paris and attempted to dictate conditions to the Dauphin Charles, then regent since his father John II had been captured by the English. Charles' supporters retook the city, and Marcel and his supporters were savagely executed. When the Dauphin became king, however, as Charles V 'The Wise' (1364-1380), mindful of the city's defiance of royal authority, he decided to transfer his residence to the safety of the Louvre. He also had a new stronghold built on the eastern edge of Paris, the Bastille.

Charles V transformed the Louvre into a royal residence, where he installed both his library and works of art. Despite the disorder in the country, the arts were still able to flourish, and at this time Parisian artisans produced peerless miniatures, tapestries, manuscripts, and objects carved in ivory or wrought in silver and gold.

The fighting, meanwhile, continued. After the battle of Agincourt in 1415 the English seemed to have won, and from 1420 to 1436 Paris was under English rule, with the Duke of Bedford as governor. In 1431, Henry VI of England was crowned King of France in Notre Dame. However, for most of this time the surrounding countryside was largely controlled by the French and the city was virtually under siege, at one time by Joan of Arc. Eventually, Charles VII of France (1422-1461) was able to retake his capital, and by the time of his death the war was over.

RENAISSANCE AND HERESY

The last decadesof the fifteenth century saw a rapid extention of royal authority, as the restored Valois monarchs sought to reaffirm their position. They also saw prosperity return to the capital, in the form of trade and the expansion of all kinds of crafts. Masons erected churches in the *Flamboyant* Gothic style, as well as an impressive array of *hôtels* commissioned by nobles, prelates and the wealthy bourgeoisie, such as the **Hôtel de Cluny** and the **Hôtel de Sens**.

The arrival of the Renaissance was reflected in Parisian homes in a variety of ways. Those of the city's bourgeois were increasingly opulent, and even in relatively humble households glass might replace greased cloth and paper in windows, and forks appear for the first time on tables. In 1473, the first printing press began work, opening up the possibility that books might no longer be the exclusive preserve of the learned and wealthy. Paris' printers published 25,000 titles during the sixteenth century.

Most spectacular figure of the Valois dynasty was Francis I (1515-1547), the epitome of a Renaissance monarch. He spent much of his time in endless wars with his great enemy the Emperor Charles V, but he also built sumptuous châteaux at **Fontainebleau** and in the Loire Valley at **Blois** and **Chambord** (*see chapter* **Trips Out of Town**), and gathered about him a glittering court of knights, poets and Italian artists, such as Leonardo and Benvenuto Cellini. He also set about making the Louvre habitable, beginning the palace that we can see today. Inside, he hung a few favourite pictures – Titians, some Raphaels, and the Mona Lisa.

All Francis' grandeur, however, was unable to prevent the arrival in France of Protestantism, first condemned by the Sorbonne in 1521. The strongholds of the Huguenots, or French Protestants, were mostly in the west; Paris, in contrast, was a citadel of virulent and often bloodthirsty Catholic orthodoxy. During the 1530s and 1540s an increasing number of heretics were sent to the stake in the place de Grève, as the Renaissance and its carefree ambience went up in smoke.

By the 1560s, the situation had degenerated into open warfare, complicated by the interwoven aristocratic squabbles between factions such as the Huguenot Prince de Condé and the Catholic Dukes of Guise. Savagery was seen on both sides, and paranoia was rife. In 1572, Paris itself was turned into a blood-bath. A rumour ran round that Huguenots were plotting to murder the royal family and sack the city; in anticipation, on 24 August, Saint Bartholomew's Day, Catholic mobs turned on anyone in Paris suspected of Protestant sympathies, killing over 3,000 people. Later, when King Henry III (1574-1589) sought to find a compromise between the two sides, Paris turned on its sovereign and forced him to flee the Louvre. In 1589 he was assassinated by a fanatical monk, bringing the Valois line to an end.

Henry III's ally Henry of Navarre, a Huguenot, was declared King of France, founding the Bourbon dynasty. He defeated Catholic armies several times, but fervently Catholic Paris continued to resist him, in a siege that dragged on for almost four years. Inside the city, people ate cats, rats, horses, donkeys and even grass. Finally, in 1593 Henry IV agreed to become a Catholic, famously declaring that *'Paris vaut bien une messe'* (Paris is well worth a mass). His agents opened the gates of the city; whatever the doubts over his sincerity, its people were exhausted, and prepared to let the 'Wars of Religion' come to an end.

Ancien Régime

The Bourbon monarchs set out to dazzle the world, and for a century the illusion was successful.

The Sun King himself, Louis XIV.

Henry IV undertook to rebuild and unify the country, and re-establish the power of France and its monarchy. In Paris, from the moment one mass made him master of the city, he set about changing the face of his ravaged capital, giving it some of its most familiar and enduring features. An equestrian bronze of the *Vert Galant* (as his subjects dubbed the lusty Henry) presides today over the **Pont-Neuf** and the **place Dauphine** on the Ile de la Cité, which he commissioned and named in honour of his heir, the future Louis XIII. Across the Seine Henry IV ordered the construction of Paris' first enclosed, geometrical square – the place Royale, now the **place des Vosges** – the creation of which set in motion the building of an entire elegant neighbourhood around it, the Marais. The central space of the place Royale was given over to festivities, jousts, bowlers and strollers. Henry also had his subjects' enjoyment in mind when he added to his own

residence: the **Louvre**'s *Galerie du Bord de l'Eau* was planned to please the eye of all who walked or sailed along the Seine.

Among his many improvements in Paris, Henry IV unfortunately never got round to improving the city's congested streets, habitually clogged with pedestrians, horses, donkeys and the latest innovation, the coach. On 14 May 1610, while caught in a bottleneck on the rue de la Ferronnerie, the King was stabbed to death by a Catholic fanatic named Ravaillac. The *ancien régime* began as it would end: with regicide.

THE CARDINAL

When Henry died his son, Louis XIII (1610-1643) was only eight years old, and Henry's widow, Marie de Medici, was installed as regent. Her idea of her own importance can be seen in the retirement home she commissioned for herself, the **Palais du Luxembourg**, and the extraordinary series of 24 panels glorifying her role in history she had painted by Rubens, now in the Louvre. In 1617 Louis XIII, still only 16, was encouraged to take over power himself. The real head of his government, however, would be a bishop who had initially been a protegé of Marie de Medici, Cardinal Richelieu, who in 1624 would formally become the king's chief minister.

Richelieu won the confidence of anxious, tormented Louis XIII, who stuck by his minister through numerous plots hatched by his Queen, Anne of Austria, his mother, assorted other royal princes and disgruntled grandees. Richelieu returned the favour by creating a strong, centralised monarchy, effectively paving the way for the the absolutism of Louis XIV, and steadily grinding down what he perceived as the two major enemies of the French monarchy: abroad, Spain, and at home the independent power of the aristocracy, and of the Huguenots in particular.

He was ably assisted by his secretary, the shadowy and much-feared Father Joseph, the man who was the origin of the phrase *éminence grise*. This is the world of intrigue that Dumas *père* found an ideal background for his Musketeers adventures.

Richelieu was also, though, one of the great patrons of the age, commissioning Jacques Lemercier to build him a palace, then known as the Palais Cardinal, later to become a royal residence as the **Palais-Royal**. The time of the Cardinal's rule was also the central period of the Counter-Reformation, and architects were given lavish commissions to create new convents and Baroque churches, such as **Val-de-Grâce** and **St-Joseph-des-Carmes**.

It was also under Louis XIII that construction fever really began in the Marais. The Parisian *hôtel particulier*, an aristocratic dwelling set between a courtyard and a garden, here flowered into a highly distinctive architectural genre.

The literary lights of France's *Grand Siècle* often found their patrons in the Marais. Salons hosted by lettered ladies (including celebrated authors like Mlle de Scudéry, Mme de la Fayette, Mme de Sévigné and the erudite courtesan, Ninon de l'Enclos) rang with saucy wit, pithy asides and political intrigue. By comparison, Richelieu's Académie Française (founded in 1634) was a fusty and rather pedantic reflection of the establishment.

Similarly elegant *hôtels* to those of the Marais were built on the Ile St-Louis, urbanised in just 20 years, and in the quarter around the Cardinal's Palais-Royal, while slightly more modest residences appeared on the Left Bank, around the rue de Seine. Everybody who was anybody in France needed a suitably modern house in Paris, and speculators were eager to provide them.

GRAND LOUIS

Richelieu died in 1642, when both Spain and the Huguenots were on the defensive. The following year Louis XIII also died, leaving once again an under-age heir, the five-year old Louis XIV. His mother, Anne of Austria, became regent, with a follower of Richelieu, Cardinal Mazarin, as chief minister. From 1648 to 1653 they were all forced to flee Paris by the *Fronde*, a rebellion of peasants

Society hostess, Marquise de Pompadour.

and some of the aristocracy against taxes and the growth in royal power. This incident has traditionally been believed to be one of the roots of Louis XIV's persistent dislike of his capital.

Mazarin died in 1661, shortly after Spain, France's enemy since the days of Francis I, had been decisively defeated. France, and its monarchy, were more powerful than ever before. The rebellions of earlier years, the *Fronde* or the Huguenots, had been silenced. The country was prosperous, and had a much larger population than any of its neighbours; also, with the old enemy defeated, it had military capacity to spare.

This was the launching pad for the personal rule of Louis XIV, who after the death of Mazarin announced that he would be his own chief minister, with the classically megalomaniac statement *'L'Etat, c'est moi'* ('The State is me'). Not only that, but as the personal embodiment of the mightiest nation in Europe, he would be the greatest monarch ever seen.

Military expansion was essential to Louis XIV's concept of greatness, and so France engaged in continual wars, with the Dutch, Austria and England. At the same time, loyal theorists developed the idea of the absolute monarchy and poured further praise upon the head of the 'Sun King'.

An essential figure in Louis's years of triumph was Jean-Baptiste Colbert, his head of finance and administration. Unlike his master, Colbert took a particular interest in Paris. Steeped in the Classics, he felt that Paris should be a 'new Rome', with grand, symmetrical vistas. Thus, new, finely proportioned squares were commissioned, such as the **place des Victoires** of 1685, and the first boulevards opened up. The Baroque city thus created functioned as a kind of grand theatre, an expression of absolute monarchy in stone to impress an already overawed populace still further.

Louis XIV, however, took little interest in Colbert's schemes. Instead, such was his aversion to Paris that from the 1670s the focus of all his interest was **Versailles**, to which he had decided to transfer the court, and into which he poured vast quantities of wealth.

The reign of the Sun King also saw a flourishing of culture and the arts. In 1659 Molière's troupe of wandering actors settled in Paris under the protection of the King, presenting plays for both court and public. After the playwright's death in 1673, they became the **Comédie Française**. Favoured composer at Versailles was the Italian Lully, who was granted sole right to compose operas – in which the King himself often appeared.

For all its endlessly-proclaimed grandeur, however, Louis XIV's regime already had within it elements of its own destruction. Its colossal spending was seemingly based on an idea that the state had infinite resources. But the royal finances were in permanent disorder, despite the best efforts of

Colbert, and as the wars dragged on, the demands of the state in taxes were reflected in growing poverty and a disastrous rise in vagrancy in the countryside. Also, endless wars left a legacy of a great many crippled veterans reduced to begging in the streets. The **Invalides**, one of the most monumental creations of Louis's reign, was built to house them, but it was never enough.

The spread of pauperisation was the reverse side of the grandeur of the Sun King. It was estimated that about a tenth of the population of Paris were vagrants, vagabonds, delinquents, women of easy virtue *et al*, and to deal with them in 1667 Colbert appointed Paris' first Lieutenant of Police, Gabriel de La Reynie. The **Salpêtrière**, a veritable city within a city, was erected to shelter women who were rounded up in Paris. Thus the administration tried to camouflage the misery of its underside – beneath domes and colonnaded façades.

France was increasingly exhausted in the last years of the Sun King's reign. Louis had lost his most able assistant with the death of Colbert in 1683, and the military triumphs of earlier years had given way to the defeats and grim struggles of the War of the Spanish Succession. Life at Versailles soured as well, under the dour, prim Mme de Maintenon, Louis's last mistress, whom he had secretly married in 1684. Nobles started to sneak away from Versailles to build handsome *hôtels particuliers* in the fashionable new Faubourg St-Germain. Louis finally died in 1715, aged 77.

Denis Diderot, the harmless drudge.

THE AGE OF ENLIGHTENMENT

Louis XIV had had several children, but within a very short time, not long before his own death, both his son and grandson had died, leaving yet again a five-year-old heir, Louis XV (1715-1774). Hardly had the Sun King disappeared over the horizon than the Regent, Philippe d'Orléans, left Versailles and moved the Court back to Paris. Parisians were more than ready for a *bon vivant* after the deprivations of the recent past. The Regent, an able general and diplomat, was also known as a drinker, blasphemer and all-round rake. Installed in the Palais-Royal, he regularly threw lavish dinners that degenerated into orgies.

The lives led by pleasure-loving courtiers and the Parisians who aped them spawned a large service population of dressmakers, jewellers, hairdressers, decorators and domestics of every degree. Tales of country youths corrupted by the city where they came to seek their fortune inspired writers from Marivaux to Rousseau, Restif de la Bretonne to the Marquis de Sade: Paris was the *nouvelle Babylone*, the modern Sodom.

The state, however, was by now chronically in debt, even though the Regent sought to avoid further military entanglements. The main form of taxation was in indirect duties on commodities, especially salt. Collection was 'farmed out' to a kind of private corporation, the *Fermiers Généraux* or 'General Farm', who passed on an amount to the state and kept a profit for themselves. This system bore down disproportionately on the poor, was riddled with corruption and never produced the resources the state needed; nevertheless, so many interests were involved in it that none of the *ancien régime*'s ministers was ever able to abolish it.

The Regent Orléans thought he had found one remedy for the state's debts when he gave his support to the plans of a Scottish banker, John Law, for an investment scheme in France's colonies. For a while, it inspired a mania of wheeling and dealing. Predictably, the bubble burst. In 1720, a run on the bank revealed that very little gold and silver was on hand to back up the paper bills. Panic ensued. Law was expelled from France, and the Regent, and to some extent royal government itself, were deeply discredited.

As soon as he was his own man, Louis XV quit Paris for Versailles, which once again saw sumptuous festivities and royal entertainments. But in the Age of Enlightenment, Paris was the real capital of Europe, the focus of intense artistic and intellectual activity, where the era's most brilliant minds met and matched wits. 'One lives in Paris; elsewhere, one simply vegetates', wrote Casanova.

It was to this lettered milieu that the King's mistress, the beautiful and cultivated Marquise de Pompadour (1721-64), belonged. She was a friend and protectress of Diderot and the *encyclopédistes*, of Marivaux and of Montesquieu; she also corresponded with Voltaire. She encouraged Louis XV to embellish his capital with monuments such as Jacques-Ange Gabriel's **Ecole Militaire**, and the same architect's Parisian masterpiece, the place Louis XV (now the **place de la Concorde**).

PRELUDE TO REVOLUTION

The great failure of Louis XV's reign was the defeat of the Seven Years' War (1756-1763), in which France lost most of its colonies in India and Canada to Britain. His successor Louis XVI (1774-93), began his reign auspiciously enough. Paris was flourishing. Across Europe, people craved Parisian luxuries: furniture by Boulle, Gobelins and Savonnerie tapestries, and Sèvres porcelain.

France in the last years of the *ancien régime* was scarcely an oppressed, backward country, even though dire poverty could easily be found both in the city and the country. Rather, it was expanding economically and culturally, and Paris in particular looked sprucer than ever. Roads were widened, lamps erected, and boulevards, gardens and promenades created. There were more places for people to meet, and Paris offered an ever-wider selection of distractions. Nobs indulged in horse racing (a taste acquired from the English) at Vincennes and the Bois de Boulogne. On the boulevard du Temple, all classes rubbed shoulders to watch dancers, singers, acrobats and trained monkeys.

Paris was obsessed with the new, whether it was ballooning (first demonstrated by the Montgolfier brothers in 1783) or the works of Rousseau, exalting 'Nature' and scorning aristocratic convention. Even French princes flirted with the new sensibilities, as when the Duc d'Orleans, developed the **Palais-Royal** as a kind of open house for different classes, entertainments and ideas (*see chapter* **Paris by Area: The Right Bank**).

The state, meanwhile, was still an entirely absolute monarchy. Louis XVI's problems were made acute by having won a war. France's intervention in the American War of Independence regained several colonies; however, it also meant giving support to rebels, and, more to the point, drove the royal finances towards total bankruptcy. Louis XVI, indecisive and dim, was his own worst enemy; as the 1780s wore on a series of ministers attempted sometimes radically different solutions to the financial situation, without ever being given adequate royal support. In 1785, at the behest of the 'Farm', a tax wall was built around Paris, supposedly to improve tax collection, but this only served to increase popular discontent (*see also* chapter **Architecture**).

Louis's only remaining option was to appeal to society for help in maintaining the national finances, in the first place through the *parlements* or regional assemblies of lawyers, and if all else failed the Estates-General, the representation of the Nobility, Clergy and Commoners, which had not met since 1614. Given the mood in the country, however, this would inevitably involve raising the the issue of the entire relationship between society and a monarchy that believed it had an absolute right to command. True to form, the embattled Louis XVI continued to prevaricate, as the year 1789 began.

Salon Society

In the era of the Enlightenment, Paris' *salons*, hosted by a select group of influential women, became the most important forums for intellectual debate. Of one of the most renowned hostesses, the Marquise Du Deffand, Montesquieu said, 'I love this woman with all my heart. You cannot be bored for a single moment with her'. Her salon, on rue de Beaune in the Faubourg St-Germain, was the most exclusive of its kind, and the conversation there the wittiest and brightest.

She may possibly have been the queen bee of salon hostesses, but a host of other unmarried or widowed women challenged her supremacy. The spontaneity of her own neice, Julie de Lespinasse, who held court on rue de Bellechasse, made her more loved, and Madame Geoffrin outdid her in terms of the numbers and variety of personalities who attended her gatherings at 374, rue St-Honoré. Her Wednesday dinners for writers attracted the likes of Voltaire and Marivaux, and Boucher, Vernet and Van Loo were regulars at her Monday sessions for artists. Their influence was such that on his arrival in the city Rousseau was told, 'You can't do anything in Paris without women'.

The role of the salon hostess was always the same: to make others shine and skilfully to direct the conversation from one guest to another. In an atmosphere of liberal urbanity, subjects might range from the ever-popular concept of 'nature' to literature and music. It was common, too, to question the justification for royal authority, and it is one of the ironies of the Revolution, which these discussions helped bring about, that it should be the cause of their disappearance.

Revolution & Empire

In less than three decades, Paris lives through the most turbulent and dramatic years of its history.

The spring of 1789 found Louis XVI increasingly isolated as unrest swept through France. In Paris, the people were suffering the results of a disastrous harvest, and there had been riots in the Faubourg St-Antoine. When he finally agreed to convene the Estates-General at Versailles in May, the King was understandably apprehensive.

The members of the Third Estate, the commoners, aware that they represented a far larger proportion of the country than the nobility and clergy, demanded a voting system of one vote per member. Discussions broke down, and a rumour went round that the King was sending troops to arrest them. On 20 June 1789, at the Jeu de Paume (tennis court) at Versailles, the Third Estate took an oath not to separate until 'the constitution of the kingdom was established'. Louis initially refused their demands; however, vacillating as ever, he backed down, and the Estates-General renamed itself the National Assembly and set about discussing a Constitution.

The debate, however, had gone beyond the confines of the Assembly into the Paris streets, among the poor *sans culottes* (literally, without breeches, as only the poor then wore long trousers). It was assumed that any concession by the King was intended to deceive. Louis had posted foreign, Swiss and German, troops around Paris; and on 11 July he dismissed his minister, Jacques Necker, considered the sole ally of the commoners in government.

In Paris, the city was full of angry bread queues, incensed by price rises, and discipline among native French troops was wavering. On 12 July an obscure lawyer named Camille Desmoulins leapt up on a café table in the **Palais-Royal** to speak. Likening Necker's dismissal to another Saint Bartholomew's Day, he called on all patriots to throw off slavery for ever. *'Aux armes!'* he exhorted the excited crowd: 'To arms!'

Desmoulins may, perhaps, have been only the most visible of many agitators around Paris, but a reaction there certainly was. A crowd stormed the **Invalides**, carrying off thousands of guns. On 14 July they moved on to the **Bastille**, symbol of royal repression. Its governor, the Marquis de Launay, refused to surrender the fortress, but the huge crowd outside were ever more aggressive. What seems to have happened next is that one of the increasingly-nervous Bastille sentries fired a shot, and within minutes they were all firing on the crowd. The mob, meanwhile, incensed, brought up cannon to storm the fortress.

After a brief battle, during which 87 revolutionaries were killed, Launay offered a conditional surrender. The crowd, however, were in no mood to be forgiving, and he was immediately killed, his head being paraded through Paris on a pike. Inside the hated Bastille the insurgents famously found only seven prisoners. Nevertheless, the Revolution now had the symbolic act of violence that marked a break with the past.

REVOLUTIONARY PARIS

With the Revolution in motion, political debate in Paris proliferated on every side, above all in the rapidly-multiplying political clubs, such as the Cordeliers, who held their meetings in the Franciscan monastery of the same name on the Left Bank, or the radical Jacobins, who had taken over another convent on the rue St-Honoré. Thousands of pamphlets were produced, read avidly by a remarkably literate public.

However, while for some, as Wordsworth put it, 'Bliss was it in that dawn to be alive', there was also a very real level of hardship among the poor, and a tension and violence that came to the surface more and more frequently. Moreover, the disruption spreading through the countryside interrupted deliveries of wheat to Paris, raising bread prices still further.

The next stage in the Revolution came in October 1789, when a huge, angry crowd of Parisian women, among them the early feminist Théroigne de Méricourt, marched to Versailles to protest at the price of bread, the incident when Marie Antoinette supposedly suggested they should try a *brioche*. They became violent, ransacking part of the palace and killing some Guards, and were only placated when Louis XVI appeared with a revolutionary red-

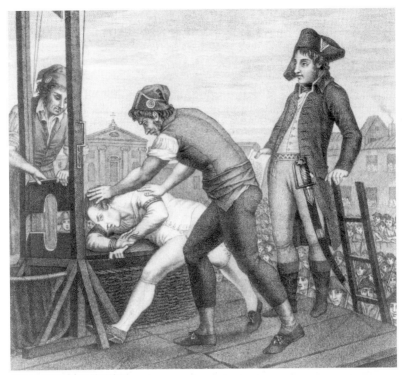

Robespierre faces the chop.

white-and-blue cockade and agreed to be taken to Paris. From then on, the royal family would be virtual prisoners in the Tuileries.

In the Assembly, the dominant tendency were initially the Girondins, who favoured some sort of agreement with the monarchy, but they were under ever-more intense attack from openly-Republican groups like the Jacobins. The cultural transformation associated with the Revolution was also proceeding apace; churches were confiscated in November 1789, to be made 'Temples of Reason' or be put to practical uses, and an 'Altar of the Fatherland' was installed on the Champ de Mars.

By 20 June 1791, Louis decided he had had enough. He and his family sought to leave Paris by night, hoping to escape from France and organise resistance from safety abroad. They got as far as the town of Varennes, where they were recognised, and were returned to Paris as captives.

The following year, the monarchies of Europe formed a coalition to save Louis and his family. A Prussian army marched into France, and the Duke of Brunswick threatened to raze Paris if the King came to any harm. Again, an underlying tension,

and paranoia, was a fundamental element in events, for not just Louis but anyone who showed sympathy for him could be accused of conspiring with foreign powers against the people. On 10 August, an army of *sans-culottes* demanded that the Assembly officially depose Louis. This was refused, and the crowd attacked the Tuileries. The royal family were imprisoned by the radical Commune de Paris, led by Danton, Marat and Robespierre, which thus became the dominant force in the Revolution.

THE TERROR

The next month, as the Prussians got closer to Paris, saw the 'September Massacres', when Revolutionary mobs invaded the city's prisons to eliminate anyone that could possibly be a 'traitor', in an orgy of bloodletting that accounted for close to 2,000 people. The monarchy was formally abolished on 22 September 1792, a day proclaimed the first day of 'Year I of the French Republic' in the radicals' all-new calendar. Almost immediately the French citizen army defeated the Prussians at Valmy. The Republic, it seemed, could be triumphant.

This was the beginning of the most radical phase of the Revolution. The Jacobins proclaimed the need to be implacable with 'the enemies within', and so Dr Guillotin's new invention took its place in the *place de la Révolution* (formerly Louis XV, now Concorde). Louis XVI was executed in January 1793, to be followed in October by Marie Antoinette.

They might have taken solace in the knowledge that the same fate awaited their executioners. In September 1793 the Revolutionary Convention, which had replaced the National Assembly, put 'terror on the agenda', in response to demands from the *sans-culottes* for more decisive action against foreign spies. An infernal machine was wound up that would claim thousands of victims before its energy expired. The Revolution, as the Jacobin St-Just said, 'devoured its own children': most of the leading Girondins, *Philippe-Egalité* of Orléans, and then even Jacobins such as Danton and Camille Desmoulins all travelled the same road from the Conciergerie to the scaffold. During the *Grande Terreur* of 1794, 1,300 heads fell in just six weeks.

FRANCE DRAWS BREATH

The collective psychosis that was the Terror was unable to sustain itself forever. In July 1794 a group of moderate Republicans led by Paul Barras succeeded in arresting Robespierre, St-Just and the remaining Jacobins. They were immediately guillotined themselves, amid expressions of generalised hatred from their erstwhile popular heroes. With this, the Terror ended.

The wealthy of Paris, among them some Revolutionary *nouveaux riches*, emerged blinking into the fashionable corners of the city. Barras and his colleagues set themselves up as a five-man 'Directory' to rule the Republic. In 1795, they were saved from a revolt in Paris by an ambitious young general called Napoleon Bonaparte.

France might no longer be the fire-breathing Republic of the Jacobins, but it was still at war with most of the monarchies of Europe. Bonaparte was sent to command the army in Italy, where he covered himself with unprecedented glory. In 1798, he took his army to Egypt, which he almost succeeded in conquering.

THE EMPEROR

When he returned to France, he found a Republic in which few had any great faith, while many were prepared to accept a dictator who had emerged from the Revolution. There had always been two potentially contradictory impulses behind the Revolution: a desire for a state that would be a democratic expression of the people, but also for one that would be an effective, powerful defender of the nation, for all Revolutionaries were intensely patriotic. Under Napoleon, the former impulse was put on hold, while France was given the most powerful centralised, militaristic state it had ever seen.

In November 1799 Bonaparte staged a coup, and in 1800 he was declared First Consul. Between continuing military campaigns, he set about transforming France with extraordinary energy – the education system (with the *Grandes Ecoles*), civil law (the *Code Napoléon*), the administration, all bear the Napoleonic stamp to this day. In 1804, he crowned himself Emperor in an ostentatious ceremony in Notre Dame.

Napoleon was also the second great megalomaniac to leave his mark on Paris, leaving his stone 'N' carved even into buildings that he had not had built, although he had much greater regard for his capital than had Louis XIV. His first additions to the city were characteristically practical: the canals, the quais along the Seine, and some fine bridges, notably the **Pont des Arts**. These projects created a great deal of employment for the city's workers, which was one reason why his regime was for a good while very popular. He also desired, though, to be master of the 'most beautiful city in the world', complete with palaces, broad boulevards, colossal monuments and temples evoking the monumental splendour of Augustan Rome – as seen in the **Madeleine** or the **Bourse**, a temple of money. The Emperor's taste can be simply summed up: big is beautiful (*'Ce qui est grand est toujours beau'*). The **rue de Rivoli** is another example of his aesthetic credo, with its grand, arcaded façade designed by Napoléon's official architects, Percier and Fontaine.

Under Napoleon Parisian society also finally regained its *brio*. A wave of Egyptomania had swept Paris after Bonaparte's oriental adventure, and this, with neo-Classicism, became an integral part of the 'Empire Style'. Monumental architecture and enigmatic sphinxes were all the rage, and fashionable women mixed transparent Greek draperies and couture *à l'égyptienne*.

But, the Napoleonic epic was inseparable from military expansion, for the Emperor never ceased to be at war. For years, he seemed invincible. In 1805, he crushed the Austrians and Russians at Austerlitz, the victory he wished to commemorate with the **Arc de Triomphe**. By 1807, he was on the borders of Russia. His victories – Wagram, Eylau, Ièna, Rivoli, Friedland – have become inseparable parts of the Paris street plan. However, even he overreached himself, in Spain, from 1808, and in the disastrous invasion of Russia in 1812. By 1813 his army was exhausted and in retreat, and in 1814 Paris was occupied for the first time since the Hundred Years' War, by the armies of the Czar.

Napoleon did of course have one last throw, with his escape from confinement in Elba, return to Paris, and the 'hundred days' that ended at Waterloo. Then, finally, the extraordinary drama that had overtaken Paris and France since 1789 was over.

Artists & Rebellions

In fifty-five years, Paris went through four regimes, and had its ancient narrow streets given an unprecedented shakeout.

In 1814, and then again in 1815, after Waterloo, the Bourbons were restored to the throne of France, in the shape of an elderly brother of Louis XVI, as Louis XVIII. Although they realised that the pretensions of the *ancien régime* were lost forever, and France now had a Constitution, he and his ministers still sought to establish a repressive, Catholic regime, that would in some way turn back the clock after the Revolution. In this they could hope to find much support in large areas of rural France, where conservative values remained strong.

Paris, however, still nurtured a strong feeling of rebellion. Over the next sixty years, a pattern would be repeated that had already been seen to some extent in the Revolution: Paris, and especially working-class districts such as the Faubourg St-Antoine or, later, Belleville, was far more radical than anywhere else in the country. The peculiar weight of Paris in the affairs of France meant that it could often be in the position of seeking to impose its radicalism on the rest of the nation, which could easily provoke a very violent reaction.

This was also the era of Romanticism, and the radicalism of Paris was fed by a progressive press, liberal intellectuals – including many Romantic artists and authors, such as Victor Hugo, Daumier, Delacroix and Lamartine – radical students and a growing, desperately poor and dangerously anarchic underclass. When provoked, this volatile coalition could explode into revolutionary violence.

In 1830, Charles X (1824-1830), yet another brother of Louis XVI, sensed a threat to the monarchy from the liberal opposition. His impolitic reaction was to dissolve the legislature, muzzle the press and control electoral procedures to suit his royal whim. Paris retorted with the Revolution of 1830, which finally ended Bourbon rule.

On 27 July 1830, government troops fired on a crowd of demonstrators. The corpse of a young woman was carried to the place des Victoires, where feeling was whipped up with an emotional plea for vengeance. There followed *Les Trois Glorieuses*, three days and nights of insurrection which swept through the capital.

France as a whole, however, was still not pre-pared to accept a Republic, and the outcome, against the wishes of the Paris crowds, was another monarchy, although it was to prove the last. As Charles X set sail for England, yet another eccentric left-over of the *ancien régime* was winched onto the throne. Louis-Philippe, Duc d'Orléans, son of *Philippe-Egalité*, was known as the 'Citizen King'. A father of eight, who never went out without his umbrella and considered it his duty to carve the Sunday roast, he was eminently acceptable to the Parisian bourgeoisie. But the workers, who had spilled their blood in 1830 only to see their quality of life worsen, simmered with rancour and frustration throughout the 'July Monarchy'.

LES MISERABLES

At the time of the Restoration and the July Monarchy, Parisians of all classes often inhabited the same streets, and sometimes the same buildings, with the well-heeled on the first floor (the *étage noble*) and the less privileged under the rafters, or in obscure alleys and culs-de-sac.

In the first half of the century, though, the population of Paris doubled to over a million, as a building boom flooded the capital with droves of

Storming the Hôtel de Ville.

workers from the provinces. After 1837, when France's first railway line was laid between Paris and St-Germain-en-Laye, there were also railway stations to build. The overflow emptied into the poorest quarters. Overcrowding brought a host of other evils: filth, disease, violence and crime. Contemporary novelists such as Balzac, Hugo and Eugène Sue were endlessly fascinated by the city's underside, and penned hair-raising accounts of dank, tomb-like hovels where the sun never shone, and of dismal, dangerous streets in central Paris whose denizens subsisted on pauper's wages.

The well-fed, complacent bourgeoisie (mordantly caricatured in Daumier's lithography) regarded this populace with fear, loathing and even perhaps a twinge of guilt. For while the bourgeoisie prospered after 1830 – when the banks flourished, as did the **Bourse**, property speculation and industry – workers under Louis-Philippe were still forbidden from forming unions or striking. Gaslight, which made city streets so much more pleasant, also enabled the working day to be extended to 15 hours or more. Factory owners pruned salaries to the limit, exploited children and were unfettered by any legislation. Unemployed or disabled workers and their families were obliged to beg, steal or starve.

A cholera epidemic in 1831 claimed 19,000 victims in just three months, and aggravated the already bitter class divisions. The rich blamed workers, beggars and immigrants for breeding disease; the poor hated the bourgeoisie who could afford to escape the city's fetid air, or move to the spacious new neighbourhoods developing in the 8th and 9th *arrondissements*. The stage was set for a battle, and it was to have an even more ferocious edge than that of 1830.

Louis-Philippe's *préfet*, Rambuteau, was no Baron Haussmann (see below), but he managed to keep busy by completing some works in progress. The Orléans monarchy, in contrast to the senior Bourbons, made a pitch to win Bonapartist support, finishing the **Arc de Triomphe** and the **Madeleine**, even though they were coyly stripped of direct references to the man who had commissioned them. Rambuteau also initiated some pro-

jects of his own, most notably of them the **Pont Louis-Philippe** and the **Pont du Carrousel**.

1848: REVOLUTION AGAIN

On 23 February 1848 nervous troops fired on a crowd on the boulevard des Capucines. Once again, demonstrators demanded blood for blood. Paris reaffirmed its right to the title *capitale des révolutions*, as barricades again covered the city. The National Guard – called out to put down the insurrection – defected to the rebels' side. In the Tuileries, Louis-Philippe abdicated, and abandoned his palace, his capital, and his country, just as Charles X had done 18 years earlier.

The workers' revolution of 1848 made France a republic again – but not for long. The Second Republic was given a progressive provisional government, which included the Romantic poet Lamartine and a mechanic – the first French proletarian to hold such a position. They abolished slavery in the colonies and the death penalty for political crimes; gave most French men (but only men) the vote and set up 'National Workshops' to guarantee jobs for all workers. Paris was euphoric. The capital, however, had not counted on the reaction of the provinces. In May 1848, general elections put a conservative commission at the head of the Republic. One of its first official acts was to liquidate the 'make work' scheme, as too costly and allied with socialism.

Desperate workers took to the streets in the 'June Days'. There were more barricades, more battles, and more blood. And this time the insurgents got the worst of it: thousands fell under the fire of the troops of General Cavaignac, and others were massacred in reprisals after the combat had ended. To justify this harsh repression, officials claimed that rebels had been responsible for the deaths of two generals and the Archbishop of Paris.

SECOND EMPIRE

At the end of 1848, to widespread surprise, new elections gave an overwhelming mandate to a new President of the Republic, Louis-Napoléon Bonaparte, nephew of the great Emperor. After a couple of years consolidating his position as President, he decided that he didn't merely want to preside, but to reign, as history repeated itself in slightly comic-opera fashion. The *coup d'état* on 2 December 1851 that gave Louis-Napoléon dictatorial powers met with little resistance. Even so, Louis-Napoléon's troops somehow contrived to fire on an unarmed crowd and kill at least 100 innocent people. A year later, in 1852, the Prince-Président moved into the Tuileries Palace as Emperor of France: *Vive Napoléon III*.

The Second French Empire was an often decadent, sometimes ramshackle affair. Many people were never quite clear on what Louis-Napoléon himself stood for, other than his

Charles Baudelaire, the perfect bohemian.

La Vie de Boheme

In 1848 a writer named Henri Murger, Paris-born but the son of a German concièrge, published his *Scènes de la Vie de Bohème* (Scenes from the Life of Bohemia), with its story of self-indulgent Rodolphe and his friends defying convention and falling in love with the frozen-handed Mimi. Murger never had another success, but nevertheless can still stand as one of the most influential hack writers in history. Previously, *Bohème* had been used in French to refer to Gypsies, who were believed to come from Bohemia; whether Murger invented the new usage is not clear, but his book certainly did most to publicise it. Within a few years, the idea of Bohemia had crossed the world. In the 1890s, Puccini would use Murger's book as the basis for *La Bohème*.

There were no real Bohemians before the Revolution; after 1815, however, the Napoleonic educational reforms, the expansion in the press, in the art market, in the bureaucracy, all made it possible for a floating, educated, intellectual class to exist. Paris, capital of freedom and the arts, was naturally a magnet for such people from all over Europe. Bohemians, living in the cheapest garrets at the top of apartment blocks, became a fixture of Paris, living for the moment, with no stable residence, working irregularly and despising all the conventions of the new bourgeois classes.

Murger possibly based his characters on the likes of Chamfleury, Nadar, Constantin Guys and Baudelaire, who frequented the Café Momus in the rue des Prêtres-St-Germain-L'Auxerrois. Ironically, Baudelaire was never a Bohemian by choice. He was born into wealth, and only after a family feud in his late twenties did he became the penniless inhabitant of dingy hotels, friend of prostitutes and avid drug user.

Another famous Bohemian, one of Paris' more unusual inhabitants, was the poet Gérard de Nerval. He could only write in the street, and had a predilection for unusual places like the quarries of Montmartre. He had several homes, but preferred to sleep amongst piles of vegetables at Les Halles. In 1841 he was put in a mental clinic for walking a live lobster through the Palais Royal on a leash, and seemed surprised that people found it stranger than walking a poodle.

desire to keep up the family name. At home, he combined authoritarianism with crowd-pleasing social welfare measures for the poor, in the Bonapartist style. Abroad, his policies included absurd adventures such as the attempt to make the Austrian Archduke Maximilian Emperor of Mexico.

Still more than his illustrious uncle, though, Napoléon III had grandiose plans for Paris, and it is they that are his most lasting legacy. His ideas included completing the Louvre, landscaping the Bois de Boulogne, constructing new, enclosed markets at Les Halles, and, above all, opening up a whole series of new boulevards. To carry out these daunting tasks he appointed an Alsatian Protestant named Baron Haussmann, Prefect of the Seine from 1853. An energetic, iron-fisted administrator, Haussmann set about his programme with unprecented energy, giving the aged, malodorous city its greatest-ever transformation (*see chapter* **Architecture**).

Haussmann's bulldozer, with its love of straight lines, naturally did not escape controversy. *Hôtels particuliers* in the Faubourg St-Germain, ancient vestiges of the Latin Quarter, and the much-loved *boulevard du crime* with its theatres, all fell before the axe. Baudelaire lamented that '*Le vieux Paris n'est plus*' (the old Paris is no more).

The new Paris was a showcase city, with the first department stores, and major events such as the International Exhibition of 1867. With so much building work, there was naturally plenty of opportunity for speculation, which Napoleon III's regime, always ready to accommodate bankers, was concerned to see taken up. During the Second Empire Paris really established its reputation as the world capital of sensual pleasure, a place where everything was for sale, and moralists again decried it as a 'New Babylon', as a means of attacking the regime. Even the unchallengeable Haussmann was not above reproach, and he was forced to resign in 1870 after it was shown that some of his projects were based on highly questionable accounts. The combination of sensuality and indulgent opulence of the Second Empire can well be seen in the regime's most distinctive single building, Charles Garnier's **Opéra**, even though Louis-Napoléon did not see it completed.

By the end of the 1860s, Napoleon III was visibly tired. In 1870, he was maneouvred into war with the German states, led by Bismarck's Prussia. At Sedan, in September, the French army was crushed, and Napoleon III abdicated, so that the Second Napoleonic interlude disappeared as quickly as it had arrived.

The Third Republic

In its belle époque Paris was at its most ebullient, but military catastrophe was looming near.

Days after Napoleon III's defeat at Sedan, on 4 September 1870, a Parisian crowd demanded and won a new Republic, proclaimed to much cheering at the **Hôtel de Ville**. A provisional government of National Defence was formed, yet within weeks Paris was under siege by the Prussians, and cut off from the rest of the nation.

Beleaguered Parisians shivered and starved through the winter. In addition to horses, dogs, cats, and rats, animals from the zoo in the Jardin des Plantes ended up in the city's butcher shops. Christmas dinner at the fashionable Restaurant Voisin featured an hors-d'oeuvre of stuffed ass's head, a *consommé d'éléphant* for the soup course, followed by *civet de kangourou* and *cuisson de loup sauce chevreuil*.

In January 1871, Prussian artillery bombarded the southern *arrondissements*. The French government negotiated a temporary armistice with Bismarck, then hastily arranged elections for a

National Assembly mandated to make peace. Paris voted republican, but the majority of successful candidates were conservative monarchists. The peace terms they agreed – a five billion-franc indemnity, occupation and the concession of Alsace-Lorraine to the newly-united Germany– disgusted Parisian patriots. When the time came for the Assembly to reconvene, the representatives spurned the left-leaning, mutinous capital and chose to set up in Versailles instead. Paris understandably regarded this *décapitalisation* as an act of hostility.

The city remained in a state of nervous agitation. Paris' National Guard formed an illegal 'federation' and refused to lay down arms. On 18 March government troops were sent to Montmartre to take away the *fédérés*' 200 cannons to Montmartre, but a furious local crowd fought off the soldiers and killed two generals. Adolphe Thiers, leader of the provisional Versailles government, evacuated the city;

Whooping it up on the 14th July, 1880 (Alfred Roll).

Paris was left in the hands of radicals who declared it a free Commune. The fuse of civil war was lit.

Karl Marx presented the Paris Commune as the first modern workers' revolt; equally, it could also be seen as the last gasp of the native Parisian revolutionary tradition that had begun in 1789. The *Communards* were able to keep control of the city until May, when, in the *Semaine Sanglante* (Bloody Week), 70,000 *Versaillais* troops marched into Paris. The *Communards* fought back street by street, but it was an unequal fight. Desperate insurgents torched the Tuileries, the Hôtel de Ville, the Finance Ministry, the Palais-Royal... The 'men of Versailles' for their part demonstrated the sheer hatred with which the Parisian revolutionary was regarded by the country's established classes, shooting thousands of *Communard* suspects without trial. On Sunday evening, 20 May, as black smoke fogged the Paris sky, the last defenders of the Commune made their final stand among the graves of **Père Lachaise** cemetery; at dawn,

soldiers shot the 147 survivors against the *mur des fédérés*, and cast the bodies into a common grave. The week claimed at least 20,000 victims – more than the revolution of 1789.

EXPOSITIONS UNIVERSELLES

The regime established after 1871, the Third French Republic, was an unloved compromise. The right detested all republics and yearned for the restoration of some kind of monarchy; on the left, the Republic was seen as tainted because of its suppression of the Commune. During its early years, its collapse was confidently predicted. Despite it all, though, the Third Republic would actually survive for 70 years, making it the longest-lasting French political system since the Revolution.

In Paris, peace permitted the restoration of all the many areas damaged in the siege and the Commune – even including the complete rebuilding of the Hôtel de Ville – and the completion of those of Haussmann's schemes that were still

City of Light

In Vive-e la France,
they're full of romance,
you'll find policemen with embroidery on their pants...
From *Fifty Million Frenchmen can't be wrong,* sung by Sophie Tucker in the 1927 show *Gay Paree.*
It is not clear just when Paris began to be regarded as the capital of the world. It was already looked on with some awe during the Second Empire. It is undeniable, though, that the city's stock has never been higher than during the years between the 1890s and 1914. Across the world, if one wanted a cast-iron pumping engine, one might send to Glasgow; if one wanted any of the finer pleasures of life, whether fine wines, fine painting, banned books or lingerie, it had to be Paris.

An Englishman, Charles Worth, had established Paris couture as the international standard for fashion. In art, the city had, naturally, long been a target for every French artist, but in the 1900s it also saw the arrival of Picasso from Spain, Brancusi from Romania, or Soutine from Russia. When Stravinsky, Diaghilev and Nijinsky unveiled *The Rite of Spring* in 1913, there was nowhere better to première it than Paris, even though it began a riot.

Paris was also naughty, a place where one could find illicit pleasures inaccessible elsewhere. In 1889, impresario Maurice Zidler opened the Moulin Rouge, which successfully

Exposition Universelle

repackaged a half-forgotten dance called the *chahut* for bourgeois audiences and the world as the can-can. In 1894 what is believed to have been the world's first strip joint opened nearby on the rue des Martyrs, the Divan Fayouac, with a routine titled *Le Coucher d'Yvette* ('Yvette Goes to Bed'). At the trial of Oscar Wilde in 1895, the mere fact that he owned 'French books' was held to be evidence against him.

The legend of Paris as the capital of pleasure was in part assiduously cultivated by those who had a vested interest in doing so; nevertheless, so powerful is it that it can be instantly summoned up today, even though you're maybe more likely to find policemen with embroidered pants elsewhere.

unfinished. Later, Paris was able to celebrate its faith in science and progress by presenting two more World Exhibitions, of which it had already hosted two during the second Empire. The Exhibition of 1889 was the first Republican exhibition, designed to mark the Centenary of the Revolution and to confirm the international respectability of the Third Republic, with festivities that combined elements of a trade fair and a patriotic paean to Republican values.

Impressionist Paris

Impressionism has been described as the first artistic movement to be organised in cafés, notably the Café Guerbois, on the avenue de Clichy. Equally, the Impressionist painters were also very much part of the modern city in their subject matter. In contrast to their immediate forerunners such as Courbet or the Barbizon school (*see chapter* **Trips Out of Town: Day Trips**), the Impressionists were fascinated by all the new developments of contemporary urban life – trains, cafés, theatres and so on.

Between 1872 and 1882, Renoir, Monet and Berthe Morisot often came to work in Paris, and Manet, Degas and Caillebotte lived in the city. Their first group exhibition took place in 1874 in the *atelier* of the photographer Félix Nadar, on the boulevard des Capucines.

From 1864, Manet lived on boulevard des Batignolles, but in 1874, he found a studio at 4, rue de St-Petersbourg. In the same area he also painted *Au café* and *La serveuse de bocks*, at the Brasserie Reichshoffen on the boulevard Rochechouart. Nearby was the symbol par excellence of modern life, St-Lazare station, which Monet depicted in a series of paintings after getting the station master to halt the trains by convincing him that he was a *Salon* celebrity. Gustave Caillebotte, meanwhile, chose the Pont de l'Europe, across the rails, as an emblem of the new Paris.

Degas was, of course, a regular at the rehearsals of the *corps de ballet* at the new Paris opera, producing wonderful backstage scenes using techniques of composition taken from Japanese woodcuts. Both he and Renoir lived on or near still semi-pastoral Montmartre, and left vivid records of *la vie montmartroise* such as *La chanson du chien*, *La chanteuse au gant*, *Le café-concert* and Renoir's classic *Moulin de la Galette*.

Renoir's sumptuous Moulin de la Galette.

It was prophecied that it would be a disaster, that French rightists would sabotage it and that the crowned heads of Europe would stay away in droves. Moreover, the centrepiece of the Exhibition was to be a giant iron structure, the **Eiffel Tower**, erected amid huge controversy and in the face of protests from groups such as the petition by artists, among them the writer Maupassant, who denounced it as a 'barbaric mass'. Nevertheless, in the event the Exhibition was a great success, while the Tower, naturally, became something without which Paris is unimaginable.

On 1 April 1900, another World Exhibition greeted the new century. On the banks of the Seine a futuristic city sprang up. Paris itself built the **Grand** and **Petit Palais**, as well as the **Pont Alexandre-III**, with its elegant arch of moulded steel and extravagant decoration. And in July 1900 the first line of the Paris métro ferried passengers from Porte Maillot to Vincennes, in the unheard-of time of 25 minutes.

The 1900 Exhibition drew well over 50 million visitors, who marvelled at the wonders of electricity, rode on the exciting new Ferris wheel, and drank in the heady atmosphere of Paris. Cafés and restaurants like **Julien**, **Le Train Bleu** at Gare du Lyon and **Pharamond** were spruced up for the occasion. At the **Ritz**, Escoffier served *homard en bellevue* to toffs who could afford it.

This was France's – and above all Paris' – *belle époque*, the 'beautiful era', a phrase coined in a wash of nostalgia in the twenties after the catastrophe of World War I, when it was looked back on as a period of untroubled confidence and *joie de vivre*. It was not by any means, though, devoid of tensions and problems seen from close to. There were intense labour conflicts. Also, France after the defeat of 1870 was intensely frustrated, with many circles obsessed with the need for 'revenge' and the recovery of Alsace-Lorraine. This frustration was also expressed in xenophobia, and especially an obsessive anti-semitism.

These strands came together in the Dreyfus case, which polarised French society for years. In 1894, a Jewish army officer, Captain Alfred Dreyfus, was accused of spying for Germany, quickly condemned and sent off to Devil's Island. As the facts emerged, though, suspicion pointed clearly at another officer on the general staff. Leftists and liberals, such as Zola, took up Dreyfus' case; rightists were bitterly opposed, sometimes taking the view that even if he were innocent it was imperative that the honour of the army should not be questioned. Such were the passions this case mobilised that fights broke out in the street; nevertheless, Dreyfus was eventually vindicated, and released in 1900.

Even with these tensions, the *belle époque* – and most of all the last ten years before 1914 – was a time of prestigious artistic activity in Paris, the world centre of painting, music, dance and almost every other art. When the Countess Greffuelhes – Proust's model for the Princesse de Guermantes in *Remembrance of Things Past* – bestowed her patronage on Debussy, Caruso, Mussorgsky, Diaghilev and his Ballet Russe, it was seen to be chic to favour avant-garde artists and musicians.

THE GREAT WAR

On 2 August 1914, France learned that war with Germany was imminent. In the streets of Paris, there was genuine rejoicing, for to many it seemed simply that the long-awaited opportunity for 'revenge' had finally come.

However, the Allied armies were steadily pushed back. Paris filled with refugees, and on 2 September the Germans were on the Marne, just 15 miles from the city. The government took refuge in Bordeaux, entrusting the defence of the capital to General Galliéni. What then occurred was later glorified as the 'Miracle on the Marne'. Troops were ferried to the front in Paris taxis, one of which is now in the **Musée de l'Armée**. By 13 September, the Germans were pushed back to the Dise, and Paris was safe. From the end of 1914, the fronts settled into the familiar image of the First World War: trenches, mud and unchanging front lines. Battles raged on, and Paris industrialised to produce weapons and chemicals.

By 1917, after the catastrophic battle of Verdun the previous year had inflicted appalling damage on the French army a strong current of defeatism emerged. Georges Clemenceau, a veteran Parisian radical, was made prime minister to restore morale. For Parisians, this was very necessary, for spirits had been sapped both by a raging epidemic of Spanish influenza, and the shells of 'Big Bertha' – a gigantic German cannon levelled at the city from over 75 miles away.

In summer 1918, the Germans were on the Marne once more, but were again pushed back. On 11 November, the shooting finally stopped. Celebrations lasted for days, but the war had cut a swathe through the male population of France.

URBAN VIOLENCE

Paris emerged from the War without the breezy confidence of the *belle époque*, but with a restless energy that was expressed in an artistic scene that in the 1920s was more dynamic, and more cosmopolitan, than ever (*see page 82* **The Jazz Age**). In the prosperity of the twenties, the city's continuing fascination with the new was seen in its enthusiastic embrace of art deco.

The Depression did not hit France until after 1930, but when it arrived, it unleashed a wave of political violence. On 6 February 1934, Fascist and extreme right-wing groups demonstrated in Paris against the Republic. Thirty thousand rightists tried to break through police cordons, and invade the **Assemblée Nationale**. Fire hoses and bullets beat them back.

Fifteen were killed, and 1,500 wounded. Not since the Commune had so much blood been shed in Paris.

On the left, these events were one of the spurs to the creation of the Popular Front, in which socialists and communists united in the face of Fascism and the economic situation. In 1936, socialist Léon Blum was elected to head a Popular Front government. Paris was paralysed by strikes, for workers were impatient to see immediate results from their government. And indeed, their demands were met, in the euphoric 'workers' spring' of 1936; they were given the right to unionise, higher salaries, a 40-hour week and, for the first time, paid holidays.

By the autumn, however, debates about the Spanish Civil War had split the coalition, and the economic situation was deteriorating thanks to middle-class non cooperation with the Popular Front. Blum's one-year-old government fell in June 1937. France seemed within an inch of revolution. The working class was disenchanted, and right-wing parties grew on the back of people's visceral fear of Communism, which to many seemed a far more immediate threat than Hitler.

War was once again upon the horizon, for by 1938 Hitler was making ever increasing demands against Czechoslovakia. Tragically, each camp of a France that was divided into right and left feared the enemy within far more than the real enemy that was waiting on its doostep.

THE SECOND WAR

Britain and France declared war on Germany in September 1939, but for months this meant only the *drôle de guerre* (phoney war), characterised by rumour and inactivity. As the storm clouds gathered, life in the City of Light continued much as before, except that curfews and black-outs put a brake on the capital's usual *joie de vivre*.

On 10 May 1940, the Germans launched their attack into France, Belgium and Holland. By 6 June, the French armies had been crushed and the Germans were already near Paris. A shell-shocked government left for Bordeaux, while archives and works of art such as the *Mona Lisa* were hurriedly hidden or bundled off to safety. Thousands of ordinary Parisians threw belongings into cars, carts, prams and bikes and began their own exodus south.

The Jazz Age

With the return of peace after 1918, the post-war era of fun, frivolity and artistic adventure began in Montparnasse. As early as 1910, avant-garde artists – Derain, Soutine, van Dongen, Chagall, Kisling, Modigliani and Picasso, the entire *Ecole de Paris* – had abandoned Montmartre for Montparnasse, and throughout the twenties the area was an international attraction. Josephine Baker may have triumphed in the Revue Nègre on the Champs-Elysées, and some painters, Braque and Utrillo, remained faithful to Montmartre, but the jazz age in Paris belonged to Kiki and her friends in Montparnasse.

They included Picasso, Brancusi, Hemingway, Matisse, Pascin, Kisling and Man Ray, who became her lover shortly after his arrival from the States in 1921. According to Marcel Duchamp, this was the first truly international colony of artists, as a third of them came from abroad, attracted by the unusual liberty of the *quartier*.

Kisling hosted lunches which lasted until 8 p.m; the surrealists flocked to Brancusi's house in the Impasse Ronsin to hear him sing Romanian folk tunes; and everyone rubbed shoulders at the legendary cafés, such as **Le Dôme**. In 1925, **Le Select** opened, the first café to stay open all night, to be joined in December 1927 by **La Coupole**, whose legendary opening party attracted the likes of Cocteau, Foujita and Vlaminck.

Bohemian Montparnasse became the white-hot centre of jazz-age nightlife. In 1923, Le Jockey opened as the area's first nightclub, with Kiki de Montparnasse as its star. The arty crowd danced the blues at La Jungle, watched the nude dancers and acrobats of La Cigogne and poured into Le Bal Nègre on the rue Blomet, where the Bal Ubu, one of the last parties of the *Folle Epoque* was held, with waiters distributing bottles rather than glasses of champagne.

Josephine Baker comes on to a tiger.

German prisoners on 25th August 1944.

By mid-June Paris had been occupied without a fight. The French cabinet voted to request an armistice, and Marshal Pétain, an elderly hero of the first war, took over the government. The Germans occupied two-thirds of France, while the French government moved to Vichy, in the unoccupied southern part of the country. Some cabinet members, disgusted by this turn of events, left for North Africa to try and set up a government-in-exile, while a young, autocratic general, Charles de Gaulle, went to London to organise a Free French movement in open opposition to the occupation. For the moment, however, they encountered little popular support, for most people were most aware of the completeness of the defeat.

THE OCCUPATION

For most Parisians, the occupation would mean going without a lot of the creature comforts they'd previously enjoyed. For the Germans, Paris was their western headquarters, and a very attractive assignment compared to, for example, Russia. They lapped up luxury goods, and swamped Paris' best nightspots, restaurants and hotels.

There was no shortage of Parisians who accepted them, and warmed to an enemy who offered a champagne lifestyle and sustained Paris' traditional glitter. In the entertainment world, Maurice Chevalier and the actress Arletty were among those who were later condemned for having performed for, or having still closer contacts with, the Germans. So too was couturier Coco Chanel.

Occupied Paris also had its share of pro-Vichy bureaucrats who preferred to work with the Germans than embrace what many saw as a futile opposition. There were also *attentistes* (the wait and see-ers), and the black marketeers, who became rich on the back of Nazi rationing. Even so, many were prepared to risk being hauled off to the torture chambers of the Gestapo at rue des Saussaies, avenue Foch or rue Lauriston. By the summer of 1941, the first executions of French underground fighters by the Germans had begun, in response to the activities of the patriots, organised from Britain. Treachery and heroism, submissiveness and resistance, co-existed in a city of torn allegiances.

There was also the rounding-up and deportation of Jews, an area in which the role of the Vichy authorities was particularly shameful, and which remains a highly sensitive issue in France to this day. The French right had been virulently anti-semitic when Hitler was a baby, and there were around the Vichy regime plenty of rabid anti-semites who eagerly introduced anti-Jewish measures even before the Germans had asked them to, and implemented them with a vigour much greater, for example, than that seen in Mussolini's Italy. In June 1942, thousands of Jews were summoned to the Vélodrome d'Hiver (the winter cycling stadium) in Paris. The Vichy Chief of Police ensured that not only Jews aged over 18, but also thousands of young children not on the original orders, were deported in what is now known as the *Vél d'Hiv*.

LIBERATION

In June 1944, a beautiful summer greeted an exhausted city, on which four years of occupation had taken their toll. Nevertheless, for those who could afford them, there was still champagne and caviar at Maxim's and the Lido, and racing at Longchamp and Auteuil. Ballet, theatre and music also survived the Nazi colonisation. While other cities burned, Paris had remained alive and largely intact.

Then came the Allied invasion of Normandy. The German troops began to retreat eastwards, and Parisians saw a real opportunity to retake their city. First came strikes – from 10 to 18 August – on public services. Parisians were bereft of métro services, gas and electricity, and there was no radio broadcasting and no news, but people began to sense that liberation was finally at hand.

On 19 August, a *Tricolore* was hoisted at the Hôtel de Ville, and the Free French forces launched an insurrection, occupying several buildings. On 23 August, Hitler ordered Von Choltitz, the German commander, to waste no more time in destroying the French capital. Von Choltitz stalled, for which inaction he would later be honoured by a grateful French government. On 25 August, General Leclerc's French 2nd Armoured Division, who had been carefully put at the head of the US forces approaching Paris in order that it would be French troops who would first enter the city, made their way into Paris by the Porte d'Orléans.

The city went wild. There were still snipers hidden on rooftops, but in the euphoria of the moment no-one seemed to care. Late in the afternoon, de Gaulle arrived to make his way down the Champs-Elysées to the Hôtel de Ville. 'We are living minutes that go far beyond our paltry lives' he cried out to an ecstatic crowd.

De Gaulle to Chirac

Since 1945, Paris has gone from a replay of its radical past to becoming an architectural showcase.

In the immediate post-war years, those who had led the fight against the Vichy government and the Germans felt that now was the time to build a new society and a new republic. The National Resistance Council's post-war programme of reforms was approved by most parties from left to right, and De Gaulle was proclaimed provisional President.

Life began to resemble normality, although there were ugly accounts to settle in those post-liberation days. Vigilante justice prevailed as neighbour turned against neighbour, and accusations of collaboration began to fly. Mock trials were set up, and severe punishments doled out to the *collabos*.

As normality was re-established, however, and the economy began to revive, post-war Paris became a magnet for thousands of French men and women for whom the capital represented a new opportunity. The population rose dramatically: in 1946, there were 6.6 million inhabitants in greater Paris, but by 1950 that number had increased by 700,000. In response, the state built *Villes Nouvelles* (new towns) and low-income housing developments. These resulted in vast concrete monoliths, made possible by the post-war use of steel, reinforced concrete and glass.

COLONIAL WAR

De Gaulle relinquished office in 1946, and the Fourth Republic was established. Thereafter, French troops were constantly engaged in a doomed policy of trying to save France's Empire from disintegration. Vietnam was lost in 1954, but after revolt broke out in Algeria in 1956 the socialist prime minister Guy Mollet sent in almost half a million French troops, the largest French expeditionary force since the Crusades.

The army was demoralised, and many of the troops sent to Algeria were young conscripts. Algeria also became a major issue for intellectuals, and it was only a matter of time before the battles were reflected in Paris.

During the winter of 1955-56, riot police prowled Paris trying to keep the peace. France, so jingoistic in the first bellicose flush of *après-guerre*, was becoming divided. Mutinous army officers, determined to oppose any 'sell-out' of the French settlers or *colons* in Algeria, took over government headquarters in Algiers. It was time, decided the Fourth Republic, to admit defeat and wheel the old demagogue out of retirement. De Gaulle came back, with the understanding that he was to be allowed to rewrite the constitution and give France the republic he thought she deserved.

DE GAULLE VICTORIOUS

Ostensibly, De Gaulle was hauled out of village retirement to deal with the Algerian crisis. The General used time-honoured tactics, appearing to promise one thing to the settlers in Algeria, while negotiating with the Algerian rebel leaders for their country's independence. The President escaped two assassination attempts, but in 1962 Algeria was proclaimed independent, and some 700,000 embittered colonists came straggling back to France. Yet De Gaulle emerged crowing victory, and the Gaullists were established as ruling the French roost.

France was at peace and economically prosperous. De Gaulle beamed down from his presidential throne like the monarch he wasn't. He commanded foreign policy, intervened in domestic policy when he felt like it, and reported to the nation by means of carefully-orchestrated press conferences or appearances on television, which had by now muscled its way into many French homes.

Television wasn't the only innovation in Parisian homes: the consumer society was making its presence felt. The state was under pressure to provide yet more new housing, and to update the métro and develop new forms of transport, such as the RER. In Paris, radical urbanisation plans were hastily drawn up. Although historic areas were considered sacrosanct,large sections of the city succumbed to the demolishing ball and chain. The 'Manhattanisation' of Paris was underway, with several totally unsuitable high-rises being built.

De Gaulle was no builder, and his monarchical tendencies stopped short of a desire to Haussmanise the capital. A hotchpotch of forgettable building styles emerged during his presidency, as in the **UNESCO** building, many of the blocks at **La Défense** or the **Tour Montparnasse**. André Malraux, however, De Gaulle's Minister of Culture, did undertake one major series of measures, to ensure the preservaton of the historic buildings of the Marais.

Political and economic stability affected the climate of Paris. The post-war mood of crisis was over, and into the breach thundered a sharp, fresh 'new wave' of cinema directors, novelists and critics – Truffaut, Godard, Resnais.

By 1968, 50 million people inhabited *l'Hexagon* – the term by which the French describe France. While intellectuals thought great thoughts, youth chaffed against their yokes, as their numbers were swelling the over-stretched French educational system. Dissatisfaction was widespread, not just with the state of education, but also with the authoritarian nature of the state and of French society – combined with the general, sixties' mood of counter-culture radicalism.

In May 1968 the students erupted, and, in the time-honoured way, took to the streets (*see page 86* **May '68**). By mid-May, workers and trade unions had joined the widening protest.

Disaster was avoided, but only just, and confidence in De Gaulle was sorely shaken. He continued to hold office for another ten months. Then, after losing a referendum, he resigned and went back to his provincial retreat, where he died in 1970 at the age of 79. In the meantime, the cobblestones in Paris were replaced and paved over, so that they could never again serve as ammunition for the mob.

POMPIDOU & GISCARD

Pom-Pom – as De Gaulle's successor was often called – didn't preside over any earth-shattering political developments during his time in office. What he did do was begin the process that changed the architectural face of Paris radically, and which affixed the state's signature on some of the most monumental building schemes since those of Haussmann and the Third Republic.

It was Georges Pompidou, a right-wing conservative, who took the decision to implant an uncompromisingly avant-garde building, the **Centre Pompidou**, in the heart of one of Paris's oldest neighbourhoods. At the time – 1968-1977 – conservatives and socialists alike condemned the project. Pompidou also gave the go-ahead to the redevelopment of **Les Halles**. This same period, not entirely unconnectedly, also saw fast food make its first appearance on the Parisian scene.

Valéry Giscard d'Estaing became president in 1974, on the sudden death of Georges Pompidou. He made clear his desire to transform France into an 'advanced liberal society'. In 1977 he inaugurated the Pompidou Centre, and promptly embarked on some projects of his own. Notable among his decisions were those to transform the **Gare d'Orsay** into a museum, and the creation at **La Villette** of a high-tech science museum in the vast old abattoirs in the north of Paris.

MITTERRAND'S *GRANDS PROJETS*

France was getting tired of the Gaullist élite. In an abrupt political turn-around, the socialists, led by François Mitterrand, swept into power in 1981. The mood in Paris was initially electric, but Socialist France turned out to be not wildly different from Gaullist France. After a few hiccups – nationalising some banks and industries – the Socialists settled into a comfortable bourgeois rule. Life in France was pretty stable and prosperous during the eighties. In Paris, these years were defined politically by the continuing feud between Mitterrand and Paris' right-wing mayor since 1977, Jacques Chirac.

St. Germain

'The word 'existentialism' only had to appear on a poster to mobilise the police, the Red Cross and the firemen', said one observer, who lived through the golden age of St-Germain-des-Prés in the forties and fifties.

If Jean-Paul Sartre was the 'pope' of Saint-Germain, then Simone de Beauvoir was the area's high priestess, and the **Café de Flore** was their headquarters. During the Occupation, the café's owner, Paul Boubal, installed a stove in the middle of his establishment. The artists who lived in the hotels of the *quartier*, out of a belief that apartments were too bourgeois, flocked in to get warm. They also avoided the **Deux Magots**, because it was a favorite with the Germans. During 1943-44, Sartre wrote *Roads to Freedom* at a table on the first floor while de Beauvoir worked away at another table.

At the end of the war, the relief felt post-Occupation was translated into an endless party atmosphere. Sartre and de Beauvoir moved on to other horizons, such as Le Montana, Le Village and La Rhumerie. The group of Communists, centred around Marguerite Duras, got together either in her apartment on the rue St-Benoît or at Le Bonaparte café. Other favourites of the era were the legendary jazz cellars such as Le Lorentais, Le Tabou and La Rose Rouge, centres of organized madness that were frequented by Cocteau, Camus, Queneau, Boris Vian and his trumpet and naturally, the existentialist 'muse', Juliette Gréco.

From the very beginning of his presidency, Mitterrand cherished very distinctive ambition for transforming the landscape of Paris. His first operation was the most daring: open-heart surgery on the **Louvre**. This in turn carried with it a corollary, the transfer of the Ministry of Finance, formerly in the Louvre, to a new office complex at **Bercy** on the Seine, the largest of its kind in Europe. Conservatives and many officials viewed the move as banishment to a Gulag.

Choice of the Bercy site was part of a vast programme for the urban renewal of eastern Paris. Mitterrand's third big scheme was also in this area, the **Opéra Bastille**. In monumental terms, though, the new triumphal arch at **La Défense**, stands head and shoulders above his other grand schemes. The *Grands Projets* have not necessarily met with universal acclaim. Even so, scarcely anyone has questioned the right of the President to devote huge sums to the contemporary embellishment of the French capital, or Mitterrand's belief that to keep Paris alive, new blood must be injected into it regularly.

THE CHIRAC ERA OPENS

The last years of the Mitterrand era were marked by the President's ill health, and a steady seeping away of his prestige. Hence, when the May 1995 elections were held, the surprise was not that the Socialists lost, but that they achieved the very respectable showing they did. The new President, Paris' long-term Mayor Jacques Chirac, is famous for being all things to all men (and women, for he makes a great play for women's votes), but he comes into power in an atmosphere very different from the expansive mood of the early eighties (*see chapter* **Paris Today**). It remains to be seen, though, whether a Gaullist President will be able to desist from leaving some sort of mark on Paris.

May '68

Even today, barely a week goes by without you hearing a French person evoke *soixante-huit*. If not a political revolution, May '68 was a cultural and social uprising. It was also the biggest strike in the history of France, when demonstrations stretched for seven kilometres through the streets of Paris.

On May 2, students at the campus of Nanterre, west of Paris, attempt to occupy a college building, and the dean of the university decide to close the entire campus down. The following day, the rector of the Sorbonne asks students to evacuate the building there, following confrontations between Trotskyist students and an extreme right group. The students refuse, and by the end of the afternoon, 2,000 students find themselves face to face with 1,500 policemen.

Paving stones are torn up, perhaps inspired by the Situationist group's slogan *'sous les pavés, la plage'* ('beneath the paving slabs, the beach'). The confrontations continue all week along boulevard St-Michel and rue Gay-Lussac. The government's reaction is to rule with an iron rod, and the violence of the police outrages the public and leads to unions calling a one-day strike action on Monday 13th.

The same day, students take over the Sorbonne and the faculty at Censier, and workers from Renault and Sud-Aviation go on strike. By the 20th, over 6 million people are on strike in France. After negotiations fail, De Gaulle's proposal to hold a referendum is rejected with the worst night of violence. However, by the end of the month, the tide begins to turn with an anti-strike demonstration on the Champs-Elysées on 30 May. By 5 June, workers begin to go back to their factories.

The May events did, in effect, topple De Gaulle, even though he managed to hang on for almost another year. Their main effect in modern France, though, has been psychological: they profoundly shook the country's institutions and its ruling classes, forcing a previously unheard-of attitude of open debate. Equally, May '68 is also the defining point of a generation, many of whom now constitute the establishment in large sections of, for example, the media, and, some would say, are as well-ensconced as any that went before them.

Paris Today

As the last of the Mitterrand-era mega-projects approaches its end, Parisians are being forced to take stock.

Perhaps more than in any other industrialised country, in France the capital city really does lead the nation. California may be a world away from Washington, and Glasgow or Manchester may revel in a disdain for London, but Paris is still the unquestioned centre of the French universe. That does not mean the French like Parisians – just watch their reaction when they see the Paris 75 number plate in the provinces – but if you are ambitious in virtually any field, Paris is your destination.

Paris' claim to lead the country is more true than ever now that the man who was mayor for nearly 20 years is President of France. Jacques Chirac became mayor in 1977, and for nearly two decades he fine-tuned a party machine which gave him almost complete control of the city. So complete was his authority that when he had to give up the job of mayor to become President, he simply nominated a successor. There were surprisingly close city council elections a month after the presidential vote, but when Jacques Chirac handed the keys of the city to his loyal but colourless lieutenant, Jean Tiberi, everyone knew he would be the new mayor.

As mayor of Paris, Chirac was unquestionably on the right, but he was also happy to spend public money. He created a special health card for poor city residents guaranteeing them free treatment in Paris hospitals. There have also been hostels for Aids sufferers, and special emergency services for the homeless. These schemes have been criticised as piece-meal and publicity-grabbing, but they have also been of real practical benefit to tens of thousands of the city's residents.

That is the good news. The downside of these years is all too obvious on the streets and underground. Nobody knows the number of homeless in Paris, but it's estimated at around 50,000. They sleep in the underground stations and under bridges along the Seine. The numbers of those the French refer to as *les exclus* – the excluded – have grown in the last few years partly because of the rise in French unemployment, but also because of the housing policies of the Paris administration.

In the 1980s, as President Mitterrand set out on his *grands projets* to glorify the French capital, Jacques Chirac and his team, for their part, took a conscious decision to try and turn Paris into a commercial and business centre to rival London. Office blocks were built all over the city to accommodate an expected business boom. To make room for them,

the city demolished large areas of old housing and moved their population out into the *banlieue*. Cheap housing inside the city dwindled, rents went up, and for the most part the offices remained unoccupied. At the same time those with empty flats in Paris preferred to keep them that way, because they didn't want to accept cheap rents, or for fear of not being able to evict unwanted tenants. It's thought that perhaps as many as 100,000 apartments are empty in Paris, either because their owners don't want to rent them, or because property companies, caught out by a fall in prices, don't know what to do with them.

To add to the general impression that something has gone badly wrong with Paris' housing policy, a number of officials and city employees have been accused of benefitting from remarkably good deals for public housing. The City of Paris owns a great many, often very desirable residences, in many cases because they were acquired compulsorily in advance of some new boulevard scheme or other development, and since then have never been put back on the market. Chirac himself and prime minister Alain Juppé are among those who have been identified as having occupied large apartments that were property of the *Mairie*, at very favourable rates.

The homeless and the excluded have become an organised pressure group, so much so that politicians, Chirac included, have had to take up some of their demands. Homeless groups have occupied empty buildings in some of the most chic areas of Paris, and then defied the authorities to evict them. The Chirac government has promised to make dealing with unemployment and 'social exclusion' their first priority, and they and the city have promised to build new housing, but homelessness is likely to remain a major and very tangible problem in Paris for years to come.

BANLIEUE BLUES

Paris is a more bourgeois city than it was 20 years ago, a fact reflected in the heavy support the city has given to the right in both national and local elections in recent years. Old working-class neighbourhoods within the city, such as Belleville in the east, have been the targets of development for flats for middle-class families, or new public housing. That means that – apart from homelessness – Paris does not have the inner-city problems or run-down neighbourhoods all too familiar in major cities in the US, Britain and elsewhere. Paris' inner

city problems are further out, in the *banlieue* that ring the French capital. It is in these bleak concentrations of tower blocks that confrontations between locals and police have flared into riots.

If the most chic neighbourhoods of Paris-proper remain the 16th in the west and the Ile St-Louis, much of the city's vibrancy is now provided by its ethnic areas. These range from the Chinatowns in Belleville and the 13th *arrondissement* in the southeast, to the African and Maghrebin neighbourhoods running from Barbès up to Clignancourt on the northern edge of the city, in the 18th. It is estimated that one-sixth of the city's population are not native to France.

Paris is home to several important communities, such as the Vietnamese, because of France's old imperial connections. It's a mark of the internationalisation of the city, however, that communities which were nothing to do with the French empire have also arrived in Paris, as the number of Indian and Pakistani restaurants demonstrates. There are large numbers of Portuguese, Lebanese, Latin Americans, Jews (both long-established French Jews and recent arrivals from North Africa) and Turks, as well as thousands of Americans, British and other Europeans.

French tradition – and the educational system – strongly favours integration over any official recognition of cultural difference, but nevertheless the multi-cultural nature of modern Paris is evident to anyone on the street. Of the most prominent non-white groups – Black Africans and Arabs – the second generation are mainly in the *banlieue*, but Paris still draws first-generation immigrants. Some are illegals who need the anonymity of the city, and who can find work in restaurants or the clothing sweatshops east of the Bourse.

The head of France's National Front, Jean-Marie Le Pen, has made much political capital out of exaggerating the numbers of immigrants in general and of illegals in particular. His pressure – along with a certain instinctive sympathy from many on the French right – has helped bring in new tougher anti-immigration laws.

It's quite normal to see police carrying out spot identity checks in immigrant areas, where the people being ordered to produce their papers will near-invariably have brown or black faces. This tension is one of the most visible aspects of the hard edge of modern Paris. It does not mean, though, that ethnic diversity will not remain as much a characteristic of the future city as the affluence of the rue du Faubourg St-Honoré.

THE BALANCE OF PARIS

Any long-term resident of Paris will lament that gentrification means the city is losing part of its character. There are more and more antique shops and burger joints, and fewer old-fashioned cheap brasseries; and often the brasseries and bistros that remain have been taken over by a chain promoting a gruesome, phoney authenticity.

Old Paris hands like to lament that things are not what they were, but, despite it all, the truth is that the French capital is still one of the most beautiful and manageable cities in the world. How many other comparable cities could you cross on foot in a day's easy walking?

Its public transport system works well, especially the Métro. The streets, particularly in the tourist areas, are spotless. They are sprayed as well as swept, and the famous special motor cycles cruise constantly to hoover up dog dirt. With basic precautions, the city is also essentially safe.

Paris has benefited from the rivalry between the city and the state. Mitterrand, President of France for longer than anyone else this century, believed that every age should leave evidence of its existence for future generations. He built the glass pyramid at the Louvre, the Opéra at the Bastille, the National Library on the banks of the Seine, and much more. Little matter that the running costs alone of the National Library will eat up almost half of the state culture budget for years to come; the city has another monumental architectural achievement on its skyline to show the world.

As mayor of Paris during these years, Jacques Chirac had to show that the *Mairie* could also play its role in beautifying the capital. His most notable embellishment was the re-modelling of the Champs-Elysées, which the French like to call the world's most beautiful avenue. He swept the cars off the pavements, widened the walkways and lined them with trees, to try and turn the avenue once again into a rendezvous where beautiful people would parade up and down on warm summer evenings. The beginning of the Chirac presidency, however, has coincided with a general feeling that the age of the *grands projets* is over, and that both state and city should use their resources for less spectacular and more socially practical purposes.

Parisians are certainly a special breed. Most are delighted to live in one of the world's most beautiful cities, but they have a brittle quality imposed by the rigours of an expensive and often unfriendly town. Like New Yorkers, Parisians see their city as the centre of the world. They all choose to go away together at the same time in August, and then probably end up next to another Parisian family on the beach in Brittany.

Bringing up a family in Paris is tough for anyone who thinks children need to be able to run around on grass once in a while. Even if you take them to one of the few public parks, the chances are the uniformed attendant will warn you off the manicured lawns. All of this perhaps makes Paris an easier city to visit than to live in – especially on a limited budget. For all the easy criticism, however, Paris has pulled off a remarkable double; a beautiful city bursting with culture and history – which works.

Architecture

Successive rulers and artists in stone and steel have expressed their grand visions in Paris.

Paris owes its elegance to a series of periods of planning, as different rulers have left their mark, whether with walls, the creation of squares and boulevards, or *Grands Projets* to develop neglected corners of the city. The city's apparent homogeneity is largely the effect of the same materials – local yellow limestone and grey slate, later zinc, roofs – having been used over the centuries. In fact, its architecture encompasses an enormous variety of styles, from Gothic churches to 1930s' schools.

The Romanesque

The medieval city was centred on the Ile de la Cité and the Latin Quarter. The main thoroughfares of the medieval, and even the modern, street plan of the area, in the rue St-Jacques and rue Mouffetard, followed those of Roman Paris. Paris had several powerful Romanesque abbeys outside the city walls, but existing remains of this simple style are sparse. The tower of **St-Germain-des-Prés**, although topped by a later spire, still has its rounded arches and something of the solid feel to the nave. The decorated capitals of **St Pierre de Montmartre**, parts of the church of St-Germain-de-Charonne behind Père Lachaise, and, north of Paris, the remains of the early church visible in the crypt of **St Denis** are other examples.

Gothic Paris

It was in the **basilica of St-Denis**, begun in 1136, under the patronage of the powerful Abbot Suger, that the Gothic trademarks of pointed arches, ogival vaulting and flying buttresses were combined for the first time. Today some of Suger's twelfth-century porch and his choir remain.

In technical terms, Gothic vaulting allowed buildings to span large spaces and let light in; this brought with it a new aesthetic of lightness and verticality and new styles of ornament. A spate of church building began with new cathedrals at Chartres, Sens and Laon, as well as **Notre Dame**, which incorporated all the features of the new style: the twin-towered west façade, soaring nave, intricate rose windows and buttressed east end.

Shortly after work on Notre Dame had commenced, in the 1190s, King Philip Augustus began the building of the first **Louvre**, with a solid defensive keep, part of which can be seen in the Louvre today. In the following century, ribbed vaulting became ever more refined and columns more slender, in the *Rayonnant* or 'High' Gothic style. One of the few master mason/architects whose name is known is Pierre de Montreuil. His masterpiece, the **Ste-Chapelle**, begun in 1248, is a supreme example of the style, virtually a wall of stained glass. An impressive example of secular building of the time is the *Salle des Gens d'Armes*, the huge vaulted hall in the **Conciergerie**, completed in 1314.

The later *Flamboyant* Gothic style of the late fourteenth century saw little structural innovation, but a wealth of decoration. The small church of **St-Séverin**, with its twisting spiral column, is particularly original. The decorated pinnacles and gargoyles of the early sixteenth-century **Tour St Jacques** and the wonderful porch of **St Germain l'Auxerrois** are also typically *Flamboyant*.

Paris's two finest surviving medieval mansions are from the end of the fifteenth century. The Hôtel de Cluny (now home to the **Musée de Cluny**) and **Hôtel de Sens** were both urban palaces, built for powerful abbots. With living quarters at the back of an enclosed forecourt, Cluny is a precursor of the domestic style of the sixteenth century. On a more humble note, the 1407 house of Nicolas Flamel, who was condemned for alchemy, at **51 rue de Montmorency** is one of the earliest surviving private houses in Paris.

The Renaissance

The influence of the Italian Renaissance came late to Paris, and when it did it seems to have been largely due to the personal impetus of Francis I. He installed Leonardo da Vinci at Amboise (*see chapter* **Trips Out of Town: Further Afield**) and brought over Rosso and Primaticcio to work on his palace at Fontainebleau. It was not until 1528, however, that he established the court in Paris and set about updating the **Louvre**, with the *Cour Carrée*, by Pierre Lescot. In the 1560s, Catherine de Medici, widow of Henry II, commissioned Philibert Delorme to begin work on another Renaissance palace at the Tuileries, later burnt down during the Paris Commune in 1871.

The hybrid church of **St Etienne-du-Mont** shows that Renaissance style remained a superficial effect. While the structure is *Flamboyant*

Gothic, the balustrade of the nave and the elaborate roodscreen, with its spiral staircases and lacy fretwork, are Renaissance. The Hôtel Carnavalet (now the **Musée Carnavalet**), altered by Mansart the following century, is Paris' only remaining example of a Renaissance mansion.

The *Ancien Régime*

France's first Bourbon king Henry IV had great plans for modernising his capital, and built the **Pont-Neuf** and laid out two major squares, the **place Dauphine** on the Ile de la Cité and the **place des Vosges** in the Marais, with new roads leading to them. Both followed a symmetrical plan, with vaulted galleries and steeply pitched roofs, and represented a clear departure from the untidy squares of medieval Paris. Their use of red brick, though, was short-lived. The place des Vosges, with its two pavillions to the north and south intended for the king and queen, seems a last flourish of the northern Renaissance in contrast with the neo-Classical stone buildings that were later built around it.

The seventeenth century, the *Grand Siècle*, was a high point in French power, and also in architecture, painting and drama. The monarchy, first of all, and in second place the aristocracy desired buildings that emphatically declared their own grandeur and greatness. The Baroque style satisfied this need perfectly. Some great architects emerged under court patronage, including Salomon de Brosse, François Mansart, Jules Hardouin-Mansart (his nephew), Libéral Bruand and Louis Le Vau, the decorator Charles Lebrun and landscape architect André Le Nôtre.

Even in its most splendid at **Versailles**, French Baroque never reaches the level of excess of decoration of the Baroque in Italy or Austria. As with Poussin's paintings, French architects followed the Cartesian principles of harmony, order and balance, with a preference for symmetry that can be seen both in royal palaces and in the plan of the grand private houses put up in the Marais.

The **Palais du Luxembourg**, built in Italianate style for Marie de Médici by Salomon de Brosse, combines simple, classic French château design with elements of the Pitti Palace in Marie's native Florence. The **Val de Grâce** is one of the best examples of Baroque architecture in Paris. It was designed by François Mansart, a perfectionist who took so long he was replaced by Jacques Lemercier, who largely followed the former's plans. In the grand monastery complex attached to the church one can see the characteristic double-pitched 'Mansart roofs', a feature of Parisian and French architecture almost ever since.

Domestic architecture also saw a boom as the nobility and *nouveaux-riches* of the royal bureaucracy flocked to build mansions for themselves. Henry IV had started the fashion in the Marais, and later the previously-unbuilt Ile-St-Louis filled up with *hôtels particuliers*. They follow a symmetrical U-shaped plan, with a secluded courtyard, combining both privacy and ostentation. Look through the archways to the *Cour d'Honneur*, where façades are richly decorated, in contrast with their street faces. The **Hôtel de Sully** has a fine façade and still has its Orangerie at the rear of the garden court; the Hôtel Salé (**Musée National Picasso**) is notable for its sphinx-adorned entrance and magnificent staircase with ornate ironwork and carved stone figures.

*The **Conciergerie**, the much-restored Gothic palace of France's medieval kings.*

Along **rue du Faubourg Saint-Antoine** a very different style of architecture developed. Most of the buildings one can see today date from the nineteenth century, but their style is much older. This was a working district, occupied by furniture-makers. The buildings they lived and worked in were tall, with arches from the street giving way to cobbled courtyards lined with workshops.

The work of Jules Hardouin-Mansart, official architect for Louis XIV, epitomises the use of architecture for the aggrandisement of the monarchy. Under Colbert, Louis's great minister, the creation of virtual stage sets to magnify the Sun King's absolute power proceeded apace. Hardouin-Mansart's 1685 **place des Victoires**, a perfect circle, and **place Vendôme** (1698), an elegant octagon of decorated arches and light Corinthian columns set off by classical pediments, were both created to show off equestrian statues of the king. At the same time, the first *grands boulevards* were cut through in place of the old city wall.

The Louvre continued to grow, and Claude Perrault created the sweeping west façade. Libéral Bruand began the military hospital of **Les Invalides**, which, in contrast to his charming house in the Marais (**Musée de la Serrurerie**), is Baroque at its most official and monumental.

Rococo & neo-Classicism

In the eighteenth century, the Faubourg-St-Germain replaced the Marais as a fashionable address. Grand mansions were built along the adjoining rues de Grenelle, rue St-Dominique and rue de Varenne. Most are now ministries or embassies, and can be viewed only from the street. Newly accessible is the Hôtel Bouchardon (**Musée Maillol**), which still has original carved panelling.

Under Louis XV, the severe lines of the previous century were softened by rounded corners and decorative detailing, such as satyr masks on doorways (as at Hôtel Chenizot, 51 rue St-Louis-en-l'Ile or the Hôtel d'Albret, 31 rue des Francs-Bourgeois). The main developments, though, came in interior decoration, with the light, frivolous French version of Rococo style. The best examples are the interiors of the Hôtel Soubise (**Musée de l'Histoire de France**), with panelling, plasterwork and paintings by the leading craftsmen and artists of the day, including Boucher, Natoire, Restout and Van Loo. Another place to see eighteenth-century panelled interiors with furnishings of the period is the Hôtel Denon (**Musée Cognacq-Jay**).

At the same time, the pomp of the *ancien régime* reached a peak with the **place de la Concorde**, Paris's largest square, created by Jacques Ange Gabriel in honour of Louis XV. Under Louis XVI, from the 1770s, curves fell still more from fashion, as the Classicism of Ancient Rome became the leading source of inspiration. Soufflot's **Panthéon**

(1755-92) was the *Grand Projet* of its day, a huge domed structure set over a Greek cross plan, inspired by the Pantheon in Rome.

One very late addition by the old regime to Paris was the tax wall, the *Mur des Fermiers Généraux*, built around the city in 1785. Some of Claude-Nicolas Ledoux's **toll gates** survive. In them he played games with pure geometrical forms; circular at Parc Monceau and La Rotonde de la Villette (place de Stalingrad), and rectangular pairs at place Denfert-Rochereau and place de la Nation.

The Nineteenth Century

In its brief span the Revolution largely confined itself to pulling buildings down or appropriating them for new purposes. Royal statues bit the dust along with the Bastille prison, and churches became 'Temples of Reason' or grain stores. Napoleon, however, soon brought Paris back to a proper sense of its grand self.

Since the Emperor naturally compared himself to the Caesars, a stern Classicism was the preferred style for great monuments and public buildings, as seen in the **Arc de Triomphe**, the **Madeleine** and the new **Bourse**. Napoleon was also very proud of his practical contributions to Paris, notably the first canals, the Canal de l'Ourcq and the Bassin de la Villette (*see chapter* **Paris by Area: The Right Bank**) and the solid banks, the *quais*, he ordered built along the Seine.

Although Napoleon left his stamp on Paris with some of its most familiar monuments, his reign was so short that he did not actually see them complet-

St-Alexandre Nevsky. *Russian cathedral.*

ed. The Arc de Triomphe and the Madeleine, for example, were only finished under the monarchy of Louis-Philippe, in awe of the Napoleonic legacy, after 1830. Their Classical style thus continued prominent on the streets of Paris, even though by the 1840s it was under challenge from a revival of Gothic, as seen in the church of **Ste-Clotilde** (1846-57) in the Faubourg St-Germain.

The Gothic revival in Paris, never as important as it was in Britain, was particularly associated with the restoration of medieval buildings. Foremost restorer-architect and standard-bearer of Gothic in France was Eugène Viollet-le-Duc, whose results were often controversial. Despite his detailed research, his critics accused him of creating a fairy-tale, romanticised notion of the Medieval, and his use of colour was felt to pollute these monuments with decoration. You can judge for yourself in the chapel of the choir of Notre Dame and the Ste Chapelle, or from the reproductions of his designs in the Musée d'Orsay.

Baron Haussmann

Under the Second Empire after 1848 Paris underwent perhaps its most radical transformation. Baron Georges-Eugène Haussmann, Napoleon III's *Préfet de la Seine* from 1853, was not an architect but an administrator, but he did most to make Paris the most modern city of its day. Straight, broad boulevards were cut through the old city, often taking the eye to a focal point such as the new Opéra, the Gare de l'Est or the Arc de Triomphe. While the Ile de la Cité was decimated, many old districts were left largely unaltered; it is estimated that 27,000 houses were demolished and some 100,000 were built during this period.

The motives for this unprecedented exercise in urban and social engineering were a mixture of authoritarianism and paternalism characteristic of Napoleon III's regime. The wide boulevards, and the removal of the narrowest, shabbiest old streets of the city centre, were in part anti-revolutionary measures, since they made the construction of barricades far more difficult. Equally, they also raised property values, enabling speculators to make a mint. However, the new streets also answered real communication and health problems in a city that had grown from a population of around 500,000 in 1789 to 1 million in 1850, was disease-ridden, and had new railway stations needing transport links. From an aesthetic viewpoint, they added the varied viewpoints, and quality of light, characteristic of Paris today. The uncompromising vision which pushed this through is best appreciated from the top of the Arc de Triomphe, where you can see 12 radiating avenues fanning out below.

There were more prosaic measures too; Haussmann constructed asylums, prisons, schools, hospitals, markets, water and sewage systems, and gave Paris an entirely new series of parks. The city also acquired the Haussmanian apartment block, which has lasted until well into this century, with some differences in decoration. It's a form that has been highly adaptable – to different styles, budgets and sites. Typically, there is a grand balcony across the façade on the second and top floors, and only small balconies on intermediate storeys. Regulations of 1859 controlled the pitch of the roof, and ratio of building height to street width.

In amongst this upheaval, one particular building went up that epitomised Second-Empire style,

Architectural Exotica

Sometimes built for a foreign community, sometimes simply expressing a love of the Orient, domes and minarets glisten above the Parisian skyline. As well as the main **Mosque** (*see chapters* **Paris by Area: The Left Bank**, **Cafés & Bars** *and* **Women's Paris**) and **La Pagode** (*see chapter* **Film**), look out for the following.

Cité Universitaire
boulevard Jourdain, 75014. RER Cité Universitaire.
This campus emerged out of an inter-war ideal of internationalism, and also due to a desire to attract foreign students to Paris. Some sections were built by native architects, such as the **Collège Néerlandais**, in purist geometrical *De Stijl*-style by Dutch architect Willem Dudok. Others were French-designed as exotic pastiches. *See also chapter* **Students**.

Galerie Ching Tsai Loo
48 rue des Courcelles, 75008. Métro Courcelles.
This stunning red edifice with a Chinese roof was built in 1926 *à la chinoise* for a dealer in Oriental art.

2 passage du Caire
75002. Métro Réaumur-Sébastopol.
Part of the Egyptian fad that followed Napoleon's Nile campaign of 1798-99. False hieroglyphics, heads of the Goddess Hathor and a Pharaonic frieze adorn this *passage*.

St-Alexandre Nevsky Cathedral
12 rue Daru, 75008 (42.27.37.34).
Métro Courcelles.
Paris' Russian Orthodox cathedral was designed partly by Kuzmin, architect at the Imperial court, and completed in 1861. Neo-Byzantine in style on a Greek cross plan, it's luxuriantly decorated inside with frescoes and icons.

St Séraphin
rue Lecourbe, 75015. Métro Sèvres-Lecourbe.
A wooden Russian church, with murals in the interior.

Villa de Beauséjour
75016. Métro La Muette.
Three Russian *dachas* built in wood by craftsmen from St Petersburg for the 1867 Exhibition on the Champ des Mars were later dismantled, and reconstructed here.

even though it was not finished until after both Napoleon III and Haussmann had fallen from power: Charles Garnier's **Opéra** of 1862-75. Its sumptuousness and exuberant (and, in their day) controversial statuary perfectly express the ostentation and ambition of mid-century Paris.

The Iron Age

As the nineteenth century progressed, engineering innovations made the use of iron frames in buildings increasingly common. Victor Baltard built market pavilions at Les Halles, now long-demolished, that proudly proclaimed their structure, but more often than not ironwork was hidden behind stone exteriors, giving spacious interiors full of light. Even such apparently massive stone structures as the Galerie d'Evolution of the **Muséum d'Histoire Naturelle** or the **Musée d'Orsay** are only shells around an iron frame.

Henri Labrouste's innovative reading room at the **Bibliothèque Ste-Geneviève**, in place du Panthéon, was one of the first, prefiguring his **Bibliothèque Nationale**. Baltard's **St-Augustin**, on boulevard Malesherbes, is one of the strangest churches in Paris – its structure is entirely in metal, and the stone exterior is only an envelope. The daring, open use of iron was most often seen in buildings erected for Paris' various great exhibitions, such as the most emphatic iron structure of them all, the **Eiffel Tower**.

Art Nouveau & Belle Epoque

Genuine art nouveau architecture in Paris is actually quite rare, although some fine interiors exist, particularly those spruced up as part of the 1900 World Exhibition, such as **Brasserie Julien**. The heavier official Beaux-Arts floral style – directly descended from the work of Garnier – continued at the same time, seen in apartment buildings and bistros or in the Gare d'Orsay. The **Grand Palais** itself has elements of the new style in its sinuous metal stairway, but the heavily-sculptured exterior is firmly within official monumental style.

Art nouveau at its most fluid and flamboyant can be be seen in Guimard's Métro stations, and the wealth of detail, especially the balconies, of his 1901 **Castel Béranger** (14 rue de la Fontaine). The entrance to the luxury apartment block at **29 avenue Rapp** is another example, by Jules Lavirotte. Rue Réamur boasts several art nouveau façades. Weirdest of all is **14 rue d'Abbeville**, with green-glazed ivy climbing up the façade.

At the same time, Henri Savage, architect of La Samaritaine, designed the unusual tiled building at **6 rue Vavin** (1911-12), using for the first time stepped-back terraces. From this he went to a bigger social housing project in rue des Amiraux, which even included a swimming pool.

Frank Gehry's radical **American Center.**

The Modern Movement

Two names stand out after World War I for their technical and aesthetic innovation, and influence – Auguste Perret and Le Corbusier. A third, Robert Mallet-Stevens, stands unrivalled for his elegance. Paris is one of the best cities in the world for examples of Modern Movement architecture, especially in houses and studios, but also in a more diluted form in public buildings and low-cost public housing. At a decorative level, the geometrical influence and love of chrome, steel and glass found its way into art deco cafés and brasseries, especially after the 1925 exhibition of decorative arts.

Perret stayed largely within a classical aesthetic, but his frank use of reinforced concrete gave scope for more varied façades than traditional load-bearing walls. Perhaps most interesting is his **Conseil Economique et Social** at place de Iéna, a circular pavilion with an open horseshoe staircase. Fortunately Paris was spared his 1922 Maisons-Tours scheme, which would have transformed the city into an avenue of skyscrapers.

Le Corbusier first tried out his ideas in early private houses such as the **Villa Jeanneret**. His Pavillon Suisse at the **Cité Universitaire** can be seen as an intermediary point between these villas and the mass housing schemes of his *Villes Radieuses*, which were to be so influential and so debased in projects across Europe after 1945.

The thirties saw a return to neo-classical monumentalism in public buildings: the **Palais de Tokyo** and **Palais de Chaillot** were lofty monumental spaces put up for Paris' 1937 Exhibition.

Post-War Paris

As France revived from the trauma of World War II, the 1950s saw the beginnings of **La Défense**, with the construction of the CNIT centre, and the 1958 **UNESCO** building, by Bernard Zehrfuss, Pier Luigi Nervi and Marcel Breuer. What was most needed at this time, however, were solutions to the problem of the shanty towns around the city, many occupied by immigrants from North Africa. In the sixties, slab-like tower blocks sprouted in the ring of suburbs and new towns that were spreading around Paris. Redevelopment in the city proper was more limited, although changes in building regulations allowed taller buildings, noticeably in Montparnasse and in the 13th and 19th *arrondissements*.

The **Centre Pompidou**, opened in 1977, was in many ways the first of the radical, large-scale building schemes that have become a trademark of modern Paris, introducing international architects into the city, and establishing the pattern of public competitions for big commissions. Buildings in glass and metal imposed within the stone fabric of Paris, tend – as Eiffel's Tower did previously – to create initial scandal, and then become quickly absorbed. The Centre Pompidou and Pei's Pyramid are two obvious examples.

The 1980s and Beyond

The eighties and early nineties have, of course, been dominated by Mitterrand's *Grands Projets*, with which the former President sought to leave his stamp on the city. The **Louvre** Pyramid, **Institut du Monde Arabe** and **Grande Arche de la Défense** each represent monuments of genuine worth, while the **Opéra Bastille,** the new **Bibliothèque Nationale** and the Bercy finance ministry are merely monumental.

Contemporary Paris also boasts interesting private commercial/cultural buildings in a multiplicity of styles, such as **Canal +** (Richard Meier) on rue de Cévennes, the **American Center** (Frank Gehry), or the **Fondation Cartier** (Jean Nouvel). Christian de Portzamparc builds with geometrical blocks – his **Cité de la Musique** looks monolithic from outside, but the inside, around a curving 'internal street', is much lighter and more varied. Paris still invests in public housing, and the roster of names is surprisingly international, with housing projects by de Portzamparc, Aldo Rossi, Renzo Piano, and young French architect Frédéric Borel.

As France comes out of recession and enters a new presidency, the time for *Grands Projets* would appear to have ended, but work continues in several development zones. Most important are those at Bercy and around the **Bibliothèque de France** across the Seine, which, it is proposed, should return the balance of Paris eastwards towards its original centre on the Ile de la Cité.

Modern Movement Houses

Maison Tristan Tzara

15 avenue Junot, 75018. Métro Lamarck-Caulaincourt.
Adolph Loos' declaration that 'ornament is a crime' became a maxim of the Modern Movement. This house in a quiet Montmartre street was designed by him in 1926 for the Dadaist writer Tristan Tzara.

Around Parc Montsouris

around avenue Reille, rue Nansouty, Villa de parc du Montsouris, 75014. RER Cité Universitaire.
To the west of parc Montsouris are several streets of small houses, many built earlier this century for artists. Villa Ozenfant, at 53 avenue Reille, is Le Corbusier's earliest building in Paris, designed in 1922 for the painter Amédée Ozenfant. Villa Guggenbuhl, at 14 rue Nansouty, with its rectangular bow window and roof terrace overlooking the park, was designed in 1926-27 by André Lurçat, who also designed Nos 3 and 4 in the nearby villa Seurat, while Auguste Perret designed 7 bis villa Seurat for sculptor Chana Orloff, and a studio at 14 rue Georges Braques for Georges Braque.

rue Mallet-Stevens

75016. Métro Jasmin.
Near to Villa La Roche is this road of six houses designed by Robert Mallet-Stevens in 1926-27. His houses were mainly designed for a restricted circle of artist and writer friends. Now slightly overgrown, the ensemble is still impressive for its severe geometry, lightened by stained glass in the stairwells and clever layering of the different storeys and terraces.

Villas La Roche & Jeanneret

8-10 square du Doctor Blanche, 75016 (42.88.41.53). Métro Jasmin. **Open** 10am-12.30pm, 1.30-6pm, Mon-Thur; until 5pm Fri. **Admission** 15F.
Of these neighbouring houses designed by Le Corbusier, Villa Jeanneret is now the library of the **Fondation Le Corbusier**, but Villa La Roche is open to the public. Built in 1923 for a Swiss banker, it has many key Corbusian features such as the *pilottis* (stilts), roof terraces and built-in furniture; the interior spaces have varied heights and openings.

Villa Savoy

82 rue Villiers, 78300 Poissy (39.65.01.06). RER line A to Poissy, then 15 min walk. **Open** *May-Oct* 10am-noon, 1.30-5.30pm, Mon-Wed; *Nov-Apr* 10am-4.30pm Mon-Wed. **Admission** free.
This house, built in 1929 for a family of rich industrialists, is perhaps Le Corbusier's most successful work, noted for its sculptural spiral staircase. It still has much of its original built-in furniture and fittings.

Paris by Area

Introduction

Look at a map and Paris, within its unchanging boundaries, seems deceptively uniform: its shape is a more or less regular oval, its boulevards form concentric rings spanning out evenly from the centre and the Seine runs through the middle in an elegant curve. Since the last century, the city has been divided into 20 *arrondissements* or districts which form a tight snail-shell spiral beginning at Notre Dame and finishing at the Porte de Montreuil, on the eastern edge of the official city limits.

Throughout Paris' history, city planners have deliberately created this sense of order and uniformity – usually in order to weed out political dissent and make the streets easier to police. But down the centuries Parisians have proved too resilient to submit entirely to such schemes, and beneath the surface their city is surprisingly diverse in style, structure and atmosphere.

Traditionally Paris is divided into two, like two halves of a brain: the practical, materialistic Right Bank, with its department stores, wholesale markets, designer shops and bustling avenues; and the intellectual, more refined Left Bank, site of university buildings, bookshops, cinemas and narrow streets stuffed with student garrets. In reality the divisions are more complex, with the grand and the intimate, the old and the new, the sacred and the profane mingling on both sides of the river.

Working out from the islands, the ancient centre of the city and now a major tourist magnet, this section explores the different themes of the city through its different districts, from the shabby streets of La Goutte d'Or to the stiff-collared bourgeois elegance of the 16th *arrondissement*. This is a city that is changing fast: the Latin Quarter and St-Germain have lost most of their students and become delightful but definitely upmarket strolling grounds, while the once down-at-heel streets north of the Palais-Royal have been spruced up to reveal a rabbit-warren of picturesque back alleys intertwined with grandiose glass-roofed arcades. Away from the centre, this famously compact city reveals individual townhouses, small but pretty parks and fine examples of avant-garde architecture.

The departure of Mitterrand from the French Presidency may well represent the end of a distinctive era for Paris – the years of his monumental *grands projets* – but work has still continued on one of his most grandiose and most criticised legacies to the city, the giant new Bibliothèque Nationale de France. It has taken shape alongside the river in the 13th *arrondissement,* a location chosen, in yet another attempt at social engineering, as part of an intended move to breathe new life into what has long been one of the most neglected corners of the city.

The Islands

The two islands in the Seine, the core of Paris, offer a fascinating contrast in atmospheres.

These islands may nestle alongside each other in the very centre of the city, but they have very divergent histories and, as a result, quite distinctive and separate characters.

Ile de la Cité

The more westerly and larger of the two islands, the Ile de la Cité, was the site of the original settlement that grew into Paris. It was first inhabited in around 250 BC by the Parisii, and when it was conquered by the Romans two hundred years later it also became the centre of their city. Today, it is most visited for two major attractions, the Sainte Chapelle and Notre Dame cathedral.

When Victor Hugo wrote *Notre Dame de Paris* in 1831, the Ile de la Cité as he described it was a bustling medieval quarter of narrow streets and hundreds of tall wooden houses: 'the head, heart and very marrow of Paris'. Baron Haussmann quickly put paid to that. During the Second Empire he supervised the expulsion of 25,000 people from the island, razing their homes, flattening churches and obliterating most of the streets. Rarely has a city centre been swept away with such ferocity. The lines of the old streets in front of Notre Dame are traced into the new *parvis*.

The people of the *Ile* were forced to resettle in slums in the east of the city, leaving behind a lot of empty space and a few large buildings — the Conciergerie, the law courts, the Hôtel Dieu, the police headquarters and, of course, Notre Dame. The island now also plays host to hordes of tour coaches during the day, but otherwise it can often seem rather sad and soulless.

The most charming spot is the western tip, where the **Pont Neuf** spans the Seine above a leafy triangular garden known as the square du Vert-Galant. With a wonderful view of the river, it can be recommended for picnics on summer evenings. In the centre of the bridge is a statue of Henry IV on his horse, first erected in 1635, destroyed in the Revolution, and then replaced in 1818 with a replica made with bronze from an out-of-favour statue of Napoleon in **place Vendôme**. On the island-side of the Pont Neuf is the strangely secluded, slightly desolate **place Dauphine**, once a haunt for lovers. It was one of the first squares commissioned by Henry IV, who named it in honour of his son, the Dauphin and future King Louis

XIII, although few of its buildings today look as they did in 1607 (no. 14 is one that does).

Moving along the *quais* towards the centre of the island, the view is dominated by the severe expanse of the **Palais de Justice** and, lining the Seine on the island's north bank, the florid medieval towers of the **Conciergerie**, where generations of prisoners were tortured and incarcerated before being executed. Among those who contemplated the next world from here were Danton, Robespierre and Marie-Antoinette.

This giant complex of buildings began life as a palace for the Roman governor in the fourth century AD, and the kings of France took up residence on the site 600 years later. It only became a prison in 1358 after Etienne Marcel's uprising caused Charles V (the Wise) to move the royal retinue into the Louvre (*see chapter* **History: Middle Ages & Renaissance**). Much of the façade is a nineteenth-century pseudo-medieval reconstruction but the original fourteenth-century clock tower, the Tour de l'Horloge, remains.

Nearby, surrounded by the Palais de Justice, is the **Sainte-Chapelle**, Pierre de Montreuil's masterpiece of stained glass and slender Gothic columns, built in the middle of the thirteenth century as a royal chapel to house the holy relics of sometimes dubious origin that were acquired at huge expense and brought back from the Crusades by France's sainted king Louis IX. The relics have since been moved to Notre Dame, but the two-tiered structure is awash with colour and light. The windows in the upper chapel, some of the finest original medieval stained glass in existence, recount stories from the Bible. Now the centre of the French legal system, the Palais de Justice slowly evolved alongside the Conciergerie, enclosing the Sainte-Chapelle and even, during some particularly thoughtless reconstruction after a fire in 1776, entirely blocking off the chapel's north side.

Across the boulevard du Palais, place Louis Lépine (another of Haussmann's empty spaces) is now filled by the city's best flower market (*see chapter* **Specialist Shops**). To the south is the impersonal façade of the Préfecture de Police, often known simply by its address, quai des Orfèvres, as immortalised in Simenon's Maigret detective novels. Straight ahead to the east is the Hôtel Dieu, site of the oldest hospital in Paris, founded in the seventh century, although the present building dates only from 1866-78. During the Middle Ages it had a reputation as the hospital from hell: if you were admitted, your chances of survival were slim. Today it is still the main hospital for central Paris, but a considerably quieter and safer place.

The eastern end of the island is dominated by the looming towers and flying buttresses of **Notre Dame**. Don't let the crowds put you off. Although heavily restored, the façade, with its three portals, remains a masterpiece of Gothic design. First begun in 1163, the cathedral was used for a string of coronations and other solemn occasions from before its completion in the 1340s, and new sections were added and alterations were made in every century since then. It was badly damaged by Revolutionaries in 1793, before being returned to its ceremonial role for the coronation of Napoleon as Emperor in 1804. Later, it was only saved from demolition by an active campaign led by Victor Hugo, and beginning in the 1840s extensive restoration was carried out by the neo-Gothic architect Eugène Viollet-le-Duc, who was responsible for much of the present-day interior. Don't miss the ascent to the roof (from the corner of rue du Cloître-Notre-Dame) to admire the wonderfully ghoulish gargoyles and fine view.

Back on *terra firma*, look for the bronze marker in front of the cathedral, showing the spot that is considered the centre of the city. This is the belly button of France, the point from which all distances are officially measured. Make sure you walk round the back of the building, too, for the best views of its structure. In the night-time floodlights, above all, the deep shadows and glowing pinnacles of its apparently wildly intertwining buttresses can make it look less like a real building than a creation of Piranesi or Universal Studios' set department.

On the very eastern tip of the island, through a pretty garden, the square de l'Ile de France, is the **Mémorial de la Déportation**, a moving memorial to the thousands, virtually all Jews, deported from France to death camps during World War II. Visitors descend a blind, prison-like staircase to river level, where there are simple, shaded chambers inscribed with the names of the deportees. One barred window looks out onto the Seine.

To the north-east of the cathedral are a few medieval streets untouched by Haussmann, such as rue Chanoinesse – built to house canons of Notre Dame – and rue des Ursins. Canon Fulbert, uncle of Héloïse and the man responsible for castrating her lover Abelard, lived at 9 quai aux Fleurs.

Ile St-Louis

Today, the Ile St-Louis is one of the most exclusive residential addresses in the city. Delightfully unspoiled, it has a mix of fine architecture, narrow streets and magnificent views from the tree-lined *quais* across the Seine.

For hundreds of years, however, the island was entirely unbuilt-up, a swampy pasture and retreat for fishermen, boaters, swimmers and lovers that was known only as the *Ile aux Vaches* ('Island of Cows'). In the fourteenth century Charles V briefly disturbed its tranquility by building a fortified canal through the middle. But its real-estate potential wasn't realised until the seventeenth century, when a speculator named Christophe Marie (after whom the Pont Marie is named) persuaded Louis XIII to let him fill in the canal and make plans for streets, bridges and fine houses. The island was renamed in honour of the King's pious predecessor, and eventually the venture proved a huge success, although Marie himself had gone bankrupt in the process. It became highly fashionable as a site for new residences from the 1630s onwards, in great part thanks to the interest shown by society architect Louis Le Vau, and by the 1660s the entire island had been filled up.

Nowadays the Ile St-Louis is like a set from a *grand siècle* period drama, without a métro or many modern shops. Instead there are quay-sides lined with plane trees and poplars, fine houses with wrought iron balconies and carved stone doorways, and, when you get hungry, some lively bars and restaurants and an important Parisian institution, **Berthillon**, by general agreement purveyor of the best ice cream in town (*see chapter* **Food & Drink**). The little baroque church of **St-Louis-en-l'Ile**, at 19 bis rue St-Louis en l'Ile, is a popular venue for classical concerts.

Among the finest buildings on the island are the Hôtel Chenizot, a few doors down from Berthillon at 51 rue St-Louis-en-l'Ile, with its doorway adorned by a bearded faun and a balcony decorated with grim-faced monsters; the Hôtel Lambert at No. 2, built by Le Vau in 1641 for Louis XIII's secretary, with its stone lions and palm trees; and the **Hôtel de Lauzun**, at 17 quai d'Anjou.

The Lauzun has an outstanding, largely original seventeenth-century interior, with superb painted ceilings and woodwork, and a fascinating history. Built by Le Vau in 1656, it once housed a salon frequented by Racine, Molière and La Fontaine. Later, in the 1840s, it was owned by a literary aficionado called Jérôme Pichon, who rented out rooms to artists and writers. Baudelaire first saw his lover and 'Black Venus' Jeanne Duval from the window of his room on the third floor, and wrote much of *Les Fleurs du Mal* here. Other Bohemians who passed through included Théophile Gautier, the *Club des Haschischins* ('Hashish-eaters') and Richard Wagner. The *hôtel* is open to the public at weekends for part of the year (Easter to November, 10am-5.30pm Sat, Sun).

Paris' beach, the quais *of the Seine.*

The Right Bank

From the grand palaces of royal Paris and the chic luxury of St-Honoré, to the quiet corners of the Marais and the hip nightlife of the Bastille.

Royal & Imperial Paris

The Louvre & the Tuileries

Finding a reliable residence in Paris was a hazardous business for France's kings and emperors. Ever fearful of street riots, they first moved off the Ile de la Cité into the area around the Tuileries in the fourteenth century, then hopped between the Louvre, the place des Vosges in the Marais, and the now destroyed Tuileries Palace for the next 500 years. Louis XIV preferred to stay outside the city altogether at Versailles. Nowadays the corner of Paris once given over to the royal and Napoleonic courts, covering much of the 1st *arrondissement*, is an elegant mixture of fine arcades and smart shops, graceful squares and gardens, interspersed with such imperial monsters as the Madeleine and the Opéra Garnier.

*Grandeur itself, the **place de la Concorde**.*

Although the main attraction of the **Louvre** is its works of art, it remains the Parisian palace *par excellence*, with its fine courtyards and long galleries stretching away towards the **Jardin des Tuileries**. One major consequence of all the renovation work undertaken in recent years has been that part of Philip Augustus' original twelfth-century fortress, which Charles V made into a royal residence in the mid-fourteenth century, can now be seen within the walls of the surrounding Renaissance palace. During the sixteenth century, succeeding monarchs built up a more luxurious residence to replace the old fortress, completing the Cour Carrée at the eastern end, perhaps the best example of Renaissance architecture in Paris, and the gallery along the Seine leading to the Tuileries Palace to the west. The northern wing, along the rue de Rivoli and the Cour Napoléon, was built by Napoleon and Napoleon III.

All around the Louvre are reminders of royal Paris. On place du Louvre, opposite the eastern façade of the palace, is the church of **St-Germain-L'Auxerrois**, once the parish church of the kings of France. It has the only original Flamboyant-style Gothic porch in Paris, built in 1435.

The Louvre was first opened to the public as a museum by the Revolutionary Convention in 1793, although the last vestige of state administration, the Finance Ministry, only moved out in 1989. It has of course been one of the great sights of Paris for centuries, but most recently the museum and its immediate surrounds have been substantially transformed yet again by becoming one of President Mitterrand's *grands projets*, in the *Grand Louvre* scheme. Its most notorious feature is the 1989 pyramid by IM Pei that now dominates the Cour Napoléon, the most provocative and possibly most successful of all the former President's architectural gifts to the city of Paris. Making no attempt to blend in with the surrounding buildings, the steel and glass structure is fascinating both for its technical brilliance and the tricks it plays with the light and water of the surrounding fountains. If you're not convinced by day, come back at night when, floodlit, it has a mesmerising, ethereal glow.

The pyramid leads to the subterranean entrances to the refurbished Louvre, and also interconnects with another radical feature of the *Grand Louvre* plan, the gleaming underground shopping mall and

First avenue for Parisian shoppers, the **boulevard Haussmann**.

exhibition centre called the **Carrousel du Louvre** (*see chapter* **Specialist Shops**). Built with a daring (and perhaps arrogance) that epitomises the spirit of the *grands projets*, it has been a great success in attracting Parisians (and not just tourists) back to this area.

Above it, back on street level, the Tuileries Palace is long gone, burned down during the Paris Commune of 1871. Still there though is the **Arc du Carrousel**, a mini-Arc de Triomphe built by Napoleon that was once the palace entrance. The Emperor placed on top of it the famous Roman bronze horses that he had made off with from Saint Mark's in Venice, but France was obliged to return them in 1815, and they were replaced with more modern replicas in 1828. Through the arch one can appreciate, almost for the first time, the extraordinary perspective all along the Champs-Elysées up to the real **Arc de Triomphe** and the **Grande Arche de la Défense**. To the west of the Arc du Carrousel, the Tuileries gardens are in the process of being entirely replanted to breathe new life into Le Nôtre's baroque gardens, grown sickly from traffic fumes and too many tourists.

Along the north side of the Louvre, the rue de Rivoli, built by Napoleon for military parades, is remarkable for its arched arcades hiding elegant shops and luxury hotels. It runs in a perfect straight line all the way to the Marais in one direction and to the place de la Concorde in the other.

Across the rue de Rivoli from the Louvre, past the giant antiques superstore the **Louvre des Antiquaires**, stands the **Palais-Royal**, origi-

nally Cardinal Richelieu's private mansion, and then used by offshoots of the royal family as a secondary residence. Now housing two major government departments, the Ministry of Culture and the Conseil d'Etat, it is cherished for its tranquil gardens flanked by eighteenth-century arcades. Within the main courtyard are Daniel Buren's black-and-white-striped column stumps, commissioned in 1986 by then culture minister Jack Lang to complement the view from his office window, and which provide some amusing places to sit.

A double colonnade leads through to the palace garden, one of the most delightful spots in central Paris. In the 1780s this was also one of the most rumbustious centres of Parisian life. The Duc d'Orléans, the future *Philippe-Egalité* of the Revolution, inherited the Palais-Royal in 1776 and turned it into a remarkable entrepreneurial venture, enclosing the gardens with arcaded buildings that were let out to house theatres, coffee houses, shops and any other kind of amusement. Described by witnesses as 'an enchanted place', it became an extraordinary, bawdy combination of early shopping mall, intellectual meeting point and pleasure palace, a place where you could find high theatre, popular farces, lace-makers and art exhibitions, alongside crowds of prostitutes and bizarre freak shows. Aristocrats and the grubby inhabitants of the *faubourgs* rubbed shoulders here in subversive abandon, and, as the private property of a Duke, it was also mostly off-limits to Louis XVI's police. The coffee houses in its arcades thus became major centres for political discussion, much frequented by future revolutionaries such as Danton, and it was here that Camille Desmoulins called the city to arms on the eve of Bastille Day.

Of the great era of the Palais-Royal only the **Grand Véfour** survives, as one of Paris' best restaurants (*see chapter* **Restaurants**). After the Napoleonic Wars, the Duke of Wellington and Field Marshal von Blücher supposedly lost so much money at the Palais's gambling dens that Parisians claimed they had won back their entire dues for war reparations. You can go through the arcades to rue de Montpensier to the west, and then explore some of the narrow, stepped passages between this street and rue de Richelieu.

On place André Malraux, on the southwest corner of the Palais Royal, is the attractive theatre housing France's oldest national theatre company, the **Comédie Française** (*see chapter* **Theatre**). The company was created in 1680 by Louis XIV, and given sole right to perform in the capital. Its repertoire still largely consists of French classics.

To the west, have a look at place des Pyramides, at the junction of the rue de Rivoli and rue des Pyramides. The shiny golden equestrian statue of Joan of Arc is one of four statues of her in the city – designed, along with Rodin's *Burghers of Calais*, to make Brits feel guilty. Just to the north on rue St-Honoré, you come to the baroque church of **St-Roch** (at No. 292), begun for Louis XIV in 1653. Unusually large, it contains many works of French religious art, but is most noticed for the bullet holes in its façade left by Napoleon's troops when they put down a royalist revolt here in 1795. The writers Corneille and Diderot, and André Le Nôtre, genius of garden design, are all buried inside. Two streets further west is the rue du Marché St-Honoré, where the lively Rubis wine bar hosts the annual scrum to taste *Beaujolais Nouveau* every November (*see chapters* **Paris by Season** *and* **Cafés & Bars**).

Place Vendôme & Place de la Concorde

A little further along the rue st-Honoré one sees to the right the eight-sided **place Vendôme**, one of the most beautiful squares in Paris and one of Louis XIV's major contributions to the city. Thanks to recent refurbishment cars now park underground, so you can once again appreciate the square's formal geometry. It is dominated by a bronze-covered column modelled on Trajan's Column in Rome, and similarly illustrated with a spiral comic-strip of military exploits. On the top is a statue of Napoleon as Caesar. The *Communards* toppled the whole column in 1871, but conservatives rushed to put it back up three years later, with a replica of the original statue.

A place Vendôme address has, perhaps, the highest snob-value in the city; the swish town houses have attracted bankers and jewellers since they were built. Cartier, Boucheron, Van Cleef & Arpels and other smart names now enjoy the company of the Ritz hotel at No. 15, the place Hemingway claimed to have personally 'liberated' in 1944 (in fact, he merely ordered a drink there after the fighting was over).

This is definitely high-class Paris. Fashion boutiques, china and silverware shops and luxury hotels fill the area. Few come grander than the Crillon, overlooking the place de la Concorde and next to the vast American Embassy, and a favourite stopping-off point for diplomats and visiting foreign ministers.

Place de la Concorde, built by Jacques-Ange Gabriel for Louis XV, is a brilliant exercise in the use of open space, with three sides open for views over the river, across the Tuileries and along the Champs-Elysées. Foreigners might quibble at André Malraux's description of it as 'the most beautiful architectural complex on this planet', but it's impossible not to recognise the grandeur of this most imposing of Paris squares, above all at sunset or at night. It was originally the *place Louis XV*, before becoming *place de la Révolution* and site for the guillotine. The name *Concorde* was introduced after the terror had ended in a suitable spirit of national reconciliation.

The obelisk in the centre comes from Luxor and, like Cleopatra's Needle in London, was a present from the Viceroy of Egypt in the 1830s. The monument has a golden inscription to the engineer who figured out how to lift it into its present position.

On the flanks of the Tuileries stand the **Orangerie**, now a small gallery of Impressionist and post-Impressionist art, and the **Jeu de Paume**, originally built for the game of real tennis. Home to Paris' main impressionist collection before the opening of the Musée d'Orsay, it's now used for temporary shows of contemporary art.

Opéra & Madeleine

Not far from place Vendôme is the wedding cake of Charles Garnier's **Opéra**, constructed between 1862 and 1875. One of Napoleon III's architectural extravaganzas, it perfectly illustrates the excesses of its reactionary patron and evokes the mood of opera at its very grandest. Outside it's covered in sculptures depicting dance and music, right up to its copper dome topped by a gaudy Apollo.

Garnier's interior is a treasure trove of frescoes, sculptures, grand stairways, marble, gold leaf and precious stones. It's not hard to see why the legend of the Phantom of the Opera started here. Since the opening of the Opéra Bastille in 1989 the old theatre has been used for ballet, but when the auditorium reopens after renovation in March 1996 the Garnier will again host occasional operatic productions. When it is reopened audiences and visitors on guided tours will again be able to admire

The streets around Beaubourg are a favourite with pavement squatters.

Chagall's 1964 ceiling frescoes, inspired by the artist's favourite operas and ballets.

The Café de la Paix (*see chapter* **Cafés & Bars**) overlooking place de l'Opéra was also designed by Garnier. Although expensive and full of tourists, its elegant interior still gives a sense of stepping back into the nineteenth century. Heading west down the boulevard des Capucines, you'll pass the venue for the Lumière brothers' first cinema show in 1895 (at No. 14). Opposite is the **Olympia** concert hall, legendary venue for performances by Edith Piaf and every other great French singer of the last hundred years (*see chapter* **Music: Rock, Roots & Jazz**). It's been declared a national monument, but nevertheless proposals have been made to knock it down and rebuild it in another location.

The classical temple at the end of the boulevard is the **Madeleine**, an only vaguely religious monument to the greater glory of Napoleon. Its regular exterior mirrors the Corinthian pillars of the National Assembly across the Seine, while the interior is cluttered with nineteenth-century kitsch. More rewarding are the gaudy shop windows of Fauchon, Paris' most extravagant delicatessen, and the other luxury foodstores that dominate the square (*see chapter* **Food & Drink**).

The *grands magasins*, or big department stores, are not far away, lined up along boulevard Haussmann. Just behind the Opéra are the nineteenth-century cupolas of Au Printemps and Galeries Lafayette, with vast floors of fashion and perfumes. There is also a large Monoprix, devoted to food, and even a branch of Marks & Spencer.

Beaubourg & the Marais

Beaubourg

Contemporary Parisian architecture started with the **Centre Pompidou**, designed by the Italo-British team of Renzo Piano and Richard Rogers. It has been the most visited site in the city since it opened in 1977, although the revamped Louvre may now be challenging its position. The building could now do with a little care and attention, and major refurbishment is due to begin in 1997. Before the building of the Centre, the site, known by its medieval name Beaubourg, was a pitiful empty space surrounded by dilapidated tenements. Now it teems with tourists, fire-eaters and buskers, not to mention trendy cafés, restaurants and cinemas.

The building itself, an international benchmark of high tech, was always intended to be as much of an attraction as its contents. The predominant use of glass gives the building its transparency, allowing visitors riding up the escalator on the western side to peer into the building on one side and take in the growing view of the city on the other. Inside, a giant public library, an arthouse cinema and the many art and exhibition spaces of different sizes all work to maintain the impression of a kaleidoscopic modern cultural emporium.

Outside you'll see a strange digital clock. Known as the Millennium clock, it is counting down the number of seconds to the end of the century in anticipation of a giant millennium party on New Year's Eve in 1999.

Around the corner is the playful **place Igor Stravinsky**, with its great fountain by Niki de Saint Phalle and Jean Tinguely that's full of multi-coloured gadgets that move and squirt water. On the south side of the square, a favourite for *al fresco* eating in the summertime, is the more sober church of **St-Merri**, with a Flamboyant-Gothic façade complete with androgynous demon leering over the doorway. Inside there is some fine vaulting, as well as the original carved wooden organ area, the oldest bell in Paris, made in 1331, and some sixteenth-century stained glass.

The area south of Beaubourg is a maze of narrow pedestrianised streets stuffed with (largely mediocre) restaurants. On the river side of the rue de Rivoli looms the neo-Gothic **Hôtel de Ville**, Paris' city hall, in which the Mayor's own vast apartment occupies an entire floor. It overlooks an enormous square of the same name, once known as the place de Grève, giving rise to the French word for strike (*grève*) because disgruntled workers used to gather here. It was also long used for executions. Many protestant heretics were burnt in the *place* during the sixteenth-century Wars of Religion, and this was there the guillotine first stood during the Revolutionary terror. From 1793, every revolutionary regime in Paris looked to the Hôtel as their seat of government.

Three-quarters of the present expanse is the result of a demolition scheme by Haussmann in the nineteenth century. The building itself was gutted by fire in the 1871 Commune, and rebuilt and considerably enlarged thereafter.

The Marais

East of the Hôtel de Ville is the Marais, a truly magical area whose narrow streets are dotted with seventeenth-century aristocratic residences (*hôtels particuliers*), art galleries, fashion boutiques and smart cafés. The big city slows down here to a gentle strolling pace, giving you time to notice the beautifully carved doorways and turrets and the early street signs carved into the stone buildings.

The Marais hasn't always been fashionable. It started life, as the name implies (*marais* means marsh), as an uninhabited piece of swampy ground near a now-submerged tributary of the Seine. Its rise as an aristocratic residential area came in the seventeenth century, but its prestige faded a century later. The current renaissance dates from 1962, when Culture Minister André Malraux slapped a preservation order on its dilapidated mansions, safeguarding many endangered buildings for use as museums. Nowadays the city's yuppies have taken over too, gradually pushing the area into the luxury bracket.

Among its idiosyncracies are a thriving gay scene, particularly at night when the bars and clubs come into their own, and Paris'oldest Jewish community, centred on the rue des Rosiers. Originally mainly made up of eastern European Jews who arrived in the last century, the community expanded greatly in the fifties and sixties with a new wave of Sephardic Jewish immigration following French withdrawal from North Africa. Consequently there are now many felafel shops

*A timeless symbol of the Marais and grand siècle Paris: the **place des Vosges**.*

alongside the kosher delicatessens, as well as several, fast-encroaching, designer clothes stores.

At the heart of the Marais is the **place des Vosges**, a magnificently symmetrical Italian-inspired square of red-brick palaces and graceful arcades. Henry IV's decision in 1605 to build the *place Royale* sparked off the building boom in the surrounding area, as aristocrats and notables hurried to commission their own grand residences in the surrounding streets. The modern name dates from the Revolutionary Wars – the Vosges was the first region of France to pay its war taxes. Nowadays it's a perfect place to linger among the linden trees that surround the central statue (of Henry's successor Louis XIII), or in the arcades, displaying antique furniture, modern art and fashion clothes. Chamber orchestras or *a cappella* choirs often perform on summer evenings. At one corner, in a house once occupied by the author, is the **Musée Victor Hugo** (*see chapter* **Museums**).

An archway leads from the south-western corner of the square to the **Hôtel de Sully**, built by one of Henri IV's ministers and one of the most elegant of all the Marais mansions. From its sunny ivy-rimmed garden you can walk through into the main courtyard, adorned with stone carvings representing the elements and the seasons, and then out onto the rue St-Antoine.

There are further fine relics of medieval and *ancien régime* Paris all around the Marais. The 1705-09 **Hôtel de Soubise** on the corner of rue des Archives and rue des Francs-Bourgeois, now home to the national archives, is a grand rococo mansion with beautiful gardens. Some of the interiors, decorated by artists like Boucher and Lemoine, are open to the public as part of the **Musée de l'Histoire de France**. The adjoining **Hôtel de Rohan** (occasionally used for temporary exhibitions) has a fine sculpture by Robert Le Lorrain, *The Horses of Apollo*, in the first courtyard on the right.

Nearby is the **Hôtel Guénégaud**, at 60 rue des Archives, built in 1654 as a residence of Louis XIV's Secretary of State by François Mansart, and now housing the **Musée de la Chasse et de la Nature**. Also easily accessible is the **Hôtel de Sens** on rue du Figuier, near the riverbank. One of the oldest private residences in Paris, built in 1475 for the Archbishops of Sens, it's a fanciful ensemble of turrets decorated with stone wolves and monsters. During the Wars of Religion of the sixteenth century the Guise brothers hatched many an anti-royalist plot within its walls. Today it leads a much quieter life as the home of the **Bibliothèque Forney**, and is also used for temporary exhibitions (*see chapter* **Museums**).

The district's two most important museums also occupy former *hôtels*. The **Musée Carnavalet** on rue de Sévigné, dedicated to the history of Paris, runs across two, the 1548 **Hôtel Carnavalet**, remodelled in 1660 by Mansart, and the later **Hôtel le Peletier**. Curiosities among the comprehensive collection include faithful reproductions of Marcel Proust's bedroom and the original Fouquet jewellery shop.

The **Hôtel Salé** on rue de Thorigny, built in 1656 for a collector of the salt tax (hence the name), has since 1985 housed the **Musée Nationale Picasso**. The mansion, which had been considerably damaged and altered, has been finely restored with a sensitive modern extension. The original elaborate staircase remains, as do two fine sphinxes in the entrance courtyard.

Every September Paris holds a weekend of *Journées Portes Ouvertes*, when usually closed-off private houses and government buildings fling open their doors to the public (*see chapter* **Paris by Season**). If you are lucky enough to be in Paris then, the Marais should be your first stop. Among the normally out-of-bounds addresses to aim for are the **Hôtel des Ambassadeurs de Hollande**, at 47 rue Vieille-du-Temple. Two huge oak doors are decorated with Medusas and medallion designs. Inside are two big sundials and stone figures of Romulus and Remus. Beaumarchais wrote *The Marriage of Figaro* here, in 1778.

Even the fire station at 7 rue de Sévigné was originally designed by François Mansard for one of Louis XIII's ministers. Also called the **Hôtel Bouthilier de Chavigny**, it hides an elegant façade around its inner courtyard. If you want to see some of these more private or official buildings during the rest of the year, your best bet is probably to join a walking tour of the district (*see chapter* **Sightseeing**).

There is much, much more besides, which is best discovered by strolling through the maze of streets. Head for the rue des Barres, a cobbled ramp leading up from the Seine behind the church of **St-Gervais-St-Protais**, itself a fine example of late French Gothic behind a classical façade added in 1616. Couperin composed several works for the organ here. Equally worth seeking out is the garden of the **Hôtel de Lamoignon**, opposite the Musée Carnavalet on the rue des Francs-Bourgeois. Built in 1585 for Diane de France, illegitimate daughter of King Henry II, this austere monumental building is now home to the **Bibliothèque Historique de la Ville de Paris** (*see chapter* **Students**).

You might also want to pay a visit to the Village St-Paul, a colony of antiques and junk sellers spread across a series of small courtyards off the rue St-Paul. On the parallel rue des Jardins-St-Paul is the largest surviving section of the **wall of Philip-Augustus**, built by the king around Paris in the twelfth century. The domed Jesuit church of **St-Paul-St-Louis** nearby on rue St-Antoine, while visible from far off in most directions, is actually a disappointing imitation of the Gesù

The *Galeries*

A little of the ambience of the Romantic era still lingers in the glass-roofed *galeries* that thread their way between Paris' boulevards. When first built these picturesque arcades were crowded with restaurants and shops, where strollers could inspect the latest novelties safe from rain, mud, and horses. Astute pedestrians can still make their way via *galeries* entirely undercover all the way from the *Grands Boulevards* to the Palais-Royal. Over 100 galeries existed in 1840; fewer than 20 remain today, but several have now been renovated and once again house fashionable shops.

Covered *galeries* and *passages* are found mainly in the 1st, 2nd and 9th *arrondissements*. As well as those listed below, also worth exploring are the **passage Verdeau**, with its superb iron-and-glass roof, and the **passage Jouffroy**, a warren of lovely, old-fashioned shops, both just north of the rue Montmartre next to the **Musée Grevin**, in the 9th; and the **passage des Princes**, nearby in the 2nd, between boulevard des Italiens and rue Richelieu.

Galerie Véro-Dodat

Between rue Croix-des-Petits-Champs and rue Jean-Jacques Rousseau, 75001. Métro Palais-Royal.
A pair of prosperous *charcutiers* – M. Véro and M. Dodat

– built this arcade during the Restoration, equipping it with gaslights and more than recouping their investment by charging their tenants astronomical rents. The *galerie*'s decoration of columns, capitals and arcades and its curious old shops are all equally worth a tour.

Galerie Vivienne

Between rue Vivienne and rue des Petits-Champs, 75002. Métro Bourse.
The prettiest and most fashionable of the *galeries*, alongside the Bibliothèque Nationale. Bright and spacious, it's decorated in neo-classical style with bas-reliefs and a beautifully crafted mosaic pavement. Jean-Paul Gaultier's innovative couture, the highly coveted fabrics of Wolff et Descourtis and a pretty tea-room, A Priori Thé, make it the ideal place for an afternoon browse (*see also chapters* **Cafés & Bars** *and* **Specialist Shops**).

Passage des Panoramas

Between rue St-Marc and boulevard Montmartre, 75002. Métro Rue Montmartre.
The evocative name is taken from the 'panoramas' – giant circular illuminated paintings of Rome, Jerusalem, London, Athens and other celebrated capitals – that were created by Robert Fulton, the American inventor, and landscape painter Pierre Prévost and exhibited here when the *passage* was first built in 1800, drawing large crowds. It's one of the oldest of the *galeries*, but enticing new shops and restaurants intermixed with its many unusual old traditional businesses have recently given the place a new lease of life. For a glimpse of how things used to look, take in the superb premises of Stern (No. 47), a smart engraving firm founded in 1830.

church in Rome, on which it was closely modelled when it was built in 1627. Inside it there is a major religious painting by Delacroix, *Christ in the Garden of Olives*.

The lower ends of the rue des Archives and rue Vieille-du-Temple are the places to go for café life and, after dark, for happening bars and good restaurants. This is also the area that's the hub of the Paris gay scene. Which venues are mainly gay-oriented is usually fairly obvious, whether you want to find them or avoid them.

The northern half of the Marais, in the 3rd *arrondissement* stretching up towards place de la République, quickly becomes more bustling and residential, and is only now becoming gentrified. There's an attractive street market on rue de Bretagne, and countless bookstores along the rue de Turenne, while behind secretive courtyard entrances along rues de Turenne, Vieille-du-Temple and Debelleyme you can find many of Paris' most avant-garde art galleries (*see chapter* **Art Galleries**).

It's even possible to humanise **Les Halles***.*

Les Halles to the *Passages*

This area is about as close as Paris gets to a backwater, not including the crowded, hamburger-filled malls of the Forum des Halles itself. For years the district was neglected, full of crumbling houses, run-down shopfronts and the downmarket strip-joints along the rue St-Denis. In recent years, however, the north-western section of the area, running up towards the *Grands Boulevards*, has undergone a revival, as the city has restored and re-opened its *passages*, elaborately designed shopping arcades that in the 1820s provided the prototype for the modern department store. Back to the east, near Les Halles proper and around the rue St-Denis, the prostitutes and neon peep-show signs have also been partly pushed back, by an energetic pedestrianisation scheme.

At the same time this remains Paris as the Parisians experience it, not some confection dressed up to impress the tourists. There are few museums, or conventional cultural attractions. Sit in a bar with the Sentier cloth wholesalers and the traders from the rue Montorgueil market, though, and you'll get a real taste of the old Paris of tight-knit neighbourhoods.

Les Halles

Few places epitomise the transformation of the entire area more than Les Halles, once the wholesale fruit and vegetable market for the city and now a miserably designed semi-sunken shopping mall. This was what Zola called the 'belly of Paris', the nerve centre of life in the capital, a giant covered market graced with Baltard's green iron pavilions. In 1969 the whole lot was moved out to a new wholesale market in the southern suburbs, leaving a giant hole that was only filled in the early eighties, after numerous political and architectural disputes about what should take its place.

The result is a compromise that has pleased nobody. The **Forum des Halles** was intended to become the new commercial heart of Paris, but this giant multi-level complex has failed absolutely to establish itself anywhere on the scale of chic, and instead has become shabbier by the year. People still flock here, for the cheap jeans or the multiplex cinemas, or because they have no alternative, since the Châtelet-Les Halles station beneath it is the unavoidable hub of both the métro and the RER. However, as 'social exclusion' has risen up as one of France's major problems the Forum has also become a mecca for the homeless, punks and junkies, the epitome of the kind of Paris seen in Luc Besson's 1985 movie *Subway*. The best things about Les Halles are the **Musée de l'Holographie** and the **Vidéothèque**.

The Les Halles gardens alongside the Forum similarly seem to be largely inhabited by the homeless. Looming over them is the sixteenth-century church of **St-Eustache**, one of Paris' largest, with a beautifully structured Renaissance interior and chunky flying buttresses on the outside. In one of the side chapels is a charming collage-cum-sculpture by British artist Raymond Mason depicting the departure of the market in 1969, with gaudily painted figures carrying outsize vegetables. On the eastern side of the garden, and now somewhat dwarfed, there is also the place des Innocents, site of the **Fontaine des Innocents**, one of the finest Renaissance fountains in Paris, and a time-honoured meeting-point.

At the other, western, end of the Les Halles gardens is the **Bourse du Commerce**, an attractive circular building in yellow stone which was once the main corn exchange, and is now a busy commodity market for coffee and sugar. It also houses a world trade centre and an office of the Paris Chamber of Commerce.

This area is now packed with smart clothes shops – Agnès B's empire extends along most of rue du Jour (*see chapter* **Fashion**), while rue Coquillière still has two 24-hour brasseries, Au Pied de Cochon and the Alsace aux Halles (*see chapter* **Nightlife**), now more geared towards tourists than market traders.

There is also a crop of trendy, expensive bars. Close to the Forum the decline of the area has been reflected in the disappearance of some high-profile drinking-holes – the 1994 closure of the giant Philippe Starck-designed Café Costes on place des Innocents could be called the end of an era in Paris – but further west others, such as Le Comptoir on the corner of rue Berger and rue Vauvilliers, are still thriving (*see chapter* **Cafés & Bars**). The pedestrianised rue des Lombards, back to the east towards the boulevard Sébastopol, is another centre for nightlife, with bars, restaurants and jazz clubs such as Le Baiser Salé and Le Sunset (*see chapter* **Music: Rock, Roots & Jazz**).

To the south, just by the Pont-Neuf, is the giant department store La Samaritaine (*see chapter* **Specialist Shops**), which retains much of its original art nouveau interior, its grand staircase and glass roof. The café at the top is worth a visit for the spectacular view it grants across the Seine, glimpsed from behind the giant neon letters proclaiming the store's name.

For something altogether weirder, go to the pest extermination shop in rue des Halles, where dead rats hang in the window. It's a surreal reminder that this was the site of the city's main burial ground, the Cimetière des Innocents, which was demolished in 1786 after flesh-eating rats started gnawing their way into peoples' living rooms.

Rue & Faubourg St-Denis

The tackiness is pretty unremitting up and down the traditional red-light avenue of rue St-Denis (and its northern continuation, the rue du Faubourg St-Denis), which snakes away northward from Châtelet and the place des Innocents. Kerb-crawlers gawp at the neon signs advertising *l'amour sur scène*, and size up the sorry-looking array of prostitutes in the doorways. Actually, the street is remarkably tame – gone are the whips and chains of former years – and likely to get more so as pedestrianisation progresses.

Amid the seediness there is also the Brasserie Julien on rue du Faubourg St-Denis, which boasts one of the finest art nouveau interiors in Paris, with stunning painted panels, mirrors and polished mahogany. Although now part of a chain, it has maintained its eternally-fashionable status (*see chapter* **Restaurants**).

At the point where the street crosses the boulevard St-Denis is the delapidated gateway of **Porte St-Denis**, erected by the city in 1672 to celebrate Louis XIV's victories on the Rhine, and once one of the main entries into Paris. North of the gate, on either side of rue du Faubourg St-Denis, there are many narrow passageways and slightly sinister

A focus for clubs, bars and eating out in the Bastille, the rue de Lappe.

cobbled courtyards. Passage Brady is a surprising piece of India, home to a small but thriving community who mainly originate from France's former Indian colony of Pondicherry, and full of cheap Indian hairdressers and tiny curry houses.

If you go from the Porte St-Denis back towards Les Halles down rue de Cléry and then rue des Petits Carreaux, you will come to rue Montorgueil, with its wonderful food market (*see chapter* **Food & Drink**). Often brightly decorated with pennants hanging from the lamp-posts, the street, with its cheap wine bars and restaurants, is an irresistible place to while away a couple of hours.

Sentier & the Bourse

Between rue des Petits Carreaux and rue St-Denis is the site of what was once the *Cour des Miracles*, so called because the paupers who came back there after a day's begging would 'miraculously' regain the use of their eyes or limbs. An abandoned aristocratic estate, it was a refuge for beggars and the underworld for decades until it was cleared out by Louis XIV's chief of police, La Reynie, in 1667.

Nowadays the surrounding area, the Sentier, is the centre of the rag trade, and the streets are filled with porters carrying long linen bundles over their shoulders. The streets north of rue du Caire, in particular, are connected by a maze of passages lined with wholesale boutiques.

The area attracts hundreds of illegal and semi-legal foreign workers, who line up in place du Caire every morning for work in the sweatshops. It's an inglorious modern-day slave market that highlights the hypocrisy of official anti-immigration drives. French governments are only too aware that their garment industry could not survive without this stream of cheap and desperate labour.

Rue Réaumur, cutting across the Sentier, was once the Fleet Street of Paris, and has some remarkable art nouveau buildings, particularly at Nos 116, 118 and 124. As in other capitals, the newspapers have today nearly all moved out of the centre of the city, although *Le Figaro* and Agence France-Presse are still based down near the **Bourse des Valeurs**, Paris' neo-classical stock exchange, commissioned by Napoleon in 1808. It still relies partly on open-floor trading.

The area around it is busy, workaday Paris, but not without its charms: head down rue Notre-Dame-des-Victoires and you come to one of the prettiest squares in town, the **place des Victoires**. Built by Hardouin-Mansart in 1685 to commemorate Louis XIV's victories against the Dutch, and featuring an inevitable statue of the Sun King, it forms an intimate circle of buildings broken only by the loud rue Etienne Marcel which breaks in on the eastern side. This is a district for serious fashion shopping; Kenzo, Jean-Paul Gaultier and Comme des Garçons all have shops in the area (*see chapter* **Fashion**). Standing on the corner of the rue d'Aboukir, you catch the best view of the smart classical Bank of France building across the square.

This is also Paris' traditional business district, with narrow streets, office blocks and restaurants where perfectly coiffed women and men in button-down shirts commune at lunchtime over a few glasses of wine. Most interesting for the casual visitor are the several *passages*, and the **Bibliothèque Nationale** on rue des Petits-Champs, with its huge iron and glass-vaulted reading room. After the library has moved to its extravagant new edifice at the end of 1996 (*see below* **The 13th Arrondissement**), the old building will be used more than today for temporary exhibitions, and so be more accessible to the public.

The *passages* or arcades were built from the 1820s onwards, and heralded the arrival of high capitalism in France, turning shopping into an exercise in style rather than the mere fulfilment of basic needs. Conspicuous consumption was born under their gaily painted glass roofs, and in the last two decades, following renovation, they have taken on a new lease of life as the domain of fashion shops, fancy knick-knack-sellers, antiques dealers and refined tea-merchants. Go during the day, as most are locked at night and on Sundays (*see page 109* **The *Galeries***).

The Bastille & Eastern Paris

Ever since the famous prison-storming that inaugurated the Revolution, the **place de la Bastille** has remained a potent symbol of popular revolt. Although the site has changed beyond recognition since the heady days of 1789, it's still a favoured spot for left-wing demonstrations and popular gatherings. Since the eighties, as the Marais and Left Bank have priced themselves out of most young people's reach, it has also become a magnet for new cafés and restaurants, art galleries and good nightclubs. The once dilapidated working-class districts stretching east from here are rapidly being renovated, making this one of the most trendy areas of the city in which to live.

Nothing remains of the Bastille fortress which served as a high-security prison and a defence for what was then the Porte St-Antoine along the city walls, although there are a few vestiges and tiled pictures of it in the métro station. After the revolutionary mob destroyed the place on 14 July 1789, in a symbolic attack on the *ancien régime*, its stones were used to construct the pont de la Concorde. One enterprising revolutionary called Palloy even made pocket-sized models of the castle – a precursor of the modern tourist souvenir – which he then sold around the country.

The site of the prison itself is now taken by a Bank of France office. The gap left by the demolished castle ramparts forms the present-day

Canal walks

It was Napoleon who gave Paris its first canals, primarily as a means of ending a chronic water shortage. Today the Canal St-Martin, now a peaceful backwater, also provides an opportunity to see some of the most atmospheric *quartiers* of nineteenth-century working-class Paris. One major attraction is the contrast they make with the monuments and more conventionally picturesque prettiness of the centre.

The canals were a means of transport as well as a water source, and warehouses sprouted up along their banks. By the 1960s, however, canal traffic had dwindled to a trickle, and a scheme was hatched to build a motorway right along the top of the canal. Somewhat surprisingly, popular protests put a stop to this plan, and the eighties saw the restoration of the canals and the opening of a small marina for pleasure boats, the Port de l'Arsenal, between the Bastille and the Seine.

The Canal St-Martin stretches for 4½ kilometres from here to the place de Stalingrad, rising 25 metres through nine locks. When first completed in 1826 the canal was open along the whole of its length, but between the Bastille and the square Jules Ferry it is now covered over with fountains and gardens. The first stretch along boulevard Richard Lenoir was covered up unusually quickly in 1859-61 in order to make it easier for troops to prevent any likely gatherings of revolutionary crowds in the proletarian *faubourgs* to the east of the canal.

If you go along the canal by boat through this stone-roofed tunnel you will see the base of the July Column in the **place de la Bastille**, as well as the grates of the crypt in which the remains of victims of the 1830 and 1848 revolutions are stored, along with the mummy of a pharaoh brought back by Napoleon from Egypt.

The canal re-emerges just north of the rue du Faubourg-du-Temple, near the place de la République métro. It's this stretch that has the most charm, lined with large shady trees and occasional small gardens, and crossed by wrought-iron footbridges. Most of the old warehouses have closed down, but the area is still semi-industrial and a bit shabby in parts, and you may even still see the odd barge puttering down the canal. There are also a few plain old canalside cafés that look as if they could have been patronised by Jean Gabin in a thirties' movie.

Between the fifth and sixth locks at 101 quai de Jemappes, in fact, is the Hôtel du Nord, which inspired Marcel Carné's classic 1938 film set in the canal district, even though most of the locations (including the footbridges) were recreated in a studio. Threatened with demolition in the early eighties, the hotel was saved as a piece of French cinematic heritage. Just east of the canal from here is the **Hôpital St-Louis**, founded in 1607 to house plague victims, and built in the form of a series of isolated pavilions in order to stop the disease spreading between its patients.

The Canal St-Martin returns underground briefly beneath the place de Stalingrad, re-landscaped in 1989 to reveal to full advantage the **Rotonde de la Villette**, an unusually grand toll house built by Claude-Nicolas Ledoux in 1784 as part of the customs wall around Paris. A large stone cylinder atop a square base, with an imposing classical portico, it's used today to house exhibitions and a display of archeological finds from the Paris area.

North-east of the Rotonde the canal widens into the **Bassin de la Villette**, built for Napoleon in 1808. During its first decades the basin, sometimes called a 'Parisian Venice', was a fashionable place for strolling, swimming, boating, and skating in the winter. All this ceased entirely when La Villette became the site of the main slaughterhouses of Paris later in the nineteenth century. But, they closed down in their turn, and since an ambitious restoration project on the *bassin* was completed in 1989 it has again become a popular place for a walk. Many of the old warehouse buildings on this northern section of the canal have also been replaced with sometimes-striking new housing.

At the eastern end of the basin is an unusual hydraulic lifting bridge, the Pont de Crimée, built in 1885. Beyond that the Canal de l'Ourcq leads away into the **Parc de la Villette** with its many and varied attractions, while another branch, the Canal St-Denis, runs north towards the Seine. The Canal de l'Ourcq runs on through the park and out into the *banlieue*, past the mills at Pantin, with a track alongside that's a favourite place for cycling. It's also possible to follow the canal all the way to its junction with the Marne.

As an alternative to walking, three companies operate boat trips along the canals. For details, *see chapter* **Sightseeing**.

square, a popular meeting point lined with cafés. The July Column at its centre commemorates a different revolution, that of 1830, when Charles X was toppled after three days of fighting.

The **Opéra Bastille** now dominates the eastern side of the square. Opened on the bicentennial of Bastille Day in 1989, it competes with the new **Bibliothèque de France** for the honour of being the most controversial of all Mitterrand's *grands projets*. It's not so much Canadian architect Carlos Ott's design that is at fault, although the curved façade and curious arch over the main entrance have attracted plenty of criticism. Intended to bring opera to the people and so symbolically built in a traditionally working class part of the city, the building has been hugely expensive to administer.

Rue de la Roquette, running off the square, the adjacent rue de Lappe and rue de Charonne are the focus for bars, restaurants and nightlife in the area; Le Balajo, for example, is a nightclub during the week, but reverts to its traditional dance hall past on Sunday afternoons (*see chapter* **Nightlife**). Walk up these streets during the day and you'll notice a tremendous amount of building work and refurbishment. A fashionable set is clearly taking over, although this is an area that still contains an interesting mix.

You can still catch a flavour of the old working-class district at the Sunday morning market on boulevard Richard Lenoir, or along the rue du Faubourg St-Antoine, with its furniture-makers' *ateliers* and many, sometimes gloriously tacky furniture stores. The street is lined with quaintly-named cobbled courtyards, dating back to the eighteenth century. Many of the courtyard workshops are now the studios of artists rather than furniture makers, and are open to the public every October during the **Génie de la Bastille** (*see chapter* **Paris by Season**).

Off the rue Daval, between rue de la Roquette and boulevard Richard Lenoir, is an engaging curiosity, the Cour Damoye, an alleyway that's been so much in demand among film companies looking to recreate nineteenth-century Paris that it's now near-permanently set up as a movie set. There's not much in the way of standard tourist sites in this area, but bags of atmosphere. Just past Ledru-Rollin métro station is the bustling North African-flavoured market of the place d'Aligre, where you can buy excellent spices and tagine pots (*see chapter* **Food & Drink**).

The **Canal St-Martin**, which begins at the Seine at pont Morland, disappears underground at place de la Bastille to re-emerge a good way to the north at rue du Faubourg du Temple. Dotted with locks and iron footbridges, the canal is a pleasant place for a stroll (*see page 113* **Canal Walks**). A new attraction near the Bastille is the **Daumesnil viaduct**, a railway viaduct, closed since 1969, that stretches along the avenue Daumesnil from place

de la Bastille. Its renovation, another project designed to raise the tone of the area, was completed only in May 1995. Officially christened the *Viaduc des Arts*, it has 60 arches that have been converted into workshops, and occupied more by designers and modern craftspersons than the district's more traditional artisans. Along the top there is a promenade lined with plants.

South of the Bastille, by the edge of the Seine, is the new Bercy development, with the Ministère de l'Economie et du Budget, the **Palais Omnisports de Paris-Bercy**, a shiny, eighties-modern sports centre and concert hall, and the dramatic **American Center**. Further east is place de la Nation, a noisy traffic junction that's interesting historically for its two square pavillions and accompanying Doric columns, remnants of the tax-collectors' wall built around Paris just before the Revolution. At the centre of the *place* is a grandiose statue titled *Triomphe de la République*, commissioned for the centenary of the Revolution in 1889 and finally inaugurated ten years later.

Ménilmontant & Père Lachaise

The main attraction of eastern Paris, a few streets north of Nation, is **Père Lachaise** cemetery. Laid out in 1804 like an English garden, it rapidly became the society cemetery of choice. Nowadays it is so full it looks like some kind of eccentric city of the dead, with mausoleums for monuments and tombstones for dwellings beneath its arching willow trees. There are maps showing who is buried where at the entrances; the most notorious grave, that of Jim Morrison, isn't hard to find, since 'Jim this way' signs have been scrawled all over the other tombstones.

The area around it is known as Ménilmontant, and it started life as a pretty village where Parisians could escape on weekends. However, it quickly turned into slumland in the mid-nineteenth century, as Haussmann cleared the working class out of the city centre and migrants flooded into Paris from the French provinces. The area has undergone constant change ever since thanks to a constant influx of immigrants: Russian Jews, Poles, Spanish Republicans, Armenians, Greeks, North Africans, and most recently, Asians. It still retains an exotic village atmosphere, although land speculators are fast tearing down characterful neighbourhood houses to make room for faceless new housing developments.

Just behind Ménilmontant métro station is rue Crespin-du-Gast, site of the small **Musée Edith Piaf**. The singer was born and began her career in the neighbourhood. A short walk away at 83 rue des Couronnes is the **Villa Calte**, one of the few fine houses in the area, with a superb wrought-iron gate, cobblestones and a charming garden used by Truffaut to film parts of *Jules et Jim*.

*One of the more unusual sights of the affluent 16th, the **Fondation Le Corbusier**.*

Belleville & La Villette

Belleville is set on the second tallest hill in Paris. Like Ménilmontant to its south it was a villagey area that was absorbed into the city during the last century. Climbing up rue de Belleville, you will find yourself in the city's newest Chinatown, where the old kebab-sellers are now out-numbered by noodle bars and Chinese supermarkets.

Up the avenue Simon Bolivar is the eccentric **Parc des Buttes-Chaumont** (main entrance rue Botzaris), one of the most attractive and least-known landscaping feats of Baron Haussmann's designers. From the small classical temple in the middle of the park lake there is a splendid view, particularly westwards towards Montmartre. Tucked away east of the park, between place des Fêtes and place de Rhin et Danube, are a number of tiny hilly streets lined with small houses and gardens that still look positively provincial.

North of avenue Jean-Jaurès are some of Paris' newest housing developments, around the **Parc de la Villette**. This ultra-modern science park, on the site of the old city abattoir, combines the technological wonders of a science museum with innovatively-designed playgrounds, fountains and eccentric sculpture. There's also the giant geodesic dome La Géode, housing a cinema, and dotted around the park, cut in two by the Canal de l'Ourcq, a real submarine, concert halls, landscaped gardens and the bright red *folies* designed by architect Bernard Tschumi. The Grande Halle is the only relic of the stockyard days.

Champs-Elysées & the West

Far away on the western side of the city centre, in the 8th, 17th and (above all) the 16th *arrondissements*, the atmosphere is very different from that found in the eastern *faubourgs*. This is smart, well-brushed Paris, preferred home of the city's *BCBG* (*bon chic, bon genre*, or in other words old money and impeccably affluent tastes) community.

The **avenue des Champs-Elysées**, the great spine of western Paris, is one of those famous streets that was not entirely planned. At first glance the near-perfect alignment of what is known as the *Grand Axe* – from the Louvre to Concorde to the Arc de Triomphe and beyond to Porte Maillot and La Défense – looks and feels like the result of a unifying architectural vision. In fact it came about bit by bit.

The Champs-Elysées – the Elysian Fields – started life as an extension to the Tuileries gardens in the seventeenth century. By the time of the Revolution, the avenue had been laid along its full stretch, but was more a place for a Sunday walk than a street. At night it was a little-frequented, dangerous place that needed intensive policing.

Things began to change at the turn of the nineteenth century when the creation of the Faubourg St-Honoré on the avenue's northern side brought fine houses, cafés and high-class prostitutes. With the industrial revolution came street lights, pavements, sideshows, concert halls, theatres and exhibition centres, plus military parades and royal processions, and the avenue of world repute was born. The completion of the **Arc de Triomphe** in 1836 also played its part. Bismarck was so impressed by the Champs-Elysées when he arrived with the conquering Prussian army in 1871 that he had a replica, the Kurfürstendamm, built back home in Berlin.

Although the modern avenue has kept some of its traditions, such as the military parade on 14 July and the annual New Year's street party, you can't help feeling the Champs-Elysées is a place whose golden age is past. Where once there were jugglers and balloonists, now there are fast-food joints, airline offices, car showrooms and multiplex cinemas. For the most part the architecture is unremarkable, and the traffic so intense that you take your life into your hands if you stray across the avenue's eight lanes for a view of the Arc de Triomphe. Only a few buildings hint at its once glorious past: Guerlain's perfume house at No. 68, its windows displaying vast bottles of *eau de Cologne*, has fine cast-iron decoration (*see also chapter* **Specialist Shops**). Nearby at No. 25, although marred by a foreign exchange bureau at the front, is the grand house built for the Marquise de Païva, one of the most celebrated courtesans of the nineteenth century, and now the smart Travellers' Club.

A huge renovation programme on the avenue was completed in 1994. Pavements were relaid in smart granite blocks and a second row of trees planted on each side, while cars were banished from the pavements to giant underground car parks. Come here during a parade when the traffic is diverted, and you can still get some idea of the avenue's former grandeur.

The best places of the Champs-Elysées are at its two ends. At the entrance to the avenue at place de la Concorde are the winged Marly horses, copies of the eighteenth-century originals by Guillaume Coustou, now wonderfully displayed in the Louvre. To the left, leading from place Clemenceau down to the Seine, is a remarkable museum complex comprising the **Grand Palais** and **Petit Palais**, both built for the 1900 World Exhibition, and still in use for major shows today. Part of the Grand Palais will be closed for renovation until 1998, but still open in one wing of the building is the **Palais de la Découverte**, a fun science museum that's a particular hit with children.

The eighteenth-century **Elysée Palace**, the official presidential residence, lurks on rue du Faubourg St-Honoré, although its large gardens extend to the northern side of the Champs-Elysées. It is, of course, closed to all but the most exclusive visitors, although if you are prepared to queue it's normally open during the *Journées Portes Ouvertes* (*see chapter* **Paris by Season**).

At the Rond-Point des Champs-Elysées, Nos 7 and 9 give some idea of the splendid fine mansions, hiding large gardens, that once lined the avenue. From here you can also stroll down the avenue

Montaigne with its array of fashion houses such as Thierry Mugler, Christian Dior and Inès de la Fressange (*see chapter* **Fashion**).

A little further west, and unavoidable, is the **Arc de Triomphe**, towering above the Champs-Elysées and the place Charles de Gaulle, still better known just as the *Etoile*. Begun to glorify Napoleon, this giant neo-classical arch was modified after his disgrace and death to celebrate the armies of the Revolution, although the Emperor could scarcely feel himself under-represented. This has always been a potent symbol of the nation, and the invading Germanic armies of Bismarck and Hitler made a point of marching through it to prove their superior might. On the right-hand side, looking west, you can admire its famous sculpture of the 1792 march of volunteers, known as the *Marseillaise*. There is a splendid view from the top, of the 12 boulevards radiating outwards in all directions.

From here you can also see a good many prize swathes of Paris real estate: the swanky mansions along the grassy verges of the avenue Foch – the widest street in the city – or the luxury hotels and prestige office buildings of avenue Hoche and avenue Wagram.

At the other end of avenue Hoche is the small, intimate **Parc Monceau** (main entrance on boulevard de Courcelles), with its Renaissance colonnade, transported here in the eighteenth century, and large, lily-covered pond. The park is usually full of neatly dressed children and nannies from this elegant and rather stuffy residential district.

South of the Arc de Triomphe, avenue Kléber leads to the group of buildings and gardens called the **Trocadéro**, from where there are spectacular views over the river to the Eiffel Tower and Champ de Mars. This is another museum-filled area: the main building, the **Palais de Chaillot**, its austere thirties' classicism typical of the vaguely fascistic architecture of the time, houses museums devoted to anthropology, marine and naval life, the cinema and French national monuments (*see chapter* **Museums**). There is also the wonderful **Cinémathèque** (*see chapter* **Film**) and the famous Chaillot national theatre company (*see chapter* **Theatre**). Along avenue du Président-Wilson at place d'Iéna is the **Musée Guimet**, with its remarkable collection of Asian art, and the **Musée d'Art Moderne de la Ville de Paris** in the Palais de Tokyo, whose permanent collection includes works by Matisse, Rouault and Dufy.

The 16th

Most of the 16th *arrondissement*, stretching southwest from Etoile and the Champs-Elysées, is as dull as it is prim and pretty. This is pearls-and-poodle country, where business executives and ambassadors make their homes in smart *belle époque* mansions. It's worth visiting, though, for a

*Archetypal Montmartre – the **place du Tertre**.*

few important curiosities, and some graceful and original architecture.

Just next to the Pont de Grenelle on the river is the circular **Maison de Radio-France** (116 avenue du Président Kennedy), the giant Orwellian home to the state broadcasting bureaucracy built in the sixties (*see chapter* **Music: Classical & Opera**). You can take guided tours round its endless corridors to learn about the history of French broadcasting; employees nickname the place 'Alphaville' after Godard's *1984*-ish film.

The southern half of the 16th, the district of Auteuil, boasts some fine art nouveau houses by Hector Guimard (better known for his métro stations), particularly on the rue La Fontaine, where you can enjoy the fluid fantasy of the Castel Béranger at No. 14 and other less ambitious works at Nos 17, 19, 21 and 60. Marcel Proust, archetypal resident of the 16th, lived in the same street. The area's other prominent architect is Le Corbusier. The **Fondation Le Corbusier** in square du Docteur-Blanche is located in two of his houses, the Villa La Roche and Villa Jeanneret (*see also chapter* **Architecture**). At the far western end of Auteuil, right on the Périphérique, a major attraction is now Paris' most important sports stadium, the **Parc des Princes**.

Among the museums in the area is the **Maison de Balzac**, at 47 rue Raynouard, where you can see the trap door beneath which he used to hide from his creditors. More worthwhile is the **Musée Marmottan**, off the Parc Ranelagh on rue Louis Boilly, which features some of Monet's best work.

To the west of the 16th, across the Périphérique, is the vast expanse of the **Bois de Boulogne**. Formerly a hunting reserve, and site of a château that housed several royal mistresses over the years, the *Bois* was made into a park by Napoleon III, although much of it is still just woodland cut by paths and roads. For all its size, it's usually packed at weekends with Parisians walking their dogs. Within there are still plenty of beautiful wooded spots, and such facilities as the Lac Inférieur, where you can hire rowing boats, the **Longchamp** and **Auteuil** race-courses and the rose gardens of the Parc de Bagatelle (*see also chapters* **Sightseeing** *and* **Sport & Fitness**). By night, the Bois perversely turns into a hang-out for kerb-crawlers and multi-national transvestites baring giant silicone breasts.

Montmartre & the Goutte d'Or

Artistic Montmartre

Montmartre, away to the north of the city's old centre, is the most unabashedly romantic district of Paris. Standing on the tallest hill in the city, it has retained much of its old village atmosphere despite the onslaught of tourists who throng around the **Sacré Coeur** and the **place du Tertre**.

Its winding streets and cosy squares have seduced generations of artists. Toulouse-Lautrec had studios nearby and patronised its raucous bars and clubs in the 1880s and 1890s, immortalising its cabarets in his posters; later it was frequented by artists of the *Ecole de Paris* like Utrillo. The *vie de bohème* of Montmartre is no longer a byword for tuberculosis and freezing winters, having been romanticised by those black and white Robert Doisneau photos of young women posing on tree-lined stone steps and in warmly lit back alleys. Montmartre hasn't entirely surrendered to modern chic, however: there's still the lurid sight of the bars, rock music venues and strip joints on the boulevards at the bottom of the hill; and, on its eastern edge, the pulsating street life of the Goutte d'Or, home to thousands of immigrant families.

For centuries, Montmartre was a quiet village packed with windmills. Then, as Haussmann and the industrial revolution sliced through the city centre, and peasant migrants poured into Paris from across France, working-class families began to move outwards from the old city in search of new accommodation. Move away from the main tourist drag, though, and peer into little alleys, steep stairways and deserted squares, or find the ivy-clad houses with gardens, and you can still catch some of its old village atmosphere.

The hill was absorbed into Paris in 1860, but remained fiercely independent. In 1871, following the capitulation to the Prussians, the new French government sought to disarm the local National Guard, distrusted by the right-wing authorities, by trying to take away its cannons, installed on Montmartre. An angry crowd led by schoolteacher and radical heroine Louise Michel succeeded in driving off the government troops and taking over the guns, thus starting the short-lived Paris Commune (*see chapter* **History: The Third Republic**). In the 1880s and 1890s artists moved in, and stayed until after World War I, when rising rents pushed them south to Montparnasse.

The best starting point is Abbesses métro station, one of only two in the city to retain their original art nouveau glass awnings designed by Héctor Guimard. Facing you across place des Abbesses as you emerge from the station is the art nouveau church of **St-Jean de Montmartre**, with its fake brick façade (actually reinforced concrete) and turquoise mosaics around the door.

Turn down the rue des Abbesses and you come to the delightful rue Lepic, packed with excellent little food shops. Off to the right in rue Tholozé is a famous cinema, Studio 28, named after the year of its opening. Buñuel's *L'Age d'Or* had a riotous première here in 1930, and you can still see the footprints made by Buñuel and Cocteau in the foyer (*see chapter* **Film**).

In the other direction from Abbesses, at 11 rue Yvonne-Le-Tac, is the **Chapelle du Martyre**, the place where, according to legend, Saint Denis picked up his head after his execution by the Romans in the third century and started walking north out of the city (*see chapter* **History: Roman Paris & the Dark Ages**). The name Montmartre probably means 'hill of the martyr' in memory of him, although it could also be derived from the temples to Mars and Mercury that stood here in Roman times. The present **Couvent des Dames Auxiliatrices** that contains the chapel dates from 1887, but has a thirteenth-century engraving of the martyrdom. The crypt of the chapel – or rather, an earlier version on the same site – is also where the Spanish soldiers Saints Ignatius Loyola and Francis Xavier founded the Jesuit Order, on 15 August 1534.

Around the corner, the pavement cafés of rue des Trois Frères are a popular place to go for an evening drink. The street leads into the place Emile Goudeau, whose staircases, wrought-iron street-lights and old houses are particularly evocative, as is the unspoiled bar Chez Camille. At No. 13 stood the **Bateau Lavoir**, named after the medieval washing stands along the Seine. Once a piano factory, it was divided during the 1890s into a warren of studios where artists lived in total penury, among them Braque, Picasso and Juan Gris. A high proportion of the great ground-breaking works of twentieth-century art, most notably Picasso's *Desmoiselles d'Avignon*, were created here. Sadly the original building burned down shortly after being declared a historical monument in 1970. The replacement still rents out space to artists, if rather more affluent ones.

Further up the hill, back on rue Lepic, are the village's two surviving windmills, or *moulins*. The **Moulin de Radet** was moved here in the seventeenth century from its original hillock in rue des Moulins near the Palais Royal, and is now an upmarket Italian restaurant. The **Moulin de la Galette** was made famous by Renoir's famous picture of an evening's revelry there, but is now closed to the public. Another legendary meeting-point for Montmartre artists when they had lain down their brushes for the evening was the cabaret **Au Lapin Agile**, further up the hill on rue des Saules, where it's still functioning today (*see chapter* **Nightlife**).

At the top of the hill, place du Tertre and the surrounding streets epitomise all that is worst about present-day Montmartre. The narrow streets are packed with souvenir shops, and the bars are expensive and soulless.

The place du Tertre itself is the worst offender of all, with dozens of so-called artists competing to sketch your portrait or trying to flog lurid sunset views of Paris. Yet it was in this square that one of the best-known French words originated: the occupying Russian soldiers who came to the taverns here in 1814 demanded to be served quickly or, as they said in their native tongue, *bistro*. In the same square you will find the large café A la Bonne Franquette, a billiards hall in the last century.

Just off the square is the oldest church in the district, **St-Pierre-de-Montmartre**, whose medieval columns have grown bent with age. Founded by

Louis VI in 1133, it is a fine example of early Gothic, and makes a striking, sombre contrast to its extravagant neighbour, the **Sacré Coeur**.

You come to Montmartre's most prominent landmark by following the tourist trail around the corner. It's the one church you can't help seeing wherever you are in Paris, since its massive white dome stands on the highest point in the city. For all its visibility, close up it's rather vulgar, the product of a nervous Catholic establishment wanting 'to expiate the sins' of France following the defeat of the Franco-Prussian war and the godless revolutionary Commune that followed it.

Though not to everyone's taste, Sacré Coeur has become one of the landmarks of the Paris skyline, and offers a panoramic view over the city. If you're climbing up to it from square Willette, it's worth avoiding the main steps, with the new funicular at the side. Try the less crowded steps of rue Foyalter or rue Maurice Utrillo on either side instead.

Back beyond the place du Tertre, on the north side, is rue Cortot and the quiet eighteenth-century manor housing the **Musée de Montmartre**, which tells the history of the area, and has some original Toulouse-Lautrec posters. Renoir, Dufy and Utrillo all had studios here. Next door, though you have to go round to rue des Saules for the entrance, is the **Montmartre vineyard**, which keeps going in memory of the scores of vineyards that used to cover this hillside. The grape-picking each September is an annual ritual (*see chapter* **Paris by Season**). Don't hold your breath for the wine itself, however. A local ditty proclaims that for every glass you drink, you pee twice as much out. And that's a polite way of putting it.

From here, a series of pretty squares leads to the rue Caulaincourt and a winding walk towards **Montmartre Cemetery**, a curiously romantic place with high stone walls and arching trees among the gravestones. It has an eminent list of residents: Stendhal, Berlioz, Théophile Gautier, Alexandre Dumas the younger, Degas, Nijinsky, Louis Jouvet and François Truffaut.

Winding down the back of the hill, the wide avenue Junot is lined with exclusive houses, among them the one built by Adolph Loos for Dadaist poet Tristan Tzara at No. 15, a monument of modernist architecture (*see chapter* **Architecture**).

Bawdy Pigalle

Along the boulevards which straddle the 9th and 18th *arrondissements* the tone suddenly changes as you enter Pigalle, which has long been the most important sleaze centre of Paris. By the end of the nineteenth century (the so-called *Années Folles*), of the 58 houses on the rue des Martyrs, 25 were cabaret venues. Today, flashing neon signs still offer live shows, and coachloads of tourists file along the rubbish-strewn pavements to inspect the

sex shops. The **Moulin Rouge**, beloved of Toulouse-Lautrec, has become a provincial tourist draw, and its befeathered dancers are no substitute for the can-can girls, La Goulue and Joseph Pujol – the *pétomane* who could fart in time to any tune – of earlier times.

But this brash area has recently become a trendy night-time spot too, and designers and advertising people are gradually moving in. New late-night bars have opened, such as Lili la Tigresse, complete with ever-popular go-go dancers. The Folies Pigalle has become a nightclub, the bar where Brel and Gainsbourg sang in the sixties has re-opened as a club and music bar, L'Erotika, and what was once the Divan Japonais, a cabaret made famous by Toulouse Lautrec, has been transformed into the Divan du Monde, one of Paris' best new music venues (*see chapters* **Nightlife** *and* **Music: Rock, Roots & Jazz**).

To the south of boulevard Clichy, large bourgeois *hôtels particuliers* remain, although many are now offices. Here, in an area dubbed the 'New Athens' in the early nineteenth century because of the number of writers, artists and composers living there, is the **Musée de la Vie Romantique** on rue Chaptal, devoted to George Sand and her circle. Further down the hill, on rue de la Rochefoucauld, is the extraordinary **Musée Gustave Moreau**, crammed with the Symbolist painter's works.

La Goutte d'Or

For an altogether different experience, head for Barbès-Rochechouart métro station and the area behind it, known as the Goutte d'Or. In Zola's day this was one of the poorest working-class districts in the city. He used it as a backdrop for *L'Assommoir*, his novel set among the district's laundries and absinthe bars, and his *Nana* grew up in the rue de la Goutte d'Or itself.

Now it's primarily an African and Arab neighbourhood, with plenty of colour to make up for the modesty of the housing. Here you'll reputedly find 37 different nationalities, speaking innumerable dialects between them. Cheap clothes, spicey food and much more are on offer on every street corner, and a lively street market is held under the overhead métro tracks on Wednesdays and Saturdays. The area also stages its own multi-national music festival each July (*see chapter* **Paris by Season**).

Unfortunately the area has also become a favourite political football for the conservative Right. In 1991 Jacques Chirac, then Mayor of Paris, made a now-notorious complaint about the 'noise and smell' of the welfare-scrounging immigrants with too many children who lived here. Since the right won power in 1993 the area's residents have been subjected to increasing police pressure, with regular random identity checks and the odd major incident of brutality.

The Left Bank

Fashion shops and tourists may have moved in on the haunts of bohemians, agitators and moody intellectuals, but the spirit of la rive gauche still lives on.

St-Germain to the Luxembourg

St-Germain-des-Prés is where the great myths of intellectual Paris were born. It was in its cafés that Verlaine and Rimbaud went drinking and, a few generations later, Sartre, Camus and de Beauvoir scribbled their first masterpieces. It is crawling with academic institutions, including Paris' main fine art school, the Ecole des Beaux-Arts, and that most finicky of national institutions, the Académie Française, which polices the French language like a jealous father trying vainly to keep his offspring free of bad influences.

For the visitor the area is irresistible. Often voted as the city's most liveable neighbourhood, it is ideal for an afternoon among the art galleries of the rue des Beaux-Arts, rue de Seine and rue Bonaparte (*see chapter* **Art Galleries**), the fine clothes shops around St-Sulpice and rue de Rennes, the jazz clubs along rue St-Benoît and rue Jacob, the classy street market on rue de Buci, or the elegant lawns and fountains of the Luxembourg gardens.

But St-Germain is not, as the myth might have us believe, full of romantically impoverished students and budding geniuses sitting hunched over their manuscripts in café windows. It has wonderful bookshops, and earnest types do still stride along the rue Jacob clutching weighty tomes, but so prestigious and therefore expensive has the district become that Gucci loafers and fur coats now outnumber cord jackets and blue berets, and any writers who inhabit the area tend to be either well-established or rich ex-pat Americans pretending to be Ernest Hemingway.

Nerve centre of the district is the place St-Germain. To the west are the famous cafés, Les Deux Magots and the Café de Flore (*see chapter* **Cafés & Bars**), which likes to think of itself as the birthplace of existentialism. The main attraction of the Flore to Sartre et al was its wood-fired stoves, which saved them a bundle in heating bills. Nowadays you can spend more on a few coffees there than you would on a week's central heating.

Earlier in the century, it was also frequented by the likes of Picasso and Apollinaire, and even today remains a writer's hang-out, especially the quiet room upstairs. The Deux Magots, named after the two statues of Chinese mandarins inside, now provides an interesting sociological cross-section of US tourists in Paris, thanks to its large pavement terrace, but can no longer boast with any conviction to be a hotbed of intellectual life.

Right across the square is the oldest church in the city, **St-Germain-des-Prés**. Its history dates back to the sixth century, and by the eighth century it was one of the most important Benedictine monasteries in France. What you see today is merely a shadow of its former glory, as it was severely damaged by a Revolutionary mob in 1792, and was scarcely better served by some of the nineteenth-century efforts at restoration. What remains mostly dates from the late twelfth century; inside the simple, somewhat truncated interior lie the remains of the founder of modern philosophy, René Descartes, who died in 1650.

Across the boulevard is the old covered market of St-Germain, once the site of the important St-Germain Fair. Following redevelopment it now houses a concert hall and an underground swimming pool (*see chapters* **Music: Classical & Opera** *and* **Sport & Fitness**).

Dawdle past the boutiques, fashion shops and high-class pâtisseries south of here and you come to **St-Sulpice**, a rather clumsy eighteenth-century exercise in classical form with uneven towers propping up its colonnaded façade. The church is redeemed, however, by Delacroix's Biblical frescoes, in the first chapel on the right, and by the square and fountain at the front. The place and rue St-Sulpice contains chic shops including branches of Yves Saint-Laurent and Agnès B, perfumier Annick Goutal and milliner Marie Mercié (*see chapters* **Fashion** *and* **Specialist Shops**).

The **Fontaine de l'Observatoire**.

The **rue de Buci**, *one of the liveliest market streets of St-Germain.*

The wide rue de Tournon, which still contains some very grand residences, opens up to the **Palais du Luxembourg** and its adjoining park, the **Jardin du Luxembourg**. Built for Marie de Medici in the early seventeenth century and given a few Tuscan touches (its ringed columns and rough-surfaced stone) to remind her of the Pitti Palace back home in Florence, the building now serves as the French Senate and is closed to the public, although it is possible to visit it as part of a walking tour on Sundays. The Luxembourg gardens are one of the most popular spots in a city generally starved of greenery, its formally laid lawns attracting walkers and joggers galore. The wilder western side of the park has tennis courts, and a children's puppet theatre (*see chapter* **Children**); leading away from the southern side of the gardens there is a long, thin extension, **Jardins de l'Observatoire**, containing one of Paris' most elaborate fountains, the **Fontaine de l'Observatoire**.

Heading back up towards boulevard St-Germain, you pass the neo-classical **Théâtre de l'Odéon**, where Beaumarchais' *Marriage of Figaro* was first performed in 1784. It is now one of Paris' leading subsidised theatres (*see chapter* **Theatre**). The attractive semi-circular place de l'Odéon was once home (at No. 2) to revolutionary hero Camille Desmoulins; the same building now houses a restaurant, La Mediterranée, that was decorated by Jean Cocteau. Back on the boulevard St-Germain at the carrefour de l'Odéon is a statue of Danton, who lived on the site when it was just

a quiet backstreet. Now it is a popular meeting point, thanks to the métro and numerous cinemas.

Straight across the boulevard is the delightful cobbled passage du Commerce St-André and its adjoining courtyards where, in the eighteenth century, Dr Joseph-Ignace Guillotin first tested out his notorious execution device. It now boasts a charming tea room and the VIA showroom of contemporary design (*see chapter* **Art Galleries**).

The parallel street, rue de l'Ancienne Comédie, is known for the Café Procope (at No.13), the oldest coffee house in Paris, where coffee was first brought to the Parisian public in 1686, following its introduction to the royal court by the Turkish ambassador. Once a favourite haunt of Voltaire, Rousseau, Benjamin Franklin and even Napoleon, it was rather over-restored in 1989, and is now a fairly undistinguished restaurant. Nearby, the rue de Buci contains a top-class food market, running into rue de Seine (*see chapter* **Food & Drink**).

From here towards the Seine is a charming web of narrow ancient streets with such names as Gît-le-Coeur ('lay down your heart'), so called because one of Henry IV's mistresses lived here. This same street also contains the hotel where William Burroughs and his Beat cohorts revised *The Naked Lunch* (*see page 122* **Penpushers' Paris**). Picasso lived in the parallel rue des Grands Augustins for 20 years.

At the top end of rue Bonaparte is the entrance to the seventeenth-century building (once a monastery) of the **Ecole Nationale des Beaux-Arts**, which is sometimes open for exhibitions. Complementing it on the quai de Conti is the giant

Penpushers' Paris

Gertrude Stein wrote that 'Paris was where the twentieth century was'. By the 1900s Paris was already a magnet for artists from around the world, and since then, above all during the twenties, many English-speaking writers have also felt the city's insistent pull. Expatriate writers became part of the mythology of Paris; equally, they also shaped all our stereotypes of what it is to be a writer.

Writers came to Paris for many reasons. Prominent among the American colony were gay women such as Gertrude Stein, the novelist Djuna Barnes and the heiress Nathalie Barney, whose salons at 20 rue Jacob became legendary. It was cheap – you could get a room and your meals for a dollar a day – and of course there was no prohibition. For the Irish eternal outsider Samuel Beckett one attraction was that in Paris cafés no one bothered if you sat in silence with your thoughts, whereas in Dublin pubs you were always obliged to keep talking.

One already-prominent writer who moved to Paris was Ezra Pound, who from 1921 lived at 70 bis rue Notre-Dame-des-Champs in Montparnasse, where at night he would read his poetry standing naked at the window holding a candle. An important institution of the twenties' literary scene appeared in 1919, when Sylvia Beach opened her bookshop Shakespeare & Company in the rue Dupuytren. Shortly afterwards the shop moved to 12 rue de l'Odéon, which Beach shared with her friend Adrienne Monnier. She published the first edition of *Ulysses* there in 1922.

Favourite cafés were in St-Germain and, especially, Montparnasse. The Dôme and La Coupole were bubbling every night, and Hemingway wrote at the Closerie des Lilas. Le Select was a great favourite of one of the most lost of the Lost Generation, Howard Stearns, whose alcoholic figure turns up thinly disguised in both *The Sun Also Rises* and *Tender is the Night*.

Since 1945 Paris has been less of a draw, but even so the city is still home today to distinguished foreign writers such as Edmund White. And, given the range of great scribblers who have passed through, there is lots of scope for a literary *hommage* – without counting French writers, for whom there has never really been any other place to be.

Oscar Wilde

Not really part of expatriate Paris, as he scarcely came here as a volunteer. Wilde first came to Paris in 1883 as an international celebrity. He stayed at the Hôtel Voltaire, at 19 quai Voltaire, and was introduced to Degas, Pissarro, Verlaine and the great actress Sarah Bernhardt. When he returned after his release from prison in 1897 he was shunned – Paris was less puritanical than London, but still not that liberal. Ill and dejected, he spent much of his time asking people he recognised for money, among them André Gide and the opera singer Dame Nellie Melba, and spent his evenings at the Café de Paris on avenue de l'Opéra. He died at L'Hôtel at 13, rue des Beaux-Arts on 30 November, 1900, shortly after he had prophetically complained 'I can't stand this wallpaper! One of us will have to go'. He is buried in Père Lachaise.

Gertrude & Alice

Gertrude Stein settled in Paris in 1903. In 1907 her soon-to-be inseparable partner **Alice B. Toklas**, author of an inimitable cookbook that is as much about history as food, joined her in their apartment at 27 rue de Fleurus. Armed with a giant sense of her own importance, Stein held court there for over three decades, following every new artistic movement and acting as guru to many of her younger compatriots. Much to be desired by anyone fresh off the boat was an invitation to the rather theatrical Saturday evening salons held at the flat, its walls covered with paintings by Cézanne, Picasso and Matisse. She once even held a lunch where she seated each painter opposite one of his own works. Stein and Toklas became a Parisian institution, and could often be seen walking their dog in the Luxembourg, or strolling along the boulevard Raspail. Stein left Paris during World War II, but returned immediately afterwards, and died in the American Hospital in 1946. She, too, is buried in Père Lachaise.

Hemingway & Fitzgerald

When **Ernest Hemingway** committed suicide in 1961 the manuscript of *A Moveable Feast*, his account of his time in Paris 'in the early days when we were very poor and very happy', lay by his typewriter. Hemingway mythologised Paris, but actually spent relatively little time here. He lived intermittently in the city from 1922 to 1927, but spent almost half of each year away on trips or journalistic assignments. He first came here during World War I, and returned in 1921 with introductions to Gertrude Stein and other Parisian figures. The first apartment he and his wife Hadley took in Paris was at 74 rue du Cardinal Lemoine, although he wrote in an unheated top-floor room around the corner at 39 rue Descartes. *The Sun Also Rises*, written in Paris and published in 1926, was his first great success. Favourite hangouts were the Closerie des Lilas café and Harry's Bar, on the Right Bank. In 1927, after he had split from Hadley, he switched his patch from Montparnasse to the boulevard St-Germain, especially the Brasserie Lipp and the Deux Magots. In March 1928 he married his second wife, Pauline, in the church of St-Honoré-d'Eylau, in the very bourgeois 16th *arrondissement*. During the thirties he left his penniless artist days behind, and when in Paris generally stayed at the Ritz, to which he made a beeline after the Liberation in 1944.

Scott Fitzgerald came to Paris in 1925 already a literary sensation, as a wealthy tourist. He was one of few American writers to stay on the Right Bank, and rented a luxurious flat at 14 rue de Tilsitt, just off the place d'Etoile. He also toured the cafés frequented by the more penniless of the Lost Generation in Montparnasse, where he met Hemingway. During a five-month trip in 1928 Fitzgerald also lived in more familiar literary territory at 58 rue de

Vaugirard, opposite the Luxembourg. He held a literary lunch once a week, attended by Hemingway, Joyce and others, and was a regular at Nathalie Barney's salon in rue Jacob. Fitzgerald was also one of the pillars of the Ritz bar and Harry's Bar, although according to Hemingway he and his wife Zelda had the problem that they both went crazy after just one drink.

Joyce & Beckett

James Joyce came to Paris in 1920 for a week and stayed for 20 years, during which time both *Ulysses* and *Finnegan's Wake* were published. His first hotel room, at 9 rue de l'Université, was so small that Joyce had to write on a suitcase perched on his lap. He and his family subsequently moved to an expensive flat at 5 boulevard Raspail, but later had many other addresses in the city, including 71 rue de Cardinal Lemoine and 8 avenue Charles Floquet, near the Eiffel Tower. An unlikely celebrity on the back of *Ulysses*, Joyce was seen around the Parisian literary scene, but confined himself increasingly to his family during the thirties, due to the worsening schizophrenia of his daughter Lucia and his own failing eyesight. The Joyce family did, however, dine together quite regularly at the plush Fouquet's in the Champs-Elysées. During the German invasion of 1940 the family fled to Zurich, where Joyce died the following year.

Samuel Beckett is of all the expatriate writers the one who stayed the longest. He first came to Paris aged 22 in 1928 as *lecteur* in English at the Ecole Normale Supérieure in the rue d'Ulm. His predecessor in the job, another Irishman called Thomas McGreevy, introduced the chronically reserved Beckett to many figures of literary Paris, among them Joyce. For a time Beckett worked devotedly as Joyce's 'unpaid secretary', running errands for the near-blind author. During his first year at the ENS Beckett had only one student, and they agreed to hold their classes in cafés, the Dôme or the Coupole. These grand cafés were often too expensive for Beckett and his Irish friends, and other Beckettian haunts were the Café du Départ on rue Gay-Lussac, the Rosebud on rue Delambre and the Café de la Mairie on place St-Sulpice (also portrayed in Djuna Barnes' *Nightwood*).

Beckett left Paris in 1930, but after several unhappy years between Dublin and London returned in 1937. The following January he was stabbed by a beggar in the avenue d'Orléans (now avenue Général Leclerc), which incident, however, led him to meet the pianist Suzanne Deschevaux-Dumesnil, who was passing by and came to his aid. They lived together almost from then on. In April 1938 they moved into a tiny seventh-floor apartment at 6 rue des Favorites, in the unfashionable Vaugirard area of the 15th *arrondissement*. During the German occupation they worked courageously as couriers for the French Resistance.

In 1946 Beckett began his most fruitful writing period. He slept during the day and wrote at night, and, when he'd had enough, went out for drinking sessions in whichever local bars were still open. Later he sometimes returned to the more fashionable cafés of Montparnasse, and during the fifties could be seen at the Dôme with Alberto Giacometti. It was during his most reclusive years, though, that he wrote *Waiting for Godot*, which catapulted him to fame when it was produced at the now long-closed Théâtre de Babylone, in rue Babylone, in 1954. In 1960 he and Suzanne Deschevaux finally moved to a larger flat, in rue St-Jacques near rue Gay-Lussac. He died on 22 December 1989, in the Hospice de la Rochefoucauld on avenue Général Leclerc.

Henry Miller

Miller arrived in Paris in 1930, an unpublished 39 year old writer, and left in 1939 an international star. The first vehicle for his success, *Tropic of Cancer*, purports to tell the story of his first years in Paris, which revolved around handouts from friends and odd jobs. He was planning an early return to the US until he met up with Anaïs Nin, already engaged in writing her steamy and semi-fictional diary. Miller used his time to get to know the seedier aspects of the city, such as the St-Antoine quartier and the dingy area around the rue de l'Ouest in the 14th *arrondissement*. A familiar face at the Brasserie Wepler in Montmartre and Le Select and Le Jockey in Montparnasse, he moved into 18 villa Seurat, off rue de la Tombe-Issoire, with Nin, and stayed until the prospect of war caused him to head for home.

James Baldwin

James Baldwin

Baldwin arrived in the French capital on a cold November day in 1948 with 'a little over $40 in [his] pocket, nothing in the bank and no grasp whatever of the French language'. The 24-year-old was whisked straight off to the Deux Magots, spent all his money in the first three days and then spent the next few years plagued by poverty and illness. However, Paris for Baldwin, Richard Wright, Chester Himes and other Black American writers meant a release from racism, and an inspiration for their writing. Baldwin used the Paris gay scene as a background for *Giovanni's Room* and met a Swiss painter, Lucien Happersberger, at La Reine Blanche bar in St-Germain. Happersberger invited him to the Alps, where he completed *Go Tell It on the Mountain*. When Baldwin needed to return to New York to meet his publisher he could only do so with a loan from an old acting friend, Marlon Brando. He left Paris for good in 1957.

The Beat Generation

In the late fifties, Allen Ginsberg, Gregory Corso, Peter Orlovsky and William Burroughs arrived in Paris and in true Bohemian style chose a headquarters which was far from a palace. The hotel at 9 rue Git-Le-Cœur had grey paint peeling from the walls, sagging beds and an often-stained cold water sink, but this did not stop them from their principal preoccupation of revising Burroughs' *Naked Lunch*. Now the Relais du Vieux Paris, the hotel makes much of its Beat associations, but is today much more neat and tidy.

*Café life goes on around the **Sorbonne**.*

Institut de France building, with its distinctive baroque dome. Built with money bequeathed by Louis XIV's minister Cardinal Mazarin, it now houses a number of eminent academies including the Académie Française. There are occasional guided tours to show you Mazarin's ornate tomb built by Hardouin-Mansart, and the rather fusty **Bibliothèque Mazarine**, France's first public library. Next door is the quirky **Hôtel de la Monnaie**, the country's mint from 1777 to 1973, and now an engrossing coin museum.

The Latin Quarter

The section of the Left Bank to the east of boulevard St-Michel is known as the Latin Quarter because Latin was the language used by the students here until the Revolution. The name, though, could equally allude to the vestiges of old Roman *Lutetia*, of which it was the heart. This was the main area to which the Romans extended their city when they moved out of their original stronghold on the Ile de la Cité. The first two streets laid by the Romans were on the site of the modern rue St-Jacques and rue Cujas; the area still boasts the best two Roman remains in the city, the 200 AD **Cluny baths**, now part of the **Musée de Cluny**, and the amphitheatre, the **Arènes de Lutèce**.

The district began its long association with scholarship and learning in about 1100, when a number of scholars, among them Peter Abelard, first came to live and teach on the Montagne St-Geneviève, now the site of the Panthéon, indepen-

dently of the established Canon school of Nôtre Dame. They began to be referred to as a *University*, then understood as a loose association of scholars who regulated themselves and issued licenses to teach. The schools of Paris rapidly established themselves as the intellectual powerhouse of the Christian world, attracting students from all over Europe, and the number of 'colleges' – really just student residences – multiplied. They gradually became more formally organised, until the University of Paris was given official recognition with a charter from Pope Innocent III in 1215. Despite the challenge it often represented to established church teaching, the university was allowed an unprecedented degree of independence from church authorities.

By the sixteenth century, however, the university – by now known as the **Sorbonne**, after the most famous of its colleges – had been co-opted by the Catholic establishment, and in 1530 a group of humanists led by Guillaume Budé founded the Collège de France to revive the study of classical authors. A century later, Cardinal Richelieu rebuilt the Sorbonne, but the place was past its heyday and slowly dwindled and slid into decay.

After the Revolution, when the whole university was forced to close and large chunks of the Latin Quarter were destroyed, Napoleon resuscitated the Sorbonne as the cornerstone of his new, centralised, exclusively French-language education system. The university rediscovered its dissident side, and the participated enthusiastically in the uprisings of the nineteenth century.

The Sorbonne was one of the seedbeds of the 1968 revolt; students battling with police ripped up the cobbles of the boulevard St-Michel (since paved over). Nowadays the university is much quieter, not least because the Sorbonne is now only one of 18 faculties of the University of Paris dotted around the city and its suburbs.

The Latin Quarter still contains a remarkable concentration of academic institutions, from research centres to *grandes écoles* such as the Ecole Normale Supérieure, and so is still an area where students congregate. However, its web of narrow medieval streets has also proved irresistible to the well-heeled, pushing accommodation prices out of most students' reach. The intellectual tradition also persists, though, in the countless specialist book stores and art cinemas around boulevard St-Germain and rue des Ecoles.

The area is highly popular with tourists, who stream down the boulevard St-Michel and its adjoining streets during the summer. The boulevard has been taken over by the fast-food giants and downmarket shoe and clothes chains, and is mostly worth avoiding, although the fountain with its statue of Saint Michael slaying the dragon in place St-Michel is an ever-popular meeting point. Down the pedestrianised rue de la Huchette or rue de la Harpe you'll find more Greek restaurants and café tables with evidence of medieval learning. Look out, though, for the rue du Chat-Qui-Pêche, the narrowest street in Paris, and the Théâtre de la Huchette, which has been playing Ionesco's *The Bald Prima Donna* every night since 1957 (*see chapter* **Theatre**).

There are also two outstanding churches. **St-Séverin** was built over 450 years, and mixes Romanesque and Flamboyant-Gothic styles. **St-Julien-le-Pauvre**, off rue Galande, was built as a resting place for pilgrims in the late twelfth century, at the same time as the initial building of Notre Dame, making it one of the oldest churches in Paris. In the later Middle Ages it was used for student assemblies that became so raucous the whole church was closed in 1524. Today it is partly ruined, but its simple Romanesque interior is relatively intact, and is often used for classical concerts (*see chapter* **Music: Classical & Opera**).

Down by the river, set back from the book and print sellers that line the *quais* and with a fine view of Notre Dame, is the illustrious second-hand English bookshop Shakespeare and Co., although no longer on the site in the rue de l'Odéon that was a daily port of call for expatriate literati in the 1920s (*see chapter* **Specialist Shops**). At 13 rue de la Bûcherie is the circular old **Faculty of Medicine**, where medieval students secretly examined corpses stolen from nearby graveyards.

Place Maubert, now a morning marketplace, was used in the sixteenth century to burn books and hang heretics, particularly Protestants. The little streets between here and the *quais* are some of the oldest in the city and retain the medieval street plan. The rue de Bièvre charts the course of the river Bièvre, which ran here in medieval times.

South of here on rue des Ecoles is the main university complex, with the **Collège de France**, whose current building dates from the late eighteenth century, and the **Sorbonne** itself, whose entrance is on rue de la Sorbonne. The present buildings are mostly nineteenth century, although the Baroque chapel, which is rarely open, still survives from the rebuilding under Richelieu. It's easy enough (unless Umberto Eco or the President is speaking) to sneak into lectures in the main amphitheatre. The biggest 'sight' in the Latin Quarter is the **Musée de Cluny**, a magnificent collection of medieval art housed in a Gothic mansion built on top of ruined third-century Roman baths. The baths are visible from boulevard St-Michel, but the entry is on place Paul Painlevé.

Climb up rue St-Jacques to the south, and to your left is the huge domed **Panthéon**, originally commissioned by Louis XV as a church for the city's patron Saint Genevieve, but converted during the Revolution into a secular temple for the 'great men of France'. Among the notables interred in the crypt are Voltaire, Rousseau, Hugo, Zola and Resistance leader Jean Moulin. In the impressive place du Panthéon, conceived by the Panthéon's

La Hune *bookshop, a Left Bank favourite.*

*The martial **Invalides**.*

famously seedy, a mixture of plain poverty and penniless bohemia. One of the narrow cross-streets off rue Mouffetard is rue du Pot-de-Fer (named after the seventeenth-century 'Iron Pot' fountain on the corner), site, at No. 6, of the hotel where George Orwell stayed during his time as a *plongeur* in Paris during 1928-29, and vividly described in *Down and Out in Paris and London* as 'rue du Coq d'Or'. Nowadays the district is much more picturesque than dingy.

To the west of this knot of narrow streets, at the bottom of rue St-Jacques, is an altogether more eminent landmark, the **Val-de-Grâce**, the least-altered, most luxurious and most ornate of all the Baroque churches in Paris, and the surrounding Benedictine monastery. The latter now houses a hospital and a museum.

The Jardin des Plantes District

West of rue Monge and rue des Fossés St-Bernard you leave the *Quartier Latin* proper behind to move into a quieter area that still contains several major academic institutions, and is also an important focus for Paris' Moslem community. Nestling behind the vile tower blocks of Paris university's campuses VI and VII (known as Jussieu) is the **Institut du Monde Arabe**, built in 1987, one of the best modern buildings in the city. Its window panels are fashioned like ancient Islamic screens, and its exhibitions focusing on different aspects of the Arab world are regularly interesting. There are fine views and a nice café up on the roof, too.

The Paris mosque is not far away, although you may want to stop off on the way at the **Arènes de Lutèce**, the Roman amphitheatre, off the rue Monge. The green-roofed **Mosquée de Paris** (2 place du Puits de l'Ermite) was built in 1922, and is now the centre of the largely Algerian-dominated Moslem community in France. Partly modelled on the Alhambra in Granada, it has a beautiful interior patio and a series of flamboyant domes. At the entrance on rue Geoffroy St-Hilaire there is a splendid Turkish *hammam*, where the baths are complemented by a very enjoyable Moorish tearoom (*see chapters* **Cafés & Bars**, **Sport & Fitness** *and* **Women's Paris**).

The mosque looks out onto the **Jardin des Plantes**, Paris' botanical garden. First established in 1626 as a garden for medicinal plants, it has an eminent history as a centre for botany. Today it's rather neglected and somewhat disappointing, but nevertheless features a charming eighteenth-century maze, a winter garden brimming with rare plant species and the assorted buildings of the **Muséum National d'Histoire Naturelle**, which has been given a new lease of life with the

architect Soufflot, is the elegant classical *mairie* of the 5th arrondissement, and the university library the **Bibliothèque Ste-Geneviève**, with a magnificent nineteenth-century iron-framed roof in the reading room.

Next to the Panthéon on rue Clovis is the more intimate and altogether prettier church of **St-Etienne du Mont**. Pascal and Racine are both buried here, as are the remains of the city's patron Saint Genevieve. Parisians still come here to ask her for favours. Further along rue Clovis is a chunk of Philip-Augustus' twelfth-century **city wall**, of which the other surviving section is in the Marais (*see above*). There is also, within the grounds of the Lycée Henri IV, the Gothic-Romanesque **Tour de Clovis**, a tower that is the only remaining part of the once-giant abbey of Ste-Geneviève. The Lycée is one of the most prestigious schools in the city, and is closed to the public, although you can admire its gardens from the swimming pool, Piscine Jean Taris (*see chapter* **Sport & Fitness**).

Nearby is place de la Contrescarpe, where there are several lively cafés. Off to the south runs rue Mouffetard, known since Roman times and one of the oldest and most characterful streets in the city. Today it's lined with cheap student-filled restaurants and neighbourhood bars, and has a busy market in its lower half, near place St-Médard (*see chapter* **Food & Drink**). This area was once

*Looming over old Paris, the **Tour Montparnasse**.*

restoration and reopening of the Galerie de l'Evolution, previously closed for 25 years. There's also a zoo, the **Ménagerie**, founded during the Revolution, and which now has some evil-looking vultures as well as big cats, bears and reptiles.

Monumental Paris

Smart townhouses spread westwards from St-Germain into the 7th *arrondissement*, but the vibrant street and café life subsides in favour of calm residential blocks and government offices. This quarter, the Faubourg St-Germain often written of by Proust as a symbol of staid, *haut-bourgeois* and aristocratic society, remains home to some of Paris' oldest and grandest families, although most of its eighteenth-century *hôtels particuliers* have now been taken over by embassies and government ministries. You can still admire their stone gateways and elegant courtyards, especially on rue de Grenelle, rue St-Dominique and rue de Varenne, among them the 1721 **Hôtel Matignon**, at 57 rue de Varenne, residence of the Prime Minister.

The eastern half of the 7th *arrondissement* is another stretch of prime shopping territory, with the famous Bon Marché on rue de Sèvres (*see chapter* **Specialist Shops**), the smart food and design shops of rue du Bac and the antiques dealers concentrated along the quai Voltaire and rue des Sts-Pères. This *arrondissement* also contains some of the most famous monuments in the city.

One of the most dynamic and interesting is the **Musée d'Orsay**, a giant converted railway station and now the city's most important museum after the Louvre. An expression of late nineteenth-century dreams of grandeur, the station was a lavish affair built to impress for the 1900 World Exhibition. No train has passed through since the fifties, because its platforms eventually proved too short. The edifice narrowly escaped demolition in the sixties to make way for a hotel and conference centre, and the idea of turning it into a museum only came to final fruition in 1986. The grandiose interior is almost as much worth seeing for itself as for the magnificent array of Impressionist and other nineteenth-century art. Recommended, too, is the roof terrace with its giant clockface and views over the Louvre.

Westwards along the Seine, facing the Pont de la Concorde and the place de la Concorde across the river, is the **Assemblée Nationale**, the lower house of the French parliament. Its pedimented neo classical façade was added in the early nineteenth century to mirror that of the Madeleine, then being constructed on the other side of the river. Visitors can attend debates (*see chapter* **Sightseeing**), and in the past you could also visit the Deligny swimming pool, a recreational fixture for Deputies and the public since the eighteenth century, which floated barge-like on the Seine behind the Pont de la Concorde. Unfortunately it sank in mysterious circumstances in July 1993.

Alongside the Assemblée is the Foreign Ministry, often referred to by its address, the quai d'Orsay. Beyond it, around the corner, stretches the long grassy esplanade leading up to the golden-domed **Invalides**, the vast military hospital complex which now houses the **Musée de l'Armée** and Napoleon's tomb. Cannons line the grand pavilions of the 196-metre (650-foot) long façade, decorated with allegorical tributes to the building's patron, Louis XIV. The place is huge, impressive and immensely impersonal.

The two churches inside – **St-Louis-des-Invalides** and the **Eglise du Dôme** – glorify the various French monarchs and their armies. Inside the Eglise du Dôme, beneath a circular balustrade, is Napoleon's tomb. The museum, meanwhile, is chock-a-block with paintings, tapestries, banners, armour and weaponry illustrating France's wartime career from Charlemagne to the present.

A far cosier place to visit is the **Musée Rodin**, housed in the Hôtel Biron, one of the most charming *hôtels* on rue de Varenne. Rodin was invited to move here in 1908 on the understanding that he would bequeath his work to the state. As a result, you can now see most of his great sculptures, including *The Thinker* and *The Burghers of Calais*, in a beautiful eighteenth-century setting. Many stand in the magnificent rose-filled garden.

Back on the other side of the Invalides, to the west is the **Ecole Militaire**, the military academy built by Louis XV and where Napoleon first graduated. Designed by Jacques-Ange Gabriel, the architect of the place de la Concorde, in 1751, it's a stern, rather unappealing building, and isn't open to the public. Opposite its south entrance, across the place de Fontenoy, is the Y-shaped **UNESCO** building, built in 1958 by a multi-national team – an American (Breuer), an Italian (Nervi) and a Frenchman (Zehrfuss) – and headquarters of the UN's Organisation for Education, Science and Culture. A giant construction in concrete and glass, it's worth visiting for the sculptures by Picasso, Arp, Giacometti, Calder and others in the lobbies (the building is open from 9am-6pm Mon-Fri).

From the north-western side of the Ecole Militaire begins the vast esplanade of the **Champ de Mars**, a former market garden converted into a military drilling ground in the eighteenth century. Now it forms a spectacular backdrop to the most famous Parisian monument of them all, the **Eiffel Tower**, tallest building in the world from 1889 until New York's skyscrapers began sprouting in the thirties. Although everyone rushes to climb as high up as they dare, the best view in many ways is from the bottom, looking up at the incredibly complex patchwork of metal soaring from its four supporting legs.

Former artists' studios on rue Campagne-Première, Montparnasse.

Fronts de Seine

Downstream from the Eiffel Tower, the 15th *arrondissement* has few mainstream tourist sites. The river-front has been mainly taken over by undistinguished seventies' tower block developments. Among recent additions are the sophisticated headquarters of the Canal + TV channel at 2 rue des Cévennes, designed by American architect Richard Meier, and a brand new public park, the **Parc André Citroën**, opened in 1992 (rue Balard). Created on the site of a former Citroën car factory, the park has been laid out as a contemporary formal garden with a geometric design, water gardens and two large glasshouses.

Montparnasse & Beyond

In the first three decades of this century Montparnasse meant artists, vibrant café life and the rowdy cabarets of the rue de la Gaîté. Artists like Picasso, Léger and Soutine, and the poet Apollinaire came to the city's 'Mount Parnassus' to escape the rising rents of Montmartre and brought a new cutting edge of intellectual life to the area. To some extent their legacy has lived on, although Montparnasse is definitely a sadder, more disparate place now. The high-rise blight of the Montparnasse Tower is only the most visible of several new building projects that have turned lively village communities into faceless residential blocks. But the area still has its attractions: the Breton crêperies of rue d'Odessa and rue Montparnasse (Gare

Montparnasse is the main point of arrival from Brittany), the cinemas and legendary brasseries of boulevard Montparnasse, and some quirky landmarks, such as the cemetery and the catacombs.

Its most eye-catching landmark today, though, is the 209-metre (688-foot) tall **Tour Montparnasse**, a steel-and-glass arrow that's Paris' tribute to Manhattan. You can use it to orientate yourself if you get lost just about anywhere in central Paris. The area around the Tower is the result of some particularly infelicitous seventies planning. The old Montparnasse railway station, where the German army signed its surrender of Paris on 25 August 1944, has been transformed into a maze of steel and glass corridors housing a shopping complex, a sports centre, a car park and any number of fast-food joints. Behind it there is now a new small garden, the **Jardin de l'Atlantique**, built above the tracks of the TGV. The tower itself is best visited as a perch from which to view the rest of the city.

The nearby rue de la Gaîté, once renowned for its cabarets and theatres, has also changed for the worse, becoming prey to strip joints and sex shops. The boulevard Montparnasse, by contrast, has retained more of its character. Such famed establishments as Le Dôme and La Coupole (*see chapter* **Restaurants**), La Rotonde, Le Select and Hemingway's favourite hangout La Closerie des Lilas (*see chapter* **Cafés & Bars**) are still in business and open day and night for beer, oysters and lively chatter. Boulevard Raspail boasts, not far from its junction with boulevard Montparnasse, Rodin's remarkable 1898 sculpture of Balzac,

Le Dôme, boulevard Montparnasse.

which caused such a furore because of its rugged, elemental rendition of the famous novelist that it wasn't displayed in public for 40 years.

There's no longer much sense of an artistic community in the area, although large windows often testify to former studios now converted into apartments, such as the strange tiled building at 31 rue Campagne Première, or around the hidden courtyard at 126 boulevard Montparnasse. The former studios of sculptors Zadkine and Bourdelle are now both interesting museums open to the public (the **Musée Zadkine** and **Musée Bourdelle**). A recent addition to the area is the gleaming glass **Fondation Cartier** on boulevard Raspail, an exhibition centre for contemporary art. The **cité Fleurie**, just into the 13th *arrondissement* at 65 boulevard Arago, is a reminder of former days that's still occupied by artists. It isn't open to the public, but you can peer through the gateway into the gardens.

It's also worth making a detour towards the Porte de Versailles to visit **La Ruche** on passage de Dantzig, the 'beehive' designed by Eiffel as a pavilion for the 1900 exhibition that from the 1900s to the 1920s was one of the great laboratories of modern art. After the exhibition it was acquired by a sculptor – himself conservative in style – called Alfred Boucher, who had it rebuilt on this site and let it as artists' studios. It had space for 140 artists,

and Chagall, Soutine, Modigliani, Brancusi and many more all worked alongside each other here. Many of the studios are still in use today.

While the rest of the neighbourhood has gone a bit downhill, **Montparnasse cemetery** has grown in status as a resting place for the famous. It's a calmer, less crowded cemetery than Père Lachaise; numbered among the eminent dead here are Baudelaire, Maupassant, Franck, Sartre and de Beauvoir, Jean Seberg and France's ultimate decadent crooner, Serge Gainsbourg.

A spookier kind of burial ground can be found at place Denfert-Rochereau (instantly recognisable from the large bronze lion which dominates the traffic junction), entrance to the Paris **Catacombs**. Some six million bones were transferred here from the over-crowded cemeteries of Paris just before the Revolution. During World War II the Resistance had a hide-out here, and more recently, in the eighties, the catacombs became popular for illicit concerts and parties. The entrance to the catacombs is next to one of the toll gates built by Ledoux in the 1780s, marking what was then the boundary of the city.

Returning towards Montparnasse along the avenue Denfert-Rochereau you will come to France's royal observatory, the **Observatoire** at 62 avenue de l'Observatoire, built by Colbert in 1668. This is where the moon was first mapped, where Neptune was discovered and where the speed of light first calculated. However, it is open to the public by appointment only, and only on the first Saturday of each month.

Alésia & Montsouris

The bulk of the 14th *arrondissement*, to the south of place Denfert-Rochereau, is a mainly residential but pleasantly spacious area. There's a small but lively street market on rue Daguerre (*see chapter* **Food & Drink**). Around rue d'Alésia there are some surprising, slightly un-Parisian-looking townhouses. At 4 rue Marie Rose is the **Maison de Lénine**, where the founder of the Soviet Union lived for four years. Once a compulsory stop for all East European dignitaries, it's now a rather forlorn place, and open by appointment only (phone 42.79.99.58). The museum inside is unspectacular unless you want to see the great man's crockery and modest furniture.

The 14th *arrondissement* also boasts a lovely large park, the **Parc Montsouris**, which has some very beautiful trees and a lake. On the park's opening day in 1878 the man-made lake suddenly and inexplicably emptied and the engineer responsible promptly committed suicide. There's a good, if expensive, restaurant, the Pavillon Montsouris, on its edge (*see chapter* **Restaurants**).

Just to the west of the park there are several small streets such as rue du Parc Montsouris and rue Georges Braque that were built up in the early years of this century with charming small villas, many by distinguished architects (*see chapter* **Architecture**). Once mainly occupied by artists, they're now more likely to be the homes of lawyers and doctors. On the southern edge of Montsouris is the **Cité Universitaire**, home to 6,000 students of different nationalities (*see also chapter* **Students**). It has 40 different pavilions, each designed in a supposedly appropriate national style. The much admired but now rather dated tower-block architecture includes the Swiss Pavilion (1935), on stilts, and the Brazilian pavilion (1959), both designed by Le Corbusier.

The 13th *Arrondissement*

Traditionally a working-class area with a strong history of political activism, this largely neglected corner of town has been undergoing massive upheaval with the building of the new **Bibliothèque Nationale de France** on the quai de la Gare, the last, most ambitious, and in many ways most troublesome of former President Mitterrand's projects for the capital. Dominique Perrault's design, personally selected by Mitterrand, has drawn down upon itself endless criticism for its impracticality, wastefulness, expense and architectural quality. As Mayor of Paris Jacques Chirac, eager to score points against the pharaonic President, tried unsuccessfully to kill off the building altogether, even planting a group of squatters on the site for a few months.

Argument has never ceased about the library's cost, a stunning 7.3 billion francs to build and another billion a year to maintain, but nevertheless the project has reached the stage where cancellation is now inconceivable, and according to official statements it's finally to open in November 1996. Mitterrand hoped the library would be the first in a series of developments to liven up this desolate part of the Left Bank, as part of a plan called *ZAC Rive Gauche*. Other features of the plan include new housing and office developments on the large stretches of land in the district formerly taken up by railway yards, the covering-over of some of the remaining rail lines, and the building of a new footbridge between the library and the equally modernistic Bercy area across the river. President Chirac and his new government are pledged to cut government spending, but, again, they are unlikely to cancel these schemes completely. One consequence of the plan will be that some other, independent developments in the area, such as **Les Frigos** art space (*see chapter* **Art Galleries**), will be threatened with closure.

The 13th also has some more established sights: the **Manufacture Nationale des Gobelins** is home to the French state's main weaving companies. The tapestries and rugs produced here on commission (usually from the government) continue a long tradition dating back to the fifteenth century. On the northern edge of the *arrondissement*, next to the gare d'Austerlitz and the Jardin des Plantes, is the huge **Salpetrière**, one of the oldest hospitals in Paris, founded in 1656. In the 1800s this was one of the first places in the world to undertake scientific treatment of the insane. Its chief architectural feature is the chapel, from 1670, designed by Libéral Bruand with eight separate naves in order to be able to separate the sick from the insane, the destitute from the debauched. The hospital is still in operation, but the chapel is regularly used for exhibitions.

Acting as a focal point for the area, the busy road intersection of place d'Italie has seen more recent developments with the Centre Commercial Italie, a slightly bizarre high-tech confection which contains the Gaumont Grand Ecran Italie, the largest cinema screen in the city, and a music venue, the Arapaho (*see chapters* **Film** *and* **Music: Rock, Roots & Jazz**) as well as the usual underground banks and shops.

To the south and west of place d'Italie is an area known as the **Butte aux Cailles**, full of old village-like houses and hilly cobbled streets centred around the rue de la Butte aux Cailles and the rue des Cinq Diamants. An area full of '68-era veterans, still with a vaguely underground atmosphere, it has fought hard to keep out the property developers, and the community is unusually close-knit. It has plenty of small, feisty bars, like La Folie en Tête (*see chapter* **Music: Rock, Roots & Jazz**), which always appear to be bursting at the seams. The rues Buot, Michal and Alphand are particularly rustic, and there's an attractive brick Arts-and-Crafts style swimming pool in place Paul Verlaine, fed by an artesian well (*see chapter* **Sport & Fitness**). Villa Daviel contains neat little villas, while the little cottages clustered around a garden square at 10 rue Daviel were one of the earliest public housing schemes in Paris.

Chinatown

South of the rue de Tolbiac is **Chinatown**, the area's other main attraction, centred in the sixties tower-blocks along avenues d'Ivry and de Choisy. The community that lives here actually comes from several Asian countries. The bleak modern architecture could make it one of the most depressing areas of Paris, but instead it's a fascinating piece of South-East Asia, with its shops and pâtisseries, and the large Tang Frères supermarket on avenue d'Ivry. It's a great place to come for excellent and cheap oriental food in big, busy restaurants like the Hawai and the Palais de Cristal (*see chapter* **Restaurants**). To see the area at its busiest, come here for the colourful floats and parades at the Chinese New Year (*see chapter* **Paris By Season**).

Beyond the Périphérique

Parisians may scorn them, but there is actually life out there in the banlieue.

Even if Paris is no longer surrounded by a city wall, its borders are still clearly circumscribed by its ring road (the *Périphérique*). Since the late nineteenth-century, however, an ever-increasing number of outlying villages have effectively been absorbed into the Parisian metropolis.

Paris' suburbs enjoy excellent transport links with the city, but nevertheless the vast majority of Parisians will do anything to keep an address within the 20 *arrondissements*. The *banlieue* do, though, contain a number of attractions, as well as **Versailles** (for which, *see chapter* **Trips Out of Town**). Several others contain châteaux, swallowed up in the suburban sprawl, and there are even some forts that once defended the city, at Aubervilliers, Mont-Valerien and Le Kremlin-Bicêtre. In addition, thanks to an official policy of cultural decentralisation, several also have dynamic cultural centres. And, as recent political discussions have shown, they are increasingly on the mind of France as much as or even more than the traditionally all-absorbing life of the capital.

The West

Paris' most desirable suburbs almost all lie to the west of the city. Between the wars, the wealthy middle classes began to build expensive properties here, and today much of the area is filled with substantial houses complete with gardens, which immediately give a quite different atmosphere from that of apartment-dominated Paris.

Neuilly-sur-Seine and **Boulogne-Billancourt**, closest to the city, are typical. Neuilly is perhaps the most sought-after residential suburb, more or less an extention of the *BCBG* 16th *arrondissement*. Expect to see lots of pearl chokers and Hermès scarves if you wander through its streets. Boulogne, to the south, used to be dominated by its film studios, recently demolished, and a Renault car factory, now closed and awaiting redevelopment. In the north of the district, however, near the Bois de Boulogne, there are elegant villas and some fine examples of twenties' and thirties' architecture. The area also has a good

museum with work by artists who lived there at that time, the **Musée de Boulogne-Billancourt**, and hosts a jazz festival each May (*see chapter* **Paris by Season**).

Just across the Seine is **St-Cloud**, site of a château that was built for Louis XIV's brother, 'Monsieur', and burnt down in the Franco-Prussian war in 1870. There remains, however, a marvellous park on a hillside overlooking the river, particularly renowned for its Grande Cascade. To the south of St-Cloud is **Sèvres**, site of the famous porcelain factory, now a museum (*see chapter* **Museums**). Back to the north is the seventeenth-century château at **Rueil-Malmaison,** closely linked with the names of Napoleon Bonaparte and Josephine (*see chapter* **Sightseeing**).

Henry II of France lived at **St-Germain-en-Laye**, further west, with his wife Catherine de Médici and his mistress Diane de Poitiers, and the Sun King Louis XIV was also born here. The château has several British connections: Mary Queen of Scots grew up here, and the dethroned James II lived here from 1689 until his death in 1701. It was restored by Napoleon III, who turned it into an archeological museum, the **Musée des Antiquités Nationales**. The château overlooks the Grande Terrasse, a popular promenade, designed by Le Nôtre in the seventeenth century, on the edge of a 3,500 hectare forest. The town of St-Germain is a smart commuter suburb, with a historic centre, upmarket shops and the **Musée Départemental du Prieuré**, former home of the Nabi painter Maurice Denis.

Maisons-Laffite, just to the north, was until recently an important horse-racing centre. It gained part of its name from the banker Jacques Lafitte, who lived at the château there in the nineteenth century.

The North & East

The suburbs around the north and east of Paris were the first to be industrialised, from the 1860s onwards, and they remain the grimmest parts of the greater Paris region. Edith Piaf laboured in a

La Défense

La Défense is only a hop, skip and a jump from central Paris, but feels like a different world. Instead of streets and houses, what you find as you emerge from the RER station are giant skyscrapers and walkways. It has been called a mini-Manhattan, but it's more antiseptic and concentrated than anything in New York. It's impressive rather than loveable, and the whole area, at least by day, has a sort of dynamism still ahead of the similar but characteristically less spectacular Docklands development in London.

La Défense has been a showcase for French business since the mid-fifties, when the triangular **CNIT** exhibition hall was built as a space for major trade shows. It was a landmark in its day, and still has the largest concrete vaulted roof in the world (a 230-metre/754-foot span), although its original open space has been divided up into shops, cafés, hotels and smaller exhibition spaces. Since then successive governments have all developed the idea of giving Paris an entirely new, separate district for modern business, and it soon proved popular with big corporations such as Elf and Fiat, who needed more space for their headquarters than a downtown location could offer.

Today, after much energetic construction and the occasional whiff of kickback scandals, over

100,000 people work on this businesspersons' reservation, and another 35,000 dwell in the ghastly futuristic blocks of flats on the southern edge. None of the skyscrapers display any great architectural distinction, although, clustered together, they are an impressive sight.

What brought La Défense most international attention was the **Grande Arche**, completed for the bicentenary of the Revolution in 1989. Composed of two 92-metre (300-foot) office blocks connected at the top, the Arche is slightly off-set from the sweeping alignment of landmarks from the Louvre through the Arc de Triomphe and beyond. The government sold most of the offices inside at cut-price rates, but ended up using the left side for its own Transport Ministry.

One can't help but be struck by the sheer amount of empty space. Outside on the giant forecourt (the *parvis*) are fountains and sculptures by artists such as Joan Miró and Alexander Calder. Even more fun are the extremely kitsch computer-controlled fountains and Takis' flashing light poles. A good introduction to the area is the 45-minute Walkman audio tour, in English and several other languages, that can be hired from the **Info-Défense** kiosk in front of the CNIT (open 10am-6pm daily). *See also chapter* **Sightseeing**.

---

boot factory in the northern suburbs before she was discovered singing on the streets. In the 1950s, huge estates full of tower blocks were built swiftly on cheap industrial land. Most famous is **Sarcelles**, considered a symbol of urban misery.

In amongst this suburban sprawl stands one of the treasures of Gothic architecture – the basilica at **St-Denis**, where most of France's monarchs were buried. Nearby a stadium is under construction for the 1998 World Cup. St-Denis has one of largest Paris' highest immigrant populations, especially from North Africa, and has become another local byword for urban blight, but it also has a lively cultural scene and hosts prestigious jazz and classical music festivals.

As well as St-Denis, **Bobigny** and **Créteil**, still resolutely working-class areas, also have excellent subsidised theatres (*see chapter* **Theatre**) and enterprising cultural programmes. More upmar-

ket residential areas are found near the Bois de Vincennes, such as **Vincennes**, **St Mandé** and **Joinville-le-Pont**, where there are villas and footpaths along the banks of the Marne.

The South-West

Much of this area was built up in the fifties and sixties, such as leafy **Sceaux** is a pleasant exception. In the seventeenth century Louis XIV's finance minister Colbert ordered the construction of a sumptuous château here. This was later destroyed, and the present building, which today houses the **Musée de l'Ile de France** (46.61.06.71), dates from 1856. It's surrounded by a park, more or less following the original design by Le Nôtre, with a Grand Canal and waterfalls. Concerts are often held in the Orangerie in summer.

On the Town

A la Carte

No need for faux pas when you know your bifteak from your faux-filet.

Abats offal. **Agneau** lamb. **Aiguillettes** (de canard) thin slices of duck breast. **Ail** garlic; **aïoli** sauce made with ground garlic. **Aloyau** loin of beef. **Ananas** pineapple. **Anchoïade** spicy paste of anchovies and black olives. **Andouillette** sausage made with pig's offal. **Aneth** dill. **Anguille** eel. **A point** medium rare. **Asperge** asparagus. **Assiette** plate.

Ballotine a piece of meat or fish boned, stuffed and rolled up. **Bar** a Mediterranean fish resembling bass. **Barbue** brill. **Bavarois** moulded cream dessert,

flavoured with vanilla and cooked. **Bavette** steak (from abdominal muscles). **Béarnaise** rich sauce of butter and egg yolks. **Beignet** fritter or doughnut. **Bien cuit** well-done. **Bifteak** steak. **Bisque** any kind of shellfish soup. **Blanquette** a 'white' stew (made with eggs and cream). **Boudin noir/blanc** black or white pudding, served grilled. **Boeuf Bourguignon** beef cooked Burgundy style, with red wine, onions and mushrooms. **Bouillabaisse** Mediterranean fish soup. **Bourride** a bouillabaisse-like soup, without shellfish. **Brebis** sheep's milk cheese. **Brochet** pike. **Brochette** kebab.

Cabillaud fresh cod. **Caille** quail. **Campagne/ campagnard** country-style. **Canard** duck.
Carbonnade a beef stew with onions and stout or beer.
Carré d'agneau rack or loin of lamb. **Carrelet** plaice.
Cassis blackcurrants, also blackcurrant liqueur used in kir. **Cassoulet** stew of haricot beans, sausage and preserved duck. **Cèpes** spongy, dark-brown mushrooms.
Cervelles brains. **Charcuterie** cold meat hors d'oeuvres, such as *saucisson* or pâté. **Charlotte** moulded cream dessert with a biscuit edge; also baked versions with fruit. **Chasseur** cooked with mushrooms, shallots and white wine. **Chateaubriand** thick fillet steak, usually served for two with a *béarnaise* sauce. **Chaud** hot. **Chaud-froid** a sauce thickened with gelatine or aspic, used to glaze cold dishes. **Chèvre** goat's cheese.
Chevreuil young roe deer. **Choucroute** sauerkraut, usually served with cured ham and sausages. **Civet** game stew. **Clafoutis** thick batter filled with fruit, usually cherries. **Colin** hake. **Confit** (de canard) preserved duck. **Coquille** scallop, or sometimes just a scallop-shaped dish. **Coquilles Saint-Jacques** scallops.
Cornichon tiny pickled gherkin. **Crème anglaise** custard sauce. **Crème brûlée** creamy custard dessert with caramel glaze. **Crème chantilly** sweetened whipped cream. **Crème fraîche** thick, slightly soured cream . **Crépinettes** small, flattish sausages, often grilled. **Crevettes** prawns (GB), shrimps (US). **Croque madame** sandwich of toasted cheese and ham topped with an egg. **Croque monsieur** sandwich of toasted cheese and ham. **Croustade** case of bread or pastry, deep-fried. **En croûte** in a pastry case. **Cru** raw.
Crudités assorted raw vegetables.

Darne (de saumon) salmon steak. **Daube** meat braised slowly in red wine or stock. **Daurade** sea bream.
Dégustation tasting or sampling. **Désossé** boned.
Dinde turkey. **Duxelles** mushrooms sautéed in butter with shallots.

Endive chicory (GB), Belgian endive (US). **Entrecôte** beef rib steak. **Epadon** swordfish. **Epinards** spinach.
Escabèche sautéed and marinated. **Escargots** snails.
Estouffade dish containing meat that has been marinated, fried and braised.

Farci stuffed. **Faux-filet** sirloin steak. **Feuilleté** literally, 'leaves' of (puff) pastry. **Filet mignon** beef tenderloin. **Fines de claire** crinkle-shelled oysters.
Fines herbes mixture of herbs. **Flambé** food flamed in a pan in burning brandy or other alcohol. **Flétan** halibut.
Foie liver; **foie gras** liver of goose or duck. **Fraise** strawberry; **fraise des bois** wild strawberry.
Framboise raspberry. **Friandises** sweets or petits fours. **Fricadelle** meat-ball. **Fricassé** meat fried and simmered in stock, usually with creamy sauce. **Frisée** curly endive. **Froid** cold. **Fromage** cheese; **fromage blanc** smooth cream cheese. **Fruits de mer** shellfish.
Fumé smoked. **Fumet** fish stock.

Galantine boned meat or fish pressed together, usually with a stuffing. **Galette** round flat cake of flaky pastry, potato pancake or buckwheat savoury *crêpe*.. **Garni** garnished. **Gâteau** cake. **Gelée** aspic. **Gésiers** gizzards.
Gibier game. **Gigot** leg of mutton; **gigot d'agneau** leg of lamb. **Gingembre** ginger. **Girolle** delicate wild mushroom. **Goujon** strips of fish, coated in egg and breadcrumbs and fried. **Granité** water-ice. **Gratin dauphinois** sliced potatoes baked with milk, cheese and a bit of garlic. **Gratiné** browned with breadcrumbs or cheese. **Grèque** (à la) vegetables served cold in the cooking liquid including oil and lemon juice. **Grenouille** (cuisses de) frogs' legs.

Hareng herring. **Haricot** bean. **Homard** lobster.
Huître oyster.

Jambon ham; **jambon cru** cured or smoked ham.
Julienne vegetables cut into matchsticks.

Langoustine Dublin Bay prawns, scampi. **Lapin** rabbit; **lapereau** young rabbit. **Lamelle** very thin slice.
Langue tongue. **Lard** bacon; **lardon** small cube of bacon. **Lièvre** hare. **Limande** flatfish, similar to sole.
Lotte monkfish. **Lyonnaise** served with onions.

Mâche lamb's lettuce. **Magret** duck breast. **Maison** (de la) of the house. **Mariné** marinated. **Marmite** small cooking pot. **Marquise** light mousse-like cake. **Mélange** mixture. **Merguez** spicy sausage. **Merlan** whiting.
Meunière fish coated with flour, sautéd (q.v.), served with lemon. **Mignon** small fillet of meat. **Moëlle** bone marrow; **os à la moëlle** marrow bone. **Morille** wild morel mushroom. **Moules** (à la) marinière mussels cooked in a sauce of white wine, shallots, parsley, thyme, butter and lemon juice. **Morue** dried and usually salted cod. **Mousseline** mixture lightened with whipped cream or egg white. **Mousseron** delicate wild mushroom.
Moutarde mustard.

Nage aromatic liquid for poaching. **Navarin** lamb and vegetable stew. **Noisettes** small round portions, usually of meat, also hazelnut. **Noix** walnut. **Nouilles** noodles.

Oeuf egg. **Oie** goose. **Onglet** cut of beef, similar to bavette. **Oursin** sea urchin.

Pain bread. **Palourde** clam. **Pamplemousse** grapefruit. **Panaché** mixture. **Pané** breaded. **Pavé** cut of steak. **Papillote** (en) cooked in paper and opened at the table (usually fish). **Parfait** mousse-like mixture, can be sweet or savoury. **Parmentier** with potato. **Pâtes** pasta or noodles. **Paupiette** a thin slice of meat, stuffed and rolled. **Pied** foot (trotter). **Pintade** guineal fowl.
Plat du jour daily special. **Poireau** leek. **Pommes Parisienne** potatoes fried and tossed in a meat glaze.
Potage soup. **Pot au feu** boiled beef with vegetables.
Poulet chicken. **Poulpe** octopus.

Quenelles light poached dumplings made with fish or meat.

Ragoût brown meat stew. **Raie** skate. **Rascasse** scorpion fish. **Rillettes** potted meat. **Ris de veau** veal sweetbreads. **Rognons** kidneys. **Rouget** red mullet.

Saignant rare. **St Pierre** John Dory. **Sanglier** wild boar. **Sauté** fried lightly and rapidly. **Seiche** squid.
Suprême (de volaille) fillets of chicken in a rich cream sauce.

Tartare raw minced steak (also tuna or salmon). **Tarte aux pommes** apple tart. **Tarte Tatin** a warm, caramelised apple tart cooked upside-down. **Tête** head; **tête de veau** calf's head, cooked in a white *court-bouillon*. **Timbale** dome-shaped mould, or food cooked in one. **Terrine** a rectangular earthenware dish or a pâté cooked in one. **Thon** tuna. **Tisane** herbal tea.
Tournedos small slices taken from a fillet of beef, sautéd or grilled. **Tripes** tripe. **Truffes** truffles – famous (and expensive) underground fungus.

Vacherin a cake of layered meringue cream, fruit and ice cream; or, a soft, cow's milk cheese, wrapped in pine bark. **Veau** veal. **Velouté** stock-based white sauce; creamy soup. **Viande** meat. **Vichyssoise** cold leek and potato soup. **Volaille** poultry.

Restaurants

Grandes tables, great seafood bars, or funky local bistros – our map of the high points in the Parisian culinary maze.

It's a fine time to come to Paris with a big appetite. Restaurateurs have finally got the message that Parisians want good quality country cooking at reasonable prices in relaxed surroundings. In response, the bistro-annexe trend, where famous chefs have been opening lower-priced branch restaurants, continues apace, which means that you can sample the cooking of even someone as exalted as **Joël Robuchon** (*see* **Le Relais du Parc** *under* **Moderate/Bistros**) for less than a quarter of what a meal would cost in his main restaurant (*under* **Haute Cuisine**). Other restaurants have reacted by offering interesting *prix-fixe* menus alongside their à la carte list too.

Many of the most popular new restaurants specialise in a French regional cuisine (*see page 144* **The French Regions**), with *provençale*, French Mediterranean, food being the big fashion of the moment. Even in places that serve a more classic bistro menu the emphasis has shifted to traditional, rustic cooking. The eighties' fad for elaborately decorated dishes has waned, and these days you'll rarely find anything on your plate without a direct relation to what you're about to eat.

Meanwhile, cafés continue to close in startling numbers, and at the other end of the scale many people are also questioning the ongoing validity of the capital's haute cuisine restaurants, many of which went rather stale during the recent recession. What's more, the formality and fussiness of these places puts off many modern diners who look to a meal as a rare oasis of relaxation.

It's also unfortunately worth noting that the often-unseen industrialisation of the French kitchen continues, whether it's in frozen *frites*, premade vinaigrette or even *sous-vide* (vacuum-packed) courses warmed up in the kitchen. The French are increasingly obsessed with 'Lite' foods, too, which is why it's becoming difficult to find a good cheese board in Paris restaurants.

The quality and variety of the city's seafood restaurants has never been better, however, and the choice of foreign eating-houses continues to widen. And, alongside them, there is still the most spectacular selection of restaurants serving wonderful French food. Contrary to much traditional propaganda, it is perfectly possible to get a lousy meal in Paris, but even if you temper your expectation with a dose of reality and common sense – avoid the most obvious tourist traps in Les Halles and the Latin Quarter, for example – the city remains the gourmet Mecca of Europe.

Below we give a few tips to help you work your way through the Paris restaurant world. For more restaurants that open through the night, *see chapter* **Nightlife**, and for a glossary of common terms, *see page 136* **A la Carte**. For suggestions specifically on how to find good food at budget prices, *see page 155* **That Good Cheap Meal**.

Restaurant customs

Booking Except in very simple restaurants, it's always wise to book ahead. For most places, this can be done the same morning or the day before, but allow more time for weekends. Tables at *grands restaurants* often need to be booked well in advance, although you stand more chance of getting in at short notice for lunch. Also, hotel receptionists will usually help in making reservations, and at the grander hotels the staff are adept at securing otherwise hard-to-book tables for the next or even the same day.

Children Dogs are almost always allowed in French restaurants; children *usually* are, although Parisians rarely take babies to classy places (*see chapter* **Children** for restaurants were children are particularly welcome).

Dress Parisians tend towards a casual but chic look when dining. Restaurants listed under **Haute Cuisine** may insist on a jacket and tie for men.

Drinks Every restaurant serves wine and other alcoholic drinks, but will normally only do so with food, or to customers waiting to be seated. Brasseries, however, usually have a café/bar area.

Smoking Specific conditions attach to smoking in French restaurants. Under a 1991 law restaurants and cafés must have designated smoking (*fumeur*) and non-smoking (*non-fumeur*) areas (unless they choose to be entirely one or the other). However, the *non-fumeur* tables are almost invariably the worst seats in the house, and non-smokers may find it more pleasant just to try and get a table in the *fumeurs* that's near a door.

Tipping All restaurants and cafés in France are obliged by law to include a 15% service charge in the bill. This amount is taxed, which is one reason why waiters often hope to get a tip as well. It's not necessary to leave anything, but if you're pleased with the service, an extra 5F-15F or thereabouts, left on the table, is always appreciated.

Averages

Prices listed are based on the cost of a starter (*entrée*), main course (*plat*) and dessert eating à la carte, but do not include drink. Menu refers to set menus, also known as *prix fixe* or *formule*, which offer a more limited choice at a set price, again usually for three courses, and sometimes include wine.

Haute Cuisine

In top restaurants the *menu dégustation* or *menu gastronomique* is almost always worth trying, with a choice of all the specialities of the house.

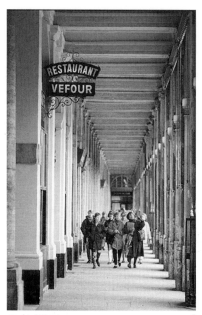

In the Palais-Royal, **Le Grand Véfour**.

L'Ambroisie

9 place des Vosges, 75004 (42.78.51.45). Métro Bastille.
Open noon-2.15pm, 8-10.15pm, Tue-Sat. Closed 3 weeks
Aug. **Average** 825F. **Credit** AmEx, EC, MC, V.
A handsome restaurant with Italianate décor spread over
two small salons in a beautifully restored house on the place
des Vosges. The refined cuisine of chef/patron Bernard
Pacaud, combined with fine, discreet service, makes this a
jewel among restaurants.
*Air-conditioning. Book one week in advance. Wheelchair
access.*

L'Arpège

*84 rue de Varenne, 75007 (45.51.47.33). Métro
Varenne.* **Open** noon-2pm, 7.30-10pm, Mon-Fri; 7.30-
10pm Sun. **Average** 750F, incl drink. **Menu** 390F (lunch
only), 790F. **Credit** AmEx, DC, EC, JCB, MC, V.
Chef Alain Passard is a rising star in the French culinary
world, and especially creative with fish and desserts. There's
an appealingly energetic atmosphere in these recently renovated dining rooms, decorated in smart but casual style with
lots of pale wood and glass. An unfortunate aspect of the renovation, though, was the creation of a dismal room in the cellar, which is to be avoided. Understand, too, that Passard's
minimalist cooking style can be a disappointment to anyone
expecting a dose of French grandeur. Excellent wine list.
Book two weeks in advance.

Gérard Besson

*5 rue du Coq-Héron, 75001 (42.33.14.74). Métro Palais
Royal.* **Open** noon-2.30pm, 7.30-10.30pm, Mon-Fri.
Average 500F. **Menu** 260F (lunch only). **Credit** AmEx,
DC, EC, MC, V.
This fine chef-owned restaurant serves a limited number of
customers in quiet, comfortable surroundings. M. Besson is
famous for his foie gras, fish and game (in season) – all pre-

pared with a strong, classic style that is unusual today. The
wine list is outstanding.
*Air-conditioning. Book one week in advance. Wheelchair
access.*

Jacques Cagna

*14 rue des Grands Augustins, 75006 (43.26.49.39).
Métro St-Michel.* **Open** noon-2pm, 7.30-10.30pm, Mon-
Fri. Closed 3 weeks Aug, 1 week Christmas-New Year.
Average 350F lunch; 550F dinner. **Menu** 260F (lunch
only). **Credit** AmEx, DC, JCB, MC, V.
Affable chef Jacques Cagna is a master at combining new
styles with classic dishes. The restaurant is located in a
lovely seventeenth-century town house, and has soft light-
ing, terracotta-coloured walls and period paintings. *See also*
La Rôtisserie d'en Face *under* **Moderate/Bistros**.
Air-conditioning. Book two weeks in advance.

Le Carré des Feuillants

*14 rue de Castiglione, 75001 (42.86.82.82).
Métro Concorde or Tuileries.* **Open** noon-2.30pm, 7.30-
10.30pm, Mon-Fri; 7.30-10.30pm Sat. Closed Sat evening
July, closed Aug. **Average** 500F. **Menu** 280F (lunch
only); *menu dégustation* 580F. **Credit** AmEx, DC, EC,
JCB, MC, V.
Chef Alain Dutournier has created an original mix of city
chic and rural cooking for his modern restaurant, where the
cuisine of south-west France is the speciality. Seasonal
dishes include hare in the style of Aquitaine. Dutournier also
owns the **Trou Gascon** (*see under* **Moderate/Bistros**).
*Air-conditioning. Book two weeks in advance. Wheelchair
access.*

Le Grand Véfour

*17 rue de Beaujolais, 75001 (42.96.56.27). Métro Palais
Royal.* **Open** 12.30-2.15pm, 7.30-10.15pm, Mon-Fri. Closed
Aug. **Average** 700F. **Menu** 305F (lunch only). **Credit**
AmEx, DC, JCB, MC, V.
Established in the Palais Royal as a coffee house in the eigh-
teenth century (*see chapter* **Paris by Area: The Right
Bank**) and often described as the most beautiful restaurant
in Paris, with a gilded interior that's distinctly *ancien régime*,
the opulent Grand Véfour provides classic French cooking,
with Savoyard touches introduced by recently-arrived chef
Guy Martin. It also has a very good wine list.
Air-conditioning. Book one week in advance.

Ledoyen

*carré des Champs-Elysées, 75008 (47.42.23.23) Métro
Champs Elysées-Clemenceau.* **Open** noon-2.30pm, 7-
10.30pm Mon-Fri. **Average** 600F **Menu** 290F lunch,
520F, 590F dinner. **Credit** AmEx, DC, EC, JCB, MC, V.
Following a sensitive restoration of the Imperial splendours
of this dining room by decorator Joseph Graf, France's top
woman chef Ghislaine Arabian now has a setting that befits
her wondrous interpretation of the northern kitchens of
Picardy and Flanders. Try her superb langoustines with
potato salad, and then go on to the delicious *côte de boeuf* in
beer sauce, or the scallops with truffles. On the ground floor
there is a grillroom, the **Cercle Ledoyen** (*47.42.76.02*),
which also offers excellent food, at more moderate prices
(average 250F; menu 160F).
Air-conditioning. Book two weeks in advance.

Lucas-Carton

*9 place de la Madeleine, 75008 (42.65.22.90). Métro
Madeleine.* **Open** noon-2.30pm, 8-10.30pm, Mon-Fri; 8-
10.30pm Sat. Closed first 3 weeks Aug, 1 week Christmas-
New Year. **Average** 1,000F. **Menu** 375F (lunch only),
menu dégustation 1,500F. **Credit** AmEx, EC, JCB, MC, V.
This *belle époque* landmark is ironically home to chef Alain
Senderens, one of the most inventive chefs in France and a
founder of *nouvelle cuisine* when the phrase was first invented. His sometimes unusual creations – people are often pas-

sionate in their love or dislike of his food – can be fabulous and are always interesting, as is the wine list. This is also one of the dressiest, and most expensive, restaurants in Paris. *Air-conditioning. Book one month in advance.*

Joël Robuchon

59 avenue Raymond-Poincaré, 75016 (47.27.12.27) Métro Trocadéro. **Open** 12.30-2pm, 7-10pm, Mon-Fri. Closed July. **Average** 1,400F. **Menu** 890F, 1,200F. **Credit** AmEx, DC, MC, V.

Ever since he moved into new quarters in an elegantly refurbished *belle époque* townhouse, Robuchon, for most critics the premier chef of France, has been threatening to retire when he turns fifty, which means in 1996. If he keeps his word, the restaurant will continue, of course, but his absence from the kitchen will surely be felt, which means that if you have your heart set on nibbling the current pinnacle of French haute cuisine you'd better act fast. Note that you usually have to book months ahead of time, too. And, you may wonder, does his food really warrant all of this fuss? Robuchon is an extraordinary cook, constructing fascinating dishes out of cream of cauliflower with caviar and John Dory with ginger, and the presentation and service are impeccable. Should you decide to invest £150 a head in this experience, however, you may arrive with impossibly high expectations, so just bear in mind that you shouldn't expect to have a vision at the table, but simply to enjoy a very fine (and very expensive) meal. *See also* **Le Relais du Parc** *under* **Moderate/Bistros.**
Air-conditioning. Book at least one month in advance.

Michel Rostang

20 rue Rennequin, 75017 (47.63.40.77). *Métro Ternes.* **Open** 12.30-2.30pm, 7.30-10.30pm, Mon-Fri; 7.30-10.30pm Sat. Closed first 2 weeks Aug. **Average** 650F. **Menu** 288F (lunch only), 520F, 720F. **Credit** AmEx, DC, EC, JCB, MC, V.

This handsome restaurant, stuffed full of silver, crystal and valuable curios, is the stage for chef-patron Michel Rostang and his sophisticated, varied cuisine blending classic and modern cooking with that of his native Isère. The friendly, attentive service front-of-house is overseen by the charming Madame Rostang. *See also* **La Bistro d'à Côté** *under* **Moderate/Bistros.**
Air-conditioning.

Guy Savoy

18 rue Troyon, 75017 (43.80.36.22). Métro Charles de Gaulle-Etoile. **Open** noon-2pm, 7.30-10.30pm, Mon-Fri; 7.30-10.30pm Sat. **Average** 700F. **Menu** 820F. **Credit** AmEx, EC, JCB, MC, V.

In a light, spacious room adorned with contemporary art, star chef Guy Savoy releases his own latest creations. Cooking becomes a real art as he ingeniously creates wonderful combinations of delicate scents, textures and flavours. His dishes are also fashionably light, with an emphasis on fish, poultry and vegetables. The menu changes every three months, and service is professional yet friendly. If you want to sample the Savoy flair at more accessible prices, note that he has become the centre of a veritable industry, with a growing chain of bistros (*see* **Les Bookinistes** *under* **Moderate/Bistros** *and* **Le Cap Vernet** *under* **Brasseries**), offering simple but still excellent food. *Air-conditioning. Book one week in advance.*

Taillevent

15 rue Lamennais, 75008 (45.63.39.94). *Métro George V.* **Open** noon-2pm, 7.30-10pm, Mon-Fri. Closed last week July, 3 weeks Aug. **Average** 800F. **Credit** AmEx, DC, EC, JCB, MC, V.

A temple of traditional haute cuisine, in the wood-panelled rooms of a nineteenth-century mansion. The perfect fusion of fine cuisine, exemplary service and elegant atmosphere means that tables here are among the hardest to book in the world. Any meal at Taillevent is a celebration. The cooking is firmly rooted in the classic French tradition, with a few contemporary touches. The wine list, too, is famously superlative (and fairly priced) and the cellars also have a retail outlet for their wines (*see chapter* **Food & Drink**). *Air conditioning. Book two weeks in advance.*

La Tour d'Argent

15 quai de la Tournelle, 75005 (43.54.23.31). Métro Pont Marie. **Open** noon-2pm, 8-10.30pm, Tue-Sun (last reservation 9.30pm). **Average** 900F. **Menu** 375F (lunch only). **Credit** AmEx, DC, EC, JCB, MC, V.

The food here provokes varying reactions, but the venerable Tour, which started life in 1582, still warrants its billing as a once-in-a-lifetime experience. The famous duck Tour d'Argent is the main attraction, but the menu also offers a contemporary selection of lighter dishes. The service, atmosphere, breathtaking view (the sixth-floor restaurant overlooks the Seine and Notre Dame) and exemplary wine cellar help keep it among Paris' most exceptional restaurants. Some of the restaurant's exclusive wines and other products can be purchased at the Tour's shop, across the street. *Air conditioning. Book two weeks in advance.Wheelchair access.*

Le Vivarois

192-194 avenue Victor Hugo, 75016 (45.04.04.31). *Métro Rue de la Pompe.* **Open** noon-2pm, 8-9.45pm, Mon-Fri. **Average** 700F. **Menu** 345F (lunch only). **Credit** AmEx, MC, V.

A quieter candidate in Paris's top-flight range of restaurants, this very pleasant place is a real find. The correct, unfailingly friendly service corresponds well to the ingeniously subtle cuisine – if you weren't relaxed, you wouldn't notice how good the food actually is. Among chef Claude Peyrot's signature dishes are red-pepper *bavaroise* in a fresh tomato sauce, lobster ravioli, red mullet on a bed of spinach and

The *élite* **Lucas-Carton**, behind these doors.

Bresse chicken cooked in vinegar. Finish up with the chestnut *parfait* and content yourself with having eaten at one of the Paris' least hyped, and best, first-class restaurants. *Wheelchair access.*

Expensive/Classic

Chiberta

3 rue Arsène-Houssaye, 75008 (45.63.72.44). Métro Charles de Gaulle-Etoile. **Open** noon-2.30pm, 7-10.30pm, Mon-Fri. Closed Aug. **Average** 450F. **Menu** 290F. **Credit** AmEx, DC, EC, JCB, MC, V.

A perennially popular restaurant off the Champs-Elysées, with striking eighties' dark-lacquered décor and beautiful arrangements of flowers. The excellent, modern cuisine is beautifully presented, and owner Louis-Noël Richard and his professional staff give diners a warm welcome.
Air conditioning. Wheelchair access.

Le Grenadin

44 rue de Naples, 75008 (45.63. 28.92). Métro Villiers. **Open** noon-2pm, 7-10pm, Mon-Fri; Oct-Mar only 8-10.30pm Sat. Closed 25 Jan, 14 Jul, 15 Aug. **Menu** 188F, 248F, 298F and 330F. **Credit** AmEx, EC, MC, V.

The menus here change frequently according to market availability, and food is cooked with care and a lightness of touch by owner-chef Patrick Cirotte, who trained with Guy Savoy. Try the *menu confiance* (where you place your trust in the chef's choice) at 330F: the several courses could include marinaded foie gras served with wafer-thin slices of melon, lobster and roast veal. For dessert, *millefeuilles* is a house speciality. Cirotte is from the Berry region, and **Berry's**, his cheaper bistro next door, specialises in regional dishes.
Air conditioning. Tables outdoors.

Le Jules Verne

Second floor, Eiffel Tower, 75007 (45.55.61.44). Métro Bir-Hakeim/RER Champ de Mars. **Open** 12.30-1.30pm, 7.30-9.30pm, daily. **Average** 800F. **Menu** 290F (lunch Mon-Fri only), 660F. **Credit** AmEx, DC, EC, JCB, MC, V.

The superb views from the strangely decorated restaurant in the Eiffel Tower – the general theme seems to be *Star Trek* – and the unequalled romance of its setting has long made the Jules Verne one of the hardest places to book in Paris (it's easier to get in for lunch). Also, chef Alain Reix has a special way with fish and vegetables, and since his arrival the cooking here has matched the heights of its location.
Air conditioning. Book 5-6 weeks in advance for dinner.

Lous Landès

157 avenue de Maine, 75014 (45.43.08.04). Métro Alésia or Mouton Duvernet. **Open** noon-2.30pm, 8-10.30pm, Mon-Fri; 8-10.30pm Sat. **Average** 300F. **Menu** 190F, 300F. **Credit** AmEx, DC, MC, V.

This long-established restaurant has always had a southwestern bent, as the name (from the flat Landes region south of Bordeaux) suggests, but chef Hervé Rumen, who took over here in 1986, has also brought sophisticated and creative skills to the region's classics. Duck, as is traditional, rules the roost, with excellent foie gras, but there's also fine Pyrenees lamb and a renowned cassoulet. If you like chocolate, order the wnderfully rich hot chocolate soufflé ahead at the start of your meal.

L'Oulette

15 place Lachambeaudie, 75012 (40.02.02.12). Métro Dugommier. **Open** noon-2.15pm, 8-10.15pm Mon-Fri; 8-10.15pm Sat. **Average** 250F. **Menu** 150F, 230F. **Credit** AmEx, EC, JCB, MC, V.

Despite a remote location in the redeveloped Bercy district, Marcel Baudis' original food draws a chic crowd who are serious about eating well. The menu features the cooking of his native Quercy, along with innovations all his own. Some find its modern décor a bit cold, but the spacious dining room is light and comfortable, and service discreetly attentive. *Tables outdoors. Wheelchair access.*

Pavillon Montsouris

20 rue Gazan, 75014 (45.88.38.52). RER Cité Universitaire. **Open** 12.15-2pm, 7.30-10pm, daily. **Menu** 255F. **Credit** AmEx, DC, EC, JCB, V.

In a romantic *belle époque* pavilion on the edge of one of Paris' most attractive and least-known parks, the Parc Montsouris, this very pretty restaurant has the distinction of having welcomed both Lenin and Mata Hari in former times. There is only a set menu, of excellent classic dishes.
Book one week in advance. Tables outdoors.

Pierre au Palais Royal

10 rue de Richelieu, 75001 (42.96.09.17). Métro Palais-Royal. **Open** noon-2.30pm, 7.-10pm, Mon-Fri. Closed Aug. **Average** 300F. **Menu** 220F. **Credit** AmEx, DC, MC, V.

Conveniently located just steps from the Palais Royal, Pierre is one of the most reliably satisfying classic bourgeois restaurants in Paris. Tables are generously spaced in the traditionally decorated dining room, and the service is a characteristically French blend of solicitous insouciance. The house foie gras served hot, *boeuf à la ficelle*, stuffed cabbage and game in season are especially good.

Le Récamier

4 rue Récamier, 75007 (42.22.51.75). Métro Sèvres-Babylone. **Open** noon-2.30pm, 7.30-10.30pm Mon-Sat. **Average** 350F **Credit** AmEx, DC, MC, V.

This venerable Burgundian restaurant has one of the best wine cellars in Paris, and attracts a *soignée* crowd of politicians, publishers and editors. On a quiet, pretty cul-de-sac, the terrace is a real midsummer night's dream, and the superb food includes a luscious lobster salad and an outstanding *boeuf bourguignon*.
Air-conditioning. Tables outdoors.Wheelchair access.

La Table d'Anvers

2 place d'Anvers, 75009 (48.78.35.21). Métro Anvers. **Lunch served** noon-2pm Mon-Sat. **Dinner served** 7-10.30pm Mon-Thur, 7-11.30pm Fri, Sat. **Average** 500F. **Menu** 160F, 250F, 340F(lunch Mon-Fri only); 230F (dinner Mon-Thur only) 520F, 680F (dinner Fri, Sat). **Credit** AmEx, EC, JCB, MC, V.

Not the prettiest of restaurants, located in the heart of Pigalle, but the Conticini brothers do prepare some of the most flavourful, interesting food in Paris (with a neat line in theme menus). The pastries are simply fabulous, and there's an unusually good choice for vegetarians.
Air conditioning. Book one week in advance for dinner, two weeks lunch.

Moderate/Bistros

See also **La Tour de Montlhéry** *in chapter* **Nightlife.**

Les Allobroges

71 rue des Grand-Champs, 75020 (43.73.40.00). Métro Maraîchers. **Open** noon-2pm, 7.30-10pm, Tue-Sat. Closed 3 weeks Aug. **Average** 200F. **Menu** 80F, 150F. **Credit** MC, V.

It's a surprise to find such a fashionably-decorated restaurant in an out-of-the-way neighbourhood, but the advantages of a low-rent location are reflected in the outstanding menus of chef Olivier Pateyron. You can feast on langoustines on a bed of ratatouille, lamb braised with garlic and brandied plums as part of the 150F menu. On the 80F menu may feature a confit of tomatoes with green-olive cream, steak with shallots, cheese and dessert. Fine setting for a tête-à-tête.
Booking essential.

Ambassade d'Auvergne

22 rue du Grenier-St-Lazare, 75003 (42.72.31.22).
Métro Rambuteau. **Open** noon-2pm, 7.30-10.30pm, daily.
Closed first 2 weeks Aug. **Average** 250F. **Menu** 160F,
300F. **Credit** AmEx, MC, V.
A family-run Auvergnat restaurant that's comfortably dusty
with age. The rich, hearty cuisine includes cassoulet, *aligot*
(mashed potatoes with Cantal cheese and garlic), and the fine
charcuterie of the region, and there's a good selection of little-
known, local wines.

Auberge Etchegorry

41 rue Croulebarbe, 75013 (44.08.83.51).
Métro Gobelins. **Open** noon-3pm, 7.30-10.30pm Mon-Sat.
Average 275F. **Menu** 130F, 165F. **Credit** AmEx, DC,
EC, MC, V.
One of only a few Basque restaurants in Paris, this cheerful
rustic dining-room offers such classics as peppers stuffed
with cod, *piperade* (scrambled eggs with tomatoes, chorizo
sausage and red and green peppers) sautéed baby squid and
a very good *confit de canard* with garlic potatoes.
Air conditioning. Tables outdoors. Wheelchair access.

Androuët

41 rue d'Amsterdam, 75008 (48.74.26.93). Métro St-
Lazare. **Open** noon-2.30pm, 7.30-10.15pm Mon-Sat.
Average 250F. **Menu** 175F lunch, 95F, 230F, 250F
dinner. **Credit** AmEx, DC, EC, JCB, MC, V.
This Mecca for cheese-lovers above the celebrated shop that
was made famous by the late Pierre Androuët (*see chapter*
Food & Drink) offers a wide variety of cheese platters and
other cheese-based dishes. The original, likeable mock-
Medieval décor has unfortunately been replaced by a strange
departure-lounge look.
Air-conditioning.

Le Bambouche

15 rue de Babylone, 75007 (45.49.14.40). Métro Sèvres-
Babylone. **Open** noon-2.30pm, 8-11pm, Mon-Fri. Closed
Aug. **Average** 230F. **Menu** 180F. **Credit** AmEx, MC, V.
Conventional wisdom has it that the wealthy 7th is an
unmarked reef for innovative restaurateurs – only the most
traditional places are expected to survive. Young chef David
van Laer, however, has so far succeeded in drawing the
locals into this intimate little restaurant with his crowd-
pleasing cuisine. Try the salad of squid and sweet peppers,
or the delicate *bourride*, a Provençal fish soup brimming with
cod, salmon and sea bass, and then try one of his excellent
grills, or, more adventurous, *tête-de-veau*. The wine list is
wisely-priced, and includes some very good buys.

La Baracane

38 rue des Tournelles, 75004 (42.71.43.33). Métro
Bastille. **Open** noon-2.30pm, 7pm-midnight, Mon-Fri, 7-
11pm Sat. **Average** 180F. **Menu** 75F, 120F, 180F.
Credit AmEx, EC, MC, V.
This shop-front space on the Bastille side of the Marais was
the original location of chef Marcel Baudis' elegant
L'Oulette (*see above* **Expensive/Classic**), now in Bercy.
Baudis retained the lease, however, and opened this very
popular place, well above the bistro norm. The menu offers
a limited but interesting choice, with the emphasis on hearty
Gascon cooking – foie gras and various duck dishes.

Au Bascou

38 rue Réaumur, 75003 (42.72.69.25). Métro Arts et
Métiers. **Open** noon-2pm, 8-11pm Mon-Fri; 8-11pm Sat.
Average 170F. **Menu** 85F. **Credit** AmEx, MC, V.
Since it was taken over by Jean-Guy Lousteau, this comfortable bistro has attracted a fashionable young crowd with
its excellent Basque-oriented modern menu and well-priced
southwestern wines. Try the lentil and bacon soup, Basque
country ham, cod with broccoli purée and baby squid.
Tables outdoors.

La Bastide Odéon

7 rue Corneille, 75006 (43.26.03.65). Métro Odéon/RER
Luxembourg. **Open** 12.30-2.15pm, 7.30-11pm Mon-Fri.
Closed first three weeks Aug. **Menu** 175F dinner, 135F
lunch. **Credit** MC, V.
Just across from the Luxembourg gardens, this sunny,
buttery-yellow dining-room with handsome oak tables is one
of the best of the many Provençale restaurants to have
opened recently in Paris. Chef Gilles Ajuelos, formerly at
Michel Rostang (*see above* **Haute Cuisine**), turns out a
superb southern French menu that's particularly strong on
fish. Start with a daily special, or maybe rabbit stuffed with
aubergines, and then try the peppered tuna steak with ratatouille or roast cod with capers. The wine list is pricey.

Le Bistrot d'à Côté
(Chez Raffatin et Honorine)

16 boulevard St-Germain, 75005 (43.54.59.10). Métro
Maubert-Mutualité. **Open** noon-2.30pm, 7.30-11pm, Mon-
Fri; 7.30-11pm Sat. **Menu** 98F lunch, 139F, 178F dinner.
Credit AmEx, EC, JCB, MC, V.
The fourth of chef Michel Rostang's (*see above* **Haute
Cuisine**) several bistros occupies a theatrical space with
white-washed stone walls and turn-of-the-century bric-à-brac
on a quiet stretch of the Left Bank's main drag. The menu
nods at classic Lyonnais cooking, with steaks and wine-
poached sausage, but also offers a good selection of seafood
such as kebabs of breaded mussels, and juicy tuna.
Air-conditioning. Tables outdoors.

Au Bon Accueil

14 rue de Montessuy, 75007 (47.05.46.11) Métro
Champs de Mars. **Open** noon-3pm, 7-10.30pm Mon-Fri, 7-
10.30pm Sat. **Average** 150F. **Credit** MC, V.
Proof that even Hermès shoppers love a bargain is found at
this very popular storefront restaurant, always packed with
well-heeled Parisians feasting on one of the best-value menus
in the city. It changes regularly, but the high-quality *cuisine
du marché* remains constant, with dishes like a terrine of
skate or a salad with St-Marcellin cheese to start, and main
courses like a superb *mignon* of veal in fresh spring vegetables, or perfectly roasted chicken. Also excellent desserts,
and well-chosen, fairly priced wines.
Booking essential. Tables outdoors.

Les Bookinistes

53 quai des Grands-Augustins, 75006 (43.25.45.94).
Métro St Michel. **Open** noon-2.30pm, 7pm-midnight Mon-
Fri, 7pm-midnight Sat. **Average** 200F. **Menu** 160F.
Credit AmEx, MC, V.
The fifth of chef Guy Savoy's successful off-shoot restaurants, in which he shows once again that he's one of the most
innovative restaurateurs in Paris (*see above* **Haute
Cuisine**). Facing the Seine, this cheery post-modern room
is painted peach, with multi-coloured wall sconces. The menu
is similarly light and modish, with such dishes as ravioli
stuffed with chicken and celery, a casserole of guinea fowl
and roasted scallops in watercress and celery juice. Desserts
are also toothsome, and service is great too. Savoy's other
bistros all offer similarly contemporary, inventive food in
chic surroundings, and, while he himself retains a
supervisory role, each has its own resident chef. **La Butte
Chaillot**, near the Trocadéro, is a hip, high-design space
reminiscent of a New York eaterie. It has particularly good
fish, but other dishes are also excellent, and there's a special
quick-lunch menu served at the bar for people in a hurry.
The three **Bistrots de l'Etoile** are smaller, and a little
cheaper. Savoy's most recent departure is a brasserie, the
Cap Vernet (*see below under* **Brasseries**).
Air conditioning.
Branches: Bistrot de l'Etoile 19 rue Lauriston, 75016
(40.67.11.16); 75 avenue Niel, 75017 (42.27.88.44); 13 rue
Troyon, 75017 (42.67.25.95); **La Butte Chaillot** 110 bis
avenue Kléber, 75116 (47.27.88.88).

Les Bouchons de François Clerc

12 rue de l'Hôtel-Colbert, 75005 (43.54.15.34).
Métro Maubert-Mutualité. **Open** noon-2pm, 7-10.30pm,
Mon-Fri; 7-11pm Sat. Closed Aug. **Menu** 215F. **Credit**
AmEx, MC, V..
A fashionable new bistro. It has a reassuringly classic 215F
menu – recent samples have included a starter of blood
sausage and leeks, *gigot de 7 heures* (lamb roasted for seven
hours), and a delicious soufflé with a sauce of spiced wine –
but what has really got people talking is its policy of offering its well-selected wines at cost price, without the usual
large restaurant mark-up. The surroundings are also
pleasant, in an old vaulted wine cellar. It's very popular, so
booking well in advance is advisable for weekends.
Branch: 22 rue de la Terrasse, 75017 (42.27.31.51).

La Cafetière

21 rue Mazarine, 75006 (46.33.76.90). Métro Odéon.
Open 12.30-2.30pm, 7.30-11pm, Mon-Sat. **Average** 230F.
Menu 100F. **Credit** AmEx, EC, MC, V.
One of the best-loved bistros in St-Germain recently changed
hands, but the wonderful collection of enamel cafetières from
which it takes its name remains. The cheery paint job is certainly and improvement, but some regulars are grumbling
about the way the menu has also been modernised. Even so,
it still offers a good terrine or vegetable platter to start – or
in a more generous portion as a main course –, and the sole
and filet of veal can be recommended to follow. The kitchen's
become a bit shakey with the sauces, so you might prefer
yours to be served on the side. Good house wines.
Air-conditioning.

Campagne et Provence

*25 quai de la Tournelle, 75005 (43.54.05.17). Métro
Maubert-Mutualité.* **Open** 12.30-2pm, 8-11pm, Mon-Thur;
8-11pm Fri, Sat. **Average** 200F. **Menu** 99F (lunch only)
Credit AmEx, EC, MC, V.

A very successful modern bistro, offering contemporary food
from Provence and the Riviera. Delicacies include vegetables
stuffed with *brandade* (purée of salt cod and garlic) and
grilled tuna steak served with polenta. The modern décor is
a bit stark, but the restaurant is very popular.
Air-conditioning.

Chez Dumonet/Josephine

*117 rue du Cherche-Midi, 75006 (45.48.52.40). Métro
Duroc.* **Open** noon-2.30pm, 7.15-10.30pm Mon-Fri. Closed
Aug. **Menu** 250F. **Credit** MC, V.
This venerable little bistro with leatherette banquettes and
frosted ceiling lamps offers a classic Parisian ambience,
which is echoed by the kitchen. The classic bistro register,
from *foie gras maison* to *boeuf bourguignon* and roast sad-
dle of lamb with artichokes, is well-prepared, and portions
are very generous, although they've recently (and very sen-
sibly) made it possible to order a half-portion of any dish. It's
very popular with affluent local residents, and the clubby
dining room is also regularly visited by show-biz personalities and politicians. There's an excellent if expensive wine
list, favouring Bordeaux.
Tables outdoors.

La Dinée

85 rue Leblanc, 75015 (45.54.20.49). Métro Balard.
Open noon-2.30pm, 7.30-10pm, Mon-Fri. Closed three
weeks Aug. **Average** 300F. **Menu** 160F (lunch), 260F
(dinner). **Credit** AmEx, MC, V.
Clever and talented young chef Christophe Chabanel has continued to grow in skills and reputation since he opened up
here at the end of 1993. Well off the beaten track, the restaurant is simple and attractive, with comfortable dark-wood
chairs and well-dressed tables. Chabanel offers one of the
most interesting takes on the classic bistro repertoire in
Paris, with dishes like chicken medallions with peppers and
a maize vinaigrette.

The French Regions

French cooking, *per se*, doesn't exist. In reality, the French
kitchen is actually an edible mosaic composed of the country's superb regional cuisines. And there's no better place
to explore all the many varieties than Paris. What's more,
regional food is now highly fashionable in the capital.
Alsace Alsatian food dominates at the city's brasseries.
Choucroute garnie, a platter of Alsatian *charcuterie* on
juniper-berry perfumed sauerkraut, is the best-known
dish, as no brasserie menu would be complete without it.
The Auvergne This region in central France is especially well-represented in Paris, because many *Auvergnats*
are café owners. Specialities are *pounti*, a rich pork loaf
that includes prunes and swiss chard, and *aligot*, a sturdy
dish of mashed potatoes, cheese and garlic. The region
also produces many of France's finest cheeses.
Basque Red peppers are a hallmark of Basque cuisine.
Piperade, scrambled eggs with peppers and tomatoes
topped with thin slices of Bayonne ham, is the classic
starter, while main courses can include tuna with a
basquaise garnish – sautéed peppers, onions, and tomatoes. For dessert, there's *gateau Basque*, a sturdy cake
filled with almond paste.
Burgundy is famous for some of the best *escargots*, *jambon persillé* (terrine of ham) and classic dishes cooked with
wine such as *boeuf bourguignon* and *coq au vin*.
Lyonnais cooking also features at a variety of Parisian
outposts. A highlight to try are *les saladiers Lyonnais*, the
assorted salads and cold plates that characteristically

begin a meal. Main courses range from *quenelles*, pike
dumplings, to local *andouillettes* (tripe sausages), and for
dessert, *cervelle de canut*, literally 'silkworker's brain', a
soft, creamy fresh cheese spiked with fresh herbs.
Normandy has a richly varied cuisine, often featuring
cider and Calvados (apple brandy). Starters may include
a salad of duck livers in cider vinegar or slabs of duck foie
gras, while main courses run to tripe with cider and veal
sweetbreads *à la Normande*, with cream and Calvados.
Camembert and Livarot star on the cheese tray.
Provençal Most people think of sun-dried tomatoes, olive
oil and garlic when they think of Provençal cooking, currently the most fashionable of all the regional cuisines. But,
beyond *ratatouille* or *bouillabaise*, dishes to try include *petit
farcis à la brandade*, baby vegetables stuffed with a garlic-
spiked purée of dried cod; *anchoiade*, a sauce of anchovies,
garlic and olive oil, often with raw vegetables for dipping;
and *soupe au pistou*, a sturdy vegetable-and-bean soup garnished with *pistou* (pesto) sauce. Beyond lamb, common
meat dishes are *daube de boeuf*, a beef stew with red wine,
onions and tomatoes, and *estouffade à la provençale*, with
beef, carrots, onions and orange zest.
The South-West If one feature dominates South
Western menus, it's *canard* (duck). Start with *salade
Quercynoise*, greens tossed with preserved duck gizzards,
and then go on to *confit de canard*, or potted duck.
Cabecous de Rocamadour, small discs of goat cheese,
make a perfect closing course.

L'Epi Dupin

11 rue Dupin, 75006 (42.22.64.56). Métro Sèvres-Babylone. **Open** noon-3pm, 7.30-10.30pm, Mon-Fri; 7.30-10.30pm Sat. **Menu** 95F (lunch only), 150F. **Credit** MC, V.
A charming, recently-opened Left Bank bistro with excellent food at very fair prices. Highlights have been a generous *salade folle* or a well-seasoned mixed green salad garnished with delicious foie gras, as starters, and then, as main courses, a tender *filet* of lamb with a huge side order of deliciously ruddy ratatouille, or a hearty filo pastry packet of oxtail accompanied by polenta. The delicious bread is made on the premises, as are all of the desserts, which change daily. Nice wine list, too.

L'Escargot Montorgueil

38 rue de Montorgueil, 75001 (42.36.83.51). Métro Châtelet-Les Halles. **Open** noon-2.30pm, 7.30-10.45pm Mon-Sat. **Average** 250F. **Menu** 140F lunch, 180F dinner. **Credit** AmEx, DC, EC, JCB, MC, V.
Supposedly, the first restaurant in Paris to serve snails. They're still a speciality, prepared in many different ways. The original 1830s-period décor is magnificent, and the chef's traditional cuisine is executed with originality.
Tables outdoors.

Les Fernandises

17-18 rue de la Fontaine au Roi, 75011 (43.57.46.25/48.06.16.96). Métro République. **Open** noon-2pm, 7.30-11pm, Tue-Sat. Closed Aug. **Average** 200F. **Menu** 100F lunch, 130F dinner. **Credit** MC, V.
A cosy, popular, family-run bistro with a wood-beamed interior which echoes the excellent, good-value Norman cooking. Highlights from the cuisine of chef-patron Fernand Asseline include scallops in cream and cider, roast lamb with garlic cream and a fine selection of cheeses. For an authentic Norman experience, try the cider instead of wine to accompany your meal.

Le Louis XIV

1 bis place des Victoires, 75001 (40.26.20.81). Métro Palais Royal. **Open** noon-2.30pm, 7.30-10.30pm, Mon-Fri. Closed Aug. **Average** 250F. **Menu** 175F, 230F. **Credit** AmEx, EC, MC, V.
The pavement tables of this venerable Lyonnais bistro are a fine perch from which to watch the comings and goings of the fashionable flora frequenting the smart boutiques round the *place*, a monument to the Sun King himself. Start with *fromage blanc* showered with herbs or *rosette de Lyon*, a well-seasoned sausage, and then try the poached turbot with hollandaise sauce. A beautifully crumbly shortbread with fresh strawberries is a good way to end the meal.
Tables outdoors.

Aux Lyonnais

32 rue St-Marc, 75002 (42.96.65.04). Métro Bourse. **Open** noon-2.30pm, 7pm-midnight, Mon-Fri; 7pm-midnight Sat. **Average** 150F. **Credit** AmEx, DC, EC, JCB, MC, V.
A beautiful art nouveau tiled interior and friendly service are the perfect complement to excellent renditions of Lyonnais classics, including salad with *lardons* (bacon strips) and poached egg and tripe. Good grills are served, too. Bursting with stock-market types at midday, this quintessential bistro is quieter in the evening.

Ma Bourgogne

19 place des Vosges, 75004 Paris (42.78.44.64). Métro St-Paul. **Open** 8am-1am daily. **Average** 220F. Closed 1 Feb-8 Mar. **Menu** 180F. **No credit cards.**
An unpretentious, busy bistro with tables spilling out under the arcades of the place des Vosges. There's simple banquette seating, a painted ceiling and cod-medieval chandeliers, and salads, steaks and strongly-flavoured Burgundian specialities on the menu.

Le Maraîcher

5 rue Beautreillis, 75004 (42.71.42.49). Métro Sully Morland. **Open** noon-2pm, Tue-Fri; 8-11pm Mon, Sat. Closed Aug. **Average** 220F. **Menu** 120F (lunch only), 175F, 295F. **Credit** EC, MC, V.
An intimate little place in the Marais, with wooden beams, exposed stone walls and considerable charm. The sophisticated modern French cuisine is based on whatever's best at the market each day, and might include warm artichoke salad, or scallop ravioli. It's very popular, and both the food and service can suffer on busy nights.

Moissonnier

28 rue des Fossés-St-Bernard, 75005 (43.29.87.65). Métro Jussieu or Cardinal Lemoine. **Open** noon-2pm, 7-10pm, Tue-Sat; noon-2pm, Sun. Closed Aug. **Average** 200F. **Credit** EC, MC, V.
A friendly 30-year-old bistro that's a perennial Left Bank favourite. Still family-run, it serves good food with Lyonnaise overtones, especially the traditional *saladiers Lyonnais* – a large assortment of hors d'oeuvres to which you help yourself.

La Niçoise

4 rue Pierre Demours, 75017 (45.74.42.41). Métro Ternes. **Open** 12.15-2.30pm, 7.30-11pm, Mon-Fri; 7.30-11pm Sat Closed Sat evenings in July or Aug. **Average** 200F. **Credit** AmEx, DC, EC, JCB, MC, V.
As the name suggests, the speciality is the cuisine of Nice, and you'll find here an interesting assortment of the sunny, herby dishes of the south of France. It's small, and filled with Tiffany glass and posters of the Côte d'Azur.

L'Os à Moëlle

3 rue Vasco-de-Gama, 75015 (45.57.27.27). Métro Balard. **Open** noon-2pm, 7.30-11pm, Tue-Sat. Closed Aug. **Menu** 140F lunch, 180F dinner. **Credit** MC, V.
There's a single *prix-fixe* evening menu at this very popular local bistro; it's usually very good, with all of six courses – perhaps white-bean soup, terrine of calf's head, scallops in orange sauce, quail, Tomme cheese with salad and a choice of desserts – in generous portions. The drawback is, that if there happens to be anything on the menu you dislike, there's no other choice. There are also good wines, at 70F a bottle. A simpler menu is available at lunchtime.
Booking essential for dinner. Tables outdoors. Wheelchair access.

Le Perroquet Vert

7 rue Cavallotti, 75018 (45.22.49.16). Métro Place de Clichy. **Open** noon-2.30pm, 7-10.30pm, Mon-Fri. Closed first three weeks Aug. **Average** 200F. **Menu** 98F lunch, 148F dinner. **Credit** MC, V.
A tiny, friendly place where the owner himself buys the produce in the market daily, hence the appealing freshness of the homey, traditional cooking. The menus are very good value, and you might start with a salad or pâté, followed by grilled salmon or chicken in cream sauce, concluding with a homemade fruit tart. Small but judiciously chosen wine list.
Tables outdoors.

Le Petit Rétro

5 rue Mesnil, 75016 (44.05.06.05). Métro Victor Hugo. **Open** 8-10.30pm Mon; noon-2.30pm, 8-10.30pm, Tue-Sat, Closed Aug. **Average** 160F. **Credit** MC, V.
A sincere greeting welcomes you into this small, spotless room with dark wood tables and beautiful art-nouveau wall tiling. The food's equally straightforward, totally traditional but absolutely delicious, as in a perfect *pavé de boeuf* in a ruddy sauce flanked by dauphinois potatoes and a fat, slightly caramelised braised endive. At noon contentedly self-important businessmen come to lunch here, while the evening sees an eclectic mix of local diners. Good wine list.
Wheelchair access.

Le Petit Zinc

11 rue St-Benoît, 75006 (42.61.20.60). Métro St-Germain-des-Prés. **Open** noon-1.30am daily. **Average** 220F. **Menu** 165F. **Credit** AmEx, DC, EC, JCB, MC, V.
A perennially popular St-Germain bistro with an art-nouveau look, and the same owners as the **Muniche** next door (*see below* **Brasseries**). It's often crowded, but remains spacious and airy. Good quality for the price, given the area. *Air-conditioning. Tables outdoors.*

Pharamond

24 rue de la Grande-Truanderie, 75001. (42.33.06.72). Métro Châtelet-Les Halles. **Open** 7.30-10.30pm; noon-2.30pm, 7.30-10.30pm, Tue-Sat. Closed 25 Dec, 1 Jan. **Average** 250F. **Menu** (lunch only) 180F, 250F. **Credit** AmEx, DC, EC, MC, V.
Prices have been rising at this grand, old-fashioned, landmark of a bistro near Les Halles, renowned for its ornate décor and gorgeous art nouveau tiles. The lunch menus, though, are still good value. Look out for Normandy specialities such as *tripes à la mode de Caen* and *andouillettes.* *Air conditioning first floor. Tables outdoors.*

La Régalade

49 avenue Jean-Moulin, 75014 (45.45.68.58). Métro Alésia. **Open** noon-2pm, 7pm-midnight, Tue-Fri; 7pm-midnight Sat. Closed 15 Jul-15 Aug. **Average** 190F. **Menu** 160F. **Credit** V.
The 160F menu here is one of the best deals in Paris, so this small, simple bistro in a residential district is always full. Chef Yves Camdeborde was second chef at the Hôtel Crillon, and his pedigree shows in dishes like his gratin of lobster and potatoes. The menu changes seasonally. Booking is essential, often three weeks in advance for dinner.

Le Relais du Parc

Hôtel Le Parc, 57 avenue Raymond-Poincaré, 75116 (44.05.66.66). Métro Trocadéro. **Open** 12.30-2.30pm, 7.30-10.30pm, daily. **Average** 300F. **Credit** AmEx, DC, EC, JCB, MC, V.
This casually chic bistro, overlooking a garden-courtyard, is one of the most popular and successful star-chef annexes in Paris. Current first chef of France **Joël Robuchon** (*see above* **Haute Cuisine**) set up the menu and the kitchens, and so this is a good opportunity to sample his cooking style ~~a~~matically lower prices than you'll find at his main ~~restau~~rant. The menu features simple but delicious dishes such as chicken leg stuffed with cabbage and foie gras, and excellent individual apple tarts. Reserve for the terrace. *Air-conditioning. Tables outdoors. Wheelchair access.*

Le Restaurant

32 rue Véron, 75018 (42.23.36.16). Métro Abbesses. **Open** 8-11pm Mon; noon-2.30pm, 8-11pm, Tue-Fri; 8-11pm Sat. **Average** 250F. **Menu** 70F lunch, 120F dinner. **Credit** AmEx, MC, V.
This simply-decorated place just off rue Lepic in Montmartre has become very popular with the creative types who still inhabit the neighbourhood. The talented young chef has worked in some of the best places in town, and his cooking is fresh and original: omelette soufflé with oysters, or lamb with fennel and black olive purée are two examples. *Air-conditioning.*

La Rôtisserie d'en Face

2 rue Christine, 75006 (43.26.40.98). Métro Odéon. **Open** noon-2.30pm, 7pm-midnight, Mon-Fri, Sun; 7-11pm Sat. Closed one week Aug. **Average** 210F. **Menu** 159F lunch. **Credit** AmEx, EC, MC, V.
A bistro-annex that's one of the most popular places in Paris: a large, homely but stylish place with a tiled floor and flowered curtains. The set menu is a bargain, compared to prices in the original, elegant restaurant of proprietor Jacques Cagna across the street (*see above* **Haute Cuisine**). Much

of the food is cooked on a rôtisserie. Try the artichoke heart salad, the spit-roasted lamb, chicken or beef and the good desserts, and note that the cheaper wines are just fine. Cagna's other rôtisseries follow a similar formula, and have been equally successful with a stylish, young crowd. *Air-conditioning.*
Branch: Rotisserie d'Armaillé 6 rue d'Armaille, 75017 (42.27.19.20); **Rôtisserie Monsigny** 1 rue Monsigny, 75002 (42.96.16.61).

Royal Madeleine

11 rue Richepance, 75008 (42.60.14.36). Métro Madeleine. **Open** noon-3pm, 6.30-10pm, Mon-Sat. **Average** 200F. **Menu** 150F, 110F. **Credit** AmEx, DC, EC, MC, V.
A homely spot – the walls are decorated with old newspapers, pewter spoons and antique scales – run by the same owners since 1943. It offers a solid gallic feed noon and night, which is why reservations are essential. In season, their oysters are excellent, but vegetable soup is also good. Follow these sturdy starters with scallops grilled on skewers, steak or the *plat du jour*, hopefully a garlicky beef stew or *brandade au morue*, purée of dried cod with milk and garlic. *Air conditioning. Tables outdoors. Wheelchair access.*

Au Trou Gascon

40 rue Taine, 75012 (43.44.34.26). Métro Daumesnil. **Open** noon-2pm, 7.30-10pm, Mon-Fri. Closed Aug. **Average** 350F. **Menu** 180F lunch, 200F, 380F *dégustation*, 280F dinner. **Credit** AmEx, DC, EC, JCB, MC, V.
This charming *belle époque* bistro in an out-of-the-way area is a popular favourite, and boasts a Michelin star. Chef-owner Alain Dutournier made his name here, but is currently more involved with **Le Carré des Feuillants** (*see above* **Haute Cuisine**), and this restaurant is now managed by his wife Nicole. They manage to find the best classic ingredients of south-western France, and serve them in original ways. Much less grand than its cousin, Au Trou Gascon is closer to the heart and to the price range of most. *Air-conditioning.*

Brasseries

Many brasseries also open very late, or through the night; for a selection, *see chapter* **Nightlife**.

Le Balzar

49 rue des Ecoles, 75005 (43.54.13.67). Métro Cluny-La Sorbonne. **Open** noon-1am daily. Closed Aug. **Average** 250F. **Credit** AmEx, EC, MC, V.
This unpretentious, very authentic brasserie is a Latin Quarter fixture. A noisy mix of students, chic arty types and tourists crowd together, enjoying simple brasserie classics such as *choucroute* (sauerkraut with pork), skate with black butter and an excellent *gigot d'agneau.*

Bofinger

5 rue de la Bastille, 75004 (42.72.87.82). Métro Bastille. **Open** noon-3pm, 6.30pm-1am, Mon-Fri; noon-1am Sat, Sun. **Average** 250F. **Menu** 169F, incl half bottle wine. **Credit** AmEx, DC, EC, MC, V.
The Bofinger claims to be the oldest brasserie in Paris, and its art nouveau décor certainly makes it one of the most beautiful. The menu is a standard list of shellfish, *choucroute* and so on. Try and sit on the ground floor under the wonderful dome – reserve a few days in advance, as no bookings are taken after 8pm. There is a bistro offshoot across the street. *Tables outdoors.*

*The art nouveau magnificence of **Julien**.*
See page 149.

Brasserie Flo

7 cour des Petites Ecuries, 75010 (47.70.13.59). Métro Château d'Eau. **Open** noon-3pm, 7pm-1.30am, daily. Closed 24 Dec. **Average** 250F. **Menu** 109F (lunch Mon-Fri and from 10pm, *'faim de nuit'*) 185F incl bottle of wine. **Credit** AmEx, DC, EC, MC, FTC, V.

Down an atmospheric, if seedy, cobbled alleyway, Flo is an authentic 1886 brasserie with a warm, jovial Alsatian ambience, and superb oysters and other shellfish, that continues to attract celebrities, tourist and all kinds of other folk. Owner Jean-Paul Bucher has also acquired several other classic brasseries (among them **La Coupole** and **Julien**, *see below*), and a similarly traditional menu is available at all of them. Alsatian wines can be ordered by the jug. *Wheelchair access.*

Brasserie de l'Ile St-Louis

55 quai de Bourbon, 75004 (43.54.02.59). Métro Pont-Marie. **Open** 11.30-1.30am Mon, Tue, Fri-Sun; 6pm-1am Thur; closed Aug. **Average** 150F. **No credit cards.**

There hasn't been any hasty modernisation at this brasserie, tucked away on the Ile St-Louis. It's popular with ex-pats (the patron is something of an anglophile) as well as an eclectic mix of locals, and the lively atmosphere makes up for the rather ordinary food – *choucroute*, cassoulet and, of course, ice-creams and sorbets from nearby Berthillon (*see chapter* **Food & Drink**). Less expensive than many brasseries. *Tables outdoors.*

La Brasserie Wepler

14 place de Clichy, 75018 (45.22.53.29). Métro Place de Clichy. **Open** 11am-1am daily. **Average** 250F. **Menu** 150F. **Credit** AmEx, DC, EC, JCB, MC, V.

A classic, bustling brasserie on the place de Clichy, once a favourite of Henry Miller and other Montmartre denizens. Fine shellfish and good value, if you can put up with the overdone décor, noise and hurried, often brusque service. *Tables outdoors.*

Cap Vernet

82 avenue Marceau, 75008 (47.20.20.40) Métro Etoile. **Open** noon-3pm, 7.30pm-midnight, daily. **Average** 200F, 100F lunch. **Credit** AmEx, MC, V.

After planting a string of bistros around the city, such as **Les Bookinistes** (*see above under* **Moderate/Bistros**), dynamic restaurateur Guy Savoy has successfully blown the dust off the brasserie format by introducing a well-priced menu at this attractive place near the Arc de Triomphe. If seafood stars on the menu – the rocket and smoked tuna salad is excellent, and they do fine trays of shellfish – the grills are good, too, and are accompanied by an appealing choice of side dishes. Light meals, such as open sandwiches or a basket of charcuterie, are served at all times, and baked-on-the-premises desserts are on offer for afternoon tea. *Booking advisable. Tables outdoors.*

La Coupole

102 boulevard Montparnasse, 75014 (43.20.14.20). Métro Vavin or Montparnasse Bienvenüe. **Open** 7.30am-2am daily. Closed 24 Dec. **Average** 250F. **Menu** 109F Mon-Fri (*'faim de nuit '* after 10pm), 87F. **Credit** AmEx, DC, EC, JCB, MC, V.

Almost a synonym for the word 'brasserie', this vast art deco establishment, opened 1927, is a Parisian monument. Over the years it's been patronised by an endless list of great names in Parisian and world culture, and today, after nearly seventy years, it still attracts movers and shakers in media, fashion and the movies. It has also taken on a new lease of life since it was extensively – some would say sacrilegiously

Chez Paul *is a Bastille favourite, for good food and atmosphere. See page 157.*

– renovated a few years ago by new owner, brasserie-magnate Jean-Paul Bucher (also of the **Brasserie Flo**, *see above*). The Coupole has the largest shellfish stand in Paris, and a lengthy menu of typical brasserie fare. The service can be maddening, and the food disappointing, but many come here as much to watch the crowds and enjoy the bustle in the vast space as they do to eat. *Tables outdoors.*

Le Grand Colbert

2 rue Vivienne, 75002 (42.86.87.88). Métro Bourse. **Open** noon-1am daily. Closed Aug. **Average** 200F. **Menu** 155F. **Credit** AmEx, DC, EC, MC, V.

You can enter this long, pretty brasserie from either the restored Passage Colbert or the rue Vivienne. The ornate, recently-restored décor, some of it from the 1830s, is impressive, and it's busy with a post-theatre crowd late at night. A classic brasserie menu, with a few unusual specialites. *Air-conditioning. Tables in Galerie Colbert.*

Julien

16 rue du Faubourg St-Denis, 75010 (47.70.12.06). Métro Strasbourg St-Denis. **Open** noon-3pm, 7pm-1.30am, daily. Closed 25 Dec. **Average** 200F. **Menu** 109F. **Credit** AmEx, DC, EC, JCB, MC, V.

Although in the heart of the red-light district, this genuine art nouveau brasserie is a perennially fashionable place to eat, and always packed. Its dazzling décor is a combination of polished wood, mirrors and superb stained glass panels. Now part of the **Flo** group (*see above* **Brasserie Flo**), it shares the familiar menu of other Bucher-owned establishments, but without the shellfish stand.

Le Muniche

7 rue St Benoît, 75006 (42.61.12.70). Métro St-Germain-des-Prés. **Open** noon-2am daily. **Average** 250F. **Menu** 125F Mon-Fri, 90F, 148F, Sat, Sun. **Credit** AmEx, DC, EC, JCB, MC, V.

A Left Bank stalwart, part of a St-Germain group that also owns **Le Petit Zinc** (*see above* **Moderate/Bistros**) and the **Layrac** *traiteur* (*see chapter* **Food & Drink**) nearby, with understated décor but truly excellent food. Superb *moules marinière*, smoked salmon and roast lamb. *Tables outdoors.*

Restaurant Marty

20 avenue des Gobelins, 75005 (43.31.39.51). Métro Gobelins. **Open** noon-2.30pm, 7-10.30pm, daily. **Average** 200F. **Menu** 185F. **Credit** AmEx, DC, MC, V.

Marty dubs itself 'the thirties' brasserie', and with its polished woodwork, stained-glass lights and old-fashioned service, it hasn't changed much since then. Little-known by visitors to Paris, it's a tranquil place to come for good classic French cooking. The 185F menu is very generous, since, unusually, most of the regular *carte* is included. Dishes vary with the season, but oysters, delicious *aiguillettes de canard* (thin slices of duck breast) in green peppercorn sauce and a *fondant de chocolat* for dessert can all be recommended. *Tables outdoors. Wheelchair access.*

Le Suffren

84 avenue de Suffren, 75015 (45.66.97.86). Métro La Motte Picquet-Grenelle. **Open** 7am-midnight daily. **Average** 150F **Menu** 102F, 169F. **Credit** MC, V.

This bustling, very popular place is a fine example of that regrettably increasingly rare species, the independent neighbourhood brasserie. As well as a full menu of shellfish, fish and grills, they also offer two extremely good-value menus both of which include a carafe of wine. Try the marinated herring and roast chicken or mussels from the cheaper menu, and smoked salmon and grilled *langouste* from the pricier. *Tables outdoors.*

The Frog & Rosbif

HONI SOIT QUI PEU Y BOIT

At Paris' only English Pub, we brew a range of traditional Real Ales.
Choose from our weekly menu of hot and cold home-cooked Pub Grub.
Brewery visits welcome.
OPEN EVERY DAY, 11am-2am

THE PARIS REAL ALE BREWERY
TEL: 42 36 34 73
116, Rue Saint-Denis, 75002 Paris
Metro: Etienne Marcel/Les Halles/Réaumur-Sébastopol

Vaudeville *provides an ornate backdrop for Bourse-employees' lunches.*

La Taverne Kronenbourg
24 boulevard des Italiens, 75009 (47.70.16.64).
Métro Opéra. **Open** 11am-1am daily. **Average** 170F.
Credit AmEx, DC, EC, MC, V.
Near the Opéra, this big, rustic-style brasserie is a fine example of the genre. A pianist plays there each evening, and it's a good place for fine shellfish and hearty Alsatian favourites. *Tables outdoors. Wheelchair access.*

Vaudeville
29 rue Vivienne, 75002 (40.20.04.62). Métro Bourse.
Open noon-3.30pm, 7pm-2am, daily.
Average 250F. **Menu** 109F lunch and after 10pm Mon-Fri, 185F dinner. **Credit** AmEx, DC, JCB, MC, V.
An animated brasserie in the **Flo** group (*see above*) opposite the Bourse. Similar menu to other Bucher brasseries – fine shellfish, excellent smoked salmon and foie gras, *plats du jour* and a large dessert selection – and classic brasserie décor – marble and mirrored furnishings, and art deco lamps. *Tables outdoors.*

Fish & Seafood

Le Bar à Huîtres
33 rue St-Jacques, 75005 (44.07.27.37). Métro St Michel or Maubert-Mutualité. **Open** noon-2am daily. **Average** 220F. **Menu** 128F, 198F. **Credit** AmEx, MC, V.
As the name suggests, the speciality is oysters, but this trio of seafood bar-restaurants also offers good fish and other shellfish. Centrepiece of the 198F menu is always lobster. *Tables outdoors.*
Branches: 33 boulevard Beaumarchais, 75003 (48.87.98.92); 112 boulevard Montparnasse, 75014 (43.20.71.01).

Charlot Roi des Coquillages
12 place de Clichy, 75009 (48.74.49.64). Métro Place de Clichy. **Open** noon-3pm, 7pm-1am, daily. Closed 24 Dec. **Average** 300F. **Menu** (lunch only) 250F, 355F (incl wine). **Credit** AmEx, DC, EC, JCB, MC, V.

Renovation in the last few years has dusted off the original thirties' décor at this bustling institution, the original Clichy oyster bar. The food has improved, too; specialities include *bouillabaisse* and, of course, copious shellfish platters. *Tables outdoors.*

Le Divellec
107 rue de l'Université, 75007 (45.51.91.96).
Métro Invalides. **Open** noon-1.30pm, 7.30-10pm, Mon-Sat. **Average** 650F. **Menu** (lunch only) 270F, 370F. **Credit** AmEx, DC, EC, JCB, MC, V.
Considered by many the best fish restaurant in Paris, with a very elegant clientele. Chef Jacques Le Divellec, from coastal Brittany, is a master at bringing out the true flavour of simply prepared fish. Particularly fine are his squid dishes, in their own ink or with a range of sauces.
Book well in advance.

Le Dôme
108 boulevard du Montparnasse, 75014 (43.35.25.81). Métro Vavin. **Open** noon-3pm, 7pm-12.45am, Tue-Sun. Closed Aug. **Average** 350F. **Credit** AmEx, DC, EC, MC, V.
The elegant Slavik-designed décor here is unstuffy because it's slightly self-mocking, and this is the key to the Dôme, like **La Coupole** (*see above* **Brasseries**) a great institution on the boulevard Montparnasse – it strives for perfection but is never stuffy about it. The oysters and other shellfish are superb, the fish, including an especially good grilled sole, is of the finest quality, and service is impeccable. Expensive, but worth it. It has two simpler bistro offshoots, with similar quality of fish, but simpler preparations and lower prices.
Air-conditioning. Tables outdoors.
Branches: Le Bistro du Dôme 2 rue de la Bastille, 75004 (48.04.88.44); 1 rue Delambre, 75014 (43.35.32.00).

Gaya Rive Gauche
44 rue du Bac, 75007 (45.44.73.73) Métro Rue du Bac.
Open noon-2.30pm, 7-11pm Mon-Sat. Closed Aug.
Average 260F. **Credit** AmEx, EC, MC, V.
The new Left Bank outpost of this excellent seafood house has a breezy modern décor with a yachting theme. The catch-

Drinks Food Live Music

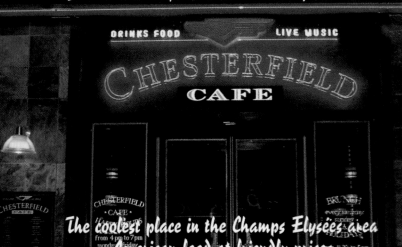

DRINKS FOOD • LIVE MUSIC

CHESTERFIELD
CAFE

The coolest place in the Champs Elysées area
American food at friendly prices
Great cocktail and fun atmosphere

LUNCH
Original american specials of the day
from 60 Frs

HAPPY HOUR
Try our great drinks
Every day from
4 p. m. to 8 p. m.
(Except saturday and sunday)
Cocktails 18 Frs Beers 8,50 Frs

New
After the band you
can party until
dawn We're open now till
5 in the morning

THE BEST LIVE MUSIC IN TOWN (no charge)
American Rock and Blues Band
from tuesday to saturday at 11.30 p. m.

COMING SOON
Omar and the Howlers. Dag .Dillon
Fence . Jan Moore . War . Ass Ponys
. Chris Duarte .Sue Foley . Gin Blossoms . Mary Lou Brandon .

by
JACQUES VABRE

Chesterfield Café
124 rue la Boetie PARIS 8e 42 25 18 06

Coffee-pot collectors will get added enjoyment at **La Cafetière**. *See page 144.*

of-the-day is impeccably fresh. All of the classic fish dishes are superb, but you can eat less expensively, and just as well, if you stick with daily specials like a *friture*, a mixed deep-fry of tiny fish, and a sautée of red mullet. Good simple desserts, and an amiable wine list. Its sister restaurant offers similar fare, near the Madeleine.

Branch: Gaya 17 rue Duphot, 75001 (42.60.43.03).

La Marée
1 rue Dauval, 75008 (43.80.20.00). Métro Ternes. **Open** noon-2.30pm, 8-10.30pm, Mon-Fri. Closed Aug. **Average** 450F. **Credit** AmEx, DC, EC, JCB, MC, V.

The menu at this venerable and elegant fish restaurant has been successfully modernised – out have gone the sauces, to be replaced with a contemporary preference for simply prepared seafood. It's now one of the best in Paris.

Paul Minchelli
54 boulevard de La Tour-Maubourg, 75007 (47.05.89.86). Métro La Tour-Maubourg or Invalides. **Open** noon-2.30pm, 8-11pm Tues-Sat. **Average** 400F. **Credit** MC, V.

Paul Minchelli, a gifted fish cook formerly at the very pricey Le Duc, has set up on his own in the former premises of one of the most enduring bourgeois restaurants in Paris, Chez les Anges. The results are refreshingly contemporary, but local blue-bloods are still comfortable bringing *grand-mère* here for lunch. Minchelli understands his clientèle too, which is why he sends out reassuring but impeccable classics like baby clams with thyme, and orange-perfumed lobster.
Wheelchair access.

L'Ostréa
4 rue Sauval, 75001 (40.26.08.07) Métro Louvre. **Open** noon-2.30pm, 7.30-11.30pm, Mon-Fri; 7.30-11.30pm Sat. **Average** 150F. **Menu** 85F lunch, 135F dinner. **Credit** MC, V.

A tiny restaurant with an aquarium filled with lobsters dividing the kitchen from the dining-room. One of the best

seafood buys in Paris, the 135F menu offers a generous serving of prawn and vegetable salad, oysters or stuffed clams followed by delicious sea bass cooked in Ricard, or a huge tuna steak garnished with capers and fried parsley or *rougets*. Excellent wines and homemade desserts too, and the only reproach to be made is that service can sometimes be painfully slow.

Port Alma
10 avenue de New York, 75116 (47.23.75.11). Métro Alma-Marceau. **Open** 12.30-2.30pm, 7.30-10.30pm, Mon-Sat. Closed Aug. **Average** 350F. **Menu** 200F (lunch only). **Credit** AmEx, DC, EC, MC, V.

One of the best fish restaurants in Paris, and certainly the best value. Chef-patron Paul Canal's contacts in the Channel fishing ports guarantee the freshest possible supplies, even on Mondays. Sea bass baked in a crust of salt is but one of his exceptional dishes, and any meal in this bright dining room with a view over the Seine is a special occasion.
Wheelchair access.

Prunier
16 avenue Victor Hugo, 75016 (44.17.35.85) Métro Etoile. **Open** noon-2pm, 7-10.30pm, Tue-Sat. Closed 15 Jul-15 Aug. **Average** 450F. **Credit** AmEx, DC, EC, MC, V.

Long one of the most glamorous restaurants in Paris, the Prunier, vintage 1925 but closed since 1989, has now reopened after renovation of its art-deco mosaics, dining room and kitchens. Its marble counters now brim again with an irresistible selection of shellfish, while the menu has been renewed by director Jean-Claude Vrinat, of Taillevent (*see above* **Haute Cuisine**). Avoiding trendiness, it still reflects a contemporary take on classic French seafood cooking. Start with a *Saintongeaise* plate, oysters with sausages as eaten in Bordeaux, or a scallop salad, and then try langoustines or a classic like Turbot in hollandaise sauce. The well-balanced wine list reflects the excellent offering at Taillevent.
Wheelchair access.

Budget

For tips on finding affordable meals, *see below* **That Good Cheap Meal**.

Astier

44 rue Jean-Pierre Timbaud, 75011 (43.57.16.35). Métro Parmentier. **Open** noon-2pm, 8-11pm, Mon-Fri. Closed end Apr-early May, Christmas-New Year, Aug. **Average** 150F. **Menu** 130F (dinner only). **Credit** MC, V.
An excellent old-fashioned bistro that's always packed. There's little in the way of decoration, but you'll love what you find on your plate, including many earthy French classics. Wines are fairly priced too.

Au Pied de Fouet

45 rue de Babylone, 75007 (47.05.12.27). Métro Vaneau. **Open** noon-2.30pm, 7-9.30pm, Mon-Fri; noon-2pm Sat;. **Closed** Aug, Christmas-New Year. **Average** 80F. **No credit cards**.
This tiny, crowded local restaurant (it seats about 16 people), mid-way between St-Germain des Prés and the more affluent Faubourg to the west, is popular with students and anyone on a tight budget. Plan on a quick meal of solid dishes, such as stews and other long-simmering recipes. Décor and service are on the minimal side, but then so is the bill. It's also non-smoking.

Bistrot d'André

232 rue St-Charles, 75015 (45.57.89.14) Métro Balard. **Open** noon-2.30pm, 7.30-10.30pm Mon-Sat; noon-2.30pm Sun. **Average** 130F. **Menu** 52F (lunch Mon-Fri only). **Credit** MC, V.
Once more or less a canteen for workers at the enormous, now shutdown Citroën factory next door, this tiny, crowded place still retains a characteristic bonhomie. Try their standards such as the roast chicken with sautéed potatoes, and the delicious cheesecake. *Tables outdoors.*

Bistro Mazarin

42 rue Mazarine, 75006 (43.29.99.01) Métro Odéon. **Open** noon-3.30pm, 7.15pm-midnight, Mon-Sat; 1-4pm, 7-11pm, Sun. **Average** 110F. **Credit** AmEx, EC, MC, V.
A convivial atmosphere, a spacious terrace and low prices combine here to create a pleasant, provincial feel. Simple, satisfying dishes are served, such as hot goat's cheese on toast with salad, lentil salad with big slices of *Morteau* sausage and a veal chop sautéed with lemon. Good house wines. *Tables outdoors.*

Le Brin de Zinc et Madame

50 rue Montorgueil, 75002 (42.21.10.80). Métro Châtelet-Les Halles. **Open** noon-2.30pm, 7.30pm-1.30pm, Mon-Sat. **Average** 160F. **Credit** EC, MC, V.
On the busy market street of rue Montorgueil, this little bistro is a real find, attracting a mix of regulars and shoppers. There's an old zinc bar at the front, and fewer than a dozen tables behind, one of which is covered with the wonderful fruit tarts made by Patrice the young owner/chef. Service can be a bit slow, but then, it's best not to hurry. *No reservations. Tables outdoors.*

Café du Commerce

51 rue du Commerce, 75015 (45.75.03.27). Métro Emile Zola. **Open** noon-midnight daily. **Average** 110F. **Menu** 85F, 110F. **Credit** AmEx, DC, EC, MC, V.
Prices have gone up a little since this multi-storey place opened in the twenties to feed local workers. Once affiliated with **Chartier**, its image has been greatly upgraded, but the quality-price ratio is still excellent. The courtyard terrace, on several levels, makes it a fine choice on a sunny day. *Tables outdoors.*

Chartier

7 rue du Faubourg Montmartre, 75009 (47.70.86.29). Métro Rue Montmartre. **Open** 11am-3pm, 6-9.30pm, daily. **Average** 80F. **Menu** 75F (Mon-Fri), 80F (Sat, Sun). **Credit** EC, MC, V.

That Good Cheap Meal

Everyone knows the image; you wander into a little, traditional Parisian bistro, and find the meal of a lifetime, all for a price that in other countries would have got you no more than a sandwich. Along with it goes the adage, still fondly believed by some, that it's impossible to have a bad French meal.

This myth has led to disappointment for many. Paris is now an expensive place, and there are plenty of mediocre restaurants around the city. That said, it is still the case that to a great extent you often get what you pay for. There's frequently a noticeable difference in quality as soon as you top the rough 180F mark for a three-course à la carte meal. Below that price, you'll be fortunate to find sophisticated cuisine, but, if you're selective – and take full advantage of the *prix fixe* set menus –, you can certainly get a good and enjoyable meal. In particularly, there a number of tips that can be kept in mind when out to eat cheaply and well.

• Make lunch your main meal, for this is when the best-value *prix fixe* or *formule* menus are available (although some restaurants offer the same menus for dinner as well). Or, follow the French; it's perfectly acceptable to have either an *entrée* and *plat*, or just a *plat* without any other courses, which will often bring the next rung of restaurant within your budget.

• Beware of putting together a 'cheap' meal in a café, as your simple lunch of omelette and a salad, with a glass of wine, and then a coffee, ordered separately, can quickly add up. However, many cafés also do remarkable value menus, and 60F-70F might get you *crudités*, salad, or herring to start, a *plat du jour* or *steak-frites* main course, and a crème caramel, chocolate mousse or fruit tart for dessert.
• Go ethnic; many of the city's foreign restaurants offer very good value for money.
• If you feel like an *aperitif*, have it in a café rather than in the restaurant; most put heavy mark-ups on drinks other than wine, and especially spirits.
• Drink the house wines, by the *pichet* (jug) or the bottle. The smallest measure of carafe wine is called a *quart*, or quarter (25 cl).
• Don't bother with bottled water; ask for a *carafe d'eau,* (jug of tap water) instead. It's safe, tastes fine and, best of all, it's free.
• Get off the beaten track. Few of the restaurants in the city's museums are any good, but if you wander just a few streets away, you'll likely find a pleasant place to eat. Moreover, since public transport is cheap and fast, restaurants in residential neighbourhoods – often markedly less expensive than those in central locations – become easily accessible.

Opened in 1995 by Graham Gooch

THE CRICKETER PUB

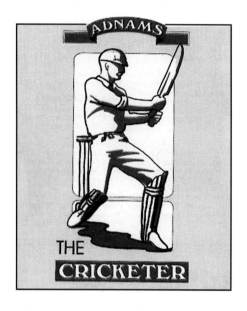

Best pint of bitter in Paris.

OPEN DAILY 11AM-2AM.

Pub food served every day.

41 rue des Mathurins, 75008 Paris
Tel: 40.07.01.45
M° St. Augustin/Havre Caumartin

A classic budget choice. Originally a *bouillon* where workers could get simple, hearty meals, this vast place (serving 1,000 meals a day) is still popular for its good value and handsome old fittings, although you shouldn't expect too much of the cuisine. Shared tables, and no bookings.

Chez Clément

123 avenue des Champs-Elysées, 75008 (40.73.87.00).
Métro George V. **Open** 8am-1am daily. **Average** 120F.
Credit MC, V.
With gentle prices and acceptably good food, this new bistro is a welcome addition to the Champs-Elysées. Start with oysters, and then choose from spit-roasted beef, pork or chicken, served on an all-you-can-eat basis. The sole meunière, too, is better than one might expect at this price. Décor is an eclectic pastiche of traditional French restaurant styles.
Tables outdoors. Wheelchair access.

Chez Paul

13 rue de Charonne, 75011 (47.00.34.57). Métro
Bastille. **Open** noon-2.30pm, 7.30pm-12.30am, daily.
Average 160F. **Credit** AmEx, EC, MC, V.
Bursting at the seams every night with a trendy, yet well-mixed crowd, this much-loved and venerable bistro is one of the institutions of the ever-changing Bastille area. The traditional bistro fare on offer includes a fine steak tartare and rabbit stuffed with goat's cheese and mint. The food can be variable, but the atmosphere's always great. A few pavement tables when weather allows.
Tables outdoors.

Chez Pento

9 rue Cujas, 75005 (43.26.81.54). Métro Cluny la-
Sorbonne/RER Luxembourg. **Open** noon-3pm, 7.30-
11pm, Mon-Fri; 7.30-11pm Sat. Closed Christmas-New
Year. **Average** 135F. **Menu** 77F lunch, 95F dinner.
Credit AmEx, EC, MC, V.
A bistro run by a former nightclub manager that's good value for the heavily-touristed Latin Quarter. The set menus include good house foie gras, snails and cured duck with lentils. Service is brusque.

Clown Bar

114 rue Amelot, 75011 (43.55.87.35).
Métro Filles-du-Calvaire. **Open** noon-3pm, 7pm-1am,
Mon-Fri; noon-3am Sat. Closed 2 weeks Aug. **Average**
150F. **No credit cards**.
This friendly neighbourhood bar is located next to the Cirque d'Hiver, and appropriately decorated with old circus posters. The menu includes a few hot dishes of the day, salads, cheese assortments and many wines by the glass.

Dame Tartine

2 rue Brise Miche, 75004 (42.77.32.22). Métro
Rambuteau or Châtelet-Les Halles. **Open** noon-11.30pm
daily. **Average** 60F. **Credit** MC, V.
A crowded, cheerful spot facing Beaubourg's whimsical Stravinsky Fountain, serving nothing but *tartines* (open sandwiches). There are starter and main course versions, hot and cold, featuring interesting combinations of ingredients. Good for lunch or a quick pre-show meal, and it's hard to spend more than 80F here.
Branches: Jardin des Tuileries, 75001 (47.03.93.00); 59 rue de Lyon, 75012 (44.68.96.95).

Les Fontaines

9 rue Soufflot, 75005 (43.26.42.80). RER Luxembourg.
Open noon-2pm, 7.30-10.30pm, Mon-Sat. Closed Aug.
Average 150F. **Credit** EC, MC, V.
For the many regulars of this café-restaurant, the disco décor makes for perfect Left-Bank anti-chic. Don't be misled, though, by the yellow neon thunderbolt on the ceiling, for the place serves an excellent traditional menu with Auvergnat leanings. Begin with fat asparagus or an endive-

and-blue cheese salad, and then have one of the excellent steaks, or maybe rolled fillet of sole with julienned vegetables and a delicious cream sauce. Fine dessert list.

Léon de Bruxelles

8 place de la République, 75011 (43.38.28.69). Métro
République. **Open** noon-12.30am daily. **Average** 110F.
Menu 65F, 98F. **Credit** AmEx, DC, EC, JCB, MC, V.
These simple, pleasant, chain restaurants play on the Belgian passion for moules – à la crème, marinière and so on – served with frites and excellent abbey-brewed beer. The other Belgian specialities on the menu are less successful, but there are acceptable grills for meat eaters.
Branches include: 3 boulevard Beaumarchais, 75004 (42.71.75.55); 63 avenue des Champs-Elysées, 75008 (43.25.96.16).

Perraudin

157 rue St-Jacques, 75005 (46.33.15.75).
Métro St-Michel/RER Luxembourg. **Open** 7.30-10.15pm
Mon, Sat; noon-2.15pm, 7.30-10.15pm, Tue-Fri. Closed last
two weeks Aug. **Average** 100F. **Menu** 63F (lunch only).
No credit cards.
An authentic turn-of-the-century bistro that has outlived fashion and continues to please a mix of tourists and local students and academics with honestly-done versions of egg mayonnaise, *boeuf bourguignon*, and roast lamb with *gratin dauphinoise*. There's a courtyard garden. No reservations are accepted.

Le Petit St-Benoît

4 rue St-Benoît, 75006 (42.60.27.92).
Métro St-Germain-des-Prés. **Open** noon-2pm, 7-10pm,
Mon-Fri. Closed first two weeks Aug, Christmas-New
Year. **Average** 80F. **No credit cards.**
A friendly St-Germain spot where the waitresses treat regulars like family, and you might easily find yourself sharing a table. The inexpensive menu features homely favourites, and changes every day. Also decent house wines, in half and full-size bottles.
Tables outdoors.

Le Petit Vatel

5 rue Lobineau, 75006 (43.54.28.49).
Métro Odéon. **Open** noon-3pm, 7pm-midnight, Mon-Fri;
noon-midnight Sat; 7pm-midnight Sun. Closed Christmas-
New Year. **Average** 80F. **Menu** 61F (lunch only). **Credit**
AmEX, EC, MC, V.
Prices have risen a bit over the years, but the tiny, excellent Petit Vatel remains a home-from-home for hungry students and budget tourists. The blackboard menu features two starters, two or three meat dishes at around 45F, and two vegetables of the day at 26F. Service is amiable, and may incline you to linger despite the cramped space and narrow bench seating.

Polidor

41 rue Monsieur-le-Prince, 75006 (43.26.95.34). Métro
Odéon/RER Luxembourg. **Open** noon-2.30pm, 7-12.30pm
Mon-Sat, noon-2.30pm, 7-11pm Sun. **Average** 90F. **Menu**
55F (lunch only), 100F. **No credit cards.**
A classic budget establishment, with lace curtains, *faux bois* columns, vintage waitresses and tables set with paper cloths. It has to be said, though, that décor, price and atmosphere are much more of a draw than the food, which can be very erratic.

Restaurant de Paris

38 rue de Ponthieu, 75008 (42.56.50.86).
Métro Franklin D Roosevelt. **Open** noon-3pm, 7pm-
midnight, Mon-Fri; 7pm-midnight Sat. **Average** 130F.
Menu 63F lunch, 75F, 120F dinner. **Credit** EC, MC, V.
Rather incongruously located in the heart of the busy, swanky 8th, this simple, friendly place offers a good feed for

those with more dash than cash. For lunch, you start with the buffet table and then have a meat or fish dish, maybe roast chicken or oven-roasted salmon. Stay with the acceptable carafe wine, and the bill will remain happily earthbound.

Thoumieux

79 rue St-Dominique, 75007 (47.05.49.75). Métro Invalides. **Open** noon-3.30pm, 6.45pm-midnight, Mon-Sat; noon-midnight, Sun. **Average** 180F. **Menu** 67F, 145F (incl wine). **Credit** MC, V.

Popular with both Parisians and tourists, this large, beautiful old restaurant has a 67F menu that is a true anomaly in this expensive area. The best dishes, though, are à-la-carte, well-prepared classics such as a giant cassoulet and a fine *blanquette de veau*. *Air-conditioning.*

Le Trumilou

84 quai de l'Hôtel de Ville, 75004 (42.77.63.98). Métro Hôtel-de-Ville or Pont Marie. **Open** noon-3pm, 7-11pm, Mon-Sat; noon-3pm, 7-10.30pm, Sun. Closed Christmas. **Average** 110F. **Menú** 65F, 80F. **Credit** EC, MC, V.

An unpretentious but classically decorated spot on the Right Bank, offering large helpings of traditional dishes like duck in prune sauce. Service can be sloppy, but the food's good. *Tables outdoors.*

Ty Breiz

52 boulevard de Vaugirard, 75015 (43.20.83.72) Métro Montparnasse **Open** 11.45am-3pm, 7-11pm, Mon-Sat. **Average** 90F. **Menu** 57F (lunch only). **Credit** EC, MC, V.

A standout among the many crêperies in this area, with a distinctly cosy, plant-filled dining room. Sweet crêpes and savoury *galettes* come in many varieties, such as *la forestière* (sautéed mushrooms, scrambled eggs, garlic and chives). *Tables outdoors. Wheelchair access.*

Le Vin des Rues

21 rue Boulard, 75014 (43.22.19.78). Métro Denfert-Rochereau. **Open** 1-3pm Tues- Sat; 9pm onwards by reservation only Wed, Fri. Closed Aug. **Average** 130F. **No credit cards**

You have to be willing to brave the moods of an incorrigibly gruff proprietor, but if your French is up to it this is a great spot for a solid, cheap meal of well-prepared Lyonnais specialities. Start with a salad, or the superb homemade terrine (you serve yourself from an earthenware dish); to follow there are two or three main courses, perhaps stuffed rabbit or roast veal. Also good are the house wines. Note the idiosyncratic system for evenings; he only opens on Wednesdays and Fridays, and usually only for prior reservations. *Tables outdoors.*

Les Zygomates

7 rue de Capri, 75012 (40.19.93.04). Métro Daumesnil. **Open** noon-2pm, 7.30-10.30pm Mon-Fri, 7.30-10.30pm Sat. Closed Aug, Christmas. **Average** 180F. **Menu** 125F **Credit** MC, V.

This funky bistro in an off-beat neighbourhood has developed quite a following with a 125F menu that changes weekly according to what's available in the markets. There are usually several fish choices, and the chicken in chive-showered cream sauce is delicate but satisfying. *Booking essential.*

International

The Americas

Anahi

49 rue Volta, 75003 (48.87.88.24) Métro Arts et Metiers. **Open** 8pm-12.30am daily. Closed 15-19 Aug. **Average** 200F. **No credit cards.**

Places frequented by a black-clad clientèle are rarely friendly or cosy, but both words apply to this little former butcher's shop. Its ceramic walls and fixtures have been retained, but it now offers a diversely Latin-American menu. Try the delicious *empanadas* or first-rate guacamole, and then the *Bife*, unbelievably tender Argentine beef. Excellent Spanish, Argentine and Chilean wines.

Chicago Meatpackers

8 rue Coquillière, 75001 (40.28.02.33). Métro Châtelet-Les Halles. **Open** 11.30am-1am daily. Closed 25 Dec. **Average** 120F. **Menu** 69F (Mon-Fri), 59F (children, lunch only). **Credit** AmEx, EC, JCB, MC, V.

A typical Yankee restaurant, serving all-meat specialities like ribs and hamburgers. The same London-based group also has several other restaurants in Paris, such as the **Chicago Pizza Pie Factory** at 5 rue de Berri, 75008 (45.62.50.23), and 9 boulevard Edgar Quinet, 75014 (43.21.73.06), offering real Chicago-style deep-dish pizza. There are cocktail bars attached, but they're also all particularly good for kids. No reservations are taken at weekends.

Chili's

114 des Champs-Elysées, 75008 (42.89.87.87). Métro George V. **Open** 11am-midnight Mon-Thur, Sun; 11am-1am Fri, Sat. **Average** 150F. **Menu** 80F (lunch only). **Credit** AmEx, DC, MC, V.

All-American grill offering burgers, bar-b-q ribs and other favourites to a mainly-young crowd.

Australian

Woolloomooloo

36 boulevard Henri IV, 75004 (42.72.32.11) Métro Bastille. **Open** noon-2.30pm, 7-11pm, Tue-Sat; noon-3pm, 7-11pm, Sun. **Average** 180F. **Menu** 120F lunch, 140F dinner. **Credit** MC, V.

Young Australian chef Bernard Plaisted is largely succeeding at the daunting goal of introducing Paris to contemporary Australian cuisine. This is a Pacific Rim story with Mediterranean references, but seasoning is more delicate than the similarly hybrid style from California. Start with duck spring rolls, and then salmon with Asian greens or ginger-glazed fillet of beef. Wonderfully sticky desserts, and a good list of Australian wines. Brunch is served on Sundays.

British

Bertie's

Hôtel Baltimore, 1 rue Léo-Délibes, 75016 (44.34.54.34) Métro Boissière. **Open** 12.30-2pm, 7.30-10.30pm Mon-Fri. **Average** 350F. **Menu** 160F lunch, 195F dinner. **Credit** AmEx, DC, MC, V.

In 1995 Bertie's won the Marco Polo award for best foreign restaurant in Paris. It's hard to credit that Parisians might get so excited about British cooking, of all things, but then, the menu here is supervised by leading London-based French chef Albert Roux. The resident chef, though, is the entirely-British David Whiffen, and much the greater part of the produce used is from Britain. Among his best dishes are a pheasant terrine with Cumberland sauce, to start, and the Angus beef, sole or roast duck stuffed with sage and apples, are impeccable. There's a fine range of British cheeses to follow. Some people might be put off by the stiff service and be-suited clientèle here, but it's still an attractive place.

Hamilton's Noted Fish & Chips

51 rue de Lappe, 75011 (48.06.77.92). Métro Bastille. **Open** 11.30am-3pm, 6pm-midnight, Mon-Sat. Closed two weeks Aug, two weeks Dec. **Average** 33F. **No credit cards.**

A British fish and chip shop, mainly for take-aways. The best of the genre in Paris, though there's no real competition.

Le Marais Cage

8 rue de Beauce, 3rd (48.87.31.20). M⁰ Arts et Métiers. Open Mon-Fri noon-2.30pm, 7-10.30pm, Sat 7-10.30pm. Credit V, Amex, DC.
A cosy atmosphere with delicious Caribbean cooking, in one of the most beautiful areas of the Marais. Avg 250F, menu 160F incl wine. Lunch menu 130F.

La Terrasse

12 rue Joseph de Maistre, 18th (44.92.34.00). M⁰ Place Clichy/Blanche. Open daily noon-2.30pm, 7-10.30pm. Credit: AmEx, Visa, DC.
Near La Butte Montmartre, a charming restaurant with relaxed prices. 120F and 160F menus. From May on, grilled meats on the roof terrace with a view over all of Paris.

Le Clocher St Germain

22 rue Guillaume Apollinaire, 6th (42.86.00.88). M⁰ St Germain-des-Prés. Open daily noon-3pm, 7pm-midnight. Credit: AmEx, Visa, DC.
An authentic French bistro in the heart of St Germain-des-Prés with old-fashioned cooking and regional specialities. Summer terrace.

La Bouteille d'Or

7-9 quai de Montebello, 5th (43.54.52.58). M⁰ Maubert or St Michel. Open daily noon-3pm, 7-10.30pm. Credit: AmEx, Visa.
From the magnificent stone-walled dining room and the shaded terrace of this incredible house (built in 1631) you can view Notre Dame, just opposite, from its loveliest angle. Clever little green dots on the varied and imaginative menu will guide you to a very reasonably priced meal (starter, main course and dessert, 130F).

Côté Seine

45 Quai des Grands Augustins, 6th (43.54.49.73). M⁰ St Michel. Open daily 7-10.30pm and Sun noon-3pm. Credit: AmEx, Visa.
One of the most pleasant bistros in Paris, on the banks of the Seine between Notre Dame and the Pont Neuf, popular with Parisians of all ages and from all walks of life. 182F menu with a choice of ten starters, ten main dishes and ten desserts, and including apéritif, wine and coffee.

Caribbean

La Théière dans les Nuages
14 rue de Cloche-Perce, 75004 (42.71.96.11) Métro St-Paul **Open** noon-2.30pm, 7-11pm Mon-Sat. Closed Aug. **Average** 150F. **Menu** 45F, 55F, 62F lunch, 88F dinner. **Credit** MC, V.
As you arrive, Henri Rousseau posters and enticing odours discreetly tip you off that what otherwise seems like a Marais tearoom is an excellent Creole restaurant. At the 'Teapot in the Clouds', try the delicious assortment of *beignets* (fritters) stuffed with fish or vegetables. and then maybe the *marmite de porc boucane*, a delicious casserole of stewed pork with red beans and rice. Good assortment of island drinks, including Corsaire beer, 26 different fruit juices and 24 different teas. Also, it's completely non-smoking.

Chinese & South-East Asian

Café Indochine
195 rue du Faubourg St-Honoré, 75008 (53.75.15.63). Métro George V. **Open** noon-2.30pm, 7.30-12.30pm Mon-Sat, 7.30-11pm Sun. **Average** 250F. **Menu** 165F (lunch only). **Credit** EC, MC, V.
This very good oriental restaurant – the menu's a mix of Thai, Chinese, Cambodian and Vietnamese dishes – is an expression of the Parisian trend for colonial chic. The walls are hung with old photos, drawings and maps of French Indochina, and in the evening the low-key lunch clientèle is replaced by a flashy show-biz crowd. Try the luscious Cambodian soup with prawn and chicken, and the pork simmered in caramelised coconut milk. *See also chapter* **Nightlife**.

Le Canton
5 rue Gozlin, 75006 (43.26.51.86).
Métro St-Germain-des-Prés. **Open** noon-2.30pm, 7-11pm Mon-Sat. **Average** 100F. **Menu** 54F, 68F lunch, 74F, 89F dinner. **Credit** MC, V.
A casual place that provides a good alternative to pizza before or after a movie in St-Germain. There are good *nems* (baby spring rolls), raviolis à la Vietnam, *bouchées* and other dim sum, as well as affordable prawn dishes.

Le Moi
5 rue Daunou, 75002 (47.03.92.05). Métro Opéra. Open noon-2.30pm, 7.30-10.30pm Mon-Fri; 7.30-10.30pm Sat. **Average** 150F. **Menu** 79F lunch. **Credit** MC, V.
An excellent Vietnamese restaurant in a handy central location. Very busy at noon, when the local office crowd comes in for the *nems*, steamed dumplings and herb-brightened salads of poultry, beef or seafood.

Mirama
17 rue St-Jacques, 75005 (43.29.66.58). Métro St Michel. **Open** noon-11pm daily. **Average** 100F. **Credit** MC, V.
The mahogany lacquered ducks hanging in the window of the small restaurant are a cue as to what you should order here for a main course. Start with one of their excellent soups, most of which have a thick tangle of noodles in broth and are then garnished, as you wish, with thin slices of savoury roast pork or shrimp dumplings. Popular, hectic and very well-priced.

Le Nioullaville
32-34 rue de l'Orillon, 75011 (43.38.95.23). Métro Belleville. **Open** noon-3.30pm, 6.30pm-12.45am, Mon-Fri; noon-1am, Sat, Sun. **Average** 120F. **Menu** 200F, 220F. **Credit** AmEx, DC, MC, V.
A sprawling, clamorous institution in Belleville – the new Chinatown of Paris – and a good place to go with a group. The 30-page menu lists a huge variety of Chinese, Thai and Vietnamese dishes, but dim sum is the speciality.

Go colonial at the **Café Indochine.**

Le Palais de Cristal
70 rue Baudricourt, 75013 (45.84.81.56).
Métro Tolbiac. **Open** noon-3pm, 6-11pm, Mon, Tue, Thur-Sun. **Average** 100F. **No credit cards**.
Originally a simple noodle shop, this place in the 13th *arrondissement* Chinatown has since been tarted up a bit. Often full of Chinese families, it serves some of the best and most authentic Vietnamese and Chinese cooking in Paris.

Indian

Maharajah
72 boulevard St-Germain, 75005 (43.54.26.07). Métro Maubert-Mutualité. **Open** 11.30am-11.30pm Mon-Thur, Sun; 11.30am-1am Fri, Sat. **Average** 150F. **Menu** 78F (lunch only), 127F, 169F. **Credit** AmEx, DC, JCB, MC, V.
One of the oldest Indian restaurants in Paris, with Mughal-style interior and very good tandoori dishes.
Air-conditioning. Tables outdoors.

Italian

Il Barone
5 rue Léopold-Robert, 75014 (43.20.87.14). Métro Raspail. **Open** noon-2.30pm, 7.30pm-midnight, daily. **Average** 160F. **Credit** MC, V.
Although this restaurant has several tables at the front, you should pass behind the velvet curtains to the larger and more convivial salon at the back. Delicious antipasti and fresh pasta come in generous quantities. Also a good wine list.

Fellini
47 rue de l'Arbre Sec, 75001 (42.60.90.66). Métro Louvre. **Open** noon-2.30pm, 7.30pm-11pm, Mon-Sat. **Average** 200F. **Menu** 110F (lunch only). **Credit** V.
An attractive Italian restaurant with a superb buffet of antipasti, including roast peppers, stuffed artichokes, sautéed baby onions, grilled aubergines, and more. It also produces a mean plate of pasta, and their *spaghetti alle vongole* (with baby clams) can be recommended.

Il Vicolo
8 rue de Jouy, 75004 (42.78.38.86).
Métro St Paul. **Open** 12.30-2.30pm, 8-11.30pm, Tue-Sat. Closed early Sept. **Average** 175F. **Menu** 100F lunch only. **Credit** MC, V.
A pleasant place that offers a discreetly sophisticated version of modern Italian cooking, with a menu that skates across the country but shows a preference for Tuscany. Start with a spicey chick-pea soup, then try *rougets* in the style of Livorno (red mullet with a savoury sauce). Good desserts, a reasonable wine list and friendly service make this a pleasant new option in the Marais.

Japanese

Isami
4 quai d'Orléans, 75004 (40.46.06.97). Métro Pont Marie. **Open** noon-2pm, 7-10.30pm Tue-Sat; 7-10.30pm Sun. **Closed** Jan, Aug. **Average** 160F. **Credit** MC, V.
Devotees of sushi and sashimi should beat a path to this small, simple restaurant which probably serves the best in the capital – the fish are astonishingly fresh, and beautifully prepared and garnished. A further indication of the quality here is the number of Japanese regulars.

Kushi Yaki
41 rue Rochechouart, 75009 (49.70.05.24). Métro Anvers. **Open** noon-2.45pm, 7-11pm daily. **Average** 135F. **Menu** 39F (kebabs), 95F (sashimi), 105F (sushi). **Credit** V.
Another address worth noting for sushi and yakitori lovers. The interior is more attractive and spacious than other Japanese restaurants in Paris, and the fish is remarkably fresh. Reasonable prices, too.

North African

Chez Hamadi
12 rue Boutebrie, 75005 (43.54.03.30). Métro St-Michel. **Open** noon-3pm, 6pm-midnight, Mon-Fri; noon-1am Sat; noon-midnight Sun. **Average** 65F. **Menu** 72F (incl wine). **No credit cards.**
A modest place serving very good couscous and Maghrebi grills, such as spicy *merguez* sausage, in the heart of the Latin Quarter. Service is friendly, but you won't be encouraged to linger too long, as there's always a queue outside.

Chez Omar
47 rue de Bretagne, 75003 (42.72.36.26) Métro Filles du Calvaire. **Open** noon-3pm, 7.30pm-midnight, Mon-Sat; 7pm-midnight Sun. **Average** 150F. **No credit cards.**
The couscous and Arab grills are excellent and the old-style décor superb, but it's the warm welcome of Omar himself – and very reasonable prices – that fills this place with young, hip Parisians every night. His success has recently spurred him to open up an offshoot in an old bistro near the Bastille, the Café Moderne. Offering a similar menu, it's quickly built up a similar popularity.
Branch: Café Moderne 11 rue Keller, 75011 (47.00.53.62).

Mansouria
11 rue Faidherbe, 75011 (43.71.00.16). Métro Faidherbe Chaligny. **Open** noon-2pm, 7.30-11pm, Mon-Sat. **Average** 150F. **Menu** 99F lunch, 164F dinner. **Credit** MC, V.
Delicate Moroccan fare is served up by owner/writer Fatima, to a dedicated clientèle of regulars. Delicious pigeon *pastilla* is a classic first course, followed by a variety of delicately balanced *tagines* (casseroles) or couscous. A refreshing antidote to an overdose of French cuisine.

Timgad
21 rue de Brunel, 75017 (45.74.23.70). Métro Argentine. **Open** noon-2.30pm, 7-11pm, daily. **Average** 300F. **Credit** AmEx, DC, MC, V.
A favourite with many Parisians, this Moroccan restaurant is famous for its couscous, as well as its *tagines*. The Moorish décor is sumptuous.

Seychelloise

Au Coco de Mer
34 boulevard St-Marcel, 75005 (47.07.06.64). Métro St-Marcel. **Open** noon-3pm, 7.30-11pm, Mon-Sat. **Average** 150F. **Menu** 135F, 170F. **Credit** DC, MC, V.
With a terrace spread with white sand, and a dining room adorned with palm crowns, the only Seychellois restaurant in Paris offers a very pleasant trip to the islands without the cost of a flight. Friendly service and tropical punch accompany such delicacies as smoked marlin and curried octopus. *Tables outdoors.*

Vegetarian

Vegetarians have a hard time in Paris. In most conventional French restaurants, you may have to make do with some crudités and chips, or a cheese course. Cafes offer omelettes, and salons de thé often do good salad-based dishes (*see chapter* **Cafés & Bars**). Italian restaurants are a good bet, or try the kosher cafés in the Marais, some of which serve delicious take-away falafel. For a good, quick meal an excellent new choice is the **Restorama** food hall in the **Carrousel du Louvre** (*see chapter* **Specialist Shops**). Among its many food stands there is an all-vegetarian wholefood stall, a cheese and wine bar, and a Middle Eastern kiosk with interesting vegetarian *mezze*.

Aquarius
40 rue de Gergovie, 75014 (45.41.36.88). Métro Pernéty. **Open** noon-2.30pm, 7-10.30pm, Mon-Sat. **Average** 80F. **Menu** 60F (lunch, Mon-Fri only). **Credit** AmEx, MC, V.
Vegetarian food doesn't enjoy a high reputation in France, but this amiable, brightly-painted place has won over many Parisians in its 15 years of life. The lunch menu generally features sustaining choices such as vegetarian chili, lasagne or couscous, as well as good seaweed and salad dishes.

Country Life
6 rue Daunou, 75002 (42.97.48.51). Métro Opéra. **Open** 11.30am-2.30pm, 7-10pm Mon-Thur. **Average** 80F. **Menu** 58F. **Credit** V.
In the centre of town, this branch of an international chain is a pleasant buffet-style place, with a bargain all-you-can-eat menu for 58F. Good for soups, salads and pastas.

Au Grain de Folie
2 rue de Lavieuville, 75018 (42.58.15.57). Métro Abbesses. **Open** 11.30am-3pm, 6-11.30pm daily. **Average** 100F. **Menu** 60F, 100F. **No credit cards.**
One of Paris' more liberal vegetarian eateries; smoking is allowed, wine (including organic) is available and portions are generous. The quality of the food, though, can be patchy. The speciality is the mixed vegetarian platter, for 65F.

Le Grenier de Notre Dame
18 rue de la Bûcherie, 75005 (43.29.98.29). Métro Maubert-Mutualité or St-Michel. **Open** noon-2.30pm, 7.15-11pm Mon-Thur, noon-3pm, 7,15-11pm Sun. **Average** 110F, **Menu** 75F, 105F, 140F. **Credit** AmEx, MC, V.
An easy-going place just across the river from Notre Dame, with a large menu and good selection of macrobiotic dishes.

Piccolo Teatro
6 rue des Ecouffes, 75004 (42.72.17.79). Métro St-Paul. **Open** noon-3pm, 7-11pm, Wed-Sun. **Average** 100F. **Menu** 85F, 110F. **Credit** AmEx, MC, V.
A relaxed wood-and-stone nook with good, fresh food, from salads to 'carrot caviar' and vegetable gratins.

La Truffe
31 rue Vieille-du-Temple, 75004 (42.71.08.39). Métro St Paul. **Open** noon-4pm, 7-11pm Mon-Fri,. noon-11pm Sat, Sun. **Average** 100F. **Credit** EC, MC, V.
An attractive duplex restaurant serving organic vegetarian food, prepared without fat or steaming – they use special cooking equipment so that the grains, mushrooms and vegetables conserve their taste and vitamins. Non-smoking. *Air-conditioning. No reservations. Wheelchair access.*

Cafés & Bars

A table in a bar in Paris: a place to write that book, catch someone's eye, have lunch, taste some wines or sup an Irish ale...

It's impossible to imagine Paris without its cafés, but nevertheless these great institutions are today under siege, with a horrendous number closing each year. Perhaps the most important threat to café life is the speed of modern Parisian life itself. If you dawdle in cafés during the day, you'll often find yourself keeping company with pensioners, students and other tourists, since most working Parisians are too busy to give themselves an hour or two over the papers and coffee.

In addition to the cafés and other kinds of bar listed here, many brasseries also have a café-bar area. This enables you to have a drink and sample the delights of places like the **Coupole** or the **Dôme** (*see chapter* **Restaurants**) for much less than it would cost to eat there.

In whichever type of bar, a consideration to be kept in mind is the difference in **prices** between, and within, Paris bars. They vary enormously, and

having a drink can be a casual operation or an expensive outing according to where you go – in famous venues such as the big cafés on boulevard St-Germain, for example, a simple beer can cost 40F. In addition, prices are noticeably higher if you sit at a table rather than stand at the bar, and higher again if the table is outside on the pavement. Many cafés also apply a surcharge after 10pm.

Cafés

Angel Café
22 rue Pierre-Lescot, 75001 (40.26.28.60). Métro Châtelet-Les Halles. **Open** 11am-2am daily. **Credit** MC, V.
Despite its tourist trap location, an eclectic collection of local musicians, students and night owls, with a large gay quotient, ensures that this minimalist café avoids banality. There's a good choice of exotic juices, reasonably priced Franco-Italian food and a DJ Thursday to Saturday nights.

L'Apparement Café
18 rue des Coutures-St-Gervais, 75003 (48.87.12.22). Métro St-Paul or Filles du Calvaire. **Open** noon-2am Mon-Fri; 4pm-2am Sat; 12.30pm-2am Sun. **Credit** MC, V.
As well as objects scoured in the flea markets, the four co-owners have brought along items of their own to give a personal touch to this nicely-designed café. Armchairs and anonymous portraits furnish the salon, while the library has board games to play and bound volumes of *Paris Match* to flick through. The effect is quietly trendy.

Le Bourbon
1 place du Palais-Bourbon, 75007 (45.51.58.27). Métro Assemblée Nationale. **Open** 7.30am-10.30pm Mon-Sat; 7.30am-6.30pm Sun. **Credit** AmEx, DC, JCB, MC, V.
A tranquil spot in front of the magnificent square in front of the Assemblée Nationale and a good place to stop on a trek to or from the Eiffel Tower.

Café Beaubourg
100 rue St-Martin, 75004 (48.87.89.98). Métro Châtelet-Les Halles or Hôtel de Ville. **Open** 8am-1am Mon-Thur; 8am-2am Fri, Sat; 8am-1am Sun. **Credit** AmEx, DC, EC, MC, V.
This stylish two-level Christian de Portzamparc-designed space is a *rendezvous obligé* for artists, famous and aspiring, because of its ring-side view of the Centre Pompidou. Good salads and a renowned dark and white chocolate mousse.

Café de Flore
172 boulevard St-Germain, 75006 (45.48.55.26). Métro St-Germain-des-Prés. **Open** 7am-1.30am daily. **Credit** AmEx.
An existentialist mecca that once played host to Sartre and de Beauvoir. The Café de Flore still has its original Deco fittings and is less touristy than **Les Deux Magots** next door (*see below*). It remains popular with the Left Bank intelligentsia, but note that a beer at an inside table (33cl, just a little larger than a *demi*) will cost you 40F.

Trés chic, the **Café Marly**. *See page 165.*

Café des Hauteurs, Musée d'Orsay

Musée d'Orsay, 1 rue de Bellechasse, 75007
(museum switchboard 40.49.48.14). Métro Solférino/RER
Musée d'Orsay. **Open** 11am-5pm Tue-Sat; 10am-9pm
Sun. **Credit** AmEx, DC, JCB, MC, V.
On the top floor of the Musée d'Orsay, this large, bright café
is a godsend for exhausted art lovers in need of a restorative cup of tea or glass of wine. The wonderful panoramic
view of Paris through the giant glass clocks is not the least
of this establishment's attractions, but one drawback is that
service is s-l-o-w.

Café de l'Industrie

16 rue St-Sabin, 75011 (47.00.13.53). Métro Bastille.
Open 11am-2am Mon-Fri, Sun. **Credit** EC, MC, V.
A hip but easy-going café, decorated with assorted can-
vasses and old lamps to give a mood of flea-market nostalgia, that makes an attractive, spacious and friendly Bastille
meeting place. They also serve good light meals.

Café de la Mairie

8 place St-Sulpice, 75006 (43.26.67.82).
Métro St-Sulpice. **Open** 8am-2am Mon-Sat; *June only*
9am-11pm Sun. **No credit cards.**
During the summer, the terrace of this local café, overlooking the lion-guarded fountain in the middle of the square, is
a favourite Left Bank rendezvous. Over the years it's been
patronised by Paul Eluard, Samuel Beckett and many other
literary eminences, and the upstairs room is a favourite place
to look meaningful with a novel.

Café Marly

93 rue de Rivoli, Cour Napoléon du Louvre,
75001 (49.26.06.60). Métro Palais-Royal. **Open** 8am-
2am daily. **Credit** AmEx, DC, MC, V.
One of the most chic cafés in Paris ever since it opened, but
then, it is in the Louvre. The food's middling and pricey, but
the décor, crowd and view are wonderful, especially during
good weather when they serve on the terrace overlooking the

Café Life

An enormous range of drinks, alcoholic and non,
and foods are available in Parisian bars – below
is a brief guide to some of the standards. On wine,
see page 171 **Wine Bars.** For more on food, tipping and other aspects of eating out, *see chapters*
Essential Information *and* **Restaurants.**

Beer

To order beer on draught ask for *une pression*. Beer is not
cheap in Paris bars, and bottled beers are particularly
pricey. Throughout the day, Parisians will indulge in a
pause for a quick *demi* (25cl glass of beer on tap), most often
a Kronenbourg, the largest French brewery. To slake a
larger thirst, specify *une grande* (large) or *un Baron*, which
is almost a pint. Choose from three colours of beer – *brune*,
blonde or the rarer *rousse*. The first is a dark, flavoursome
brew; the second is lager; and the third more like bitter. A
panaché (beer and lemonade shandy) is also popular.

Coffee

Ever since Le Procope (today an indifferent restaurant)
opened as the capital's first café in 1686, coffee has been
the mainstay of café life. French coffee-drinking habits
change throughout the day. People only drink coffee with
milk, the classic *café au lait* (also called *café crème*), in the
morning, preferring to end meals or jolt themselves during the day with an *express*, or expresso (which is what
you'll get if you just ask for a café). Really flagging, they
might order a *café serré*, a high-voltage expresso made
with half the normal amount of water, or a *double express*,
a double expresso. On the other hand, they might order a
décaféiné or *déca*, a decaffeinated expresso, or a *café*
allongé, a weak expresso, often accompanied by a jug of
hot water for further thinning out.

Food

As well as serving drinks, Paris cafés serve a wide range
of food. Café standards include the *croque monsieur* (toasted ham and cheese sandwich) and the *croque madame* (the
same, with a fried egg on top). Many also serve salads,
sandwiches, and plates of charcuterie. Note, though, that if
you order several things separately, and sit at a table, prices
can soon add up, especially in certain parts. The best bet if
you want to keep prices down is to find a good *prix fixe*
menu, which many cafés offer at lunchtime for around 70F.

Juices, water & soft drinks

Apart from Coca-Cola, the processed juice *Orangina* is the
most popular French soft drink; few cafés serve diet
(called lite) sparkling drinks, but they have good plain
lemonade (*limonade*). If you ask for fruit juice (*jus*), you
will get Orangina or a similar product unless you request
orange pressé (freshly-squeezed orange juice), a *citron*
pressé (fresh lemon juice, served with water and sugar,
and which you then make up to your taste), and so on.
Fruit and vegetable juices, especially *un jus de tomate*,
often served with a shaker of celery salt, and Perrier,
which the French never drink with meals (too gassy), are
the most popular non-alcoholic *apéritifs*.

Spirits & *apéritifs*

The French rarely drink spirits before a meal, believing
that it numbs the taste buds. They prefer a glass of champagne; a *kir* – white wine with a dash of *cassis*, blackcurrant liqueur – or one of the vast range of sometimes
curiously coloured and mysterious aperitifs you'll see on
shelves behind the bar. Many are Vermouth- or wine-
based; some of the most common are Dubonnet, Noilly
Prat and Byrrh. Pastis, Pernod and similar aniseed drinks
have long been so out of fashion that they've become popular again, especially during the summer, when trendy
Parisians order *une tomate*, pastis with a splash of grena-
dine syrup, or *un perroquet*, pastis with mint syrup; both
are acquired tastes. Fashionable bars also offer a wide
range of cocktails, which also are not cheap.

Tea, chocolate & related herbs

Tea is drunk almost exclusively at the end of the afternoon, while hot chocolate, *un chocolat chaud*, is a local
treat consumed through the day. After dinner, many
Parisians favour a *tisane*, or herbal tea; the most popular
include *tilleul*, or linden flowers and leaves, *verveine*, ver-
bena, and camomile.

Etiquette

It's actually rude to call the waiter *Garçon*; say *S'il vous*
plaît, madame/mademoiselle/monsieur, instead. Also, note
that most cafés still have telephones that take coins, if you
find yourself without a telephone card, and are also good
places to find toilets. This is true even if you haven't
ordered anything, although it's polite at least to have a coffee. You can always pretend you're going to use the phone.

*Taking the air at the **Café de la Mairie**. See page 165.*

Pyramid, or late at night when the dramatic deep red walls are shown to advantage. It's run by the Costes brothers (of **Café Beaubourg**, *above*). *See also chapter* **Nightlife**.

Café Mouffetard

116 rue Mouffetard, 75005 (43.31.42.50). Métro Censier Daubenton. **Open** 7am-9pm Tue-Sat; 7am-3.30pm Sun. Closed Sept 1995, July other years. **No credit cards.**
This café overlooking the open-air market in villagey rue Mouffetard is a favourite with students and writers (and featured in Kieslowski's *Three Colours: Blue*). Excellent croissants and crusty bread are made on the premises, and the *plats du jour* offer a real taste of French home-cooking.

Café Noir

65 rue Montmartre, 75002 (40.39.07.36). Métro Sentier. **Open** 7am-2am Mon-Sat. **No credit cards.**
This intimate but busy old café has very friendly bar staff and a lively Anglo-French clientele. Prices are well below average, and live blues or jazz is served up once a week.

Café Orbital

4 rue du Quatre Septembre, 75002 (42.80.24.74). Métro Opéra. **Open** noon-midnight Tue-Sat; noon-8pm Mon, Sun, public holidays. **Credit** MC, V.
The Internet has been the mania of 1995 and this is the first online café in town. It was opened by a bunch of recent converts above a high-tech sandwich bar: here you can eat, drink and hire a computer terminal (35F for 30 minutes/60F per hour). There's always someone on hand to help, so why not ask them to look at the *Time Out* site at www.timeout.co.uk?

Café de la Paix

12 boulevard des Capucines, 75009 (40.07.30.20). Métro Opéra. **Open** *terrace* 10-1.30am daily; *bar* noon-1am daily. **Credit** AmEx, DC, EC, JCB, MC, V.
A Parisian landmark, haunted by the ghosts of Oscar Wilde and the boulevardiers of the naughty nineties. The interior is by Charles Garnier, best known for his Opéra across the street, and decorated with Second Empire frescoes. Outside, on the covered terrace, you can enjoy a wide-angle view of

the bustling boulevards. It's expensive (25F a coffee), and packed with tourists, but charming all the same.

Café des Phares

7 place de la Bastille, 75004 (42.72.04.70). Métro Bastille. **Open** 7am-4am daily. **No credit cards.**
From outside there's nothing unusual about this little café that almost seems to be constructed within the Banque de France on the place de la Bastille. But every Sunday, between 11am and 1pm, the room at the back becomes the seat of an animated philosophy debate (in French). Proof that the French intellectual tradition lives on. Arrive early.

Le Café Zephyr

12 boulevard Montmartre, 75009 (47.70.80.14). Métro Rue Montmartre. **Open** 9am-2am daily.
With its traditional wicker chairs, billiard table and neo-colonial atmosphere, this is one of the rare places along the boulevard that still feels local, which is to say Parisian. They only serve light snacks, but the mood is very languid and very French in a part of town that's increasingly neither.

Les Deux Magots

170 boulevard St Germain, 75006 (45.48.55.25). Métro St-Germain-des-Prés. **Open** 7.30am-1.30am daily. Closed 3rd week of Jan. **Credit** AmEx, DC, MC, JCB, V.
Named after the two wise Chinamen inside the entrance, Les Deux Magots still glories in its long list of deceased clients – Mallarmé *et al*. Today's customers are less literary, possibly because they have to shell out 21F for an espresso, although it has to be said it's a little cheaper than the **Flore** (*see above*). Also, the coffee's good, as is the rich hot chocolate, best savoured indoors in one of its great old mahogany booths.

Le Flore en L'Ile

42 quai d'Orléans, 75004 (43.29.88.27). Métro Pont-Marie. **Open** 9am-2am daily. **Credit** EC, MC, V.
Real brewed tea, honey cakes, Berthillon ice-creams and fine *plats du jour* are reason enough to visit this popular café-cum-tea room on Ile St-Louis. Great views of the Seine.

The **Café de la Paix**. *See page 167.*

Le Fouquet's

99 avenue des Champs-Elysées, 75008 (47.23.70.60).
Métro George V. **Open** 8am-1.30am daily. **Credit** AmEx,
DC, EC, JCB, MC, V.
A favourite with showbiz types, politicians, wealthy Arabs
and, long ago, James Joyce. Fouquet's (pronounce the 't')
managed to obtain landmark status in 1989 to save it from
the wrecking ball. Expensive (42F a *demi* beer).

Le Gutenberg

64 rue Jean-Jacques Rousseau, 75001 (42.36.14.90).
Métro Louvre-Rivoli. **Open** 7.30am-7.30pm Mon-Fri. **No**
credit cards.
A wonderfully authentic (and cheap) old Paris café not far
from the Louvre. The big bar, mosaic floor and coloured tiles
look much as they must have done a century ago, and
haven't (yet) suffered either over-modernisation or over-
restoration.

The Lizard Lounge

18 rue du Bourg-Tibourg, 75004 (42.72.81.34).
Métro Hôtel de Ville. **Open** noon-2am daily; *food served*
noon-2.20pm, 7.30-11pm. **Credit** MC, V.
The upstairs gallery is excellent for checking out the crowd
at this popular new Anglo-American bar-café. Good beers,
fancy long drinks and NY-style deli food.

Le Nemrod

51 rue du Cherche-Midi, 75006 (45.48.17.05).
Métro Sèvres-Babylone. **Open** 6.30am-10.30pm Mon-Fri;
6.30am-8pm Sat. **Credit** DC, MC, V.
This bustling neighbourhood café at a busy crossroads does
much better food than most, and is a good stop for lunch.

La Palette

43 rue de Seine, 75006 (43.26.68.15).
Métro Mabillon. **Open** 8am-1.30am Mon-Sat. Closed Aug.
No credit cards.
Popular with students from the nearby Ecole des Beaux-Arts,
this unpretentious turn-of-the-century artists' bar has plenty
of tables inside and out, and serves good sandwiches.

Pause Café

41 rue de Charonne, 75011 (48.06.80.33).
Métro Ledru-Rollin. **Open** 9am-2am Tue-Sat; 9am-9pm
Sun. **Credit** EC, MC, V.
A relaxed café favoured by Bastille hipsters. It has large win-
dows, red and yellow formica tables and exhibitions of paint-
ings on the walls. Great pavement terrace, and cheap.

La Perla

26 rue François-Miron, 75004 (42.77.59.40). Métro Hôtel
de Ville. **Open** noon-2am daily. **Credit** AmEx, EC, V.
Connoisseurs of tequila and killer margaritas pack this popular Mexican spot. Weaker constitutions can settle for a
bottle of Mexican beer and an array of Mexican snacks.

Le Petit Fer à Cheval

30 rue Vieille-du-Temple, 75004 (42.72.47.47).
Métro St-Paul. **Open** 9am-2am daily. **No credit cards.**
A young international crowd cosies up to the horse-shoe
shaped bar, where there are good beers on tap. Fine vintage
décor, and great *plats du jour.*

La Rouquet

188 boulevard Saint-Germain, 75007 (45.48.06.93).
Métro St-Germain-des-Prés. **Open** 7am-10pm Mon-Sat.
No credit cards.
Just a few steps from the very pricey, world-renowned duo
at St-Germain des Prés, this pleasant café is frequented by
locals who'd be appalled to pay 45F for a glass of wine. The
atmosphere is charmingly fifties, with neon lighting fixtures
and a wrap-around phone box. The deep, canopied terrace
is a fine place to write a letter.

Le Royal Turenne

24 rue Turenne, 75003 (42.72.04.53). Métro St-Paul.
Open 7.30am-10.30pm Mon-Fri, Sun. **Credit** MC, V.
A busy corner café, just a few metres from the place des
Vosges. Moustachioed Michel is the classic Paris waiter, and
in the winter he'll serve you a wonderful onion soup; in the
summer there's a pavement terrace from which to watch the
96 bus go by (made famous by Polanski in *Bitter Moon*).

Le Sancerre

35 rue des Abbesses, 75018 (42.58.08.20). Métro
Abbesses. **Open** 7.30am-1.30am daily. **Credit** V.
This thriving old café bar halfway up the Butte Montmartre
has a mermaid on the ceiling and an arty, young, leather-
clad crowd packing it out every evening. Good (recorded)
music. Hot dishes served at lunchtime only.

Le Select

99 boulevard du Montparnasse, 75006 (42.22.65.27).
Métro Vavin. **Open** 7am-2.30am daily. **Credit** EC, MC, V.
Eccentrics, non-conformists and other colourful characters
prefer the Select to glitzier Montparnasse watering holes. One
of the rare Montparnasse cafés not to have been over-
renovated inside, it retains something of the bohemian feel of
the area's twenties heyday, especially if you sit inside rather
than on the terrace, which is a contemporary add-on. Good
beers (26F a *demi*); plenty of malt whiskies.

Bars

L'Academie de la Bière

88 bis boulevard Port-Royal, 75005 (43.54.66.65). RER
Port-Royal. **Open** noon-2am Mon-Thur; noon-4am Fri,
Sat. **Credit** EC, MC, V.
You can 'study' a huge range of international beers at this
lively Port Royal bar – ten on tap, and around 150 in bottles,
with Belgian specials like *moules frites* and *Carbonnade*
Flamande (beef stewed in beer) to sop up the booze.

L'Aréa

10 rue des Tournelles, 75004 (42.72.96.50). Métro
Bastille. **Open** 7pm-2am Tue-Sun; *happy hour* 7-10pm
daily. **Credit** MC, V.
Be prepared for the intoxicating qualities of the *caipirinha*
house cocktail at this bar-café. Brazilian and Lebanese dishes
are served, and there's occasional live music or entertainment on Wednesday nights (at least from the clientèle).

Bar Belge

75 avenue de St-Ouen, 75017 (46.27.41.01). Métro Guy-
Môquet. **Open** 11am-3am daily. **Credit** V.
The oldest Belgian beer house in Paris is well off the usual
nightlife circuit, but true amateurs willingly make the trip.
Sample any of the 50 Belgian brews on offer, along with some
excellent Flemish charcuterie, in a warm, jolly atmosphere.

Le Baretto
Hôtel de Vigny, 9 rue Balzac, 75008 (40.75.04.39).
Métro George V. **Open** 7am-1am daily.
Credit AmEx, DC, MC, V.
One of the most handsome recent openings in Paris, this quiet place features big mocha-leather chairs and lots of pale wood to create a Milanese mood. Good sandwiches and Italian wines by the glass. Expensive.

Bar des Ferrailleurs
18 rue de Lappe, 75011 (48.07.89.12). Métro Bastille.
Open 5pm-2am daily. **Credit** MC, V.
Yet another long, dimly lit, quirky Bastille dive, but crowded and noisy, whereas **L'Entrepot** (*see below*) is more relaxed. As the name suggests (it means scrap-metal merchants) everything here seems to be made from rusting metal. The action takes place on uncomfortable stools around a long bar.

Pubs

Paris' pubs are homes-from-homes for wandering Anglophones, and also draw in young Parisians eager to catch a taste of life in Dublin, Sydney or Ashby-de-la-Zouche. For Irish pubs with music, *see chapter* **Music: Rock, Roots & Jazz.**

Café Oz
184 rue St-Jacques, 75005 (43.54.30.48). RER Luxembourg. **Open** 11am-2am daily. **Credit** EC, MC, V.
There's not always enough room to swing a koala in Paris' first Australian bar, complete with grinning stuffed crocodile and boomerangs. It offers Fosters on draught, cocktails, snacks, and good, if pricey, Aussie wines.
Branch: 18 rue St-Denis, 75001 (40.39.00.18).

Connolly's Corner
12 rue de Mirbel, 75005 (43.31.94.22).
Métro Censier-Daubenton. **Open** noon-2am Mon-Fri; 4pm-2am Sat, Sun. **Credit** MC, V.
A popular and boisterous Irish pub with Guinness, Kilkenny, Tennant's, Bass and other beers on tap, a busy darts board and Christmas decorations that seem to stay up all year. Tie wearers beware.

The Cricketer Pub
41 rue des Mathurins, 75008 (40.07.01.45).
Métro Havre-Caumartin. **Open** noon-2am daily; *happy hour* 10pm-midnight daily. **Credit** MC, V.
Oak-panelled English pub. Adnams beers delivered weekly from Suffolk make it a draw for real ale fans. City types reign till 9ish, when younger ex-pats flock in for the unusually late happy hour. Traditional English roast every Sunday lunch.

Finnegan's Wake
9 rue des Boulangers, 75005 (46.34.23.65). Métro Cardinal Lemoine. **Open** 11am-1am Mon-Fri; 4pm-1am Sat, Sun. **No credit cards.**
Irish pub in a tavern that's seen 400 years of student revelling. Poetry nights and folk music often on offer.

The Frog & Rosbif
116 rue St-Denis, 75002 (42.36.34.73).
Métro Etienne Marcel or Les Halles. **Open** noon-2am daily. **Credit** MC, V.
This English corner pub offers real ale brewed on the premises, plus ploughman's lunches, jacket potatoes and other pub grub, a darts board and loads of knees-up entertainment.

James Joyce Pub
71 boulevard Gouvion-St-Cyr, 75017 (44.09.70.32).
Métro Porte Maillot. **Open** noon-1am Mon-Thur, Sun; noon-2am Fri, Sat. **Credit** MC, V.
Brought to you by the same team as **Kitty's** (*see below*), this noisy Irish pub is devoted to the great Dubliner who left Ireland committed to 'silence, exile and cunning'. Stained-glass scenes of Dublin and Joycean memorabilia add intellectual depth to your Guinness. There a restaurant upstairs.

Kitty O'Shea's
10 rue des Capucines, 75002 (40.15.00.30). Métro Opéra. **Open** noon-1.30am Mon-Thur, Sun; noon-2am Fri, Sat. **Credit** AmEx, EC, MC, V.
The pub décor in this convivial watering-hole – embossed wallpaper, wooden booths and stained glass – has been imported from Ireland, as are the (expensive) Guinness and Kilkenny draught beers. Food prepared by the Irish chef includes excellent breads and smoked salmon.

Pub 64 WE
64 rue Charenton, 75012 (44.75.39.55). Métro Ledru-Rollin. **Open** noon-2am daily. **Credit** AmEx, DC, MC, V.
A friendly English-style pub with Guinness and McEwan's on tap. Breton owner Jean-Paul blasts out good music from indie rock to the Doors.

Tap into a tinnie at **Café Oz.**

Bar Vendôme (The Ritz)

Hôtel Ritz, 15 place Vendôme, 75001 (43.16.30.30).
Métro Concorde. **Open** 11am-1am daily.
Credit AmEx, DC, EC, JCB, MC, V.
Perhaps the best way to sample the luxury of the Ritz and
the elegance of its service is by visiting its bar, where fine-
ly-wrought examples of the barman's art are priced at 100F.
Big spenders can shell out several times that sum for a snifter
of old Armagnac (something over 900F).

Le Bélier (l'Hôtel)

L'Hôtel, 13 rue des Beaux-Arts, 75006
(43.25.27.22). Métro St-Germain-des-Prés. **Open** 6am-
2am daily. **Credit** AmEx, DC, EC, MC, V.
Cross the unusual lobby of this Left Bank hotel where Oscar
Wilde lived – and died – to discover one of the city's most
romantic bars. Sleek, chic creatures exchange murmured
conversation over expertly-mixed cocktails. Not as pricey as
one might expect. *See also chapter* **Accommodation**.

Birdland

20 rue Princesse, 75006 (43.26.97.59). Métro
Mabillon. **Open** 7pm-6am Mon-Sat; 10pm-6am Sun.
Credit AmEx, DC, MC, V.
Just down the street from the super-exclusive Castel nightclub, this democratic bar is open to nighthawks of all ages
and persuasions who appreciate moderately priced libations,
low lights and judiciously chosen recorded jazz.

Chez Richard

37 rue Vieille-du-Temple, 75004 (42.74.31.65).
Métro St-Paul. **Open** 5pm-2am daily; *happy hour* 5-
8.30pm. **Credit** EC, MC, V.
A fashionable but relaxed Marais bar where a well-dressed
young crowd go for an after-work drink or a cocktail en
route for **Les Bains** (*see chapter* **Nightlife**). At the back
there's a warren of little corners, but best vantage point is
at the bar – once you've mastered the strange, slithery green
bar stools. Good cocktails, but don't bother with the tapas-
style snacks.

China Club

50 rue de Charenton, 75012 (43.43.82.02).
Métro Ledru-Rollin. **Open** 7pm-2am Mon-Thur, Sun;
7pm-4am Fri, Sat. **Credit** EC, V.
From an inconspicuous street behind the Bastille opera, this
beautiful people's hangout transports you to colonial Hong
Kong. Downstairs, a hardwood bar runs the length of the
place, but best is the lacquered *fumoir chinois* upstairs,
where the barman shakes up one of the best cocktails in
Paris. Dim sum-type bar snacks are served.

La Closerie des Lilas

171 boulevard du Montparnasse, 75006
(43.26.70.50). Métro Vavin/RER Port-Royal. **Open**
11.30am-2am daily. **Credit** AmEx, DC, MC, V.
This Montparnasse classic is rather quieter than in its
literary heyday – recalled by little brass plaques on the
tables telling you which celebrity sat where, including
Hemingway and Gertrude Stein. White-jacketed barmen
nonchalantly shake cocktails, a pianist tinkles in the background – it's hard to believe that this place started life in
the last century as a *guinguette* dancehall. When it's fine,
you can sit outside on the large pavement terrace, enclosed
by hedges.

Le Comptoir

37 rue Berger/14 rue Vauvilliers, 75001 (40.26.26.66).
Métro Châtelet-Les Halles. **Open** noon-2am Mon-Thur,
Sun; noon-4am Fri, Sat. **Credit** AmEx, EC, MC, V.
A lively, postmodern, and expensive designer café-bar which
regularly attracts an interesting assortment of night owls.
There's usually dancing on Friday and Saturday nights, with
a DJ from 10.30pm.

L'Entrepot

14 rue de Charonne, 75011 (48.06.57.04). Métro
Bastille. **Open** 4.30pm-2am daily; *happy hour* 5.30-
8.30pm. **Credit** MC, V.
One of the longer-running of the dimly-lit Bastille nooks,
with an artfully distressed interior – half the plaster has
fallen from the ceiling, a faded ad can be glimpsed on the
much-patched wall, spiral stairs lead to doors on an internal
courtyard that must have come from a film set, and the cellar
looks like a métro station. Cocktails (45F) are fine, but happy
hour here means not half-price but rather that the second
drink is free.

Le Forum

4 boulevard Malesherbes, 75008 (42.65.37.86).
Métro Madeleine. **Open** 11.30-2am Mon-Fri; 5.30pm-2am
Sat, Sun. **Credit** AmEx, EC, V.
Since 1930, the Forum's resident chemists have delighted
Parisians with their ingenious inventions. Pick your chosen
potion from a list of 150 cocktails and a superb collection of
premium whiskies, then enjoy it ensconced in a comfortable
chair. The bar is at its best at cocktail hour, around 7pm.

Au Général Lafayette

52 rue La Fayette, 75009 (47.70.59.08).
Métro Le Peletier or Cadet. **Open** 8am-4am Mon-Sat.
Credit EC, MC, V.
This friendly, spacious address for serious beer drinkers has
beautiful, turn-of-the-century woodwork and *trompe l'oeil*.
An excellent selection of draught and Belgian abbey beers
are preferred in appropriate vessels.

Harry's New York Bar

5 rue Daunou, 75002 (42.61.71.14). Métro Opéra.
Open 10.30am-4am daily. **Credit** AmEx.
A famous American ex-pat watering-hole (and birthplace of
the Bloody Mary), where expert mix-masters concoct anything under the sun. Their speciality, the *Pétrifiant*, needs
no further description.

Le Mustang Café

84 boulevard du Montparnasse, 75014
(43.35.36.12). Métro Montparnasse-Bienvenüe. **Open**
9am-5am daily. **Credit** DC, MC, V.
Always packed with teenagers, this lively ranch-style Tex
Mex is one of the latest openers in Montparnasse. Budweiser
on tap and nachos, steaks, brownies and the rest served well
into the night, for those who like eating to deafeningly loud
music. Theme party with DJ every Thursday night.
Branch: 20 rue de la Roquette, 75011 (49.23.73.73).

Le Piano Vache

8 rue Laplace, 75005 (46.33.75.03).
Métro Maubert Mutualité. **Open** noon-2am Mon-Fri;
9pm-2am Sat, Sun. **No credit cards.**
A dark, narrow hole with theatre and concert posters plastered on every available inch of the walls, and a mostly student crowd.

Le Requin Chagrin

10 rue Mouffetard, 75005 (44.07.23.24). Métro Monge.
Open noon-2am Mon-Thur; noon-4am Fri, Sat; noon-2am
Sun; *happy hour* noon-9pm. **Credit** AmEx, DC, MC, V.
A student-packed bar on the busy place de la Contrescarpe
with a melancholy shark (*requin chagrin*) hanging from the
ceiling. Good selection of draught and bottled beers.

Le Rosebud

11 bis rue Delambre, 75014 (43.35.38.54). Métro Vavin.
Open 7pm-2am daily; *closed* Aug. **Credit** MC, V.
This dimly-lit Montparnasse bar is a relic of more debauched
days. Today it's a middle-aged pick-up joint – it seems the
stools by the bar are the place to linger for strangers-in-the-
night encounters. Jazz records crackle in the background.

Sans Sanz
49 rue du Faubourg-St-Antoine, 75011 (44.75.78.78).
Métro Bastille. **Open** 8.30am-2am daily. **Credit** MC, V.
In the evening, Parisian yoof clamours at the door to get in
despite the rather mean-looking meat guarding it, but beers
are cheap and the chatter loud. At midday, the character is
quite different, as Bastille trendsters sprawl in a rag-bag
selection of chairs for lunch.

Le Sous-Bock
49 rue St-Honoré, 75001 (40.26.46.61).
Métro Pont-Neuf. **Open** 11am-5am Mon-Sat; 3pm-5am
Sun. **Credit** EC, MC, V.
We've heard some sturdy souls are working their way
through all 400 beers and 200 whiskies in this bar's stock.
Cocktails are also on hand (37F), along with stomach-lining
dishes like chilli, goulash and Irish stew. A giant video
screen, golden oldies, country music and a darts club may
or may not add to your heart-burn.

Le Train Bleu, Gare de Lyon
entrance inside Gare de Lyon, first floor,
or 20 place Louis-Armand, 75012 (44.75.76.57). Métro
Gare de Lyon. **Open** 10am-10pm daily.
Credit AmEx, DC, EC, MC, V.
If you have a train to catch, it's worth turning up early just
to take a look at the extravagant carved and painted ceiling,
complete with cherubs, at this, possibly the most ornate station café in the world. One of the most fabulous interiors in
Paris, it was designed to give a stylish welcome to visitors
to the 1900 Exhibition. The restaurant is expensive, but take
a seat in one of the Chesterfield sofas in the bar area for a
luxurious drink.

Le Violin Dingue
46 rue de la Montagne-Ste-Geneviève, 75005
(43.31.78.77). Métro Maubert Mutualité. **Open** noon-
2am Mon-Fri; 9pm-2am Sat, Sun. **No credit cards**.
The 'crazy violin' is part of a venerable Latin Quarter duo,
with the 'gormless piano', **Le Piano Vache**. It's hugely popular with a young foreign crowd, cruising for a good night
out. Beer, note, is served in pints only.

Wine Bars

Wine bars offer the perfect opportunity to investigate different grapes and vintages, as you can
sample by the glass as well as by the bottle. Take
advantage of the patron's expertise to try some of
the smaller châteaux, or underrated areas, such as
the less-celebrated Côtes de Bourg in Bordeaux, or
the wines of the Loire or Alsace. There are any
number of such bars spread throughout the city,
often tiny, eccentric places with bizarre opening
hours. Look for signs saying *bistro à vins* or *dégus-*
tation de vins de propriété (wine tastings), and the
great accolade of *Coupe du Meilleur Pot* for the
annual Best Cup of Wine Trophy.
   Wine bars are also good places for light meals,
often specialising in regional charcuterie and farmhouse cheeses, and many offer *tartines* (open sandwiches). Many open outside standard restaurant
hours, but may offer hot dishes at midday only.

Aux Négociants
27 rue Lambert, 75018 (46.06.15.11).
Métro Château-Rouge or Lamarck-Caulaincourt. **Open**
noon-10.30pm Mon; noon-midnight Tue-Fri. Closed Aug.
No credit cards.

Behind the Sacré-Coeur, where tourists rarely go, is an
appealing little *bistro à vins* in the true Montmartre tradition. To eat there's sturdy country fare, washed down by fine
Bourgueil and Beaujolais and fruity white Jasnières.

Les Bacchantes
21 rue Caumartin, 75009 (42.65.25.35).
Métro Havre-Caumartin. **Open** 11.30am-6pm daily.
Credit AmEx, MC, V.
One of the very best wine bars in Paris – and reasonably
priced –, its superb offerings include a remarkable
Minervois. A very high-quality cheese board, charcuterie and
delicious daily specials accompany the wines.

Le Baron Rouge
1 rue Théophile-Roussel, 75012 (43.43.14.32).
Métro Ledru-Rollin. **Open** 10am-2pm, 5-10pm, Tue-Fri;
10am-10pm, Sat; 10am-2.30pm Sun. **Credit** MC, V.
This tiny, old-style local wine bar is a far cry from all the
pricey eighties upstarts, and its very authenticity has
brought it back into fashion again. Huge barrels fill the shop
area at the front, and at the back you can sample a wide
choice of wines by the glass, from simple Touraines at 7F to
grand crus, accompanied by a plate of cheese or charcuterie.

Le Café du Passage
12 rue de Charonne, 75011 (49.29.97.64). Métro
Bastille. **Open** 6pm-2am Mon-Sat. **Credit** AmEx, MC, V.
This bar, connected to a restaurant (Le Passage), is an excellent place for nocturnal oenophiles to come for a good bottle
and a light meal (30F-50F). The sophisticated atmosphere is
created with indirect lighting, dark walls, wicker chairs and
banquettes. Browse the fine selection of wines (especially
good bottles from Burgundy and the Loire), and sup on a good
salad, *andouillette* poached in wine, cheese or charcuterie.

La Cave Drouot
8 rue Drouot, 75009 (47.70.83.38).
Métro Richelieu-Drouot. **Open** 7am-9pm Mon-Fri;
7.30am-7pm Sat; **closed** Sat July-Sept. **Credit** V.
Appraisers and auctioneers from the Hôtel Drouot (*see chapter* **Art Galleries**) and the mischievous Basque patron Jean-
Pierre Cachot create a good atmosphere in this colourful
bistro. Best bets from the wine list are the superb Burgundies
– order a copious Basque *plat du jour* to go with them, and
finish up with a portion of sheep's milk cheese.

A la Cloche des Halles
28 rue Coquillière, 75001 (42.36.93.89).
Métro Châtelet-Les Halles. **Open** 8am-10pm Mon-Fri;
10am-4pm Sat. **No credit cards**.
Beaujolais is the speciality of this bustling and well-
established place, named after the bell that once tolled the
opening and closing of the market at Les Halles.

Le Coude Fou
12 rue du Bourg-Tibourg, 75004 (42.77.15.16). Métro
Hôtel de Ville or St-Paul. **Open** noon-2am Mon-Sat; 6pm-
2am Sun. **Credit** AmEx, MC, V.
Wines from Burgundy, Bordeaux, the Côtes du Rhône or the
Loire can be sampled here with traditional French cooking.
There's a 110F lunch menu that gives three courses and two
glasses of wine, but you can also just stop by for a drink.

Le Crétois
19 rue Treilhard, 75008 (45.63.34.17).
Métro Miromesnil. **Open** 7.30am-7pm Mon-Fri.
Credit AmEx, MC, V.
Opened in 1994, this has become a great spot for lunch, a
snack or a glass of wine after work. There's a friendly atmosphere along the long bar, where you can get a plate of freshly cut Auvergnat ham with country bread or a cheese plate
with a glass of excellent red Saint-Joseph. The good wine list
favours Beaujolais and Côtes du Rhône.

L'Ecluse

*15 quai des Grands-Augustins, 75006
(46.33.58.74). Métro St-Michel.* **Open** noon-1.30am daily.
Credit AmEx, V.
This bar was the first link in the l'Ecluse chain, that now has
a presence in many parts of the city. Bordeaux wines are
showcased here, with some 70 châteaux represented. They
are always first-rate, as are the pricey little dishes (foie gras,
carpaccio, San Daniele ham) that accompany them.
Branches: too numerous to list; consult the telephone
book for your nearest.

Jacques Mélac

*42 rue Léon-Frot, 75011 (43.70.59.27).
Métro Charonne.* **Open** 9am-5pm Mon; 9am-midnight
Tue-Fri. Closed Aug. **Credit** EC, V.
The jovial Jacques Mélac takes pride in offering one of Paris'
most original wine lists, with a particularly good selection
of Côtes du Rhône. There are hot dishes, Auvergne specialities and an excellent cheese board.

Juveniles

*47 rue de Richelieu, 75001 (42.97.46.49). Métro Palais-
Royal.* **Open** 11am-midnight Mon-Sat. **Credit** MC, V.
This unpretentious wine bar attracts a sophisticated clientele. It's run by the same two Brits as **Willi's** (*below*) and is
a great spot to sample lesser-known French wines and an
international choice from Spain and Australia. The bar
serves tapas-style snacks, as well as hot and cold dishes.
There's even farmhouse cheddar or Stilton alongside the brie.

Les Pipos

*2 rue de l'Ecole Polytechnique, 75005 (43.54.11.40).
Métro Maubert-Mutualité.* **Open** 7.30am-9.30pm Mon-
Fri; 9am-3am Sat. **No credit cards.**
Jean-Michel Delhomme, the friendly owner of this Left Bank
hideaway, will enthusiastically suggest his latest finds and
answer questions about the very good selection of bottles.
Good light meals include salads, cheese plates and *tartines*.

Le Rallye

*6 rue Daguerre, 75014 (43.22.57.05).
Métro Denfert-Rochereau.* **Open** 8.30am-8.30pm Tue-Sat;
9am-2pm Sun. **Credit** MC, V.
A friendly wine bar with plenty of little tables on the pedestrianised rue Daguerre market street, where you can benefit from
the knowledge of its patron Peret, who also owns the wine shop
next door. It's reasonably priced, and as well as the house selection of Bordeaux and Beaujolais, you can also try good specimens from lesser-known areas such as Valençay in the Berry.

Le Rouge Gorge

8 rue St-Paul, 75004 (48.04.75.89). Métro St-Paul.
Open noon-2am Mon-Sat; noon-8pm Sun. **Credit** EC, V.
This pleasant bar near the antique dealers' enclave at St-Paul
has a wide-ranging selection of wines, including a huge num-

Trotsky woz here. **La Tartine.**

ber of Sauvignons from different regions. The selection
changes every two weeks. The food is traditional French,
and includes home-made terrines and puddings.

Le Rubis

*10 rue du Marché-St-Honoré, 75001 (42.61.03.34).
Métro Tuileries.* **Open** 7am-10pm Mon-Fri; 9am-4pm Sat.
Closed Aug. **No credit cards.**
An old-fashioned no-nonsense wine bar on a quaint side-
street with a faithful following, a friendly meeting place
where you can try 30 wines by the glass, and 50 by the bottle.
In the summer, drinkers cascade into the street where they
chat while eating the *tartines* that are the speciality of the
house. Hot dishes are also served, but only at lunch-time. The
bar's annual moment of fame comes on Beaujolais Nouveau
day in November, when Le Rubis is the scene of a drunken
riot that spills out into neighbouring streets.

Le Sancerre

*22 avenue Rapp, 75007 (45.51.75.91).
Métro Alma Marceau.* **Open** 8am-9pm Mon-Fri; noon-
4.30pm Sat. **Credit** MC, V.
One of the best kept wine bars in Paris, Le Sancerre – right
by the Eiffel Tower – is a showcase for the red, white and
rosé Sancerre wines chosen by Alphonse Mellot. The menu
runs to omelettes, cheeses and salads.

Le Sauvignon

*80 rue des Sts-Pères, 75007 (45.48.49.02).
Métro Sèvres-Babylone.* **Open** 8.30am-9.30pm Mon-Sat.
No credit cards.
This minuscule *bistro à vins*, decorated with colourful soft-
porn murals and a collection of caricatures, is a favourite
with sophisticated locals. The choice of wines is small but
very reliable, with a good house Burgundy and Sancerre and
Quincy wines from the Loire. Delicious if pricey sandwiches of cheese and charcuterie on Poilâne bread are served.

La Tartine

*24 rue de Rivoli, 75004 (42.72.76.85).
Métro Hôtel de Ville.* **Open** 8.30am-10pm Mon, Thur-Sun;
noon-10pm Wed. Closed Aug. **No credit cards.**
Ever-fashionable bar on the upper reaches of the rue de
Rivoli, a favourite with everyone from Trotsky, when he
lived around the corner, to today's leading fashion designers.
Delicious *tartines* accompany the changing selection of
wines by the glass (from 7.50F to 14F), chosen from a cellar
of over 3,000 bottles.

Taverne Henri IV

*13 place du Pont-Neuf, 75001 (43.54.27.90).
Métro Pont-Neuf.* **Open** noon-10pm Mon-Fri; noon-4pm
Sat. Closed three weeks in Aug. **No credit cards.**
On the tip of the Ile de la Cité, the tiny Taverne is a good spot
for snacks of cheese, charcuterie, *tartines* and a variety of
wines by the glass or bottle, with an emphasis on Beaujolais.

Willi's Wine Bar

*13 rue des Petit-Champs, 75001 (42.61.05.09). Métro
Pyramides.* **Open** noon-11pm Mon-Sat. **Credit** MC, V.
The British duo of Williamson and Johnston have put togeth-
er one of the best wine lists in Paris with an ever-changing
and innovative assortment of wines from around the world.
Bistro dishes are served next door to a fashionable crowd.

Salons de Thé

Tea rooms abound in trendy areas like the Marais
and in the covered galleries (*see chapter* **Paris by
Area: The Right Bank**). They're usually pret-
tily-decorated places, where you can have teas, coffee or a (often rather expensive) light lunch.

Ladurée Royale, *a palace for macaroons.*

A la Cour de Rohan
59-61 rue St-André-des-Arts, 75006
(43.25.79.67). Métro Odéon. **Open** noon-7.30pm Mon-
Thur, Sun; noon-10pm Fri, Sat. Closed last two weeks
Aug. **No credit cards**.
A quiet salon near the boulevard St-Germain. Cosy and stylish, with a wide range of teas and pastries. No smoking.

Angélina
226 rue de Rivoli, 75001 (42.60.82.00).
Métro Tuileries. **Open** 9am-7pm Mon-Fri; 9am-7.30pm
Sat, Sun. **Credit** AmEx, EC, V.
A place to visit with your grandmother, to appreciate the old-
fashioned service, marble tables and classical columns. The
hot chocolate is sublime; the queues can be enormous.

L'Arbre à Cannelle
57 passage des Panoramas, 75002 (45.08.55.87).
Métro Rue Montmartre. **Open** 11am-6.30pm Mon-Sat.
Credit EC, MC, V.
A pretty salon de thé occupying a decorative former
chocolatier in this glass-roofed passage – the first to be
built in Paris. A wide choice of salads and savoury flans
and good fruit juices, as well as the usual cakes, tarts and
sundaes.

Brocco
*180 rue du Temple, 75003 (42.72.19.81). Métro
République.* **Open** 8am-8pm daily. **Credit** EC, V.
Marble, mirrors and sculptured mouldings adorn this tea
room near the place de la République. Prices are more in
keeping with the downscale neighbourhood than with the
lush décor, so take a seat at one of the triangular marble
tables and stuff yourself with delicious, inexpensive pastries. Try the rich *Malgache au chocolat*, and they also
serve great coffee, too.

Café de la Mosquée de Paris
39 rue Geoffroy-St-Hilaire, 75005 (43.31.18.14).
Métro Censier-Daubenton. **Open** 10am-10pm daily.
Closed Aug. **No credit cards**.
Sweet mint tea, authentic *loukoums* and sticky pastel pastries are served in a leisurely fashion at the Paris mosque.
You can sit either in a little courtyard or in the atmospheric
interior, among carved wood, cushions and brass trays For
the mosque's Moorish baths, *see chapter* **Women's Paris**.

Les Deux Abeilles
*189 rue de l'Université, 75007 (45.55.64.04). RER Pont
de l'Alma.* **Open** 9am-7pm Mon-Sat. **No credit cards**.
A fashionable but friendly spot not far from the Eiffel
Tower, but mostly untroubled by its crowds. The décor
has an attractive country feel, with rose wallpaper and
antiques, and the menu is similarly rustic, with white
asparagus tarts, ravioli in herb sauce, apple crumble and
excellent lemon scones.

Ladurée Royale
16 rue Royale, 75008 (42.60.21.79).
Métro Madeleine. **Open** 8.30am-7pm Mon-Sat; 10am-7pm
Sun. **Credit** AmEx, EC, JCB, V.
Come here to enjoy a late breakfast of wonderful croissants
and coffee, or better still, a tea-time treat of Ladurée's
renowned raspberry, chocolate and vanilla macaroons.

Lindsay's Tea Room
4 rue Yvonne-le-Tac, 75018 (42.52.74.09).
Métro Abbesses. **Open** 11.30am-7pm Mon, Wed-Sun.
Credit EC, MC, V.
A peaceful English tea room on a quiet street not far from
the foodie shops of rue Lepic. Lindsay serves homemade
scones, tea and light snacks, such as beans on toast and
Welsh rarebit that will take you back to the nursery.

Mariage Frères
30 rue du Bourg-Tibourg, 75004 (42.72.28.11).
Métro Hôtel de Ville. **Open** noon-7pm daily. **Credit**
AmEx, EC, MC, V.
Hundreds of rare and exotic teas perfume the air of this extraordinary shop. The salon de thé produces mediocre light
lunch dishes, but the pastries served with, for example, a cup
of golden-tipped Grand Yunnan are delicious.
Branch: 13 rue des Grands Augustins, 75006
(40.51.82.50).

Muscade
*36 rue de Montpensier, 75001 (42.97.51.36). Métro
Palais-Royal.* **Open** *restaurant* noon-3.15pm, 7-9pm, *tea
and pastries* 3.30-6pm, daily. **Credit** AmEx, EC, MC, V.
The meals here are generally disappointing, but the setting
– amid the flowers and fountains of the Jardin du Palais
Royal – is superb, especially in summer.

La Nuit des Thés
22 rue de Beaune, 75007 (47.03.92.07).
Métro Rue du Bac. **Open** 11.30am-7pm Mon-Sat; 11am-
4pm Sun. **Credit** MC, V.
An elegant salon with mirrors, marble and gilt trim and a
suitably elegant 7th *arrondissement* crowd. A good selection
of teas and light meals, and delicious *tarte au fromage blanc
caramelisée* (cheesecake with a crunchy caramel topping).

La Pagode
57 bis rue de Babylone, 75007 (36.68.75.07).
Métro St-François Xavier. **Open** 4-9.45pm Mon-Sat; 2-
8pm Sun. **No credit cards**.
A truly exotic tea room within the beautiful oriental pagoda
cinema. You don't have to see a film to visit this peaceful
spot, which opens on to a courtyard garden. Good cakes,
brownies and a wide choice of teas. *See also chapter* **Film**.
Branch: 4 rue St Honoré, 75001 (40.39.93.99).

A Priori Thé
35-37 galerie Vivienne, 75002 (42.97.48.75).
Métro Bourse. **Open** noon-6pm Mon-Fri; 12.30-6.30pm
Sat; 1-6pm Sun. **Credit** EC, MC, V.
This stylish salon de thé in the most elegant of the *galeries*
is a long-popular call-in for shoppers touring the nearby
fashion boutiques. There's an interesting range of English
teas and French and American-style pastries, set out for
your inspection or temptation. Lunches and weekend
brunches are also served.

Tea Follies
6 place Gustave-Toudouze, 75009 (42.80.08.44).
Métro St-Georges. **Open** 9am-8pm Mon-Sat; 9am-7pm
Sun. **Credit** AmEx, EC, MC, V.
On a shady square just south of Pigalle, you can indulge in
scones and tea, or the rather more calorific *Ardèchois* (a
chocolate and chestnut confection). A good selection of wines
is available by the glass. Brunch is served on Sundays.

Nightlife

Dance cheek to chic in the hippest haunts or frolic to old tunes on the banks of the Seine.

There are many ways to trip the City of Light fantastic. Party people hit the town *en masse* around previews, fashion weeks, movie premières and the like. One-off parties rave on, and annual musts include Mardi Gras, the Fireman's Balls on 13 July (*see chapter* **Paris by Season**) and the summer Gay Party on quai de la Tournelle, usually also on the eve of Bastille Day, although dates may vary in future. In recent years Summer Balls have also been organised in outlying châteaux, where fairground rides spin, the music pumps and the champagne flows. August, on the other hand, sees one-offs on hold, as stalwarts of the scene head south.

Meanwhile Parisian *boîtes de nuit* thrive, notably three dynasties. Hubert Boukobza and Philippe Fatien own the perennially trendy **Les Bains**, new institution **Queen** and the recently-revamped **Bus Palladium**. Régine still holds court and has lately been throwing her nightclubbing know-how behind recent aquisitions **Le Palace** and it's hipper basement **Le Privilège/Kit Kat**. Septuagenarian Hélène Martini controls the pick of the Pigalle haunts, **Moloko**, **Shéhérazade** and **Folies Pigalle**.

Despite the oligarchy, though, there's no shortage of new entrepreneurs ready to light your fire. After a sabbatical club queen Martine Meyer is back for weekly rendezvous at **La Casbah** and **Décadence**. Also watch out for jungle/ragga/acid jazz nights promoted by the Semi Shade, House Keeper, Jellybabies or What's Up teams.

There is now too an expanding number of club-bars (known as *Dance Bars*) for a half way house before you really party down. **Club Club** is a recent opener in Pigalle, while **Moloko** and **Lili La Tigresse** continue packing them in down the road. In the Bastille, **What's Up** has made its mark with a London-ish formula.

Big stomping additions to the scene are the major Dance Parties organised by rival radio stations NRJ and Fun, held at **Bercy** and **Zénith** (*see chapter* **Music: Rock, Roots & Jazz**). Also peculiarly Parisian are the club barges along the Seine, which during summer in particular pump out salsa, reggae and ragga 'til dawn. Paris's most famous French DJ Albert can be found aboard a Mississippi steamboat moored in front of the Eiffel Tower playing tunes as cool as the night air.

As well as all these crucial spots there are naturally other things to do in Paris *de nuit*. Newly

restored to popularity as summer venues are the *guinguettes*, traditional French dance halls, ideal for a laid-back good time (*see below* **Guinguettes**). And, of course, the kind of Nite-life Paris invented and for which it's famous from Tokyo to Timbuktu continues to strut its stuff, despite every prophecy of its disappearance (*see page 179* **Boobs & Boas**). There are too several smaller cabarets, offering entertainment from sophisticated to kitsch (*see below* **Cabaret & Turns**).

Essential Info

What's On

One-nighters are notoriously subject to change or cancellation, and even established clubs have been known to vanish from one week to the next, so it's worth phoning ahead, or checking the *Time Out Paris* listings in *Pariscope* or the hip magazine *Nova*. Tune in to **Radio Nova** (101.5 MHz) at around 6pm daily for last minute club, concert and rave details, or at 7.15pm to the Gay station **Radio FG** (98.2 MHz) (*see chapter* **Media**). Party flyers can be found at hip bars and at indie record stores such as **Rough Trade** (*see chapter* **Specialist Shops**). The Minitel services 3615 Party News and 3615 Rave also have handy information.

Drink: Have a Care

Once you're in, the next issue is *la consommation* – drink. Hopefully at least one will be included in the entry price, but with a humble can of beer at 50F-100F, drinking in clubs is for the loaded. Rather than beer you might as well go for spirits, which are sloshed into the glass, or even buy a bottle, which at 1,000F may strike you as insane, but with endless mixers thrown in and a table to sit at it makes sense if you are four or more.

Getting Home

The best way to get home is usually by taxi. Night buses do run every hour all night, but some parts of the city are very poorly served (*see chapter* **Getting Around**).

Groovy

Le Balajo

9 rue de Lappe, 75011 (47.00.07.87). Métro Bastille. **Open** *disco-musette* 3-6.30pm Fri-Sun; *disco* 11pm-5am Mon, Thur-Sat. **Admission** 100F. **Credit** V.
Although permanently-cool DJ Albert, under whose tutelage the Balajo became *the* hip alternative club of the mid-eighties, moved on to other venues a while ago his spirit lingers, and this period venue still looks the part. The bizarre, colourful West-Side-Story interior is as eyecatching as when it opened in 1936, and, they claim, unchanged apart from a lick of paint and a few light bulbs. It's also ever popular. Monday and Thursday are still the nights for assorted groovers to get down to a mix of rumba, cha cha cha, samba and those smooth fifties' classics. The classic atmospheric dancehall.

*Getting it on at **La Casbah**.*

Le Bataclan

50 boulevard Voltaire, 75011 (47.00.39.12/47.00.30.12).
Métro Voltaire. **Open** 11am-dawn Thur-Sat. **Admission**
80F Fri, Sat. **No credit cards.**
Run by David Guetta and friends, late of **Queen** and **Folies
Pigalle.** They've turned the end of the week club nights here
into a camp dance machine for a mixed/gay following. A
sizeable place with large dancefloor and surrounding tables
and chairs for spectating, it has played host to a range of
celeb and fashion events too. Also a fine venue for live music
(*see chapter* **Music: Rock, Roots & Jazz**).

La Casbah

18-20 rue de la Forge Royale, 75011
(43.71.71.89). Métro Faidherbe-Chaligny or Ledru-Rollin.
Open *bar* 9pm-4am daily; *disco* 9pm-4am Tue-Sat.
Admission free Mon-Thur, Sun; 100F Fri, Sat; *drinks*
60F-90F. **Credit** AmEx, DC, V.
Visit North Africa without splashing out on a ticket in this
Bastille venue with décor inspired by the classic movie *Pépé
le Moko.* The trendy clientèle sip cocktails with exotic names
('Fez' and 'Laziza' are among the best), and outlandish prices.
After a quiet period the place is coming alive again, with a
series of one nighters. Door policy can be snooty.

Cristal Palace

43 boulevard de Sébastopol, 75001 (42.36.45.59).
Métro Châtelet-Les Halles. **Open** 6pm-4am daily.
Admission 30F Mon-Thur, Sun; 50F Fri, Sat. **Credit**
AmEx, DC, MC, V.
After a number of false starts this sprawling ex-shop is set
to become a major venue. It's on three floors, with dancing
in the basement to music *à la mode*, a video wall, billiards
and three bars. From the upstairs window you can look down
at the streetlife, or take five in the lounge in one of the multi-
coloured armchairs and play some backgammon.

Divan du Monde

58 rue des Martyrs, 75018 (42.55.48.50). Métro Pigalle.
Open 8pm-dawn Mon-Sat; 3pm-dawn Sun. **Admission**
30F-100F. **Credit** MC, V.
As painted by Toulouse Lautrec, when it was the Divan
Japonais, one of the most legendary Montmartre cabarets of
the 1890s. It's now one of Paris' most sparky live music
venues, but has also quickly made the crossover to become
a happening place for various DJ's and MC's Expect the
latest acid-jazz, fusion funk and ragga. The accent is
definitely street and multi-racial; décor is straight out of the
latest trendy beer commercial. Despite the obvious commercial touch it has built up a strong reputation in a short time
(*see also chapter* **Music: Rock, Roots & Jazz**).

Folies Pigalle

11 place Pigalle, 75009 (48.78.25.56).
Métro Pigalle. **Open** 11am-7am Thur-Sat. **Admission**
100F (incl drink). **Credit** AmEx, DC, MC, V.
A raunchy old cabaret on two floors: survey the action from
the intimate theatre balcony. DJs David Guetta and Kien and
hot hostess Sylvie Chateigner have upped sticks to
Bataclan, but weekend parties still attract a lively, gayish,
crowd. Garage and progressive house predominate.

El Globo/La Décadence

8 boulevard de Strasbourg, 75010. (El Globo 42.41.55.70;
La Décadence 46.59.29.29). Métro Strasbourg St-Denis.
Open *El Globo* 11pm-dawn Fri; *Décadence* 11pm-dawn
Sat. **Admission** 100F. **No credit cards.**
For years a no-nonsense favourite student venue for Friday
nights, this place has now emerged from obscurity thanks
to David Callister's Friday *El Globo* slot and Martine Meyer's
Saturday night *Décadence* session. Glittering show girls à la
Ru Paul, candlelight and drapes create an atmosphere of
bordello chic.

Niel's

*27 avenue des Ternes, 75017 (47.66.45.00). Métro
Ternes.* **Open** *restaurant* 9pm-midnight, *disco* 12.30am-
dawn, daily. **Admission** free Mon-Wed, Sun; 100F Thur-
Sat; *drinks* 100F. **Credit** AmEx, DC, MC, V.
Like **L'Arc** (*see below* **Classic**), Niel's aims for an exclusive
clubby atmosphere, as can be seen in its wood panelling and
leather armchairs reminiscent of New York's Nell's, which
allegedly served as a model. A favourite of the showbiz and
fashion set, with a selective door policy.

Le Privilège/Kit Kat

3 cité Bergère, 75009 (47.70.75.02).
Métro Rue Montmartre. **Open** *Le Privilège* 11.30pm-
dawn Tue-Sun; *Kit Kat* 6am-noon Fri-Sun. **Admission**
60F. **Credit** AmEx, MC, V.
Linked to the next-door **Palace** (*see below* **Classic**) this
cavernous vaulted cellar is one of Paris' best looking
nightspots. Le Privilège attracts a glamorous lesbian crowd
for the first half of the night (Tue-Sun). Kit Kat (from 6am)
is mostly gay male, and it's probably the hottest, most flamboyant weekend spot in town. Selective door policy; dress
outrageous. See also *chapter* **Gay & Lesbian**.

Le Queen

102 avenue des Champs-Elysées, 75008 (42.89.31.32).
Métro George V. **Open** midnight-dawn daily.
Admission free Mon-Thur, Sun; 80F (incl drink) Fri, Sat.
Credit AmEx, DC, V.
Now firmly claiming hippest nightspot status. Though
certain events are male-only, such as its *Les Mousses* (foam
parties), it appeals across the board. On Saturday night it
starts the evening with mainly gay, and later a young
straight crowd invades to finish off their night, although girls
unaccompanied by a beautiful man may find it hard to get
in. Seventies disco happens on Monday; otherwise it's house
all the way. See also *chapter* **Gay & Lesbian**.

Le Rex Club

5 boulevard Poissonnière, 75002 (42.36.83.98). Métro Bonne-Nouvelle. **Open** 11.30pm-6am Thur, Fri, Sun; 11pm-5.30am Sat. **Admission** 60F Thur, Fri; 100F Sat (incl first drink); 70F Sun. **Credit** (bar only) MC, V.

Long the temple of grunge, the Rex Club stays firmly anchored within the techno-trance orthodoxy. It has followed a young crowd by presenting the latest DJ's and MC's. Formerly Manchester-based star DJ Laurent Garnier still puts in a guest appearance once a month.

Classics

L'Arc

12 rue de Presbourg, 75016 (45.00.45.00). Métro Charles de Gaulle-Etoile. **Open** club 11.30pm-dawn daily; *restaurant* 9pm-1am daily. **Admission** free. **Credit** AmEx, DC, MC, V.

A high-class establishment overlooking the Arc de Triomphe that offers the ultimate jet set setting for a swanky night in Paris. It's in a former gaming den, with the plush still in place, and also has a garden where you can stroll in summer. Dancing goes on downstairs in the basement. Drawing an upmarket crowd, it's a favourite spot for the likes of Naomi and her guru Azzedine Alaïa. Of late, too, they've been doing a roaring trade hosting mega-parties on the film and fashion world calendar. The door staff can sometimes claim it's members only, depending on their mood.

Les Bains

7 rue du Bourg-l'Abbé, 75003 (48.87.01.80). Métro Etienne-Marcel. **Open** club midnight-6am daily; *restaurant* 9pm-1am daily. **Admission** club free Mon-Thur, Sun; 140F (incl drink) Fri, Sat. **Credit** AmEx, DC, MC, V.

These premises were once Turkish baths, and so where Marcel Proust steamed you can now roast in the crowded disco downstairs, surrounded by models and older men with fat wallets. Successfully surviving nightlife trends, Les Bains has recently built up a reputation for its hip restaurant, and dining here handily circumvents legendary doorstep dragon Marilyn's tyrannical door policy. There are special rock'n'roll and disco evenings.

Top Tables

In France meeting up to eat is a central part of a night out, and bars and restaurants considered *mondain* are as much a part of the Paris scene as any club. Say, however, that you've arrived in town *without* your invite to share a table with Jean-Paul G. Don't despair: old standards such as **La Coupole** or **Julien** (*see chapter* **Restaurants**), and the even older Brasserie Lipp on boulevard St-Germain regularly host the *demi-monde*, and there are plenty of other Parisian restaurants where the whiff of celebrity is never far away.

404

69 rue des Gravilliers, 75003 (42.74.57.81). Métro Arts et Métiers. **Open** noon-3pm, 8pm-midnight, daily. **Average** 200F. **Credit** AmEx, DC, MC, V.

Casbah style, a Mecca for the in-crowd offering off-beat North African dishes. A good choice for low-key high-power soirées where you just might happen to see photographer Mario Testino with Mme Lacroix.

Barfly

49 avenue George V, 75008 (53.67.84.60). Métro Alma-Marceau. **Open** noon-3pm, 7.30pm-2am daily. **Average** 250F. **Credit** AmEx, DC, EC, MC, V.

Looks set to corner the celeb market well into 1996, having opened describing itself unblushingly as *très branché* (hip). Eat from the Franco-Italian menu or, as the name says, prop up the bar, with assorted models, tennis stars (in season, May-June) and Roman Polanski. DJ arrives around midnight. Door policy can be selective, so book.

Café Marly

93 rue de Rivoli, Cour Napoléon du Louvre, 75001 (49.26.06.60). Métro Palais-Royale. **Open** 8am-2am daily. **Average** 170F. **Credit** AmEx, DC, MC, V.

Sphinx-like inscrutable trendies in Japanese designer fatigues contemplate Pei's pyramid. In the evening, it's booked out with creative and media types, with their occasional trophy star. *See also chapter* **Cafés & Bars.**

Davé

39 rue St Roch, 75001 (42.61.49.48). Métro Tuileries. **Open** noon-2pm, 7.30-11pm, Mon-Fri; 7.30-11pm Sat, Sun. **Average** 250F. **Credit** AmEx, DC, MC, V.

Ebullient Davé (pronounced Darvey) is the life, soul and the law here where he hectors and badgers customers according to status. Expect to have your food – Chinese and Vietnamese – chosen for you, and to be jostled by supermodels in this tiny corner of extreme trendiness.

La Maison

1 rue de la Bûcherie, 75005 (43.29.73.57). Métro St-Michel. **Open** 7-11.15pm, Tue-Sun. **Average** 200F. **Menu** 110F (lunch), 167F (dinner). **Credit** MC, V.

Intimate, chic and with a *nouvelle*-ish menu that makes it popular with visiting Californian media clout. A secluded terrace also makes it a summer favourite.

La Maison Blanche

15 avenue Montaigne, 75008 (47.23.55.99). Métro Alma-Marceau. **Open** noon-2pm, 8-10.30pm, Mon-Fri; 8-10.30pm Sat. **Average** 250F. **Credit** AmEx, EC, MC, V.

One for the upper echelons of avenue Montaigne's *mode* movers and shakers. A big favourite of Christian Lacroix, who has thrown many a party up here.

Natacha

17 bis rue Campagne-Première, 75014 (43 20 79 27). Métro Raspail. **Open** 8.30pm-1am Mon-Sat. **Average** 250F. **Credit** AmEx, MC, V.

Très rock chic. Regulars include Mickey Jagger and Madonna, plus rock wannabees Johnny Depp and Mickey Rourke. Verdant ferns and closed black blinds ensure discretion, and for total intimacy there's the basement.

Le Télégraphe

41 rue de Lille, 75007 (40.15.06.65). Métro Rue du Bac. **Open** noon-2.30pm, 7.30pm-2am, daily. **Average** 300F. **Menu** 125F, 185F. **Credit** AmEx, MC, V.

A Left Bank gem that's a tasteful art deco setting for laid back dinners; afterwards, you can repair to the piano bar for a snifter until late. A favourite of the fashion crowd.

A bal that's seen them come and go, **Le Balajo.** *See page 174.*

Bus Palladium

6 rue Fontaine, 75009 (53.21.07.33/53.21.02.31).
Métro Pigalle. **Open** 11pm-2am Mon-Sat. **Admission**
100F. **Credit** AmEx, MC, V.
This Pigalle venue has been taken over by the owners of
Queen and **Les Bains**, who have installed the latest sound
system to answer the complaints which plagued it
previously. Now it can belt out the hits of Joan Jett, Jo Jo
Gunne and other guitar rock anthems to its heart's content
and to the obvious pleasure of the partying crowd.

Castel's Princess

15 rue Princesse, 75006 (43.26.90.22). Métro Mabillon.
Open 11pm-5am Mon-Sat. **Admission** disco 'members
only'; *restaurant* 9pm-4am Mon-Sat. **Credit** AmEx, MC, V.
A trendy haunt which prides itself on being notoriously difficult to get into. If you care enough to try, inside you'll find
a gourmet restaurant, a disco and seventies décor setting off
the clientèle of tacky showbiz types and jaded aristos.

La Comédie

5 rue du Mont-Cenis (place du Tertre), 75018
(42.62.89.99). Métro Abbesses. **Open** 10pm-dawn daily.
Admission free (drinks 50F). **Credit** MC, V.
Perched at the top of the town in the tourist heart of
Montmartre, the newest Parisian club is mixing middle of
the road and très risqué during the week. Theatrical décor
means that even if the music isn't your bag checking out the
frescoes will while away the time.

La Coupole (Le Salon)

102 boulevard du Montparnasse, 75014 (43.20.14.20).
Métro Montparnasse-Bienvenüe or Vavin. **Open** 9.30pm-
2am Tue-Thur, Sun; 9.30pm-4am Fri, Sat. **Admission** 90F
(incl drink) Fri, Sat; 80F Tue-Thur, Sun. **Credit** MC, V.
The glitzy basement club of the famous art deco brasserie –
a notorious haunt of gigolos in the thirties – mainly spins
retro and disco. *Mambo Mania* nights on Tuesdays have all
sorts of trendies cha-cha-chaing to a 15-piece live band. They
offer lessons to those lacking latin toes, and there are also
occasional one-nighters. *See also chapter* **Restaurants**.

La Locomotive

90 boulevard de Clichy, 75018 (42.57.37.37). Métro
Blanche. **Open** 11pm-6am Mon-Thur, Sun; 100F Fri, Sat. **Credit** AmEx, DC, MC, V.
A mammoth three-storey venue next to the Moulin Rouge. The
spacious first floor offers live music, while the muted

'American Bar' above is the haunt of the lounge lizard and the
dancefloor-inept. Below, rap, house and the inevitable James
Brown remix pound out in a converted boiler room packed with
a teen crowd. A few interesting one-offs on Monday nights.

La Main Jaune

place de la Porte Champerret, 75017 (47.63.26.47).
Métro Porte de Champerret. **Open** 10pm-dawn Fri, Sat,
day before public holiday. **Admission** *disco* 70F; *drinks*
15F; *rollerskate rental* 15F. **No credit cards**.
A huge venue with post-modern glitzy Philippe Starck décor,
pool tables, two dance floors, two bars and plenty of stuccoed
nooks. The real action happens in the central roller-rink
where young dudes zoom around the fibreglass rock forma-
tions at a vertiginous speed to rap, soul and funk.

Le Palace

8 rue du Faubourg Montmartre, 75009
(42.46.10.87). Métro Rue Montmartre. **Open** 11.30pm-
6am Tue-Sat; *gay tea dance* 5-11pm Sun. **Admission**
50F-100F. **Credit** AmEx, MC, V.
Having emerged from the doldrums of the late Eighties and
become part of the Regine stable, this place trades shame-
lessly on past glories, like the highly successful men-only
gay Sunday tea dance. Suburban theatricality still reigns on
the small dance floor, where poseurs vie for the podiums.
These antics are upstaged only by those who can afford the
1,000F-plus drinks bottles, reclining on 'reserved' couches.

Le Saint

7 rue St-Séverin, 75005 (43.25.50.04). Métro St-Michel.
Open 11pm-5am Tue-Sun. Admission 50F (incl drink)
Tue-Thur, Sun; 80F Fri, Sat. **Credit** MC, V.
Three communicating thirteenth-century cellars in which
well-bred students and au pairs dance the night away to an
eclectic mix from French pop oldies to house numbers. Very
Left Bank-studenty, with drinks a bargain at 10F to 50F.

La Scala

188 rue de Rivoli, 75001 (42.60.45.64). Métro Palais-
Royal. **Open** 10.30pm-6am daily. **Admission** 80F (incl
drink) Mon-Fri, Sun; 90F Sat; free for women Mon-Thur,
Sun, day before public holidays. **Credit** MC, V.
An enormous venue (with no fewer than eight bars) and light
shows, lasers and video screens, La Scala pulls in 40,000 punters a month. The clientèle is predominantly teen. Swedish
tourists and girls in their mothers' stilettos vie for the attention of crew-cut soldier boys on leave.

Shéhérazade

3 rue de Liège 75009 (42 85 53 78).
Métro Europe. **Open** 11pm-6am Fri, Sat. **Admission**
100F. **Credit** JCB, MC, V.
The Russian red and gold columns of this Jules Verne grotto
alone make this intimate venue worth a visit. It's home to a
series of one-nighters and parties for discerning Parisians,
and the rest of the time it's a disco for the *BCBG* student
crowd. Complaints from the neighbours mean it's currently
only operating on Friday and Saturday, but there are hopes
that it will go back to opening six nights a week at some
point in the future.

Afro/Latin

Café de la Plage

59 rue de Charonne, 75011 (47.00.91.60/47.00.35.39).
Métro Ledru-Rollin. **Open** *bar* 8pm-2am Mon-Wed, Fri,
Sat; 10pm-2am Thur; *cellar* 11pm-3am Tue-Thur; 11pm-
dawn Fri, Sat. **Admission** free Tue-Thur; 100F Fri, Sat
with first drink. **Credit** MC, V.
There are two sections, the upstairs bar, and downstairs
where the music happens. Caribbean, African, funk and salsa
all get a look in. It's usually packed at the weekends.

La Chapelle des Lombards

19 rue de Lappe, 75011 (43.57.24.24). Métro Bastille.
Open disco 10.30pm-dawn Tue-Sat; *live show* 8pm Tue-
Thur. **Admission** 100F (incl drink) Tue-Thur; 120F Fri,
Sat. **Credit** AmEx, MC, V.
Like the **Balajo** (*see above* **Classics**) one of the institutions
of the Bastille's rue de Lappe, this club has been pumping
out the hot dance sounds of 'all that is tropical' for over 15
years now. Unaccompanied gents may run into trouble at
the door, and they also don't like trainers, especially white
ones, so you have been warned. Salsa, samba, zouk,
merengue and Afro-Cuban beats fill the dance floor, and the
excellent live concerts include salsa, Caribbean blues and
Réunionaise *malagache* (*see also chapter* **Music: Rock,
Roots & Jazz**).

La Java

*105 rue du Faubourg du Temple, 75011
(42.02.20.52). Métro Belleville.* **Open** 11pm-5am Thur;
9.30pm-5am Fri, Sat; 9pm-5am Sun; *OAP tea dance* 2-
7pm Mon, Sun (free). **Admission** 80F Thur; 60-90F
Thur; 80F Sat; 40F Sun. **Credit** MC, V.
Edith Piaf and Maurice Chevalier made their names at this
place when it was a *musette*-style dance hall – now it's a retro
fetish night-spot which majors on Brazilian and Latin
themes, with live bands and DJs. Great fun.

Keur Samba

*79 rue La Boétie, 75008 (43.59.03.10). Métro Franklin D
Roosevelt.* **Open** midnight-dawn daily. **Admission** free,
first drink 120F. **Credit** AmEx.
A stylish venue popular with monied Africans and Lebanese,
as the row of Jaguars and Mercedes outside will tell you. The
'exclusive' entrance policy demands smart dress and liquid
assets. Once inside, those expensive silk ties are loosened as
the contagious mix of African and Antilles music pounds its
way into the bloodstream, along with the heady rum punch.

Le Tango

*13 rue au Maire, 75003 (42.72.17.78). Métro Arts et
Métiers.* **Open** 11pm-5am Thur Thur-Sat; *musette* 2-6pm
Sat, 2-8pm Sun. **Admission** 100F (with free drink) Thur;
60F Fri, Sat. **No credit cards.**
Funky, laid-back Afro-Caribbean club, full of hedonists dancing to music that goes from zouk and soul to reggae, salsa
and Argentinian tango. Mouth your way through karaoke
on Thursdays; and stop in for a proverbial 'last tango' in
Paris on a Saturday or Sunday afternoon.

Club Bars

Club Club

3 rue André Antoine, 75018 (42.54.38.38).
Métro Pigalle. **Open** 7.30pm-2am daily. **Admission** free.
Credit MC, V.
Buzz your way into this laid-back world on two levels by
hosts architect Tex and Nicholas. It offers an arty fashion
ambience, and a number of happenings take place each week.
Past attractions have included jazz recitals and poetry
readings, though Friday and Saturday it reverts to a quality DJ. Drinks cost from 10F before 9.30pm, 20F thereafter.

Lili la Tigresse

98 rue Blanche, 75009 (48.74.08.25).
Métro Pigalle. **Open** 8pm-2am daily. **Admission** free
Mon-Thur, Sun; 50F Fri, Sat. **Credit** MC, V.
Pigalle's post-modern spot has made its avant garde mark.
The deep scarlet, orange, gilt and all-round plushness of the
décor mean it's in demand as much as a location for films
and videos as a place to drink. Scantily-clad go-go girls and
boys prowl the bar top in a range of bijou fetish outfits (with
whips), and shimmy up and down ladders. Jean-Paul
Gaultier threw a notable little soirée for the Madonna here.

Le Moloko

26 rue Fontaine, 75009 (48.74.50.26).
Métro Blanche or Pigalle. **Open** 10pm-5am daily.
Admission free Mon, Tue, Thur, Fri, Sun; 20F Wed; 40F
Sat. **Credit** AmEx, DC, MC, V.
This ground-breaking Pigalle venue has settled down as a
regular stop-off for the bright young things of Paris. The
crucial clientèle sip tequila cocktails and nibble tapas in
spacious surroundings that have been funkily made-over. In
a power-to-the-people move, the DJ has been replaced with
a jukebox holding 1,200 tunes. Meanwhile on the door, it's
power-to-the-bouncers, so easy does it if you want to get in.

Le Satellit' Café Musical

44 rue de la Folie Mericourt, 75011 (47 00 48 87).
Métro Oberkampf. **Open** 6pm-2am Mon-Thur; 6pm-
dawn Fri-Sun. **Credit** MC, V.
World-music fare washed down with decent wines, a rarity
in similar trendy spots where the accent is on the discs not
the drinks. A cool but friendly crowd.

What's Up Bar

15 rue Daval, 75011 (48.05.88.33). Métro Bastille.
Open 8pm-2am daily. **Credit** MC, V.
Opened in 1994 to lots of fuss as the new designer music bar,
What's Up resembles a sparse concrete bunker inside. This
is a hipster's hangout, fronted by deeply cool cats from the
UK. DJs every night spin hard sounds, and their own pro-
motions bring in the latest bands. This and a selective door
policy make it a halfway-point between bar and club,
although finding enough space to dance can be a challenge.

Guinguettes

Very much in vogue, *les guinguettes* are a dance
hommage to France's rustic past of gingham, red
wine and the accordion. Sited on the riverbank,
they cluster along the Marne valley south-east of
Paris and are easily accessible by RER. Folksy
classics, often pepped up by a bit of swing, prove
irresistible to the feet – a live combo is best, but
the record selection rarely disappoints. Few stay
seated even if they can't equal the fanciest foot-
work, and plates of traditional food and the obligatory red wine welcome you back to your table.

Boobs & Boas

Those high-kicking flagships of Paris cabaret are hitting high seas. The lights have all but gone out at the Folies Bergère, the flamboyant owner of Crazy Horse has committed suicide, the venerable Moulin Rouge is getting over an unhappy association with LaToya Jackson and the Left Bank's Paradis Latin has just changed hands.

Despite all these dramas, though, the shows go on. Leading the way is the Lido, which has just undergone a multi-million franc refit to renew the lustre of the Bluebell Girls. Busty damsels remain the hit formula in any language.

La Belle Epoque
36 rue des Petit Champs, 75002 (42.96.33.33).
Métro Pyramides. **Show** 10.30pm daily; *dinner* 9.30pm daily. **Admission** 330F (incl ½ bottle champagne).
Credit AmEx, MC, V.
Josephine Baker once trod the boards of this faded glory hole, where now they present the *Naughty Nineties* – twentieth century style. Older couples spin unself-consciously round the stage before the show to a diet of showtunes, until the curtain rises on topless *Legs & Co* going through their glitzy paces, and acrobats and conjurers who do their best to amaze.

Crazy Horse Saloon
12 avenue George V, 75008 (47.23.32.32). Métro Alma-Marceau. **Show** 8.45pm, 11.15pm Mon-Fri; 8pm, 10.30pm, 12.50am Sat. **Admission** *standing at bar* 195F (incl one drink, 2nd drink 50F); *seated* 350F-530F (incl 2 drinks), 590F (incl half bottle champagne).
Credit AmEx, DC, EC, JCB, MC, V.
Impresario Alain Bernardin, who lovingly created this temple of 'tasteful' erotica, took his own life in 1994, but the family are carrying on the tradition, despite a fierce squabble between wife Lova Moor (that is her name) and his offspring. The formula remains; saucy antics by icecold beauties with names like Bulba Butterfly and Funky Big Bang, of identical height and vital statistics, with one or two who are more amply endowed thrown in for 'special interest' viewers. Is that real pubic hair, or a toupée?

Folies Bergère
32 rue Richer, 75009 (42.46.77.11). Métro Cadet.
The quintessential Paris cabaret has lately been hosting a sixties'-nostalgia show called *Les Années Twist*, and proposes only to present its traditional girly shows for private corporate functions. Major corporations only need apply.

Le Lido
116bis avenue des Champs-Elysées, 75008 (40.76.56.10). Métro George V. **Show** 10pm, 12.15am daily. **Admission** *dinner* 760F-900F (incl half bottle champagne); *show only* 510F (incl half bottle champagne). **Credit** AmEx, DC, EC, JCB, MC, V.
The 60 Bluebell Girls shake their endowments in the current show *C'est Magique*, in routines that are certainly athletic, if none too innovative. Ranks alongside the Crazy Horse as one of the most glitzy revues in town, with extravagant special effects such as an ice rink, skaters and a waterfall. Ever-popular with Japanese businessmen.

Moulin Rouge
82 boulevard de Clichy, 75018 (46.06.00.19).
Métro Blanche. **Show** 8pm (dinner & dance), 10pm, midnight, daily. **Admission** *dinner & show* from 720F per person (incl half bottle champagne); *show only* from 495F per person (incl half bottle champagne).
Credit AmEx, DC, MC, V.
The high temple of kitsch. For two hours, the 'Doriss Girls' can-can across the stage, with the skill, energy, flair and synchronisation necessary for so much pounding flesh in such a small space. Showstoppers include a tank of live crocodiles, but they overreached themselves when they engaged leading curiosity Miss LaToya Jackson. Her unhappy run ended early.

Paradis Latin
28 rue du Cardinal Lemoine, 75005 (43.25.28.28).
Métro Cardinal Lemoine. **Show** 8pm (dinner), 9.45pm Mon, Wed-Sun. **Admission** *dinner* 670F (incl half bottle of Bordeaux); *show only* 465F (incl half bottle of champagne). **Credit** AmEx, DC, EC, JCB, MC, V.
Reputedly the oldest big show in town, in a theatre designed by Gustave Eiffel. Under new ownership, and a glittering new no-expense-spared show is planned for October '95.

*A touch of the old France at **Chez Gégène**.*

Chez Gégène
162 quai de Polangis, Joinville-le-Pont (48.83.29.43).
RER line A to Joinville-le-Pont. **Open** *Apr-mid Oct* 9pm-2am
Tue-Sat, 3pm-midnight Sun; *Oct-Mar* 9pm-2am Fri, Sat,
3pm-midnight Sun. **Admission** 50F. **Menu** 150F. **Credit**
AmEx, V.
The classic *guinguette*, unaltered for decades except for a
coat of paint and new lacquer on the dancefloor. Elderly
French dance fiends, families and young Parisians pack the
place every weekend. Live band Fri-Sun.

Le Martin-Pêcheur
41 quai Victor-Hugo, Champigny-sur-Marne
(49.83.03.02). RER line A to Champigny.
Open *Apr-end Oct* 8pm-2am Tue-Sat; noon-midnight
Sun. *Nov-Mar* 8pm-2am Fri, Sat; noon-midnight Sun.
Admission from 40F. **Credit** V.
The youngest and hippest of the *guinguettes*. You have to
pully yourself across on a raft to reach this tiny island in the
middle of the Marne. Your efforts will be rewarded by great
music, cute young trendies trying to look like Jean Gabin and
Edith Piaf, and a live band from Friday to Saturday.

Cabaret & Turns

Paris' cabaret tradition survives in small-scale
venues that mainly offer the kind of niche kitsch
that brings the faithful back year after year.
Expect impressionists, puppets, drag, magicians
and of course a Piaf, Chevalier or Brel medley. In
amongst them all, there are also some subversive
modern interlopers. *See also* **Café-Théâtres** *in*
chapter **Theatre**.

L'Ane Rouge
3 rue Laugier, 75017 (45.62.52.42).
Métro Ternes. **Show** 10pm; *dinner* arrive at 8pm for
8.30pm daily. **Admission** *dinner* 200F-350F Mon-Fri,
Sun; extra 50F Sat; *show only* 200F. **No credit cards**.
All the ingredients of a typical Parisian cabaret: a choice of
menu, a restaurant crowded with French provincials and foreign business people, and a tiny stage. The emphasis is on
laughs – the formula is singer, magician, comedian, followed
by a ventriloquist, and audience participation is *de rigueur*.

Le Canotier du Pied de la Butte
62 boulevard Rochechouart, 75018 (46.06.02.86). Métro
Anvers. **Open** 10.30pm-4am daily. **Admission** 190F
before midnight, 80F after. **Credit** EC, MC,.V.
This tiny old-fashioned Pigalle cabaret was frequented by
Piaf, Jacques Brel and Maurice Chevalier in the old days, and
now welcomes modern French variety stars such as Patrick
Sebastien. Performers from neighbouring cabarets tend to
come along after their shows, sometimes joining in on the
tiny stage. Acts change frequently, but include accordion-
ists, some good Piaf-style singers, impressionists and magicians. It's highly recommended, and a particular find is their
version of Jacques Brel.

Caveau de la Bolée
25 rue de l'Hirondelle (place St-Michel),
75006 (43.54.62.20 after 6pm). Métro St-Michel. **Show**
9pm (dinner), 10.30pm. **Admission** *dinner* 230F; *show*
only 100F. **Credit** MC, V.
A cosy bar in a basement, where the formula of 'singalong-
Piaf' means that punters get to hear the resident chanteuse
singing touching ballads or bawdy community songs. The
acts change every three or four months, but the formula
remains the same.

Caveau des Oubliettes
11 rue St-Julien-le-Pauvre, 75005 (43.54.94.97).
Métro St-Michel. **Show** 9pm Mon-Sat. **Admission** 70F.
No credit cards.
A medieval-style, tiny, vaulted cellar piano bar where Anne-
Marie Belin interprets Piaf and Gérard Delord plays the
hurdy-gurdy. Expect to be entertained by minstrels, trouba-
dours and serving wenches. After the show, the audience can
take part in a guided tour of the dungeons to see a guillotine,
a chastity belt and a collection of weapons from the days
when the cellar was part of the prison of Petit Châtelet.

Chez Madame Arthur
75 bis rue des Martyrs, 75018
(42.64.48.27/42.54.40.21). Métro Pigalle. **Show** 9pm
(dinner), 10.30pm daily. **Admission** *dinner from* 295F;
show only 165F (incl one drink, 2nd drink 95F). **Credit**
AmEx, DC, EC, JCB, MC, V.
A non-stop show of drag artists and transsexuals, who mime
to female singers or camp-up historic scenes. The make-up
is as heavy as the *doubles entendres*, and the (recorded) music
is so loud and the speakers so worn out that you are pre-
vented from commiserating with your neighbour. However,
Madame Arthur does have camp value, and does his best to
insult everyone equally; those of a sensitive disposition, bald
men and people who wear specs should refrain from sitting
at the front.

Chez Michou
80 rue des Martyrs, 75018 (46.06.16.04).
Métro Pigalle. **Show** 10.30pm daily; *dinner* (reservation
only) 8.30pm daily. **Admission** *dinner* 550F (incl
cocktail & wine). **No credit cards**.
Visit Michou if you're looking for a French drag and parody
show that's very funny, very high camp and has impressive
costumes. High-pressure enjoyment is the order of the day,
and the biggest laughs come when towering trannies make
a bee line for the businessmen. Essential to book in advance.

Kentina

54 bis rue de Clichy, 75009 (47.82.91.35). Métro Trinité.
Show 8.30pm Sat. **Admission** 100F. **Credit** MC, V.
A dance school in the week, on Saturday nights this place turns into a cabaret as Ken's private floorshow takes to the catwalk. Attractions range from shadow drag theatre to tacky chanteuses. The 100F entry includes a Thai meal, and a table in the same room as *Tout Paris*, but not drinks, bought separately from the bar. Be warned; it can and does run dry.

Au Lapin Agile

22 rue des Saules, 75018 (46.06.85.87).
Métro Lamarck Caulaincourt. **Show** 9pm Tue-Sun.
Admission 110F (incl one drink, second drink 30F); 80F students, except Sat. **No credit cards.**
The Agile Rabbit first became a revue bar in 1860, when it was a favourite meeting place for Montmartre's more bohemian residents, who paid with the sketches and poems on the walls. The artists have now been replaced by a team of well-intentioned performers who warmly invite you in for a programme of songs, poetry and comic turns.

Pau Brasil

32 rue de Tilsitt, 75017 (42.27.31.39).
Métro Etoile. **Show** 10pm daily. **Admission** *dinner & show* 350F-450F. **Credit** AmEx, DC, V.
If meat from a sword and exhibition lambada-ing are your bag, then the noisy, rumbustious Pau Brasil is for you, but

don't sit near the front if you value your hearing. The star turns at this big, glitzy venue (once a swimming pool) don't fail to impress, and the regulation snap with the resident Carmen Miranda is worth the ticket price for her grin alone.

René Cousinier – La Branlette

4 impasse Marie Blanche (2nd left off rue Lepic), 75018 (46.06.49.46). *Métro Blanche.* **Open** 10pm-1.30am Tue-Sat; closed end July, Aug. **Admission** free; obligatory drink starts at 99F. **No credit cards.**
A grubby little cellar bar where René Cousinier, a living legend, will, if your French is up to it, keep you chuckling for a good hour and a half. If his nickname means anything to you (slang for wanking), you'll already have a good idea of his humour. Vulgar, truculent and very funny, he's full of pertinent observation and philosophical – even poetic – charm.

Au Vieux Paris

72 rue de la Verrerie, 75004 (no telephone).
Métro Châtelet-Les Halles. **Open** 3pm-4am Tue-Sat, singing starts around 8pm. **Admission** free; obligatory drink starts at 15F. **No credit cards.**
There's no admission fee; just ring the bell. If Madame Françoise likes the look of you, she'll let you in. Inside, Mexican accordionist extraordinaire Sergio Valagez plays and invites you to sing your heart out (photocopied handouts of classic French ballads are provided, then quickly snatched up). A real taste of old Paris.

Late Eats

Paris has plenty of cafés and brasseries open through the night. You'll find a choice of places open late-night on the Champs-Elysées, boulevard St-Germain, boulevard Montparnasse, and at Pigalle, Les Halles and the Bastille.

L'Alsace aux Halles

16 rue Coquillière, 75001 (42.36.74.24). Métro Châtelet-Les Halles. **Open** 24 hours daily. **Average** 250F. **Credit** AmEx, DC, EC, MC, V.
A brasserie with Alsatian specialities around the clock, and a large terrace for sitting out on summer nights. Excellent *choucroute* with cured pork and sausages, goose confit or fish.

Café de la Bastille

8 place de la Bastille, 75011 (43.07.79.95).
Métro Bastille. **Open** 24 hours daily. **Average** 100F. **No credit cards**
An ordinary café from the outside, but inside this has been given the Jonathan Amar treatment – he of **Les Bains** fame. The bar food is plentiful, if you get the night-time munchies. The surcharge of 3F after 11pm, and cappuccinos are a hefty 33F.

La Cloche d'Or

3 rue Mansart, 75009 (48.74.48.88)
Métro Blanche. **Open** 7pm-4am Mon-Sat. **Average** 170F. **Credit** AmEx, DC, MC, V.
Popular with journalists and Montmartre cabaret types, a Pigalle institution with fusty old-fashioned charm. Traditional dishes and good grills, and a superb wine list.

Le Dépanneur

27 rue Fontaine, 75009 (40.16.40.20). Métro Blanche. **Open** 24 hours daily. **Average** 100F. **Credit** V.
A 24-hour café-bar done up like an American diner, where prices go up a little at night and the food is basic salads

and sandwiches. Assorted Pigalle trendies keep on drinking here after the clubs close.

La Juventus

10 place de la Bastille, 75011 (43.43.18.33).
Métro Bastille. **Open** 24 hours daily. **Average** 150F
Menu 55F incl one beer. **Credit** MC, V.
The place to drop off after a hard night's clubbing for a meal, a pizza or *moules*. 6F surcharge after 11pm, Fri, Sat.

Planet Hollywood

78 avenue des Champs-Elysées, 75008 (45.63.02.86).
Métro Franklin D Roosevelt. **Open** 11am-2am daily.
Average 150F. **Credit** AmEx, DC, MC, V.
Arnie, Bruce and Sly's Parisian outpost is in a building that was once the Lido. Concessions to local feelings include 'classic French dishes' on the menu and movie memorabilia such as Depardieu's hat from *Cyrano*.

Pub St-Germain

17 rue de l'Ancienne Comédie, 75006 (43.29.38.70).
Métro Odéon. **Open** 24 hours daily. **Average** 150F.
Credit AmEx, DC, EC, MC, V.
This vast five-storey enterprise is part pub, part restaurant serving *steak-frites* brasserie staples, plus a huge selection of beers. After hours, ring the bell to get in.

La Tour de Montlhéry

5 rue des Prouvaires, 75001 (42.36.21.82).
Métro Châtelet-Les Halles. **Open** 24 hours Mon-Fri (closes 7am Sat). Closed also 15 July-15 Aug. **Average** 200F. **Credit** EC, MC, V.
A near-legendary old bistro (also known as *chez Denise*) with good house wines, many from barrels by the door, and wonderful food. The walls are stained with cigarette smoke, sausages dangle overhead, and a clientèle mixing celebs and unknowns moves in and out. Usually packed, so book.

'Paris Canaille'

Women's Fashion

Large choice of dresses,
skirts and pullovers.

70's high-heeled shoes.

Prices 100 - 1,300F.

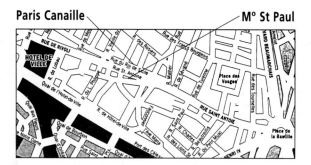

**26 rue du Roi de Sicile
75004 Paris. M° St-Paul.
42.77.74.11. Credit: V.**

Open Mon-Sat 1-8pm, Sun 3-8pm.

*20% discount with your copy of
the Time Out Paris Guide.*

Shopping & Services

Fashion

From plastic platforms to diamond tiaras, the fashion capital has everything for the determined dresser.

French ready-to-wear designers such as Agnès B and Sonia Rykiel – or Jean-Paul Gaultier if you want something more funky – continue to enhance Paris' position as the fashion capital of the world. And, despite a reputation for chauvinism, the governing bodies of French fashion have also opened their doors to established names and new hopefuls from Italy, Japan, Britain and elsewhere. Consequently, the twice-yearly forums that are the Fashion Weeks have stretched into fortnights.

Grunge, an anomalous import that was never really at home here, has given way to archetypal Parisian glamour, causing retailers to breathe a sigh of relief. The recent craze for recycled clothing and salvage wear has even been gussied up. As proof, there's the Malian designer Xuly Bët (real name Lamine Kouyaté), whose trademark patched clothing, complete with exposed seams and hanging threads, has gained the establishment recognition of a boutique in **Au Printemps** (*see chapter* **Specialist Shops**) and a design partnership with sports giant Puma. And he's not the only one: former renegade designer **Tim Bargeot** saw the writing on the wall in 1993, when he abandoned his flea-market T-shirt stand and opened a Barbie-doll sized boutique selling clubwear that's coquettish and techno by turns. For men, *le style anglais* remains popular, with both imported lines – **Paul Smith** is a top seller – and the French version, found in stores such as **Façonnable**.

WHERE TO SHOP

Individual boutiques are the backbone of retailing in Paris, alongside French chains like Naf Naf, Chipie and Kookaï, and international groups such as Benetton and Esprit. For a whiff of the luxurious, *grande dame* Paris shopping that conjures up clichés of a chic Parisienne stalking past with her poodle, head for the rue du Faubourg-St-Honoré and the avenue Montaigne (1st and 8th *arrondissements*). Place Vendôme is best for fine jewellery.

Fashion victims should make straight for the area to the north of Les Halles, along rue Etienne-Marcel to place des Victoires, and along rue du Jour and rue J-J Rousseau (1st and 2nd). **Absinthe** and **Maria Luisa** (*see below* **Designer Boutiques**) are good places to catch up on the latest designers. The trendy Marais is bursting with small one-off shops, especially along rue des Francs-Bourgeois and rue des Rosiers, where cutting-edge boutiques and American-style jeaneries are incongruously sandwiched between old-world delis and Jewish religious artefact shops. There's a growing number of shops too in the Bastille area, where Gaultier has recently opened a spectacular new outlet.

On the Left Bank, the area between boulevard St-Germain and place St-Sulpice (6th *arrondissement*) is particularly good for clothes, while the rue du Cherche-Midi and rue de Grenelle (6th and 7th) are known for top-quality shoes and leather goods.

SALES & HOLIDAYS

Most shops are open from Monday to Saturday; some close for lunch and on Mondays. Some Marais shops open on Sundays, although this has been under legal dispute, so occasional swoops mean they can be closed. All shops close on 1 January, 1 May, 14 July and 25 December, but most stay open on other public holidays. As with everything else in Paris, many shops close for all or part of August. Seasonal sales (*soldes*) are held in early January and the beginning of July, and can offer very good discounts, typically of 30 to 50 per cent.

Détaxe (Tax refunds)

Non-European Union residents can reclaim value-added tax (15.68% of the purchase price) if they have spent more than 2,000F **in any one shop**. At the shop ask for a *bordereau de vente* form, and when you leave France have it stamped by customs. Then send a stamped copy back to the shop, who will refund the tax in francs. To speed up the process you can use the **Cashback** company (48.27.24.54), who will handle the bureaucracy for you, for a fee. *Détaxe* does not cover food, drink, medicine, unset gems, antiques and works of art, cars (and their parts) or commercial purchases.

L'Eclaireur. *See page 186.*

Paris Cuts

Strangely enough, haute couture – that epitome of French style and artistry – was invented by an Englishman. When Charles Frederick Worth hung up his dressmaker's shingle on the rue de la Paix in 1858, he showed the French how it was done. Haute couture reached its pinnacle in the thirties, led by sleek couturiers Madeleine Vionnet, Coco Chanel and Elsa Schiaparelli. It was briefly revived after World War II by Christian Dior's New Look, but at the end of the 1950s many couture houses closed their doors, making way in the early sixties for the rise of *prêt-à-porter* (ready to wear) collections. Nowadays, with laboriously crafted garments costing 20,000F to 50,000F or more, it's not surprising that the market for original couture is restricted to a few thousand women in the world.

At the end of the eighties the wit and opulence of Christian Lacroix gave haute couture a boost, while Karl Lagerfeld has injected the Chanel name with such irreverence and street-cred that his couture has almost ceased to be considered elitist. With the recession receding, couture clients are again turning up at the Paris presentations, and justifying shelling out for one outfit the amount of money it would take to build a school in a third-world country. Dior, one of couture's most successful houses, recently released order figures for one season totalling 150 suits, 100 ball gowns and six wedding dresses.

Even in haute couture's darkest days, received wisdom held that the show must go on in order to give the house's *prêt-à-porter* ranges, accessory spin-offs and perfume lines the glamour rub-off necessary for huge sales and lucrative licensing agreements. And all couturiers will tell you that haute couture is their laboratory of ideas, elements of which are incorporated into ready-to-wear.

Couture houses are grouped around the Champs-Elysées, in particular along avenue Montaigne and rue du Faubourg St-Honoré. Most spectacular to look at are Chanel, Nina Ricci and Valentino on avenue Montaigne, Lacroix and Versace on rue du Faubourg St-Honoré, and Christian Dior on the rue François Ier.

The entire fashion world descends on Paris for the couture shows in January and July, and the *prêt-à-porter* collections in March and October. As part of the *Grand Louvre* plan the **Carrousel du Louvre** exhibition hall was supposed to become the sole centre for the fashion weeks, and it does now hold the largest number of shows. However, many designers dislike it and prefer more atmospheric venues around town. All events are strictly invitation only, but those not on the list can always hang around outside to catch a glimpse of the celebs and the razzmatazz; determined liggers can even try to cadge themselves an invite.

Designer Boutiques

Absinthe
74-76 rue Jean-Jacques Rousseau, 75001 (42.33.54.44). Métro Châtelet-Les Halles or Etienne Marcel. **Open** 11am-7.30pm Mon-Sat. **Credit** MC, V.
Owner Marthe Desmoulins tracks down and nurtures fresh international talent, and clothes by Dries Van Noten, Christophe Lemaire, Julie Skarland, Yoneda Kasuko, Costume National, Fred Sathal, Mieke Cosyn and Osamu Maeda can all be found here. Also stocked are attention-getting hats by Jacques Lecorré, clever bags by Jamin Puech, made-to-measure shoes by Andres Hombach and ex-votive jewellery by Wouters & Hendrix.

Agnès B
2, 3, 6, 10 rue du Jour, 75001 (women 45.08.56.56/men 42.33.04.13). Métro Châtelet-Les Halles. **Open** 10am-7pm Mon-Sat. **Credit** AmEx, EC, MC, V.
There's an Agnès B boutique for everyone on rue du Jour: women's wear at No. 6, men's wear at No. 3, Lolita for teens at No. 10, children's wear at No. 2 and at No. 19 she offers her own bags, sunglasses and watches, along with knick-knacks she has picked up in her exotic travels. There's even a gallery showing contemporary art and photography at No. 6 (*see chapter* **Art Galleries**). Her style is casual, modern and wearable, using lots of neutral colours and natural fabrics: cotton shirts cost around 560F, silk shirts from 920F and soft knitted cotton tops from around 300F. **Agnès B Beauté**, upstairs in the women's shop, stocks make-up and perfume. **Branches include:** 83 rue d'Assas (Lolita), 75006 (43.54.69.21); 13 rue Michelet (women), 75006 (46.33.70.20); 6 rue du Vieux Colombier, (women, beauté, children), 75006 (44.39.02.60).

A.P.C.
3 (men) and 4 (women) rue de Fleurus, 75006 (42.22.12.77). Métro St-Placide. **Open** 11am-7.30pm Mon-Sat; 11am-7pm Sat. **Credit** AmEx, EC, MC, V.
A hip collection of jackets, A-line minis, drainpipe trousers and skinny rib knits inspired by the film *A Bout de Souffle* and St-Germain in May '68. APC is a favourite with the students at the nearby universities, and young fashion editors. **Branch:** 25 bis rue Benjamin Franklin, 75016 (45.53.28.28)

Au Vrai Chic Parisien
8-10 rue Montmartre, 75001 (42.33.15.52). Métro Châtelet-Les Halles. **Open** 10.30am-7.30pm Mon-Sat. **Credit** AmEx, EC, JCB, MC, V.

A retro shop evoking the heady joys of the Liberation. Women's clothes have a girlish charm: chunky-knit little cardigans are paired with skimpy gingham frocks or peddle-pushers. There's also a smattering of men's casual pieces, and a small collection for children.
Branch: 47 rue du Four, 75006 (45.44.77.00)

Azzedine Alaïa

7 rue de Moussy, 75004 (42.72.19.19).
Métro Hôtel-de-Ville. **Open** 10am-7pm Mon-Sat.
Credit AmEx, DC, EC, MC, V.
Never one to go with the flow, Alaïa gives a sneak-peek of his collection only after all the fashion editors and buyers have gone home. Hence, only the style cognoscenti have first access to his curve-hugging dresses for about 3,000F, and forties-style shoes for 1,500F. Alaïa groupies include Grace Jones, Tina Turner and all the supermodels.

Barbara Bui

23 rue Etienne-Marcel, 75001 (40.26.43.65).
Métro Etienne Marcel. **Open** 11am-7pm Mon-Sat.
Credit AmEx, MC, V.
This boutique has been newly expanded for Barbara Bui's romantically detailed, tailored collection, which appeals to working women who want to strike that balance between looking fashionable, feminine and professional.
Branches: 414 rue St-Honoré, 75008 (42.60.86.69); 35 rue de Grenelle, 75007 (45.44.85.14).

Bonnie Cox

38 rue des Abbesses, 75018 (42.54.95.68). Métro Abbesses. **Open** 10.30am-8pm Mon-Sat; 11am-7pm Sun.
Credit AmEx, MC, V.
Owner Ludovic Lainé was first to discover Xuly Bët a few years ago, and is currently grooming Hilda Heim, whose elongated brocade and satin dresses are leading the shop away from its kitsch image. Average price for a dress is 500F.

Chachnil

68 rue Jean-Jacques Rousseau, 75001 (42.21.19.93).
Métro Châtelet-Les Halles or Etienne Marcel. **Open** 11am-7pm Mon-Sat. **No credit cards.**
Entering this boutique, tucked at the back of a courtyard, is like stepping into one of the Pierre & Gilles photos that adorn the walls. Owner-designer Chachnil creates colourful fairy-tale clothes, and dresses stars such as Marc Almond, Nina Hagen and famous French transvestite Marie France.

Christian Lacroix

2/4 place St-Sulpice 750026(46.33.48.95). Métro St-Sulpice. **Open** 10am-7pm Mon-Sat. **Credit** AmEx, DC, EC, JCB, MC, V.
The ebullient couturier from sunny Arles has recently inaugurated his newest Paris boutique to house his *prêt-à-porter* line, his signature symbolic jewellery and accessories, the new casual line, Bazar, and a range of sheets and towels.
Branches: 73 rue du Faubourg St Honoré, 75008 (42.65.79.08); 26 avenue Montaigne, 75008 (47.20.68.95).

Comme des Garçons

40 (men) and 42 (women) rue Etienne-Marcel, 75002 (women 42.33.05.21/men 42.36.91.54). Métro Etienne Marcel. **Open** 11am-7pm Mon-Sat. **Credit** AmEx, DC, EC, JCB, MC, V.
Rei Kawakubo, known for her severe minimalism and androgynous styles, has of late crafted mannish suits for women in pristine white, with her trademark dramatic draping. The two stores have an art-brut design of glass and bare concrete to match. Prices start at around 7,000F for men's suits, 2,000F for women's dresses. Also in the women's shop are her less expensive, made-in-Italy Comme des Garçons line and the quirky, colourful collection of her protégé Junya Watanabe.

Détails

15 rue du Jour, 75001 (40.26.75.65). Métro Châtelet-Les Halles. **Open** noon-7.15pm Mon; 10.30am-7.15pm Tue-Sat. **Credit** AmEx, MC, V.
Détails carries the work of trendy recycled clothing designers: Xuly Bët's Funkin' Fashion (layers of cut-up shirts and jumpers don't come cheap), and Olive, who makes clothes from old post-office sacks, among other things. Saner styles are stocked downstairs: Irène van Ryb coordinates, girlish dresses and knits from Jerôme L'Huillier, and good accessories, including Emma Luna velvet hats, D. Lavilla suede bags and Philippe Model shoes.

L'Eclaireur

3 rue des Rosiers, 75004 (48.87.10.22). Métro St-Paul. **Open** 2-7pm Mon; 10.30am-7pm Tue-Sat. **Credit** AmEx, DC, MC, V.
Cutting-edge fashion and furnishings cleverly displayed in a lofty, skylit boutique. Fornasetti's playful ceramics and fabrics printed with neo-classical designs form a backdrop for clothing by Dolce e Gabbana, Prada, Ann Demeulemeester, Vivienne Westwood, Dries Van Noten and Martin Margiela, among other fashion renegades, plus decorative jewellery by Slim Barrett and Chrome Hearts.
Branches: 26 avenue des Champs-Elysées, 75008 (45.62.12.32); 24 rue de L'Echaude, 75006 (43.29.58.01).

Equipment

46 rue Etienne-Marcel, 75002 (40.26.17.84).
Métro Etienne-Marcel or 4 Septembre.
Open 11am-7pm Mon; 10.30am-7pm Tue-Sat. **Credit** AmEx, EC, DC, JCB, MC, V.
Nothing but shirts are sold here, in a stylish storefront. Only a small part of the vast choice is folded on the shelves, but the assistant will willingly pull out drawers to reveal much more, available in both fitted ladies' and a larger unisex cut.
Branches: 203 boulevard St-Germain, 75007 (45.48.86.82); 5 avenue Victor Hugo, 75016 (45.01.20.29).

Et Vous

25 rue Royale, 75008 (47.42.31.00). Métro Madeleine.
Open 10.30am-7.15pm Mon-Sat. **Credit** AmEx, DC, EC, JCB, MC, V.
To update their image, Et Vous have recruited as consultant Koji Tatsuno, the avant-garde designer known for inventive textiles, and commissioned Andrée Putman to design this 1,200-square metre flagship store. Their own suits, sold as separates, dresses, trousers and accessories, are rounded out by Equipment shirts and Patrick Cox shoes; average price for a jacket is 1,500F. The store is always full of customers, and caters for an urban, dynamic clientèle.
Branches: 62 (men) rue de Rennes, 75006 (45.48.56.93); and 64 (women) rue de Rennes, 74006; 15 rue des Francs-Bourgeois, 75004 (48.87.48.98).

Inès de la Fressange

14 avenue Montaigne, 75008 (47.23.08.94). Métro Alma-Marceau. **Open** 10am-6.30pm Mon-Sat. **Credit** AmEx, DC, JCB, MC, V.
Former Chanel star model Inès de la Fressange proved that she has brains as well as beauty when she opened this shop, decorated like a circus tent. Here she displays her own clothing line, which is not terribly original but very chic: less-is-more clothes and accessories in a choice of colours and sumptuous fabrics. Suits start at around 4,000F, dresses 1,800F-2,000F and shoes from about 1,000F. Items for the home now include china, glass, bed-linen, towels and lamps.

Irié

8 and 10 rue du Pré-aux-Clercs, 75007 (42.61.18.28).
Métro Rue du Bac. **Open** 10am-7pm Mon-Sat; closed first three weeks Aug. **Credit**, EC, MC, V.
Fashion editors and chic Parisians make a bee-line for this Japanese designer's twin boutiques. Long silhouette trouser

From the **Maison de la Fausse Fourrure.**

suits, new-classic jackets, printed knit tops and lots of graphic black and white.

Jean-Paul Gaultier

30 rue de Faubourg St-Antoine, 75012 (44.68.84.84) Métro Bastille. **Open** 11am-7.30pm Mon,Sat; 10.30am-7.30pm Tue-Fri. **Credit** AmEx, DC, EC, JCB, V.
Once the *enfant terrible* of French fashion, lovable Euro-pixie Gaultier now seems destined for Renaissance manhood. His witty, irreverent clothes have become icons for the stylish, and are cleverly displayed in his new shop alongside the clubby JPG diffusion line and Gaultier Jeans. Check out his latest fashion show on the video screens inlaid in the blue mosaic floor, the changing celestial signs on the fibre-optic ceiling and the fun-fair mirrors.
Branch: 6 rue Vivienne, 75002 (42.86.05.05).

Jil Sander

52 avenue Montaigne, 75008 (44.95.06.70). Métro Franklin D Roosevelt. **Open** 10am-6.30pm Mon-Sat. **Credit** AmEx, DC, EC, JCB, MC, V.
German designer Jil Sander opened her vast Paris outpost in autumn 1992 to a wave of publicity. The double-height space, behind the façade of the 1890s mansion (occupied by couturier Madeleine Vionnet in the twenties), matches the perfect beauty and high price tags of her modern, well-cut, simple suits, separates and sweaters.

Kashiyama

147 boulevard St-Germain, 75006 (46.34.11.50). Métro St-Germain-des-Prés. **Open** 11am-7pm Mon; 10am-7pm Tue-Sat. **Credit** AmEx, DC, EC, JCB, MC, V.
Buyer Christine Weiss has an eye for hot fashion blood, having scooped up Martin Margiela's first collection and adding Ann Demeulemeester, Rifat Ozbek, Jean-Paul Gaultier and Dries Van Noten into the mix. Her latest discoveries to watch

for are fresh-from-design-school Kim Roffy and Marc LeBihan. Downstairs is devoted to brides, as well as fabulous lingerie by La Perla, Rien and André Sarda. Shoes by Sara Navarro, Ann Demeulemeester and Dries Van Noten and hats by Jacques Lecorré punctuate fashion's last word.
Branch: 80 rue J-J Rousseau, 75001 (40.26.46.46).

Kenzo

3 place des Victoires, 75001 (40.39.72.87). Métro Palais-Royal. **Open** 10am-7pm Mon-Sat. **Credit** AmEx, DC, EC, JCB, MC, V.
Kenzo is a master of colour and pattern. Kenzo Jungle is the less-expensive line, which still carries sharp jackets and leggings, and exotic prints. Women's items go from sophisticated suits to pretty flower dresses and rich brocade jackets. A rainbow range of shirts and extravagant ties are the highlights for men. The shops also sell a range of household goods, although their own-brand *Kenzo-Maison* line is currently not available.
Branches include: 16 (women/home) and 17 (men) boulevard Raspail, 75007 (women 42.22.09.38/men 45.49.33.75); 60-62 rue de Rennes, 75006 (45.44.27.88)

Maison de la Fausse Fourrure

34 boulevard Beaumarchais, 75011 (43.55.24.21). Métro Bastille. **Open** 14-7.00pm Mon; 11am-7pm Tue-Sat. **Credit** AmEx, DC, EC, JCB, MC, FTC, V.
The 'House of Fake Fur' pays tribute to our furry friends with synthetic teddy-bear coats, animal-print minis and bags, hats and scarves in your choice of chic 'leopard' or cheeky 'monkey'. There are also bolts of fake fur fabric and furniture covered with the stuff to decorate your lair.

Magic Circle

25 rue Etienne-Marcel, 75001 (42.33.39.99). Métro Etienne Marcel. **Open** 11am-7pm Mon-Sat. **Credit** AmEx, EC, MC, V.
A kitschy throwback to the 70s, this is a crucial stop before nightclubbing (if only to get you in the mood). Labels featured are Xuly Bët, Dolita, No Such Soul, de rigueur patent T-strap stilettoes by Rodolphe Menudier and high-heel trainers by Cyd Jouny. Prices range from 100F to 4,000F.

Maria Luisa

2 rue Cambon, 75001 (47.03.96.15). Métro Concorde. **Open** 10.30am-7pm Mon-Sat. **Credit** AmEx, DC, JCB, MC, V.
Venezuelan Maria Luisa Poumaillou is like a godmother to every talented young designer, and one of Paris' original stockists for Helmut Lang, Ann Demeulemeester, John Galliano and Martine Sitbon. New labels to discover here are Hannoh, Andrew Gn and Dirk Bikkembergs. There are shoes from Sara Navarro and Paul Harnden, as well as handbags and jewellery.

Mosaïque

17 rue de Sèvres, 75006, (45.48.53.06). Métro Sèvres Babylone. **Open** 11am-7pm Mon; 10am-7pm Tue-Sat. **Credit** AmEx, DC, JCB, MC, V.
A recent shake-up has made this shop into a haven for women looking for designer labels, such as Michel Klein, Enrica Massei, D&G, Martine Sitbon, G Gigli, Sportmax and 22 Octobre, which are edited into stylish, easy looks.

Myrène de Prémonville

38 rue du Bac, 75007 (45.49.46.96). Métro Rue du Bac. **Open** 2-7pm Mon; 10am-7pm Tue-Sat. **Credit** AmEx, DC, JCB, V.
De Prémonville's proves that feminine, fashionable career-dressing isn't a contradiction in terms. Hervé van der Straeton's fantasy-fixtures shows off evening wear: swinging, neo-sixties cocktail dresses shot with jet beads, feathers and satin ribbons.
Branch: 32 avenue George V, 75008 (47.20.02.35).

Plantation Issey Miyake

17 boulevard Raspail, 75007 (45.48.12.32). Métro Rue du Bac. **Open** 10am-7pm Mon-Sat. **Credit** AmEx, MC, V.
Futurist designer Miyake's Plantation line, based on androgynous Japanese workers' clothes and reinterpreted in modern fabrics, is accessible to those who aspire to his lofty look, but at more down-to-earth prices.

Plein Sud

17 rue du Cygne, 75001 (42.33.49.95). Métro Etienne-Marcel. **Open** 11am-7pm Mon-Sat. **Credit** AmEx, EC, V.
Plein Sud is the unabashedly sexy, slightly costume-y collection signed by Fayçal Amor. Styles range from the dandy look of long-waisted riding jackets and ankle-length *décolleté* velvet dresses, to born-again sixties minis for girls who think cellulite is a male phone.
Branches: 21 rue de Sevigné, 75004 (42.72.10.60); 70bis rue de Bonaparte, 75006 (43.54.43.06).

River

66 rue Bonaparte, 75006 (43.26.35.74). Métro St-Germain-des-Prés. **Open** 10am-7pm Mon-Sat. **Credit** AmEx, DC, MC, V.
In a theatrical setting, with red velvet drapes and gilt mirrors, is a very large selection of Moschino's three lines: Couture, Cheap & Chic and Jeans, along with their crucial matching handbags. Also found here is a smattering of the Ozbek and D&G labels.

Romeo Gigli

46 rue de Sévigné, 75003 (48.04.57.05). Métro St-Paul. **Open** 11am-7pm Tue-Sat. **Credit** AmEx, MC, V.
Come here for clothes in wonderful colours, shapes and luxurious fabrics by the Italian designer. It's more like an art show in a beautiful sun-drenched loft than a shop.

Sonia Rykiel

175 boulevard St-Germain, 75006 (49.54.60.60). Métro St-Germain-des-Prés. **Open** 10am-7pm Mon-Sat. **Credit** AmEx, DC, EC, JCB, V.
The sum of all this designer's parts make up total Parisian style. Her signature knitwear has become a staple in many wardrobes, and berets, scarves, shoes, bags, luggage, stockings, household items and cosmetics complete the Rykiel universe at her flagship boutique. The rue d'Alésia store sells last season's line at half price.
Branches: 70 rue du Faubourg St-Honoré, 75008 (49.54.61.95); 64 rue d'Alésia, 75014 (43.95.06.13).

Tehen

5 bis rue des Rosiers, 75004 (40.27.97.37). Métro St-Paul. **Open** 2-7pm Mon, Sun; 11am-7pm Tue-Sat. **Credit** AmEx, EC, JCB, MC, V.
A comely collection of knitted, jersey and natural fabrics. Designs come in greys, blacks and neutral shades, with fluid draping and minimalist details. Prices are reasonable: no more than 1,500F for a two-piece outfit.
Branches: 30 rue Montmartre, 75001 (40.26.86.23); Les 3 Quartiers (Centre Commercial) 23 boulevard de la Madeleine, 75001 (42.96.10.96); 28 rue de Grenelle, 75007 (45.44.80.42).

Trussardi

21 rue du Faubourg St-Honoré, 75008 (42.65.11.40). Métro Madeleine or Concorde. **Open** 10am-7pm Mon-Sat. **Credit** AmEx, DC, EC, JCB, V.
This family-owned Italian leather goods house has left behind its classic country-squire look to become more urban and streamlined. The mainstay is still high-quality leather and suede, but they've added more experimental materials such as laminated linen, metallic shot silk and neoprene. Women's wear and leather handbags are on the ground floor, and men's suits, along with the more techno Trussardi Action and Jeans lines, are upstairs.

Y's

69 rue des Sts-Pères, 75006 (45.48.22.56). Métro St-Germain-des-Prés. **Open** 10.30am-7pm Mon-Sat. **Credit** AmEx, DC, EC, JCB, V.
Yohji Yamamoto, whose starting point for his garments is the kimono, stocks his simpler, less expensive second line at this shop, for men and women. The fashion crowd make much of his zipped black leather wallets in three sizes.
Branch: 25 rue du Louvre, 75001 (42.21.42.93)

Cheap & Cheerful

Apart from the ubiquitous Kookaï, Etam and Morgan chains, here are a few individual options for up-to-the-minute fashion at *pas cher* prices.

Patricia Louisor

16 rue Houdon, 75018 (42.62.10.42). Métro Abbesses or Pigalle. **Open** 11am-8pm daily. **Credit** EC, MC, V.
Walk in as a customer and leave as a friend of this energetic, talented designer and her two sisters, who sell original clothes you'll wear for seasons to come. The tiny boutique, between Pigalle and the Butte Montmartre, has a party atmosphere – and the best part is nothing costs over 600F.

La Rue est à Nous

28 rue Rochechouart, 75018 (42.55.13.09 ext 242). Métro Barbes-Rochechouart. **Open** 10am-7pm Mon; 9.30am-7pm Tue-Fri; 9.15am-7pm Sat. **Credit** V.
One of the Tati stores, a Parisian institution (*see chapter* **Specialist Shops**). Their super-cheap junior basics (T-shirts 30F, a jersey dress 90F) are designed by Gilles Rosier and Claude Sabbah, whose own line, GR816, is urban and edgy.

Mon Ami Pierlot

3 rue Montmartre, 75001 (40.28.45.55). Métro Châtelet-Les Halles. **Open** 10.30am-7pm Mon-Sat. Closed 28 July-28 August. **Credit** AmEx, EC, MC, FTC, V.
Claudie Pierlot's less expensive, basics line for women, men and children. The predominant fabric is cotton, and shapes are simple and squared off: drawstring pants, Chinese jackets and apron dresses.

Zara

2 rue Halévy, 75009 (44.71.90.90). Métro Opéra. **Open** 10am-7.30pm Mon-Sat. **Credit** AmEx, JCB, MC, V.
Well-known in Spain for à la mode bargains, this chain has taken Paris by storm. For women, jackets run from 429-649F and dresses are 269-329F. Accessories, men's and children's wear are also available.

Jeans, Sports & Casual Wear

Autour du Monde

8 and 12 rue des Francs-Bourgeois, 75003 (42.77.16.18). Métro St-Paul. **Open** 2-7.30pm Mon; 11am-7.30pm Tue-Sat; 2-7pm Sun. **Credit** AmEx, EC, MC, V.
Serge Bensimon began in the surplus clothing business, and soon created a traveller's outfitters which stocks timeless, authentic casual wear at good prices and for all ages. The look is wholesome and pastoral, with lots of plain colours and natural fabrics. No. 10 also stocks children's wear, and the American colonial household shop at No. 8 is full of patchwork quilts and painted folk furniture.
Branch: 54 rue de Seine, 75006 (43.54.64.47).

Chevignon Trading Post

49 rue Etienne-Marcel, 75001(40.28.05.77). Métro Etienne-Marcel. **Open** 10.15am-7pm Mon-Sat. **Credit** AmEx, DC, EC, JCB, V.

Yohji Yamamoto's **Y's**.

Can't make a trip to Santa Fe? Guy Azoulay, the alter-ego of his fictional hero Charles Chevignon, has created his own little piece of the American West, stocking Chevignon jeans and jackets, duvet covers and horse blankets, pottery, books, trinkets and foodstuffs.

Go Sport
10 place de la République, 75011 (48.05.71.85). Métro République. **Open** 10.30am-7pm Tue-Sat, noon-7pm Mon. **Credit** AmEx, MC, V.
This is probably your best address to find Paris' most complete selection of name-brand active wear and equipment for just about any sport imaginable, often at discounted prices.
Branches include: Forum des Halles, Level 3, Porte Lescot, 75001 (45.08.92.96); 110 boulevard Diderot, 75012 (43.47.31.17); 68 avenue du Maine, 75014 (43.27.50.50).

Hagen + Ratz
5 rue de Turbigo, 75001 (40.26.07.00). Métro Châtelet-Les Halles. **Open** 10.30am-7.30pm Mon-Sat.
Credit EC, MC, V.
Street-wise clothes by Soochi, Velvet Monkees, and Onyx and shoes by Caterpillar, Adidas and Puma, lined up with acid-jazz, funk and techno music. They've recently expanded to include kids' clothes.

Harley Davidson
61 boulevard Beaumarchais, 75003 (40.29.96.90). Métro Chemin Vert. **Open** 10am-7pm, Tue-Sat.
Credit AmEx, MC, V.
Clothes, bikers boots and accessories for Hells' Angels, or anyone who loved Brando in *The Wild One*.

Pôles
17 rue du Jour, 75001 (45.08.93.67). Métro Les Halles. **Open** 10am-7pm Mon-Sat. **Credit** AmEx, EC, MC, V.
Pôles first established itself selling soft, over-sized sweaters, but has added matching coloured jeans with a great French

fit for women. It also sells sensibly-priced sweat shirts, dresses and trainers for home or weekend wear.

WSN
3 rue d'Argout, 75002 (40.28.95.94). Métro Etienne-Marcel. **Open** 11am-7pm Mon-Sat. **Credit** MC, V.
A market-like space with a collection of individual outlets, where you might even run into Tank Girl sampling the second-skin sport fashion of Daniel Poole, Lady Soul and Sexy Space Girl. For surfers (waves, concrete or Internet), there's the critical Stüssy line, Urban Outfitters, Trigger Happy, Dosse Posse and Carhartt industrial wear.

Lingerie

Capucine Puerari
63 rue des Sts Pères, 75006 (42.22.14.09). Métro St-Germain-des-Prés. **Open** 10am-7pm Mon-Sat.
Credit AmEx, DC, MC, V.
Capucine Puerari graduated from modern, sexy and fashionable lingerie and swimwear to a ready-to-wear collection in the same spirit. Her evening wear is particularly enticing.

Chantal Thomass
1 rue Vivienne, 75001 (40.15.02.36). Métro Palais-Royal. **Open** 11am-7pm Mon; 10am-7pm Tue-Sat. **Credit** AmEx, MC, V.
Paris' best-known lingerie designer. She also designs clothes and accessories, but it's the luxurious, modern lingerie that has made her reputation, all fancifully displayed in an elegant three-floor boutique that gives frou-frou a good name.

Ci-Dessous
48 rue du Four, 75006 (42.84.25.31). Métro St-Sulpice **Open** 10.30am-1.30pm, 2.30-7.30pm, Mon-Fri, 11am-7.30pm Sat. **Credit** AmEx, EC, MC, V.
Mostly cotton, softly coloured, comfortable underwear which appeals to young women. Recycled packaging reinforces the natural image.

Laurence Tavernier
7 rue du Pré-aux-Clercs, 75007 (49.27.03.95). Métro Rue du Bac. **Open** 10am-7pm Mon-Sat. **Credit** EC, MC, V.
The last word in comfortable pyjamas (around 800F), wool and cashmere bathrobes (1,800F) and slippers (900F), all designed by the sister of film director Bertrand Tavernier.

La Storia
4 rue de Sèvres, 75006. (45.48.20.04). Métro Sèvres-Babylone or St-Sulpice. **Open** 10.30am-7.30pm Mon-Sat.
Credit AmEx, EC, MC, V.
Fancy Italian lingerie by Vera Donna, Cotton Club and the cheaper La Perla lines, Sognando and Occhi Verdi.

Sabbia Rosa
73 rue des Sts-Pères, 75006. (45.48.88.37). Métro St-Germain-des-Prés. **Open** 10am-7pm Mon-Sat. **Credit** AmEx, EC, MC, V.
Incredibly beautiful, sexy lingerie in subtle, sensual colours, designed by a true artist. Everything is made in the boutique. Bras costs 200F-2,000F, silk slips around 2,000F, and you can also buy slippers and Sabbia Rosa jasmin perfume.

Mainly Men

Anthony Peto
12 rue Jean-Jacques Rousseau, 75001 (42.21.47.15). Métro Palais-Royal. **Open** 11am-7pm Wed-Fri. **Credit** AmEx, DC, EC, JCB, MC, V.
Going to the Prix de Diane, Longchamps or Ascot? Stop here first for the top hat or boater and all the accoutrements you'll need to look like a gentleman at the races.

Façonnable

9 rue du Faubourg St-Honoré, 75008 (47.42.72.60).
Métro Concorde. **Open** 10am-7pm Mon-Sat. **Credit**
AmEx, DC, EC, JCB, MC, V.
A male *BCBG* haven where new suits smell like old money.
Upstairs you'll find urbanely executive suits averaging
4,500F, as well as shoes and luggage. The ground floor
stocks hunting jackets, jeans, an impressive range of silk ties
(325F) and there's a whole showcase of Liberty-print boxer
shorts (200F).
Branch: 174 boulevard St-Germain, 75006 (40.49.02.47).

Le Garage

23 rue des Francs-Bourgeois, 75004 (42.71.96.94).
Métro St-Paul. **Open** 2-7pm Mon; 11am-7pm Tue-Sat.
Credit AmEx, DC, JCB, MC, V.
Hip and expensive shirts for pale night owls in yet another
Marais boutique, occupying a former *boulangerie-pâtisserie*.
Virtually everything on display here is in black and white,
the plainest designs start at around 600F – more elaborate
ones with zips and a variety of silver detailing go up to
around 1,500F.

Hackett

17 rue des Sèvres, 75006 (45.49.18.93).
Métro Sèvres-Babylone. **Open** 2-7pm Mon; 10am-7pm
Tue-Sat. **Credit** AmEx, EC, MC, V.
Another Brit-import for the quintessential Savile Row style
the French male covets. Terry Haste, the tailor from
Hackett's Sloane Street and Jermyn Street locations, is in res-
idence here on the second Tuesday of every month. The fine
gentleman's treats that are regularly in stock include shirts,
ties, cufflinks, sportswear, luggage and an entire series of
Hackett grooming products.

Loft Design By

12 rue du Faubourg St-Honoré, 75008 (42.65.59.65).
Métro Concorde or Madeleine. **Open** 10am-7pm Mon-Sat.
Credit AmEx, DC, EC, MC, V.
The sporting yuppie look is peddled here – sweatshirts,
jumpers, shirts and nice scarves – in lots of grey and navy.
Shirts cost around 300F and there's some women's wear,
such as leggings (350F) and shirts.
Branches: 12 rue de Sévigné, 75004 (48.87.13.07); 56 rue
de Rennes, 75006 (45.44.88.99); 175 boulevard Pereire,
75017 (46.22.44.20).

Paul Smith

22 boulevard Raspail, 75007 (42.84.15.75). Métro Rue
du Bac. **Open** 11am-7pm Mon; 10am-7pm Tue-Sat.
Credit AmEx, DC, EC, JCB, MC, V.
Le style anglais in a wood-panelled interior. Smith's great
range of suits and classic shoes are on the upper floor, while
women's wear gets a funkier, more irreverent space below.

Rykiel Homme

194 boulevard St-Germain, 75006 (45.44.83.19). Métro
St-Germain-des-Prés. **Open** 10am-7pm Mon-Sat. **Credit**
AmEx, DC, EC, JCB, V.
Sonia Rykiel's menswear designs are classic, with just
enough originality to make them special without being ostentatious. Her silk ties are wonderful, with discreet but amusing motifs.

Vintage & Discount Clothes

Second-hand clothes aren't cheap in Paris, but
check out discounts on designer names. In particular, the rue d'Alésia, in the 14th, is packed with
discount factory outlets (look for 'Stock' next to the
name). Among the best are **Chipie Stock**, at No.
82 (jeans and casual wear), **SR** (Sonia Rykiel) at

No. 64 and **Diapositive Stock** at No. 74. *See also*
Flea Markets *in chapter* **Specialist Shops**.

Alternatives

18 rue du Roi-de-Sicile, 75004 (42.78.31.50). Métro St-
Paul. **Open** 11am-1pm, 2.30-7pm, Tue-Sat. **Credit** MC, V.
Owner Martine Bergossi accepts only the most trendy labels
in top condition, such as Jean-Paul Gaultier, Hermès, Dries
Van Noten and Comme des Garçons, from 400F-3,000F.

L'Apache

45 rue Vieille-du-Temple, 75004 (42.71.84.27). Métro St-
Paul. **Open** 2-7.30pm Mon; 11am-7.30pm Tue-Sat.
Credit EC, MC, V.
A huge selection of quality clothes and accessories from the
thirties to the fifties, sold by staff dressed to match. Not as
cheap as a flea market, but the clothes are in much better
shape, and well selected.

Catherine Baril

14 (women) and 25 (men) rue de la Tour, 75016
(45.20.95.21/45.27.11.46). Métro Passy. **Open** 2-7pm
Mon; 10am-7pm Tue-Sat; *July, Aug only* closed Mon and
noon-2pm. **Credit** JCB, MC, V.
Catherine Baril collects Saint Laurents, Chanels and
Givenchys and passes them on for a (relative) pittance. Look
out for Armani and Ralph Lauren in the new men's shop.

Derrière Les Fagots

8 rue des Abbesses, 75018 (42.59.72.53). Métro
Abbesses. **Open** 10am-1pm, 2.30-7.30pm, Tue-Sat.
Credit MC, V.
The window display of twenties' and thirties' kitchen gadgets, lamps and vintage handbags will draw you in. Antique
clothing in good condition is wedged into this sweet little
shop, along with a lot of great hats to inspire your outfit.

Shoes at **Roger Vivier.** *See page 193.*

L'Habilleur

44 rue de Poitou, 75003 (48.87.77.12). Métro St-Sébastien-Froissart. **Open** 11am-8pm Mon-Sat. **Credit** MC, V.

Wait a season or two and that Galliano dress may show up at this shop, which buys past-season designer merchandise from manufacturers or other stores, showcasing it lovingly.

La Ville du Puy

36 rue Tronchet, 75009 (47.42.25.69). Métro Havre-Caumartin. **Open** 9:45am-7pm Mon-Sat. **Credit** AmEx, DC, EC, JCB, MC, V.

The ground floor is like a bargain basement of cheap clothes, but as you climb higher, coat labels like Max Mara, Apara and Ramosport, and suit collections like Irene Van Ryb and Teenflo, greet you (not at sale prices). At the very top, old-season Moschino Cheap & Chic, Sate of Claude Montana, Mani and Genny are half-price.

Le Mouton à Cinq Pattes

19 rue Grégoire de Tours, 75006 (43.29.73.56). Métro Odéon. **Open** 10.30am-7.30pm Mon-Fri; 10.30am-8pm Sat. **Credit** AmEx, MC, EC, JCB, V.

Most clothes in these jumble sale-like stores are *dégriffées* (have had had their label cut out), and you need to know what you're looking for to recognise the Gaultier, Jasper Conran, Claude Montana, Helmut Lang, Sybilla, Mugler and Martine Sitbon pieces that can be found here. Stock changes frequently; avoid Saturdays.

Branches include: 15 rue Vieille du Temple, 75004 (42.71.86.30); (men, women, children) 8, 10, 14-18 and 48 rue St-Placide, 75006 (45.48.86.26); 138 boulevard St-Germain, 75006 (43.26.49.25).

Quai des Marques

8 quai du Châtelier, 93450 L'Ile St Denis, (42.43.70.20/recorded info 36.68.48.38). Métro Mairie de St-Ouen, plus bus 137N or 138. **Open** 11am-8pm Wed-Fri; 10am-8pm Sat, Sun.

Opened in February 1995, this equivalent to an out-of-town discount shopping mall is the first of its kind in the Paris region. Some 35 different factory outlets offer recent- or current-season models with a discount of 30% or more against normal retail prices. The men's, women's and children's wear includes Apostrophe, Karl Lagerfeld, Kenzo and Montana, and there are also shoes and some household goods.

Réciproque

89, 92, 95, 97, 101 and 123 rue de la Pompe, 75016 (47.04.82.24/47.04.30.28). Métro Rue de la Pompe. **Open** 10.30am-7pm Mon-Sat. Closed last week July, all Aug. **Credit** EC, MC, V.

Réciproque's side-by-side second-hand boutiques are the answer for those with couture taste and no cash. Alaïa, Thierry Mugler, YSL and many other designers' wares all turn up here. No. 92 specialises in leather clothes, No. 97 is the depot for leaving clothes if you have anything you want to sell, and No. 101 is for men.

Thank God I'm A V.I.P.

60 rue Greneta, 75002(40.28.43.14). Métro Réamur-Sébastopol. **Open** 11am-8pm Mon-Sat. **No credit cards.**

The name of the shop and the bright, multi-ethnic and second-hand clothes from the forties to the seventies are irresistible to kitschophiles.

Jewellery & Accessories

Alexis Lahellec

14-16 rue Jean-Jacques Rousseau, 75001 (42.33.40.33). Métro Palais-Royal. **Open** 11am Mon-Fri, noon-7pm Sat. **Credit** AmEx, DC, EC, MC, JCB, V.

Jewellery and objects for the house, made by a young lawyer-turned-designer. Pedro Almodóvar used his fun teapot-motif jewellery in the movie *Women on the Verge of a Nervous Breakdown.*

Branches: 17 rue St-Florentin, 75008 (42.61.07.17); 14 rue Bernard Palissy, 75006 (45.48.71.98).

Biche de Bere

71 rue de Rennes, 75006 (42.97.47.36). Métro St-Sulpice. **Open** 10am-7.30pm Mon-Sat. **Credit** AmEx, DC, JCB, MC, V.

Biche de Bere probably translates into cheap & cheerful in some language. Earrings, bracelets and necklaces to coordinate with whatever you're wearing – the bestseller is a set of three interchangable earrings for 269F.

Branches: 348 rue St-Honoré, 75001 (42.97.49.27); 34 rue du Commerce, 75015 (45.75.94.36); 113 avenue Victor-Hugo, 75016 (45.53.00.53).

Cartier

13 rue de la Paix, 75002 (42.18.53.70). Métro Opéra. **Open** 10.30am-7pm Mon; 10am-7pm Tue-Fri; 10.30am-1pm, 2-7pm, Sat. **Credit** AmEx, DC, EC, JCB, MC, V.

Looking for a tiara? Cartier is the favoured jeweller to the rich and royal for diamonds, gold pens, scarves, watches, cigarette lighters and elegant little bags and purses.

Branches include: 7 place Vendôme, 75001 (44.55.32.50); 23 place Vendôme, 75001 (44.55.32.20); 23 rue du Faubourg St-Honoré, 75008 (44.94.79.81).

Galerie Hélène Porée

31 rue Daguerre, 75014 (40.47.80.60). Métro Denfert-Rochereau. **Open** 11am-7.30pm Tue-Sat, or by appointment. **Credit** AmEx, MC, EC, V.

A gallery with an international roster of well-chosen contemporary artist-designed jewellery. British artists Cynthia Cousens, Susan Cross and Allison Evans are stocked here along with work by their counterparts from Germany, Holland and Italy. A far cry from the glitzy gold chains and large fake pearls that commonly characterise Paris costume trends.

Hermès

24 rue du Faubourg St-Honoré, 75008 (40.17.47.17). Métro Concorde. **Open** 10am-1pm, 2.15-6.30pm, Mon, Sat; 10am-6.30pm Tue-Fri. **Credit** AmEx, DC, EC, JCB, MC, V.

Hermès trademark silk scarves come in hundreds of bordered prints for about 1,200F. For men, there are John Lobb custom-made shoes and riding boots. There's a vast jewellery department upstairs. Hours may vary during July and August, and at sale times.

Lunettes Beausoleil

28 rue du Roi-de-Sicile, 75004 (42.77.28.29). Métro St-Paul. **Open** 9am-6.30 pm; preferably by appointment. **Credit** EC.

Frederic Beausoleil designs glasses on a grand scale. His client list reads like an all-star band: Stevie Wonder, Ray Charles, Tania Marie and even Jean-Michel Jarre. Once you spot his special series of tortoiseshell and antique frames (from 450F to over 1,000F for customised orders), other specs will seem to be of the Thunderbirds-Brains variety.

Marie Mercié

56 rue Tiquetonne, 75002 (40.26.60.68). Métro Etienne Marcel. **Open** 11am-7pm Mon-Sat. **Credit** AmEx, DC, EC, MC, V.

Marie Mercié hand-makes about 160 hats a year, and sells them from this boutique, complete with charming striped hat boxes. There are colourful felt hats in winter, straw and silks in summer, in styles that go from classic to theatrical. One-offs cost from 2,000F, the season's lines 500F-1,200F.

Branch: 23 rue St-Sulpice, 75006 (43.26.45.83).

Les Montres

58 rue Bonaparte, 75006 (46.34.71.38). Métro Mabillon or St Germain-des-Prés. **Open** 10am-7pm Mon-Sat. **Credit** AmEx, DC, EC, MC, V.

Status-symbol watches for any occasion, amongst Swiss and American models for men and women. There are also collectors' watches, such as vintage Rolexes from the twenties. **Branches**: 7 rue Castiglione, 75001 (42.60.65.88); 6 rue Gustave Courbet, 75016 (47.04.85.06).

Miu Miu

10 rue du Cherche-Midi, 75006 (45.48.63.33). Métro Sèvres Babylone. **Open** 10.30am-7pm Mon-Sat. **Credit** AmEx, DC, JCB, MC, V.

The less expensive line from Prada is young and sweet, but still pricey. Patent or tanned leather bags cost 1,500F-2,500F. 'Baby' shoes with a heel and featherweight linen slip dresses are bought by flower children with a hefty allowance.

Optique Josette Poux

40 rue du Four, 75006 (45.48.61.33). Métro St-Germain-des-Prés. **Open** 2-7pm Mon; 9.30am-7pm Tue-Sat. **Credit** AmEx, DC, EC, MC, V.

A small shop packed with one of the best selections of spectacle frames in Paris. For 35 years, this father-daughter business has drawn in discriminating customers; among their designers are Gaultier, Oliver Peoples, Persol and Ray Ban.

Philippe Model

33 place du Marché St-Honoré, 75001 (42.96.89.02). Métro Pyramides or Tuileries. **Open** 11am-7pm Mon-Sat. **Credit** AmEx, MC, V.

Model's fantasy hats get the most double-takes at Paris race meetings. Precious handbags, flirty, lady-like gloves and fancy footwear with tapered silhouettes and shapely heels display his other talents. Also men's and children's shoes. **Branch**: 25 rue de Varenne, 75007 (45.44.76.79).

Prada

5 rue de Grenelle, 75006. (45.48.53.14). Métro Sèvres-Babylone. **Open** 10.30am-7pm Mon-Sat. **Credit** AmEx, DC, EC, JCB, MC, V.

A large corner store just opened to accompany the two adjacent tiny shops selling the best in Italian-made leather bags, shoes and sleek-chic clothing. Buying a Prada bag could mean you skip paying the rent, but the quality, design and status of owning one just may skew your priorities.

Scooter

10 rue de Turbigo, 75001 (45.08.50.54). Métro Etienne Marcel. **Open** 2-7pm Mon; 10am-7pm Tue-Fri; 11am-7pm Sat. **Credit** AmEx, EC, MC, V.

A haunt for models and art students. The costume jewellery here might be chunky ethnic bangles, glitzy 'ruby' earrings, hair clasps or fun dinosaur and fish motif necklaces. There's a colourful junior range called *Mademoiselle Zaza*, and clothes and shoes too. **Branch**: 29 boulevard Raspail, 75007 (45.48.24.37); 10 rue Guichard, 75016 (45.08.50.54).

31 Fèvrier

2 rue du Pélican, 75002 (42.33.48.27). Métro Palais-Royal. **Open** 11am-7pm Tue-Sat. **Credit** AmEx, MC, EC, V.

Wonderfully witty bags, belts and gloves designed by Hélène Népomiatzi and Marc Gourmelen. Their shopping baskets on wheels, covered in seductive sequins or fuschia fake fur have graced fashion pages around the world.

Têtes en L'Air

65 rue des Abbesses, 75018 (46.06.71.19). Métro Abbesses. **Open** 10.30am-7.30pm Tue-Sat. **No credit cards.**

A quirky, colourful storefront with hand-made hats to top off a look *à la parisienne*. Prices are reasonable.

Pick up some elegant headgear at **Phillippe Model.**

Shoes

Accessoire Diffusion
*6 rue du Cherche-Midi, 75006 (45.48.36.08). Métro
Sèvres-Babylone or St Sulpice.* **Open** 10am-7pm Mon-Sat.
Credit AmEx, V.
A French chain selling well-made fashionable styles at reasonable prices. The Détente range, with canvas uppers and
rubber soles, is more casual and less expensive.
Branches include: 8 rue du Jour, 75001 (40.26.19.84); 36
rue Vieille-du-Temple 75004 (40.29.99.49); 9 rue Guichard
75016 (45.27.80.27).

Charles Jourdan
*86 avenue des Champs-Elysées, 75008 (45.62.29.28).
Métro Franklin D Roosevelt or George V.* **Open** 10am-
7.45pm Mon-Sat. **Credit** AmEx, DC, EC, JCB, MC, V.
Charles Jourdan strikes an ideal balance between fashion
fads and classic styling. The Bis line has cheaper, younger
lines; the Jourdan-designed Karl Lagerfeld collection, with
spike or fan-shaped heels, is an engineering feat for the foot.
Branch: 5 boulevard de la Madeleine, 75001
(42.61.15.89).

Christian Louboutin
*19 rue Jean-Jacques Rousseau, 75001. (42.36.05.31).
Métro Palais-Royal or Louvre-Rivoli.* **Open** 11am-7.30pm
Mon-Sat. **Credit** AmEx, DC, EC, MC, V.
Louboutin's luxurious footwear, costing 1,400F-2,300F for
handmade shoes with gold details, are sophisticated, dressy
and much sought by the younger of the *beau monde.*

Kabuki
*13 rue de Turbigo, 75002 (42.36.44.34). Métro Etienne-
Marcel.* **Open** 10am-7pm Mon-Sat. **Credit** AmEx, DC,
EC, JCB, MC, V.
One of the few multi-mark shoe stores in Paris, they stack
designer footwear from Dolce & Gabbana, Vivienne
Westwood, Prada, and Michel Perry and Cesare Paciotti.

Mare-France
*4 rue du Cherche-Midi, 75006 (45.44.55.33).
Métro Sèvres-Babylone.* **Open** 10-7.30pm Mon-Sat.
Credit AmEx, EC, DC, JCB, MC, V.
Made in Italy shoes 'in the style of' Ann Demeulemeester and
Patrick Cox, but cheaper.

Roger Vivier
*24 rue de Grenelle, 75007 (45.49.95.83). Métro Sèvres-
Babylone or Rue du Bac.* **Open** 2-7pm Mon; 10am-1pm, 2-
7pm, Tue-Sat. **Credit** AmEx, EC, MC, V.
This octogenarian shoe master began his career fashioning
exquisite footwear to accompany Christian Dior's New Look.
Re-editions of Vivier's couture shoes and new styles are
available to the few: prices start at 1,500F for ballerina flats,
1,900-2,900F for leather and 8,900F for crocodile.

Patrick Cox
*62 rue Tiquetonne, 75002 (40.26.66.55). Métro Etienne-
Marcel.* **Open** 10am-7pm Mon-Sat. **Credit** AmEx, MC, V.
Cox's covetable, much-photographed shoes, at 800F to about
1,400F, are snapped up by trendy Parisian couples. He's now
added leather goods, separates and coats to his range.

Shoe Bizz
*42 rue du Dragon, 75006 (45.44.91.70). Métro St-
Germain-des Prés.* **Open** 2-7.30pm Mon; 10.30am-7.30pm
Tue-Sat. **Credit** AmEx, EC, JCB, V.
Their bizz is to zero in on the most fashionable shoe shapes
of the season, and recreate them at about 30% cheaper than
their competitors. There are also tried and true classic court
shoes for women and English-style brogues for men.
Branches include: 48 rue Beaubourg, 75003
(48.87.12.73).

Stephane Kélian
*13bis rue de Grenelle, 75007 (42.22.93.03). Métro
Sèvres-Babylone.* **Open** 10am-7pm Mon-Sat. **Credit**
AmEx, EC, MC, V.
Women's shoes from the sublime to the sensational, with
prices to match (1,000F upwards), plus men's and children's
shoes, too. Kélian also designs for Gaultier, Claude Montana
and Martine Sitbon.
Branches include: 6 place des Victoires, 75002
(42.61.60.74); 36 rue de Sévigné, 75003 (42.77.87.91); 26
avenue des Champs-Elysées, 75008 (42.56.42.26).

Tim Bargeot
*75 rue Quincampoix, 75003 (40.29.93.42). Métro
Rambuteau or Châtelet-Les Halles.* **Open** 2-7pm Tue-Fri;
1.45-7pm Sat. **Credit** AmEx, MC, V.
Just the place if you're searching for lime green and lemon
striped plastic platforms, this shop sells extraordinary sixties' and seventies' shoes, as well as Bargeot's seventies-inspired clothes.

Children's Clothes

See also above **Agnès B, Autour du Monde, Au
Vrai Chic Parisien, Détails, Mon Ami
Pierlot, Hagan + Ratz** *and* **Kenzo**.

Bonpoint
*67 rue de l'Université, 75007 (45.55.63.70). Métro
Solférino.* **Open** 10-7pm Mon-Sat. **Credit** AmEx, DC, EC,
JCB, V.
The kiddie's shop to the French gentry, but don't be intimidated – it's fun just to see the charming children's dress-up
clothes, all embroidered and be-ribboned. No. 86 has lacy
christening gowns, and fanciful clothes for flower girls. At
7 rue Solférino there is furniture and nursery accessories.
Branch: 64 avenue Raymond Poincaré, 75016
(47.27.60.81); 184 rue de Courcelles, 75017 (47.63.87.49.

Dipaki
75 rue Rocher, 75008 (45.22.03.89). Métro St-Lazare.
Open 10am-7pm Mon-Sat. **Credit** MC, V.
One of Paris's best addresses for inexpensive, easy-to-care-
for baby and kids' clothing in bold primary colours. Cheaper
still is the Dipaki old-season stock shop, at 98 rue d'Alesia.
Branches include: 22 rue Cler, 75007 (47.05.47.62); 46
rue de l'Université, 75007 (42.97.49.89); (45.25.51.38); 18
rue Vignon, 75008 (42.66.24.74).

Gaspard de la Butte
*10 bis rue Yvonne Le Tac, 75018 (42.55.99.40). Métro
Abbesses.* **Open** 10am-7pm daily. **Credit** MC, EC, V.
Little rompers and knits for babies and toddlers up to 6 years
are all hand-made with tender loving care. These are hand-
me-downs that will last and look adorable for generations.

Du Pareil au Même
*59 rue de Commerce, 75015 (48.28.86.76). Métro Emile
Zola.* **Open** 10am-7pm Mon-Sat. **Credit** EC, JCB, MC, V.
A keenly-priced chain selling good, plain but attractive
basics for babies and children up to age 14.
Branches include: 15-17 rue des Mathurins, 75008
(42.66.93.80).

Pom d'Api
*13 rue du Jour, 75001 (42.36.08.87). Métro Châtelet-Les
Halles.* **Open** 10am-7pm Mon-Sat. **Credit** AmEx, DC, EC,
MC, V.
Good quality, comfortable, miniature versions of Doc
Martens, desert boots and other classics in bright colours for
babies and pre-teen children.
Branch: 28 rue du Four, 75006 (45.48.39.31).

Specialist Shops

The latest destinations for big spenders and window shoppers alike.

There are shops in Paris which reflect every facet of the city's self-image, from the proliferation of book shops on the Left Bank, to the perfumeries which contribute to the Parisian chic ideal, or the traditional toy shops conjuring up a vision of French childhood. Here we've tried to include the ordinary and the luxurious, as well as those useful places relied on by Parisians themselves.

Most shops are open until at least 7pm, but some close for lunch and on Mondays, and many close for all or part of August. For information on the détaxe tax refund scheme, *see chapter* **Fashion**.

Department Stores

BHV (Bazar de l'Hôtel de Ville)
Shop: 52-64 rue de Rivoli/DIY hire annexe 40 rue de la Verrerie, 75004 (shop 42.74.90.00/DIY hire 42.74.97.23). Métro Hôtel de Ville. **Open** 9.30am-6.30pm Mon, Tue, Thur, Fri; 9.30am-9pm Wed; 9.30am-6pm Sat. **Credit** AmEx, EC, MC, V.
A haven for DIY-ers, the BHV is the central Paris alternative to the warehouse superstores ringing the edge of town, with a vast range of paints, electrical goods, furnishings, tools and car parts. It also stocks classic clothes and accessories on the ground floor, and perfunctory health and beauty aids. *See also chapter* **Services**.

Le Bon Marché
38 rue de Sèvres, 75007 (44.39.80.00). Métro Sèvres-Babylone. **Open** 9.30am-7pm Mon-Sat. **Credit** AmEx, DC, EC, MC, V.
The 'good bargain' was the first department store in Paris, and Gustave Eiffel is said to have had a say in the design of its iron-framed structure, long before he moved on to skyscraping. Less touristy than its boulevard Haussmann rivals, it's still a refuge for refined Left Bank ladies. As well as the celebrated food hall (*see chapter* **Food & Drink**), Shop 2 contains an antiques arcade. Shop 1 has added its fashion and accessories, providing contemporary looks on a budget; menswear is smart-casual. Excellent kitchen and household departments. *Gift vouchers. One-hour photo service. Restaurants. Watch & shoe repair. Travel agency. Wedding lists.*

Galeries Lafayette
40 boulevard Haussmann, 75009 (42.82.34.56/ fashion show reservations 42.82.30.25). Métro Chaussée d'Antin/RER Auber. **Open** 9.30am-6.45pm Mon-Wed, Fri, Sat; 9.30am-9pm Thur. **Credit** AmEx, DC, EC, JCB, MC, V.
The Louvre of department stores has over 75,000 brand names, including concessions for Christian Lacroix's diffusion line Bazar, Azzedine Alaïa, Comme des Garçons and Yohji Yamamoto, plus John Galliano and Vivienne Westwood. Cheaper alternatives include Agnès B, The Gap and Galeries Lafayette's own labels Jodhpur (classic work styles), Avant Première (quick translations of catwalk looks) and Version Originale (natural cotton basics). As well as an entire floor devoted to lingerie, there are enormous depart-

ments celebrating the *arts de la table* – porcelain, crystal and every kitchen gadget under the sun. Phone to book a place at the free fashion show-cum-breakfast at 11am Wednesday. *Baby and wedding lists. Bureau de change. Car park. One-hour photo service. Restaurants. Travel & theatre ticket agency. Watch & shoe repair.*
Branch: Tour Montparnasse Complex, 22 rue du Départ, 75014 (45.38.52.87).

Marks & Spencer
35 boulevard Haussmann, 75009 (47.42.42.91). Métro Havre-Caumartin/RER Auber. **Open** 9.30am-7pm Mon, Wed, Fri, Sat; 10am-7pm Tue; 9.30am-8pm Thur. **Credit** EC, MC, V.
A branch of the British chain that's every bit as good for underwear and jumpers as you'd expect, but priced about 50% higher than in the UK. The food hall is a great hit with French shoppers – cox's apples, scones and chicken tikka masala are best-sellers.
Branch: 88 rue de Rivoli, 75004 (44.61.08.00).

Monoprix/Uniprix
Branches all over Paris. **Open** generally 9.30am-7.30pm Mon-Sat; some branches open till 9pm. **Credit** MC, V.
Sooner or later you're bound to come into a branch of dependable Monoprix, for food, shampoo, a notepad or a pair of socks. Some are just supermarkets, bigger branches have delicatessens and even wet fish counters, and the largest have entire fashion floors. The branch at 21 avenue de l'Opéra is a destination for cheap junior clothing and a wide selection of colourful cosmetics. *See also chapter* **Services**.
Photobooths. Photocopying.

Au Printemps
64 boulevard Haussmann, 75009 (42.82.50.00). Métro Havre-Caumartin/RER Auber. **Open** 9.35am-7pm Mon-Wed, Fri, Sat; 9.30am-10pm Thur. **Credit** AmEx, DC, EC, JCB, MC, V.
All the big names of fashion under one roof – Romeo Gigli, Martine Sitbon, Dolce & Gabbana, Issey Miyake or Martin Margiela. Rising stars like Jean Colonna, Xüly Bet and Véronique Leroy are on the fourth floor *rue de la Mode*. Lower floors carry mainstream but fashionable labels such as Ralph Lauren and APC. Kitchenware, china and stationery are worth a look too. In the adjacent building you'll find a plethora of beauty labels, albeit in an atmosphere that's a bit like a self-service duty-free shop.
Baby and wedding lists. Bureau de change. 24-hour shopping pick-up. Gift vouchers. Repair to own goods. Restaurants. Travel & theatre ticket agency. Watch repair.
Branches: 30 avenue d'Italie, 75013 (40.78.17.17); 25 cours de Vincennes, 75020 (43.71.12.41).

La Samaritaine
19 rue de la Monnaie, 75001 (40.41.20.20). Métro Pont Neuf. **Open** 9.30am-7pm Mon-Wed, Fri, Sat; 9.30am-10pm Thur. **Credit** AmEx, DC, EC, JCB, MC, V.
La Samaritaine has somehow never acquired the status of Galeries Lafayette or Printemps, but it does have a faded charm, a superb location on the Seine and one of the best views over Paris from the rooftop terrace of building 2 (lift to the ninth floor, then stairs to the viewing platform). You can find just about anything in the five-store complex, from fashion and

sporting goods to household goods and nuts'n'bolts hardware, and the biggest toy department in Paris at Christmas.
Baby and wedding lists. Bureau de Change. Gift vouchers. Restaurants. Watch repairs.

Tati

4 boulevard Rochechouart, 75018 (42.55.13.09). Métro Barbès-Rochechouart. **Open** 10am-7pm Mon; 9.30am-7pm Tue-Fri; 9.15am-7pm Sat. **Credit** AmEx, DC, MC, V.
As much a Paris institution at the bottom end of the scale as Galeries Lafayette at the top. The shops are a chaos of tights' and underwear boxes, and the crowd uses rugby scrum tactics. Tati has a 'designed' range **La Rue est à Nous**, aimed at streetwise younger buyers (*see chapter* **Fashion**).
Branches: 13 place de la République, 75003 (48.87.72.81)*;* 140 rue de Rennes, 75006 (45.48.68.31).

Antiques & Retro

Antiques shops tend to be clustered along the quai Voltaire (the 'quai des Antiquaires') and in the neighbouring streets of the Carré Rive Gauche –

rues de Lille, de Beaune, des Saints-Pères and de l'Université (all 7th *arrondissement*). There are also many tiny specialist collectors shops in the old *passages* and *galleries* off boulevards Montmartre and Poissonnière. For smart Art Deco visit the shops of St-Germain, while if it's fifties and sixties retro you're after, try rue de Charonne in the Bastille.

Look out, too, for open-air antiques and collectors fairs, known as *Brocante*. As most dealers come from out of town, prices are often lower than at regular flea markets (*see page 201* **Markets**). They're usually advertised with banners and posters in the street, or you can contact SADEMA (*86 rue de Lille, 75007; 40.62.95.95*) for details. If you're interested in old books and prints, take a look at the *Bouquinistes* – the celebrated green boxes lining the banks of the Seine. For auctions, *see chapter* **Art Galleries**.

The Carrousel du Louvre

The underground shopping complex created in the *Grand Louvre* has succesfully contrived to avoid becoming tacky, thanks not just to its splendid address, but also to its dramatic design and the interesting variety of stores that have opened there. Moreover, it's open on Sundays. Services provided include bars, restaurants – with a good choice for vegetarians –, photo developing and a bureau de change. Most shops follow the opening hours of the museum, and accept the forms of payment listed here.

Carrousel du Louvre

99 rue de Rivoli, 75001 (46.92.47.47). Métro Palais Royal-Musée de Louvre. **Open** 10am-10pm Mon, Wed; 10am-8pm Thur-Sun. Closed Tue. **Credit** AmEx, DC, JCB, MC, TC, V.

Aridza Bross

(47.03.98.50).
Inexpensive clothing and accessories for juniors. Pick up on the latest trends in two face-to-face shops.
Branch: 4 place des Victoires, 75001 (42.36.31.84).

Bodum

(42.60.47.11).
Modern Scandinavian transparent or bright design for kitchenware. Stop at the coffee bar for what some consider the best espressos in town.

Courrèges

(40.15.05.85).
Octogenarian André Courrèges continues to dress women into the next millenium with his unique, futuristic vision. Vinyl go-go boots and see-through plastic umbrellas are surprisingly low-priced, fun additions.
Branches: 49 rue de Rennes, 75006 (45.48.08.71); 46 rue du Faubourg St-Honoré, 75008 (42.65.37.75); 40 rue François 1er, 75008 (53.67.30.73); 10 avenue Victor-Hugo, 75016 (45.01.70.18).

Cravatterie Nazionali

(42.86.82.35).
One of two shops here specialising in ties (Tie Rack is the other), this carries top French and Italian labels like Christian Dior, Valentino, Yves Saint Laurent and Moschino.

Esprit

(42.60.51.41).
Young, casual clothes, bags and shoes for men and women. In stock is the planet-friendly Ecollection, designed by Royal College grad Linda Gross.
Branch: 9 place des Victoires, 75002 (40.29.00.95).

Lalique

(42.86.01.51).
In her eighties, René Lalique's daughter Marie Claude is still at the creative helm of this august French institution, and has added to the classic crystal tableware and furnishings a new image of colourful jewellery and collectable figurines.

Metropolitan Museum of Art

(40.20.58.50).
The granddaddy of all relics-to-wear museum shops, New York's MET has installed itself in Paris' Louvre.

Nature & Découvertes

(47.03.47.43).
Always crowded and for a good reason: there's something here for nature-lovers of every age, from cheap little gadgets, toys and stickers to science kits to animal sound effects and sophisticated surveillance equipment.
Branches: Forum des Halles, 75001 (40.28.42.16); Les Trois Quartiers, 23 boulevard de la Madeleine 75001 (49.27.07.58); Italie 2-Grand Ecran, 75013 (45.88.28.28); 61 rue de Passy, 75016 (42.30.53.87).

Tout Ranger

(42.60.10.85).
Racks, pouches and hangers for every room in the house. One for truly obsessive compulsives.

Art Depôt
3 rue du Pont-Louis-Philippe, 75004 (42.77.99.02).
Métro Pont-Marie or Hôtel de Ville. **Open** noon-8pm
Tue-Sun. **Credit** AmEx.
A tiny shop crammed with classy kitsch from the thirties to
the fifties – 1957-vintage TVs, Cobra telephones, advertising memorabilia and a heap of stylish thirties chrome lamps.

Di Maria
45 rue des Francs-Bourgeois, 75004 (42.71.02.31).
Métro St-Paul. **Open** 10.30am-7pm Mon-Fri; 10.30am-
7pm Sat. **Credit** AmEx, DC, MC, V.

A packed little store that buys, sells and also appraises
antique posters, postcards, books, documents, photographs
and ephemera of all kinds.

Kitsch
3 rue Bonaparte, 75006 (43.29.76.23). Métro St-
Germain-des-Prés. **Open** 2-7pm Mon-Sat. **Credit** AmEx,
DC, MC, V.
What else could they have called this shop with the loudest
ceramic fish lamps, floral-shaded sconces and curlicue vases
in creation? Collectors will also recognise ceramics from
sought-after manufacturers from the thirties to the fifties.

Parfums de Paris

Few varieties of shop are more distinctively
Parisian than the city's lavish *parfumeries*. With
delightful, often ornate window displays and
endless ranges of rare fragances on offer, they
are fascinating places to visit even if you don't
necessarily feel inclined to buy.

Creed
38 avenue Pierre 1er de Serbie, 75008 (47.20.58.02).
Métro Alma Marceau or Georges V. **Open** 2.30-7pm
Mon; 10am-9pm Tue-Sat. **Credit** AmEx, MC, V.
Empress Eugenie patronised Creed, and the hoi polloi can
buy the Jasmin and Angélique Encens fragrances she
inspired today. Their green Irish Tweed and Erolfa are
particulary desirable scents for men.

Détaille
10 rue St Lazare, 75009 (48.78.68.50). Métro Notre-
Dame de Lorette. **Open** 10am-1.30pm, 2-7pm, Mon-Fri;
2-7pm Sat. **Credit** AmEx, EC, MC, V.
Founded in 1905 by the Comtesse de Presle to protect her
skin from the pollution of the new automobiles. The range
is now quite sophisticated, but boutique and bottles retain
a turn-of-the-century charm.

Annick Goutal
14 rue de Castiglione, 75001 (42.60.52.82).
Métro Concorde. **Open** 10am-7pm Mon-Sat. **Credit**
AmEx, DC, EC, MC, V.
Annick Goutal is a talented 'nose' and one of few women
prominent in the perfume business, producing fragrances
that are rare combinations of glamour, delicacy and luxury. The ivory and gold-leaf décor is echoed in the delicate
and luxurious packaging.
Branches: 12 place St-Sulpice, 75006 (46.33.03.15); 16 rue
Bellechasse, 75007 (45.51.36.13).

Guerlain
68 avenue des Champs-Elysées, 75008 (45.62.52.57).
Métro Franklin D Roosevelt. **Open** 9.45am-7pm Mon-
Sat . **Credit** AmEx, EC, MC, V.
One of the last vestiges of the golden age of the Champs-
Elysées. Many of the Guerlain fragrances for women and
men were created with royal or Proustian inspirations,
and the company's cosmetics are renowned the world
over. There's a beauty treatment salon upstairs in the
Champs-Elysées branch only (*see chapter* **Services**).
Branches: 2 place Vendôme, 75001 (42.60.68.61); 47
rue Bonaparte, 75006 (43.26.71.19); 35 rue Tronchet,
75008 (47.42.53.23); Centre Maine-Montparnasse, 75015
(43.20.95.40); 93 rue de Passy, 75016 (42.88.41.62); 29
rue de Sèvres, 75006 (42.22.46.60).

L'Occitane
55 rue St-Louis-en-l'Ile, 75004 (40.46.81.71).
Métro Pont-Marie. **Open** 2.30-7pm Mon; 10.30am-7pm
Tue-Sun. **Credit** MC, V.
Natural treatments for the body and hair made from essential oils in Provence. Gift packs are ready-made for shaving and travelling; homely scents include vervain, honey
and milk.

Octée
53 rue Bonaparte, 75006 (46.33.18.77).
Métro St-Germain-des Prés. **Open** 11-7pm Mon-Sat.
Credit AmEx, MC, V.
A large selection of ingeniously packaged fragrances.
There's also a skin treatment range.

Les Salons du Palais Royal Shiseido
142 galerie de Valois, 75001 (49.27.09.09).
Métro Palais-Royal. **Open** 9am-7pm Mon-Sat. **Credit**
AmEx, DC, EC, MC, V.
An oriental treasure trove of exotic scents created by
Serge Lutens, in the arcades of the Palais-Royal. The interior pays homage to the beautiful arcades of the era of
Colette; if you have an appointment, you can climb the
spiral staircase to the beauty treatment salon above.

Shu Uemura
176 boulevard St Germain, 75006 (45.48.02.55).
Métro St-Germain-des-Prés. **Open** 11am-7pm Mon;
10am-7pm Tue-Sat. **Credit** AmEx, DC, MC, V.
Professional make-up artists swear by this Japanese line of
skin-care and cosmetics which come in peacock shades as
well as more subdued colours. Eyebrow raising price-tags.

*The fine products of **Annick Goutal**.*

Louvre des Antiquaires
2 place du Palais-Royal, 75001 (42.97.27.00). Métro Palais Royal. **Open** 11am-7pm Tue-Sun.
A notably upmarket, purpose-built antiques centre behind an old facade, home to 250 dealers. Louis XV furniture, tapestries, Chinese porcelain, silver and antique jewellery can all be found here, at a price.

Salle de Vente Saint Honoré
214 rue du Faubourg St-Honoré, 75008 (43.59.68.63). Métro Charles de Gaulle-Etoile. **Open** noon-7pm Mon-Sat.
Depôt-ventes are sale rooms where you can leave objects to be sold at a fixed price. As befits the superior location, this is one of the most reliable for antiques, repro and works of art, although you'll find others dotted around Paris.

Books

See also **FNAC** *and* **Virgin Megastore** *in* **CDs, Records, Cassettes & Hi-Fi** *below.*

Abbey Bookshop
29 rue de la Parcheminerie, 75005 (46.33.16.24). Métro St-Michel. **Open** 10am-7pm Mon-Sat. **Credit** AmEx, MC, V.
This small Canadian-run bookshop has an extensive section of Canadian writers (including Québecois), as well as English and American titles. They will take special and mail orders for books, and happily serve coffee to browsers.

Artcurial
9 avenue Matignon, 75008 (42.99.16.16). Métro Franklin D Roosevelt. **Open** 10.30am-7.15pm Tue-Sat. **Credit** AmEx, DC, EC, MC, V.
A definitive art bookshop for glossy, coffee-table books on twentieth-century art, photography and design. You can also lose yourself in the contemporary jewellery and gift shop, and the cavernous gallery spaces above and below (*see also chapter* **Art Galleries**).

Brentano's
37 avenue de l'Opéra, 75002 (42.61.52.50). Métro Opéra. **Open** 10am-7pm Mon-Sat. **Credit** EC, MC, V.
A good address for American classics, modern fiction and best-sellers. English language books are at the front; magazines in the far corner; children's books are in the basement. In one alcove there's always a table of reduced-price books.

Entrée des Artistes
161 rue St-Martin, 75003 (48.87.78.58). Métro Rambuteau. **Open** 11am-9.30pm Mon-Sat. **Credit** DC, EC, JCB, MC, V.
A veritable shrine to celluloid, from the most obscure movies to box-office blockbusters. Every inch of space is packed with film posters, photo stills, and an impressive selection of film books in French and English.

Galignani
224 rue de Rivoli, 75001 (42.60.76.07). Métro Tuileries. **Open** 10am-7pm Mon-Sat. **Credit** EC, MC, V.
Reputedly the first English-language bookshop in continental Europe, Galignani's dark, woody décor lends it a traditional atmosphere. Fine art, decorative arts and garden books in French and English are at the front; English literature is tucked away at the back.

Gibert Joseph
26 boulevard St-Michel, 75006 (44.41.88.88). Métro Odéon or Cluny-La-Sorbonne. **Open** 9.30am-7.30pm Mon-Sat. **Credit** V.
Best known as a bookstore and a place to flog your old text books, the Gibert empire stretching along the boulevard St-Michel also has a vast stationery department that stocks an encyclopaedic range of office and writing accessories.

Institut Géographique National
107 rue de la Boëtie, 75008 (43.98.85.00). Métro Franklin D Roosevelt. **Open** 9.30am-7pm Mon-Fri; 10am-12.30pm, 2-5.30pm, Sat. **Credit** EC, MC, V.
Paris' best map shop, which also stocks guidebooks to all regions of France, posters and a great selection of globes.

La Hune
170 boulevard St-Germain, 75006 (45.48.35.85). Métro St-Germain-des-Prés. **Open** 10am-11.45pm Mon-Sat. **Credit** AmEx, DC, EC, MC, V.
A Left Bank classic, this well-organised bookshop is open until nearly midnight, and always busy.

Shakespeare & Co
37 rue de la Bûcherie, 75005 (43.26.96.50). Métro Maubert-Mutualité/RER St-Michel. **Open** noon-midnight daily. **No credit cards.**
A Parisian legend, if no longer on the same site as Sylvia Beach's famous shop. New, used and antique books are idiosyncratically arranged – mainly on the floor – and it's still packed with would-be Hemingways. Some love it, others would prefer a shop where they could find what they want.

Super Héros
175 rue St-Martin, 75003 (42.74.34.74). Métro Rambuteau. **Open** 11.30am-8pm Mon-Sat. **Credit** AmEx, EC, MC, V.
Comic books are serious business here. Alongside characters such as Tintin and Batman, the nihilistic strips of Enki Bilal are on sale, plus second-hands, posters and gadgets.

Tea & Tattered Pages
24 rue Mayet, 75006 (40.65.94.35). Métro Duroc. **Open** 11am-7pm daily. **No credit cards.**
A gentle American-style tea salon where you can browse at leisure through new editions and over 10,000 second-hand, mainly paperback, books (average price per book: 25F).

Le Verre et L'Assiette
1 rue du Val-de-Grâce, 75005 (46.33.45.96). RER Port-Royal. **Open** 2-7pm Mon; 10am-12.30pm, 2-7pm, Tue-Sat. **Credit** AmEx, DC, MC, V.
A haven for cooks and wine lovers with cook books, some in English, plus decanters, corkscrews and other gadgets.

Village Voice
6 rue Princesse, 75006 (46.33.36.47). Métro Mabillon. **Open** 2-8pm Mon; 11am-8pm Tue-Sat; *June, July* 12.15-6pm Sun. **Credit** AmEx, DC, EC, MC, V.
Odile Hellier supports alternative literature by stocking little-known writers as well as the tried and true. She also holds literary events and play and poetry readings.

WH Smith
248 rue de Rivoli, 75001 (44.77.88.99). Métro Concorde. **Open** 9.30am-7pm Mon-Sat. **Credit** AmEx, MC, V.
A long-established branch of the British chain. Paperback bestsellers, classics, travel guides, cookery books and videos are on the ground floor. There are also good reference and business departments, and a comprehensive English language-teaching section. London *Time Out* is available here.

Children's Toys & Books

Attica 3
64 rue de la Folie Méricourt, 75011 (48.06.17.00). Métro Oberkampf. **Open** 2-7pm Mon; 10am-7pm Tue-Sat. **Credit** DC, EC, JCB, MC, V.
Attica's slogan is 'literature for pleasure', for English speakers or those wanting to learn English. As well as a large stock of TEFL literature, you'll find all the British children's classics and English translations of French comics.

Au Nain Bleu

406-410 rue St-Honoré, 75008 (42.60.39.01).
Métro Concorde. **Open** 9.45am-6.30pm Mon-Sat. **Credit**
AmEx, EC, JCB, MC, V.
The most prestigious toy shop in France, dating from 1836,
and with a huge stock of toys from all around the world.
There's a dazzling collection of dolls and dolls' houses, musical instruments, and the latest in electronic toys and gadgets
for under 50F. Also to be found is a large games section, on
the upper floors.

Chantelivre

13 rue de Sèvres, 75006 (45.48.87.90). Métro Sèvres-
Babylone. **Open** 1-6.50pm Mon; 10am-6.50pm Tue-Sat;
closed one week mid-Aug. **Credit** EC, MC, V.
Over 10,000 titles cover books for infants to adolescents, as
well as health and psychology and publications for expectant
parents. With them there's also a wide selection of cassettes,
videos, toys, games and party supplies. Children can be left
in the play or reading area.

Corvinus

16 rue des Halles, 75001 (42.33.68.97).
Métro Châtelet-Les Halles. **Open** 2.15-7pm Mon; 10.45am-
7pm Tue-Sat. **Credit** AmEx, EC, JCB, MC, V.
Tiny, detailed dolls' houses – available in kits from 650F to
3,000F – and their furnishings. Other old-fashioned toys
include kaleidoscopes, marionettes and Victorian paper dolls.

Il était une fois

1 rue Cassette, 75006 (45.48.21.10).
Métro St-Sulpice. **Open** 10am-7.30pm Mon-Sat. **Credit**
AmEx, EC, JCB, MC, V.
A delightful children's toy box filled with marionettes,
Tintin and Babar dolls, toys, games and small wooden
gadgets. There are fancy clothes for boys and girls up to 12.

The groovy and wacky **Hilton McConnico.**

Si Tu Veux

68 galerie Vivienne, 75002 (42.60.59.97). Métro Bourse.
Open 10.30am-7pm Mon-Sat. **Credit** MC, V.
An old-fashioned, toy store in this nineteenth century *galerie*
that stocks skipping-ropes, wendy-houses and other traditional toys. They also have a good selection of fancy-dress
outfits, masks and other party gear.

Design & Furniture

Conran Shop

117 rue du Bac, 75007 (42.84.10.01). Métro Sèvres-
Babylone. **Open** noon-7pm Mon; 10am-7pm Tue-Sat.
Credit AmEx, EC, MC, V.
Sir Terence Conran opened this branch of the London furniture and accessories shop at the end of 1992 in an elegant
building just next to the Bon Marché. Wonderful kitchen
gadgets, candlesticks and handkerchiefs.

En Attendant Les Barbares

50 rue Etienne-Marcel, 75002 (42.33.37.87). Métro
Etienne Marcel. **Open** 10.30am-7pm Tue-Fri; 11am-
6.30pm Sat. **Credit** AmEx, EC, MC, V.
A showcase for the pick of irreverent, contemporary designers, who blend baroque, tribal and salvage styles. Pick up
resin lampstands (1,500F) and soap dishes (350F) in boiled-
sweet colours by Jarrige, as well as Thierry Wagner's bul-
bous furniture or Carl Schmitt's wrought iron and glass
console tables.

Etat de Siège

1 quai de Conti, 75006 (43.29.31.60). Métro Pont-Neuf.
Open 11am-7pm Tue-Sat; closed 10 days in August.
Credit AmEx, EC, MC, V.
This shop specialises in chairs, covering every epoch from
Louis XIII to today, including re-editions of Biedermeier,
Eileen Gray, Mies van der Rohe and Gaudi, and contem-
poraries like Oscar Tusquets.
Branches: 94 rue du Bac, 75007 (45.49.10.20); 21 avenue
de Friedland, 75008 (42.56.64.75); 45 rue de Lyon, 75012
(43.43.25.97).

Galérie Joyce

168-173 galérie de Valois, 75001 (40.15.03.72). Métro
Palais-Royal. **Open** 2.30-6.30pm Mon; 11am-6.30pm Tue-
Sat. **Credit** MC, V.
Joyce Ma, whose Hong Kong empire of fashion is world-
renowned, has opened a furniture-art gallery in Paris' Palais-
Royal, showing designers' *objets de maison.*

Galerie Néotu

25 rue du Renard, 75004 (42.78.96.97).
Métro Hôtel de Ville. **Open** 10am-7pm Mon-Fri; 11am-
1pm, 2-6pm, Sat. **Credit** AmEx, MC, V.
Exhibitions of avant-garde furniture by the likes of Garouste
et Bonetti, Martin Tzekely and Pucci di Rossi. Great fun.

Hilton McConnico

28 rue Madame, 75006 (42.84.32.22). Métro St-Sulpice.
Open 10am-7pm Tue-Sat. **Credit** AmEx, DC, JCB, MC, V.
This Tennessee transplant is a design star in Paris for his
film sets (he won a César for *Diva*) and exhibitions. In his
shop you'll find favourite themes such as chilli peppers, cac-
tuse, cats and dogs, all applied to such things as china,
towels, rugs and bathrobes.

Meubles et Fonction

135 boulevard Raspail, 75006 (45.48.55.74). Métro
Vavin. **Open** 9.30am-12.30pm, 2-7pm, Mon-Fri; 10am-
12.30pm, 2-7pm, Sat. **No credit cards.**
Contemporary furniture by designers and architects such as
Antonio Cittério and Paolo Navarre showing Italian design
flair. Lots of elegant glass, wood and metal.

Volt et Watt

29 boulevard Raspail, 75007(45.48.29.62). Métro Sèvres-Babylone. **Open** 10am-7pm Mon-Sat. **Credit** MC, V.
Plenty of trendy contemporary lighting. There's more colour these days, after years of matt black and chrome.

Fabrics & Trimmings

La Droguerie

*9 rue du Jour, 75001 (45.08.93.27).
Métro Châtelet-Les Halles or Etienne-Marcel.* **Open** 2-6.45pm Mon; 10.30am-6.45pm Tue-Sat; 1-6.45pm Tue-Sat in Aug. **No credit cards.**
Baubles, beads and buttons in all conceivable colours and shapes, to be selected individually or by the scoopful. Also ribbons, feather boas and knitting yarns galore.

Marché St Pierre

Dreyfus, *2 rue Charles Nodier, 75018 (46.06.92.25);*
Tissus Reine, *5 place St-Pierre (46.06.02.31);* **Moline**, *1 place St-Pierre (46.06.14,66). Métro Anvers.* **Open** 1.30-6.45pm Mon; 9.30am-6.30pm Tue-Fri; 9.30am-6.45pm Sat. **Credit** MC, V.
Join the scavengers in the five stories of the Marché for a truly Parisian experience. Top floors have linens; the middle, silks and luxury fabrics; the first, wool and synthetics; and the ground floors are littered with a little of everything.

Mokuba

*18 and 26 rue Montmartre, 75001 (40.13.81.41).
Métro Châtelet-Les Halles.* **Open** 9.30am-6.30pm Mon-Fri; closed Aug. **Credit** MC, V.
Row after row of ribbons, cords and braids in satin, velvet, taffeta, organza, netting and silk.

Souleiado

*78 rue de Seine, 75006 (43.54.62.25).
Métro Mabillon.* **Open** 10am-7pm Mon-Sat. **Credit** AmEx, DC, EC, JCB, MC, V.
Specialises in the bright Provençal prints that go to make French country interiors as warm as the sun on the Côte d'Azur. There are also bags and clothing.
Branches: 7 rue Lobineau (professional showroom), 75006 (44.07.33.81); 83 avenue Paul Doumer, 75016 (42.24.99.34).

Wolff et Descourtis

*18 galerie Vivienne, 75002 (42.61.80.84).
Métro Bourse.* **Open** 11am-7pm Mon-Fri; 1-7pm Sat. **Credit** AmEx, DC, EC, JCB, MC, V.
This shop has supplied couturiers with exotic and sumptuous materials and fabrics since 1875. Sumptuous silks range from 200F to 600F per metre.

Florists & Garden Fittings

See also chapter **Services**.

Baptiste

*27 rue des Sts-Pères, 75006 (42.60.11.90/
42.60.11.45). Métro St-Germain-des-Prés.* **Open** 8.30am-9pm Mon-Sat. **Credit** MC, V (in person only).
A miniscule shop with beautiful blooms. Simple, garden-variety flowers are elevated to fairy-tale heights.

Jardins Imaginaires

*9 bis rue d'Assas, 75006 (42.22.90.03).
Métro Sèvres-Babylone.* **Open** 10.30am-1pm, 2-7pm, Tue-Sat. **Credit** AmEx, EC, MC, V.
The perfect addition to the elegant back yard. Pots in terracotta or blue Oriental ceramic come in all shapes, sizes and prices, plus beautiful dried flowers and hand-woven baskets.

Christian Tortu

6 carrefour de l'Odéon, 75006 (43.26.02.56). Métro Odéon. **Open** 9am-8pm Mon-Sat. **Credit** MC, V.
This 'new-age' florist sculpts exotic flowers, foliage, twigs and moss into imaginative, gravity-defying wildernesses.

Gifts

Cir

*22 rue St-Sulpice, 75006 (43.26.46.50).
Métro Odéon.* **Open** 10am-12.30pm, 1.30-7pm, Mon; 10am-7pm Tue-Sat. **Credit** V.
Candles of every imaginable form, from waxen images of the Eiffel Tower to scented ones that keep insects away at night.

L'Entrepôt

*50 rue de Passy, 75016 (45.25.64.17).
Métro La Muette.* **Open** 10.30am-7pm Mon-Thur; 10am-7pm Fri, Sat. **Credit** MC, V.
Gifts for everyone: party supplies, home accessories, kitsch kitchenware, tools for the serious gourmet and clothing.

Marais Plus

*20 rue des Francs-Bourgeois, 75004
(48.87.01.40). Métro St-Paul.* **Open** 10am-7.30pm daily. **Credit** AmEx, EC, MC, V.
A friendly tea room/toy shop/gift shop, with fun novelty teapots including some on wheels by Domart. It's also a good place for inexpensive jewellery, and fine-art T-shirts.

Robin des Bois

*15 rue Ferdinand Duval, 75004 (48.04.09.36).
Métro St-Paul.* **Open** 2-7.30pm Mon-Sat; 1.30-7.30pm Sun. **Credit** EC, MC, V.
Everything is made with recycled or ecologically sound products – bottle-top jewellery and buttons; ear-rings made from vegetal ivory; attractive recycled notepaper.
Branch: 35 rue du Bourg-Tibourg, 75004 (48.04.95.78).

Home Accessories/Kitchenware

Au Bain Marie

*10 bis rue Boissy d'Anglas, 75008 (42.66.59.74).
Métro Concorde.* **Open** 10am-7pm Mon-Sat. **Credit** AmEx, DC, EC, JCB, MC, V.
An emporium dedicated to the art of fine dining, with elegant displays of new or perfectly preserved old tableware, linens, crystal, silver, bar accessories and knick-knacks.

La Chaise Longue

*8 rue Princesse, 75006 (43.29.62.39).
Métro St-Germain-des-Prés, Mabillon.* **Open** 11am-7pm Mon-Sat. **Credit** AmEx, EC, MC, V.

Baroque accessories at **Au Bain Marie**.

Treasures of the Orient at the **Compagnie Française de l'Orient et de la Chine**.

Glasses, ceramics and real old-fashioned, painted tin plates, plus re-editions of gadgets from the thirties, forties and fifties, such as polished oak picture frames and whirring black electric fans. The rue des Francs-Bourgeois branch is also open 2-7pm on Sundays.
Branches: 30 rue des Croix des Petits Champs, 75001 (42.96.32.14); 20 rue des Francs-Bourgeois, 75003 (48.04.36.37).

Compagnie Française de l'Orient et de la Chine (CFOC)

170 boulevard Haussmann, 75008 (45.62.12.53).
Métro St-Philippe-du-Roule. **Open** 10am-8pm Mon-Fri; 10am-7.30pm-Sat. **Credit** AmEx, EC, MC, V.
The newest and most impressive of the several branches of this store, known to Parisians as the CFOC. The company sells high quality imported goods from the Far East, such as tableware, textiles and clothing. Don't miss the lower level, where you'll not only find a wealth of often-rare Chinese furniture, but also some fine original Lalique Art Deco lighting in the ceiling.
Branches: 24 rue St-Roch, 75001 (42.60.65.32); 163 & 167 boulevard St-Germain, 75006 (45.48.00.18 & 45.48.10.31); 260 boulevard St-Germain, 75007 (47.05.92.82); 65 avenue Victor-Hugo, 75016 (45.00.55.46); 113 avenue Mozart, 75016 (42.88.36.08).

E Dehillerin

18 rue Coquillière, 75001 (42.36.53.13). Métro Châtelet-Les Halles. **Open** 8am-12.30pm, 2-6pm, Mon; 8am-6pm Tue-Sat. **Credit** EC, MC, V.
Dehillerin has supplied many of the great European chefs since 1820, and the shop is an Aladdin's cave of every kind of cooking utensil you could think of, including huge and unusual cooking vessels and equipment – gargantuan casseroles and ladles big enough to serve 50.

Kitchen Kitsch

15 rue des Ecouffes, 75004 (42.72.74.02). Métro St-Paul. **Open** 2-7pm Tue-Sun. **Credit** AmEx, JCB, MC, V.

The name perfectly describes the shop, filled with a bizarre selection of household Americana, including mint-condition Osterizer blenders, toasters, and mixers that look like they might have been pinched from a 1950s suburban situation comedy, the perfect accessories for Post-Moderns just longing to recapture that genuine Doris Day atmosphere. To top it off, with most items you'll also get a genuine Pillsbury Bake-Off cookbook.

Laïmoun

2 Rue de Tournon, 75006 (43.54.68.00).
Métro Mabillon or Odéon. **Open** noon-7pm Mon; 10am-7pm Tue-Sat. **Credit** AmEx, MC, V.
Richly ornamented fabric, cushions and easy-to-wear, pyjama-like clothing imported from different countries around the Middle East.

Geneviève Lethu

95 rue de Rennes, 75006 (45.44.40.35).
Métro St-Placide. **Open** 2-7pm Mon; 10.15am-7pm Tue-Sat. **Credit** EC, MC, V.
A high-class tableware shop between Montparnasse and St-Germain, with china, glass and silverware all in the best possible taste, both in the plain 'pop' range and more decorative styles. A good place to look for classy gifts, and popular for wedding lists.
Branches include: 91 rue de Rivoli, 75001 (42.60.14.90); 28 rue St-Antoine, 75004 (42.74.21.25); 1 avenue Niel, 75017 (45.72.03.47); 317 rue Vaugirard, 75015 (45.31.77.84).

Maison de Famille

29 rue St-Sulpice, 75006 (40.46.97.47).
Métro St-Sulpice. **Open** 10.30am-7pm Mon-Sat. **Credit** AmEx, DC, EC, JCB, MC, V.
Irresistible furniture, linen, crockery and utensils deck the shelves of this shop, the kind of things you might expect (or hope) to find in charming French farmhouses. The upper floors consist of a labyrinth of lofts, containing a well-stocked bed and bath shop, some gardening accessories and a range of men's and women's casual clothing.

Markets

Paris' three main flea-markets occupy sites next to the thundering *périphérique*, as they originally developed outside the *portes* (gateways) to Paris so that rag and bone men from outside the town could avoid paying duty.

Marché aux Fleurs/Oiseaux

place Louis-Lépine, Ile de la Cité, 75004.
Métro Cité. **Open** *flower market* 8am-4pm Mon-Sat;
bird market 8am-4pm Sun.
Blossoms and plants are brought here every day, fresh from the French Riviera, Holland and exotic locales. Prices are cheaper, on average, than at florists'. On Sunday, it's partly transformed into a bird market, which some may find unpleasant.

Marché aux Fleurs

Place de la Madeleine, 75008. Métro Madeleine.
Open 8am-7pm Tue-Sat.
Place des Ternes, 75017. Métro Ternes.
Open 8am-8pm Tue-Sun.
Flowers are in ready-made bouquets at these charming markets, or they'll make one to order.

Marché aux Livres

Parc Georges Brassens, rue Brancion and rue des Morillons, 75015. **Open** 9am-6pm Sat, Sun.
Antiquarian and second-hand books. Arrive early and get ready for some hard haggling.

Marché aux Puces de Montreuil

Outside Métro Porte de Montreuil, 75020. **Open** 7.30am-7pm Mon, Sat, Sun.
Expect second-hand clothing, contraband videos and loads of miscellaneous junk. The site is threatened with closure for redevelopment. More anarchic than Clignancourt.

Marché aux Puces Clignancourt

outside Métro Porte de Clignancourt, 75018. **Open** 5am-6pm Mon, Sat, Sun.
This enormous market, reputedly the largest flea market in Europe, with 2,000 stands, is made up of arcades of semi-permanent shops (past the clothes stalls). There are definitely rare and high-quality pieces to be found here, but at a price. The whole complex is divided into various different 'Marchés', most of which run off the rue des Rosiers in St-Ouen, such as the Marché Serpette specialising in art nouveau and art deco; Marché Biron, less grand than it used to be but still the place for an ormolu candelabra or Louis XV chairs; Marché Jules-Vallès, the most eccentric and prestigious antechambers; Marché des Rosiers, smallest with more affordable goods such as antique baby clothes; Marché Paul Bert, good for up-market decorating; and Marché Vernaison, the largest and most chaotic. Many of the *brocs* (merchants) will restore or customise your purchases, and will also help organise delivery. Arrive early for any hope of a bargain, and give yourself a good few hours to get round the whole lot.

Marché aux Timbres

corner of avenue Marigny and avenue Gabriel, 75008. Métro Champs-Elysées-Clemenceau. **Open** 10am-sunset Thur, Sat, Sun, public holidays.
Vintage stamps and postcards from around world, as well as the curiously tradeable modern phone cards and little enamel pins.

Marché aux Puces de Vanves

avenue Georges Lafenestre (on bridge after Périphérique) and avenue Marc Sangrier 75014. Métro Porte de Vanves. **Open** 7.30am-7pm Sat, Sun.
Smaller than St Ouen or Montreuil, and perhaps the friendliest and most informal of the markets. You probably won't find great treasures here, but it can be a good source of small decorative or household items.

Catherine Memmi

32-34 rue St-Sulpice, 75006 (44.07.22.28).
Métro St-Sulpice. **Open** 12.30am-7.30pm Mon; 10.30am-7.30pm Tue-Sat. **Credit** AmEx, EC, JCB, MC, V.
Comfy, natural furnishings for home and bath: textiles in undyed linen and towelling in honeycomb cotton, unusual candles and cedarwood home fragrances from Miller & Bertaux.

Records, CDs, Cassettes & Hi-Fi

Blue Moon Music

7 rue Pierre Sarrazin, 75006 (46.34.63.89). Métro St-Michel. **Open** 11am-7pm Mon-Sat. **Credit** EC, MC, V.
Specialists in reggae, rap, ragga, salsa, African and Caribbean music. Very friendly and a good place for flyers.

Crocodisc

40-42 rue des Ecoles, 75005 (43.54.47.95).
Métro Maubert-Mutualité/RER Luxembourg. **Open** 11am-7pm Tue-Sat. **Credit** EC, MC, V.
Good value new, second-hand and off-beat records: pop, rock, funk, Oriental, African and country music; everything, in fact, except classical. Crocojazz specialises in jazz, blues and gospel.
Branch: Crocojazz 64 rue de la Montagne-Ste-Geneviève, 75005 (46.34.78.38).

FNAC

Level –3, Forum des Halles, 1-7 rue Pierre Lescot, 75001 (40.41.40.00). Métro Châtelet-Les Halles. **Open** 10am-7.30pm Mon-Sat. **Credit** AmEx, EC, MC, V.
The giant FNAC emporia are one-stop shops for books, music, electronics and computers, stereo, videos and photography gear, and also develop film and sell tickets for just about every major event in Paris (the ticket service is Alpha-FNAC). Try to avoid going there on Saturdays, when pandemonium generally reigns at every FNAC branch. *See also* chapters **Services** *and* **Theatre**.
Branches: 136 rue de Rennes, 75006 (49.54.30.00); 26-30 avenue des Ternes, 75017 (44.09.18.00); 24 boulevard des Italiens, 75009 (open till midnight, music only) (48.01.02.03); 4 place de la Bastille, 75012 (music and records only) (43.42.04.04).

Parallèles

36 rue des Bourdonnais, 75001 (42.33.60.00).
Métro Châtelet-Les Halles. **Open** 10am-7pm Mon-Sat.
Credit MC, V.
Buys and sells records, cassettes, CDs and books. This branch specialises in jazz and classical records, cinema, cookery and sci-fi books, posters and rock'n'roll postcards. The rue St-Honoré branch stocks rock music, literature, political and comic books, fanzines and badges.
Branch: 47 rue St-Honoré, 75001 (42.33.62.70).

Rough Trade

30 rue de Charonne, 75011 (40.21.61.62).
Métro Ledru-Rollin. **Open** noon-7pm Mon, Tue; 11am-
8pm Wed, Fri, Sat; 11am-7pm Thur. **Credit** MC, V.
This offshoot of the famed London shop opened in 1993. It
stocks plenty of indie labels, with lots of noise, techno and
ambient, plus more dance music in the basement. There are
occasional instore gigs on Saturday afternoons. A good place
to pick up fanzines and party flyers.

USA Imports

20 rue des Tournelles, 75004 (42.71.52.33). Métro
Bastille. **Open** 2-8pm Mon-Sat. **No credit cards**.
Hip French DJ Laurent Garnier (formerly of Manchester's
Hacienda and now a regular at the **Rex Club**) is one of the
owners of this store, which explains the house music bias.

Virgin Megastore

52-60 avenue des Champs-Elysées, 75008 (49.53.50.00).
Métro Franklin D Roosevelt. **Open** 10am-midnight Mon-
Thur; 10am-1am Fri, Sat; noon-midnight Sun. **Credit**
AmEx, DC, EC, JCB, MC, V.
The huge flagship of the Virgin empire in France creates the
occasional roadblock when a headline band turns up for a
record signing. The video department on the top floor has a

Out of Hours Shopping

Areas considered *touristique* are given the green light
to open on Sunday. This situation is subject to rapid
changes and occasional crackdowns,but they generally include sections of rue de Rivoli near the Louvre,
rue des Francs-Bourgeois and place des Vosges, and
avenue des Champs-Elysées. Bookshops **La Hune**
and **Shakespeare & Co**. both stay open until midnight, as does the **Virgin Megastore**.

Champs Disques

84 avenue des Champs-Elysées, 75008
(45.62.65.46). Métro Franklin D Roosevelt. **Open**
10am-midnight Mon-Sat; noon-8pm Sun. **Credit**
AmEx, DC, EC, MC, V.
A large store selling CDs and cassettes.

Drugstores Publicis Etoile

133 avenue des Champs-Elysées,
75008 (44.43.79.00). Métro Charles de Gaulle-
Etoile. **Open** 9am-2am daily. **Credit** AmEx, DC,
EC, MC, V.
The Publicis advertising agency opened this chain in
the swinging sixties. The Drugstores are late-night
convenience stores stocking a great variety of often
top-quality goods: food, gifts, cigarettes, alcohol and
books. There's also, as the name suggests, a chemist's,
as well as a café and restaurant.
Branches: 149 boulevard St-Germain, 75006
(42.22.92.50); 1 avenue de Matignon, 75008
(43.59.38.70).

Prisunic

109 rue de la Boétie, 75008 (42.25.27.46). Métro
Franklin D Roosevelt. **Open** 9am-midnight Mon-
Sat. **Credit** EC, MC, V.
One of the few places where you can buy clothes at
night. Groceries are in the basement.

decent selection of non-dubbed English films. The new
Carrousel du Louvre branch is much less hectic.
Branch: Carrousel du Louvre, 99 rue de Rivoli, 75001
(47.03.91.17).

Stationery & Art Supplies

Comptoir des Ecritures

82 rue Quincampoix, 75003 (42.78.95.10).
Métro Rambuteau. **Open** 11am-1.30pm, 3-7pm, Tue-Sat.
Credit MC, V.
A tiny shop specialising in calligraphy, with inks, pens
and an incredible range of hand-made papers from Asia.

Marie-Papier

26 rue Vavin, 75006 (43.26.46.44). Métro Vavin. **Open**
10am-7pm Mon-Sat. **Credit** DC, EC, MC, V.
Marie-Paule Orluc designs elegant but simple paper
products, dossiers and photo albums. Prices are high.

Papier +

9 rue du Pont-Louis-Philippe, 75004
(42.77.70.49). Métro St-Paul or Pont-Marie. **Open** noon-
7pm Mon-Sat. **Credit** EC, MC, V.
Crayons in an infinite array of shades come in attractive
boxes alongside stacks of hand-cut paper.

Oddities

Catastrophe

(47.34.91.57). **Open** by appointment only,
call Eric Dahyot.
A collective of five young women who transform urban
debris into collectables: old 33-rpms are recycled into café
tables and lamps; bottle caps are rescued to cover frames;
copper, brass and steel bits are welded to form garden tables
and chairs. Exhibitions are held wherever they squat.

Deyrolle

46 rue du Bac, 75007 (42.22.30.07). Métro Rue du Bac.
Open 9am-12.30pm, 2-6pm, Mon-Fri; 9am-12.30pm, 2-
5.30pm, Sat. **Credit** EC, MC, V.
This dusty shop, established 1831, overflows with stuffed
animals, ranging from a polar bear and a horse to exotic
birds. You can also have your own household pets lovingly
stuffed here, for 3,000F and upwards.

Madeleine Gély

218 boulevard St-Germain, 75007 (42.22.63.35). Métro
Rue du Bac. **Open** 10am-7pm Tue-Sat. **Credit** EC, MC, V.
It's probably safe to say that this shop, spilling over with
umbrellas and canes, hasn't changed much since it first
opened in 1834. Short or long, plain or fancy, there's an
umbrella or cane here for everyone.

Ophir

8 cité Véron, 75018 (42.64.58.40/42.57.74.45).
Métro Blanche. **Open** 9.30am-1pm Mon-Fri; afternoons
by appointment. **Credit** MC, V.
A narrow cobblestone passage near the Moulin Rouge leads
to this jumble of unusual gifts, accessories and other treasures, assembled by owner Jacqueline Marcovivi from across
the five continents.

Des Pieds et des Mains

22 passage Molière, 75003 (42.77.53.50).
Métro Châtelet-Les Halles. **Open** 2-5.30pm Fri, Sat.
No credit cards.
A bizarre shop where you can have your hand or foot
enshrined in plaster. A fascinating window is crammed with
hands and feet of past customers, from a baby of 57 minutes
to a hardy 98-year old.

Food & Drink

Handmade breads, superb cheeses, succulent pastries and the best of wines – a brief guide to gourmet heaven.

On the food counters of Paris you won't see earthy local specialities such as you might find in provincial French towns, but you will benefit from the centralising force of a city that brings in fine foods from all over the country – melons and tomatoes from the Midi, artichokes from Brittany, chickens from Bresse, hams from Bayonne and *saucisson* from the Auvergne. And, in this world capital of luxury food, you'll be able to sample an endless variety of subtle delicacies that are hard – or impossible – to find anywhere else.

When shopping, look for signs such as *fabrication maison*, *artisanale* or *à l'ancienne*, indicating that products are made on the premises following traditional methods. This is particularly important at a *traiteur*, who sells pâtés and ready-to-eat prepared dishes, and for bakers. There is even talk of introducing an *appellation contrôlée* for the baguette, to highlight the additives put in some supermarket bread and catch out treacherous bakeries that simply warm up pre-baked loaves.

Bakeries & Pâtisseries

Coquelin Aîné
1 place de Passy, 75016 (45.24.44.00). Métro Muette or Passy. **Open** 9am-7.30pm Tue-Sat; 9am-1pm Sun. **Credit** V.
Since 1900 the Coquelin family have been making mouth-watering *grandes classiques* in this chic shopping area – coffee and strawberry macaroons, almond madeleines, chocolate truffle cakes and exquisite handmade chocolates. On warm days you can sit outside to enjoy the shop's pastries with excellent coffee, and then sample their delicious ice cream. Light lunches are also served.

Paul Bugat – Pâtisserie Clichy
5 boulevard Beaumarchais, 75004 (48.87.89.88). Métro Bastille. **Open** 8.30am-8pm Tue-Sat; 8am-7.30pm Sun. Closed Aug. **Credit** AmEx, V.
Master pastry chef Paul Bugat creates a full range of traditional French cakes, chocolates and ice-creams. A little tearoom adjoins the shop, founded in 1892. Specialities include *Le Paris*, a blend of chocolate mousse and meringue, and the marrons glacés (November to January only) are superb.

Sacha Finkelsztajn
27 rue des Rosiers, 75004 (42.72.78.91). Métro St-Paul. **Open** 10am-2pm, 3-7pm, Wed-Sun. **No credit cards.**
The best of Russian and central European Jewish specialities, in the heart of Paris' most traditional Jewish quarter. The cheesecake and chocolate *sachertorte* melt in your mouth, and also on offer are delicious deli favourites such as potato latkes and rye and challah breads.
Branch: 24 rue des Ecouffes, 75004 (48.87.92.85).

Bernard Ganachaud
150-152 rue de Ménilmontant, 75020 (46.36.13.82). Métro St-Fargeau. **Open** 2.30-8pm Tue; 7.30am-8pm Wed-Sat; 7.30am-1.30pm Sun. Closed Aug. **No credit cards.**
Dapper, white-haired M. Ganachaud, first baker in the country to win the coveted *Meilleur Ouvrier de France* award, has now gone into semi-retirement, but Jean Jeudon continues his shop's grand tradition. The wood-fired ovens produce 1,000 loaves a day, in 30 different shapes and varieties of bread. Try the wonderful *bostock* (brioche made with almonds), or the *pain aux noix*, full of walnuts.

Bernard Legrand
28 rue Legendre, 75017 (45.74.41.26). Métro Porte Maillot or Argentine. **Open** 7.30am-8pm Mon-Fri. **No credit cards**
Customers often leave this luxurious *boulangerie* already nibbling at their newly-bought baguettes. Still more tempting than the many breads may be the generous portions of *tarte normande* that explode with apples and calvados (13.70F) or the mile-high *millefeuilles*, which in summer contain crème Chantilly and fresh strawberries (10.20F). Legrand also prepare fine seasonal specialities at Christmas and Easter.

Le Moule à Gâteaux
17 rue Daguerre, 75014 (43.22.61.25). Métro Denfert-Rochereau. **Open** 8am-7.30pm Mon-Sat; 8am-1.30pm Sun. **No credit cards.**
The name translates as 'the cake tin', and these shops specialise in excellent, reasonably-priced fresh fruit tarts, savoury flans and cakes, all made on the premises. Both branches are on lively street markets.
Branch: 111 rue Mouffetard, 75005 (43.31.80.47).

Jean-Luc Poujauran
20 rue Jean Nicot, 75007 (47.05.80.88). Métro Invalides or Latour-Maubourg. **Open** 8am-8.30pm Tue-Sat. Closed Aug. **No credit cards.**
Jean-Luc Poujauran is the superstar baker of Paris. His honey-coloured, chewy *baguette biologique*, made with organically grown, stone-ground flour, is a hot favourite among the range of 15 different breads. Others to try are the sensuous fig bread (best eaten with foie gras) and the apricot bread, delicious with cheese. Poujauran can never make enough of his mini fig-and-raisin breads (3.90F). There's also a fine vegetable pie, *tourte landaise aux légumes*.

Lionel Poilâne
8 rue du Cherche-Midi, 75006 (45.48.42.59). Métro Sèvres-Babylone or St-Sulpice. **Open** 7.15am-8pm Mon-Sat. **No credit cards.**
Make new friends in the queue for the speciality *pain Poilâne*, which has won its maker celebrity status. It's made by hand each morning from stone-ground flour in a wood oven built by his father, and each giant round loaf (20F per kg - ask for a half or a quarter) is still made to the original recipe with pungent sourdough yeast and sea salt. No two batches are ever the same, and this heavy bread is an acquired taste. Poilâne also offers fine nut bread and apple tarts (11F) and presentation baskets of *sablés* (shortbreads – 109F per kg)
Branch: 49 boulevard de Grenelle, 75015 (45.79.11.49).

Pâtisserie Stohrer

*51 rue Montorgueil, 75002 (42.33.38.20). Métro
Châtelet-Les Halles or Sentier.* **Open** 7.30am-8.30pm
daily. **Credit** V.
When the Polish Princess Marie Leszczynska married Louis
XV in 1725 she brought along her personal chef, M. Stohrer.
In 1730 he opened his own pâtisserie, which to this day
makes his legendary *babas au rhum, Puits d'Amour* (flakey
pastry and crème patissière with caramelised sugar on top)
and feather-light *feuilletés* of vegetables.

René-Gérard Saint-Ouen

*111 boulevard Haussmann, 75008 (42.65.06.25). Métro
Miromesnil.* **Open** 8am-7.30pm Mon-Sat. **No credit cards.**
Parisians call M. Saint-Ouen 'the Michelangelo of bakers'.
Using flour from Chartres and olive oil from Provence, in a
secret recipe, he makes unique edible sculptures – Eiffel
Towers, Dali-esque suns, vintage cars, and even a Noah's
Ark of animals (all from 50F). No less than 73 different
varieties of bread are available, plus delicious sticky seasonal
fruit tarts and pizzas, quiches and baguette sandwiches.

Chocolate & Confectionery

Christian Constant

26 rue du Bac, 75007 (47.03.30.00). Métro Rue du Bac.
Open 8am-8pm daily. **Credit** EC, MC, V.
The aroma of chocolate perfumes the air of the rue du Bac,
leading you to Constant's temple of chocolate. Here you'll
find irresistible chocolate jewels made from *ylang-ylang* flowers, *vétiver* (from La Réunion) and jasmin, among imaginative cakes, marshmallows and fresh fruit jams. The
Bitter-Plus low-sugar chocolate bars (30F), are a particular
favourite of such Parisian celebrities as Karl Lagerfeld,
Gérard Depardieu and Sonia Rykiel, although some may find
them too bitter.
Branch: 37 rue d'Assas, 75006 (45.48.45.51).

Debauve & Gallais

*30 rue des Saints-Pères 75007 (45.48.54.67). Métro St
Germain-des-Prés or Rue du Bac.* **Open** 10am-7pm Mon,
Sat; 9am-7pm Tue-Fri. **Credit** AmEx, DC, EC, MC, V.
This shop was originally the pharmacy of a M. Debauve,
who recommended chocolate to Louis XVI as a panacea for
fevers and other ailments. It's expensive and very touristy,
but worth a look for its old-world charm. The pharmacy
counter now dispenses rich chocolate truffles (420F per kg),
and the famous *boule d'antin* pralines, made to the same
recipe for 200 years.

Jadis et Gourmande

*88 boulevard Port-Royal, 75005 ((43.26.17.75). RER
Port-Royal.* **Open** 1-7pm Mon; 9.30am-7pm Tue-Sat.
Credit MC, V.
A good mix of both sophisticated and novelty chocolates.
There are chocolate champagne bottles, Arcs de Triomphe
in various sizes (from 48F) and letters of the alphabet, which
all make fun presents. For inscriptions written in white
chocolate, order a few days in advance (15F extra).
Branches: 39 rue des Archives, 75004 (48.04.08.03); 49
bis avenue Franklin D Roosevelt, 75008 (42.25.06.04); 27
rue Boissy d'Anglas, 75008 (42.65.23.23).

Lenôtre

44 rue du Bac, 75007 (42.22.39.39). Métro Rue du Bac.
Open 9am-7.30pm Mon-Sat; 9am-1pm Sun. Closed Aug.
Credit AmEx, DC, V.
The Lenôtre shops are perhaps best known for their cakes
and catering service, but their intensely flavoured chocolate
truffles and *palettes d'or* are simply not to be missed. There
are several branches around the city.
Branches include: 15 boulevard de Courcelles, 75008
(45.63.87.63).

Réné-Gérard Saint-Ouen.

La Maison du Chocolat

*225 rue du Faubourg-St-Honoré, 75008 (42.27.39.44).
Métro Ternes.* **Open** 9.30am-7pm Mon-Sat.
Credit MC, V.
A mecca for chocolate lovers. There are incredibly rich cocoa-
coated truffles, simple slabs of the *maison's* own chocolate,
wicked-looking eclairs (at 20F a piece) and chocolate cakes
with names like the *Brasilien* and the *Andalusie*.
Branches: 8 boulevard de la Madeleine, 75001
(47.42.86.52); 52 rue François 1er, 75008 (47.23.38.25)
(open Aug); 19 rue de Sèvres, 75007 (45.44.20.40).

A la Mère de Famille

*35 rue du Faubourg-Montmartre, 75009 (47.70.83.69).
Métro Cadet or Rue Montmartre.* **Open** 8.30am-1.30pm,
3-7pm, Tue-Fri; 8.30am-12.30pm, 3-7pm, Sat. Closed Aug.
Credit MC, V.
Traditional confections from all regions of France (*calis-
sons d'Aix, pralines de Montargis, macarons de
Mortmorillon*), are sold in this shop, founded in 1761. Also a
dizzying assortment of boiled sweets, jams and biscuits.

Richart

*258 boulevard St-Germain, 75007 (45.55.66.00). Métro
Solférino.* **Open** 11am-7pm Mon, Sat; 10am-7pm Tue-Fri.
Credit MC, V.
Designer chocolate for the year 2000. This sleek, shiny
brown-and-white store offers unusual assortments such as
tiny four-gramme chocolate squares filled with malt whisky
and other surprises, all stylishly presented in a suitably post-
modern manner. There is also an excellent selection of teas,
jams and desserts, and you can even become a member of
the *Club Richart*.

Cheese

There is no better city in which to discover new cheeses than Paris. Every quartier has dozens of pristine *fromageries*, each offering an incredible seasonal selection. The sign *Maître Fromager Affineur* identifies master cheese merchants who buy in young cheeses from farmers and then age them themselves, on the premises, following a complex and sensitive process (*affinage*).

Maturing cheeses need daily attention to develop character and texture and have to be periodically turned. Washing them with beer or brine, or home-made *eau-de-vie* spirit, gives each its distinctive aroma. *Affineurs* all have their own techniques, and know when each cheese will be ripe. Don't be surprised if you're asked when you intend to eat this work of art.

Specify raw milk cheese by asking for *fromage fermier* or *au lait cru*. The perfect cheese board should have five or six cheeses. One of goats' milk (such as a Sainte-Maure de Touraine), one with a pressed curd (Laguiole), one hard (Cantal), one veined (Fourme d'Ambert) and one soft cheese with a washed rind (Chaource). As well as compatability with the meal, you should always consider seasonal variations. The following is a brief guide to the seasonal quality of some of the varieties available.

Good all year round: Camembert, Cantal, Chabichou, Coulommiers, Reblochon, Saint-Nectaire, Saint-Paulin, Tomme.
Best between mid-April and mid-November: Goats' milk cheeses such as Banon, Cabecou, Chevrotin, Crottin de Chavignol. Also creamy, strong perfumed cheeses such as Epoisses, Fontina, Livarot, Maroilles, Mont d'Or, Roquefort, Saint-Maure and Saint-Marcellin.
Best between mid-November and mid-April: Banon (ewes' milk), Beaufort, Brie, Brousse, Feuille de Deux, Pont-l'Eveque, Vacherin and Vendôme.

Alléosse
13 rue Poncelet, 75017 (46.22.50.45). Métro Ternes. **Open** 9am-1pm, 4-7.15pm, Tue-Sat; 9am-1pm Sun, public holidays. **Credit** V.
People come for miles to this large shop for the range of cheeses ripened in its cellars. They include wonderful farmhouse Camemberts, delicate St-Marcellins and a very good choice of *chèvres*.

Androuët
41 rue d'Amsterdam, 75008 (48.74.26.90). Métro Liège. **Open** 10am-1.30pm, 2.30-7.30pm, Mon-Sat. **Credit** AmEx, DC, V.
Perhaps the most celebrated Parisian *fromagerie*. Pierre Androuët himself died some time ago, but it's still highly reliable. It claims to stock over 200 varieties, and there's even a restaurant upstairs (*see chapter* **Restaurants**). Pungent Epoisses, Munsters and Maroilles mature in a warren of cellars beneath the shop, and display cases overflow with farmhouse brie and triple-cream Lucullus.

Barthélemy
51 rue de Grenelle, 75007 (45.48.56.75). Métro Rue du Bac. **Open** 8.30am-1pm, 3.30-7.30pm, Mon-Fri; 8.30am-1.30pm, 3-7.30pm, Sat. **Credit** V
Roland Barthélemy has been in this charming shop for 23 years. A native of the Auvergne, his own favourites are his mountain cheeses – the Mont d'Or from the Jura and the alpine Beaufort are both superb. Try too the beautiful brie de Malesherbes, and the Banon from Alpes-de-Haute-Provence. Also to be had are *plateaux de folies* to take home as gifts, and an assortment of cheese-related porcelain.

Marie-Anne Cantin
12 rue du Champ-de-Mars, 75007 (45.50.43.94). Métro Ecole Militaire. **Open** 2.30-7.30pm, Tue-Sat; 8.30am-1pm Sun. **Credit** V.
To savour authentic French farmhouse cheeses expertly ripened and sold at the peak of their form, head for this charming *fromagerie* and sample the St-Marcellin, or the buttery Fourme d'Ambert.

Alain Dubois
80 rue de Tocqueville, 75017 (42.27.11.38). Métro Malesherbes or Villiers. **Open** 7.30am-1pm, 3.45-7.45pm, Tue-Sat; 9am-1pm Sun. **Credit** V.
Difficult to choose from the bewildering display, including some 70 different varieties of goats' cheese. M. Dubois, who has built a separate cellar to age his prize St-Marcellin and St-Félicien, is the darling of the super-chefs, his cheeses appearing on the menus of many Paris restaurants. He also holds frequent cheese tastings, and happily ships orders.

Fromagerie de Montmartre
9 rue du Poteau, 75018 (46.06.26.03). Métro Jules-Joffrin. **Open** 8.45am-1pm, 4-7.30pm, Tue-Fri; 8.45am-1pm, 3-7.30pm, Sat. **No credit cards.**
Hundreds of cheeses, many of them matured on the premises, are attractively presented in this bright shop on the northern side of Montmartre, in a street full of good food shops.

Lillo
35 rue des Belles-Feuilles, 75116 (47.27.69.08). Métro Victor Hugo or Trocadéro. **Open** 8am-1pm, 4-7.30pm, Mon-Sat. **Credit** DC, V.
Jean-Claude Lillo is a specialist in cooked cheeses, selling delicious tarts, *croustades*, gnocchi and crêpes, all prepared with a multitude of different cheeses. He does not age his cheeses on the premises, but many of the 200 varieties in stock are carefully 'finished' in the cellar below the shop. You can also buy unpasteurised milk, cream and yoghurts, and an interesting home-made milk jam (*confiture de lait*).

Select a sublime sandwich and the perfect pickle at **Chez Marianne.**

Delicatessens & Traiteurs

Chedeville
18 place du Marché St-Honoré, 75001 (40.15.01.92).
Métro Pyramides. **Open** 8am-1.30pm, 3-6.30pm, Mon-Fri.
Credit AmEx, EC, V.
A busy market *charcuterie* with over 100 years' experience, and an impressive list of regular clients. Particularly excellent are the *andouillette* and Lyon sausages, hams and the house speciality *pieds farcis aux herbes* (stuffed pigs feet).

Chez Marianne
2 rue des Hospitalières-St-Gervais, 75004 (42.72.18.86).
Métro St Paul. **Open** 11am-midnight daily.
Credit MC, V.
Funky Marais residents nip in here for the best falafel sandwiches in the city (20F). All the flavours and aromas of Europe are combined together – stuffed vine leaves, pickled vegetables, *caviar d'aubergines*, sticky nut brittle and natural, unfermented olives, kept in barrels. Everything can be bought to take away or enjoyed in the bustling, atmospheric restaurant at the back of the shop. There's also a wide choice of wines, and miniature bottles of rare spirits.

A la Cigogne
61 rue de l'Arcade, 75008 (43.87.39.16). Métro St-Lazare. **Open** 8am-7pm Mon-Fri; 9am-6.30pm Sat; closed Aug. **Credit** AmEx, V.
A vast array of robust Alsatian specialities, from sausages to sumptuous sweets such as bilberry, cherry or plum tarts, *kugelhopf* (currant cake), sweet pretzels and *sachertorte*.
Branches: 17 rue Tronchet, 75008 (42.66.04.78); 2 quai de Grenelle, 75015 (45.75.94.51); 48 rue de Flandre, 75019 (40.36.87.46).

Le Fin Gousier
50 rue des Morillons, 75015 (40.43.19.00). Métro Porte de Vanves or Convention. **Open** 4.30pm-8.30pm Mon; 10.30am-2pm, 4.30-8.30pm, Tue-Sat. **Credit** MC, V.
The charming, English-speaking Mme Legagneur will help you select a takeaway supper or gifts from her world-wide selection of exotic goodies. The range includes home-made pasta dishes and desserts, *rillettes* (potted meat made from pork or goose) and *rillons* (chopped pork cooked in fat, served

cold) and violet mustard from Brives. Prices are reasonable, and there's an impressive selection of beers.

Flo Prestige
42 place du Marché St-Honoré, 75001 (42.61.45.46).
Métro Pyramides. **Open** 8am-11pm daily.
Credit AmEx, DC, MC, V.
Everything you might need for an impromptu de luxe picnic or midnight snack: wines and champagnes, smoked salmon and all sorts of cold meats, cheeses and desserts. They also have a delivery service (*see chapter* **Services**).
Branches include: 36 avenue de la Motte-Picquet, 75007 (45.55.71.25); 211 avenue Daumesnil, 75012 (43.44.86.36); 352 rue Lecourbe, 75015 (45.54.76.94); 61 avenue de la Grande Armée, 75016 (45.00.12.10); 102 avenue du Président Kennedy, 75016 (42.88.38.00).

La Galoche d'Aurillac
41 rue de Lappe, 75011 (47.00.77.15). Métro Bastille.
Open *café and delicatessen* 9.30am-2am, *restaurant* noon-2.30pm, 7-11.30pm, Tue-Sat. Closed Aug.
No credit cards.
Authentic Auvergne *charcuterie* and cheeses to sample on the spot or take with you to enjoy later. Especially worth trying are the *pounti* (a rustic meatloaf), the dried *saucisses de Marcolès*, earthy wines and *eaux-de-vie*.

Gourmet Goodies

Berthillon
31 rue St-Louis-en-l'Ile, 75004 (43.54.31.61). Métro Pont-Marie. **Open** 10am-8pm Wed-Sun.
No credit cards.
A winding queue announces this legendary *glacier* on the Ile St-Louis. There are more than 70 flavours of ice creams and sorbets to choose from (prices start at 9F per scoop), among them amandine, *pain d'épice* (honey cake), chestnut, whisky and, soothing on a hot summer's day, Earl Grey Tea.

Fauchon
24-30 place de la Madeleine, 75008 (47.42.60.11). Métro Madeleine. **Open** *shop* 9.40am-7pm, *traiteur* 9.40am-8.30pm, Mon-Sat. **Credit** AmEx, DC, MC, V.

Wine Buying

All French wines are classified into one of four categories, shown on the label. *Vins de Table* are wines for daily consumption, and not subject to any special quality control. *Vins de Pays* are wines made from specified vines produced in a particular region, and which have satisfied a tasting panel. Above them are *Vins Délimités de Qualité Supérieure* (VDQS), now being phased out. At the top are *Vins d'Appelations d'Origine Contrôlées* (AOC), France's finest, whose production is strictly controlled. The only classic French wine that does not have to state AOC on its label is champagne, but the divisions between the categories are not as absolute as they once were, and the quality of many *Vins de Pays*, in particular, has improved enormously in recent years.

Wines and winemaking have their fashions and France is no exception. Currently Côtes du Rhône is a popular favourite. Look for St Joseph, Cornas, or Crozes-Hermitage 1988 and 1989. Wines from Provence, too, have been through a revolution in the last ten years. Many vineyards are now producing organic wines with techniques called *Biodynamie*. Château-Vignelaure, Saint Simone, Domaine de Trévallon and Domaine Tempier are all good, and Bellet white from the hills behind Nice is a delight.

A buzz has also grown up around the new generation of white, red and sparkling wines from the Languedoc-Roussillon area, where foreign winemakers have been helping to produce full-bodied, fruity vintages. Labels to look for are Blanquette de Limoux, Clairette de Languedoc and 1993 Fitou.

Les Caves Augé
116 boulevard Haussmann, 75008 (45.22.16.97). Métro St Augustin or Miromesnil. **Open** 1-7.30pm Mon; 9am-7.30pm Tue-Sat. **Credit** AmEx, MC, V.
Marcel Proust was a regular customer at this, one of the oldest wine stores in the city. A qualified *sommelier* is always on hand to give help and advice to clients. Prices range from the Côtes de Gascogne (22F) to a Romanée-Conti for 3,000F. In between, there is a large range of organic wines (Domaine Gramenon), and rare ports, cognacs and whiskies. Good opportunities for bulk buying are provided by Augé's weekly and monthly specials.

Caves de Georges Duboeuf
9 rue Marbeuf, 75008 (47.20.71.23). Métro Alma Marceau. **Open** 9am-1pm, 3-7pm, Tue-Sat. Closed Aug. **Credit** EC, MC, V.
Georges Duboeuf is the dynamic King of Beaujolais, responsible for making the celebrations of *beaujolais nouveau* every November a world-wide event. He also stocks a good selection of Rhône valley and Côte Rôtie wines.

Les Caves Taillevent
199 rue du Faubourg St-Honoré, 75008 (45.61.14.09). Métro Charles de Gaulle-Etoile or Ternes. **Open** 2-8pm Mon; 9am-8pm Tue-Fri; 9am-7.30pm Sat. **Credit** AmEx, DC, JCB, MC, V.
Choose from half a million bottles of wine in a modern space dedicated to serious oenophiles. It's linked to the exalted Taillevent restaurant (*see chapter* **Restaurants**). Helpful salesmen will guide you through the comprehensive selection. Young wine lovers of Paris gather here every Saturday morning, when chief *sommelier* of both shop and restaurant Didier Bordas presents about 50 different wines, all selected by him, for an informal wine tasting. No appointment is necessary, and prices start at 22F.

Nicolas
31 place de la Madeleine, 75008 (42.68.00.16). Métro Madeleine **Open** 9am-8pm Mon-Sat. **Credit** AmEx, EC, MC, V.
The flagship store of the group with 111 branches in and around Paris. As well as French there are plenty of Spanish, New World and even Swiss wines, plus three floors of wine-related goodies and gifts, and a highly informative catalogue.
Branches: 111 branches in Paris and area.

Le Repaire de Bacchus
112 rue Mouffetard, 75005 (47.07.39.40). Métro Censier-Daubenton. **Open** 9.30am-1pm, 3.30-8pm, Mon-Thur; 9.30am-8pm Fri, Sat; 9.30am-1pm Sun. **Credit** AmEx, JCB, V.
Bacchus would feel right at home in this lair among the superb Burgundies and interesting choice of inexpensive, lesser-known country wines. Also in stock are over 50 beers, and some curiosities such as a Breton whisky.
More than 15 branches including: 88 rue Montorgueil, 75002 (42.36.17.49); 40 rue Damrémont, 75018 (42.52.27.78).

Le Savour Club
125 bis boulevard Montparnasse, 75014 (43.27.12.06). Métro Vavin. **Open** 10am-8pm Tue-Sat; 10am-12.30pm Sun. **Credit** AmEx, V.

A wine store oddly situated on one side of an underground car park (the Parking Montparnasse-Raspail) – which, though, means that the temperature is ideal, and makes life easy for purchasers with cars. Top chefs Paul Bocuse, Pierre Troisgros, Marc Meneau, Joël Robuchon and Georges Lepré, *sommelier* of the Ritz, have all put their noses together to approve all the wines, and quality is very high. You can expect to find both interesting labels and good advice, and it's assumed that you will taste before you buy. If you buy in quantity you can obtain substantial discounts, and members of the 'club' receive a regular catalogue.
Branch: 11 rue Gros, 75116 (42.30.94.18).

The most famous food store in Paris, a temple of culinary luxury. The service can be haughty, the prices are high, but the fabulous window displays are an education in the *traiteur*'s art. Equally renowned are its exotic fruits, excellent *pâtisseries*, wine cellar, ready-packaged goods and enormous charcuterie section. There's a luxury cafeteria at no. 30.

Foie Gras Import
34 rue Montmartre, 75001 (42.33.31.32). Métro Etienne Marcel. **Open** 6am-1pm, 2.30-7pm, Tue-Sat. **Credit** V.
Foie gras from south-west France in all its forms, both duck and goose, from raw liver and *mi-cuit* to tins of pâté. Also snails, caviar, dried mushrooms and truffles.

Out of Hours

You'll find local shops that stay open until around 10pm in most parts of the city. At other times, or if you're looking for something special, the shops listed here can all help placate the midnight or Sunday afternoon munchies.

L'An 2000
82 boulevard des Batignolles, 75017 (43.87.24.67). Métro Rome. **Open** 7pm-midnight Mon-Sat; 11am-midnight Sun, public holidays. **Credit** AmEx, MC, V.
A *traiteur* where the house speciality, paella, is always on the menu, as well as a daily-changing selection of cooked dishes to take away, usually in two-person portions.

Boulangerie de l'Ancienne Comédie
10 rue de l'Ancienne Comédie, 75006 (43.26.89.72). Métro Odéon. **Open** 24 hours Mon-Sat; closed 6am-9pm Sun. **Credit** AmEx, V.
Bread, pâtisseries, *viennoiseries* and sandwiches to deal with that empty feeling just before dawn, plus a variety of hot and cold snacks, served in the bar-restaurant.

Chez Salem
20 boulevard de Clichy, 75018 (46.06.60.03). Métro Pigalle. **Open** 24 hours Tue-Sun. **No credit cards.**
A call-in for essentials and Arab food products.

Layrac
29 rue de Buci, 75006 (43.25.17.72). Métro Odéon. **Open** 10am-midnight Mon-Thur; 10am-1am Fri, Sat; 10am-11pm Sun. **Credit** AmEx, DC, EC, MC, V.
A high-quality *traiteur* where you can find everything you need for a full-scale meal: first course, main course, dessert, wine and any other drinks. Home deliveries are available until midnight (last orders 11.45pm). Good, but expensive.

Noura
27 avenue Marceau, 75016 (47.23.02.20). Métro Ièna or Alma Marceau. **Open** 7am-midnight daily. **Credit** AmEx, DC, EC, MC, V.
This up-market Lebanese *traiteur-épicerie* claims to stock 'all that is refined in life' – prepared *mezze*, cheeses, *charcuterie*, bread, wines and cognacs. Local deliveries are free.

La Grande Epicerie de Paris
Le Bon Marché (shop 2), 38 rue de Sèvres, 75007 (44.39.81.00). Métro Sèvres-Babylone. **Open** 9.30am-7pm Mon-Sat. **Credit** (minimum 200F) EC, JCB, V.
Magasin 2 of the department store Le Bon Marché (*see chapter* **Specialist Shops**) is a vast gourmet supermarket-cum-*traiteur*, where smart French housewives and career women buy ready-made goodies to enhance their dinner parties. Take home tins of *confit de canard*, *tisanes* (herb teas), bottled or dried mushrooms, or any of the full range of Fauchon products (*see above*). The bakery is one of Paris' best.

Hédiard
21 place de la Madeleine, 75008 (43.12.88.88). Métro Madeleine. **Open** 9.30am-9pm Mon-Sat. **Credit** AmEx, DC, V.
Across the *place* from Fauchon (*see above*), Paris' second most famous foodstore offers the best of just about everything you might want to buy. It's expensive, but the selection is vast, and their excellent jams and spices make good gifts. They also deliver (*see chapter* **Services**).
Branches include: 126 rue du Bac, 75007 (45.44.01.98); 70 avenue Paul Doumer, 75016 (45.04.51.92); 6 rue Donizetti, 75016 (40.50.71.94).

La Maison du Caviar
Restaurant & shop *1 rue Vernet, 75008 (47.23.53.43). Métro George V.* **Open** noon-1am daily. **Shop only** *21 rue Quentin, 75008 (40.70.06.39).* **Open** 10am-9pm daily. **Credit** AmEx, V.
The finest Iranian caviars, Beluga, Ossetra and Sevruga (from 250F per 40g), can all be found here, along with smoked salmon from different countries, and salmon, mullet and trout caviar. You can buy them in the boutique, or try them straight away in the restaurant. Also available in the shop are vodka, blinis, and fine crystal and silverware.

La Maison du Miel
24 rue Vignon, 75008 (47.42.26.70). Métro Madeleine or Havre-Caumartin. **Open** 9am-7pm Mon-Sat. **Credit** MC, V.
Founded in 1898, this shop stocks 28 different French honeys with names such as *châtaigner*, *aubépine*, *tilleul*, *lavande* and *thym*, as well as others from around the world. Prices

Get oiled **A L'Olivier.** *See page 209.*

begin at 16F for a jar, and you are expected to taste before you buy. You can also find honey-based products such as *pain d'épice* (a spicy honey cake), *hydromel* (fermented honey to drink), royal jelly, pollen, soaps and beauty products.

Maison de la Truffe
19 place de la Madeleine, 75008 (42.65.53.22). Métro Madeleine. **Open** 9am-9pm Mon-Sat; *December only* 9am-9m daily. **Credit** AmEx, DC, JCB, MC, V.
With Périgord truffles (available from November to March only) at 9,520F a kilo, you might want to do no more than take a look inside this store for the seriously rich, just for a sniff. The staff, however, rarely mind. More affordable items include truffle vinegar (38F), and tinned truffle sauce (95F). There's also a tiny, shiny restaurant offering truffle and foie gras-related dishes, such as a fluffy *omelette aux truffes*.

Marquise de Sévigné
1 place Victor Hugo, 75116 (45.00.89.68). Métro Victor Hugo. **Open** 9.30am-7pm Mon-Sat. **Credit** AmEx, V.
An elegant shop which began life as a letter in 1705, when the Marquise de Sévigné wrote to her daughter on the health-giving properties of chocolate. You can experience the same

feel-good factor today with the shop's gold-wrapped chocolate coins (19F) and *déjeuner de la Marquise*, chocolate granules, for 70F, gift boxes (from 21F) and tins of foie gras, all in exquisite packaging featuring the Marquise herself.
Branch: 32 place de la Madeleine, 75008 (42.65.19.47).

A L'Olivier
23 rue de Rivoli, 75004 (48.04.86.59). Métro St-Paul or Hôtel-de-Ville. **Open** 9.30am-1pm, 2-7pm, Tue-Sat.
Credit MC, V.
L'Olivier's walls are lined with the company's own attractively bottled olive oils (in various strengths of fruitiness), together with other exotic oils and wine vinegars. There's also a good range of olives.

Soirée Gourmande
16 boulevard Richard Lenoir, 75011 (43.38.99.11). Métro Bastille. **Open** 10am-7pm Mon-Sat. **Credit** V.
The house motto is 'Madeleine quality at Bastille prices'. In other words, the same fine foods – caviar, foie gras, smoked salmon, champagne, and more – that are sold in the luxury emporia of the 8th *arrondissement* are available here for sometimes half the price.

Food Markets

Paris still has 13 covered and 57 open-air markets, each with lovingly-stacked fruits, meat, fish, aromatic fresh herbs, household accessories and much more. Except where stated, the markets listed below, by *arrondissement*, are permanent, and are open 8am-1pm and 4-7pm from Tuesday to Saturday and on Sunday morning. There are also several markets that function only one or two mornings each week. Among those worth checking out are **boulevard Richard Lenoir** near the Bastille (11th) on Thursday and Sunday, **boulevard Port-Royal** (5th) on Tuesday, Thursday and Saturday and, for an Arab/African flavour, **boulevard de la Chapelle** at Barbès-Rochechouart (18th) on Wednesday and Saturday. There is also a fine selection of food shops, if not a market, along **rue Lepic** in Montmartre (18th).

Les Halles: rue Montorgueil
75001. Métro Châtelet-Les Halles.
The street has now been pedestrianised, but the last remnant of Paris' old central market of Les Halles is still brash and noisy, and continues to supply many Paris restaurants. There are several *fromageries* – **La Hutte** is highly recommended for its ewe's milk cheeses – as well as the historic Pâtisserie Stohrer (see p204).

Latin Quarter: rue Mouffetard
75005. Métro Monge.
A lively market on the narrow street that winds up the hill from place St-Médard. Go in the morning to see fruit impressively displayed, and there are also several good *traiteurs* and *charcuteries*. Buy a hot roast chicken for a picnic from one of the butchers, or try the Café Mouffetard for its excellent croissants (see chapter **Cafés & Bars**). On Sunday mornings, an accordionist hands out song sheets for you to join in his *chansons* – it's touristy but fun.

St-Germain: rue de Buci
75006. Métro Mabillon.
A busy market that runs up rue de Seine from boulevard St-Germain and into rue de Buci, spilling off the pavements and into the road. Pricey but good cheese, fruit and flower stalls, and some noted, chic, pâtisseries and *traiteurs*.

Odéon: Marché Biologique
boulevard Raspail, between rue de Rennes and rue du Cherche-Midi, 75006. Métro Rennes. Sun morning only.
An expensive outlet for organically grown or reared produce. There's a non-organic market here on Tuesdays and Fridays.

Bastille: place d'Aligre
75011. Métro Ledru-Rollin. Tue-Sun mornings only.
One of the cheapest food markets, with a strong North African flavour and a wide range of ethnic products. The covered hall has good cheese and *charcuterie* stalls, and there's also a junk, old clothes and bric-à-brac section.

Belleville: boulevard de Belleville
75011. Métro Belleville or Couronnes. Tue and Fri only
A lively gathering place for the African, Asian and French local inhabitants with a wide range of international foods on display, alongside everything from hardware to underwear.

Denfert-Rochereau: rue Daguerre
75014. Métro Denfert-Rochereau.
The southern, pedestrian end of rue Daguerre is given over to a busy market with several pavement cafés. There's an excellent fishmonger, a stall with Auvergne hams, and a branch of Le Moule à Gâteau (see p203). In October, the greengrocer has a huge display of wild mushrooms.

Ternes: rue Poncelet
75017. Métro Ternes.
A classier-than-usual street market in an affluent location, with a Viennese pastry shop, excellent bakeries such as Paul and the Fournil de Pierre, and the cheese shop Alléosse (see p205). Nearby, at place de Ternes, is a small flower market.

Services

Places to book a ticket, hire your outfit for the ball, or to order a gourmet meal brought to your door.

As well as the services below, there are several help numbers, often starting with *SOS* or *Allô*, listed in the *Pages Jaunes* (Yellow Pages). Many *SOS* numbers are non-profit-making agencies. However, there are also commercial enterprises that preface their name with SOS to connote speedy service (and may charge exorbitant rates). Emergency numbers are listed in *chapter* **Survival**. For babysitting and child-minding services, *see chapter* **Children**.

All-Purpose Services & Repairs

Many branches of the **Monoprix/Uniprix** supermarkets contain a range of useful services such as photocopiers, clothes repairers and photo booths (*see chapter* **Specialist Shops**).

BHV (Bazar de l'Hôtel de Ville)
Shop: *52-64 rue de Rivoli, 75004 (42.74.90.00)*/DIY hire annexe: *40 rue de la Verrerie, 75004 (42.74.97.23)*. *Métro Hôtel de Ville.* **Open** 9.30am-7pm Mon, Tue, Thur-Sat; 9.30am-10pm Wed. **Credit** AmEx, EC, MC, V.
The leading department store for camera cleaning and repair, shoe repair, photocopying, car parts and equipment hire. The basement is a fix-it-yourselfer's dream.

James
12 rue Dupetit-Thouars, 75003 (42.78.17.00/fax 42.78.18.88). Métro Temple/République. **Open** 9am-7pm Mon-Sat. **Credit** AmEx, MC, V.
A service for those who don't feel like queuing at the post office, figuring out French income tax or making dinner for eight – they will take on almost any domestic need. Subscription 70F per month, interventions from 30F to 180F.

Car & Bike Hire

Car Hire

To hire a car you must be aged 21 or over and have held a licence for at least a year. Take your licence and passport with you. Most places prefer that you pay by credit card; otherwise, they may demand a huge cash deposit. If you're coming from the US, it's cheaper to arrange car hire before you leave.
Hire companies: Ada: Central reservations: 46.58.01.52. Credit AmEx, DC, MC, V. **Avis**: Central reservations: 46.10.60.60. Credit AmEx, DC, MC, V. **Budget**: Central reservations: 05.10.00.01. Credit AmEx, DC, MC, V. **Eurodollar**: Central reservations: 49.58.44.44. Credit AmEx, DC, MC, V. **Europcar**: Central reservations: 30.43.82.82. Credit AmEx, DC, EC, MC, V. **Hertz**: Central reservation 47.88.51.51. Credit AmEx, DC, MC, V. **Rent-a-Car**: Central reservations 46.82.60.60. Credit AmEx, MC, V. **Valem**: 88 rue de la Roquette, 75011 (43.55.81.83). Credit MC, V.

Most of the companies listed here offer special reduced-rate deals at weekends (usually Friday to 9am Monday) – Ada, Rent-a-Car and Valem generally have the best offers. Prices for a basic group A-type car (Peugeot 106, Ford Fiesta, Renault Clio) with insurance range from about 210F-995F a day, to 1,795F-3,650F for a week, depending on mileage.

Chauffeur-driven Cars

International Limousines
182 boulevard Péreire, 75017 (53.81.14.14). Métro Porte Maillot or Ternes. **Open** 24 hours daily. **Credit** AmEx, DC, MC, V.
Modest cars, luxury limousines or something in between from 249F/hour. All come with an English-speaking driver.

Cycles, Scooters & Motorbikes
See also chapter **Sport & Fitness**.

Agence Contact Location
10 bis avenue de la Grande Armée, 75017 (47.66.19.19). Métro Charles de Gaulle-Etoile. **Open** 9.30am-1pm, 2-6.30pm, Mon-Fri; 9.30am-1pm Sat. **Credit** AmEx, DC, MC, V.
Rent a scooter (50cc) for 230F a day, 850F a week or 2,400F a month; motorbike, 320-950F per day or 1,350-3,900F per week (including accessories). Weekend rates (Fri-Mon) work out best. A 7,000F-30,000F refundable deposit is required (credit card preferred). A car drivers' licence is enough for all engines under 1,000cc. Insurance included.

Bicloune
7 rue Froment, 75011 (48.05.47.75). Métro Bréguet-Sabin. **Open** 10.30am-1pm, 2-7pm, Tue-Fri; 10am-1pm, 2-6.30pm, Sat. **Credit** MC, FTC, V.
Cycle rentals from 100F per day, as well as a large selection of new and vintage bicycles and hard-to-find parts.
Branch: 93 boulevard Beaumarchais, 75003 (42.77.58.06).

Maison du Vélo
11 rue Fénélon, 75010. (42.81.24.72). Métro Gare du Nord or Poissonnière. **Open** 10am-7pm Tue-Sat. **Credit** MC, V.
Cycles for hire, new and used bikes for sale, along with repairs and accessories. The rendezvous for English-speaking cyclists.

Paris-Vélo
2 rue du Fer-à-Moulin, 75005 (43.37.59.22). Métro Censier-Daubenton. **Open** 10am-12.30pm, 2-7pm, Mon-Sat; *summer only* 10am-2pm, 5-7pm, Sun. **Credit** EC, MC, V.
Mountain bikes and 21-speed models for hire by day, month or weekend (baby-carrying seats also available).

Sovemat
206 boulevard Bineau, 92200 Neuilly sur Seine (47.7.60.67). Métro Anatole France.
Open 8am-noon, 2-7pm, Mon-Sat. **Credit** MC, V.
Scooters for hire for 212F first day, 106F each day thereafter; 10,000F refundable deposit required. Includes helmet, lock and insurance.

Clothing & Accessories

Cleaning & Repairs

Dry-cleaners go by a variety of names – *nettoyage à sec, pressing, teinturerie* – and, like laundrettes (*laverie libre service*), they can be found in every neighbourhood. **5 à Sec** is a reliable chain of same-day dry cleaners. Many dry-cleaners do alterations and repairs (*retouches*), and most fashion shops also offer an alterations service.

ARGA Executive Laundry Service

6 rue Martel, 75010 (42.46.40.22/fax 47.70.01.975). Métro Château d'Eau. **Open** 9am-6pm Mon-Fri. **No credit cards**.
Dirty laundry picked up from home or office and returned within 72 hours. 24-hour service available, plus shoe repair.

Legrand Tailleur

27 rue du Quatre Septembre, 75002 (47.42.70.61). Métro Opéra. **Open** 10am-6pm Mon-Fri; 10am-5pm Sat. **Credit** AmEx, DC, MC, V.
Expert alterations and repairs at 160F per hour.

Nestor Pressing

6 bis rue Jonquoy, 75014 (freephone 05.05.10.05). Métro Plaisance. **Open** 8.30am-9pm Mon-Fri; 8.30am-6pm Sat. **No credit cards**.
Full-service cleaning, ironing, shoe repair and even film developing for those in western Paris and Neuilly, Levallois and Boulogne. Home pick-up (until 10.30pm).

Costume Hire

Costumes de Paris

21 bis rue Victor Massé, 75009 (48.78.41.02). Métro Pigalle. **Open** 1-7pm Tue-Fri; 10am-7pm Sat. **Credit** EC, MC, V.
Over 20,000 outfits, from fancy dress to designer cocktail and evening dresses. Rental is 600F-750F for a weekend.

Mucha Costumes

17 rue La Bruyère, 75009 (49.95.04.42). Métro St-Georges. **Open** 11am-7pm, 2.30-7pm, Mon-Thur; 11am-8pm Fri; 11am-5pm Sat. **Credit** MC, V.
A huge choice of fancy dress costumes, with a strong music hall element. Owner Monika Mucha works with theatres, and is loved by nightclubbers. Hire prices average 200F-400F.

A la Poupée Merveilleuse

9 rue du Temple, 75004 (42.72.63.46). Métro Hôtel de Ville. **Open** 10am-1.30pm, 2.30-7pm, Mon-Sat. **Credit** MC, V.
An outlandish collection of practical jokes and Hallowe'en decorations. Slip into disguise for 175F-800F (48-hour rental).

Sommier

3 passage Brady, 75010 (42.08.27.01). Métro Chateau d'Eau. **Open** 10am-6.30pm Tue-Fri; 10am-6pm Sat; open Mondays in December. **Credit** MC, V.
Fulfil a Fellini fantasy. All costumes are pre-1925. The cost is 150F-1200F for a weekend rental.

Formal Wear Rental

L'Affaire d'un soir

147 rue de la Pompe, 75016 (47.27.37.50). Métro Rue de la Pompe. **Open** 2-7pm Mon; 10.30am-7pm Tue-Sat. **Credit** EC, MC, V.
Rents out fashionable gowns, specially created by designer Sophie de Mestier, for 700F-1,000F (48-hour rental).

La Femme Ecarlate

42 avenue Bosquet, 75007 (45.51.08.44). Métro Ecole Militaire. **Open** 11am-7pm Tue-Sat. **No credit cards**.
Traditional women's evening attire, for 600F-1,600F per night. For something borrowed, wedding dresses by the week cost from 1,000F to 3,000F.

Latreille

62 rue St-André-des-Arts, 75006 (43.29.44.10). Métro Odéon or St-Michel. **Open** 2-7pm Mon; 9.45am-7pm Tue-Sat. **Credit** AmEx, DC, EC, MC, V.
Its staff will suit any gent up *en penguin*, preferably eight days before the occasion. Rental is 395F-1,695F (Fri-Tue).

Leather, Watch & Jewellery Repair

Try **Topy** or **Talons** minute counters for on-the-spot shoe repairs – they're in many métro stations (eg, Châtelet-Les Halles and Franklin D Roosevelt).

L'Épée de Cuir

2 rue des Patriarches, corner of rue de l'Épée-de-Bois, 75005 (43.37.43.88). Métro Censier-Daubenton. **Open** 9.30am-12.30pm, 2-7pm, Tue-Sat. **No credit cards**.
Repairs of leather cases, bags, wallets, satchels and belts.

Horloger Artisan/Jean-Claude Soulage

32 rue St-Paul, 75004 (48.87.24.75). Métro St-Paul. **Open** 9.30am-noon, 3-7pm, Tue-Fri; 9.30am-noon Sat. **No credit cards**.
Meticulous repairs and restoration for expensive or antique watches, clocks and fine jewellery.

Feasts & Flowers

Florists

Interflora

23 boulevard Berthier, 75017 (freephone 05.20.32.04 credit card orders). **Open** 8am-8pm Mon-Sat. **Credit** AmEx, DC, MC, V.
The head office of Interflora. Prices start at 270F for a standard bouquet delivered in Paris.

Lachaume

10 rue Royale, 75008 (42.60.57.26). Métro Concorde or Madeleine. **Open** 9am-7pm Mon-Fri; 9am-6pm Sat. **Credit** AmEx, EC, MC, V.
Probably Paris' most regal flower shop, founded 1845, with staff as grand as their exquisite arrangements. Call before 2pm for same-day delivery in Paris or the nearby suburbs.

Monceau Fleurs

11 boulevard Henri IV, 75004 (42.72.24.86). Métro Sully-Morland. **Open** 9am-8pm Mon-Sat; 9am-1.30pm Sun. **Credit** MC, V.
A large selection at some of the lowest prices in town. Mix and match fresh flowers from the buckets along the pavement, then pay inside. Say *pour offrir* and they will arrange your blossoms in a presentable bouquet at no extra charge.
Branches: 84 boulevard Raspail, 75006 (45.48.70.10); 92 boulevard Malesherbes, 75008 (45.63.88.23); 60 avenue Paul Doumer, 75016 (40.72.79.27); 2 place Général Koening, 75017 (45.63.88.23).

Food & Drink Delivery

Allô Champagne

11 rue Ambroise Paré, 75010 (44.53.93.33). **Open** 24 hours daily (reserve in advance). **No credit cards**.
Monsieur Foucher stocks some 50 labels, from a Mumm Cordon Rouge at 149F, to a Dom Perignon at 499F a pop.

When you're suddenly in need of a gourmet takeaway, call **Flo Prestige**.

Allô Couscous

70 rue Alexandre Dumas, 75011 (43.70.53.82). **Open** 6-10pm Mon; 11am-2pm, 6-10pm, Tue-Sun. **No credit cards**.
The Halimi family will deliver this North African – but now quintessentially French – dish piping hot in a *couscousier* double pot for a minimum of two people. Lamb, beef, chicken, meatballs, mutton and spicy *merguez* sausage cost 60F per person. Delivery charge is 20-50F, depending on the area.

Coq o'Dac

15 rue Saussure, 75017 (44.40.22.50).
Open 10.30am-2.30pm, 6.30-10.30pm, Mon-Fri; 6.30-10.30pm Sat, Sun. **No credit cards**.
Roast chicken delivered to your home by moped and in a polystyrene helmet packaging, with tubs of mayonnaise or gravy on the side. Allow 45 minutes for delivery.

Flo Prestige

42 place du Marché St-Honoré, 75001 (42.61.45.46).
Métro Opéra or Pyramides. **Open** for deliveries 8am-9pm daily. **No credit cards** on deliveries.
From the cooks who made Brasserie Flo an institution, the fast food equivalent: delectable dishes from six take-away outlets. They'll deliver to your door with two hours notice. Gourmet meal plates cost from 50F-150F. The delivery charge is 100F until 6pm, and 130F thereafter. *See also chapters* **Restaurants** *and* **Food & Drink**.
Branches: 36 avenue de la Motte-Picquet, 75007 (45.51.91.36); 211 avenue Daumesnil, 75012 (43.44.86.36); 352 rue Lecourbe, 75015 (45.54.76.94); 61 avenue de la Grande Armée, 75016 (45.00.12.10); 102 avenue du Président Kennedy, 75016 (42.88.38.00).

Hédiard

21 place de la Madeleine, 75008 (43.12.88.88).
Métro Madeleine. **Open** 9.30am-7pm Mon-Sat.
No credit cards on deliveries.
This upmarket grocer's has sold luscious sweets and gourmet dishes since 1854 (*see chapter* **Food & Drink**). You can order the delicacies by phone (70F delivery charge).

Intermagnum

(Phone orders 05.00.50.20). **Open** 9am-1pm, 2.30-7pm, Mon-Sat. **Credit** AmEx, MC, V.
Instead of saying it with flowers, why not a bottle of champagne, or one of any number of other liquid alternatives. Place a booze order by phone, or visit any branch of the drinks chain Nicolas (*see chapter* **Food & Drink**) to arrange for the delivery of a gift-boxed bottle, with personal message if required, within 48 hours.

Ly-Weng

(For the 8th, 16th, 17th, Neuilly and Levallois 47.64.44.44). **Open** 10am-2.30pm, 6-11pm, Mon-Fri; 6-11pm Sat, Sun. **No credit cards**.
Billed as 'the true Chinese cuisine', this delivery service specialises in lunch plates delivered in 45 minutes. The minimum order is 50F. They also do supper menus.

Matsuri Sushi Service

(40.26.12.13). **Open** noon-2.30pm, 7-10.30pm, Mon-Fri; 7-10.30pm Sat. **No credit cards**.
As the excellent sushi and sashimi of this Japanese home delivery service are made to order, it usually takes an hour to reach you. The wait is worth the expense (250F minimum).

Hair & Beauty
Beauty Salons

Guerlain Institut de Beauté

68 avenue des Champs-Elysées, 75008 (47.89.71.80).
Métro Franklin D Roosevelt. **Open** 9am-6.30pm Mon-Sat (last appointment 5pm). **Credit** AmEx, EC, MC, V.
Art Deco touches by Cocteau and Giacometti surround the 15 cabins where miracles occur – including skin purification, exfoliation or massage from 360F. Facials from 570F. The famous fragrances are sold in the ground floor boutique.
Branch: 29 rue de Sèvres, 75006 (42.22.87.96).

Institut Payot

10 rue de Castiglione, 75001 (42.60.32.87).
Métro Concorde or Tuileries. **Open** 9.30am-6.30pm Mon-Sat. **Credit** AmEx, DC, EC, MC, V.
Separate salons provide facials (about 450F), make-up application for day and evening (165F-245F), eyelash and brow tinting (from 150F) and body massage (340F/45 minutes).

Institut Yves Saint-Laurent
32 rue du Faubourg-St-Honoré, 75008 (49.24.99.66).
Métro Concorde. **Open** 8.30am-8.30pm Mon-Fri; 8.30am-
7.30pm Sat. **Credit** AmEx, EC, MC, V.
Among the myriad treatments on offer are *soin régénération*
– a two-hour facial with gravity defying results – or you can
be made up for the evening (*maquillage du soir*, 420F).

Hairdressers

Alexandre de Paris
3 avenue Matignon, 75008 (42.25.57.90).
Métro Alma Marceau. **Credit** AmEx, EC, MC, FTC, V.
Mr. Glamour himself tends to your locks and those of stars
like Catherine Deneuve, Jodie Foster and Vanessa Paradis:
coupe création, a unique hairdo (from 570F); *chignon création*, an artfully knotted plait (600F); or *balayage*, added
highlights (600-980F). He does not hold court at the branch
salon, 23 boulevard Madeleine, 75001 (49.26.04.59).

Béati-Corpus
(48.74.14.84). **Open** 24 hours daily.
Around the clock in-home appointments. Emerge with a
wash, cut and style (from 300F) or satisfy that midnight craving for a pedicure (from 300F). Add 50F for hotel visits.

Jacques Dessange
37 avenue Franklin D. Roosevelt, 75008 (43.59.31.31).
Métro Franklin D Roosevelt. **Open** 9.30am-6.30pm Mon-
Sat (last appointment 5.45pm). **Credit** EC, MC, V.
Women's cuts 400F; men's 300F. Women can brave a 40F
haircut at Dessange's Ecole de Coiffure, but only if at least
3-4cm is to be cut. Call a week ahead for an appointment: 24
rue St Augustin, 75002 (47.42.24.73). 15 branches in Paris.
Branches include: 52 boulevard Sébastopol, 75003
(42.71.45.23); 2 rue de la Bastille, 75004 (40.29.98.50); 1 rue
de l'Odéon, 75006 (43.26.39.93).

Jean-Claude Biguine
47 branches in Paris.
You're never far from a branch of one of Paris' largest (and
cheapest) salons. Trendy young clippers will shampoo, cut
and style your hair at prices beginning at 150F for women,
110F for men.

Ecole Jean-Louis David
5 rue Cambon, 75001 (42.97.51.71). Métro Concorde.
Open 9.30am-1.30pm, 2.30-6pm, Mon-Fri.
Free snip or curl by fledgling hairdressers practising new
techniques from this ubiquitous chain. First-timers must
show up to go on the client list (hair type permitting).

Salon Vendôme
*5 rue Rouget de Lisle, 75001 (42.60.80.07). Métro
Concorde.* **Open** 9.30am-6.30pm Mon-Sat. **Credit** MC, V.
Women have recently been admitted to this clubby salon,
but it remains a predominantly male preserve. Distinguished
gentlemen can have a haircut (200F), a shave (150F), or get
their ears plucked (60F).

Spas

Villa Thalgo
*218-220 rue du Faubourg St-Honoré, 75008
(45.62.00.20). Métro George V.* **Open** 9am-8.30pm Mon;
8.30am-8.30pm Tue-Thur; 9am-7pm Fri; 9am-6pm Sat.
Credit AmEx, EC, MC, V.
Discover the restorative properties of thalassotherapy,
whether it's *balnéothérapie*, an hour's bath (350F), or *envelope-
ment*, a seaweed wrap (350F). Join for a month and enjoy water
gymnastics in a pool of reconstituted sea water (700F, includes
fluffy bathrobe and slippers).

Les Bains du Marais
31-33 rue des Blancs-Manteaux, 75004 (44.61.02.02).
Métro Rambuteau. **Open** 10am-7pm Mon, Wed, Fri, Sat;
10am-10.30pm Tue, Thur. **Steam bath/sauna** *women*
Mon-Wed; *men* Thur-Sat; 180F (includes towel rental).
Credit EC, MC, V.
Morrocan décor for a steam bath or *massage à l'arabe* (180F).

Tattooists

Bruno
4-6 rue Germain-Pilon, 75018 (42.64.35.59).
Métro Pigalle. **Open** 10am-7pm Mon, Tue, Thur-Sat. **No
credit cards.**
Indelible work by the master starts at 350F.

Hélianthe
*37 avenue Victor-Hugo, 75016 (45.00.91.59). Métro
Charles de Gaulle-Etoile.* **Open** 4-7pm Mon, Wed; 4-8pm
Fri; 10am-8pm Sat. **No credit cards.**
Temporary, one-year tattoos for the less committed.

Opticians

Alain Afflelou
*43-45 avenue des Ternes, 75017 (42.27.10.14). Métro
Ternes.* **Open** 9.30am-7pm Mon-Sat. **Credit** AmEx, MC, V.
The largest of 30 Parisian branches: over 1,000 different
styles. Prescription glasses can be ready within one hour.

SOS Optique
(48.07.22.00). **Open** 8am-10pm daily. **Credit** MC, V.
Glasses repaired at your home by a certified optician. The
mobile repair shop will correct your vision within 30 minutes.

Packing & Shipping

For courier services, *see chapter* **Business**.

Hedley's Humpers
*6 boulevard de la Libération, 93284 St-Denis
(48.13.01.02). Métro Carrefour Pleyel.*
Open 8am-7pm Mon-Fri. **Credit** MC, V.
An English company specialising in transporting goods
between France and the UK. Lorries depart twice weekly.

Logistic Air/Sea France
14 rue Morand, 75011 (48.62.80.42/fax 48.62.80.44).
Métro Couronnes. **Open** 8.30am-7.30pm Mon-Fri; 9am-
noon Sat. **Credit** MC, V.
Shipping worldwide for roughly 12F per kg (45kg minimum), plus a 500F pick-up charge for packages up to 100kg.

Photocopying & Faxing

The chains **Alpha Top** and **Copy Top** have
branches all over Paris. Copiers are also found in
many large stores, and at post offices.

Graphic Procédé
4 rue de Buci, 75006 (43.26.55.05). Métro Odéon.
Open 9am-8pm Mon-Fri. **Credit** V.
Probably the best in town for specialised copying work.

Sara Photo
128, rue de Vaugirard, 75006 (45 48 13 12).
Métro Montparnasse Bienvenüe. **Open** 10am-6pm Mon-
Fri. **Credit** V.
A full-service copy shop: 500 copies for 175F, or 35c a copy.

Photographic

FNAC Service
*1 rue Pierre Lescot, 75001 (40.41.40.00). Métro
Châtelet-Les Halles.* Service Rapide: *136 rue de Rennes,
75015 (49.54.30.00). Métro Montparnasse-Bienvenüe.*
Open 10am-7.30pm Mon-Sat. **Credit** MC, V.
Probably the most reliable for general work. Overnight
developing (36 exp) averages 105F. For same-day service of
higher calibre, try FNAC's Espace Image at 12 boulevard de
Sébastopol, 75004 (42.77.19.00), or the FNAC Service at 136
rue de Rennes, 75015 (49.54.30.00). 50 branches in Paris.

Pro Service
*85 boulevard du Port-Royal, 75013 (43.31.83.00). Métro
Gobelins.* **Open** 9am-6pm Mon-Fri. **Credit** MC, V.
Fine-quality camera repairs and sales, new and second-hand.

Ticket Agencies

It's advisable to book for all concerts, theatres and
sporting events. *See also chapter* **Theatre**.

FNAC
*entrance 1/5 rue Pierre Lescot, 3rd level down (-3),
Forum des Halles 75001 (40.41.40.00). Métro Châtelet-
Les Halles.* **Open** 10am-7.30pm Mon-Sat. **Credit** MC, V.
Branches: at Ternes, rue de Rennes or the Bastille (*see also
chapter* **Specialist Shops**); or book by Minitel 3615 FNAC.

Gibert Joseph
*26 boulevard St-Michel, 75006 (44.41.88.60). Métro
Odéon.* **Open** 9.30am-7.30pm Mon-Sat. **Credit** MC, V.

Virgin Megastore
*53 avenue des Champs-Elysées, 75008 (49.53.50.00).
Métro Franklin D Roosevelt.* **Open** 10am-mid-night Mon-
Thur; 10-1am Fri, Sat; noon-midnight Sun. **Telephone
bookings** 10am-6pm Mon-Fri. **Credit** AmEx, DC, MC, V.
Branches: Carrousel du Louvre, 75001 (47.03.91.17).

Travel & Transport
Hitch-hiking

Allô Stop
*84 passage Brady, 75010 (42.46.00.66).
Métro Château d'Eau.* **Open** 9am-7.30pm Mon-Fri; 9am-
1pm, 2-6pm, Sat. **Credit** MC, V.
For nearly 35 years, this company has been putting passengers in touch with drivers. There's an initial fee (30-70F
depending on the distance), plus petrol costs (max charge 20
centimes per km). Call a week ahead.

Hot Air Balloons

France Montgolfières
*76 rue Balard, 75015 (40.60.11.23/fax 45.58.60.73).
Métro Balard.* **Open** 9am-7pm Mon-Sat.
Credit AmEx, MC, V.
Weather permitting, flights daily from the countryside. The
total trip lasts three to four hours, with 1-1½ hours in the air.

Travel Agencies

Access Voyages
*6 rue Pierre Lescot, 75001 (40.13.02.02/fax
42.21.44.20/Minitel 3615 Access Voyages). Métro
Châtelet-Les Halles.* **Open** 9am-7pm Mon-Fri; 10am-6pm
Sat. **Credit** AmEx, DC, MC, V.

Cash and Go
*54 rue Taitbout, 75009 (44.53.49.49/Minitel 3615
CashGo). Métro Chaussée d'Antin.* **Open** 8.30am-7pm
Mon-Fri. **Credit** MC, V.

Maison de Grande Bretagne
*19 rue des Mathurins, 75009 (44.51.56.20).
Métro Havre-Caumartin/RER Auber.* **Open** 9.30am-6pm
Mon-Fri; 10am-5pm Sat.
Houses a number of organisations specialising in travel to
and within the UK, including the British Tourist Office:
British Rail *(44.51.06.00/Minitel 3615 BR).* Credit MC,
V. **Brittany Ferries** *(44.94.89.00).* Credit MC, V.
Edwards & Edwards *(42.65.39.21).* For theatre
tickets in the UK. **Sealink** *(44.94.40.40).* Credit AmEx,
DC, MC, V. **Le Shuttle** *(44.94.88.80).* Credit MC, V.

Nouvelles Frontières
*5 avenue de l'Opéra (42.60.36.37/fax
40.15.03.75/Minitel 3615 NL).* **Open** 9am-8pm Mon,
Wed-Fri; 9am-9pm Tue; 9am-7pm Sat. **Credit** DC, MC, V.
Branches throughout Paris. Phone 41.41.58.58 for details.

Travelstore
*14 boulevard de la Madeleine, 75009
(53.30.50.00). Métro Opéra or Madeleine.* **Open**
10.30am-7.30pm Mon-Wed, Fri, Sat; 10:30am-10pm Thur;
2-7pm Sun. **Credit** AmEx, MC, V.
A recently-opened establishment with a large number of
independent travel agents together under one roof. A good
place to find discount fares, and also very convenient if you
suddenly need to book a trip on a Sunday.

USIT
*6 rue de Vaugirard, 75006 (43.29.85.00/telephone
bookings only 30.75.30.00). Métro Cluny-La Sorbonne.*
Open 9.30am-6pm Mon-Fri; 1-4.30pm Sat. **Credit** MC.
Coach, air and train tickets for the under-26s.
Branches: 12 rue Vivienne, 75002 (42.96.06.03); 31 bis
rue Linné, 75005 (44.08.71.20).

Video & Cassette Rental
Reels on Wheels
*35 rue de la Croix Nivert, 75015 (45.67.64.99). Métro
Cambronne.* **Rates** 70F for three nights (35F, members).
Open 11.30am-10.30pm daily. **Credit** AmEx, MC, V.
Ian, a Scot, stocks over 3,500 films (in English or with sub-
titles, if in a foreign language). The subscription fee is 500F
per year, 250F for three months (or 1,200F for life). Movies
can be delivered. Note that unless your VCR and TV are
PAL-SECAM you'll have to view films in black and white.
Luckily, he can rent you a PAL-SECAM VCR. Added bonus:
Tex Mex or Indian food deliveries.

V.O. Only
*25 boulevard de la Somme, 75017 (43.80.70.60). Métro
Porte de Champerret.* **Open** 4-10pm Mon-Sat. **Rates** 35F
per day. **Credit** AmEx, DC, EC, MC, V.
Their rental library includes 1,000 PAL videos and laserdiscs
in non-subtitled English – mainly new releases but with a
fair share of classics and concert videos. Also for sale: a selection of 10,000 laser discs (200F-1000F, with a 35F delivery
charge), as well as VCR and VHS Pal/Ntsc, laserdisc players, TVs and 5-speaker Surround Sound Systems.

Perfect Video Duplication
*20 avenue André Malraux, 92300 Levallois
(47.48.91.32/fax 47.48.93.14). Métro Porte de
Champerret.* **Open** 9am-7pm Mon-Fri, or other times by
appointment. **Credit** AmEx, EC, MC, V.
This video lab converts American and British videos to the
French Secam standard. 245F to convert a 90-minute tape.

Galleries & Museums

Museums

Whether you're a culture vulture, an art herbivore or a fairground fan, Paris has got a collection to suit.

In one of the great museum capitals of the world, it's always difficult to know where to start. Paris is positively packed with museums. In the past twenty years, moreover, new ones have sprouted up in delapidated Marais mansions, or high-tech edifices such as the **Cité des Sciences et de L'Industrie** or the **Institut du Monde Arabe**. Most recently, however, it has been the grandaddy of them all, the **Louvre**, that has again demanded centre stage. Although it opened as a museum over 200 years ago in 1793, it has been given a dynamic new lease of life through the *Grand Louvre* project and the opening of the new Richelieu wing, a programme that will not be finally completed until 1997.

Most major museums are in central Paris, so transport is not a problem. You can quite easily walk from the **Centre Pompidou** to the **Louvre**, and across the Seine to the **Musée d'Orsay**. The cluster of museums in the Marais includes the **Musée National Picasso** and the **Musée Carnavalet**, chronicling the history of Paris, as well as the more recent magic museum, the **Musée de la Curiosité**.

*From the **Maison de Balzac**. See page 229.*

Two museums which opened in early 1995 commemorate important figures of World War II: **General Leclerc**, commander of the French troops who liberated Paris in 1944, and resistance hero **Jean Moulin**. Another important addition to Paris' mass of museums is the exquisite **Musée Maillol,** which consists of the collection of twentieth-century art belonging to the late sculptor Maillol's model, Dina Vierny. The renovated **Muséum d'Histoire Naturelle** (Natural History Museum) and new **Musée des Arts Forains** (Fairground Museum) are perfect for entertaining kids, and it's also worth going to see the newly-renovated gardens of the **Musée Rodin**.

Note that **most museums are closed on either Monday or Tuesday**. To avoid queues, try to visit major museums and exhibitions during the week; on Sundays, when rates are often reduced, they get very busy. Late-night openings and lunch-time visits are another way of avoiding the crowds. Last tickets are generally sold 45 minutes before closing time.

Guided tours in English tend to be available only in the larger museums. There are reduced admission charges for some categories of people (pensioners, students), but make sure you have an up-to-date identity card or a passport proving your status if you don't want to have to pay the full price. The staff at ticket counters are often inflexible and rarely open to persuasion, and in some cases even valid documents, such as non-French Senior-Citizen identity cards, may not be accepted.

Paris Carte-Musées et Monuments
Price one day 60F, three days 120F, five days 170F.
This card gives free entry into 65 museums and monuments in and around Paris, and also allows you to jump queues. Very good value if you're in Paris for a few days and plan to do some intensive museum visiting, although you do have to pay extra for special exhibitions. It can be bought at museums, monuments, tourist offices (*see chapter* **Essential Information**) and principal métro and RER stations.

Decorative Arts

Manufactures des Gobelins
42 avenue des Gobelins, 75013 (44.08.52.00). Métro Gobelins. **Open** *by guided tour only,* 2pm Tue-Thur.
Admission 37F adults; 27F students, over-60s, 7-18s; 5F under-18s; free under 7s. **No credit cards.**
Named after Jean Gobelin – a fifteenth-century dyer – this working museum occupies the site where state tapestries,

carpets and furniture have been made since the seventeenth century, although the current buildings are much more recent. The factory was at its wealthiest under Louis XIV and his successors, favoured by a string of royal commissions. In this century, sales figures have fallen steadily, and there are still threats to shift most of the work elsewhere. Apart from witnessing the laborious process of tapestry weaving, visitors can also tour the workshops, where Savonnerie carpets are still made in the traditional way (tours in French only).

Musée des Arts Décoratifs

107 rue de Rivoli, 75001 (44.55.57.50).
Métro Palais-Royal. **Open** 12.30-6pm Wed-Sun.
Admission 25F adults; 16F under-25s, over-60s.
Credit (shop only) AmEx, MC, V.
A fascinating museum in the north-west wing of the Palais du Louvre, which displays the treasures of France's rich tradition of decorative arts. The five upper floors contain objets d'art, furniture and furnishings from the Middle Ages, via sixteenth-century Limoges enamels, Louis XV cabinets and the extravagances of the rococo to the present day, including an impressive collection of porcelain and some marvellously self-important Empire creations. The ground floor twentieth-century galleries display wonderful art nouveau and art deco works, plus a fun array of more modern pieces by Niki de St Phalle and Philippe Starck. Don't miss the art nouveau bedroom set, carved in pear-tree wood, designed by Héctor Guimard, creator of the legendary métro entrances. Jeanne Lanvin's jungle-décor bathroom, with zebra-skin toilet seats and fixtures carved in the shapes of exotic birds, is guaranteed to send you into a swoon. Certain sections, such as textiles and wallpaper, can only be viewed by appointment with the Curator. There are also varied temporary exhibitions. As part of the Louvre complex the museum is affected by the many alterations undertaken in the building, and at some point in 1996-7 will expand into a larger section of the part of the building formerly used by the Finance Ministry. This may lead to temporary closure of some sections.
Reference library. Shop. Wheelchair access.

Musée des Arts de la Mode et du Textile

107 rue de Rivoli, 75001 (44.55.57.50).
Métro Palais-Royal. **Open** during exhibitions only 12.30-6pm Wed-Sun. **Admission** from 35F adults; 25F under-25s, over-60s. **Credit** (shop only) V.
Opened in 1986, the Museum of Fashion has presented some imaginative temporary exhibitions of both historical and contemporary creations, from shoe designs to perfumes to film costumes. However, like the **Musée des Arts Décoratifs** (*see above*), it is affected by the *Grand Louvre* project, and will be closed for renovation from 1995 until late 1996. The museum inherited a rich collection of historical garments representing the highlights of Paris' couture heritage, but at all times a written application must be made in advance to see the permanent collection.
Reference library (by appointment only). Wheelchair access.

Musée du Cristal Baccarat

30 bis rue de Paradis, 75010 (47.70.64.30). Métro Poissonière . **Open** 9am-6pm Mon-Fri; 10am-5.30pm Sat. **Admission** 10F. **Credit** (shop only) MC, V.
Essentially the showroom of celebrated glass-maker Baccarat, with a museum attached. The greatest interest here is in seeing which fallen head of state or deposed monarch used to drink out of Baccarat glasses. There are also some supremely kitsch but technically magnificent pieces produced for the great exhibitions of the last century. Baccarat moved its glass workshops here in 1832, and this street is still the one to visit for glassware outlets.
Shop.

Musée Christofle

9 rue Royale, 75009 (49.22.41.15).
Métro Concorde. **Open** by appointment only, phone in advance. **Admission** 40F. **Credit** (shop only) AmEx, DC, EC, JCB, MC, V.
In this chic street running from Concorde to the Madeleine you can browse round the showroom and small museum where the accomplishments of Christofle – the man who first gave the world silver-plated cutlery – are celebrated. By promoting the use of silver-plate rather than solid silver, Christofle not only enabled the new middle classes of the last century to acquire ornately designed items, but also made himself a fortune. The display spans 150 years of silver work; look for the marrow-shaped samovar of 1880, the water-lily tray and the carrot vase.
Shop.

Musée de la Mode et du Costume

Palais Galliéra, 10 avenue Pierre 1er de Serbie, 75116 (47.20.85.23). Métro Iéna or Alma-Marceau.
Open *during exhibitions only* 10am-5.40pm Tue-Sun. Closed **Mon. Admission** 35F adults; 25F students; free under-7s. **No credit cards.**
Not far from the city's **Musée d'Art Moderne de la Ville de Paris** (*see below* **Fine Art & Architecture**) in the Palais de Tokyo, this elegant nineteenth-century mansion hosts a varied series of temporary exhibitions of clothes and accessories devoted to historical periods, themes or individual designers.
Library (by appointment only).

Musée National de Céramique de Sèvres

place de la Manufacture, 92310 Sèvres (41.14.04.20).
Métro Pont de Sèvres. **Open** 10am-5pm, Mon, Wed-Sun. Closed **Tue. Admission** 20F adults; 18F 18-25s, over-60s; free under-18s. **Credit** (showroom only) MC, V.
Founded in 1738 as a private concern, the Sèvres porcelain factory was soon taken over by the State. On display are finely painted, delicately-modelled pieces that epitomise French rococo style, together with ceramics and porcelain from other European centres including Saxe, Delft and Nevers. Italian majolica and Spanish ceramics from the Middle Ages and some superb early Islamic pieces are also on show. Sèvres is in the western suburbs, between Paris and Versailles; while you're here, visit the Parc de St-Cloud next door.
Shop and showroom. Wheelchair access.

Musée Nissim de Camondo

63 rue de Monceau, 75008 (45.63.26.32).
Métro Monceau or Villiers. **Open** 10am-5pm Wed-Sun. **Admission** 27F adults; 18F 6-25s, over-60s; free under-6s. **No credit cards.**
The Camondos were a rich banking family who moved to Paris from Constantinople in 1867. The collection put together by Count Moïse de Camondo exploits to the full a love for fine French furniture and ceramics, as well as loudly patterned Italian marble, and is named after his son Nissim, who died in the First World War (the rest of the family died at Auschwitz). Moïse replaced the two family's houses near Parc Monceau with this palatial residence in 1911-14, and lived here in a style quite out of his time. A succession of rooms is crammed with furniture by leading craftsmen of the Louis XV and Louis XVI eras, including Oeben, Riesener and Leleu, and there are silver services and sets of Sevres and Meissen porcelain large enough to feed an army. All are set off by superb carpets and tapestries (Gobelins, Aubusson, Savonnerie, Beauvais), which are mostly in extremely good condition, so that some rooms appear to contemporary tastes a real riot of colour. Most remarkable is the circular Salon de Huet, overlooking the Parc Monceau and adorned by eighteenth-century pastoral scenes.

The Louvre

As the *Grand Louvre* unfolds, the Louvre is emerging as a glorious setting for its vast collections, and paradoxically one of Paris' most modern museums, with almost double its former exhibition space. Until the project is completed in 1997 there will unfortunately be some ongoing disruption, with collections being moved or rehung, and departments occasionally closed for refurbishment. Nevertheless, the main features of the renovated Louvre are now in place. Many may feel daunted by the idea of tackling the mother of all museums, but with a bit of planning it's possible to discover within it some of the greatest treasures in world art, and many less familiar wonders.

The collections are based around the original royal collections, augmented by revolutionary seizures and later acquisitions. It's important to be selective, for the museum is truly huge, and you could easily spend days or even weeks just gazing at French or Italian painting, not to mention the rich reserves of Classical sculpture, Ancient Egyptian, Islamic and Medieval works of art.

The museum is organised into wings – Richelieu (along the rue de Rivoli), Sully (around the Cour Carrée) and Denon (along the Seine) – which lead off on three sides from beneath the entrance pyramid. They are further subdivided into *arrondissements*, and each section is colour coded and labelled, but it is almost impossible not to get lost at some point while exploring this treasure trove. Always pick up one of the free orientation leaflets at the entrance. For details of closures and updates on the state of the restoration, call 40.20.53.17 (9.15am–9.45pm Mon, Wed, Sun) or consult the Minitel on 3615 Louvre. As well as the pyramid, the Louvre now also has attached to it a smarter-than-average shopping mall, the **Carrousel du Louvre** (*see* chapter **Specialist Shops**).

French Sculpture

Richelieu, ground floor.
The most dramatic features of the Richelieu wing, opened in November 1993, are its two magnificent sculpture courts. A high-tech glazing system lets light flood into these covered courtyards, casting warm shadows around the monumental pieces here. The Cour Marly gives pride of place to Guillaume Coustou's two giant horses the *Chevaux de Marly* of 1745, being restrained by grooms in a freeze-frame of rearing struggle. Coustou used live models to achieve this degree of naturalism, which contrasts with the courtly correctness of the two winged horses opposite, *Fame* and *Mercury*, created by Coysevox, Coustou's uncle, for Louis XIV in 1706. In the Cour Puget, admire the four bronze captives that originally adorned a statue in the place des Victoires. Spacious side rooms are devoted to French sculpture from medieval tombs

The Lacemaker, *by Vermeer.*

and the original Renaissance reliefs by Jean Goujon for the Fontaine des Innocents in Les Halles to pompous eighteenth-century busts. A remarkable piece is the fifteenth-century *Tomb of Philippe Pot*, with an effigy of this Burgundian aristocrat supported by eight ominous black-cowled figures.

Northern Painting

Richelieu, second floor.
The Dutch, Flemish and German schools have been given new breathing space, and the 24 canvases painted by Rubens for Marie de Medici are displayed together for the first time in the new Galerie Médicis. Since she commissioned the work for the Luxembourg palace to celebrate her own virtues and successes, you'd hardly expect an objective view. Despite all the re-hanging, there are still some major works tucked away in small rooms – look out for masterpieces such as Bosch's *Ship of Fools*, the series of penetrating self-portraits by Rembrandt, and Vermeer's exquisitely delicate *Lacemaker* and *The Astronomer*.

French Painting

Richelieu, Sully, second floor, and Denon, first floor.
The collection starts with late Medieval and Renaissance work, including the striking *Diana the Huntress* by an unknown artist, thought to be an idealised portrait of Diane de Poitiers, Henry II's mistress. There are fine portraits by Clouet and landscapes by Claude Lorraine, as well as Biblical and mythological canvases by Poussin. The peasant scenes of Le Nain and strikingly-lit religious works of Georges de la Tour from the 1640s give way to the eighteenth-century frivolity of Watteau, Fragonard and Boucher, although Watteau's *Pierrot* strikes a dreamily sombre note, despite possibly being intended as a café sign for a former actor.

Look for portraits by the successful court painter of the 1780s Elizabeth Vigée-Le Brun, one of only two women painters represented in the main collection of the Louvre (the other is a student of hers, Marie-Guillaumine Benoist). Severe Revolutionary-era images by David follow, along with the sensuous odalisques of Ingres, whose *Turkish Bath* creates an opulent bordello atmosphere. Corot's misty pastoral scenes have a nostalgic charm, and provide a bridge to the era of Impressionism.

The wonderfully flamboyant large Romantic paintings are still housed in the long gallery of the Denon wing. There's Géricault's *Raft of the Medusa*, inspired by a shipwreck that was a *cause celèbre* at the time, as the survivors resorted to cannibalism. David's monumental representation of the coronation of Napoleon looks suitably restrained by contrast, unlike one of the Louvre's most famous images, Delacroix's *Liberty Leading the People*, celebrating the Revolution of 1830.

French Objets d'Art
Richelieu, first floor.
Highlight among the medieval jewels, gold and ivories is the Treasure of St-Denis. There are also Renaissance enamels, furniture and early clocks.

Italian Painting
Denon, first floor.
The crowds lead you to it: *Mona Lisa* (*La Joconde*). Just nearby you can look un-jostled at Leonardo's *Virgin on the Rocks* and *The Virgin, The Child and Saint Anne*. There are also masterpieces of the Venetian school to watch out for, including works by Titian and Tintoretto. Don't miss Veronese's huge and magnificent *The Marriage at Cana*, its jewel-bright colours glowing after a recent clean, or Uccello's *The Battle of San Romano*.

Spanish Painting and Sculpture
Denon, Pavillon de Flore.
One of the last of the Louvre's sections to be rehung, the Spanish collection includes works by El Greco, Zurbarán and Goya.

Non-French European Sculpture
Denon, basement, ground floor.
Italian sculpture including pieces by Donatello, Della Robbia terracottas, and neo-Classical works by Canova. Michelangelo's *Dying Slave* and the *Rebel Slave*, created for the tomb of Pope Julius II in 1513-1515, are perhaps the best known works in the Louvre's post-Classical sculpture

The Cour Marly in the Richelieu wing.

collection, despite being unfinished; you can make out the marks he left in the marble with stonemason's tools. There are also some Spanish and northern European works.

Greek, Etruscan and Roman Antiquities
Denon, Sully, ground floor.
The collection of Greek vases has lately been closed, but the greatest treasures, including the magnificent *Winged Victory of Samothrace* and the *Venus de Milo*, discovered by a Greek peasant in 1820, are still on view. The unusual Etruscan *Sarcophagus of a Married Couple* in terracotta depicts a couple happily reclining together at a banquet. There are also mosaics from Carthage, Pompeii and Antioch.

Egyptian Antiquities
Sully, ground and first floors.
This extensive collection had its beginnings in Napoleon's Egyptian adventure of 1798. The department will be closed until the end of 1996, but certain works will be on display elsewhere.

Oriental Antiquities
Richelieu, ground floor.
Pieces from Anatolia, Iran and Mesopotamia are now grouped around a magnificent reconstruction of the courtyard of Khorsabad, with breathtaking Assyrian winged bulls. The remarkable *Law Code of Hammurabi* (circa 1750 BC) could be the original tablet of stone, although not laws but royal pronouncements are carved on the basalt stele.

Islamic Art
Richelieu, basement.
The Islamic collections include early glass, ceramics, inlaid metalwork, carpets and funerary stele.

The Medieval Louvre
Sully.
One unexpected feature of the new Louvre is that a section of the massive walls of Philip-Augustus' first keep, hidden beneath the Cour Carrée, can now be seen. It's not necessary to pay for admission to the museum to do so.

The Nineteenth-Century Louvre
Richelieu, second floor.
The opulent apartments of Napoleon III (used until 1989 by the Ministry of Finance for receptions) have been preserved with their glittering chandeliers and splendid crimson upholstery intact.

Musée National du Louvre
entrance through Pyramid, Cour Napoléon, 75001 or via Carrousel du Louvre (40.20.50.50/recorded information 40.20.51.51). Métro Palais Royal-Musée du Louvre. **Open** *permanent collection* 9am-9.45pm Mon (only the *Aile Richelieu*) & Wed; 9am-6pm Thur-Sun; *temporary exhibitions* 10am-10pm Mon, Wed-Sun; *Medieval Louvre & bookshop* 9am-9.45pm Mon, Wed-Sun. Closed **Tue** & 1 Jan, 16 Apr, 1 May, 4 June, 1 Nov, 25 Dec. **Admission** *permanent collection* 40F (until 3pm)/20F (after 3pm & Sun); free under-18s; *temporary exhibitions* admission varies. **Credit** (bookshop only) AmEx, EC, MC, V.
Souvenir & bookshop. Bureau de change. Café-restaurant. Guided tours in English. Nursery. Post office. Wheelchair access.

The Musée d'Orsay

The Musée d'Orsay occupies a fine Beaux-Arts train station which escaped the wrecking ball in the seventies to become Paris' museum of the nineteenth century, devoted to the art of the pivotal years 1848-1914, and incorporating the collection formerly housed in the **Jeu de Paume**. Milanese architect/designer Gae Aulenti did a superb job of remodelling the station's interior, creating vast galleries running either side of a central canyon and carefully managing the mix of natural and artificial light to ensure optimal display of the art works.

Since its opening in 1986, most of its visitors have come to see the impressive selection of works by Impressionists such as Monet, Manet, Degas, Renoir and Van Gogh, but the museum's collection actually covers all of the important art movements from 1848 to 1914, including late Romantics, Realists, Symbolists, Pointillistes and Nabis. The only drawback of the design may be that it gives rather too much space and prestige to the *artistes pompiers* of the nineteenth century, while the Impressionists are rather crammed together on the upper floors. It can appear that there are whole rooms of what could be described as Second-Empire soft porn – the languidly gasping nudes of Cabanel, Auguste and Couture – and grand history paintings such as those of Meissonier or Chassériau. Even so, this does mean that the museum gives a very authentic impression of the art of the period, for these artists were highly regarded in their lifetimes, and one of the Orsay's distinctive attractions is that it is such a grand compendium of every aspect of nineteenth-century art.

The museum is planned so that one can follow a more-or-less chronological route around the exhibits. Starting in the mid-nineteenth century, the collection allows you to see both the continuities between the Impressionists and their forerunners, such as the Realists, Millet and landscape painters like Corot, and appreciate the true revolutionary effect of their use of light and colour.

On entering the museum, the central aisle is dominated by French nineteenth-century sculptures, with many works by Jean-Baptiste Carpeaux, including his respresentation of the four corners of the earth for the Fontaine de l'Observatoire near the Luxembourg, and the controversial *La Danse*, from the facade of the Opéra Garnier, which shocked nineteenth-century sensibilities with its abandoned naked dancers. Up on the first floor terraces are bronzes by Bourdelle and Maillol, as well as some powerful busts by Rodin and his original *Gates of Hell*, *Balzac* (other casts of which are in the Musée Rodin) and *Ugolin*.

The first rooms to the right of the central aisle on the ground floor are dedicated to the Romantics and history painters. There are some typically classical portraits by Ingres, contrasting with the Romantic passion of Delacroix's North African period. The rooms across the central aisle are given over to the work of the Barbizon school such as Corot and Daubigny. Millet's idealised depictions of rural virtue are represented, including his *Angelus*. Make sure you also see the set of clay figures by Daumier caricaturing notables of his time, some of the most searing social satires ever produced.

Further on, you will find early Impressionist masterpieces and Fantin-Latour's *Un atelier aux Batignolles*, which shows a group that includes Zola, Renoir, Bazille and Monet gathered around Manet at his easel. On the left side of the Seine gallery, there is a room dedicated to Gustave Courbet, with his monumental *Burial at Ornans*, and other galleries with fine Pissarros, pastels by Degas, early works by Van Gogh such as *The Potato Eaters*, Boudin seascapes and some striking paintings by Orientalists such as Guillaumet. Also on the ground floor there is a room dedicated to the early works of Manet, including his famously scandalous *Olympia*, which refuses to idealise or prettify the model, who to contemporaries clearly appeared to be a prostitute.

In the rooms opposite there are some examples of the early output of Degas, as well as melancholically mystical works by the Symbolists

Degas' dancers are stars of the Orsay.

A window on the city at the museum café.

Gustave Moreau and Puvis de Chavannes. Decorative Arts from 1850-1880 are on show to the right of the central area. Plans and maquettes for the Opéra Garnier and other contemporary buildings occupy a small gallery at the far end. The Pavillon Amont, in the far left corner, has architectural drawings and Arts-and-Crafts furniture, including items by William Morris.

Escalators whisk you straight up to the third floor, where under an ample sprinkling of the Impressionists' most crucial ingredient – light – you can take in the major masterpieces by Pissarro, Monet, Renoir and Degas, and then the post-impressionists Van Gogh, Cézanne, Gauguin, Toulouse-Lautrec, Seurat and the Nabis movement, although you have to go downstairs again for Bonnard and Vuillard. Manet's controversial *Déjeuner sur l'Herbe*, possibly the most famous picnic in history, which opened the door to the Impressionist revolution, fittingly now opens the Orsay's Impressionism section. A few rooms on there's an equally familiar image, *Whistler's Mother*. In Monet's series of paintings of Rouen cathedral, he explored the changing qualities of light at different times of the day; his paintings of his garden at Giverny (*see chapter* **Trips Out of Town**) immortalise his green fingers.

As well as taking their easels outside, the Impressionists ranged across new subject matter. Degas' depictions of ballet dancers backstage surrounded by client-admirers are taken further by Toulouse-Lautrec, who as well as capturing the vivid characters of the Moulin Rouge went backstage and beyond to sketch the prostitutes he befriended in the brothels of Montmartre. A woman artist such as Berthe Morisot, however, was still more restricted by good taste in her subject matter, and concentrated on domestic scenes, such as *The Cradle*, showing a woman watching her baby. The riches go on: there are

landscapes by Sisley and Picasso, still lives by Cézanne, the artistic mavericks Redon and Douanier Rousseau, and a room of hallucinatory Van Goghs, full of day-glo colours, boiling, wriggling brushwork and distorted perspective. On the west side of the third floor are works by Gauguin, Toulouse-Lautrec, the pointillistes Seurat and Signac, and Vuillard.

Down on the middle level is the fine Kaganovitch collection which includes paintings by Cézannes, Gauguin, Van Gogh, Daumier and Vlaminck, and several rooms with works by the Nabi painters, such as Bonnard, Vallotton and Maurice Denis. A number of rooms on the left of this level are given over to the decorative arts, with a mouth-watering collection of art nouveau furniture, but there are still a few more fine paintings, by Munch and Klimt among others.

The Orsay also contains a large photographic collection. Finally, it is worth taking a look at the reception room, with its ornate columns, painted ceiling and swanky chandeliers, formerly part of the vast 370-room hotel that was incorporated into the station. Equally impressive is the museum's Café des Hauteurs, with a wonderful view through the clock. *See also chapters* **Sightseeing** *and* **Cafés & Bars**.

Musée d'Orsay
1 rue de Bellechasse, 75007 (40.49.48.14/recorded information 45.49.11.11). Métro Solférino/RER Musée d'Orsay. **Open** *museum* 10am-6pm Tue, Wed, Fri, Sat; 10am-9.45pm Thur; 9am-6pm Sun. Closed **Mon.** *bookshop only open* 10.30am-6.30pm Mon, Wed-Sun. **Admission** 36F adults; 24F 18-25s, over-60s, and all visitors Sun; free under-18s. **Credit** (bookshop only) AmEx, EC, MC, V. *Bookshop. Café-restaurant. Concerts. Guided tours. Library. Wheelchair access.*

The Centre Pompidou

Designed by Piano and Rogers as a truly poly-valent cultural space, the Pompidou hosts an enormous variety of activities – dance, cinema and music, as well as art shows. Major temporary exhibitions coming up between 1995 and 1997 include theme shows on art, gender and sexuality, and retrospectives of Francis Bacon and Fernand Léger. 1997 will be the Centre's twentieth anniversary, to be marked by several special exhibitions; after then the building will undergo large-scale renovation until the year 2000, so it's probably best to catch it now.

The third and fourth floors are home to the **Musée National d'Art Moderne**, which has over 30,000 works covering art from 1905 to the present. Only some 1,500 can be seen at any one time. The works on show are changed roughly every six months, and here we can only give an overview of the collection.

The fourth floor covers all the major movements up to 1965, starting with the violent colours of the *Fauves* ('wild beasts') and the bright gouache cut-outs of Matisse's later years. The Cubist revolution of the 1900s is seen in the shape of Braque, Picasso, Gris and Picabia.

The north side of the fourth floor moves towards abstraction, with Kandinsky, Malevitch and Brancusi. Pure abstraction can also be seen in the work of Sonia and Robert Delaunay, well represented here. The dream-scapes of Chagall's floating figures then contrast with the portraits of German expressionist Otto Dix, which serve as a prelude to Dada and Surrealism, and pieces by Duchamp, Man Ray, Magritte, Miró and Ernst.

The post-World War II work shown on this floor includes the primitivism of Dubuffet, and Giacometti's unsettling sculptures. There's a brief representation of American art of the period, including Abstract Expressionism by Jackson Pollock and Willem de Kooning and colour-field paintings by Rothko and Barnett Newman.

On the third floor works by artists of the post-1960s generations are shown – the 'salvage art' of the French New Realists, Pop Art, Minimalism, Conceptual Art and Italian *Arte Povera*. Nearly always on show are Joseph Beuys' piano covered in felt, *Insulation Homogen for Gran Piano*, and *Ben's Store*, a giant assemblage of found, junk objects by French Fluxus-group artist Ben.

There are several other exhibition spaces in the Pompidou. The south mezzanine (and sometimes the ground floor) is used by **Galeries Contemporaines** for exhibitions from big retrospectives to small showcases for young artists. Other sections with regular displays and shows are the **Revue Virtuelle**, featuring the latest computer and interactive video technology, and the **CCI** (Centre de Création Industrielle) devoted to industrial design and architecture. The **Grandes Galeries** on the fifth floor are used for major twentieth-century retrospectives and theme shows.

The Centre also contains a giant public library, and hosts contemporary concerts, in association with IRCAM (*see chapter* **Music: Classical & Opera**), and lectures. There are also excellent book- and gift shops. About the only part not worthy of a visit is the fifth-floor cafeteria, except perhaps for its view. The Centre is least crowded in the evenings. *See also chapters* **Sightseeing**, **Dance**, **Film**, **Children** *and* **Students**.

Centre Pompidou – Musée National d'Art Moderne

Centre National d'Art et de Culture Georges Pompidou/Musée National d'Art Moderne, rue Beaubourg, 75004 (44.78.12.33/recorded information 42.77.11.12). Métro Châtelet-Les Halles or Rambuteau. **Open** noon-10pm Mon, Wed-Fri; 10am-10pm Sat, Sun, holidays. Closed **Tue** & 1 May. **Admission** *Musée National d'Art Moderne* 35F adults; 24F 18-25s, over-60s and all visitors Sun and public holidays; free under-18s, unemployed. *Grande Galerie* 45F adults, 30F 18-25s; *Galeries Contemporaines & CCI* 27F adults, 20F 18-25s, free under-13s. *Day-pass to museum and all exhibitions* 60F adults; 40F 13-25s, over-60s; free under-13s. **Guided tours** 2.30pm Sat, Sun. **Credit** (bookshop/exhibitions 100F minimum) MC, V. *Bookshop & design shop. Café-restaurant. Cinema. Reference library. Slide, video and record libraries; specialist design library. Wheelchair access.*

Ethnography & Tribal Art

Musée des Arts d'Afrique et d'Océanie

293 avenue Daumesnil, 75012 (44.74.84.80).
Métro Porte Dorée. **Open** 10am-5.30pm Mon, Wed-Fri;
10-6pm Sat, Sun, public holidays. Closed **Tue.**
Admission 36F adults; 27F 18-25s, over-60s; free under-
18s. **Credit** (shop only, from 100F) MC, V.

Housed in a building that reeks of colonialism, this is a
wonderful collection of tribal art, often deserted except for
art students and parties of schoolchildren. The museum, on
the east of Paris just by the entrance to the Parc de
Vincennes, was actually designed for the 1931 *Exposition
Coloniale*, and as well as the astonishing bas-relief of the
façade there is some remarkable art deco furnishing inside.
The tribal art, especially the African masks in the upper galleries, is stunning. In addition, there are fabrics and embroidery from the Maghreb and artefacts from the Pacific.
Surprisingly, the basement contains an enormous aquarium
– a great hit with children – full of tropical fish and crocodiles, with a dark section for luminous sea-bed species.
Bookshop. Wheelchair access.

Musée des Arts et Traditions Populaires

6 avenue du Mahatma Gandhi, 75116
(44.17.60.00). Métro Les Sablons. **Open** 9.45am-5.15pm
Mon, Wed-Sun. Closed **Tue. Admission** 20F adults; 13F
18-25s, over-60s; free under-18s. **Credit** (shop only, from
100F) EC, MC, V.

This important centre of French folk art is located close to
the Bois de Boulogne. As a break from the cycle of palaces
and aristocratic collections, it gives a wide overview of 'peasant' France in those halcyon, pre-industrial days. All the
activities of rural life – work and leisure – are explained and
illustrated with tools, objects, furniture, reconstructed
interiors and models. Don't miss the waffle irons, skittles and
early toys. Demonstrations are given of certain craft techniques, and audio-visual material supplements the exhibits.
*Auditorium. Bookshop. Library & archive material.
Record collection.*

Musée Dapper

50 avenue Victor Hugo, 75116 (45.00.01.50).
Métro Victor Hugo. **Open** during exhibitions only, 11am-
7pm daily. **Admission** 20F adults; 10F students,
schoolchildren, over-60s; free under-12s, all visitors Wed.
No credit cards.

An attractive museum which exhibits some superb pieces of
African art, in rotation and according to a chosen theme or
region. It was set up by a Dutch foundation in 1986, in a
limited but beautifully designed space with a verdant garden that sets the tone perfectly. Two or three exhibitions are
arranged every year; while they go on performances of
African tales relating to the exhibition are staged (Wed
mornings for children, Sun evening for adults; phone for a
reservation). The museum is closed between exhibitions.
Library (by appointment).

Musée de l'Homme

Palais de Chaillot, place du Trocadéro, 75116
(44.05.72.72). Métro Trocadéro. **Open** 9.45am-5.15pm
Mon, Wed-Sun. Closed **Tue. Admission** 25F adults; 15F
students,under 25s, over-60s; free under-4s. **Credit**
(bookshop only) AmEx, EC, MC, V.

Through costumes, weapons, jewellery, sculpture and other
ornamental artefacts, the museum traces the development of
the human race. The African and European displays are on
the first floor; Asia, the Americas and the Pacific are on the
second. The *Salon de la Musique* displays a weird and
wonderful collection of musical instruments, while a series
of recordings – some as rare as the exhibits themselves – act
as background music for visitors. Some fantastic objects are
shown here, in rather dusty displays, ranging from Maori

earrings to African masks. Gory highlights of the tribal past
include the life-sized King Béhanzin, 'shark-man', in the
African section, an Easter Island head and a selection of 'dec-
orative' human skulls, with reconstructed faces, from the
Pacific. There's also an exhibition devoted to human biolo-
gy. A number of activities are arranged for children.
*Café. Cinema. Concerts. Lecture room. Library.
Wheelchair access.*

Fine Art & Architecture

Atelier-Musée Henri Bouchard

25 rue de l'Yvette, 75016 (46.47.63.46). Métro Jasmin.
Open 2-7pm Wed-Sun; by appointment for groups at
other times; closed last two weeks of March, June, Sept
and Dec. **Admission** 25F adults; 15F students, under
25s; free under-7s, over 60s. **No credit cards.**

This small studio museum displays the work of sculptor
Henri Bouchard (1875-1960). He undertook many official
commissions, and his work is dotted around town, including the tomb of Cardinal Dubois in Notre-Dame. The
museum, if not a prime destination for many visitors, has an
amusingly genteel character, and you will be well looked
after by the sculptor's son and daughter-in-law, who run it.
Wheelchair access.

Espace Dalí Montmartre

*11 rue Poulbot, 75018 (42.64.40.10). Métro Anvers or
Abbesses.* **Open** *Sept-June* 10am-6pm daily. **Admission**
35F adults; 25F students; free under-6s. **No credit cards.**
The black-walled interior, artistically programmed lighting
and specially composed soundtrack make it clear that this
is a high-marketing presentation of an artist's work. The collection runs to over 300 works, but don't come expecting to
see Dali's celebrated Surrealist paintings: the museum concentrates on sculptures – mainly bronzes from the seventies,
at the tacky end of Dali's over-long career. There are also
plenty of reproductions of his book illustrations, an area in
which he could fully exploit his taste for the fantastic and
the sexual; they include La Fontaine's fables, Freud,
Casanova, de Sade, Dante – and *Alice in Wonderland*.
Bookshop.

Fondation Le Corbusier

10 square du Docteur Blanche, 75016
(42.88.41.53). Métro Jasmin. **Open** 10am-12.30pm, 1.30-
6pm, Mon-Thur; 10am-5pm Fri. Closed Aug. **Admission**
8F. **No credit cards.**

Tucked away in the 16th *arrondissement*, this house,
designed by Le Corbusier for a Swiss banker and art collector and completed in 1923, provides a good opportunity to
see the architect's ideas in practice, and also contains a collection of his drawings, paintings, sculpture and furniture.
The adjoining Villa Jeanneret – also by Le Corbusier – houses the Foundation's library (*see also chapter* **Architecture**).
Bookshop. Library (1.30-6pm).

Musée d'Art Moderne
de la Ville de Paris/ARC

Palais de Tokyo, 11 avenue du Président Wilson, 75116
*(53.67.40.00/recorded information 40/70/11/10). Métro
Iéna.* **Open** *permanent collection* 10am-5.30pm Tue-Fri;
10am-7pm Sat, Sun; *temporary exhibitions* 10am-7pm
Tue-Sun. Closed **Mon. Admission** *permanent collection*
27F adults; 14.50F students; free under-7s; *temporary
exhibitions* 40F adults, 30F students; free under-7s;
combined ticket 45F adults; 35F students; free under-7s.
Credit (bookshop only) AmEx, DC, EC, MC, V.

This monumental museum was built as the Electricity
Pavilion for the 1937 *Exposition Universelle*, and Dufy's vast
mural *Electricité* can still be seen in a curved room. Today
the building holds the municipal collection of modern art,
which is particularly strong on the Cubists, the *Fauves*,

Rouault, the Delaunays, Gromaire, Soutine, Modigliani and the *Ecole de Paris*. Contemporary artists such as Boltanski, Lavier, Ange Leccia, Sarkis and Buren are also represented, and there are some recently-discovered panels from an early version of Matisse's *La Danse*, alongside his later reworking of 1932-33. The contemporary department, ARC (*Animation, Recherche, Confrontation*), puts on some of the most ambitious and adventurous contemporary art exhibitions in Paris, ranging from established names to the first museum shows of young artists.

Bookshop. Café-restaurant (tables outdoors). Concerts. Wheelchair access.

Musée de Boulogne-Billancourt

26 avenue André Morizet, 92100 Boulogne-Billancourt (47.12.77.39). Métro Marcel Sembat.
Open 9am-noon, 1.30-5.30pm, Mon, Wed, Thur; 9am-4.30pm Fri; 10am-noon, 2-5.30pm, Sat, Sun. Closed **Tue. Admission** 15F adults; 10F over-60s, artists, disabled; free students. **No credit cards.**

This western suburb of Paris was home to a number of artists back in the twenties, and this modest museum holds a collection of their work. There are paintings by Gris, Denis, Bernard, Carrière, Huet, Masson and Lipska, and sculptures by Bouchard, Poupelet and Muller, among others. An architectural section contains plans, drawings, photos and maquettes of buildings in the area, and the museum is also rich in other designs from the same period, exhibiting work by Mallet-Stevens, Perret, Le Corbusier and Lurçat. The museum is due to be moved to a new building during 1996, where it will reopen as the *Musée des Années 30.*
Wheelchair access.

Musée Bourdelle

16 rue Antoine-Bourdelle, 75015 (45.48.67.27). Métro Montparnasse-Bienvenüe or Falguière. **Open** 10am-5.40pm Tue-Sun. Closed **Mon** and public holidays. **Admission** 17F (27F during exhibitions) adults; 9F (19F during exhibitions) students, over-60s; free under-7s. **No credit cards.**

An interesting museum devoted to the sculptor Antoine Bourdelle, a pupil of Rodin who produced several monumental works including the friezes at the Théâtre des Champs-Elysées (*see chapter* **Music: Classical & Opera**). Housed in a mix of buildings around a small garden, the museum includes the artist's studio and apartments, a fifties' extension revealing the evolution of Bourdelle's monument to a General Alvear in Buenos Aires, and an impressive new wing added by Christian de Portzamparc, with smaller bronzes and maquettes.
Reference library (by appointment only). Wheelchair access.

Musée Cognacq-Jay

Hôtel Denon, 8 rue Elzévir, 75003 (40.27.07.21). Métro St-Paul. **Open** 10am-5.40pm Tue-Sun. Closed **Mon. Admission** 17F adults; 9F students, over-60s. **No credit cards.**

Put together by the founders of the Samaritaine department store, Ernest Cognacq and his wife Louise Jay, this collection, which moved into this Marais mansion in the eighties, concentrates on paintings, furniture and ceramics of the eighteenth century. They are displayed in different panelled interiors from the period, some of which already belonged to the Hôtel Denon, and others which were collected by Cognacq himself. There are paintings by Boucher, Chardin, Canaletto, Fragonard and Greuze, and pastels by Quentin de la Tour.
Bookshop.

Musée Delacroix

6 place Furstenberg, 75006 (43.54.04.87). Métro St-Germain-des-Prés. **Open** 9.45am-5pm, Mon, Wed-Sun. Closed **Tue. Admission** 15F adults; 10F 18-25s, over-60s; free under-18s. **No credit cards.**

The elderly Delacroix moved to the tiny place Furstenberg in 1857, to be nearer to the church of St-Sulpice where he was painting the murals which can still be seen there (*see chapter* **Sightseeing**), and lived here until his death in 1863. You'll have to go to the Louvre and the Musée d'Orsay to see his major paintings, but the collection displayed in the three rooms of his apartment and the cube-shaped studio he had constructed in the garden does include several small oil paintings (a self-portrait as Hamlet, and a portrait of his governess among others), some wonderfully free pastel studies of skies and sketches for larger works, and still conserves some of the atmosphere of the studio as it must have been. Other displays relate to his friendships with George Sand and Baudelaire. There are plans to extend the museum.

Musée Départmental du Prieuré

2bis rue Maurice Denis, St-Germain-en-Laye 78100(39.73.77.87). RER St-Germain-en-Laye. **Open** 10am-5.30pm Wed-Fri; 10am-6.30pm Sat, Sun. **Admission** 25F adults; 15F students. **No credit cards.**

Out in the elegant commuterland of St-Germain-en-Laye, this former royal hospital became home and studio to Nabi painter Maurice Denis in 1915. The remarkable collection, housed in ancient wards and attics, comprises paintings, prints and decorative objects by the Nabis (a group that including Denis himself and Sérusier, Bonnard, Vuillard, Roussel and Valloton). There are also paintings by their forerunners Gauguin and the Pont-Aven school, and by Toulouse-Lautrec. The collection is, not surprisingly, especially rich in works by Denis, who also painted the frescoes and designed the stained glass in the small chapel.

Musée Jacquemart-André

158 boulevard Haussmann, 75008 (42.89.04.91). Métro Miromesnil or St-Philippe du Roule.
Open phone for details.

Another impressive example of a marital team amassing an aesthetic hoard of no mean proportions (*see above* **Musée Cognacq-Jay**). This collection, housed in a nineteenth-century mansion and due to re-open after a revamp early in 1996, was assembled at the end of the last century and concentrates on eighteenth-century French paintings and furnishings, seventeenth-century Dutch and Flemish paintings and works from the Italian Renaissance, including Uccello's *St George* and a number of della Robbia terracottas.

Musée Maillol

59-61 rue de Grenelle, 75007. (42.22.59.58). Metro Rue du Bac or Sèvres-Babylone. **Open** 11am–6pm Mon, Wed-Sun (last tickets at 5.15pm). Closed **Tue. Admission** 40F adults; 26F students and over-60s; free under-18s. **No credit cards.**

This eighteenth-century *hôtel particulier* on the rue de Grenelle is especially famous for the Fountain of the Four Seasons decorating its façade, and inside some of its original panelling has also been preserved. The romantic dramatist Alfred de Musset once lived here. After several years of preparation it has recently been opened as a museum by the Dina Vierny foundation. Vierny met the artist Aristide Maillol (1861-1944) at the age of 15, and became his model for the next ten years. Some of Maillol's best known sculptures, such as *The Mountain, Air* and *River,* resulted from the collaboration. Several of his bronzes grace the Tuileries gardens, but this museum displays his work in a variety of media – drawings, pastels, ceramics, engravings, painting and sculpture. Also on show is the exceptional private collection of Vierny, who posed for Matisse, Bonnard and Dufy before opening a gallery in St-Germain after World War II. There are works by Picasso, Rodin, Gauguin, Bonnard, Degas, Cézanne, Dufy and Kandinsky. In the basement is an installation by the contemporary Russian artist Ilya Kabakov titled *The Communal Kitchen,* recreating the atmosphere and sounds of a shared Russian kitchen.
Cafeteria 11am-5pm. Bookshop.

From the **Musée Maillol**.

or a mould – whether mural, gargoyle or stained glass – allowing you to admire the stained-glass of Chartres or the portals of Vézelay cathedral without leaving Paris.
Shop. Wheelchair Access.

Musée Gustave Moreau
14 rue de la Rochefoucauld, 75009 (48.74.38.50). Métro Trinité. Open 11am-5.15pm Mon, Wed; 10am-12.45pm, 2-5.15pm, Thur-Sun. Closed **Tue**. Admission 17F adults; 11F students over-60s; free under-18s. **No credit cards**.
The most eccentric of all the one-man museums in Paris. The enormous double-height studio, with a further storey above reached by an impressive spiral staircase, is literally crammed wall to wall with Moreau's paintings – many unfinished – and there are thousands more of his drawings and watercolours to pull out from shutters on the walls. Here the Symbolist painter Gustave Moreau (1825-1898) lived, worked and taught his art to the likes of Matisse, Rouault and Puy. The museum will transport any visitor back into the mystical and dreamily abstract artistic movement that peaked in the late nineteenth century. Moreau developed a personal mythology, filling his fantasically detailed canvases with images of Salomé, St John the Baptist, St George, griffins and unicorns, using jewel-like colours that, like those of his near contemporaries the English Pre-Raphaelites, owed much to the rediscovery of the early Italian masters. Don't miss the small private apartment, crammed with furniture and ornaments, where Moreau lived with his parents.
Bookshop. Library (by appointment only).

Musée National Hébert
85 rue du Cherche-Midi, 75006 (42.22.23.82). Métro Sèvres-Babylone. Open 12.30-6pm Mon, Wed-Fri; 2-6pm Sat, Sun and public holidays. Closed **Tue**. Admission 12F adults; 8F students, over-60s; free under-18s. **No credit cards**.
The now largely forgotten Ernest Hébert (1817-1908) painted landscapes of Italy and figurative subjects, bending to the fashion of the time whether in pious portraits and sentimental shepherdesses in mid-century or brightly coloured Symbolist-influenced female muses, Ophelias and Impressionist-tinged ladies towards the end of his career. The endless watercolours and oils are mostly unremarkable, if an interesting testament to nineteenth-century taste. The rather run down house is strangely appealing though: a curious mix of marble additions, and some fine rooms on the second floor which still have their original early eighteenth-century panelling.
Shop.

Musée National Jean-Jacques Henner
43 avenue de Villiers, 750017 (47.63.42.73). Métro Malesherbes/Monceau. Open 10am-noon, 2-5pm, Tue-Sun. Closed **Mon**. Admission 20F adults; 15F students, over-60s; free under-15s. **No credit cards**.
A surprising one-man museum north of the Parc Monceau, with more than 700 paintings, sketches and drawings by the prolific Henner (1829-1905), a rather modest, solitary character, never satisfied with the official honours that were lavished on him. The collection is interesting not so much for the quality of the works, but as an illustration of how obsessively he reworked and transformed the same subjects. Look out for the Islamic balcony in the first floor drawing room.

Musée National Picasso
Hôtel Salé, 5 rue de Thorigny, 75003 (42.71.25.21). Métro Chemin Vert or St-Paul. Open 9.30am-5.30pm Mon, Wed-Sun. Closed **Tue**. Admission 27F adults; 18F 18-25s, students, over-60s, and all visitors Sun; free under-18s. **No credit cards**.
The *grand siècle* mansion, lushly decorated with stone carvings, is alone worth the trip here, as are the wrought-iron fixtures and furnishings designed by Diego Giacometti. Opened in 1985 in a renovated Marais *hôtel*, the Musée Picasso possesses an unparalleled collection of paintings represent-

Musée Marmottan
2 rue Louis-Boilly, 75016 (42.24.07.02). Métro La Muette. Open 10am-5.30pm Tue-Sun. Closed **Mon**. Admission 35F adults; 15F 8-25s, over-60s; free under-8s. **No credit cards**.
Originally simply a private collection of furniture, objects and paintings from the Napoleonic period, this museum achieved fame with Michel Monet's bequest of 165 works by his father, including a breathtaking series of late water-lily canvases, advantageously displayed in a special basement room. Sit and absorb the intensity of viridian green and electric blue: these wonderful exercises in pure colour show Monet at his most original. There are also Impressionist canvases by Sisley, Renoir, Pissarro, Berthe Morisot and Caillebotte, among others, as well as some by the nineteenth-century Realists. The collection also contains Monet's *Impression Soleil Levant* – the painting that gave the Impressionist movement its name, and which hangs on the stairs. In 1987 the museum also acquired the Duhem donation, with works by Gauguin, Renoir, Corot and Sisley. Apart from these major pieces, you can see the magnificent Wildenstein collection of 230 medieval illuminated manuscripts, displayed on the recently redecorated first floor.
Shop.

Musée des Monuments Français
Palais de Chaillot, place du Trocadéro, 75016 (44.05.39.10). Métro Trocadéro. Open 10am-6pm Mon, Wed-Sun. Closed **Tue**. Admission 36F adults; 24F under-25s, over-60s; under-13s. **Credit** (shop only) EC, MC, V.
Another inhabitant of the imposing Palais de Chaillot, this museum was first founded by the Gothic revivalist Viollet-de-Duc as an exercise in collecting celebrated counterfeits of French sculpture and architecture. Everything here is a copy

ing all phases in the master's long and varied career, acquired by the French state in lieu of inheritance taxes. Many of the paintings Picasso could not bring himself to part with are on display here. The result is a collection spanning six decades of creativity, including not only his famous gaunt blue figures and harlequins, but also the boldly drawn and unabashedly ribald pictures he produced in his later years, wonderful beach pictures and portraits of his favourite models Marie-Thérèse and Dora Maar. The drawings for the pivotal *Demoiselles d'Avignon* are on display, as well as prints and ceramics that demonstrate the amazingly versatile nature of Picasso's genius. What stands out above all is the sculpture: from the vast head on the staircase to a girl skipping. Look closely at the sculpture of an ape – you'll see that its face is made out of a 2CV. Picasso stands out for his continual inventiveness and, surprisingly rare in great art, his wonderful sense of humour. Also there is Picasso's collection of tribal art – interestingly juxtaposed with the 'primitive' wood figures he carved himself – and of paintings, including works by Matisse and Douanier Rousseau. *Bookshop. Wheelchair access.*

Musée de l'Orangerie

Jardin des Tuileries, 75001 (42.97.48.16). Métro Concorde. **Open** 9.45am-5.15pm Mon, Wed-Sun. **Closed Tue. Admission** *permanent collection* 27F adults; 18F 18-25s, over-60s, all visitors Sun; free under-18s; *temporary exhibitions* 40F adults; 30F 18-25s, over-60s. **Credit** (shop only) EC, MC, V.

Across the Tuileries Gardens from the Jeu de Paume is the Orangerie, home of Monet's *Water Lilies* (*see also above* **Musée Marmottan**), as well as the collections of Jean Walter and Paul Guillaume. The eight gigantic panels of Water Lilies were conceived for these oval rooms, and left as a 'spiritual testimony' by Monet. Presented to the public in 1927, a year after his death, they still have an extraordinary freshness and depth. The Walter-Guillaume collection on the floor above has some big names such as Soutine, Cézanne, Renoir, Sisley, Picasso, Derain, Matisse, Rousseau and Modigliani, but benefits little from slightly run-down suroundings. *Shop. Wheelchair access.*

Musée du Petit Palais

avenue Winston Churchill, 75008 (42.65.12.73). Métro Champs Elysées-Clemenceau. **Open** 10am-5.40pm Tue-Sun. **Closed Mon** & public holidays. **Admission** *permanent collection* 27F adults; 14.5F 7-18s, students; free under-7s; *temporary exhibitions* 40F adults; 30F students. **Guided tours** 2.30pm Thurs, Sat. **Credit** (bookshop only) V.

Standing sedately across the road from the Grand Palais (*see below* **Exhibition Centres**), the Petit Palais contains rather a hotchpotch of private collections donated to the city, including Greek pottery, Chinese porcelain, Beauvais tapestries, French furniture and paintings by Millet, Delacroix, Géricault, Daumier, Courbet, Odilon Redon and a good selection of Impressionists and works by Vuillard and Bonnard. It's most often visited, however, for temporary exhibitions, including some fine ones devoted to the decorative arts. *Bookshop. Guided tours Tue 12.30pm, 2.30pm. Library. Wheelchair access.*

Musée Rodin

Hôtel Biron, 77 rue de Varenne, 75007 (47.05.01.34). Métro Varenne. **Open** 9.30am-6.45pm Tue-Sun. **Closed Mon. Admission** *museum & gardens* 27F adults; 18F 18-25s, over-60s, all visitors Sun and public holidays; free under-18s, art students; *gardens only* 5F. **Credit** (bookshop only) AmEx, JCB, MC, V.

Deep in thought in the gardens of the **Musée Rodin.**

One of Paris' most pleasant museums, the Rodin occupies the stately *hôtel* in the Faubourg St-Germain where Rodin actually lived and sculpted. His arrestingly dramatic works in marble and bronze fill its rooms, themselves decorated with exquisite panelling and mirrors, and adorn the lovely gardens. The famous *Kiss*, the moving *Cathedral*, formed by two hands that hold each other tenderly without touching, Rodin's studies of *Balzac* and other pieces of note occupy the rooms indoors, accompanied by several works by Rodin's mistress and pupil-cum-tutor Camille Claudel, and paintings by Van Gogh, Monet, Renoir and Rodin himself. In the gardens, there is the tragically moving *Burghers of Calais*, the elaborate *Gates of Hell*, the final proud portrait of Balzac, and the eternally absorbed – and absorbing – *Thinker*. The gardens have recently been replanted to create more of an eighteenth-century naturalistic feel. The central alley behind the hôtel leads down to a pond, with flower beds and small fountains down the side, behind which there are sandpits for children. To the left, there is a shady stretch of trees in which Rodin's *Orpheus* is displayed. During the summer months, Rodin fans can also visit the **Villa des Brillants** at Meudon (45.34.13.09), where he worked from 1895. On display are sculptures, as well as numerous plastercasts and sketches for his major works (Apr-Oct only: 1.30-6pm Fri–Sun). *Bookshop. Cafeteria (in garden). Wheelchair access.*

Musée Zadkine

100 bis rue d'Assas, 75006 (43.26.91.90). RER Port Royal. **Open** 10am-5.40pm Tue-Sun. **Closed Mon. Admission** 17F adults; 9F students. **No credit cards.**

Arresting works in wood and stone by the Russian-born Cubist sculptor Ossip Zadkine are displayed in the tiny house and garden he inhabited from 1928 – when Montparnasse was the centre of the artistic world – until his death in 1967. The house and studio now contain well designed exhibition spaces setting off numerous drawings, gouaches and sculptures and preparatory studies. In the garden are his largest sculptures, much as they were during his lifetime.

History

Hôtel des Monnaies

11 quai de Conti, 75006 (40.46.55.35). Métro Pont-Neuf. **Open** *museum* noon-7pm Tue, Thur; noon-9pm Wed; 10am-7pm Sat, Sun; *workshop* 2.15-2.45pm Tue, Fri. **Admission** 20F adults; 15F students, all visitors Sun; free under 16s. **No credit cards.**

The National Mint and its museum are found in this spectacular Louis XVI edifice overlooking the Seine. Coins and medals from all epochs are displayed, as are drawings, models and relevant tools and objects. The workshops themselves can be visited on Tuesday and Friday only. *Wheelchair access.*

Mémorial du Maréchal Leclerc de Hauteclocque et de la Libération de Paris & Musée Jean Moulin

23, allée de la DB, Jardin Atlantique (above the Grandes Lignes tracks of Gare Montparnasse), 75015 (40.64.39.44). Métro Montparnasse Bienvenüe. **Open** Tue-Sun 10am–5.40pm **Closed Mon. Admission** 17.5F adults (27F during exhibitions); 9F students, over-60s (19F during exhibitions); free under-8s. **No credit cards.**

In March 1995, less than a year after the fiftieth anniversary of the Liberation of Paris, these two museums opened dedicated to men who played a large part in the event. General Leclerc commanded the French Division that was the first Allied unit to enter Paris; Moulin was a Communist resistance martyr. Both are full of war memorabilia, such as photos, posters and newspapers of the time. The Memorial also incorporates a videotheque with material on the war. *Bookshop.*

Musée de l'Armée

Hôtel des Invalides, Esplanade des Invalides, 75007 (44.42.37.67). Métro Varenne or Latour-Maubourg. **Open** *April-Sept* 10am-6pm daily; *Oct-March* 10am-5pm daily. **Admission** (valid for 2 consecutive days) 35F adults; 25F under-18s, students, over-60s; under-7s, soldiers in uniform, free. **No credit cards.**

Apart from housing the monolithic tomb of Napoleon, the Musée de l'Armée is a feast for young and not-so-young boys prone to war fantasies. Military history is explained through prints, paintings, diagrams, maps, plans, uniforms, weapons and armour (with and without bullet holes), from paleolithic times up to World War II. The museum is vast, and there are miles of exhibits devoted to the Napoleonic era alone. A cinema screens simulations and rare footage of French battles from World Wars I and II. A 'temporary' exhibition of large models of French forts, built between the seventh and nineteenth centuries, is still in the *Galerie des Plans en Relief*, despite plans to move it to a separate museum. A ticket to the Musée de l'Armée will allow you free entry. *See also* **Les Invalides** *in chapter* **Sightseeing**.

Cinema (films on World War I at 2.15pm; World War II 4.15pm). Shop. Wheelchair access to half the museum.

Musée de l'Assistance Publique

Hôtel de Miramon, 47 quai de la Tournelle, 75005 (46.33.01.43). Métro Cardonal Lemoine. **Open** 10am-5pm Tue-Sat. Closed **Mon** & Aug. **Admission** 20F; 10F students, over-60s. **No credit cards.**

The history of Paris hospitals, from the days when they were receptacles for abandoned babies to the beginnings of modern medicine with anaesthesia, is explained in surprisingly lively fashion through paintings, prints, various grisly medical devices and a reconstructed ward and pharmacy, although texts are unfortunately in French only. Recent temporary exhibitions have ranged from Daniel Spoerri's artworks using prints of skin diseases to displays on childbirth.

Musée du Cabinet des Médailles

Bibliothèque Nationale, 58 rue de Richelieu, 75002 (47.03.83.30). Métro Bourse. **Open** 10am-5pm Mon-Sat; noon-7pm Sun. **Admission** 20F adults; 12F students, over-60s; free under-12s. **Credit** (shop only) EC, MC, V.

This major collection of coins and medals is kept on the first floor of the Bibliothèque Nationale. It's a place for the initiated: there are some 400,000 specimens, including the world's largest collection of cameos and intaglios. If your eyes begin to blur after focusing on such small exhibits, there are also some works of art. Of particular interest is the Merovingian King Dagobert's throne, as well as items of silverwork and a selection of paintings, with works by Boucher and Van Loo.

Shop.

Musée Carnavalet

23 rue de Sévigné, 75003 (42.72.21.13). Métro St-Paul. **Open** 10am-5.35pm Tue-Sun. Closed **Mon**. **Admission** 27F adults; 14.5F students, teachers; free under-18s. **Credit** (bookshop only) AmEx, V.

If the history of Paris given at the Musée Grévin (*see below*) is a little lightweight for you, head for this comprehensive museum housed in two connected Marais mansions. The Hôtel de Sevigné, where writer Madame de Sévigné lived from 1677 to 1696, houses the displays covering the history of Paris and its arts and crafts from the sixteenth century onwards. You can also see Madame's desk, and samples of her famous letters. In 1989 the museum was extended into the neighbouring Hôtel Le Peletier de St-Fargeau, giving space to display archeological collections from the Gallo-Roman period and medieval works of art. The rich collection of paintings, furnishings and architectural elements ranges from gilded panelling to tavern signs, engravings, maps and some topographical models that provide a fascinating glimpse of what the city looked like in various centuries. A special section devoted to the Revolution displays bizarre memorabilia, such as a miniature of the Bastille prison carved out of one of its stones and some superb gouaches by Hubert Robert painted during his imprisonment, and also gives a wealth of information on the complex history of the Revolution and subsequent Terror. You can also see Napoleon's cradle, a number of fascinating room reconstructions that include Proust's bedroom, and a luxurious art nouveau shop.

Bookshop. Guided tours Wed, Sat (phone for details). Reference section. Wheelchair access.

Musée de Cluny (Musée National du Moyen Age)

6 place Paul-Painlevé, 75005 (43.25.62.00). Métro St-Michel or Cluny-La Sorbonne. **Open** 9.15-5.45pm Mon, Wed-Sun. Closed **Tue**. **Admission** 27F adults; 18F 18-25s, over-60s, and all visitors Sun; free under-18s. **No credit cards.**

Occupying the fifteenth-century Hôtel du Cluny, the Paris mansion of the abbots of Cluny, which was built into the partly restored ruins of third-century Roman baths, this intriguing museum of medieval art and artefacts retains a domestic scale suitable for the small-scale intimacy of many of its treasures. Its most famous pieces are the *Lady and the Unicorn* series of tapestries, depicting convoluted allegories of the five senses, beautifully displayed in a special circular room. The *millefiore*-style tapestry, filled with rabbits and flowers, is wrought in exquisite colour and detail. Elsewhere there are displays of wonderful enamel bowls and caskets from Limoges, carved ivories and gold reliquaries and church plate, medieval books of hours to leaf through, wooden chests and locks. There are also early fabrics, including ancient Coptic weaving from Egypt and heavily embroidered bishop's copes, medieval sculpture with capitals from churches all over France, and heads of the kings of Judea from Notre Dame, which had been destroyed in the Revolution under the mistaken belief that they represented the kings of France, and were discovered by chance (minus their noses) in 1979. *See also chapter* **Sightseeing**.

Bookshop. Concerts.

Musée Grévin

10 boulevard Montmartre, 75009 (47.70.85.05). Métro Rue Montmartre. **Open** *term-time* 1-6pm daily; *school holidays* 10am-7pm daily. **Admission** 50F adults; 34F 6-14s; free under-6s. **Credit** (from 130F) MC, V.

Paris's wax museum is over 100 years old, and was originally inspired by Madame Tussaud's in London. It gives a quick, animated overview of French history. On the ground floor you can keep up with the latest hot news on the personality front; the current Prime Minister, for example. Needless to say, children love it. An annexe in the Forum des Halles presents scenes of Paris in the 1900s – complete with *son et lumière* light relief.

Branch: Level 1, Grand Balcon, Forum des Halles, rue Pierre Lescot, 75001 (40.26.28.50).

Musée de l'Histoire de France

Hôtel de Soubise, 60 rue des Francs-Bourgeois, 75004 (40.27.62.18). Métro St-Paul. **Open** 1.45-5.45pm Mon, Wed-Sun. Closed **Tue**. **Admission** 15F adults; 10F students, teachers, over-60s; free under-18s. **No credit cards.**

Expand on your knowledge gained at the Carnavalet (*see above*) by visiting this museum of French history – part of the National Archives. There's a permanent display of 200 historical documents relating to the social and political history of France, from King Dagobert to the end of World War II, while further rooms are used for temporary exhibitions. The Hôtel de Soubise also contains the finest rococo interiors in Paris, the apartments of the Prince and

Princess de Soubise, which were decorated in the early eighteenth century with superb plasterwork, panelling and paintings by prominent artists of the period such as Boucher, Natoire, Restout and Van Loo.

Musée de la Marine

Palais de Chaillot, place du Trocadéro,
75016 (45.53.31.70). Métro Trocadéro. **Open** 10am-6pm Mon, Wed-Sun. Closed **Tue**. **Admission** 34F adults; 22F under -26s, over-60s, soldiers, sailors; free under-5s.
Credit (bookshop only) EC, MC, V.
A favourite among mariners craving the smell of the sea or the pull of the tides, the museum has one of the largest maritime collections in the world. Apart from Vernet's imposing series of 13 paintings of the ports of France (1754-1765), the collection boasts the Emperor's barge, built when Napoleon's delusions of grandeur were reaching their zenith in 1811. There are also carved prows, numerous models of ships, old maps, antique and modern navigational instruments, underwater equipment and a model of a nuclear submarine, as well as more romantic maritime paintings, mainly from the eighteenth century. There are regular temporary exhibitions on related themes.
Lectures. Shops.

Musée de Vieux Montmartre

12 rue Cortot, 75018 (46.06.61.11). Métro Lamarck-Caulaincourt. **Open** 11am-6pm Tue-Sun. Closed **Mon**.
Admission 25F adults; free under-8s. **No credit cards**.
If you're up in the heights of Montmartre and want a rest from the tourist junk and hustlers, visit this quiet seventeenth-century house and its small garden next to the Montmartre vineyard. It's mainly used for temporary exhibitions of artists associated with Montmartre, but the permanent collection consists of a room devoted to Modigliani, who lived in rue Caulaincourt, the study of composer Gustave Charpentier, some original Toulouse-Lautrec posters and a homage to the famous local bistro the Lapin Agile (*see chapter* **Nightlife**).

Literary

Maison de Balzac

47 rue Raynouard, 75016 (42.24.56.38).
Métro Passy. **Open** 10am-5.40pm Tue-Sun. Closed **Mon**.
Admission 17.5F adults; 9F students, over-60s; free under-7s. **No credit cards**.
Although Balzac was always moving from house to house, this pretty little house and garden in a quiet corner of Passy managed to keep the writer at home from 1840 to 1847, and in his ground-floor apartment he churned out most of the volumes of *La Comédie Humaine*. It makes a charming one-man museum, providing background colour in the form of portraits of Balzac and his beloved *étrangère* Eva Hanska. There are walking-sticks, engravings, letters, an extensive library, the desk over which he brooded and publications by many of his contemporaries. The highlight of the visit is the trapdoor under which Balzac hid from his creditors; he could also slip out through a corridor to the lane below. The upper floors are used as archive and exhibition spaces.
Library.

Maison de Victor Hugo

Hôtel de Rohan-Guéménée, 6 place des Vosges, 75004 (42.72.10.16). Métro Bastille or St-Paul. **Open** 10am-5.45pm Tue-Sun. Closed **Mon**. **Admission** 17.50F adults; 9F under 25s; free under 18s, over-60s. **No credit cards**.
One of the most Parisian of all the great nineteenth-century novelists, Victor Hugo lived in this seventeenth-century townhouse on the place des Vosges from 1832 until he was forced to flee – first elsewhere in Paris and then to Guernsey – following the 1848 revolution. The luxurious apartment witnessed the writing of part of *Les Misérables*

and a number of poems and plays. When not writing, the author kept himself busy drawing, decorating, carving much of the furniture is his work – and engraving. The interior is much altered, but the collection includes typical period portraits of Hugo and his large family, his own drawings and some of the strange Oriental-influenced furniture he designed himself. One room is devoted to the then new middle-class hobby of photography.

Musée de la Vie Romantique

16 rue Chaptal, 75009 (48.74.95.38). Métro Pigalle.
Open 10am-5.30pm Tue-Sun, Closed **Mon**. **Admission** 17F (27F during exhibitions) adults; 9F (19F during exhibitions) over-60s, students. **No credit cards**.
When artist Ary Scheffer lived in this villa, this area south of Pigalle was known as the New Athens because of the concentration of writers, composers and artists living here. George Sand (1804-76) was a frequent guest at Scheffer's soirées, and the house is now a little museum devoted to the writer, her family and her intellectual circle, which included Chopin, Delacroix and the composer Charpentier. Quietly charming, the museum reveals little of her writing or proto-feminist ideas, nor her affairs with Chopin (represented by a marble bust) and Alfred de Musset; rather it presents a typical bourgeois portrait in the watercolours, lockets and jewels she left behind. In the courtyard is Scheffer's studio.

Music, Cinema & Media

Musée du Cinéma Henri Langlois

Palais de Chaillot, place du Trocadéro, 75116 (45.53.74.39). Métro Trocadéro. **Open** guided tours only 10am, 11am, 2pm, 3pm, 4pm, 5pm Wed-Sun. **Admission** 25F. **No credit cards**.
Cinema really is a religion in Paris, and this museum is testimony to the devotion of its highest priest Henri Langlois, who devoted his life to assembling the truly miraculous collection of the **Cinémathèque**. Rather than just show memorabilia of the stars or clips of favourite movies, the museum concentrates on the technical inventions of the early years. You pass from precursors of the silver screen, such as Chinese silhouettes, through the history of photography to the first animated cartoons, and the development of different cameras. There is a video (in French) about Démeny, who filmed simple movements before the Lumière brothers invented cinema, film posters, photos of early stars such as Lilian Gish and Mary Pickford, costumes and reconstructions of film sets, including one for the Expressionist masterpiece *The Cabinet of Doctor Caligari*. There's also a reconstruction of Meliès' studio. The guided tour includes some film screenings. There are also plans for tours in English on Saturdays and Sundays during the summer months. For the adjoining Cinémathèque and its rich daily programme of screenings, *see chapter* **Film**.

Musée Edith Piaf

5 rue Crespin-du-Gast, 75011 (43.55.52.72).
Métro Ménilmontant. **Open** by appointment only.
Admission voluntary donation. **No credit cards**.
The small private Edith Piaf museum in the working class *faubourg* where she grew up, dedicated to Paris' famous 'little sparrow', who died in 1963. Her clothes, tiny shoes, letters and posters, as well as photos and paintings of the singer are displayed and maintained with Gallic devotion. All the recordings she ever made and a collection of 8,000 photos can be scanned, but the museum is only opened by prior appointment with the devoted curator.

Musée de l'Opéra

1 place de l'Opéra, entrance on rue Auber side of Opéra, 75009 (40.01.24.93). Métro Opéra. **Open** 10am-4.30pm daily. **Admission** 30F adults; 18F students; free under10s. **No credit cards**.

Between gazing at Charles Garnier's extravagant opera house and shopping at the Galeries Lafayette you might want to drop in on this little museum. It's squeezed in next to the huge Opéra library, which contains the scores of all operas and ballets performed at the Opéra, as well as drawings and photos of costumes and sets. At the museum you can see some nineteenth-century scale models of opera sets and other opera-related memorabilia such as Debussy's desk, Nijinsky's sandals, Pavlova's tiara and portraits of other less eminent patrons. *See also chapters* **Sightseeing**, **Dance** *and* **Music: Classical & Opera**.

Musée de Radio-France

116 avenue du Président Kennedy, 75016 (42.30.21.80). Métro Ranelagh/RER Quai Kennedy. **Open** *guided tours only* 10.30am, 11.30am, 2.30pm, 3.30pm, 4.30pm, Mon-Sat. **Admission** 15F adults; 10F students. **No credit cards.**
On the second floor of this building, the giant headquarters of France's national radio stations, is a museum of communications. Starting a fair way back with Roman fire beacons (clumsy but cost-effective), it takes you through Chappe's telegraph, a number of Marconi originals, crystal receivers from the twenties, those imposing thirties art deco radios, early television sets and the latest colour models. *See also chapter* **Music: Classical & Opera**.

Oriental Arts

Institut du Monde Arabe

1 rue des Fossés St-Bernard, 75005 (40.51.39.53). Métro Jussieu. **Open** *museum* 10am-6pm Tue-Sun; *library* 1-8pm Tue-Sat; *temporary exhibitions* 10am-6pm Tue-Sun. Closed **Mon**. **Admission** 25F adults; 20F students, 18-25s, over-60s; free under-18s. **Guided tours** 3pm Tue-Fri; 2pm, 4pm, Sat, Sun; 40F. **Credit** (shop only) AmEx, DC, EC, MC, V.
Opened in 1987, the Institute of the Arab World is yet another Mitterrandian *grand projet*. The permanent collection was put together from various Parisian museums, including the Louvre. It's shown off well by the high-tech setting, and extends from pre-Islamic archaeological finds through ancient pages from the Koran up to contemporary fine and decorative art. There are particularly fine Hispano-Moorish ceramics, Syrian metalware and early scientific instruments. Since it opened, the museum has been struggling to exact payment from the 20 Arab countries that initially pledged funding to the project, but it still manages to put on some impressive temporary exhibitions.
Bookshop. Café-restaurant (noon-3pm, 8pm-midnight Tue-Sat; noon-3pm Sun). Cinema. Lectures. Library. Wheelchair access.

Musée Cernuschi

7 avenue Velasquez, 75008 (45.63.50.75). Métro Villiers or Monceau. **Open** 10am-5.40pm Tue-Sun. Closed **Mon**. **Admission** 17F adults (27F during exhibitions); 9F 18-25s (17F during exhibitions); free under 18s. **No credit cards.**
Often nearly deserted, this collection of Chinese art ranges from neolithic terracottas (from several millenia BC) to Han and Wei dynasty funeral statues – in which Chinese potters displayed their inventiveness to the full by creating entire legions of animated musicians, warriors, dancers, animals and other lifestyle accessories to take to the next world. Other highlights include a T'ang spitting vessel, and a superb stoneware leaf-form pillow from the Sung dynasty. The collection was originally built up at the end of the last century by a private collector, who frantically scoured the East for more pieces. However, it is still being expanded today, and among the recent additions there is some contemporary Chinese painting. It is next to the entrance to the Parc Monceau, and close to the Nissim de Camondo museum (*see above* **Decorative Arts**).

Musée Kwok-On

57 rue du Théâtre, 75015 (45.75.85.75). Métro Emile Zola. **Open** 10am-5.30pm Mon-Fri. **Admission** 15F adults; 10F under-12s, students under 25, over-60s. **No credit cards.**
This fantastically colourful private collection of objects relating to the Asian performing arts was first built up in Hong Kong before being brought to Paris. Since then it has been enlarged by a number of private organisations, and is now arranged according to the origins of the pieces. The Japanese showcase contains some perfectly sculpted heads used for doll theatre, exclusive to Japan, and the elaborate costumes from the Peking Opera are unrivalled in their rich fabrics and complex embroidery. It was formerly in the Marais, and another move is planned, so phone to check before visiting. *Documentation centre. Library. Wheelchair access.*

Musée National Guimet

6 place d'Iéna, 75016 (47.23.61.65). Métro Iéna. **Open** 9.45am-5.45pm Mon, Wed-Sun. **Admission** *permanent collection* 27F adults; 18F students, over-60s, all visitors Sun; free under-18s; *temporary exhibitions* 35F adults; 26f students; free under 18s. **Credit** (shop only) EC, MC, V.
The Guimet has long been one of the great lesser-known treasures of Paris. This national collection of Oriental art contains work from Afghanistan, India, Nepal, Thailand, Cambodia, Vietnam, China, Korea and Japan, all represented by pieces that are stunning both in scale and quality. The most spectacular pieces are from the former French colonies in Indochina, in the shape of Cambodian Khmer sculptures from the civilisation of Angkor Wat, each Buddha's countenance more enigmatic than the next. Also in the museum, however, there are exuberant pieces from Indonesia, ornate statues and a fine series of mandala wall hangings on the life of Buddha from Tibet, and much fine work from India (marble bas-reliefs, stone sculpture, bronzes, and fine gouaches from the Mogul and Rajput periods) as well as wonderful painting, porcelain and other artefacts from China and Japan. However, the Guimet is also another Paris museum for which the hour of renovation has struck: major rebuilding work is due to begin at the end of 1995, and the museum will be closed for a period of about two years, so anyone who wishes to see it should catch it while they can. *Bookshop. Library. Photographic reference section. Wheelchair access.*

Religion

Musée d'Art Juif

42 rue des Saules, 75018 (42.57.84.15). Métro Lamarck-Caulaincourt. **Open** 3-6pm Mon-Thur, Sun. Closed Aug, Jewish holidays. **Admission** 30F adults; 20F students, under-16s. **No credit cards.**
Founded in 1948, this friendly, slightly ramshackle sanctuary of Jewish art and artefacts above a Jewish social centre possesses some rare pieces: a beautiful wooden eighteenth-century tabernacle from Italy, ornamental plaques, incense burners and candlesticks. A collection of model Central European synagogues is another rarity. The art collection contains photos, prints, sculpture and paintings, with works by Chagall, Benn, Mane-Katz and Lipschitz. *Library.*

Musée de la Franc-Maçonnerie

16 rue Cadet, 75009 (45.23.20.92). Métro Cadet. **Open** 2-6pm Mon-Sat. Closed public holidays. **Admission** free.

The natural world has a new showcase at the **Muséum National d'Histoire Naturelle.** *See page 233.*

A hands-on approach at the **Musée des Arts Forains** *fairground museum. See page 233.*

Situated at the back of the Masonic Temple, this museum displays insignia, paintings glorifying the brotherhood, objects used in ceremonies and documents relevant to the Society's past. While trying to fathom what all this esotericism is about, beware the six-fingered handshake.

Science & Technology

Cité des Sciences et de l'Industrie

Parc de la Villette, 30 avenue Corentin-Cariou, 75019 (40.05.12.12/recorded information 36.68.29.30). Métro Porte de la Villette. **Open** 10am-6pm Tue-Sat; 10am-7pm Sun. Closed **Mon**. **Admission** *Cité Pass* (includes Explora aquarium, planetarium, 3-D film) 45F adults; 35F students, schoolchildren; free under-7s; *Cité/Géode Pass* 90F adults; 75F children; not valid weekends or holidays. **Credit** EC, MC, V.

Set within the complex of the **Parc de la Villette** (*see chapter* **Sightseeing**), the Cité des Sciences, an ultra-modern science museum, has been riding high since its opening in 1986 and pulls in over five million visitors a year. The Cité started out as a modern abattoir, a huge poured concrete structure designed to replace the old La Villette stockyards. In mid-construction, the expensive project was wrecked by the realisation that stockyards *intra muros* in Paris were an antiquated concept. To save face, the government decided to transform the structure into a gigantic, state-of-the-art science museum, with a futuristic rooftop lighting system designed to follow the sun across the sky. With clever design, and plenty of money, the Cité's architects and directors managed to pull off the transformation with great bravado, and to watch the youngsters frolicking from one exhibit to another you'd never guess the site's original purpose. **Explora**, the permanent show, occupies the upper three floors, whisking the visitor through 30,000 square metres (323,000sq ft)

of 'space, life, matter and communication', where scale models of satellites including the Ariane space shuttle, planes and robots make the journey an exciting one. There's a special section **La Cité des Enfants** for children under 12, and an impressive array of interactive exhibits on the language and communication floor enable you to learn about sound waves, try out different smells, and see what you'd look like wearing different styles of clothing. The new **Techno-Cité** allows you to get to grips with yet more aspects of modern technology in a user-friendly manner, and there are also displays on climate, ecology and the environment, and health. Other sections feature energy, agriculture, the ocean and volcanoes. The lower floors house temporary exhibitions and a documentation centre. The Louis Lumière cinema shows films in 3-D, and there's a restored submarine moored outside next to the Géode. *See also chapters* **Film** *and* **Children**. *Bookshop. Café. Cinema. Conference centre. Library (multimedia). Wheelchair access & hire.*

Musée Nationale des Techniques

292 rue St-Martin, 75003 (40.27.22.20/recorded information 40.27.23.31). Métro Arts et Métiers. **Open** 10am-5.30pm Tue-Sun. Closed **Mon**. **Admission** free. **No credit cards.**

As we went to press, most of this museum was due to remain closed until 1997, although one room is still open. Occupying the ancient church and abbey of St-Martin-les-Champs, it's a historic science museum with a wealth of objects relating to great inventions from the sixteenth century onwards. They include Foucault's pendulum (Umberto Eco's novel of the same name begins in the chapel where it hangs) and the plane in which Blériot crossed the channel in 1909. When the museum re-opens it will be rearranged into seven sections covering different aspects of science and technology, with visits ending in the twelfth-century chapel. *Library (1-8pm Tue-Sun). Wheelchair access.*

Musée de l'Holographie

Level 1, Forum des Halles, 15-21 Grand Balcon, 75001 (40.39.96.83). Métro Châtelet-Les Halles. **Open** 10am-7pm Mon-Sat; 1-7pm Sun and holidays. **Admission** 32F adults; 27F students, under-18s, over-60s; free under-8s. **Credit** (shop only) AmEx, DC, EC, MC, V.

Located in the depths of the Forum des Halles shopping centre, this small museum colours the air with illusory 3-D images and makes a fun stop for kids. However, lasers and holograms, having appeared on beer-taps, credit cards and in night clubs, have lost much of the exotic appeal they had when the museum opened in 1980. The examples shown here are not over-stimulating, but new developments may perhaps make for more inventive displays in the future.
Shop.

Muséum National d'Histoire Naturelle

57 rue Cuvier, 75005 (40.79.30.00).
Métro Jusssieu/Gare d'Austerlitz. **Open** 10am-6pm Mon, Wed, Fri-Sun; 10am-10pm Thur. Closed **Tue.**
Admission (varies depending on choice of exhibitions) 25F-40F; discounts for under-14s. **No credit cards.**

The *Grande Galerie* of the Muséum National de l'Histoire Naturelle reopened in June 1994 after being closed for over 25 years. The restoration has been a huge success, and the museum hit one million visitors in its first eleven months. Architect Paul Chemetov has successfully integrated modern design into the nineteenth-century glass and iron structure, creating very agreeable surroundings for the displays of skeletons and stuffed animals. As you enter, you will be confronted with the 13.66 metre-long skeleton of a whale: the rest of the ground floor is dedicated to other sea creatures. Don't miss the unpleasant-looking swordfish, or the narwhal with its two metre-long tusk. On the first floor are the big mammals, organised by habitat, with video screens showing species in the wild, and interactive computer screens. Glass-sided lifts take you up through suspended birds to the second floor, which deals with man's impact on nature and considers demographic problems and pollution. The third floor traces the evolution of species. Striking a neat balance between fun and education, the museum is popular with kids, with a 'discovery' room for the under-12s and laboratories for teenagers. Also not to be missed is Louis XVI's rhinoceros. Other sections of the museum on geology and other earth sciences are housed in separate pavilions in the Jardin des Plantes (*see chapter* **Sightseeing**).
Bookshop. Café. Auditorium for film projections and conferences.

Palais de la Découverte

Grand Palais, avenue Franklin D Roosevelt, 75008 (40.74.80.00)/recorded information 43.59.18.21).
Métro Franklin D Roosevelt. **Open** 9.30am-6pm Tue-Sat; 10am-7pm Sun. Closed **Mon** & 1 Jan, 1 May, 14 July, 15 Aug, 23 Dec. **Admission** *Palais* 25F adults; 15F under-18s, over-60s; *with planetarium* 40F adults; 25F under-18s, over-60s. **No credit cards.**

Paris' original science museum, housing works and designs from Leonardo da Vinci's extraordinary inventions onwards. Replicas, models, audio-visual material and real apparatus are used to bring the displays to life. Permanent displays cover man and his biology, light and the thrills of thermodynamism. One of the latest additions is a room dedicated to all you could ever possibly want to know about the sun, including the reassuring information that it has enough energy to shine for a few billion years yet. The panels are all written in French, but it you go behind the model of the sun, there is recorded information in English. There is also a new theatre, where demonstrations of electrostatics are presented at 11am, 1pm, 3pm and 5pm. Members of the audience are electrocised so that their hair stands on end, or so that they can create long sparks. Housed at the back of the Grand Palais, it is far more conveniently located than the Cité des Sciences, if a bit old-fashioned by comparison, and teems

with young children. The Planetarium has shows up to six times a day, depending on the time of year (ring for details) and films are screened in the cinema at 2pm and 4pm. For budding genetic engineers, scientific experiments are conducted at 11am and 3pm.
Bookshop. Cinema. Guided tours.

Eccentricities

Musée de la Contrefaçon

16 rue de la Faisanderie, 75016 (45.01.51.11).
Métro Porte Dauphine. **Open** 2-5pm Mon-Thur; 9.30am-noon Fri. **Admission** 10F. **No credit cards.**

Any designer will tell you that the counterfeit industry is big business these days, and, although the West is hardly in the same league as Taiwan or Hong Kong, an impressive selection of fakes awaits you at Paris' 'museum of forgery'. It shows how this lucrative business dates back to 200 BC – with fake wine from Narbonne – and continues in Portugal with Audak (Kodak) cameras and in Italy with countless handbags (Louis Vuitton is ever-popular). Big-name labels now have enormous 'defence' budgets to try to prevent these ingenious counterfeits, and the museum takes care to underline the penalties awaiting you in case you're tempted.

Musée de la Chasse et de la Nature

Hôtel Guénégaud, 60 rue des Archives, 75003 (42.72.86.43). Métro Hôtel de Ville. **Open** 10am-12.30pm, 1.30-5.30pm, Mon, Wed-Sun. Closed **Tue. Admission** 25F adults; 12.5F students. **No credit cards.**

Devoted to hunting rather than nature, this exceptional collection – exhibited over three floors of a delightfully-proportioned mansion of 1654 by François Mansart, and set against a garden that can, unfortunately, only be admired from inside the museum itself – contains weapons, from ivory cross-bows to ebony halberds and etched silver daggers, hunting trophies and stuffed and mounted beasties from across the continents that mournfully oversee the proceedings. As firearms were a way of displaying wealth and status, many pieces are magnificently decorated with inlay or engraving. To finish off, there's a superb collection of paintings by Cranach, Brueghel, Rubens, Oudry and Chardin and hunting scenes by the eighteenth-century court painter François Desportes.

Musée de la Curiosité

11, rue Saint-Paul, 75004 (42.72.13.26).
Métro Saint-Paul/Sully Morland. **Open** Wed, Sat & Sun 2pm–7pm. **Admission** 45F adults, 30F under-14s. **No credit cards.**

A new museum of magic at the heart of the Marais, with a show of card tricks, a talk (in French) on the history of magic going back to Egyptian times and displays of a whole range of objects such as magic wands, a cabinet for cutting people in half, optical illusions and posters. The welcome is warm and enthusiastic, and you'll be guided through the collection by specialists whose passion for their art is absolutely contagious. They might even teach you a magic trick or two.

Musée des Arts Forains

50, rue de l'Eglise, 75015 (45.58.31.76). Métro Félix Faure or Charles Michel. **Open** Sat & Sun 2pm-7pm. **Admission** 42F adults, 35F over-60s, 25F 3-25s; free under 3s. Family rate 120F (two adults, two children). **Guided tours** 2.30pm, 4pm and 5.30pm. **No credit cards.**

Depending on when you visit this collection of fairground rides and shows, it may either seem like a museum or a kid's birthday party. Occupying a warehouse-like building that used to be part of the Citroën plant, it covers the history of fairgrounds from 1850 to the present day. There are several old roundabouts – some of which are operational – a tincan alley, shooting range, the façade of an old bar and a display of pieces from rides of the past. Children can also be entertained by a magic show, which is given three times a day.

Musée de la Poste

34 boulevard de Vaugirard, 75015 (42.79.23.45).
Métro Montparnasse-Bienvenüe. **Open** 10am-6pm Mon-
Sat. **Admission** 28F adults; 14F 18-25s, over-60s; free
under-18s. **No credit cards.**
Although postage stamps must be among the smallest possible exhibits a walk around this museum is quite an undertak-
ing, as its 15 rooms cover five floors. On display are drawings
by artists such as Miró, Dali and Buffet, examples of different
methods of communication including pigeons and metal balls
floated down the Seine during the Prussian seige in 1870, and
transport, postmen's uniforms, letter-boxes, stamps and their
printing methods, and a miscellaneous collection of related
instruments and tools. Recent developments in technology and
future projects are also covered. At time of writing, the museum
was closed for refurbishment, but it is expected that this will
not be as long-drawn out as in some Paris museums.
Shop.

Musée de la SEITA

12 rue Surcouf, 75007 (45.56.60.17). Métro Invalides or
Latour-Maubourg. **Open** 11am-7pm Mon-Sat.
Admission free. **No credit cards.**
Though this museum smacks of propaganda, in it you'll at
least be able to trace the development of the lowly weed that
came from relative obscurity to becoming a household name
in most hospitals throughout the world at this, the official
museum of the French state-run tobacco company SEITA.
In France, all thanks to Jean Nicot, who in 1561 first introduced it to the country in his diplomatic bag. Smoking paraphernalia from around the world, some with literary
connotations, such as Georges Sand's favourite pipe, or astro-
logical links, such as a model pipe engraved with Zodiac
signs are featured. Since the thirties SEITA has sponsored
artists and designers – including Max Ponty, the creator of
that famous blue silhouette adorning the Gitanes packet –
in an attempt to keep its image clean. It's a small museum
that makes interesting and amusing viewing. Surprisingly,
smoking is forbidden inside. The museum also has an adventurous programme of temporary art exhibitions seemingly
unrelated to smoking, with subjects as varied as Nijinsky,
Otto Dix and Jean-Michel Basquiat.

Musée de la Serrurerie

Musée Bricard, 1 rue de la Perle, 75003
(42.77.79.62). Métro St-Paul. **Open** 2-5pm Mon; 10am-
noon, 2-5pm, Tue-Fri. **Admission** 30F adults; 15F
students, over-60s. **No credit cards.**
Yet another museum housed in an old Marais mansion,
designed by Libéral-Bruant for himself, this one specialises
in locks and keys from Roman times onwards, many of them
notable for their size. Watch out for the lion-mask lock which
bites the hands of unauthorised intruders. It also displays
other objects in wrought iron.

Musée du Vin

5 square Charles Dickens, 75016.
Métro Passy (45.25.63.26). **Open** 2-6pm daily.
Admission 30F. **No credit cards.**
Of the many small specialist museums in Paris, this has to
be one of the most convivial. Housed in medieval cellars, it
has scenes showing the wine-making process, as well as
corkscrews, bottles, and other wine-related objects. End a
visit by sampling a glass or two in the restaurant.

Exhibition Centres

As one of the great art showcases of the world
Paris has a great many exhibition spaces for
temporary shows, run by the state, other public
bodies or private foundations. Temporary exhibitions are also presented at most museums.

Still Life No. 28, *by Tom Wesselmann, as*
seen at the **Fondation Cartier.**

American Center

51 rue de Bercy, 75012 (44.73.77.77). Métro Bercy. **Open**
noon-8pm Wed-Sat; noon–6pm Sun. **Admission** free.
Frank Gehry's new building for the US cultural centre in
Paris, opened in 1994, is perhaps the most spectacular recent
addition to the city's arts scene, with large-scale exhibition
and gallery spaces, an ultra-comfortable, state-of-the-art
cinema and a theatre. The exhibitions presented by the
centre tend to be highly contemporary and innovative, and
feature a catholic mix of US and international artists. The
largest exhibition space is on the fifth floor, and opens up
onto an airy terrace. In the basement, meanwhile, there's an
all-black video space. Another piece of good news is that all
exhibitions at the centre are free. *See also chapter*
Sightseeing.

Bibliothèque Forney

Hôtel de Sens, 1 rue du Figuier, 75004
(42.78.14.60). Métro Pont-Marie. **Open** 1.30-8pm Tue-
Fri; 10am-8.15pm Sat. **Admission** 20F adults; 10F under
12s, students, over-60s. **No credit cards.**
Set in the turrets and Gothic vaulting of this medieval
mansion – the oldest in the Marais – the library specialises
in the applied and graphic arts, and has a wing given over
to temporary displays.

Bibliothèque Nationale

Galerie Mansart, 58 rue de Richelieu, 75002
(47.03.81.26)/Galerie Colbert, 6 rue Vivienne, 75002
(47.03.81.26). Métro Bourse. **Open** 9am-8pm Mon-Fri;
9am-5.30pm Sat. **Admission** *Galerie Mansart and*
Mazarine: both galleries 35F adults; 24F students, over
60s and under 26s; *one gallery* 22F adults; 15F students.
Galerie Colbert free. **No credit cards.**
Even after the 'world's biggest library', the **Bibliothèque de**
France, is opened in south-east Paris, the grand nineteenth-
century edifice of the old Bibliothèque Nationale will continue
to be used for temporary exhibitions. Its Galerie Mansart has
regularly hosted exhibitions that range from Indian miniatures
to contemporary etchings, while the Galerie Colbert, situated
in the library annexe, hosts contemporary photography and
print displays. *See also chapter* **Sightseeing.**

Centre National de la Photographie

Hôtel Salomon de Rothschild, 11 rue Berryer, 75008
(53.76.12.31). Métro Charles de Gaulle-Etoile. **Open**
noon-7pm Mon, Wed-Sun. **Admission** 30F adults; 15F
10-25s, over-60s; free under-10s. **No credit cards.**
Excellent exhibitions covering the work of both contemporary photographers and great photographers of the past are
presented at this official centre. Don McCullin, Sebastião
Salgado and theme shows on Beirut and fashion photography have all been featured. This is a temporary home, but the
centre should be here until 1997 at the earliest.
Shop.

Ecole Nationale des Beaux-Arts

14 rue Bonaparte, 75006 (47.03.50.00).
Métro Saint-Germain-des-Prés. **Open** 1-7pm Mon, Wed-Sun. **Admission** 20F adults; 10F students, over-60s.
Credit (bookshop only) AmEx, EC, MC, V.
The exhibition halls of France's central art college are used regularly for thematic exhibitions which vary considerably in both scale and content. Enormous banners, easily legible from across the Seine, announce forthcoming events. *See also chapter* **Sightseeing**.
Bookstore.

Espace Photographique de Paris

Nouveau Forum des Halles/4, 8 Grande Galerie,
place Carrée, 75001 (40.26.87.12). Métro Châtelet-Les Halles. **Open** 1-6pm Tue-Fri; 1-7pm Sat, Sun.
Admission 10F. **No credit cards.**
This space presents the work of world-famous photographers as well as more obscure French and international names. If it's anyone you haven't heard of, the glass panelling conveniently makes it possible to see what's showing before paying the admission fee.
Wheelchair access.

Fondation Cartier

261, boulevard Raspail, 75014 (42.18.56.72/
42.18.56.51 recorded information). Métro Raspail.
Open noon-8pm Tue, Wed, Fri-Sun; noon-10pm Thur.
Admission 30F/20F students, over-60s, under-25s; free under 10s, unemployed. **Credit** (shop) MC, V.
The building that houses the new Fondation Cartier is as much a work of art as any of the items and artefacts you might see in the exhibitions of contemporary painting, photography, sculpture, video and design that are presented there. Built on the site of the former building of the American Center, now moved on to grander premises elsewhere (*see above*), and opened in May 1994, Jean Nouvel's glass and steel structure is surrounded by a rather desolate-looking garden conceived by Lothar Baumgarten. There are 1,200 square metres of exhibition space on the ground floor, although its total transparency means that artists often seem happier with the white basement space. Theatre, concerts and dance are presented in the *Soirées Nomades* at 8pm every Thursday between September and June.
Bookshop

Grand Palais (Galeries Nationales)

avenue Winston Churchill, avenue du Général Eisenhower, 75008 (44.13.17.17). Métro Champs-Elysées-Clémenceau. **Open** 10am-8pm Mon, Thur-Sun; 10am-10pm Wed. **Admission** 42F adults; 29 students, all visitors Mon; *both exhibitions* 63F adults; 43F students, all visitors Mon. **Credit** (shop) V.
The Grand Palais is a striking leftover from the 1900 Exhibition, and its galleries have long been one of Paris' most prestigious venues for large-scale fairs and exhibitions. They host important historical shows – Géricault, Picasso and Titian are some of the masters to have been featured, as well as grandiose theme exhibitions on the Vikings, or twentieth-century design. The central glass-domed hall of the building is normally used for various salons and fairs, but is currently closed for restoration. (*see also chapters* **Paris by Season** *and* **Sightseeing**).
Café & bookstore in section on avenue Général Eisenhower. Wheelchair access.

Institut Français d'Architecture

6 rue de Tournon, 75006 (46.33.90.36).
Métro Odéon. **Open** (during exhibitions only) 12.30-7pm Tue-Sat. **Admission** free.
A must for anyone with even a fleeting interest in architecture: the exhibitions on individual architects or aspects of the built environment are always imaginatively presented.
Wheelchair access.

Jeu de Paume

place de la Concorde, 75001 (42.60.69.69).
Métro Concorde. **Open** noon-9.30pm Tue, noon-7pm Wed-Fri; 10am-7pm Sat, Sun. **Admission** 35F, 25F students, over-60s. **No credit cards.**
When the Impressionist museum moved from here to the Musée d'Orsay, this former real tennis court – once part of the Tuileries Palace – was redesigned by Antoine Stinco, re-opening as a space for contemporary art exhibitions with an impressive retrospective of Jean Dubuffet. Its record has been mixed, with slightly disappointing shows of new work, but some excellent retrospectives. There's a basement cinema used for artists' film and video series.
Bookshop. Café. Cinema. Wheelchair access.

Pavillon de l'Arsenal

21 boulevard Morland, 75004 (42.76.63.46).
Métro Sully-Morland. **Open** 10.30am-6.30pm Tue-Sat; 11am-7pm Sun. **Admission** free.
This centre presents urban design and architectural projects, in the form of drawings, plans, photographs and models. There's an illuminated 50-square metre (165ft) model of Paris, and a permanent exhibition on the *grands projets*.
Bookshop. Guided tours. Wheelchair access.

Pavillon des Arts

101 rue Rambuteau, 75001 (42.33.82.50).
Métro Châtelet-Les Halles. **Open** 11.30am-6.30pm Tue-Sun. **Admission** 30F adults; 20F students, over-60s; free under-6s. **No credit cards.**
Next to the Forum des Halles, this first-floor gallery hosts four exhibitions a year. They might cover anything from sculpture to photography, with little apparent continuity.
Wheelchair access.

Renn Espace d'Art Contemporain

7 rue de Lille, 75007 (42.76.33.97) Métro Rue du Bac.
Open varies depending on exhibitions. **Admission** varies depending on exhibitions. **No credit cards.**
A well-designed space for exhibitions of modern art, opened in 1991, which has mainly hosted retrospective-style exhibitions, lasting six to nine months, devoted to modern masters such as Yves Klein and Sol LeWitt. It's owned by film director Claude Berri.

Cultural Centres

The national cultural centres listed here also regularly host interesting temporary exhibitions.

Centre Culturel Canadien

5 rue Constantine, 75007 (45.51.35.73). Métro Invalides.
Open 9am-7pm Mon-Sat.

Centre Culturel Calouste Gulbenkian (Portugal)

51 avenue d'Iéna, 75016 (47.20.86.84).
Open 9am-12.30pm, 2-6pm, Mon-Fri.

Centre Culturel Suisse

32 rue des Francs-Bourgeois, 75003 (42.71.44.50).
Métro St-Paul. **Open** 2-7pm Wed-Sun.

Centre Culturel Wallonie-Bruxelles

7 rue de Venise, 75004 (42.71.26.16). Métro Rambuteau.
Open 9.30am-6.30pm Tue-Sun.

Goëthe Institut (Germany)

31 rue de Condé, 75006 (43.26.09.21). Métro Odéon/RER Luxembourg. **Open** noon-8pm Mon-Fri.

Maison de l'Amérique Latine

217 boulevard St-Germain, 75007 (49.54.75.00).
Open 10am-7pm Mon-Fri.

Art Galleries

In smart galleries and warehouse spaces, Paris retains a dynamic and international contemporary art scene.

The Paris art world is still recovering from the shock of a deep recession that saw many galleries go out of business, as private collectors retrenched and public arts budgets were cut. Survivors continue to seek out new artists and develop projects with their established ones, and it's in such galleries that you'll discover adventurous new work before it makes its way into the public exhibition spaces. At the same time, there's also a surprising flourishing of trendy new art and multi-media magazines with titles like *Purple Prose*.

The current trend is towards informal collaborations between groups of young artists, critics and galleries. Work shown in such galleries as **Air de Paris**, **Jennifer Flay**, **Jousse-Seguin** and **Anne de Villepoix** is often seen as neo-conceptualist but, instead of the black and white/image-text orthodoxy of the sixties, their artists often have no definable style. There is a plurality of approaches, stemming from eighties' appropriation and renewed interest in spiritual forefather Duchamp. Many pieces are self-reflectory on art and/or concerned with current issues – in the AIDs

era, mutilation, identity and gender are high on the agenda, clothes and the body common materials.

For new and innovative work head for the northern part of the Marais, along rues Vieille-du-Temple and Debelleyme, where galleries often occupy former industrial spaces hidden at the back of historic courtyards. There are also numerous small galleries around the Bastille, which with the exception of heavyweights **Durand-Dessert** and **Claire Burrus** mainly present young artists. The galleries around St-Germain-des-Prés, home of the avant-garde in the fifties and sixties, now confine themselves to traditional sculpture and painting.

ALTERNATIVE SPACES & OPEN STUDIOS

The circuit of alternative spaces is less developed in Paris than in some cities, but shows do occasionally take place in disused garages, empty blocks of flats, cafés or even private apartments. Curator Hans-Ulrich Obrist recently held a show with works by seventy artists all in a fairly small hotel bedroom.

The Parisian art world's favourite fridge, **Les Frigos**, *threatened by redevelopment.*

Paris may no longer be centre of the art world, but it continues to attract artists of all nationalities, who work here aided by studio projects such as the **Cité Fleurie** on boulevard Aragó in Montparnasse. There are also a number of alternative studio complexes, often originally art squats, which come and go. The best known, the **Hôpital Ephémère**, occupying a vast former hospital in the 18th *arrondissement*, has finally been closed for redevelopment, but a new **Ephémère** is planned elsewhere. A similar complex is **Les Frigos**, at 91 quai de la Gare in the 13th (44.24.96.96), in some magnificent former refrigerated railway warehouses. They too are under threat, due to the development surrounding the new **Bibliothèque Nationale de France**.

There are several chances each year to visit artists' studios. The **Génie de la Bastille** (*see chapter* **Paris by Season**) is the best known, but there are also '*portes ouvertes*' events in Belleville, Ménilmontant, the 18th and 13th *arrondissements* and the suburbs of Montrouge, Montreuil and Ivry-sur-Seine. Dates vary, but they often take place over a weekend at the beginning of October. Check local listings magazines for details.

FIAC & THE SALONS

The annual contemporary art fair in October, the **Foire Internationale de l'Art Contemporain (FIAC)**, provides rich pickings drawn from galleries world-wide. There are also several annual salons, although they no longer have the influence they had in the last century. Among the most important are the **Salon des Indépendants**, the **Salon de Mai** and **Nouvelles Réalités**. Before its sudden closure for essential repairs they and FIAC were held at the **Grand Palais**, but they have temporarily been transferred to a marquee-type space on the quai Branly.

INFORMATION

International art magazines are widely available in Paris. Major local publications include *Beaux Arts*, which tends toward the historical and the main art market, and the bilingual *Art Press*, which covers contemporary art.

Only a selection of the hundreds of galleries in Paris can be listed here. For information on current shows, look for the leaflets *Galeries Mode d'Emploi* (for the Marais/Bastille) and the foldout published by the *Association des Galeries* (Left and Right Bank shows), available at many galleries. Virtually all galleries are closed in August. Ring to check, too, in late July and early September.

Beaubourg & the Marais

Air de Paris

5 bis rue des Haudriettes, 75003 (48.87.45.27). Métro Rambuteau. **Open** 11am-1pm, 2-7pm, Tue-Sat.
Named after Duchamp's famous bottle of air, this tiny gallery

gives a taste of a new generation of artists, among them Philippe Parreno, Pierre Joseph and Liam Gillick, who use varied media to play witty games with the concepts and language behind contemporary art.

Gilbert Brownstone

26 rue St-Gilles, 75003 (42.78.43.21). Métro Chemin-Vert. **Open** 2-7pm Tue-Fri; 11am-1pm, 2-7pm, Sat.
Elegant artists, often with a minimalist aesthetic, including John Armleder, photographer Seton Smith and shopping addict Sylvie Fleury are shown in this glass-roofed warehouse-like space.

Farideh Cadot

77 rue des Archives, 75003 (42.78.08.36). Métro Arts-et-Métiers. **Open** 10am-1pm, 2-7pm, Tue-Fri; 11am-1pm, 2-7pm, Sat.
Farideh Cadot helped pioneer the art scene's shift to the Marais. Among artists shown are Joël Fisher, Daniel Trembley, Marcus Raetz and Connie Beckley.

Chantal Crousel

40 rue Quincampoix, 75004 (42.77.38.87). Métro Rambuteau or Châtelet-les-Halles. **Open** 11am-1pm, 2-7pm, Tue-Sat.
One of the longest-standing Marais galleries, formerly known as the Galerie Crousel-Robelin. It continues to host a cohesive programme of internationally-known artists, including Sigmar Polke, Tony Cragg, Thomas Ruff, Annette Messager and Sophie Calle, reinforced by younger figures such as Marie-Ange Guilleminot, whose installations with little fabric dolls are based on parts of the body.

Jean Fournier

44 rue Quincampoix, 75004 (42.77.32.31). Métro Rambuteau or Châtelet-Les-Halles. **Open** 10am-1pm, 2-7pm, Tue-Sat.
A beautiful, spacious gallery hidden in a courtyard. French seventies' movement *Support-Surface* is well represented, with Claude Viallat and Pierre Buraglio, plus independents like Simon Hantaï and US West Coast abstract painters Sam Francis and Jean Mitchell. Also a well-stocked bookshop.

Froment & Putman

33 rue Charlot, 75003 (42.76.03.50). Métro Filles-du-Calvaire. **Open** 10.30am-1pm, 2-7pm, Tue-Sat.
Froment and Putman's highly individualistic tastes complement each other, resulting in eclectic shows mainly of sculpture and installation. Artists are both French and international, including James Turrell, Fabrice Hybert, Anne-Marie Jugnet and Huang Yong Ping.

Galerie des Archives

4 impasse Beaubourg, 75003 (42.78.05.77). Métro Rambuteau. **Open** 11am-1pm, 2-7pm, Tue-Fri; 2-7pm Sat.
An interesting mix of mainly young artists are shown, including the installations of Thomas Shannon, paintings by Lydia Dona and the photos/videos of Florence Paradeis.

Galerie Jacques Barbier

58 rue de l'Hôtel-de-Ville, 75004 (48.87.56.14). Métro Pont-Marie. **Open** 2-7pm Tue-Sat.
Jacques Barbier shows mainly French artists, often independents such as Jean-Luc Mylayne and Olivier Hucleux, and occasional short shows by new young artists.

Galerie Beaubourg

23 rue du Renard, 75004 (42.71.20.50). Métro Hôtel-de-Ville. **Open** 10.30am-1pm, 2.30-7pm, Tue-Sat.
The Galerie Beaubourg was very active in the eighties, but a new offshoot in a château at St Paul-de-Vence near Nice suggests that the owner's interests have turned more to museum-style presentation in the sunny south. French pop sculptors Arman and César remain the gallery's backbone.

Galerie Jennifer Flay

Ground floor, 7 rue Debelleyme, 75003
(48.87.40.02). Métro St-Sébastien-Froissart. **Open**
10.30am-7pm Tue-Sat.
Private views are always packed out here, as New Zealander
Jennifer Flay has a special talent for picking up on interest-
ing young artists. Among those on her books are Americans
Sean Landers and John Currin, British sculptor Cathy de
Monchaux and up-and-coming French names Xavier
Veilhan, Claude Closky and Dominique Gonzalez-Foerster.

Galerie de France

54 rue de la Verrerie, 75004 (42.74.38.00).
Métro Hôtel-de-Ville. **Open** 10am-7pm Mon-Sat.
An influential gallery which puts on interesting shows cov-
ering all aspects of twentieth-century art. Artists presented
recently include Derain, Matta, Pierre Soulages, Jean-Pierre
Bertrand, Suzanne Laffont and Braco Dimitrijevic.

Galerie Karsten Greve

5 rue Debelleyme, 75003 (42.77.19.37).
Métro St-Sébastien-Froissart. **Open** 10am-1pm, 2.30-7pm,
Tue-Fri; 10am-7pm Sat.
Three floors of an historic Marais building converted into a
gallery by Karsten Greve in 1992, as a Parisian outpost of
his Cologne space. Since then he has held impressive retro-
spectives of major international artists such as Cy Twombly,
Louise Bourgeois, John Chamberlain and Lucio Fontana.

Galerie Ghislaine Hussenot

5 bis rue des Haudriettes, 75003 (48.87.60.81). Métro
Rambuteau. **Open** 11am-7pm Tue-Sat.
Hussenot has a strong stable of high-profile names, usually
well-presented in a two-level warehouse space. You might
find the conceptual date paintings of On Kawara, knitted
toys by Mike Kelley, glossy monochrome panels by Adrian
Scheiss or the cool *simulacra* of Katharina Fritsch.

Galerie du Jour Agnès B

6 rue du Jour, 75001 (42.33.43.40). Métro Châtelet-Les-
Halles. **Open** 10am-7pm Tue-Sat.
A former butcher's shop amid **Agnès B**'s clothing empire
(*see chapter* **Fashion**) houses a choice of artists reflecting
her interests in the Third World, the environment and AIDS
– such as mandala-like watercolours by Indian artist Vyakul
or the neo-Pop of young French painter Aurèle.

Galerie Laage-Salomon

57 rue du Temple, 75004 (42.78.11.71). Métro
Rambuteau. **Open** 2-7pm, Tue-Sat.
This gallery has close links with several German galleries
and represents German neo-Expressionists such as Georg
Baselitz, but has recently made a conscious move towards
including newer trends in painting as well.

Galerie Maeght

12 rue St-Merri, 75004 (42.78.43.44). Métro Hôtel-de-
Ville. **Open** 9am-1pm, 2-7pm, Tue-Sat.
Prints at *42 rue du Bac, 75007 (45.48.45.15). Métro*
Rue du Bac. **Open** 9.30am-1pm, 2-7pm, Tue-Sat.
One of the most famous gallery names in Paris, Maeght
recently moved into a beautiful sixteenth-century Marais
mansion. Still a sure place to find painting and works on
paper by modern masters – Braque, Matisse, Miró,
Giacometti – plus a few contemporary artists such as Tàpies
and the late Gérard Gasiorowski. They also continue the tradition of beautifully-produced artists' books, printed in their
own workshops, and publish their own art monographs.

Galerie Nikki Diana Marquardt

9 place des Vosges, 75004 (42.78.21.00). Métro St-Paul
or Chemin Vert. **Open** 12.30-7pm Tue-Sat.
This surprising former industrial space is reached through
a courtyard from the place des Vosges. As well as projects

with artists such as Dan Flavin, Marquardt also works with
the association *Project for Europe*, which aims to build relationships between artists throughout the wider Europe.

Galerie Gabrielle Maubrie

24 rue Ste-Croix-de-la-Bretonnerie, 75004 (42.78.03.97).
Métro Hôtel-de-Ville. **Open** 2-7pm Tue-Sat.
In a Marais apartment, this gallery shows an international
range of socially or politically committed artists, including
Dennis Adams, Alfredo Jaar and Kryzysztof Wodkiczko.

Galerie Jacqueline Moussion

110 rue Vieille-du-Temple, 75003 (48.87.75.91). Métro
Filles du Calvaire. **Open** 10am-7pm Mon-Sat.
Unusual and varied young French artists feature here, such
as Anne Ferrer, whose satin pigs touch lightly on feminism
and sexuality, and Pierrick Sorin, who plays with both video-
making and autobiography with a rare, melancholy humour.
He's recently won international recognition.

Galerie Natkin-Berta

124 rue Vieille-du-Temple, 75003 (42.74.42.16).
Métro Filles-du-Calvaire. **Open** 2-7pm Mon, Sat; 11am-
7pm Tue-Fri.
A small, corner-shop space founded in 1992 that shows contemporary classics like Sol LeWitt and younger mixed-media
artists Thomas and Michel Delacroix, alongside some brave
if not always wholly successful ventures into the risky area
of new technology/computer art.

Galerie Nathalie Obadia

8 rue de Normandie, 75003 (42.74.67.68). Métro Filles-
du-Calvaire. **Open** 11am-7pm Tue-Sat.
This gallery is very supportive of young artists, such as
French painter Pascal Pinaud, and put on the first Paris show
of new British abstractionist Fiona Rae.

Galerie Roger Pailhas

36 rue Quincampoix, 75004 (48.04.71.31).
Métro Rambuteau or Châtelet-Les Halles. **Open** 11am-
1pm, 2-7pm, Tue-Sat.
An offshoot of a Marseilles gallery known for its influential
work with Dan Graham and Jeff Wall. The smaller Paris
space shows a lot of photo-based work, plus works on architecture and space by artists such as Langlands and Bell.

Galerie Gilles Peyroulet

1st floor, 7 rue Debelleyme, 75003 (42.74.69.20). Métro
St-Sébastien-Froissart. **Open** 11am-7pm Tue-Sat.
Peyroulet's eye generally seems to be stronger for sculptors,
with Canadian Ronald Jones and young German Udo Kochor,
or artists like Marie-Claire Jezequel, where the work borders
on architecture, than for painters. Also some photo-based
artists, including Markus Hansen and Marin Kasimir.

The influential **Galerie de France.**

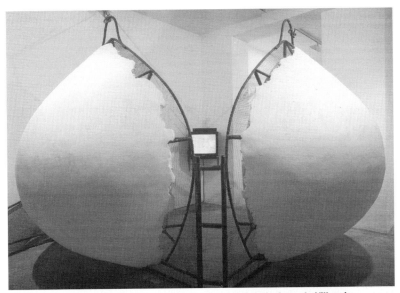

Vito Acconci's Adjustable Wall Bra, *a major success at* **Galerie Anne de Villepoix.**

Galerie Philippe Rizzo

9 rue St-Gilles, 75003 (48.87.12.00). Métro Chemin-Vert.
Open 11am-1pm, 2-7pm, Tue-Fri; 11am-7pm Sat.
Until very recently Bastille-based, Philippe Rizzo presents international artists in all media, and is particularly strong on women artists who have a broadly feminist slant, such as Sue Williams, Sarah Charlesworth, Laurie Simmons and Tania Kovats.

Galerie Thaddaeus Ropac

Ground floor, 7 rue Debelleyme, 75003 (42.72.99.00). Métro St-Sébastien-Froissart. **Open** 10am-7pm Tue-Sat.
A large, two-level space in which Austrian gallerist Ropac presents established international names such as Italian *transavanguardia* painter Sandro Chia, British sculptors Antony Gormley and Anish Kapoor, or American Pop and neo-Pop artists, with a few younger additions such as young photographer Wolfgang Tillmans.

Galerie Samia Saouma

16 rue des Coutures-St-Gervais, 75003 (42.78.40.44). Métro St-Sébastien-Froissart. **Open** 2-7pm Tue-Sat.
A small gallery that often features works on paper by high calibre artists. Recent shows have included Albert Oehlen, Jean-Pierre Bertrand and Robert Gober.

Galerie Toner

33 rue du Faubourg-Poissonnière, 75009 (48.24.22.14). Métro Bonne Nouvelle. **Open** 2-6pm Mon-Fri.
Off the well-worn gallery track, this place specialises in photocopier art. The results are surprisingly varied – often group shows arranged by theme, from voyages to flowers.

Galerie Anne de Villepoix

11 rue de Tournelles, 75004 (42.78.32.24). Métro Bastille. **Open** 11am-7pm Tue-Sat.
Anne de Villepoix usually shows quite difficult work in varied media. She mixes established, older generation figures such as veteran American photographer John Coplans and conceptual artist Vito Acconci (one of whose *Adjustable Wall Bras* virtually filled the gallery in one stunning show) with new wave, younger generation artists such as Beat Streuli and Sylvie Bossu.

Galerie Reno Xippas

108 rue Vieille-du-Temple, 75003 (40.27.05.55). Métro Filles du Calvaire. **Open** 11am-7pm Tue-Sat.
In an unusual U-shaped space that actually runs beneath and around the sides of **Yvon Lambert**, this gallery presents artists as varied as Thomas Demand, Nancy Dwyer, Joan Hernández Pijoan and some names from Xippas' native Greece. A recent group show entitled *Paysages* (Landscapes) showed how contemporary vitality can be injected into a well-worn theme.

Yvon Lambert

108 rue Vieille-du-Temple, 75003 (42.71.09.33). Métro Filles du Calvaire. **Open** 10am-1pm, 2.30-7pm, Tue-Fri; 10am-7pm Sat.
A Paris heavyweight. In a gigantic, warehouse-like space well-suited to large-scale works, Lambert exhibits familiar names from across the Atlantic, including Carl André, Sol LeWitt, Andrés Serrano and Julian Schnabel, major European painters such as Francesco Clemente, Niels Toroni and Miquel Barceló, and some French artists like Philippe 'small is beautiful' Favier.

Le Monde de l'Art

18 rue de Paradis, 75010 (42.46.43.44). Métro Château d'Eau. **Open** 2-7pm Mon; 1-7.30pm Tue-Sat.
Well north of the main gallery concentration, in a wonderful art-nouveau tiled former ceramics factory, this space is very popular with fashion designers for their shows. The gallery opened in 1993 intending to represent 'new countries which have not yet found a place on the map of contemporary art', but has since turned towards a more general, international range of painters.
Branch: 35 rue Guénégaud, 75006 (43.54.22.40).

Claudine Papillon

59 rue de Turenne, 75003 (40.29.98.80).
Métro Chemin Vert. **Open** 2-7pm Tue-Sat.
Claudine Papillon is committed to important contemporary European artists such as Tony Carter, Erik Dietman, Raymond Hains, Michael Craig-Martin, Sigmar Polke, Berndt and Hilda Becker and Dieter Roth.

Emmanuel Perrotin

3rd floor, on left, 26 rue Beaubourg, 75003
(40.27.85.57). Métro Rambuteau. **Open** 2-7pm Tue-Sat.
Perrotin's gallery is in his own flat opposite the **Centre Pompidou**. He puts on a varied selection of young artists, many of whom are exploring portraiture and/or autobiography, including Maurizio Cattelan, Mark Wallinger, Alix Lambert and photographer/videomaker Noritoshi Hirakawa.

Le Sous Sol

12 rue du Petit Musc, 75004 (42.72.46.72).
Métro Sully Morland. **Open** 2.30-7pm Tue-Sat.
A huge basement space opened in 1992, this is one of the newer generation of galleries that aims to shows groups of very young artists who aren't otherwise part of the established gallery circuit, or shows proposed by young curators.

Daniel Templon

30 rue Beaubourg, 75003 (42.72.14.10). Métro
Rambuteau. **Open** 10am-7pm Mon-Sat.
After a brief stay in chic avenue Marceau, Templon returned to his old rue Beaubourg haunt. One of the best-known galleries in Paris, it shows big-name European painters such as German neo-Expressionist Jörg Immendorff and Italian *transavanguardia* artists Paladino and Cucchi. French artists include Jean-Michel Alberola and Vincent Corpet.

Bastille

Claire Burrus

16 rue de Lappe, 75011 (43.55.36.90). Métro Bastille.
Open 2-7pm Tue-Fri; 11am-7pm Sat.
Claire Burrus was one of the first to set up in the Bastille area. Behind the blank-glass window she shows mainly British and North American artists working in a range of media. Negative-space sculptor Rachel Whiteread had her first Paris solo show here; Angela Bulloch, Hirschl Perlman, Charles Ray, Thomas Hüber and Paul Graham all crop up too. Younger French names recently featured are Didier Trenet and Véronique Verstraete.

Durand-Dessert

28 rue de Lappe, 75011 (48.06.92.23).
Métro Bastille. **Open** 11am-1pm, 2-7pm, Tue-Sat.
A powerhouse of the French art scene. Long committed to artists associated with *arte povera*, Kounellis, Pistoletto and Mario Merz, but major French artists such as François Morellet, Gérard Garouste and Bertrand Lavier and German sculptor Ulrich Rückriem are also shown. Newer talents such as Dijon-based Chinese painter Ming occasionally reinforce their stable of big names. There's an excellent art bookshop.

Espace d'Art Yvonamor Palix

13 rue Keller, 75011 (48.06.36.70). Métro Bastille.
Open 2-8pm Tue-Sat.
A Mexican gallerist who moved to Paris from Madrid in 1993. Her slickly presented artists mainly use photography and/or new technology, and include Sandy Skogland, Calum Colvin, Joseph Nevchatel, Maryvonne Arnaud and interesting Spanish artist Paloma Navares, whose photoworks incorporate famous female nudes from art history.

Galerie Lavignes-Bastille

27 rue de Charonne, 75011 (47.00.88.18). Métro Bastille
or Ledru Rollin. **Open** 11am-7pm Tue-Sat.

This three-tiered gallery shows approachable, often flamboyant, figurative work, for a fashionable clientele of private collectors. Among artists represented are Bedri Baykam, Libessart, Calum Fraser, Rosaz and Jean-Claude Maynard.

Galerie Météo

4 rue St-Nicolas, 75012 (43.42.20.20). Métro Ledru-Rollin.
Open 2.30-7.30pm Tue-Fri; 11am-1pm, 2-7.30pm, Sat.
Look for young artists working in new directions, such as the wood and sound installations of Nathalie Elémento and the casual snapshots of Dominique Forest.

Galerie Praz-Delavallade

10 rue St-Sabin, 75011 (43.38.52.60).
Métro Bastille. **Open** 2-7pm Tue-Sat.
Founded at the end of the eighties, this small white space presents young artists of all nationalities.

Galerie Jousse Seguin

34 rue de Charonne, 75011 (47.00.32.35). Métro Bastille
or Ledru-Rollin. **Open** 11am-1.30pm, 2.30-7pm, Mon-Sat.
Committed to progressive new art, this dynamic gallery has hosted a series of wacky group shows, curated by editors and writers of cutting edge art mags *Documents, Bloc Notes* and *Purple Prose*. A hangar-like second space round the corner at 5 rue des Taillandiers is devoted to furniture and ceramics by architects and designers of the thirties to fifties such as Charlotte Perriand and Jean Prouvé.

Champs-Elysées

Artcurial

9 avenue Matignon, 75008 (42.99.16.16). Métro
Franklin D Roosevelt. **Open** 10.30am-7.15pm Tue-Sat.
Fairly traditional modern painting and sculpture, a print gallery, limited edition artist-designed carpets, jewellery, furniture and ceramics, and an excellent art bookshop can all be found here (*see also chapter* **Specialist Shops**).

Louis Carré

10 avenue de Messine, 75008 (45.62.57.07). Métro
Miromesnil. **Open** 10am-12.30pm, 2-6.30pm, Mon-Fri.
A historic venue, now run by the grandson of its founder, focusing on contemporary French artists such as *nouvelle figuration* painter Hervé di Rosa.

Galerie Lelong

13 rue de Téhéran, 75008 (45.63.13.19). Métro
Miromesnil. **Open** 10.30am-6pm Tue-Fri; 2-6.30pm Sat.
First employed by Aimé Maeght (*see above* **Beaubourg & the Marais**), Lelong has been running this gallery since the eighties. It shows major twentieth-century artists such as Alechinsky, Miró, Kounellis, Tàpies, Chillida and Kirkeby.

Galerie Gerald Piltzer

16 avenue Matignon, 75008 (43.59.90.07). Métro
Franklin D Roosevelt. **Open** 10am-7pm Mon-Sat.
Pltzer shows garish examples of very commercial American New Painting, or the strange neo-classical mythologies of Norwegian Odd Nerdrum. Also, occasional historic shows devoted to the Russian avant-garde also feature, including impressive assemblies of works by Chagall and Malevitch.

St-Germain-des-Prés

Berggruen & Cie

70 rue de l'Université, 75007 (42.22.02.12). Métro
Solférino. **Open** 10am-1pm, 2.30-7pm, Tue-Sat.
At the western end of the St-Germain circuit, Berggruen is known for its stock of drawings and prints by modern and Surrealist masters, including Braque, Léger, Picasso, Ernst and Masson, and contemporaries such as Raysse and Polke.

Boulakia et Cie

20 rue Bonaparte, 75006 (43.26.56.79).
Métro Mabillon or St-Germain-des-Prés. **Open** 2.30-7pm
Mon; 10.30am-1pm, 2.30-7pm, Tue-Sat.
Fabien Boulakia shows high-quality twentieth-century paintings, from abstracts by the likes of Serge Poliakoff, Sam Francis and Olivier Debré to Pop Art collages by Tom Wesselman and the Italian *transavanguardia* painters of the eighties. Next door (43.26.56.79), Philippe Boulakia shows young painters such as Côte d'Ivoire-born Outtara.

Jeanne Bucher

53 rue de Seine, 75006 (43.26.22.32). Métro Mabillon
or St-Germain-des-Prés. **Open** 9am-1pm, 2-6.30pm, Tue-Fri; 10am-12.30pm, 2-6.30pm, Sat.
One of the first galleries to set up on the Left Bank, in 1925. It now occupies a lovely, very simple, airy space hidden in a courtyard, and specialises in post-war abstract and *Cobra* painters such as Aguayo, Dubuffet, Bissière, Jorn and De Staël, with a few contemporary artists.

Galerie 1900-2000

8 rue Bonaparte, 75006 (43.25.84.20).
Métro Mabillon or St-Germain-des-Prés. **Open** 10am-12.30pm, 2-7pm, Mon-Sat.
Marcel Fleiss presents an eclectic range of twentieth-century art with a strong predilection for Surrealism, Pop and the *Fluxus* movement. A second space, the former Galerie de Poche at No 3, has now been converted into a suitably lurid shop called **Kitsch** (*see chapter* **Specialist Shops**).

Galerie Claude Bernard

7 rue des Beaux-Arts, 75006 (43.26.97.07). Métro
Mabillon or St-Germain-des-Prés. **Open** 9.30am-12.30pm,
2.30-6.30pm, Tue-Sat.
This large gallery shows mostly realist, figurative paintings from the sixties to the present, by the likes of Peter Blake, David Hockney, Xavier Valls and Balthus.

Galerie Di Meo

9 rue des Beaux-Arts, 75006 (43.54.10.98).
Métro Mabillon or St-Germain-des-Prés. **Open** 10am-1pm, 2.30-7pm, Tue-Sat.
Italian owned, and specialising in Italian abstract artists such as Pizza Cannelli, Nunzio and Luigi Mainolfi.

Galerie Jean-Jacques Dutko

13 rue Bonaparte, 75006 (43.26.96.13).
Métro Mabillon or St-Germain-des-Prés. **Open** 2.30-7pm
Mon; 10.30am-1pm, 2.30-7pm, Tue-Sat.
This gallery combines the preoccupations of St-Germain to effect, with an impressive display of superb quality art deco furniture, African tribal art and abstract paintings.

Galerie Loft

3 bis rue des Beaux-Arts, 75006 (46.33.18.90).
Métro Mabillon or St-Germain-des-Prés. **Open** 10am-1pm, 2.30-7pm, Tue-Sat.
Another space in a courtyard, showing a mixed bag of contemporary artists, from the comic strip paintings of Philippe Druillet to former street artist Jerôme Mesnager, whose trademark footprints lead the visitor up to the first-floor gallery.

Galerie Montenay

31 rue Mazarine, 75006 (43.54.85.30). Métro Odéon.
Open 10am-1pm, 2.30-7pm, Tue-Sat.
This expansive sky-lit gallery, which started life as a garage, is now used for exhibiting a mixed selection of contemporary artists. Malcolm Morley, Keith Sonnier, Erró and Eric Dalbis have all been shown here recently.

Galerie de Paris

6 rue du Pont de Lodi, 75006 (43.25.42.63). Métro
Odéon. **Open** 2.30-7pm Tue-Sat.

An adventurous gallery that shows a range of established and younger artists, including many of the *lettristes*, and continues to plough an independent course in an increasingly staid area, often putting on interesting themed group shows.

Galerie Denise René

196 boulevard St-Germain, 75007 (42.22.77.57).
Métro Rue du Bac. **Open** 11am-1pm, 2-7pm Mon; 10am-1pm, 2-7pm Tue-Sat.
Something of an institution, Denise René has remained firmly committed to kinetic art and geometrical abstraction ever since Tinguely first presented his machines here in the fifties.
Branch: 22 rue Charlot, 75003 (48.87.73.94).

Galerie Darthea Speyer

6 rue Jacques Callot, 75006 (43.54.78.41).
Métro Mabillon or St-Germain-des-Prés. **Open** 2-7pm
Tue-Fri; 11am-7pm Sat.
Often colourful, representational painting and sculpture are the speciality here. It's sometimes fairly kitsch, but at best features the politically-committed expressionism of Leon Golub and the Californian dreams of Ed Paschke, a regular.

Galerie Stadler

51 rue de Seine, 75006 (43.26.91.10).
Métro Mabillon or St-Germain-des-Prés. **Open** 10.30am-12.30pm, 2-7pm, Tue-Sat.
Not the most beautiful (the black walls are a matter of taste), but consistently one of the most interesting galleries in the area. Stadler opened in the fifties in what was then the heart of avant-garde Paris, and in the sixties was one of the first to present the *art corporel* (body art) of Gina Pane, Urs Lüthi, Hermann Nitsch and others. It still does, along with abstract art by painters such as Sigrid Glöerfelt and Arnulf Rainer.

Galerie Vallois

41 rue de Seine, 75006 (43.29.50.84).
Métro Mabillon or St-Germain-des-Prés. **Open** 10.30am-1pm, 2-7pm, Mon-Sat.
With the recent opening of a new gallery for contemporary figurative painting at No. 36, the Vallois domain now extends to three spaces on the rue de Seine. Its core lies in its range of sculpture, from 1920s Cubism onwards, and superb array of art deco furniture by the likes of Ruhlmann, at No. 41. At No. 38 son of the house Georges-Philippe Vallois also concentrates on sculpture, with a more contemporary bent.

Galerie Lara Vincy

47 rue de Seine, 75006 (43.26.72.51).
*Métro Mabillon or St-Germain-des-Prés.***Open** 2.30-7.30pm Mon; 11am-12.30pm, 2.30-7.30pm, Tue-Sat.
Lara Vincy is one of the more eccentric characters of the area and one of the few to retain a sense of the seventies' *Fluxus*-style 'happenings'. She puts on interesting theme shows, such as *Salon de Musique*, which included sound pieces as well as works on paper, and the interventions/performances of Slovak artist Mlynarcik.

Samy Kinge

54 rue de Verneuil, 75007 (42.61.19.07).
Métro Rue du Bac. **Open** 2.30-7pm Tue-Sat.
This small venue in the antiques district is active in promoting European artists working in the Surrealist tradition, such as Victor Braunen, plus some younger names like Greek sculptor Lydia Venieri.

Pièce Unique

4 rue Jacques-Callot, 75006 (43.26.54.58).
Métro Mabillon or St-Germain-des-Prés.
Open 2.30-7pm Tue-Sat.
This Italian-owned gallery invites artists to create one piece which is displayed in the space visible from the street. They often plan the 'show' to coincide with museum shows, and recently have featured Boltanski, Kounellis and Immendorf.

VIA Diffusion

4-8 cour du Commerce St-André, 75006 (44.07.00.36). Métro Odéon. **Open** *9.30am-7pm Mon-Fri; 9.30am-1.30pm, 2-7pm Sat.*

The best place in town for an overview of French contemporary design, promoting furniture and objects by torch-bearers such as Philippe Starck and Jean Nouvel as well as new young designers. Also a branch in the **Viaduc des Arts**, near the Bastille (*see chapter* **Paris by Area**).

Photo Galleries

Photoworks can also be found in many other galleries, and FNAC branches (*see chapter* **Specialist Shops**) mount surprisingly erudite photography shows. The biennial **Mois de la Photo** (due in autumn 1996) sees a vast range of photo exhibitions in different venues across the city.

Galerie Bouqueret + Lebon

69 rue de Turenne, 75003 (40.27.92.21). Métro Chemin Vert. **Open** *2-7pm Tue-Sat.*

An interesting selection of work, from rediscovered avant-garde pioneers, to contemporary photographers like Dörte Eissfeldt and Gerd Bonfert and theme shows.

Michèle Chomette

24 rue Beaubourg, 75003 (42.78.05.62). Métro Rambuteau. **Open** *2-7pm Tue-Sat.*

This second-floor Beaubourg gallery exhibits historical and contemporary photographic work, from Man Ray to Alain Fleischer, Eric Rondepierre, Lewis Baltz and Tromeur.

Galerie Contrejour

96 rue Daguerre, 75014 (43.21.41.88). Métro Gaîté. **Open** *1-7pm Tue-Fri; 2-8pm Sat.*

Outside the gallery circuit, Contrejour specialises in living photographers, mainly French and Italian, selected for their personal vision. The gallery also publishes its own catalogues and books, and has darkroom facilities.

Agathe Gaillard

3 rue du Pont Louis-Philippe, 75004 (42.77.38.24). Métro Pont-Marie. **Open** *1-7pm Tue-Sat.*

Ms Gaillard was one of the first people to open a photography gallery in Paris, specialising in classic masters such as Ralph Gibson, Cartier-Bresson and André Kertesz.

Zabriskie

37 rue Quincampoix, 75004 (42.72.35.47). Métro Rambuteau or Châtelet-Les Halles. **Open** *2-7pm Tue-Fri; 11am-7pm Sat.*

Alongside the classic pioneers of art photography, such as Eugène Atget, Lee Friedlander and Alfred Stieglitz, Zabriskie also features contemporary artists who work with photography such as Joan Fontcuberta and Pascal Kern.

Alternative Spaces

Musée-atelier Adzak

3 rue Jonquoy, 75014 (45.43.06.98). Métro Plaisance. **Open** *by appointment, otherwise depends on show, usually 3-7pm daily.*

The eccentric house and studio built by the late Roy Adzak himself resounds with traces of this conceptual artist's work, notably his plaster body columns and dehydrations. Now a registered charity, it gives (mainly foreign) artists a first chance to exhibit in Paris. An annual print show gathers artists from all five continents.

Confluences

190 boulevard de Charonne, 75020 (40.24.16.34). Métro Philippe-Auguste. **Open** *11am-7pm, Mon-Sat*

A multi-disciplinary space founded in 1975, with a gallery, artists' studios, a theatre/cinema, film editing rooms and bar.

Procréart

Lavoir Moderne Parisien, 35 rue Léon, 75018 (42.52.09.14). Métro Château-Rouge. **Open** *6-8pm daily.*

The former wash rooms of this old laundry now house a theatre, while in the drying spaces there's a gallery and video-making facilities. It's mainly concerned with video art.

Under the Hammer

A spiky aluminium and marble-clad concoction is the unlikely setting for the hub of France's secondary art market. The architects Biro and Fernier, who designed it in the early eighties to replace the crumbling former premises, had wanted to achieve a 'surrealist interpretation of Haussmann'. Inside, shiny escalators whizz you upstairs to a number of small salerooms, where at any one time medieval manuscripts, eighteenth-century furniture, perfume bottles, Japanese netsuke, Old Masters, contemporary paintings and fine wines may be up for sale.

The auction system in France is quite different from those in London or New York. Indeed, although Sotheby's and Christie's both have offices in Paris they are not allowed to hold sales here, due to a law that's been hotly disputed within the supposedly-open European Union.

Most Paris auctions take place at **Drouot**, but are actually held by one of any number of small firms of expert-valuers (*commissaires priseurs*), who have both legal and art expertise. Even if you're not interested in buying, Drouot makes for a great free exhibition, with pieces of all levels of quality often crammed in together. Works usually go on public view the day before auction, or earlier for important sales. Details of auctions here and all over France are published every Friday in *La Gazette de l'Hôtel Drouot* (13F, from newsstands).

Hôtel Drouot

Drouot-Richelieu, 9 rue Drouot, 75009 (48.00.20.20/recorded information 48.00.20.17). Métro Richelieu-Drout. **Open** *11am-6pm Mon-Sat.* **Branches**: *Drouot-Montaigne, 15 avenue Montaigne, 75008 (48.00.20.80);. Drout Nord, 64 rue Doudeauville, 75018 (48.00.20.90).*

Arts & Entertainment

Media

High brow to low brow: French media run from one to the other, with not much in between.

The Press

In France the idea of a national press is not well-established. Only 17 per cent of French people read the Parisian dailies: the most-read French paper is the regional daily, *Ouest-France*. The major papers do not have Sunday editions, but this is balanced by a wide choice of news magazines, which are published on Thursdays.

French newspapers tend to be serious, expensive (6 or 7 francs) and reflect an abiding passion for politics. Formats are pretty stolid, and there is no real equivalent to British or American scandal sheets, thanks to a combination of strict privacy laws and an easy acceptance of extra-marital affairs. There is also little tradition of investigative journalism, and the major revelations of the 1995 presidential campaign – on the finances of Jacques Chirac and Edouard Balladur – appeared in the satirical weekly *Le Canard Enchaîné*.

Newspapers

Le Figaro

A long-established right-wing morning broadsheet (founded 1866), *Le Figaro* remains the choice vehicle for economic news (*Fig-Eco* on pink paper) and property ads. On Fridays, there is a job ads supplement, while on Wednesdays, *Figaroscope* gives weekly listings of Paris arts and entertainment events, plus restaurant reviews. The Saturday edition comes with a women's magazine, *Madame Figaro*, a news magazine, *Figaro Magazine*, and a TV guide.

France Soir

If *Le Figaro* is for educated conservatives, then the Hersant group's other daily *France Soir* is for the rest. It consciously seeks a non-political image, carrying very little hard news and lots of consumer affairs. A broadsheet, its layout is messy, with loads of colour. Much-read by horse racing fans.

L'Humanité

Still sub-titled 'The Organ of the Communist Party', *L'Humanité* has kept going despite the collapse of the Party's colleagues outside France. Publishes *Humanité Dimanche* magazine on Sunday (out on Saturday).

InfoMatin

The new news kid on the block. Launched in January 1994, *InfoMatin* has broken new ground with its small size, all-colour layout and cheap price (3.80F). All the news in brief for those who want to keep informed, but have not got the time to plough through the more hefty papers. Perfect métro reading. No Saturday edition.

Libération

The cult paper of the post-'68 generation, *Libé* has mirrored the evolution of its core readers into today's affluent middle class. It was founded in the early seventies as an extreme-left paper, by a group that included Jean-Paul Sartre and Simone de Beauvoir, at a time when in France this meant the mainstream. More recently, it has been hit by declining circulation and financial problems. In 1994 it changed its format, but sales have continued to fall. The launch of a weekend magazine was also abandoned after only six months. The modified layout is still hard to get around at times, but it's the most wide-ranging paper in its news treatment, with a separate *Métro* section on Paris and the suburbs, and excellent arts coverage.

Le Monde

Paris' most-read newspaper, by far the best written, and also the most influential, because of its status with politicians and top businessmen. Created in 1944 by Resistance leaders and owned by its journalists, it has retained its humanist ideology. Its painstaking thoroughness does not always make for easy reading; articles, complete with footnotes, can run over several days, and though the layout was recently modified, it remains extremely dense. The front page sticks to tradition and is illustrated only by a Plantu cartoon; even inside, there are very few photographs. Out in Paris at around 2pm (with the next day's date).

Le Parisien

The closest that a French daily comes to British tabloid. It has a healthy dose of Parisian news, a strong sports section and even colour photos on the front and back pages.

L'Equipe and Paris-Turf

Two for the sports fan. *L'Equipe* is an excellent, comprehensive sports daily; *Paris-Turf* is the horse-racing paper.

La Tribune Desfossés & Les Echos

Daily financial papers with little general news coverage. *La Tribune* is more left-wing; *Les Echos* more to the right.

Satirical Newspapers

Le Canard Enchaîné, Charlie Hebdo

Despite an old-fashioned look, the venerable *Canard* still regularly carries influential scoops on political, judicial and economic scandals. You're unlikely to understand much if you are not up-to-date with national current events or familiar with French politicians. The acid *Charlie Hebdo* is mainly bought for its cartoons.

Magazines

If the French are not great newspaper consumers, they make up for it with vast numbers of magazines. There is a huge range of women's glossies: French *Elle* appears weekly, and is probably the best fashion magazine. Style magazines for men are harder to find. As befits a country obsessed with the cinema, there is a whole range of cinema mags, from *Cahiers du Cinéma* for serious reviews to *Première* and *Studio* for gossip.

Le Nouvel Observateur, Le Point, L'Express, L'Evénement du Jeudi

France has a strong tradition of heavyweight weekly news magazines, of various political complexions, that come out on Thursdays. *Le Nouvel Observateur* is furthest to the left, although it's rather lost the influence it held in the seventies. *Le Point* and *L'Express* are both centre-right and serious, while *L'Evénement du Jeudi* is more iconoclastic.

Nova Magazine

Linked to Radio Nova, this monthly A to Z of Paris life has swiftly distinguished itself as the trendsetter's bible. It covers the latest places to be seen and the latest things to do: 72 pages, with a guide to upcoming cultural events, for only 5F.

Paris Match

A French institution: no one admits to buying it, but everyone seems to have read it. Lots of photo-stories, syrupy celebrity interviews and gossip, plus the occasional scoop.

Voici

France's only really juicy scandal sheet is a weekly which comes out on Mondays and often sells out the same day. Generally photo-led, it is full of the usual paparazzi photos of celebrity weddings and film openings, and favours catching female stars naked on the beach. Full of scoops, and it was the publication in *Voici* of an article about Richard Gere and Cindy Crawford's marital problems which led to their 'everything's fine-and-dandy, honest' letter in *The Times*.

Listings Magazines

See also **Le Figaro** *and* **Nova** *above.*

L'Officiel des Spectacles

Weekly listings mag with cinema and theatre information.

Pariscope – une semaine à Paris

Wednesday-to-Tuesday listings of all cultural events are found in this pocket-sized weekly, the bible of the Parisian cinema-goer. The eight-page *Time Out Paris* section inside gives you a more critical selection of exhibitions, events and restaurant suggestions – in English.

Every French politician dreams of being quizzed by Anne Sinclair on **TF1**.

Télérama

Out on Wednesday, this surprisingly high-brow TV listings magazine has good arts and entertainment features and excellent reports on international affairs. Its Paris edition has a local listings insert.

Television
French TV

TF1

France's first TV channel to be privatised, and the most successful chain with its largely mass-market programming policies. The 8pm evening news has star anchors Patrick Poivre d'Arvor (PPDA) and Claire Chazal. In the high-profile *Sept sur Sept* on Sunday evenings star interviewer Anne Sinclair grills celebrities, usually politicians, but much of the early evening schedules are taken up with teen sitcoms, with titles like *Les Garçons de la Plage* and *Les Nouvelles Filles d'à Côté*. Broadcasts 24 hours.

France 2

Since the privatisation of TF1, France 2 has been France's leading public service channel, watched by around a quarter of the population. It's funded, like France 3, by a mix of advertising and *la redevance*, the French licence fee. Early evening viewing includes the game show *Que Le Meilleur Gagne*, hosted by the omnipresent Nagui, and Michel Drucker's talk show *Studio Gabriel*. Weightier fare includes *Envoyé Spécial* and *Géopolis*, both internationally-oriented documentary series. The successful late-night cultural chat show *Le Cercle de Minuit*, hosted by Laure Adler and Bernard Pivot's *Bouillon de Culture*, show that an intellectual audience does exist out there somewhere. Also 24-hour.

FR3

France 3 is regarded as the more serious of the two state channels. Its charter as the 'regional' channel ties it to a heavy itinerary of local programming. Late Sunday night *Cinéma de Minuit* offers film classics in their original language. *La Marche du Siècle* debates social issues every Wednesday and the popular *Thalassa* has weekly documentaries about the sea. The sports coverage is strong.

Canal +

A subscription channel – most programmes can only be viewed if you have paid for a special signal *décodeur*. Created in 1983, Canal + had a tough infancy, but a major turning point came with its introduction of late-night porn. Now highly profitable, it's also generally the best channel for recent movie releases, shown in their original language. Canal + is available unscrambled to non-subscribers in the early morning, at lunchtime and in the early evening. Other regulars include the early-evening talk show *Nulle Part Ailleurs* and the satirical puppets *Les Guignols*.

La Cinquième

This channel started broadcasting its daily feast of educational programmes in December 1994. Its mixture of language, science and history programmes are broadcast until 7pm, when the less didactic **Arte** takes over.

Arte

This peculiar Franco-German hybrid began broadcasting on the French airwaves in 1992, after the demise of La Cinq. It offers some excellent programmes, including the lively magazine show *Confettis*, co-hosted by the English Alex Taylor. Its devotion to themed evenings – with subjects as varied as Piaf, Liverpool or gender – can produce fascinating, but also often turgid, viewing. Films are often in VO. The news slot at 8.30pm gives an interesting counterpoint to the French-dominated news on the main channels.

M6

Popular and mass-market, M6 was created in 1987 and is now highly successful. M6's mix features afternoon music videos, broadcast under the title *Boulevard des Clips*, late-night soft porn and lots of ageing British and American shows (dubbed), but there's also some excellent and imaginative series such as the Sunday night *Culture Pub*, a programme all about advertising. Broadcasts 24 hours.

Cable TV

The Paris-Cable Franchise began hooking up Paris homes to its network in the mid-eighties. Most major hotels are already equipped. The basic package (148F per month, plus connection fee) provides 15 channels, including Eurosport (in French) and CNN. BBC Prime, specialised movie channels and several others are also available for an extra charge.

Radio

Deregulation in 1981 saw an explosion of private radio stations, and France now has some of the most crowded FM wavelengths in the world. Despite official proclamations of a 40 per cent quota for French music, most chains remain dominated by Anglo-Saxon current hits and oldies. A recent fad has been the vogue for highly up-front phone-ins on sexual problems, aimed at the teens.

Chante France (90.9 MHz FM): 100% French music, with a French cockerel for a mascot.

Europe 1 (104.7 MHz FM): News bulletins, sports, business, gardening and music. Its news-heavy breakfast time show is less irritating than France Info's.

Europe 2 (103.5 MHz FM): An almost constant programme of easy-listening French and Anglo music.

FIP (90.4 MHz FM): Useful in the car, as it tells you why you're stuck in a 4km traffic jam, interspersed with news of what's on in Paris, and a musical mix of jazz, classical, world and pop. Famous for the voices of its female presenters, nicknamed *'Les FIPettes'*.

France Culture (93.5/93.9 MHz FM): State-owned high-brow culture station: literature, poetry, history, cinema and music. Tough going.

France Infos (105.5 MHz FM): This 24-hour programme of international news, economic updates and sports reports is useful if you want to catch up on the latest headlines, but as everything gets repeated roughly every 15 minutes, it's guaranteed to drive you mad.

France Inter (87.8 MHz FM): State-run, it broadcasts mostly MOR music and international news. Also known for Bernard Lenoir's Black Sessions of indie rock and the wit of Laurent Ruquier on the cultural *Rien à Cirer*.

France Musique (91.7 MHz; 92.1 MHz FM): The national classical music channel offers concerts, live orchestras and top jazz.

Fun Radio (101.9 MHz FM): Popular with teenagers for its sexual problems phone-in with the 'Doc' and 'Difool' every weekday evening (7-10pm).

Radio FG 98.2 (98.2MHz FM): Gay station. Techno music, rave announcements and very explicit lonely hearts.

Radio Latina (99 MHz FM): Great mix of Latin and salsa music.

Radio Nova (101.5 MHz FM): At the forefront of musical style. The talk is very hip and sometimes incomprehensible, especially on *La Grosse Boule*, which is presented by Ariel Wizman and Edouard Baer. *Bon plans* are announced every day between 6–7pm.

RFM (103.9MHz FM): The ultimate in easy listening. Sixties legend Françoise Hardy presents the horoscopes.

Rire et Chansons (97.4 MHz FM): A bizarre feature of the local scene. A non-stop diet of jokes – racist, sexist, crude, and often just plain lousy – interspersed with fairly corny music. Who said the French are always chic?

RTL (104.3 MHz FM): By far the most popular French station. Mix of music and talk programmes. *Grand Jury* on Sunday is a heavyweight debate between journalists and top politicians. Also, classic rock on Saturday nights, country on Sundays.

Skyrock (96MHz FM): Trendy pop station with a phone-in show for teenagers to rival the Doc on **Fun Radio**, presented by former porn star, Tabatha Cash.

English Language Media

The hallowed, Paris-based *International Herald Tribune* is on sale throughout the city. The best places to find other English-language press are the **Virgin Megastore**, **Brentano's** and **WH Smith** (*see chapter* **Specialist Shops**). Major British dailies and *USA Today* are now widely available on the day of issue, especially at larger kiosks in the city centre. English Sunday papers are also increasingly easy to find (at a price).

FUSAC (France-USA Contacts)

3 rue Larochelle, 75014 (45.38.56.57). Métro Gaîté. **Open** 10am-7pm Mon-Fri.
A small-ads free-sheet in English, with flat rentals, job ads and appliances for sale. You can find it at US- and Britisn-oriented enterprises such as bookshops, travel agencies, bars and restaurants.

The Paris Free Voice

A free monthly English-language paper with reasonable arts coverage, available at English-language bookshops.

Time Out Paris

Eight pages of selected movies, exhibitions, events, restaurants and other news about what's on in Paris, reviewed in English and contained in each week's *Pariscope* (*see p246* **Listings Magazines**).

Radio

BBC World Service (648 KHz AM): Continuous English-language broadcasting, with international news, current events, pop, drama. Also on 198KHz LW, from midnight to 5.30am daily. At other times this frequency carries **BBC Radio 4 (198 KHz LW)**: British news and talk directed at the home audience. **BBC Radio 5 Live** (news and sport) can be picked up on **693 KHz AM**.

TV

Canal +, **FR3** and **Arte** are the main local channels that show movies in VO. For news, **Canal +** shows the previous night's *CBS Evening News* every Mon-Fri at 7am, and **La Cinquième** shows undubbed news from Britain and several other countries at 6.30pm, Mon-Fri, in its *Eurojournal* language-learning slot. CNN and several more English-language channels are available on cable.

Dance

The French dance scene has spread around the country, but Paris remains a showcase for classic and contemporary dance.

Carolyn Carlson, a frequent visitor to the **Théâtre de la Ville**.

Dance is one area of French cultural life where official cultural decentralisation policies have worked a dream. There is now a large number of subsidised companies in France, but most are based outside Paris. Thus, innovative choreographer Jean-Claude Gallotta can be found in Grenoble, Roland Petit is in Marseilles, Joëlle Bouvier, Régis Obadia and their company L'Esquisse are at the Centre National de Danse Contemporaine in Angers, and even the outstanding younger choreographers Michel Kelemenis, Josef Nadj and Angelin Preljocaj have of late left the Paris region for residencies in other parts of the country. Even so, while these companies may be based elsewhere, an appearance in the capital is still an essential part of their annual programme.

The **Ballet de l'Opéra National de Paris** remains the focus of the classical ballet world in Paris, whether at the Bastille or the Garnier, but major French and foreign companies also appear at other venues across the city. Big name productions may be put on at the **Palais des Congrès**, or north

of town at **MC93** in Bobigny (*see chapter* **Theatre**), while traditional dance from around the world can be caught at **Centre Mandapa**. The **American Center** (*see chapters* **Sightseeing** *and* **Museums**) also hosts dance performances. Innovative dance companies tend to appear at the **Théâtre de la Ville** and **Théâtre de la Bastille**. Stylistically, the expressionistic work of Pina Bausch, Japanese *butoh* dance and rap-influenced works all continue at the height of fashion in Paris.

Dance Venues

Ballet de l'Opéra National de Paris

Opéra Garnier, place de l'Opéra, 75009 (40.01.17.89/telephone bookings 47.42.53.71). Métro Opéra **Box office** open 14 days in advance: *by telephone* 11.30am-6.30pm Mon-Sat; *in person* 11am-6.30pm Mon-Sat. **Tickets** 30F-370F (reductions for some matinées). *Opéra de Paris Bastille, place de la Bastille, 75012 (telephone bookings 44.73.13.00/recorded information 43.43.96.96). Métro Bastille.* **Box office** 11am-6.30pm Mon-Sat. **Tickets** 60F-570F. **Credit** AmEx, EC, V.
The glittering Palais Garnier, with its sweeping staircase and immense stage, has been used almost exclusively by the Ballet de l'Opéra de Paris since the opening of the Opéra Bastille in 1989, and has also hosted visiting companies. However, the Garnier has recently been closed for restoration, and the ballet company has also had to move into the Bastille. When the Garnier reopens in Spring 1996 it will again become their main house, but it is expected that some large-scale productions will be presented at the Bastille, and similarly that some opera will feature at the Garnier. Current stars in the ballet company include Laurent Hilaire and Fanny Gaïda. Some of the details listed above may change when the Garnier reopens. *See also chapter* **Sightseeing**. *Wheelchair access at Bastille, notify when booking.*

Centre Mandapa

6 rue Wurtz, 75013 (45.89.01.60). Métro Glacière. **Box office** open 30min before performance. **Tickets** 80F; 60F students. **No credit cards.**
Dedicated to traditional dance forms. Companies from India, China, the Middle East, North Africa and Eastern Europe visit regularly. It also houses a school of Indian dance.

Centre Pompidou

19 rue Beaubourg, 75004 (44.78.12.33/box office 44.78.13.15). Métro Rambuteau. **Box office** from noon on day of performance. **Tickets** 70F-90F. **No credit cards.**
The Centre Pompidou was conceived as a true multi-media centre, and the *Grande Salle* in the basement is sometimes used by visiting contemporary dance companies. Maguy Marin visits from Créteil (*see below*). Bookings should be made well in advance, but standbys are available on the day. *See also chapters* **Sightseeing** *and* **Museums**). *Wheelchair access.*

Châtelet – Théâtre Musical de Paris

1 place du Châtelet, 75001 (40.28.28.40).
Métro Châtelet-Les Halles. **Box office** *telephone bookings* 10am-7pm; *in person* 11am-7pm daily. **Tickets** 55F-190F. **Credit** MC, V.
Mainly used for opera and classical concerts, Châtelet sometimes plays host to visiting ballet companies. William Forsythe and Ballet Frankfurt will continue their annual residency here until the end of 1997. *See also chapter* **Music: Classical & Opera**.

Théâtre de la Bastille

76 rue de la Roquette, 75011. (43.57.42.14). Métro Bastille. **Box office** 10am-7pm Mon-Fri; 2.30-7pm Sat. **Tickets** 100F; 70F over-60s, students. **No credit cards**.
A young, adventurous dance programme. Two spaces are used for theatre (autumn) and dance (spring). The theatre makes a point of searching out experimental young choreographers for new productions. *See also chapter* **Theatre**. Wheelchair access.

Théâtre des Champs-Elysées

15 avenue Montaigne, 75008 (49.52.50.00).
Métro Alma Marceau. **Box office** *telephone bookings* 10am-noon, 2-6pm, Mon-Sat; *in person* 11am-7pm Mon-Sat. **Tickets** 40F-500F. **Credit** V.
Mainly a classical music venue, this elegant 1,900-seat theatre attracts a well-heeled crowd for visits by prestige companies like the Royal Ballet and the New York City Ballet. *See also chapter* **Music: Classical & Opera**.

Théâtre de la Ville

2 place du Châtelet, 75004 (42.74.22.77).
Métro Châtelet-Les Halles. **Box office** 11am-6pm Mon; 11am-8pm Tue-Sat; *telephone bookings* 9am-7pm Mon; 9am-8pm Tue-Sat. **Tickets** 80F-190F; 70F-120F under-25s. **Credit** DC, EC, MC, V.
The leading contemporary dance venue. This 1,000-seat modern theatre with a historic façade has excellent sight lines (but poor leg room) and a strong policy of co-productions to aid the creation of challenging new pieces. Claude Brumachon, Mathilde Monnier, Jan Fabre, Pina Bausch, Japanese *butoh* company Sankai Juko and Californian Carolyn Carlson all make regular appearances. *See also chapters* **Music: Classical & Opera, Music: Rock, Roots & Jazz** *and* **Theatre**.

Out of Town

Some venues and events on the outskirts of Paris and easily reachable by public transport should be kept in mind.

Ferme du Buisson

77 allée de la Ferme, 77437 Noisiel (64.62.77.77).
RER line A to Noisiel. **Box office** 2-7pm Tue-Sat. **Tickets** 100F; 70F under-20s, unemployed, students. **Credit** EC, MC, V.
A very pleasant venue, with a restaurant, on the western edge of the Paris suburbs. The highlight of its varied dance programme is the Spring festival *Danses d'Avril*, which presents the most stimulating of the French and European avant garde, with a focus on young choreographers.

Biennale de Danse en Val-de-Marne

Information *(46.86.17.61).* **Open** 9.30am-noon, 2-6pm, Mon-Fri.
The next edition of this festival, which features a great variety of performers and is held in different venues east of Paris, will be in March-April 1997. For most events, shuttle buses run from central Paris. There are also many more performances by national and international companies in this area, dotted throughout the year.

Maison des Arts et de la Culture de Créteil

place Salvador Allende, 94000 Créteil (45.13.19.19).
Métro Créteil-Préfecture. **Open** 10.30am-7pm Mon-Sat. **Tickets** 100F; 70F unemployed; 55F students. **Credit** V.
Choreographer Maguy Marin is based in Créteil, an unprepossessing south-eastern Paris suburb. She shot to international fame with her *Cendrillon*, devised for the Lyon Opera Ballet in 1985. Praised for her daring and dark humour, Marin's performances are well worth the long métro ride, but Parisians are reluctant to make the trek, so her productions are sometimes transferred to a more central venue. This centre now also hosts the annual **Festival Exit** or different performance styles (*see chapter* **Paris by Season**).

Classes & Information

Centre de Danse du Marais

41 rue du Temple, 75004 (42.77.58.19).
Métro Hôtel de Ville. **Open** 9am-9pm Mon-Fri; 9am-8pm Sat; 9am-7pm Sun. **Classes** 80F; 300F for 14 classes, 500F for 18 classes.
Courses at all levels in every conceivable type of dance, from classical ballet and contemporary dance to tap, rock 'n' roll, African, salsa, funk and flamenco, as well as gym, yoga and mime classes. Some teachers are English-speaking. Also classes for children, from about four years old.

Fédération Française de Danse

12 rue St Germain l'Auxerrois, 75001 (42.36.12.61).
Métro Châtelet-Les Halles. **Open** 9am-5pm Mon-Fri.
The federation has information on classes, studio rentals, auditions, festivals and workshops throughout France. It also has a database of dance teachers, both for those looking for work and for schools searching for teachers.

Rock'N Roll Dance Center

6 impasse Lévis, 75017 (43.80.90.23). Métro Villiers.
Open 10am-10.30pm Mon-Fri; 2-6pm Sat. **Classes** 10 lessons for 650F.
Do the jitterbug: classes in jive, samba, tango, waltz, rap and other groovy styles. They also run theme evenings at **Aquaboulevard** and **Gymnase Club d'Italie** (*see chapter* **Sport & Fitness**).

Salle Pleyel

252 rue du Faubourg St-Honoré, 75008 (45.61.53.00).
Métro Ternes. **Open** 9am-6pm Mon-Fri.
Various dance schools and individual teachers give classes at the Salle Pleyel concert hall. Telephone the number above or pick up leaflets at the Salle Pleyel to contact the different organisations. Courses include classical ballet, contemporary, tap and jazz dance for adults and children, at all levels.

Stanlowa

250 rue du Faubourg St-Honoré, 75008 (45.63.20.96).
Métro Ternes. **Open** 10am-7pm Mon-Sat. **Credit** V.
Shoes, practice wear and costumes for all dance disciplines.

Théâtre Contemporain de la Danse (TCD)

9 rue Geoffroy l'Asnier, 75004 (42.74.44.22).
Métro Pont Marie. **Open** 10.30am-6.30pm Mon; 9.30am-6.30pm Tue-Fri.
The TCD promotes contemporary dance in association with venues such as the **Théâtre de la Ville** and the **Théâtre de la Bastille** (*see above*), offering tickets to subscribers for selected events at 240F for three shows (180F, under-20s). Subscribers can also attend meetings with choreographers and free performances given in the centre's own small studio space. Professional dancers who are members have access to courses and a Documentation Centre.

Film

Welcome to movie fan utopia, with every kind of film on view every single week.

Acknowledged world capital of serious cinema, Paris is a seventh heaven for lovers of the Seventh Art. With over 300 films screened each week, there's everything from blockbusters to Buñuel. After years of generous support during the Mitterrand era it also has a state-of-the-art cinema infrastructure. Official patronage looks set to continue under Jacques Chirac, for support for the film industry is accepted on all sides in France. This approach, despite a lot of misses, has produced a fair few hits, and also generates the greatest number of first films by new directors in Europe.

Paris offers an unparalled range of publicly funded venues, which are proliferating all the time. The new national library will house a modern auditorium, and official support is also likely for a new cinema centre at place de Clichy, an initiative planned by Jean-Jacques Beineix to showcase the best of leading edge auteur talent. Another cinema venue recently opened its doors at the new **American Center** (*see chapters* **Sightseeing** *and* **Museums**), offering the latest technology and acoustics, and with ambitious plans for the future. In addition, Parisian audiences enthusiastically support a string of festivals throughout the year, and especially major celebrations have been going on during 1995 to mark the centenary of cinema.

PARISIAN MOVIEGOING

Details of current programmes can be found in *Pariscope* and *l'Officiel des Spectacles*. Programmes change on Wednesdays. Films shown in their original language, with French subtitles, are identified as VO (*version originale*). A good many cinemas specialise in VO, but the largest number still screen *version française* (VF) copies, dubbed into French. A sign of the times are *version anglaise* (VA) films, made by French directors, but in English, such as Luc Besson's *Leon*.

The big boys of commercial movie distribution in France are UGC and Gaumont, both of whom have recently undertaken impressive refurbishment programmes in many of their complexes. To see the latest blockbuster, head for screens marked *Gaumontarama*, *Grande Salle* or *Salle Prestige*, where comfort, a wide screen, Dolby sound and air conditioning come guaranteed with the ticket. Paris also has a wealth of repertory theatres showing movie classics, themed series and non-stop retrospectives, almost invariably in VO.

BARGAIN VIEWING

Tickets usually cost about 45F, but 25F-35F bargains can be had at mid-day performances, and all day on Mondays and/or Wednesdays, at many cinemas. Student discounts (*réduction étudiante/tarif réduit*) are available at early shows at most venues during the week but rarely on Friday nights, at weekends or on public holidays. Tipping is no longer required in first-run cinemas, but you may find art cinema ushers expect a franc or two.

There are also some special dates for bargains. The popular **Fête du Cinéma** in June mobilises thousands in search of multiple cheap admissions. Another fixture of the Parisian year is the **18 heures 18F** week in February, when all screenings nearest 18h (6pm) can be seen for a mere 18F, but again, be prepared for long queues. *See also chapter* **Paris by Season**.

Discount Cards & *Cartes de Fidelité*

The Gaumont and UGC chains both issue discount cards valid at all their cinemas which are a good buy for first-run film-going. The UGC card – valid for 60 days – represents four admissions for one person (130F) or six admissions for one or two people per show (195F). It also lets you jump the queue. The Gaumont card, also for 60 days, gives five entries for 165F, and can be used by more than one person. Also, several independents and mini-chains offer their own *carte de fidelité*, stamped at each show. After a certain number of screenings (from six to ten, according to the cinema) you are entitled to another film free of charge.

Allô Ciné

(40.30.20.10).
A free, 24-hour film information service. A computerised voice (in French only) details films by category or area (including the nearest métro stations and forthcoming programmes in your vicinity).

Cine Showcases

Dôme IMAX

1 place du Dôme, 92095 Paris la Défense. (46.92.45.45). Métro Grande Arche de La Défense, exit H. **Tickets** 55F; 45F unemployed, students.
The Dôme IMAX in La Défense offers a 1,114 square metre OMNIMAX screen, similar to **La Géode**. The ideal locale for experiencing such startling cinema-in-the-round as the 90-minute Rolling Stones show, a regular feature. *Wheelchair access.*

La Géode

26 avenue Corentin Cariou, 75019 (36.68.29.30/same day booking 42.05.50.50). Métro Porte de la Villette. **Tickets** 55F; 40F unemployed, students, disabled.
An OMNIMAX cinema housed in a glorious geodesic dome

in the Villette complex. The 386-seat auditorium is tipped at a 30° angle to the horizon, and the hemispherical screen (1,000square metres, 26m in diameter) wraps around the viewer. Shot in fish-eye perspective, corrected by the curvature of the screen, most films feature dizzying 3-D plunges through dramatic natural scenery. Booking is advisable, through Minitel on 3615 Villette, or at the Virgin Megastore. *Wheelchair access.*

Le Grand Rex
1 boulevard Poissonnière, 75002 (42.36.83.93) Métro Bonne Nouvelle. **Reduced price** Mon; discount card.
Paris lacks many palatial thirties' cinemas, but the Rex, a listed Art Deco monument that doubles as a concert venue, has a grandeur and scale that all other Parisian picture palaces lack. With no fewer than 2,600 seats, it claims to be the biggest first-run movie house in Europe. Films are shown in *version française*.
Wheelchair access.

Gaumont Grand Ecran Italie
30 place d'Italie, 75013 (45.80.77.00/36.65.70.13). Métro Place d'Italie. **Reduced price** Wed; under-12s; Gaumont discount card.
Great for big screen extravaganzas, as it has the largest screen in Europe (24m by 10m). Worth the price of admission alone is the awesome 'Galaxie Gaumont' laser show, featuring top-drawer 3D special effects, as well as movie excerpts floating by on screen in ambient bubbles and THX sound. The two smaller screens are to be avoided.
Wheelchair access.

Gaumont Kinopanorama
60 avenue de la Motte-Picquet, 75015 (43.06.50.50/ 36.68.75.15). Métro La Motte-Picquet Grenelle. **Reduced price** Wed; under-12s; Gaumont discount card.
A splendid 550-seat establishment with a balcony, a huge curved screen (18m by 9m) and six-track Dolby stereo sound.

Max Linder Panorama
24 boulevard Poissonnière, 75009 (48.24.88.88/ 36.68.00.31). Métro Rue Montmartre. **Reduced price** Mon, Wed.
A great state-of-the-art screening facility in a house founded in 1919 by the great comic Max Linder. Ideal vantage points are the first row on the mezzanine, or either balcony.
Wheelchair access.

La Pagode
57 bis rue de Babylone, 75007 (36.68.75.07). Métro St-François-Xavier. **Reduced price** Wed; Gaumont discount card.
An extravagant pagoda built in 1896, with a framework and wooden ornamentation from Japan, while most of the lavish glass and ceramic detailing was created in Paris. A cinema since 1931, and an official historic monument since 1982. The exotic main auditorium is exquisite; the utilitarian small screen is distinguished only by the arthouse films on show. *Salon de thé (4-10pm Mon-Sat; 2-8pm Sun). Wheelchair access to Salle Japonaise.*

The Left Bank Cine Village

The art cinemas crowded in the 5th and 6th *arrondissements* make up a truly unique collection of screens all within walking distance of each other. Quaint, even rundown, they offer the most diverse programming in the world.

Action
Reduced price Mon; 6-7pm Mon-Fri; discount card.
An independent mini-chain founded in 1967 that prides itself

The oriental splendour of **La Pagode**.

on obtaining the negatives of old movies and striking fresh prints. Their showpiece, the Grand Action, is billed as 'the panoramic big screen of the Latin Quarter'. Action excels in showing forties' and fifties' Hollywood, and theme retrospectives. The late summer two-for-the-price-of-one special is one of the best offers in town. *See also* **Other Art Cinemas: Mac Mahon.**
Action Ecoles 23 rue des Ecoles, 75005 (43.25.72.07/36.65.70.64). Métro Maubert-Mutualité.
Action Christine 4 rue Christine 75006 (43.29.11.30, 36.65.70.62). Métro Odéon.
Grand Action 5 rue des Ecoles, 75005 (43.29.44.40/36.65.70.63). Métro Cardinal-Lemoine.
Wheelchair access to at least one screen.

L'Arlequin
76 rue de Rennes, 75006 (45.44.28.80). Métro St-Sulpice. **Reduced price** Mon, Wed.
The most modern left-bank theatre in 1934, the 400-seat Arlequin was owned by Jacques Tati in the fifties, and completely overhauled in 1993. Films run the gamut from reruns of historic French movies to quality *exclusivités*, such as Cannes *Palme d'Or* selections.

Europa Panthéon
13 rue Victor Cousin, 75005 (43.54.15.04). Métro Cluny La Sorbonne/RER Luxembourg. **Reduced price** Mon, Wed.
Founded in 1907 in the Sorbonne gymnasium, this is the oldest movie house in Paris, although the seating has recently been revamped. Screenings range from Rossellini to Russian movies to just-released art films by young French directors.

Quartier Latin
9 rue Champollion, 75005 (43.26.84.65). Métro Cluny La Sorbonne/RER St Michel. **Reduced price** Mon, Wed; noon shows; discount card.
Once a theatre, and retaining some kitsch vestiges of its past, this house is committed to world cinema, such as Chinese, Arab and African films, and festivals on political themes.
Wheelchair access to ground floor.

14 Juillet Parnasse

11 rue Jules Chaplain, 75006 (43.26.58.00/36.68.69.02).
Métro Vavin. **Reduced price** Mon; unemployed,
students, Mon-Thur, Fri up to 7pm.
A cinema with a policy of running films considered 'diffi-
cult', such as Dreyer and Mizoguchi line-ups, or Tom Kalin's
Swoon. Also shows children's programmes at weekends.

St-André-des-Arts

30 rue St-André-des-Arts, 75006 (43.26.48.18) & 12 rue
Gît-le-Coeur, 75006 (43.26.80.25). Métro St-Michel.
Reduced price Mon, Wed; *carte de fidelité.*
A two-screen renowned for its quality programming – Mike
Leigh, Bergman, Kieslowski, classic retrospectives, and a
range of shorts. Wim Wenders had such faith in this cinema
that he would show up without knowing what was playing.
Wheelchair access to salle 2.

Studio Galande

42 rue Galande, 75005 (43.26.94.08/36.65.72.05).
Métro St-Michel. **Reduced price** Wed; *carte de fidelité.*
A hole-in-the-wall institution that holds high the tradition of
The Rocky Horror Picture Show, every Friday and Saturday
at 10.30pm and 12.30am. Cult followers flock in, suitably
dressed (only 2 litres of water and a small bag of rice per per-
son, lighters forbidden). It also regularly shows *A Clockwork*
Orange, amid a wide range of art movies. Only one screen.

Studio des Ursulines

10 rue des Ursulines, 75005 (43.26.19.09/08).
RER Luxembourg. **Reduced price** Mon, Wed; *carte de*
fidelité.
One of the original arthouses, first opened in 1926. It went
on to screen incendiary avant-garde films, but now offers a
repertory programme. The balcony has excellent sightlines.
Wheelchair access.

Les 3 Luxembourg

67 rue Monsieur le Prince, 75006
(46.33.97.77/36.63.93.25). Métro Odéon/RER
Luxembourg. **Reduced price** Mon, Wed; noon shows;
carte de fidelité.
Not too comfortable, but a superb selection of international
movies. Highlights have included Claude Lanzmann's *Shoah,*
tributes to Cassavetes and Godard and a German
Expressionism festival highlighting Marlene Dietrich.

Other Art Cinemas

Auditorium du Louvre

entrance through Pyramid, Cour Napoléon, 75001
(40.20.54.55). Métro Palais Royal. **Tickets** 25F-100F;
15F students.
Like the Louvre pyramid, this 420-seat auditorium was
designed by IM Pei. Film seasons parallel art exhibitions –
past themes have included Frank Lloyd Wright, King Vidor
and Pier Paolo Pasolini. It's also a good venue to see silent
movies with musical accompaniment, as the acoustics are
splendid. The **Musée d'Orsay** also shows films, often musi-
cally-accompanied silents such as Abel Gance's *Napoléon.*
Wheelchair access.

Le Balzac

1 rue Balzac, 75008 (45.61.10.60). Métro George V.
Reduced price Mon, Wed; *carte de fidelité.*
An independent arthouse that scores highly for both design
and programming. It shows French and international films
and documentaries, such as its recent Marcel Pagnol season.

Denfert

24 place Denfert-Rochereau, 75014 (43.21.41.01).
Métro/RER Denfert-Rochereau. **Reduced price** Mon,
Wed; *carte de fidelité.*

The slightly down-at-heel Denfert is a valiant little place with
a hugely eclectic repertory programme, from *Arsenic and*
Old Lace to Eric Rohmer and new animation.
Wheelchair access.

Elysées Lincoln

14 rue Lincoln, 75008 (43.59.36.14/36.68.81.07). Métro
George V. **Reduced price** Mon and up to 6.30pm Tue-
Fri; *carte de fidelité.*
One of a limited number of right-bank arthouse cinemas. It
shows smaller-scale and independent films, and also organ-
ises frequent meet-the-director screenings.

L'Entrepôt

7-9 rue Francis de Pressensé, 75014 (45.43.41.63).
Métro Pernéty. **Reduced price** Mon, Wed; discount
card; *carte de fidelité.*
Based in a former warehouse, L'Entrepôt offers three bare
screening rooms, a cinema bookshop and a restaurant and
bar. Programmes have featured new or Third World directors, shorts, and retrospectives of Stroheim and Lang.
Air-conditioning. Wheelchair access to Salle 1.

Escurial Panorama

11 boulevard du Port-Royal, 75013 (47.07.28.04). Métro
Gobelins. **Reduced price** Mon, Wed; noon shows.
The ultimate in kitsch: red velvet seats in the *Grande Salle,*
and a lobby with brass, neon trim and portraits of the stars.
First-runs are shown, except during the summer season,
when it's revival favourites all the way.
Wheelchair access.

Le Latina

20 rue du Temple, 75004 (42.78.47.86).
Métro Hôtel de Ville. **Reduced price** Mon, Wed; *carte de*
fidelité. Closed Aug.
Le Latina (established 1913) screens films from Spain,
Portugal and Latin America. There are also Latin-themed
dances, a gallery and a Latin American restaurant.

Mac Mahon

5 avenue Mac Mahon, 75017 (43.29.79.89/36.65.70.48).
Métro Charles de Gaulle-Etoile. **Reduced price** 6-7pm
Mon-Fri; discount card. Closed Aug.
A quaint local, part of the **Action** mini-chain (*see above* **The**
Left Bank Cine Village) that screens revivals and clas-
sic American flicks, such as a Howard Hawks season. Old
newsreel footage is often shown instead of pre-film adverts
as part of the programme.

Passage du Nord-Ouest

13 rue du Faubourg Montmartre, 75009 (36.68.03.32).
Métro Rue Montmartre. **Reduced price** unemployed,
students; *carte de fidelité.*
The only café-concert-cinema space in Paris now screens
films more irregularly. There are more concerts than movies,
but it's worth noting for its idiosyncratic style. Watch for
special 80F all-nighters, featuring the likes of 'fantastic'
Italian movies, Japanese erotica and rare restored films. It's
also the only Paris cinema where smoking is allowed. *See*
also chapter **Music: Rock, Roots & Jazz**.

Le Ranelagh

5 rue des Vignes, 75016 (42.88.64.44). Métro La Muette.
Reduced price Wed.
An elegant cinema in the *seizième* that shows classics, and
hosts plays and concerts. A historical monument.
Facilities for people with hearing difficulties. Wheelchair
access.

St Lambert

6 rue Péclet, 75015 (45.32.91.68/48.98.78.87). Métro
Vaugirard. **Reduced price** Wed.
A family-run, deco-style local cinema that shows an enor-

mous range of second-run and revived movies in VO and VF. Morning shows – generally in VF – feature kids' films such as *Tintin* or *Astérix*.

Studio 28

10 rue Tholozé, 75018 (46.06.36.07). Métro Abbesses or Blanche. **Reduced price** discount card. Closed Aug.
Part of the history of avant-garde Paris, the Montmartre movie house where Buñuel premièred *L'Age d'Or* in 1930. It's decorated with souvenirs and posters, and the entrance is embedded with footprints of the great. Family-run, the Studio offers a repertory mix of classics and recent movies.

Museums & Film Theatres

La Cinémathèque Française

Palais de Chaillot, 7 avenue Albert-de-Mun, 75116 (47.04.24.24). Métro Trocadéro. **Admission** 25F; 15F students. Closed Mon.
Founded in 1936 by film fanatics Georges Franju and Henri Langlois, and the model for public film theatres across the world, the Cinémathèque is a magnificent institution that played a seminal role in shaping the New Wave directors at the end of the fifties, and is still today a great meeting point for devoted *cinéphiles*. As well as offering an on-going range of conferences and courses, this bastion of film buffery shows double bills, retrospectives (Chaplin, Borzage) and series (film noir, films on 'Ruins', French *policiers*) and holds theme nights. Until the opening of the Cinémathèque's film reference library and stills collection at nearby Palais de Tokyo, planned for late 1995, Cinémathèque programmes are also shown at the **Reflet République** *18 rue du Faubourg du Temple, 75011 (48.05.51.33). Métro République.*

Musée du Cinéma-Henri Langlois

Palais de Chaillot, 7 avenue Albert-de-Mun, 75116 (45.53.74.39). Métro Trocadéro. **Open** 10am-6pm Wed-Sun. **Admission** 25F; 15F students.
A brilliantly eclectic vision of the evolution of moving images. Langlois (1914-77) initially amassed this peerless display of over 5,000 film-related items from all over the world (costumes, set designs, cameras and props) as an entirely private collection. The museum also regularly hosts temporary exhibitions on special topics.
One-hour tours in English on request, 10am, 11am, 2pm, 3pm, 4pm.

Salle Garance – Centre Pompidou

Centre Pompidou, rue Beaubourg 75004 (42.78.37.29). Métro Châtelet-Les Halles or Rambuteau. **Tickets** 20F. Closed Tue.
The Pompidou Centre's cinema presents comprehensive two-to five- month cycles of films, linked to exhibitions in the Centre, recently-published books, and so on. One of the most complete has been an exhaustive series on Pathé, the first great French film producer, for the 1995 cinema centenary. *Air-conditioning.*

Vidéothèque de Paris

2 Grand Galerie: Porte St-Eustache – Forum des Halles, 75001 (40.26.34.30). Métro Châtelet-Les Halles. **Open** 12.30-8.30pm Tue, Wed, Fri-Sun; 12.30-10pm Thurs. **Admission** 30F per day; membership available.
A public archive which acts as an image-bank of the city. No matter how brief the clip – the Eiffel Tower scene in *Superman II* or the letter of introduction scene in *Babette's Feast* –, if Paris is on film, it's here. A Star Trek-like consultation room has 40 video consoles with Minitel-style keyboards to access computerised data by theme, year or author. This 4,850-film library (calculated at 3,000 watchable hours) accumulates nearly 500 new titles each year. The two auditoria show themed series of films and videos featuring Paris.

Festivals & Special Events

Each year there are any number of movie festivals, large and small, in Paris, such as the open-air **Nuit des Court-Métrages** in August, when short films are screened against the wall of the church of St-Eustache in Les Halles, the women's film festival at Créteil in March (*see chapter* **Women's Paris**) or the discount periods **18 heures 18F** in February and the **Fête du Cinéma** in June (*see chapter* **Paris by Season**). The cinema listings of magazines such as *Pariscope* also include permanent sections on *Festivals*, generally meaning short seasons on themes, directors, countries and so on that are organised independently by different cinemas. Listed here are only some of the regular and easily accessible events.

Cinéma du Réel

Salle Garance, Centre Pompidou, rue Beaubourg 75004 (42.78.37.29). Métro Châtelet-Les Halles or Rambuteau. **Dates** March. **Admission** 27F per film; 60F per day; 250F per week.
Despite its billing as an 'ethnographic and sociological' festival, this international documentary survey is an extraordinary compilation of impressive, fascinating or off-putting films. Screenings are in the **Salle Garance** or smaller *salles*. Directors are usually available for post-film Q&A sessions.

La Nuit des Publivores

Palais des Congrès, 2 place de la Porte Maillot, 75017 (40.68.22.22). Métro Porte Maillot. **Dates** March. **Admission** 180F.
An all-nighter for commercial freaks, featuring a mind-boggling array of more than 500 adverts, brand new and vintage, from across the world. It's held at the 4,000-seat Palais des Congrès, with ice-cream on the house, a mainly-teenage audience and an atmosphere like a pop show. It's often sold out, but postal bookings can be made from December at the Palais des Congrès.

Côté Court

104 avenue Jean Lolive, 93500 Pantin (48.46.95.08). Métro Eglise de Pantin. **Dates** 2nd, 3rd weeks of June. **Admission** 32F per film, 160F per week; 24F, 135F, students.
A major festival of short films, running from 30 seconds to 30 minutes, from serious to comic, and from experimental to golden oldies.

Cinéma en Plein Air

Prairie du Triangle, Parc de la Villette, 75019 (40.03.75.00/30.03.75.00). Métro Porte de Pantin. **Dates** mid-July-mid Aug. **Admission** free; 40F with chair.
Open-air cinema in the park at La Villette, where families picnic while watching epics, musicals and spaghetti westerns. Projection quality and acoustics aren't bad, but not all films are shown in VO.

CinéMémoire

29 rue du Colisée, 75008 (45.63.07.83). **Dates** late Nov-Dec. **Admission** 15F-120F.
This remarkable five-week festival shows rare, restored and recently rediscovered films as they were intended, at the right speed and often with orchestral accompaniment. Almost 150 restored films culled from 20 film archives worldwide are shown in a dozen architecturally stunning locales throughout Paris. Themes are wide-ranging, and the 1995 edition will celebrate the centenary of cinema in special style.

We'll always have Paris...

Only New York rivals Paris as the world's most-filmed city. The Hôtel de Ville gladly accommodates film crews, and Parisians indulge the disruption they cause, which only enhances the chic of their town. Recent Hollywood movies that have set up here include Laurence Kasdan's *French Kiss*, in which Meg Ryan and Kevin Kline clinch in front of Notre-Dame-des-Blancs-Manteaux in the Marais, closely followed by Sydney Pollack directing Harrison Ford and Julia Ormond in a remake of *Sabrina*, using the real city instead of the backlot seen in the original with Audrey Hepburn. Both succumbed to the ultimate cliché – the view of the Eiffel Tower from the Trocadéro. But for every shot of the tower, there is an off-beat Parisian nook immortalised on celluloid that's worth discovering.

Boudu Sauvé des Eaux (Boudu Saved from Drowning, 1932)

French master Jean Renoir made many films in Paris. One of his most striking images was the leap from the **Pont des Arts** by Michel Simon, who as the tramp Boudu goes on to become the houseguest from hell. Another star bridge nearby inspired Léos Carax' 1991 *Les Amants du Pont Neuf,* although most shooting was done on a giant set.

Hôtel du Nord (1938)

Even though most scenes of this hotel by the **Canal St-Martin** were actually shot in a studio it's now a national monument, as was leading lady Arletty in this Marcel Carné film. In front of the hotel by the lock our shrill heroine uttered scathingly those words 'Atmosphere! Atmosphere!'

Charade (1953)

Audrey Hepburn was in her home from home filming in Paris, where she made a number of films including *très-fashion Funny Face*. But one of her most glamorous scenes was in the **Ritz** Bar, for that famous rendezvous with Cary Grant – 'Meet me in the Ritz'.

Gigi (1958)

Another film to keep up the image of Paris was this MGM classic musical. Her quaint courtyard is no longer a thoroughfare, but still visible is the balcony *Chez Gigi* above the gate in **Cour du Commerce-St-André**, in the 6th.

A Bout de Souffle (Breathless, 1959)

Godard's classic tale of girl-meets-vagabond lovingly observed Jean Seberg at work as the cutest Trib vendor on the Champs-Elysées. The offices where she picked up her daily copies have since moved to more prosaic Neuilly, but you can pitch up like Seberg at their former building at **21 rue de Berri**, in the 8th. Otherwise, stand significantly in the middle of **rue Campagne-Première** in Montparnasse to relive a timeless image of Belmondo.

Zazie dans le Métro (1960)

A real Paris imagefest. Louis Malle's third film offers the ultimate New Wave Paris tour in the company of little Zazie. The whole city is featured, but the star of the show is the **Eiffel Tower**, scene of some truly breathtaking images.

Jules et Jim (1961)

Are they coming or going from the wrong side of the tracks? Jeanne Moreau and her two suitors in the most famous still from Truffaut's *nouvelle vague* classic are on the bridge behind **Gare de l'Est** off rue de l'Aqueduc.

What's New Pussycat? (1965)

This fabled Sixties psychedelic cult film was largely set in Paris. Woody Allen in goggles and a three-wheeled car scatters the tables and customers of the famed **Closerie des Lilas** in Montparnasse (*see chapter* **Cafés & Bars**).

Last Tango in Paris (1972)

Bertolucci traversed the city, including the memorable crossing of the **Pont Bir-Hakeim** by métro. Brando heads for a steamy rendezvous with Maria Schneider in a Passy apartment, overlooking the métro station of the same name.

Diva (1981)

The trigger for this operatic drama is the misdirection of a cassette into the pouches of the young postman on his moped. Revisit the bloody scene at the post office at the rear entrance to **Gare St-Lazare**, on rue d'Amsterdam.

Subway (1985)

Enfant terrible Luc Besson's notorious subterranean world of hustlers and hassle, a million miles from the cute postcard world of Paris. Christophe Lambert and Isabelle Adjani most frequently turn up at the RER in La Défense and Les Halles. Hold onto your handbag.

Bitter Moon (1992)

One of Roman Polanski's most personal films, starring his young wife Emmanuelle Seigner. Her fateful meeting with Peter Coyote is aboard the 96 bus between Odéon and the rue de Rennes. Don't forget your ticket.

Three Colours: Blue (1993)

One of the prettiest swimming pools in Paris, the **Piscine de Pontoise** (*see chapter* **Sport & Fitness**) was dressed up for the occasion for the Blue part of Kieslowski's trilogy. You can still see the sellotape marks on the walls.

Jean and Jean-Paul catch their breath.

Music: Classical & Opera

While operatics continue offstage and on at the Opéra Bastille, challenging programming is the keynote elsewhere.

Classical music in Paris continues to enjoy a level of official subsidy that's remarkable in the post-Cold War era. Orchestras, venues, festivals and composers all feed from a deep trough provided by both city and national authorities. The strategy behind this support has been to ensure that Paris retains some of its former prominence in music, the same way that it has in the art market. It will never recapture the glory days of the twenties, when the city was home to *Les Six* and brilliant Russian virtuosi fleeing the revolution, but it's hoped that Paris can at least remain a vibrant international centre for classical music and opera.

The downside of such institutionalised generosity is a level of political interference unthinkable in most music capitals, the most famous example of which is the squabbling that besets the **Opéra Bastille**. Even so, politics can sometimes be made to work for the benefit of the repertoire. Rivalry between a Socialist government and Chirac's city administration played a significant role in helping to produce an opera revival in the early nineties. While Myung-Whun Chung did his best to restore a level of dignity to the Bastille opera, the **Châtelet – Théâtre Musical de Paris** introduced a daring series of modern works culminating in *Wozzeck*, a brilliant production conducted by Daniel Barenboim, the man so unceremoniously sacked from the directorship at the Bastille. The quality at Châtelet continued in 1995, with a fine *Peter Grimes* and a sumptuous production of Purcell's *King Arthur, The English Worthy*. Now that Gaullists are in control in both the city and the state it remains to be seen if this fruitful rivalry will continue.

Apart from the election of a new government and the consequences it may have for funding, the most significant recent changes on the music scene have been the firing of Chung by the Opera's new director, Hugues Gall, who replaced him with James Conlon, and the opening of the **Cité de la Musique**, a prestigious new concert facility that's the final stage in the music complex in the giant La Villette development in north-east Paris (*see chapters* **Sightseeing** *and* **Paris by Area: The Right Bank**).

Young composers, many of them foreign, are still drawn to Paris because of the excellence of its conservatoires and the munificence of public support. As with so much in France, however, work depends on contacts. Composers linked to IRCAM, the contemporary music centre opposite the Centre Pompidou founded by Pierre Boulez, tend to do particularly well in terns of commissions for new compositions. Octogenarian Marcel Landowski is the only composer in town who rivals Boulez for influence, although Henri Dutilleux and Iannis Xenakis are also greatly respected and well-connected. For information on courses and lectures given at IRCAM write to: *1, place Igor Stravinsky, 75004, Paris (44.78.48.17/ fax 44.78.48.23.)*.

BOOKING AHEAD

To find out what's on, turn to *Pariscope* and *L'Officiel des Spectacles*. The monthly *Le Monde de la Musique* and *Diapason* also list classical concerts, and best of all is the free monthly *Cadences*, distributed outside concert halls prior to performances. *The Paris New Music Review*, printed six times a year, features music news and is available at English-language book shops for 12F.

Despite all the funding, tickets are still not always easily affordable. Also, many venues have large numbers of subscribers who have first preference for tickets, so that seats can be difficult to come by at the last moment. Most venues offer special cut-rate tickets to students (aged under 26) an hour before the performance, subject to availability. Other than concert series in churches, few concerts are held in late July or August. One good time to hear music in Paris, though, is in January, when during two-weeks every concert ticket bought will get you a second one free, a gift from the City of Paris (*see chapter* **Paris by Season**). For ticket agencies, *see chapters* **Services** *and* **Theatre**.

Jeunesses Musicales de France

20 rue Geoffroy L'Asnier, 75004 (44.61.86.86). Métro Pont Marie or St-Paul. **Open** 10am-7pm Mon-Fri. **Membership** 150F over-30s; 100F 18-30s; 20F under-18s. Membership gives the equivalent of student discounts at various theatres, and the organisation has a reciprocal arrangement with its British equivalent, 'Youth and Music' at 28 Charing Cross Road, London, WC2H 0DB (0171 379 6722).

Orchestras & Ensembles

As well as the main ensembles listed below, others to look out for in Paris include William Christie's magnificent **Les Arts Florissants**, almost always to be found at the Châtelet – Théâtre Musical de Paris, and the **Ensemble 2E2M** chamber orchestra, specialising in modern music. London's **Philharmonia Orchestra** takes up a short residence at the Châtelet every year. On a much smaller scale, a group of young professionals called the **Péniche Opéra** (42.45.18.20) perform regularly on a barge on the river, at 200 quai de Jemmapes. Two subscription orchestras, the **Orchestre Pasdeloup** (45.61.53.00) and the **Orchestre des Concerts Lamoureux** (45.63.60.62) offer concerts of a nineteenth-century repertoire. They're made up mostly of students, retired musicians and amateurs, and it's sometimes hard to justify paying the prices they ask.

Ensemble InterContemporain
Based at the Cité de la Musique.
This world famous outfit begun by Pierre Boulez and now directed by American David Robertson is dedicated entirely to modern and contemporary music. No longer as controversial as it used to be: it has found its audience, and preaches mainly to the converted.

Ensemble Orchestral de Paris
Based at the Salle Pleyel.
New music director Jean-Jacques Kantorow has introduced a more adventurous repertoire for this chamber orchestra with essays into the works of twentieth-century composers such as Kordaly, von Dohnanyi, Ives, Landowski and Copland, alongside more traditional works.

At the **Cité de la Musique**. *See page 256.*

Orchestre Colonne
Based at the Salle Pleyel.
Once a force to be reckoned with, the Orchestre Colonne is now a shadow of its former self, offering only a handful of performances each season, and without the star soloists it used to attract even a decade ago. To compensate, its repertoire, although still firmly rooted in the nineteenth century, does sometimes stretch to include lesser-known works.

Orchestre National de France
Based at the Maison de Radio France *and* Théâtre des Champs-Elysées
Perhaps because the claim that Montreal possessed the finest French-speaking orchestra in the world struck a nerve, Radio France appointed its chief, Charles Dutoit, as director of the Orchestre National de France in 1991. He arrived at a time of low morale, replacing a too-often absent Lorin Maazel. Today the orchestra is a more unified outfit, with specific themes such as Slavic Music helping to hone its direction. Opera now plays a more important role, thanks in large part to principal guest conductor Jeffrey Tate. Regular guest soloists include Gideon Kremer and Yo Yo Ma; regular guest conductors include Leonard Slatkin and Evgeni Svetlanov.

Orchestre de Paris
Based at the Salle Pleyel *and* Châtelet – Théâtre Musical de Paris
Generally considered France's leading orchestra, it has had trouble maintaining its audience since the departure of Daniel Barenboim in 1989 and sadly no longer features the astonishing number of brilliant soloists he used to attract. New director Semyon Bychkov has chosen to concentrate on a Russian and French repertoire, trying to restore the traditional French orchestral sound. He has been able to maintain the orchestra's old links to Solti, Giulini, Sanderling, Von Dohnanyi and Georges Pretre, but one wonders who will replace these maestros in the years to come.

Orchestre Philharmonique
Based at the Maison de Radio France *and* Salle Pleyel.
Its many devotees maintain that the Orchestre Philharmonique is the finest in the land. Certainly its long-serving musical director Marek Janowski continues to push it into demanding territory, whether it's a complete cycle of The Ring or rediscoveries of neglected French music.

Orchestre Symphonique Français
Based at the Salle Pleyel.
The average age in this independent orchestra is 29, and their youth is reflected in a programming policy that highlights contemporary works alongside nineteenth century classics. The pricing policy is exemplary: 50F-80F per concert.

Concert Halls

Châtelet – Théâtre Musical de Paris
1 place du Châtelet, 75001 (40.28.28.40/ recorded information 42.33.00.00). Métro Châtelet-Les Halles. **Open** *box office* 11am-7pm daily; *telephone bookings* 10am-7pm Mon-Sat. **Tickets** phone for details. **Credit** AmEx, MC, V.
This nineteenth-century theatre has a refined, slightly worn interior with cramped seating, and poor sight lines on the sides. The repertoire is slanted towards the last century and neglected older works, but its ever-expanding opera programming has been consistently more adventurous than the Opéra Bastille's, winning it an extremely loyal audience. This makes it difficult to get seats. Abbado, Barenboim, Boulez, Chailly, Christie and Rattle are some of the conductors who have appeared there in recent seasons. It also hosts ballet performances (*see chapter* **Dance**). *Wheelchair access.*

Cité de la Musique

221 avenue Jean-Jaurès, 75019 (44.84.45.45/24-hour recorded information 44.84.45.00/reservations 44.84.44.84). Métro Porte de Pantin. **Open** *box office noon-6pm Wed-Sun; noon-8pm, performance days. telephone bookings noon-6pm Mon, Sun; noon-8pm Tue-Sat.* **Tickets** 60F-160F; *reduced price over-60s, unemployed.* **Credit** (in person only) MC, V.

The verdict is still out on this new performance space as far as the acoustics are concerned. Visually and technically it's an impressive venue – the seats can be easily separated and re-arranged, to create varying performance spaces. The emphasis is on the contemporary repertoire, although baroque and ethnic music have also been highlighted, and special programmes are devised for the young. Featured composers have included Steve Reich and the ubiquitous Pierre Boulez. It's possible to attend rehearsals for free; reservations can be made up to three weeks in advance. There is also a music museum, with another small concert space. *Wheelchair access.*

Maison de Radio France

116 avenue du Président Kennedy, 75016 (42.30.22.22/42.30.15.16 concert information/42.30.33.83 guided tours). Métro Ranelagh or Passy/RER Kennedy Radio France. **Open** *guided tours 10.30am, 11.30am, 2.30pm, 3.30pm, 4.30pm, Mon-Sat; box office 11am-6pm daily.* **Tickets** *concerts phone for details; guided tour 15F.* **Credit** (in person only) MC, V.

Within the largest broadcasting complex on earth, Radio France sponsors a daring range of concerts, often connected to specific themes. It's worth writing in advance to ask for the programme guide, especially as quite a few events are free. The **Salle Olivier Messiaen** is the main venue for larger concerts. Radio France is generous to young musicians, and admirably open towards foreign performers.

Opéra Comique/Salle Favart

5 rue Favart, 75009 (42.96.12.20). Métro Richelieu Drouot. **Open** *box office 11am-7pm Mon-Sat; telephone bookings (42.86.88.83) 11am-1pm, 2-6pm, Mon-Fri.* **Tickets** 50F-490F. **Credit** EC, MC, V.

The list of French operas that have had their premières in this charming, jewel box-sized theatre is impressive. *Carmen* was first performed here, as were *The Damnation of Faust*, *The Tales of Hoffmann*, *Pelléas et Mélisande*, Delibes' *Lakmé*, Massenet's *Manon*, Ravel's *L'Heure Espagnole* and dozens more. The building is a relic from a previous age; the light opera season (usually performed in French), and occasional concerts respect the history of the place. *Wheelchair access.*

Opéra National de Paris Bastille

place de la Bastille, 75012 (44.73.13.00/recorded information 43.43.96.96). Métro Bastille. **Open** *box office 11am-6pm Mon-Sat.* **Tickets** 60F-570F. **Credit** AmEx, EC, MC, V.

If ever a big idea has gone adrift, it's the Opéra Bastille. It was originally conceived by President Mitterrand as a venue where ordinary people could afford to go to the opera, but today it is extremely difficult, and expensive, to get tickets (although some unsold tickets are put on sale, to personal callers only, two weeks before the date of performance). Worse still, the many resignations and firings which have taken place here have made it Paris' favourite object of derision. New director-Czar Hugues Gall ruffled feathers with the abrupt way he dismissed popular music director Myung-Whun Chung, but he may be the man to make the place work: he's actually had the courage to propose moving many of the smaller opera productions back to the Palais Garnier, keeping the Bastille for ballet and large-scale productions, which makes a lot of sense. While the Bastille's acoustics are a great disappointment, the interior is large, the seating comfortable and the sightlines excellent throughout. *Wheelchair access.*

Opéra National de Paris Garnier

place de l'Opéra, 75009 (47.42.53.71). Métro Opéra. **Open** *box office 11am-6.30pm Mon-Sat; telephone bookings 11.30am-6.30pm Mon-Sat. Tickets 30F-370F.* **Credit** AmEx, MC, V.

With its perfect accoustics, huge stage area and gorgeous interior the decison to ban opera from this Second-Empire venue was always inexplicable. Closed since the summer of 1994, the most famous theatre in Paris reopens to the public on 1 March 1996 with a production of *Don Giovanni*, ironically the opera which was originally slated to open the Opéra Bastille before heads began to roll. Hopefully the revovations will have improved the cramped seating. It is expected that the Palais Garnier will again become the city's primary venue for opera by the 1996-97 season. Some of the details listed here may change when the theatre reopens.

Salle Gaveau

45 rue La Boétie, 75008 (49.53.05.07). Métro Miromesnil. **Open** *box office 11am-6pm Mon-Fri; 11am-4pm Sat; Sun when concerts on.* **Tickets** *phone for details.* **Credit** AmEx, MC, V.

This well-known concert hall named after the famous French pianomakers has a charming, old-world atmosphere, reflected in its choice of programming. As you'd expect, there's a strong emphasis on piano recitals, with Chopin, Liszt, Débussy and Fauré frequently represented. While the pianists are sometimes as famous as Marta Argerich, they more often tend to be bright young prizewinners or unknown musicians from the former Eastern block. Chamber music is regularly featured, with mainly duos and quartets. The other great focus of the hall is vocal recitals, featuring such figures as Gwyneth Jones, Katia Ricciarelli, Maria Ewing, Ruggiero Raimondi, Renata Scotto and Montserrat Caballé. *Wheelchair access.*

Salle Pleyel

252 rue du Faubourg St-Honoré, 75008 (45.61.53.00). Métro Ternes. **Open** *box office 11am-6pm Mon-Sat.* **Tickets** 75F-360F. **Credit** MC, V.

This concert hall, which is home to several orchestras including the **Orchestre de Paris**, has absolutely nothing to do with the famous venue of the same name where Chopin played his last recital. Completely redesigned nearly 15 years ago, it is a high-ceilinged, rather chilly space, and while the acoustics aren't nearly as bad as you'd expect for big orchestral sound, they're less forgiving for recitals, which is unfortunate since it hosts an excellent piano subscription series, featuring giants such as Pollini, Perahia and Brendel. Far better to hear the many regular star soloists, such as Radu Lupu and Anne-Sophie Mutter, who perform alongside the Orchestre de Paris. The audience tends to be the most bourgeois of all the major concert halls, and is not afraid to show its indifference to newly-commissioned works by yawning and coughing loudly. *Wheelchair access*

Théâtre des Champs-Elysées

15 avenue Montaigne, 75008 (49.52.50.00/recorded information 49.52.50.51/telephone booking 49.52.50.50). Métro Alma Marceau. **Open** *box office 11am-7pm Mon-Sat; telephone booking 10am-noon, 2-6pm, Mon-Fri.* **Tickets** 40F-750F; *cheaper matinée 3pm or 5pm Sun.* **Credit** AmEx, DC, EC, MC, V.

This beautiful theatre, with its exterior bas-reliefs by Bourdelle, has won a place in the history of modernism as the site of the première of Stravinsky's *Le Sacre du Printemps* on 29 May, 1913, and the subsequent riot. The interior is well preserved, with the famous ceiling by Maurice Denis dominating the auditorium, but the seating is cramped in the upper levels and many seats on the sides have restricted visibility. The audiences are the best dressed in town. The home of the **Orchestre National de France**, it presents a popular series of chamber concerts on Sundays.

Some people take to the **Opéra Bastille.**

Théâtre de la Ville

2 place du Châtelet, 75004 (42.74.22.77). Métro Châtelet-Les Halles. **Open** *box office and telephone booking* 11am-6pm Mon; 9am-8pm Tue-Sat. **Tickets** 80F. **Credit** (above 100F) MC, V.

A huge concrete amphitheatre, far too steeply inclined for comfort, has been placed inside the stately shell of this theatre opposite the Châtelet – Théâtre Musical de Paris. Mainly used for contemporary dance, it also offers bi-monthly concerts featuring ethnic music and avant-garde classical music. *See also chapter* **Dance.**
Wheelchair access.

Museums

Paris' museums make charming places to attend an intimate concert. *See also chapter* **Museums.**

Musée de Cluny
(Musée National du Moyen Age)

6 place Paul-Painlevé, 75005 (43.25.62.00). Métro Cluny-La Sorbonne. **Concert times** 12.30pm Fri; 4pm, 6.30pm or 8.30pm Sat; 6.30pm or 8.30pm Sun. **Tickets** 25F, plus entrance to museum (27F adults, 18F concessions).

Musée du Louvre

cour Napoléon, 75001 (40.20.50.50/auditorium 40.20.59.29). Métro Palais-Royal. **Open** *box office* 9.30am-7.30pm Mon-Sat. **Tickets** 25F-130F.
Wheelchair access.

Musée d'Orsay

1 rue de Bellechasse, 75007 (40.49.49.92). RER Musée D'Orsay/Métro Solférino. **Open** *box office opens 30 mins before each concert.* **Concert times/rates** 12.30pm (60F), 6.45pm (60F), 8pm (130F, 100F students). **Tickets** 90F-130F.

Churches

The absence of good halls in Paris in the past meant that churches were regularly used as a substitute. It can be difficult to find out when church concerts are planned, but *L'Officiel des Spectacles*

or *Pariscope* will let you know what's on in the immediate days ahead. Predictably enough, organ recitals are frequent fare, but choral and chamber-symphonic concerts and even gospel are not unusual. At the Sunday-evening recitals in Notre-Dame and St-Eustache some spectacular sounds are produced on their mighty instruments, and St-Eustache also has a summer festival of organ recitals on alternate Thursday evenings. The Madeleine is a popular venue for choral concerts. **Concerts Boeringer** *21 rue Messageries, 75010 (48.01.91.35)* and **Concertsolo** *(44.62.70.87)* are two agencies that both regularly organise church concerts. If you have difficulty reaching a church by phone, call the tourist office (*see chapter* **Essential Information**) for programme information. Tickets generally cost 80F-180F.

Cathédrale Notre-Dame de Paris

place du Parvis-Notre-Dame, 75004 (42.34.56.10). Métro Cité or St-Michel.

Eglise de la Madeleine

place de la Madeleine, 75009 (42.65.52.17). Métro Madeleine.

Eglise St-Eustache

2 impasse St-Eustache, 75001 (42.36.31.05). Métro Châtelet-Les Halles.

Eglise St-Germain-des-Prés

3 place St-Germain-des-Prés, 75006 (43.25.41.71). Métro St-Germain-des-Prés.

Eglise St-Julien-le-Pauvre

1 rue St-Julien-le-Pauvre, 75005 (43.54.52.16). Métro Cluny-La Sorbonne or St-Michel.

Eglise St-Louis-en-l'Ile

19 rue St-Louis-en-l'Ile, 75004 (46.34.11.60). Métro Pont-Marie.

Eglise St-Séverin

1 rue des Prêtres St-Séverin, 75005 (43.25.96.63). Métro Cluny-La Sorbonne or St-Michel.

Eglise de la Trinité

place Estienne d'Orves, 75009 (48.74.12.77). Métro Trinité.

Sainte-Chapelle

4 boulevard du Palais, 75001 (43.54.30.09). Métro Cité.

Festivals

For the **Festival Chopin à Paris** and **Fête de la Musique**, *see chapter* **Paris By Season.**

Festival St-Denis

(48.13.06.07). **Dates** June-early July.
A large-scale celebration of classical music, this festival draws top flight musicians who perform in several locations ,including St-Denis's famous Gothic basilica (*see chapter* **Sightseeing**).

Festival d'Art Sacré

(48.74.12.77). **Dates** Mar-April, Oct-Dec.
Mostly held in churches, these festivals celebrate religious music in the periods leading up to Christmas and Easter.

Music: Rock, Roots & Jazz

Is Paris hip? Does Johnny Halliday wear tight trousers?

For years, French officialdom has tried to control the music scene in Paris. Events such as the June **Fête de la Musique** and some facilities and venues receive lavish subsidies, but are subject to bureaucratic controls that do nothing for spontaneity, while other venues are harrassed through anti-noise laws and restrictive licensing. Recently, however, two grass roots movements have emerged to buck this trend: the rise of independent musical life in the Pigalle area, and the growth of live music in cafés.

Up until the end of World War II, Pigalle was the centre of popular music in Paris. This changed in the 1960s, as the old music halls were converted into porn cinemas, but now the process is being reversed. The **Divan du Monde** and **L'Erotika** are the largest of the most recent additions, but there are also many smaller studios and cafés showing live music, and by Christmas '95 a new blues club at 6 boulevard de Clichy, former site of the Ritz porno cinema, will open its doors.

The success of the café live music scene is even more surprising, given the battles cafés have waged over the years against Paris' tough anti-noise laws. A network of over 100 cafés presenting music has been built up by an association called **Life, Live in the Bar**, dedicated to freedom of musical expression and affordable live concerts.

In general, Paris venues don't present just one style of music, so audiences are constantly crossing town to follow the style of music they prefer. Still hugely popular is *nouvelle guinguette* or *rock musette*, an infectious music that mixes rock with traditional French styles. Pioneers Les Négresses Vertes have survived the death of former leader Helno, and there is a good crop of new groups on the scene such as La Tordue, with vibrant singer Juliette. French rap groups continue to multiply, and, while world music in Paris is no longer as dynamic as it was a few years ago, the city is still a major centre for *rai* music, and there are plenty of opportunities to catch good musicians from Africa and the Caribbean.

The best source of information on all non-classical concerts is a free booklet, *LYLO*, with monthly listings of around 1,000 concerts. It's available from most of the venues below and from ticket agencies. *Pariscope* and *L'Officiel* have concert listings, as does the daily *Libération*. Tickets for major venues, such as the **Zénith**, that do not have their own box offices can be bought through ticket agencies (*see chapter* **Services**). For the festivals Paris Quartier d'Eté, Banlieues Bleues, Fête de la Musique, La Goutte d'Or en Fête, Halle that Jazz and Boulogne-Billancourt Jazz Festival, see *chapter* **Paris by Season**.

Large-Scale Venues

Auditorium du Châtelet
Forum des Halles, Porte St-Eustache, 75001 (42.36.13.90). Métro Châtelet-Les Halles. **Box office** 11am-start of concert. **Admission** 100F-180F. **Credit** AmEx, MC, V.
This modern auditorium has cramped, too-steeply pitched seating but good acoustics and innovative programming including flamenco, *chanson française* and world. It hosts two jazz concerts a month as part of the *Jazz au Forum* series.

La Bataclan
50 boulevard Voltaire, 75011 (47.00.55.22). Métro Oberkampf. **Box office** 10.30am-7pm Mon-Sat. **Admission** 100F-150F. **No credit cards**.
An attractive, horseshoe-shaped former theatre that's a fixture on the Parisian nightlife scene and, musically, one of the most interesting venues in town, hosting everything from Oasis to Ute Lemper. Fin-de-siècle murals, warm colours, a large dancing area in front of the stage and a bar with good sight-lines also make it one of the most popular. Three nights a week it's a disco (*see chapter* **Nightlife**).

Casino de Paris
16 rue de Clichy, 75009 (42.85.26.27/box office 49.95.99.99). Métro Trinité/RER Auber. **Box office** 11am-6pm Mon-Sat. **Admission** 250F. **Credit** MC, V.
This comfortable venue just down from Pigalle is one of the last of the old-style Paris music halls. When not featuring traditional *variété française* or show-biz acts, it hosts figures like David Byrne and PJ Harvey and festivals such as the *Paris New Orleans Follies* and *La Nuit Sidney Bechet*.

La Cigale
120 boulevard Rochechouart, 75018 (49.25.81.75). Métro Pigalle. **Box office** one hour before performance. **Admission** 120F-160F. **No credit cards**.
An old horseshoe-shaped vaudeville house near Pigalle, with a slightly nihilistic air thanks to its grey and black colour scheme. There's still seating upstairs, but everyone heads for the cleared orchestra area, which can get a little too crowded for comfort. The most unpleasant bouncers in town.

A multi-varied musical mix has taken the place of chanson *at* **L'Erotika.**

Elysée Montmartre
72 boulevard Rochechouart, 75018 (42.55.81.47/
44.92.45.49). Métro Anvers. **Box office** 10am-6pm
Mon-Fri; concerts 7.30pm most nights. **Admission** about
130F. **No credit cards.**
The leader of the musical action in the Pigalle-Montmartre
area. With its art nouveau façade, moulded ceiling and wood-
en floors, it has retained its authentic music-hall character
while consistently presenting an imaginative mix of music
including Portishead, Sheryl Crow and Boyz II Men. Recently
launched was *Le Bal,* a twice-monthly party of many musical styles, including *nouvelle guinguette,* r'n'r and java.

Olympia
28 boulevard des Capucines, 75009 (47.42.82.45/
telephone bookings 47.42.25.49). Métro Opéra.
Box office 10am-7pm Mon-Sat; 11am-7pm Sun.
Admission 150F-240F. **No credit cards.**
A sentimental favourite of Parisians, but if it wasn't for its
history it would be hard to see why: the fabled interior was
blandly remodelled several years ago. It may be knocked
down, and rebuilt in a new location on the same street.

Palais Omnisports de Paris-Bercy
8 boulevard de Bercy, 75012 (booking 43.46.12.21/
44.68.44.68). Métro Bercy. **Box office** 11am-6pm Mon-
Sat. **Admission** from 170F. **Credit** MC, V.
Bercy is like a cursed cooking pot: no matter what ingredients go in, the results are never satisfying. Unlike the sporting events which take place here, at least the rock concerts
can fill some of this 16,000-seat indoor stadium with smoke
and light, but nothing can help the acoustics.

Zénith
211 avenue Jean-Jaurès, 75019. Métro Porte de Pantin.
No box office (see Introduction). **Admission** from 160F.
The only thing this unatmospheric La Villette venue with
notoriously poor acoustics has going for it is that it's not
Bercy. Still, almost everyone plays here, from reclusive
French singer Francis Cabrel to Megadeth, by way of Bryan
Ferry and Suicidal Tendencies.

Small/Medium-Sized Venues

Arapaho
Centre Commercial Italie II, 30 avenue d'Italie, 75013
(53.79.00.11). Métro Place d'Italie. **Box office** from 8pm
daily. **Admission** 60F-100F. **Credit** V.
This two-year old club without a door sign (look for silver
portholes to the left of the Printemps store) has become a
quality rock venue, although it's cramped, and about a third
of the space has very poor sight-lines. Dour door muscle.

La Chapelle des Lombards
19 rue de Lappe, 75011 (43.57.24.24/48.06.91.82).
Métro Bastille. **Open** occasional concerts, 8pm; disco
10.30pm-dawn, Tue-Sat. **Admission** 100F Tue-Thur;
120F Fri, Sat, incl. one drink. **Credit** AmEx, MC, V.
At the hub of Bastille nightlife, and the programming generally has a Latin/World edge to it, although *nouvelle
guinguette* groups like Les Voleurs des Poules also get a look-
in. *See also chapter* **Nightlife.**

Le Divan du Monde
75 rue des Martyrs, 75018 (42.55.48.50). Métro Pigalle.
Open 7pm-5am daily. **Credit** MC, V.
Once the Divan Japonais, made famous by Toulouse-Lautrec,
this auditorium has retained none of its original decor. By
way of compensation it boasts some of the most original programming in Paris at very reasonable prices, with everything from Syrian Whirling Dervishes to Alvin Lee. Friendly
staff and an eclectic, young crowd create a vibrant atmosphere and the Sugar Black evenings attract a wild mix of
gays and heteros. *See also chapter* **Nightlife.**

L'Erotika
2 rue Coustou, 75018 (46.06.26.25). Métro Blanche or
Place de Clichy. **Box office** from 8pm on the night.
Jacques Brel, Brassens and Serge Gainsbourg all performed
here when it was a celebrated venue for *chanson française.*
Now hosting funk, rai, salsa, acid jazz and Planet Rock's
Friday indie rock sessions, it's been jazzed up with a sleek
bar and a low stage.

Espace Reuilly

21 rue Hénard, 75012 (44.74.90.96); Métro Montgallet.
These halls are rented out by independent promoters, and often a good bet for discovering new African bands.
Branches: Espace Hérault, 8 rue de la Harpe, 75005 (43.29.86.51); **Espace Voltaire,** 4 rue Camille Desmoulins, 75011 (40.24.02.48).

Les Etoiles

61 rue du Château d'Eau, 75010 (47.70.60.56). Métro Château d'Eau. **Admission** 100F at 9.30pm for meal and concert; 50F at 11pm for concert. **No credit cards.**
This claims to be the oldest venue to have continuously presented live music in Paris, and one of the first in the world to have exhibited motion pictures. It looks like it could have come out of an early Martin Scorsese film, with arching ceilings and a community hall feel. Salsa is the staple of the menu, but jazz, r'n'b and funk are also served up.

Flèche d'Or

102 bis rue de Bagnolet, 75020 (43.72.42.44.). Métro Porte de Bagnolet. **Open** *café* from 6.30pm, *concerts* from 8pm, daily. **No credit cards.**
A big café in a former train station, as the locomotive motifs suggest. The nightly concerts are free, and usually light electric or acoustic. Some films and plays are staged.

Le Gibus

18 rue du Faubourg-du-Temple, 75011 (47.00.78.88). Métro République. **Open** 8pm-5am Tue-Sat. **Admission** 50F, 70F with drink. **Credit** AmEx, DC, MC, V.
A giant top hat advertises this venerable basement club located in a slightly funky part of the République area. With very low ceilings and a very loud sound system it's perfect for hard metal and psychobilly groups.

Java

105 rue du Faubourg du Temple, 75010 (42.02.20.52). Métro Belleville. **Admission** average 80F, incl. one drink.
Many films are shot here, and it's easy to see why: Java has perfectly preserved its old-world atmosphere down to the Morocco leather booths from 1928, the year it opened. It attracts a lively Spanish-speaking crowd, and every Thursday features Cuban music, and every Sunday Brazilian; the other evenings are given over to *bal musette*. *See chapter* **Nightlife**.

La Lola

8 rue Rouget de l'Isle, 93520, Pantin (48.10.93.91.). Métro Eglise de Pantin. **Admission** 40F. **No credit cards.**
A centre for indies, with its own recording facilities and newspaper. Electric gigs take place in the studio, acoustic in the large hall. All styles except jazz; cabaret 6pm Sun.

New Moon

66 rue Pigalle, 75009 (40.16.94.25). Métro Pigalle. **Open** from 9pm Tue-Thur; from 11pm Fri, Sat. **Admission** 30F Tue-Thur; 40F Fri, Sat. **No credit cards.**
Across the road from Pigall's, and not to be confused with the strip joint of the same name next door, this trippy club has psychedelic décor, a low stage and polite door staff. The eclectic music is mainly booked by Life, Live in the Bar (*see below*), with a jungle beat session every Saturday night.

New Opus Café

167 quai de Valmy, 75010 (40.34.70.00/40.05.08.08). Métro Louis Blanc. **Open** 8pm-4am Mon-Sat. **Admission** 100F incl first drink. **Credit** V.
Once a British army mess hall, this place was a classical music venue before being transformed into a chic candlelit club. Tables are clustered round the dance floor or perched on the first floor balcony, above the attractive bar. Programming runs the spectrum of Latin music, *chanson* and standards, with torch singers like Julie Pietri and Karibo.

Passage du Nord-Ouest

13 rue du Faubourg Montmartre, 75009 (36.68.03.22/ 43.07.69.07). Métro Rue-Montmartre. **Box office** two hours before concert. **Admission** 80F-120F. **No credit cards.**
A relative newcomer, but quickly established because of its adventurous programming mix of jazz, world and indie music. Once a cabaret, it has café tables in the old stalls and excellent sight lines from the sides. Also a cinema (*see chapter* **Film**).

Pigall's

77 rue Pigalle, 75009 (42.80.52.52). Métro Pigalle. **Music** 8.30pm-4am Fri, Sat. **Admission** 50F. **No credit cards.**
A good night here will be the closest you'll get to living in an Antonioni film. The over-the-top interior, with mirrors, gilt edging and *trompe d'oeil* ceiling, has good acoustics, and the staff are friendly and bar prices low. Currently there's music only on Fridays and Saturdays, with rock, funk or fusion at 8.30pm. A separate club event starts around midnight and lasts way past dawn. *See also chapter* **Nightlife**.

Sentier des Halles

50 rue d'Aboukir, 75002 (42.36.37.27). Métro Sentier. **Box office** 10am-6.30pm Tue-Sat; shows 6.30pm, 8.30pm, 10.30pm. **Admission** 50F-80F. **No credit cards.**
A superb small venue with about 100 seats clustered inside a medieval vaulted cellar. Acoustic artists favour the space, but you can also find jazz, *chanson*, rock, cabaret and theatre.

Other Venues

The giant **Grand Rex** cinema (*see chapter* **Film**) has welcomed major international acts in the past, but lately has been under-utilised. Big-name French and international stars also appear at the vast, echoing **Palais des Congrès** (*see chapter* **Business**), and a range of concerts, some free, are held in the also-cold **Maison de Radio France** (*see chapter* **Music: Classical & Opera**). The **Théâtre de la Ville** regularly presents world and avant-garde music, and the small **Théâtre du Tourtour** *chanson française* (*see chapter* **Theatre**).

Jazz

Le Baiser Salé

58 rue des Lombards, 75001 (42.33.37.71). Métro Châtelet-Les Halles. **Open** 9pm-4am daily; concert room opens 10.30pm. **Admission** free. **Credit** MC, V.
The least interesting of the jazz venues along this street, with a programme that relies too heavily on jam sessions, despite the occasional interesting musician from Africa. A narrow bar leads you upstairs to the small, slightly spacey jazz club.

Caveau de la Huchette

5 rue de la Huchette, 75005 (43.26.65.05). Métro St-Michel. **Open** 9.30pm-2.30am Mon-Fri; 9.30pm-4am Sat, Sun. **Admission** 60F Mon-Thur, Sun; 70F Fri, Sat. **Credit** DC, V.
This Left Bank jazz club, located in a twelfth-century cellar with an appealing upstairs bar, looks like a set from one of Audrey Hepburn's Paris films, and the resident dancers are straight out of Central Casting. Billie Holiday's favourite trumpeter, Harry 'Sweets' Edison, is a regular here, as are some of Count Basie's former sidemen, including Butch Reynolds, but most of the time the music is uninspired trad.

Au Duc des Lombards

42 rue des Lombards, 75001 (42.33.22.88). Métro Châtelet-Les Halles. **Open** 6pm-4am daily; music 10pm. **Admission** 50F-100F, plus 28F first drink. **Credit** MC, V.
Known as 'the bar that Bobby built' by American musicians because brilliant pianist Bobby Few first introduced live music here back in the 1970s. Since enlarged, it feels more like

Mid-set at the **Passage du Nord-Ouest.**

a corner café than a jazz club, with large windows and wooden furniture. Programming, however, is often disappointing.

Hot Brass

Parc de la Villette, 211 avenue Jean-Jaurès, 75019 (42.00.14.12). Métro Porte de Pantin. **Open** *doors* 8pm, *concerts* 9.30pm, Wed-Sun. **Admission** 100F, 70F students. **Credit** AmEx, MC, V.
In only two years, the Hot Brass at La Villette has set an impressive track record, showcasing major figures such as Roy Hargrove, Steve Coleman, Kenny Garrett and James Carter. There's a dynamic, young audience and regular monthly hip hop and acid sessions. Terrible ventilation makes it off-limits to anyone remotely allergic to smoke.

Houdon Jazz Club

5 rue des Abbesses 75018 (46.06.35.91.). Métro Abbesses. **Jazz** from 9.30pm Fri, Sat. **Admission** free.
A friendly neighbourhood café in the heart of Montmartre which turns into a jazz club every Friday and Saturday. You can catch some surprisingly impressive names up here.

Instants Chavirés

7 rue Richard Lenoir, 93100 Montreuil (42.87.25.91). Métro Robespierre. **Open** 8pm Tue-Sat; concerts 8.30pm. **Admission** 30F-80F. **No credit cards.**
A friendly, vital club in Montreuil. Apart from avant-garde local talent, it has often hosted challenging international musicians, and has a connection with the Knitting Factory in New York. If you turn up late, you may be locked out.

Latitudes

7-11 rue St-Benoît, 75006 (42.61.53.53). Métro St-Germain-des-Prés. **Open** *piano bar* 6pm-2am daily; *concerts* 10.30pm-2am Tue-Sat. **Admission** free, first drink 120F. **Credit** AmEx, DC, MC, V.

A stylish club in St Germain, with good seating throughout, except for a terrible section by the stairs. Unfortunately, programming is less impressive, and rarely good enough to justify the drink prices.

Lionel Hampton Jazz Club

at Hôtel Le Méridien-Etoile, 81 boulevard Gouvion-St-Cyr, 75017 (40.68.34.34). Métro Porte Maillot. **Open** *bar* 7pm-2am daily; *music* 10.30pm-2am. **Admission** free, first drink after 10pm 130F, refills 70F. **Credit** AmEx, DC, EC, JCB, MC, V.
One of the most impressive venues in terms of facilities, it is also the leading soul, gospel and rhythm'n'blues venue in Paris. Because of audience chit chat, it's vital to book a table close to the stage and to avoid Friday and Saturday nights.

New Morning

7-9 rue des Petites Ecuries, 75010 (45.23.51.41/bookings 42.31.31.31). Métro Château d'Eau. **Open** *advance booking* through agents or 5-7pm daily; concerts most nights 9pm. **Admission** usually 110F. **No credit cards.**
A world-famous jazz club that single-handedly kept quality jazz alive in Paris during the dark days of the early 1980s. Archie Shepp has now replaced the late Chet Baker as unofficial resident musician, but virtually every significant name in jazz has played there over the last fifteen years. As well as jazz, New Morning boasts powerful blues and Latin programming. The best seats are down in the centre or on the raised sections on either side. The staff are reliably friendly and relaxed, and the audiences are great.

Petit Journal Montparnasse

13 rue du Commandant-Mouchotte, 75014 (43.21.56.70). Métro Montparnasse-Bienvenüe or Gaîté. **Open** 9pm-2am Mon-Sat. **Admission** first drink 100F. **Credit** DC, MC, V.
If it weren't for the neon trumpeter, it'd be hard to find this large, modern club, in a bleak part of Paris. The best tables at the front are reserved for diners. Most gigs feature quality French artists, but beware occasional slip-ups such as dreadful local C&W band The Bunch.

Petit Journal St-Michel

71 boulevard St-Michel, 75005 (43.26.28.59). Métro/RER St Michel. **Open** 10pm-3am Mon-Sat. **Admission** 100F, includes first drink. **Credit** MC, V.
A cellar club that's inexplicably popular considering it has one of the worst layouts of any in Paris, with most seats providing a limited view. The music is dixieland.

Petit Opportun

15 rue des Lavandières-Ste-Opportune, 75001 (42.36.01.36). Métro Châtelet-Les Halles. **Open** 9pm-2am Tue-Sat; concerts 10.45pm. **Admission** 100F, incl first drink. **No credit cards.**
This charming warren of 13th century cellars puts on quality local talent. Come early, or you may have to sit in a back cellar, with no view. The bar upstairs is a musicians' hangout.

Quai des Blues

17 boulevard Vital Bouhot, 92200 Neuilly sur Seine (46.24.22.00). Métro Porte de Champerret, then bus 164 or 165. **Open** *music sets* 10.30pm, midnight, Thur-Sat. **Admission** 80F. **Credit** MC, V.
A new club dedicated to blues, soul, gospel, boogie-woogie and r'n'b. There's a good restaurant, but it's a hike from the nearest métro if you don't have a car.

Le Slow Club

130 rue de Rivoli, 75001 (42. 33.84.30). Métro Châtelet-Les Halles or Pont-Neuf. **Open** 10pm-3am Tue-Sat. **Admission** 60F. **Credit** MC, V.
The Right-bank sister club of the **Caveau de la Huchette.** Fewer tourists, and popular with a young, media crowd.

Studio des Islettes
10 rue des Islettes, 75018 (42.58.63.33). Métro Barbès-Rochechouart. **Open** jamming 7-10.30pm Mon-Fri; concerts from 7.30pm Sat, Sun. **Admission** 50F concerts, jamming free.
Off an old courtyard in the heart of the Goutte d'Or, this small studio is a jazz co-operative, with weekend concerts featuring local expatriate talent as well as French musicians. There are jam sessions during the week, and it's a good place for visiting musicians to meet Paris-based players.

Le Sunset
60 rue des Lombards, 75001 (40.26.46.60/restaurant 40.26.21.25). Métro Châtelet-Les Halles. **Open** 9.30pm-dawn daily; *concerts* from 10pm; *restaurant* 8pm-2am. **Admission** 78F, incl one drink. **Credit** EC, MC, V.
A friendly basement spot where serious jazz fans are often found, the Sunset offers a good diet of talented but neglected Americans, with the very best of French jazz, such as the Belmondo Brothers quintet or Babik Reinhardt, Django's son.

La Villa
29 rue Jacob, 75006 (43.26.60.00). Métro St-Germain-des-Prés. **Open** *bar* from 6pm daily; *concerts* from 10.30pm Mon-Sat (three sets). **Admission** 120F Mon-Thur, 150F Fri, Sat, incl one drink. **Credit** AmEx, DC, JCB, MC, V.
The only club in St-Germain continuing the area's tradition of excellence in jazz, La Villa is also the most intimate club in town. While the club sometimes features visiting outfits, it usually presents famous brass players with consistently excellent local rhythm sections. Von Freeman had a sensational run here. Drinks are cheaper Mon-Thur.

Music & Dining

Arbuci Jazz Club
25-27 rue de Buci, 75006 (44.41.14.14). Métro Mabillon or Odéon. **Open** 7pm-1am Tue-Sun; jazz from 11pm Thur-Sun. **Admission** free; drinks 50F-70F. **Credit** AmEx, MC, V.
Walk through the traditional brasserie-style ground floor restaurant to the basement, where the tables have more space and the setting is warmer.

Milonga
18 rue Guisarde, 75006 (43.29.52.18). Métro Mabillon. **Open** 7.30pm-12.30am Mon, Thur; 7.30pm-1am Fri, Sat; concerts from 9pm Fri, Sat. **Credit** AmEx, EC, MC, V.
Currently the only venue in Paris which regularly presents tango, performed by well-known Argentinian musicians. Tables upstairs can hear the music just fine; the cellar can get cramped. The restaurant specialises in Argentinian food.

Life, Live in the Bar

A selection from over 100 venues currently presenting live music through the Life, Live in the Bar association. For further information, contact Julien, who speaks English, at Life, Live in the Bar, 196 rue du Faubourg Saint-Antoine, 75012 (43.72.27.28).

Ailleurs
13 rue Jean Beausire, 75004 (44.59.82.82). Métro Bastille. **Concerts** from 9.15pm daily; doors open 8pm.
A major centre for traditional French *chanson*.

L'Archipel
50 rue Basfroid, 75011 (44.93.71.01.). Métro Voltaire. **Open** 2pm-2am daily; concerts 7pm Tue, Wed, 9.30pm Mon, Thur-Sun. **Admission** free-60F. **Credit** MC, V.
A comfortable venue with very good bands playing all types of music. There's a restaurant on the first floor.

Les Blues Heures
97 bis rue Championnet, 75018 (42.57.30.66.). Métro Clignancourt. **Open** 8pm to late Thur-Sat. **Admission** 20F. **Credit** AmEx, EC, MC, V.
A *café-musicale* that's a social and community centre as well as a music venue. Music tends to be rock, rai and reggae.

La Liberté
196 rue du Faubourg St Antoine, 75012 (43.72.11.18.). Métro Faidherbe Chaligny. **Music** 7-10pm Fri.
Acoustic jazz and folk café. Also some art exhibitions.

L'Oreille Cassée
6 rue de la Main d'Or, 75011 (49.23.05.91). Métro Ledru-Rollin. **Concerts** 8.30pm Wed, Sat.
A tiny, picturesque little café with good sound given over to *chanson française* and sometimes jazz.

Wait & See
9 boulevard Voltaire, 75011 (48.07.29.49.). Métro République. **Concerts** 9pm Tue-Sat.
A scruffy bar that's a good place to pick up flyers and info on gigs all around Paris. Old-style r'n' and ragga.

Floating Musical Bars

La Guinguette Pirate
Quai de la Gare, 75013 (54.41.10.09.). Métro Quai de la Gare. **Open** 6pm-2am Mon-Sat; noon-11pm Sun; concerts from 8.30pm. **Admission** free.
A re-converted old Chinese junk given over to theatre, *chanson française* and *rock musette*. Food and drink served.

Le Kiosque Flottant
Quai de Montebello, 75005 (43.54.19.51). Métro St-Michel. **Music** 9pm Fri, Sat.
A large barge, on the quai opposite Nôtre Dame. Meals and drinks available.

Peniche Le Calife
Quai de Montebello, 75005 (46.55.66.15.). Métro St-Michel. **Music** 10.30pm-2am Fri-Sun.
This reconverted river barge right opposite Nôtre Dame has live music in the downstairs bar. Drinks or meals available.

Other Bars

Le Bistrot d'Eustache
37 rue Berger, 75001 (40.26.23.20). Métro Châtelet-Les Halles. **Open** 9am-2am daily; music 10.30pm-2am Thur-Sat. **Admission** free. **Credit** MC, V.
Small, pretty bar; lively crowd; acoustic jazz every Fri, Sat.

Au Café Chantant
36, rue Bichat, 75010 (42.08.83.33.). Métro Goncourt. **Open** from 8pm, music 8.30pm, Tue-Sat. **Admission** free Tue; 40F Wed, Sat. **No credit cards.**
Devoted mainly to *chanson française*. Tuesdays the stage is open to all-comers, as long as they don't sing in English.

Chesterfield Café
124 rue de La Boétie, 75008 (42.25.18.06). Métro Franklin D Roosevelt. **Open** 9am-2am daily; music 11.30pm Tue-Sat. **Admission** free.
Certainly not *chanson*, but a giant, recently-opened all-American bar with Americana-theme décor that hosts good-quality rock, blues and r'n'b bands from the USA.

La Folie En Tête
33 rue de la Butte-aux-Cailles 75013 (45.80.65.99). Métro Place d'Italie. **Music** 9pm Thur, Fri.
A bustling bar on one of Paris' most picturesque streets.

Paris Jazz

One of this century's best-known cultural love affairs has been that between jazz and the city of Paris. For many American artists, Paris has acquired a mythic allure. Von Freeman speaks of playing 'April in Paris' as a kid with tears in his eyes, dreaming of escape from the ghettos of Chicago to the City of Light. Joshua Redman says he hopes the last gig he plays before he dies will be in Paris.

It is the audiences which make Paris a wonderful place to hear great jazz. Parisian audiences are knowledgeable, appreciative and passionate. They have a soft spot for hard luck stories, and can give big boosts to artists at the end of their careers, such as Chet Baker and Jimmy Scott.

Jazz first took Paris by storm just after World War I: the rich danced to the giddy syncopation of Louis Armstrong at the Paris Lido and the Embassy Club, while Josephine Baker's phenomenal success popularised jazz and exposed audiences to people like Percy Johnson and Henry Goodwin. The 1930s saw a change in jazz audiences which reflected harsher economic times. Jazz lost its popular appeal, and was followed by smaller, more critical audiences. For the first time local musicians became real stars, with the emergence of Django Reinhardt and Stephane Grappelli. The shift to smaller, less ostentatious club venues during the 1930s made it easier for jazz to survive the years of Nazi occupation, when it was banned as a supposedly 'decadent' art form.

The second golden age of Paris jazz coincided with the post-War rise of the St Germain des Prés area. With local residents Picasso, Dora Maar, Sartre and de Beauvoir giving the revolutionary bebop enthusiastic support, a number of famous clubs opened, including the Club St-Germain. It was the defection to Paris of two famous figures in the 1950s which consolidated the hold the music had on Paris. Drummer and founding member of the Modern Jazz Quartet Kenny 'Klook' Clarke and brilliant pianist Bud Powell, the model for the tragic Dexter Gordon character in Bertrand Tavernier's film *'Round Midnight*, gave Paris two thirds of a world-class rhythm section, and hornmen such as Lester Young spent long periods playing with them. Other regular visitors included Dizzy Gillespie, Lee Morgan and Art Blakey.

Black American jazz musicians were accorded a status they had never received in their home country. During the fifties Paris also experienced its second wave of American expatriate artists. Along with writers such as William Styron, and James Jones were many African American artists such as James Baldwin and Chester Himes, and their presence contributed to a unique feeling of community. At the end of the decade there was a craze, too, for featuring American jazz artists on the soundtracks of

nouvelle vague films, such as Louis Malle's *L'Ascenseur pour l'Echafaud*, featuring Miles Davis and a bright young French sax star, Barney Wilen.

Although some notable French musicians appeared at this time – Wilen, pianist Claude Bolling – by and large the French went in more for talking about than playing jazz. Two world-class journals did emerge from the French critics, *Jazz Hot*, now over 60 years old, and *Jazz Magazine*, celebrating its 40th anniversary in 1995. A new quality magazine, *Jazzman*, has also recently been launched.

The scene changed again in the 1960s when clubs closed and gigs grew scarce. De Gaulle's decision to expel the American forces when he quit NATO is often cited as a cause of the decline, but it was also Rock'n'Roll and TV that were to blame for jazz's diminishing popularity. Moreover, when the Socialists came to power in 1981 pressure from disgruntled French musicians led to it becoming more difficult for foreigners to play, and stay, in France.

The situation has since improved once again, and today there are probably more jazz clubs in Paris than ever before. The neo-con movement launched by people like Wynton Marsalis has done a lot to bring Parisians back to jazz, attracting younger audiences.

Among expatriate musicians currently living in Paris, the most famous is Steve Lacy, the great innovator of the soprano sax. Drummer Sunny Murray, cornetist Graham Haynes, alto sax player Steve Potts, trumpeter Mra Oma and tenor star Johnny Griffin are either based here or stay for much of the year, and keep an eye out too for singers Liz McComb, Tommy Garrett and Henry Soul. Among the French contingent, watch out for violinists Didier Lockwood and Jean-Luc Ponty, pianists Michel Petrucciani, Olivier Hutman and Laurence de Wilde, and Italian drummer Aldo Romano.

Practical matters

To get the most out of a jazz club always book, and arrive thirty minutes before the show to make sure you get a table close to the stage and away from the noise of the bars. Admission commonly includes one drink, and subsequent drinks are cheaper. Try to avoid Fridays and Saturdays, when you often get large groups more interested in talking than listening. If you're going to a venue like **New Morning** or **Hot Brass**, where you pay at the door, get your tickets in advance, either at the venue or an agency, as you'll get priority of entry. Otherwise, don't be surprised if you turn up to a venue five minutes before the doors open and find three hundred people ahead of you. They may get the best seats, but at least you know they'll be a dynamic audience.

Aux Noctambules

24 boulevard de Clichy, 75018 (46.06.16.38.). Métro Pigalle. **Music** from 10pm Tue-Sat. **Credit** EC, MC, V.
If John Cassavetes had ever shot a film in Paris, he would have made it in this bar, packed with eccentric regulars and refugees from various bygone eras. The music, mainly *chanson française*, begins at 10pm and never stops before 4am, even if you want it to.

Utopia

79 rue de l'Ouest, 75014 (43.22.79.66 recording). Métro Pernéty. **Open** phone for details; music from 10.30pm Tue-Sat. **Credit** MC, V.
Relaxed café in an alternative neighbourhood: homegrown blues and folk are served along with a wide variety of beer.

Irish Pubs

For more Irish bars in Paris, *see chapter* **Cafés & Bars**.

The Quiet Man

5 rue des Haudriettes, 75003 (48.04.02.77). Métro Rambuteau. **Music** from 9pm daily.
Irish traditional music nightly, except for singalong Wed.

Tigh Johnny

55 rue Montmartre 75002 (42.33.91.33.). Métro Sentier or Les Halles. **Music** 9.30pm Mon, Wed, Sun.
A venue without much atmosphere, but it makes up for it with reputedly the best Irish musicians in Paris.

Sport & Fitness

Tear yourself away from la table and tuck into a healthy sporting feast.

Keeping Informed

The *Figaroscope* supplement that comes with *Le Figaro* every Wednesday includes a calendar of sporting events in the Paris region. To follow the French sporting scene, buy the popular all-sports daily *L'Equipe* (*see chapter* **Media**).

Allô-Sports
(42.76.54.54). **Open** 10.30am-5pm Mon-Thur; 10.30am-4.30pm Fri.
Helpful municipal phoneline giving information on sports and sporting events in the Paris area. The staff speak English.

Maison des Associations de Paris
14 Grande Galerie, Forum des Halles, 75004 (42.33.74.00). Métro Châtelet-Les Halles. **Open** 10am-7pm Tue-Sat.
General information on sports clubs and associations in Paris. Located next to the pool on the third level below ground in the Forum des Halles complex.

The Two Main Parks

See also chapter **Sightseeing**.

Bois de Boulogne
Métro Porte d'Auteuil, Porte Dauphine, Porte Maillot or Les Sablons. **Open** dawn-dusk daily.
This 865-hectare area of wooded parkland is a favourite place for Sunday *promeneurs* and sports-minded Parisians, although a lot of its tennis courts, equestrian centres and swimming pools belong to private clubs. The famous red clay courts at **Stade Roland Garros** are here, but are never open to the public. Good jogging tracks can be found around the Lac Inférieur and the gates of the **Longchamp** and **Auteuil** race tracks (*see* **Spectator Sports: Horse Racing**). The latter is also a popular spot for serious cyclists. A 2.5km (1½ mile) fitness course begins near the intersection of avenue de St-Cloud and the route de la Seine à la Butte Mortemart. You can rent bicycles near the Jardin d'Acclimation (Métro Porte Maillot) and just north of the Lac Inférieur. Both stands are open from 10am to 7pm, mid-Apr to mid-Oct (*information* 47.47.76.50). During winter months, the stands are open only on Wednesdays and weekends. Not far from the Lac Inférieur bicycle stand is a dock where you can rent rowing boats from the end of Feb until 15 Nov (51F an hour with a security deposit of 200F; *information* 45.25.44.01). There's also a weekly all-comers softball game on Sunday, near the Jardin de Bagatelle.

Bois de Vincennes
Métro Château de Vincennes, Porte de Charenton, Porte Dorée/RER Fontenay-sous-Bois or Joinville. **Open** dawn-dusk daily.
On the east side of the city is the 995-hectare Bois de Vincennes. Less chic than its sister-park on the other side of Paris, it is nonetheless every bit as crowded at the weekends, and almost as charming, with fewer roads breaking up its spaces. As in the Bois de Boulogne, you can rent rowing boats on the two lakes or jog around them. There's the

Shoot pool late-night at the **Académie de Billard Clichy-Montmartre***. See page 267.*

Vélodrome Jacques Anquetil (club members only) and several football and rugby fields, as well as the only baseball field in Paris (built by Americans and named after the World War I American general, John 'Blackjack' Pershing). The Bois de Vincennes has the best municipal tennis facility in Paris: 21 public courts at the **Centre Sportif La Faluère** in the plaine de St-Hubert (*see below* **Tennis**). You can rent bicycles at the Porte Dorée entrance to the park and near the banks of the Lac des Minimes.

Activities

Basketball

Residents serious about team play should contact the **French Basketball Federation** (49.23.34.00) and ask for a list of clubs. Visitors and those looking for a less structured environment can try an increasing number of outdoor possibilities. French teenagers frequent two newish courts under the Métro tracks near the Glacière stop in the 13th *arrondissement*. There's also a single hoop in the Jardin du Luxembourg in the 6th. One of the best outdoor courts for all ages is in the same municipal sporting complex as the **Emile-Anthoine** swimming pool in the 15th arrondissement (*see below* **Swimming Pools**). For free throws, rebounds and the occasional pick-up game try the **American Church** (*see chapter* **Survival: Religion**) on Tuesday nights at 9.30-10.30pm), where it's bring-your-own basketball.

Boulodromes

A stroll through almost any park on a fair day makes it clear that any level patch of dirt will do, but the city provides fourteen official spots to play *pétanque* (*boules* is the name for the balls used in the game). The most popular is at the square des Arènes-de-Lutèce in the 5th *arrondissement*.

Bowling

At last count, the Paris region had over 25 bowling centres. The two listed below are among the most pleasant. Both rent out shoes and have restaurants and games rooms.

Bowling-Mouffetard

13 rue Gracieuse, 75005 (43.31.09.35). Métro Monge.
Open 11.30am-2am daily. **Prices** 18F per game Mon-Thur, after 8pm 20F; 18F per game Fri, after 8pm 30F; 30F Sat, Sun, public holidays. **Credit** MC, V.
Eight lanes and a lively atmosphere.

Bowling de Paris

Jardin d'Acclimatation, Bois de Boulogne, 75016 (40.67.94.00). Métro Porte Maillot, Sablon. **Open** 11am-2am daily. **Prices** 20F per game Mon-Fri; 33F after 9pm and Sat, Sun (discounts for members of French and other bowling federations). **Shoe hire** 10F. **No credit cards.**
Inside the Jardin d'Acclimatation, so you have to pay a 10F entry fee to get into the complex. The centre has 24 lanes.

Climbing

The French are among the world's best free climbers. If you can't make it to the Alps, Paris offers five outdoor *murs d'escalade*. Though usually reserved for schools and climbing clubs, facilities are open to individuals who have a one-month membership (available from any location for 15.60F, photo and proof of insurance required) and their own gear.

Centre Sportif Poissonnier

2 rue Jean-Cocteau, 75018 (42.51.24.68). Métro Porte de Clignancourt. **Open** to public for climbing noon-2pm Mon-Fri; noon-4pm Sat, Sun. **Height** 21 metres.
The ochre-coloured climbing cliff is designed to imitate nature's challenges – it even has chimneys. For climbers at every skill level, it is the city's tallest and most popular wall.

Cricket

Château de Thoiry Cricket Club

rue Pavillion de Montreuil, 78770 Thoiry. Autoroute 13 direction Rouen exit St-Quentin en Yvelines.
Information men (47.43.19.01), women (45.31.11.83).
A relaxed club where players at all levels rally under the motto 'hit and run'. Matches are usually held on weekends and public holidays. The season runs from April to October with 45 matches for men and a growing 15 for women. All are welcome to play. The château is also home to a zoo.

Standard Athletic Club

Route Forestière du Pavé de Meudon, 92360 Meudon-la-Forêt (46.26.16.09).By train SNCF from Gare Montparnasse to Meudon-Bellevue, then 20-minute walk/By car N116 or D2. **Open** 9am-11pm daily.
This private, non-profit-making club open to Britons living in Paris (with a quota system for those from other countries) fields two sides. The season runs from May to September

and includes friendlies against six local teams. The club also has eight tennis courts, two squash courts, a heated outdoor pool, men's and women's hockey, football and rugby.

Cycling

For cycle hire companies, *see chapter* **Services**.

Vélodrome Jacques Anquetil

Bois de Vincennes, 75012 (43.68.01.27). Métro Liberté.
Open 8am-8pm Mon-Sat. **Membership** 15F a month (bring a photograph for your membership card).
The only velodrome in Paris which is open to cyclists on an occasional basis (you still must belong to a cycling club and have a membership card for the velodrome). The cement track is a bit worn but still functional. There's an excellent restaurant, La Cipale.

Diving

ASCAN Plongée

(42.21.18.14/40.63.61.86).
Well-qualified, experienced scuba instructors offer courses, in English, aimed at a variety of underwater interests – basic to advanced scuba diving, first-aid and diver rescue, underwater photography and even elementary marine biology. Courses are held Wed nights at the Marché St-Germain pool in the 6th *arrondissement*. Beginner's courses including text books, insurance and scuba gear rental, and cost 1,890F.

Golf

Now that tennis has been thoroughly democratised, golf has become the French status-seeker's sport of choice. There are no courses in Paris, but scores in the Paris region, many of them open to non-members. Green fees are usually much cheaper during the week. For a full list of courses, contact the **French Golf Federation** (69 avenue Victor-Hugo, 75016/tel 44.17.63.00).
Golf Clément Ader *Domaine du Château Péreire, 77220 Gretz Armainvilliers (64.07.34.10). SNCF from Gare de Lyon to Gretz Armainvilliers.* **Open** 8.30am-7pm Mon-Wed, Fri-Sun. **Fee** 200F Mon-Fri; 450F Sat, Sun.
Challenging, Japanese-designed course with plenty of water hazards.
Golf Disneyland Paris *Marne-la-Vallée, 77777 Marne-la-Vallé (60.45.68.04). RER Marne-la-Vallé/Chessy then free shuttle.* **Open** 9am-dusk Mon-Fri; 7.40am-dusk Sat, Sun. **Fee** 150F Mon-Fri; 250F Sat, Sun. Mickey's course has the lot: 27 holes, great clubhouse, American professional, buggies for hire, even Mouse-shaped bunkers.
Golf du Réveillon *Ferme des Hyverneaux, 77150 Lesigny (60.02.17.33). SNCF from Gare de Lyon to Pontault-Combault.* **Open** 8am-6pm Mon-Fri; 7.30am-7.30pm Sat, Sun; reduced winter hours. **Fee** 160F Mon-Fri; 240F Sat, Sun. An attractive, 36-hole public course.

Health & Fitness

Health clubs hit Paris in the late eighties and they continue to proliferate. Clubs fill up at lunchtime and on weekday evenings, so stick to off-peak hours. Paris residents might consider joining a municipal club with a weights room (*contact* **Allô-Sports** or the **Maison des Associations** for information; *see above* **Keeping Informed**).

Club Quartier Latin

19 rue de Pontoise, 75005 (43.54.82.45). Métro Maubert-Mutualité. **Open** 9am-midnight Mon-Thur; 9am-10pm Fri; 9.30am-7pm Sat, Sun. **Membership** *annual* 2,900F; *monthly* 600F; *daily* (health club and pool only) 60F. **Squash courts** 20F-25F per hour for members. **No credit cards.**

It doesn't look like much from the outside, but inside there's a 30m/33yd art deco pool, four squash courts, a weights room and an exercise studio, not to mention dance classes and a restaurant. This club is very popular among anglophones.

Espace Vit'Halles
place Beaubourg, 48 rue Rambuteau, 75003 (42.77.21.71). Métro Rambuteau. **Open** 8am-10pm Mon-Fri; 10am-7pm Sat; 11am-4pm Sun. **Membership** *annual* 3,900F; *student* 2,900F; *day pass* 80F. **Credit** MC, V.
Bills itself as the only New York-style gym in Paris, and the dress is scantier here than in other Paris gyms. No pool.

Gymnase Club
19 locations in Paris and environs, contact 44.37.24.24 or 46.51.88.16 for full list. The most central are: **Gymnase Club Palais Royal** *147 bis rue St-Honoré, 75001 (40.20.03.03). Métro Palais Royal.* **Gymnase Club Champs-Elysées** *26 rue de Berri, 75008 (43.59.04.53). Métro George V.* **Gymnase Club Grenelle** *8 rue de Frémicourt, 75015 (45.75.34.00). Métro Cambronne.* **Membership** *annual* 3,600F (reductions for company membership and students); *one month* 650F; *ten visits* 600F; *day pass* 140F. **Credit** AmEx, MC, V.
The biggest and best-known chain in France. A membership card gives access to every club in the chain. Some of the clubs have pools; some give martial arts classes; all have plenty of Stairmasters, pulse-checkers, treadmills, machines, free weights and other instruments of torture.

Thermes du Royal Monceau
Royal Monceau Hôtel, 38 avenue Hoche, 75008 (42.25.06.66). Métro Charles-de-Gaulle-Etoile. **Open** 7am-11pm daily. **Membership** *annual* 16,000F; *Sept-Dec* 5,700F; *daily* 900F. **Credit** AmEx, DC, V.
A private club that's one of the *plus cher* in Paris. Not big, but certainly luxurious: steam baths, fitness classes, massage, weights room, squash court, swimming pool, pedicures, manicures and tanning salon. There's also a gym at the **Ritz** on the place Vendôme (20,000F per year, 600F daily).

Vitatop
Vitatop Plein Ciel *Hôtel Sofitel, 8 rue Louis Armand, 75015 (45.54.79.00). Métro Balard.* **Vitatop Porte Maillot** *1 place du Général Koenig, 75017 (40.68.00.21). Métro Porte Maillot.* **Membership** *annual* 5,600F (plus 800F entry fee). **Credit** AmEx, MC, V.
The two Vitatop outlets aim for the top of the market, but membership also gives access to all 19 Gymnase Clubs. Both Vitatops have pools, Jacuzzis and the most modern equipment, and the Porte Maillot branch, on the 22nd floor of a hotel, has cliff-scaling and a small roof-top pool with a body-bronzing area.

Horse Riding

If you frequent the Bois de Boulogne or Bois de Vincennes, you will see plenty of elegantly dressed riders on well-mannered mounts. To ride in either Bois, you must belong to a riding club. Some are exclusive, others accept new members, among them: **La Société d'Equitation de Paris** (45.01.20.06); the **Centre Hippique du Touring** (45.01.20.88) and the **Cercle Hippique du Bois de Vincennes** (48.73.01.28). Also try:

Haras de Jardy
boulevard de Jardy, 92430 Maine-la-Coquette (47.41.97.84). Autoroute 13 direction Rouen, exit Versailles-Vaucresson. **Open** 9am-noon, 2-9pm, Mon-Fri; 9am-7pm Sat, Sun.
This lovely equestrian centre, which also includes a nine-hole golf course and 20 tennis courts, rents by the hour (100F) to riders who have passed an exam with its instructors. You must still ride with a group.

Poney Clubs du Relais
next to the Parc de Pré-Catelan, Bois de Boulogne (45.27.54.65). Métro Porte Maillot, then bus 244. **Open** 9am-7.30pm daily.
Rents ponies by the half-hour (80F per person) but still requires riders to be accompanied by a monitor.

Ice Skating

For an outdoor turn, head for the Jardin des Tuileries where from December to April a rink is set up at the **Carré du Sanglier** (near the place de Concorde) attracting crowds from all over the city. If the temperature drops extremely low and the park's staff posts signs declaring the ice safe, there is also skating on the Lac Superieur in the Bois de Boulogne. Otherwise, go to:

Patinoire de Boulogne
1 rue Victor Griffuelhes, Boulogne-Billancourt (46.21.00.96). Métro Marcel Sembat. **Open** 3.45-6.30pm Mon, Thur; 3.45-6.30pm, 9-11.30pm, Tue, Wed, Fri; 10am-12.30pm, 2pm-5.45pm, 9.15pm-midnight, Sat; 9.45am-12.30pm, 2.30-6pm, Sun. **Admission** 29F; 18F skate hire.
French Olympic skater Surya Bonaly trains here.

Roller Skating

La Main Jaune
place de la Porte-de-Champerret, 75017 (47.63.26.47). Métro Porte-de-Champerret. **Open** 2.30-7pm Wed, Sat, Sun; 10pm-dawn Fri, Sat, eve of public holidays. **Admission** 40F Wed, Sat, Sun, skate hire 10F; 70F Fri, Sat, eve of public holidays, skate hire 15F.
A nightclub and a roller-skating rink, all in one.

Rowing & Watersports

The Seine is too full of Bateaux-Mouches to leave any room for sculls in central Paris, but the **French Rowing Federation** (48.74.43.77) counts over 30 rowing clubs in the Paris region. One of the closest is the **Athletic Club de Boulogne-Billancourt**, 4 quai du Quatre Septembre, 92100 Boulogne Billancourt (46.05.27.17).

Base Nautique de la Villette
15-17 quai de la Loire, 75019 (42.40.29.90). Métro Jaures. **Open** *children* 9am-noon, 2-5pm, Wed; *adults* (16 and over) 9am-4pm Sat.
Children and adults can row, canoe and kayak in the 600m x 65m (656yd x 71yd) basin at La Villette. Equipment is provided, and children may row free on Wed from 9am-noon and 2-5pm. For adults (16-and-over), the centre is open on Saturdays for free courses beginning at 9am and running every hour until 4pm (12F per month registration fee).

Rugby

If you want to play on a French-speaking team, call the **Comité d'Ile de France** (43.42.51.51). If you prefer to ruck and maul with Anglophones, try the **British Rugby Club of Paris**, run by Graham Spensby (42.68.08.08/42.94.29.26). The Club runs two Saturday sides near Versailles and trains once a week in Meudon at the **Standard Athletic Club** (*see above* **Cricket**).

Running

Parisians usually jog in the city's parks or along the *quais*. There are two big races: the Paris Marathon in April and the Paris-Versailles in late September. To enter the Marathon, call 53.17.03.10/fax 53.17.03.13 or write to 17 rue de Sévigné, 75004 Paris. For the Paris-Versailles, a popular 16-kilometre race, call 30.21.10.25 to register in Aug or early Sept.

Snooker/Billiards

The French have their own brand of (pocketless) billiards, and many halls here have only French or American pool tables. The few snooker facilities include the **Bowling de Paris** (*see above* **Bowling**), which has three tables.

Académie de Billard Clichy-Montmartre
84 rue de Clichy, 75009 (48.78.32.85).
Métro Place de Clichy. **Open** 11am-3am Mon-Thur, Sun; 11am-5.30am Fri, Sat. **Rates** 53F-68F per hour.
Gilt mirrors and high ceilings give this parlour plenty of atmosphere. French and American tables as well as snooker and a bar. Fun for a late night.

Blue-Billard
111 rue St-Maur, 75010 (43.55.87.21). Métro Goncourt.
Open 11am-2am daily. **Rates** 60F-65F per hour.
French and American tables; relaxing atmosphere; a bar.

Hôtel Concorde St-Lazare
108 rue St-Lazare, 75007 (40.08.44.44). Métro St Lazare. **Open** 11am-2am daily. **Rates** 50F-65F per hour.
The most elegant setting for playing French billiards, American pool or snooker in Paris. The vast turn-of-the-century salon has recently been redone by Sonia Rykiel.

Swimming Pools

Paris has 35 swimming pools open to the public: 26 municipal, seven run by private organisations and two privately owned (there used to be three, until the famous Piscine Déligny sank into the Seine in 1993). Opening times vary tremendously and change frequently, especially between term times and school holidays. For a serious swim, try first thing in the morning or midday, and avoid Wednesday afternoons and Saturdays when local school kids are unleashed.

Admission to the municipal pools is 13F for adults and 6F50 for children. Privately run or owned pools cost a bit more (20F-25F for adults, 16F-18F for children). Some pools now require swimmers to wear racing suits (no shorts or trunks). For further information, contact **Allô-Sports** (*see above* **Keeping Informed**). The following are in order of *arrondissement*:

Piscine Suzanne-Berlioux
10 place de la Rotonde, 75001 (42.36.98.44).
Métro Châtelet-Les Halles.
Inside the Forum des Halles is an Olympic-size pool with pyramidal skylights. It's open until 10pm on Tue, Thur, Fri. The pool is clean and crowded and has a tropical greenhouse with 700 species of plants. Young and trendy clientele.
Indoor. Pool: 50 x 15m.

Piscine St-Merri
18 rue du Renard, 75004 (42.72.29.45).
Métro Rambuteau or Hôtel-de-Ville.
Centrally located behind the Centre Pompidou in an ugly piece of seventies architecture. It's often reserved for school kids.
Indoor. Solarium. Pool: 25 x 10m.

Piscine de Pontoise
19 rue de Pontoise, 75005 (43.54.82.45).
Métro Maubert-Mutualité.
This old pool with thirties-style glass roof and retro tiles has a dynamic health and fitness programme (*see above* **Club Quartier Latin**). Also classes for children and expectant mothers. Open till midnight Mon-Thur (evening swim, 40F).
Indoor. Solarium. Pool: 33 x 15m. Café.

Piscine Jean Taris
16 rue Thouin, 75005 (43.25.54.03). Métro Cardinal-Lemoine.
Look out onto the Panthéon and the Lycée Henri IV gardens as you paddle in this lovely pool. Equipped for disabled swimmers.
Indoor. Two pools: 25 x 15m, children's pool 25 x 6m.

Piscine du Marché St-Germain
7 rue Clément, 75006 (43.29.08.15). Métro Mabillon.
A rather small, underground pool in the recently-redeveloped complex around the old St-Germain market site.
Indoor. Pool: 25 x 12.5m.

Piscine Reuilly
13 rue Hénard, 75012 (40.02.08.08). Métro Montgallet.
This bright, friendly municipal facility has the two newest pools in Paris (both opened in 1992). Large bay windows on three sides give a view out over a park. Closed Sundays.
Indoor. Solarium. Two pools: 25 x 15m; 12.50 x 5m.

Piscine Roger-LeGall
34 boulevard Carnot, 75012 (44.73.81.12).
Métro Porte de Vincennes.
Almost in the suburbs, on the edge of the Bois de Vincennes, this rather calm pool is covered with a tent every winter that comes off during the hot months.
Outdoor. Solarium. 50 x 15m.

Piscine Butte-aux-Cailles
5 place Paul-Verlaine, 75013 (45.89.60.05).
Métro Place d'Italie.
Built in 1910 and renovated in 1924, the main indoor pool has delightful Italian tiles and an art deco, vaulted ceiling. Two outdoor pools are open in the summer.
One indoor pool: 33 x 12m; two outdoor pools: 25 x 12.5m and 12.5 x 6m.

Aquaboulevard
4 rue Louis-Armand, 75015 (40.60.10.00). Métro Balard/RER Boulevard Victor. **Open** 9am-11pm Mon-Thur; 9am-midnight Fri; 8am-midnight Sat; 8am-11pm Sun. **Admission** *Aquatic Park* 68F adults for 4 hours; 49F 3-12s; free under-3s; 10F each additional hour. *Aquatic Park plus gym* 140F.
If you want a big, splashy time with your children, this might be the place to come. Aquaboulevard has tennis courts, a gym, a bowling alley and a putting green, but its main focus is swimming. The 70,000 square feet of indoor-outdoor water sports facilities include a tropical lagoon, wave pool, water slides and hot baths. There are also 10 bars, and several restaurants.

Piscine Armand-Massard
66 boulevard du Montparnasse, 75015 (45.38.65.19).
Métro Montparnasse-Bienvenüe.
A vast underground swimming complex under the reviled Montparnasse skyscraper. Renovated in 1993, the complex has three pools, one of which is for beginners.
Indoor. Three pools: 33 x 15m, 25 x 12.5m, 12.5 x 6m.

Piscine Emile-Anthoine
9 rue Jean-Rey, 75015 (45.67.10.20). Métro Bir-Hakeim.
A very modern pool with an outdoor jogging track and a view of the nearby Eiffel Tower. Maybe that's why it's so crowded. The pool is ideal for the disabled.
Indoor with terraced garden. Two pools: 25 x 12.5m and 12.5 x 6m.

Piscine Henry-de-Montherlant
32 boulevard Lannes, 75016 (45.03.03.28).
Métro Porte-Dauphine.
A modern pool with a very chic clientele. It's popular but never oppressive. Open until 8.30pm on Tuesday.
Indoor with large outdoor tanning area. Two pools: 25 x 15m, 15 x 6m.

Piscine Hébert
2 rue des Fillettes, 75018 (46.07.60.01).
Métro Marx-Dormoy.
A lovely (but crowded) pool with a retractable roof.
Indoor. Two pools: 25 x 15m, 14 x 12m.

Piscine Georges-Hermant

6, 10 rue David d'Angers, 75019 (42.02.45.10).
Métro Danube.
The biggest pool in the capital, complete with a sliding roof that is opened in the summer. A diving area is reserved for clubs. Open Friday until 8.30pm.
Indoor with sliding roof. Pool: 50 x 20m.

Piscine Georges-Vallerey

148 avenue Gambetta, 75020 (40.31.15.20). Métro Porte des Lilas.
The first pool to hold swimming competitions as an Olympic sport (in 1924). It was here that Johnny Weismuller swam to gold and glory. Today, the pool remains a regular site for top competition and is in mint condition. The roof comes off May to Sept. Open Tue and Thur evenings until 9.15pm.
Indoor with sliding roof. Solarium. Pool: 50 x 18m.

Piscine de Plein Air du Parc du Sceaux

148 bis avenue du Général de Gaulle, 92160 Antony (43.50.39.35). RER line B to Croix de Berny.
Open dawn to dusk May-Sept.
Located next to a regional forest, just 10 minutes from central Paris by RER, this park has four outdoor pools, including an uncluttered, 50m Olympic-size pool, separate deep diving tank with high- and medium-level diving boards and a children's pool. There's also a spacious lawn with plenty of sunbathing and picnic space. The sports park next door has 10 tennis courts (open to the public during the week only).

Tennis: Public Courts

If you want to use any of the 170 city-operated courts, you can either show up and hope for the best (which can mean waiting for hours) or, if you are a resident, using the city's computerised reservation system. To register for this service, pick up an application form from one of the city's 43 tennis centres. After mailing in the form, with a copy of your identity card and two passport-size photos (but no fee), you will have to wait a little over a month to get a reservation number. With this you can then reserve municipal courts by Minitel 3615 Paris (*see chapter* **Survival**). Whether you use the Minitel or simply show up, the price is the same: 33F per hour, 48F per hour with lights.
You can also join a club and play on municipal courts. The cost depends on how long you're staying in Paris. Some clubs cost only 500F in membership fees, plus the 22F court rental fee. Compared to a private club, this is a bargain. For a list, contact **Allô-Sports** (*see above* **Keeping Informed**).

Centre Sportif La Faluère

Route de la Pyramide, Bois de Vincennes, 75012 (43.74.40.93). Métro Château de Vincennes.
Open (with lights) 7am-10pm Mon-Sat; 8am-8pm Sun.
A pleasantly landscaped complex with 21 hard courts in relatively good condition, although many are reserved for club use. Turn up on a weekday morning or early afternoon and you may get a game. The hitting wall costs 4F15 per ½ hour.

Centre Sportif Henry-de-Montherlant

30-32 boulevard Lannes, 75016 (45.03.03.64).
Métro Porte-Dauphine. **Open** 7am-10pm Mon-Sat; 8am-7pm Sun (lights).
On the edge of the Bois de Boulogne, this complex with swimming pool and six hard courts gets a lot of use from college students and clubs. Best to make a reservation. Free hitting wall for those without a partner.

Jardin du Luxembourg

75006 (43.25.79.18). Métro Notre-Dame-des-Champs or RER Luxembourg.
Six of the best public courts in Paris in one of the city's loveliest parks. The trick is getting a chance to play on them. There is a same-day sign-up sheet, so arrive early.

Tennis: Private Clubs

There are some lovely private clubs in and around Paris, but they're very expensive and have very long waiting lists. Courts, though, are generally in superb condition and you don't have to figure out the Minitel to get a reservation.

Club Forest Hill

Eleven clubs in the Paris region (46.30.00.30).
Membership *annual* 3210F (235F a month, plus 300F entry fee the first year); *non-members* 200F per hour.
Credit V.
An affordable alternative, even if most of its locations are beyond the Périphérique. In addition to tennis and squash, several of its clubs have body-building, muscle-toning equipment and instruction. A Forest Hill membership also gives access to **Gymnase Club** and **Aquaboulevard** (*see above*).

Stade Jean Bouin

20-24 avenue du Général-Sarrail, 75016 (46.51.55.40).
Métro Porte d'Auteuil. **Membership** *annual* 5,295F (plus 3,000F entry fee the first year); *15 Apr-15 Oct* 2,650F (plus 1,000F entry fee the first year). **No credit cards.**
The site of the men's qualifying tournament for the French Open: 21 red clay courts (10 indoors).

Tennis de Longchamp

19 boulevard Anatole-France, 92100 Boulogne (46.03.84.49). Métro Jean-Jaurès. **Membership** *annual* 5,300F (plus 2,200F entry fee the first year); *daily* 180F (includes gym). **Credit** MC, V.
The club has 20 well-maintained hardcourts along with a new complex that includes weights and a sauna.

Spectator Sports
Multi-Purpose Venue

Palais Omnisports de Paris-Bercy

8 boulevard de Bercy, 75012 (40.02.61.67/44.68.44.68).
Métro Bercy. **Box office** 11am-6pm Mon-Sat.
Admission from 170F **Credit** MC, V.
A giant, futuristic eighties' sports hall that hosts some major competitions such as indoor tennis tournaments, and a bizarre selection of other events – indoor windsurfing, mountain biking, indoor beach volleyball. Also used for large-scale rock concerts (*see chapter* **Music: Rock, Roots & Jazz**).

Athletics

Every year, in early June, the athletes of the moment assemble in the northern suburb of St-Denis for the **IAAF Humanité Meeting** at the Stade Auguste-Delaune (9, avenue Roger-Semat. Métro St-Denis-Basilique). Information: 49.22.73.73. Tickets cost 90F-120F, available by post or in person at 32 rue Jean-Jaurès, 93528 St-Denis.

Basketball

The French professional leagues are still light years behind the NBA, but the level is fairly high. Racing PSG and Levallois are two of the better teams in the French Pro A division. Matches take place from early Sept to late May.

Levallois Sporting Club Basket

Palais des Sports Marcel Cerdan, 141 rue Danton, 92300 Levallois-Perret (47.58.15.92/47.39.21.20). Métro Pont de Levallois. **Tickets** 60F, 80F.

Racing PSG Basket

Stade Pierre de Coubertin, 82 avenue Georges Lafont 75016 (45.27.79.12). Métro Porte de St-Cloud.
Tickets 20F, 60F.

The French get desperate with the flower of Scotland at the Parc des Princes.

Cycling

It might not hold quite the same sway over the nation as it did during the golden eras of Eddie Merckx and Bernard Hinault, but the **Tour de France** remains France's definitive sporting event. The three-week race, born as a publicity stunt in 1903, follows a different route every July, but always finishes on a Sunday in the Champs-Elysées.

For cycling fans who want to avoid huge crowds, there are four other major events that begin in Paris: *Paris-Nice* in March, *Paris-Roubaix* in April, *Paris-Brussels* in September and *Paris-Tours* in early October. For information call the **Fédération Française du Cyclisme** on 49.35.69.00.

Football

Paris St-Germain F.C.

Parc des Princes, 24 rue du Commandant-Guilbaud, 75016 (ticket info 49.87.29.29). Métro Porte d'Auteuil. **Matches** late July-early May.
With the World Cup coming to France in 1998, a new stadium is being built in St-Denis. Until then the 50,000-seat Parc des Princes remains the epicentre of football attention. It's home to PSG, and a shrine for fans who make the pilgrimage draped in the team's red, white and blue. Lately they've been rewarded with a string of victories in French and European competitions. Tickets to a garden-variety match are not hard to get, but for a major like PSG-Nantes it's a bit of a scramble. Season tickets are available from the stadium (360F-2,040F). Occasional believers can get tickets for most games a month in advance at the ground and from two weeks in advance at FNAC or Virgin (*see chapter* **Services**). Matches draw a passionate but generally well-behaved crowd.

Golf

There are three top-flight professional tournaments in the Paris region, all of which attract the first-rank European players. Tickets(50F-100F) are available in advance from the organisers or on the day of competition at the gate.

Tournoi Perrier de Paris, Golf de St-Cloud, *60 rue du 19 Janvier, 92380 Garches. RER Garches.* **Dates** April. **Information** (47.95.18.19).
Peugeot Open de France, Golf National de Guyancourt, *2 avenue du Golf, 78280 Guyancourt. RER Guyancourt and look for shuttle buses.* **Dates** late June. **Information** (47.72.28.10).
Trophée Lancôme, Golf de St-Nom-la-Brétèche, *rue Henri Frayssineau, 78860 St-Nom-la-Brétèche. Directions: A13 toward Rouen, exit at Versailles Ouest, take RN 307 and follow signs.* **Dates** mid-Sept. **Information** (45.03.85.03).

Horse Racing

The Paris region is abundantly provided with race tracks. There are no private bookmakers in France, so all betting proceeds go back into the race course, where you'll find facilities are very well-maintained. Placing a bet is not complicated. Video monitors at the track list the name, number and odds for each horse. As an example, if you bet 10F at 5.2 odds you win 52F. In the UK, this would be 4.2 to 1 against. You can bet to win (*gagnant*) or to place (*gagnant placé*). The minimum wager is 10F. If you can't make it out to the track, do what one in seven French citizens do on a regular basis: march into a tabac and place a wager with France's Pari-Mutuel-Urbain (PMU), one of the largest off-track betting systems in Europe. If you really want to look like a regular, pick up a copy of *Paris Turf* or *Tiercé Magazine*.

Hippodrome d'Auteuil

Bois de Boulogne, 75016 (45.27.12.25). Métro Porte d'Auteuil. **Admission** 30F.
Steeplechase and the annual *Prix du Président de la République* in mid-April.

Hippodrome de Chantilly

Bois de Boulogne, 60631 Chantilly (16.44.57.02.54). SNCF from Gare du Nord to Chantilly. **Admission** 25F Mon-Sat; 40F Sun (Prix de Diane Hermès 50F).

The Sporting Year

January
Horse racing: Prix d'Amérique trotting race, Vincennes (49.77.17.17).
February
Rugby: Five Nations Cup, Parc des Princes (42.30.03.60).
Tennis: Open Gaz de France, Stade Pierre-de-Coubertin (45.03.85.03).
March
Cycling: Paris-Nice (49.35.69.00).
Football: Coupe de France, Parc des Princes (42.30.03.60).
Gymnastics: Internationaux de France, Palais Omnisport de Paris-Bercy (43.46.12.21).
Windsurfing: Super Fundoor, Palais Omnisport de Paris-Bercy (43.46.12.21).
April
Athletics: Paris Marathon, finishes avenue des Champs-Elysées (42.77.17.84).
Cycling: Paris-Rouaix (49.35.69.00).
Golf: Tournoi Perrier de Paris, Golf de St-Cloud (47.95.18.19).
Horse racing: Prix du Président de la République, Auteuil (45.27.12.25).
May
Sailing: Trois Heures de Paris race on the Seine.
Swimming: Cross-Paris Swim, Pont d'Austerlitz-Pont de Grenelle (40.36.54.15).

Rugby: French Cup Final, Parc des Princes (42.30.03.60).
Tennis: French Open, Stade Roland Garros (47.43.48.00).
June
Athletics: IAAF Humanité Meeting, Stade Auguste-Delaune, St-Denis (49.22.73.73).
Golf: French Open, Golf National de Guyancourt (47.72.28.10).
Horse racing: Prix de Diane Hermès, Chantilly (16.44.57.02.54).
July
Athletics: IAAF Mobil Grand Prix BNP (49.35.69.00).
Cycling: Tour de France, finishes avenue des Champs-Elysées (49.35.69.00).
September
Cycling: Paris-Brussels (49.35.69.00).
Golf: Trophée Lancôme, Golf de St-Nom-la-Brétèche (45.03.85.03).
October
Cycling: Paris-Tours (49.35.69.00).
Horse racing: Prix de l'Arc de Triomphe, Longchamp (44.30.75.00).
November
Tennis: Open de Paris, Palais Omnisport de Paris-Bercy (43.46.12.21).
December
Showjumping: International Showjumping, Palais Omnisport de Paris-Bercy (43.46.12.21).

Races have been held here since 1834. The second Sunday in June sees the *Prix de Diane Hermès*, the 'French Derby', when odds run on what to wear as much as on the horses.

Hippodrome de Longchamp
Bois de Boulogne, 75016 (44.30.75.00). Métro Porte d'Auteuil, then shuttle bus on race days. **Admission** 30F Mon-Sat; 40F Sun (Arc de Triomphe 50F).
Hosts one of the top flat races in the world, the *Prix de l'Arc de Triomphe* in early October, also a top event for top hats.

Hippodrome de St-Cloud
1 rue du Camp Canadien, 92210 St Cloud (47.71.69.26). RER line A to Reuil-Malmaison. **Admission** 25F Mon-Fri; 35F Sat, Sun.
A lovely track in a southern suburb; has flat-racing but a much longer season than Longchamp.

Hippodrome de Vincennes
Bois de Vincennes, 75012 (49.77.17.17; restaurant 43.68.64.94). RER line A to Joinville-le-Pont, then 10 minute walk or free shuttle bus. **Admission** 15F.
East of Paris, this course specialises in *le trot*. Its major event, the *Prix d'Amérique*, is held on the last Sunday in January.

Rugby

Most French Rugby Union teams are concentrated in southwestern France with Paris (and Grenoble) merely outposts. But to catch a good local scrum, hop on bus 164 out to Stade Yves du Manoir (12 rue François Faber, 92700 Colombes) where **Racing Club de France** hosts its rivals a dozen or so times a year. Tickets are from 30F to 110F and games are well attended. For the team schedule ring 45.67.55.86. Five Nation matches and the French cup final (in mid-May) are held at the **Parc des Princes** (*see above* **Football**).

Tennis

Open Gaz de France
Stade Pierre-de-Coubertin, 82 avenue Georges-Lafont, 75016 (45.27.79.12). Métro Porte de St-Cloud.
Information (45.03.85.03). **Dates** mid-Feb. **Tickets** can be booked 3 months in advance 80F-180F.
Big-name women players like Graf and Pierce compete for more fame and a lot more fortune in this WTA indoor event.

Tournée Roland Garros/French Open
Fédération Française de Tennis, Stade Roland Garros, 2 avenue Gordon Bennett, 75016 (47.43.48.00). Métro Porte d'Auteuil. **Dates** end May-early June.
The second leg of the Grand Slam, always referred to by the name of the stadium, Roland Garros. Garros was a French aviation pioneer and rugby player who died in World War I, and became inextricably linked with tennis when some of his friends decided to name a new stadium after him. The Open is held during the last week of May and first week of June. Getting tickets is difficult but not impossible, especially if you are not after centre court seats during the second week. To reserve, write for a reservation form before the end of February. Unsold tickets go on sale at the stadium two weeks before the Open starts. Count on spending at least 150F for a decent seat. In 1995 *entrée stade* and *billet courts annexes* were introduced, cheaper tickets to watch the lesser, unseeded players volley away from the centre court (45F-75F). As a last resort, you can try buying from touts, who are always present in large numbers (don't be afraid to bargain hard).

Open de Paris
Palais Omnisport de Paris-Bercy, 8 boulevard de Bercy, 75012 (43.46.12.21). Métro Bercy. **Dates** early Nov.
Tickets can be booked 6 months in advance 72F-292F.
Boris, Stefan and Goran have all won this indoor tournament.

Theatre

*The avant-garde is alive and well in the Parisian theatre world,
sharing centre stage with timeless classics and circus wonders.*

Paris prides itself on being the city with the greatest number of theatres of any in the world, and the theatre scene here is highly internationally-oriented. For anglophones, though, appreciating the French theatrical tradition itself may require a cultural leap. Two streams dominate – subsidised and private theatres. The former are funded by public bodies, especially the Ministry of Culture, on the basis of the artistic and intellectual content of their work. To foreign eyes some of their productions can seem almost wilfully heavy, and the French intellectual tradition is reflected in a taste for very long performances (three hours with no interval is not uncommon). Private theatres, meanwhile, offer star performers and lighter fare.

A good indicator of quality are the Molière Awards, presented in early Spring, and widely advertised. Many good, innovative productions also reach Paris as part of the **Festival d'Automne** (*see chapter* **Paris by Season**), or after having been premiered in France's major theatre festival in Avignon in the summer. Much anticipated in France currently is the return to theatre work of director Patrice Chéreau, after his foray into the cinema with *La Reine Margot.*

If you don't feel like handling a performance in French, take a look backstage. Many theatres are steeped in history and are architectural landmarks. The Comédie Française and both Opéra Houses offer guided tours (*see also chapters* **Sightseeing, Dance** *and* **Music: Classical & Opera**).

AT THE CIRCUS

One special French current that contrasts spectacularly with the wordiness of some local drama is 'Alternative Circus'. Best-known internationally through the group *Arkaos,* it dispenses with skinny tigers and tired lions to incorporate mime, music and magic. For an extraordinary experience try the *Théâtre Equestre Zingaro,* a blend of dashing horsemanship and theatrical effects. They tour most of the time, and legendary cloaked ringmaster Bartabas leads his unique troupe into their wooden circus ring in the Paris suburb of Aubervilliers for only a couple of months each year. Check *Pariscope* to see when one of their haunting spectacles might be coming up (at **Zingaro**, 176 avenue Jean-Jaurès, 93 Aubervilliers, 44.78.25.02). Look out too for other roving troupes such as the surreal *Cirque de Plume.*

Booking Tips

Few theatres are open on Monday or Sunday evenings, and many close in July and August. For full details of current programmes check local listings magazines. You can book theatre tickets by Minitel, on Access code 3615 THEA. Private theatres offer 50% reductions on previews, which are widely advertised. Also, there is a special two-tickets-for-the-price-of-one event at all theatres in May (*see chapter* **Paris by Season**). The agencies below specialise in theatre tickets; for general ticket agencies, *see chapter* **Services**.
Agence Chèque Théâtre *2nd floor, 33 rue Peletier, 75009 (42.46.72.40). Métro Le Peletier.* **Open** 10am-7pm Mon-Sat. **Credit** V.
Kiosque Théâtre *across from 15 place de la Madeleine, 75009. (no phone). Métro Madeleine.* **Open** 12.30-8pm Mon-Sat; 12.30-4pm Sun. **Credit** V. Same-day tickets at half-price, plus 16F commission per seat.
Branches: Forum des Halles, 75001; In front of Gare Montparnasse, 75015.

National Theatres

Comédie Française – Salle Richelieu
2 rue de Richelieu, 75001 (40.15.00.15). Métro Palais-Royal. **Box office** 11am-6pm daily. Closed Aug.
Tickets 50F-170F. **Credit** AmEx, EC, MC, V.
The most established theatre in France, founded by Louis XIV. A mixture of French classics (Molière, Racine) and lesser-known works, often presented by important directors.
Guided tours. Wheelchair access.

Comédie Française – Théâtre du Vieux Colombier
21 rue du Vieux-Colombier, 75006 (44.39.87.00). Métro St-Sulpice. **Box office** 11am-7pm Tue-Sat; 1-6pm Sun. Closed 2 July-1 Sept, Closed for guided tours Aug.
Tickets 130F; 95F over-60s, unemployed; 60F under-25s, students under 27 (available 45min before performances). **Credit** V.
Reopened in 1993 as a branch of the Comédie Française, offering contemporary plays and small-scale classical works. *Guided tours. Wheelchair access.*

Odéon – Théâtre de l'Europe
1 place de l'Odéon, 75006 (44.41.36.36). Métro Odéon/RER Luxembourg. **Box office** 11am-6.30pm Mon-Sat; *telephone bookings only* 11am-7pm Sun. Closed mid July-mid Sept. **Tickets** *main space* 30F-170F; *Petit Odéon* 50F-70F. **Credit** EC, MC, V.
One of Paris's most acclaimed theatres. The main house and the 80-seat Petit Odéon both present seasons centred on a specific country, in French and the original language. *Wheelchair access.*

Théâtre National de Chaillot
1 place du Trocadéro, 75016 (47.27.81.15). Métro Trocadéro. **Box office** 9am-7pm Mon-Sat; 11am-5pm Sun. *Telephone bookings* 11am-7pm Mon-Sat; 11am-5pm Sun. Tickets 150F; 110F under-25s, over-60s; 80F students, 30min before show. **Credit** *in person only* V.

Well-staged and flamboyantly directed plays with the emphasis on entertainment, often by star artistic director Jérôme Savary. Mythical choreographer Maurice Béjart and his dance company are regularly invited to perform here. *Wheelchair access.*

Théâtre National de la Colline
15 rue Malte-Brun, 75020 (44.62.52.52). Métro Gambetta. **Box office** 11am-6pm Sun; 11am-8pm Tue-Sat. Closed 25 June-Sept. **Tickets** 150F; 110F over-60s, students. **Credit** AmEx, DC, EC, MC, V.
The newest theatre in Paris, entirely devoted to international contemporary drama. Argentinian Director Jorge Lavelli's programmes have a socio-political slant.

Subsidised Theatres

Bouffes du Nord
37 bis boulevard de la Chapelle, 75010. (46.07.34.50). Métro La Chapelle. **Box office** 11am-6pm Mon-Sat. Closed July-Aug. **Tickets** 100F-30F; 70F students. **No credit cards.**
Peter Brook's acclaimed experimental productions ensure this remains at the forefront of the Paris theatre world. The nineteenth-century building is itself worth a visit; actors perform amid flaking walls and a dirt floor. Note that the métro station is not *Porte de* la Chapelle.

Cartoucherie
route de Champ-de-Manœuvres, 75012 (reservations for all theatres 47.00.15.87). Métro Château de Vincennes, then shuttle bus or bus 112.
A multi-theatre complex in the Bois de Vincennes, opened in 1970 by theatre pioneer Ariane Mnouchkine, who still directs the **Théâtre du Soleil** often considered the most avant-garde theatre in Paris. The **Théâtre de l'Epée de Bois** hosts a bilingual Franco-Spanish troupe.
Wheelchair access at all theatres, but warn when booking.
Atelier du Chaudron
(43.28.97.04). **Box office** 2-5pm daily. **Tickets** 110F; 80F over-60s, unemployed; 50F students. **No credit cards.**
Théâtre de l'Aquarium
(43.74.99.61). **Box office** 10am-6pm Mon-Fri; 2-6pm Sun. **Tickets** 50F-110F. **No credit cards.**
Théâtre de l'Epée de Bois
(48.08.39.74). **Box office** 10am-6pm Mon-Sat; 10am-4pm Sun. **Tickets** 110F; 80F over-60s, unemployed, students. **No credit cards.**
Théâtre du Soleil
(43.74.87.63/reservations 43.74.24.08). **Box office** 4-7pm daily. **Tickets** 120F; 100F over-60s, students. **No credit cards.**
Théâtre de la Tempête
(43.28.36.36). **Box office** 2-6pm Mon, Sat; 11am-1pm, 2-7pm, Tue-Fri. **Tickets** 110F; 80F over-60s, unemployed, students. **No credit cards.**

Théâtre de la Bastille
76 rue de la Roquette, 75011. (43.57.42.14). Métro Bastille. **Box office** 10am-7pm Mon-Fri; 2.30-7pm Sat. **Tickets** 100F; 70F over-60s, students. **No credit cards.**
An innovative theatre which promotes risk-taking new theatre and dance (*see also chapter* **Dance**).
Wheelchair access.

Théâtre de l'Athénée Louis Jouvet
4 square Opéra-Louis Jouvet, 75009. (47.42.67.27). Métro Opéra. **Box office** 11am-7pm Mon-Fri. **Tickets** 30F-140F; 70F students, under-20s. **No credit cards.**
A delightful mock-Rococo theatre where literary plays, from Sophocles to Kleist, are presented by challenging directors. Highly recommended.

Théâtre de la Ville
2 place du Châtelet, 75004 (42.74.22.77). Métro Châtelet-Les Halles. **Box office** 11am-6pm Mon; 11am-8pm Tue-Sat; *telephone bookings* 9am-7pm Mon; 9am-8pm Tue-Sat. **Tickets** 80F-190F; 70F-120F under-25s, students. **Credit** DC, EC, MC, V.
Funded by the City of Paris, this major dance theatre also presents a couple of plays a year, varying from excellent to highly controversial. *See also chapters* **Dance, Music: Classical and Opera** *and* **Music: Rock, Roots & Jazz**).

Théâtre du Rond Point – Compagnie Marcel Maréchal
2 bis avenue Franklin D Roosevelt, 75008. (44.95.98.00). Métro Franklin-D-Roosevelt. **Box office** 10am-7pm Mon-Fri. **Tickets** details unavailable at time of writing.
Home for many years to two French theatre legends, Madeleine Renaud and Jean-Louis Barrault, this nineteenth-century former circus has recently been renovated to host the earthy Marcel Maréchal and his company. It is due to reopen in Autumn 1995.

Suburban Theatres

Thanks to an official policy of cultural decentralisation there are several major public theatres in the Paris suburbs, which serve as a base for some top directors, such as the Freudian Brigitte Jacques at Aubervilliers, responsible for bringing Tony Kushner's *Angels in America* to France, and Bernard Sobel in Gennevilliers. They often present high-profile productions, and are easily accessible by métro or RER, and so are not to be dismissed.

Howard Barker's The Castle *at the* **Odéon – Théâtre de l'Europe**.

Aubervilliers/Théâtre de la Commune
2 rue Edouard Poisson, Aubervilliers, Seine St-Denis 93300 (48. 34.67.67). Métro Aubervilliers-Pantin-4 Chemins. **Box office** 9am-6.30pm Mon-Fri, Closed Aug. Tickets 120F; 70F under-26s. **No credit cards.**
Re-opening Jan 1996

Bobigny/MC93
La Maison de la Culture, 1 boulevard Lénine, Bobigny, Seine St-Denis 93000(48.31.11.45). Métro Bobigny-Pablo Picasso. **Box office** 10am-7pm Mon-Sat. Closed mid July-mid Aug. **Tickets** 95F-130F. **Credit** AmEx, MC, V

Gennevilliers/Théâtre de Gennevilliers
Centre Dramatique National, 41 avenue des Grésillons, Gennevilliers (41. 32. 26.26). Métro Gabriel Péri. **Box office** 1-7pm Tue-Sat. Closed mid July-mid Aug. **Tickets** 130F; 110F under-25s. **Credit** V

Nanterre/Théâtre des Amandiers
7 avenue Pablo Picasso, Nanterre 92022 (46.14.70.00). RER line A to Nanterre Préfecture, then free shuttle bus every quarter hour to theatre. **Box office** noon-7pm Tue-Sat. Closed Aug. **Tickets** 130F; 100F over-60s, unemployed, students (110F, 70F Mon, Thur only). **Credit** AmEx, MC, V.

St-Denis/Théâtre Gérard Philipe
59 boulevard Jules Guesde, St-Denis 93207 (42.43.17.17). RER line D to St-Denis, then follow the arrows (5 min)/Bus 155 from Porte de Clignancourt. **Box office** 12.30-7pm Mon-Sat. Closed Aug. **Tickets** 110F; 80F over-60s, students under 26; 60F unemployed. **Credit** *in person only* MC, V.

Private Theatres

Antoine-Simone Berriau
14 boulevard de Strasbourg, 75010 (42.08.77.71/ 42.08.76.58). Métro Strasbourg-St-Denis. **Box office** 11am-7pm daily. **Tickets** 80F-220F; 110F students. **Credit** EC, MC, V.
An elegant theatre with a glorious past, famous for introducing Ibsen to France. It now mainly stages classic and modern French works.
Wheelchair access.

Atelier
Place Charles Dullin, 75018 (46.06.49.24). Métro Anvers. **Box office** 11am-7pm daily. **Tickets** 50F-250F. **Credit** EC, MC, V.
At the foot of Montmartre, another theatre with a rich history, and today a noticeable preference for literary works. A recent hit, directed by film and stage star Laurent Terzieff, was TS Eliot's *Murder in the Cathedral.*

Comédie des Champs Elysées
15 avenue Montaigne, 75008 (47.23.37.21; bookings 47.20.08.24). Métro Alma-Marceau. **Box office** 11am-6pm Mon; 11am-7.30pm Tue-Fri; 11am-4pm Sat. **Tickets** 110F-250F. **Credit** EC, MC, V.
Refined theatre presenting quality hits. A major success has been its production of *Art* by Yasmina Reza, winner of two Molière awards in 1995.

Edouard VII Sacha Guitry
10 place Edouard VII, 75009 (47.42.59.92). Métro Opéra. **Box office** 11am-6.30pm daily. **Tickets** 80F-290F; half-price over-60s, students, on Sun only. **Credit** AmEx, DC, EC, MC, V.
An attractive old theatre offering a mainstream repertoire, in a smart neighbourhood.
Wheelchair access (limited numbers).

Marais
37 rue Volta, 75003 (42.78.03.53). Métro Arts-et-Métiers. **Box office** 10am-7pm Mon-Sat; *telephone bookings* 9.30am-7pm. **Tickets** 150F; 100F students (not Sat). **No credit cards.**
A small 80-seater that generally offers serious contemporary drama.

Mogador
25 rue de Mogador, 75009 (48.78.04.04). Métro Trinité. **Box office** 11am-7pm Mon-Sat; 11am-4pm Sun. **Tickets** 150F-250F. **Credit** V.
The popular Mogador often houses high-quality productions from the national theatres after they have finished their initial runs. Thanks to its giant size (all of 1,700 seats) it's often used for musicals too.
Wheelchair access.

Montparnasse
31 rue de la Gaîté, 75014 (43.22.77.74). Métro Gaîté. **Box office** 11am-7pm Tue-Sat. Closed Aug. **Tickets** *large theatre* 90F-230F; *small theatre* 130F. **Credit** EC, MC, V.
Two auditoria that stage a variety of solid imported pieces and recent-ish French works. Lunch and wine are served before shows in the larger theatre.

Palais-Royal
38 rue Montpensier, 75001 (42.97.59.81). Métro Palais-Royal. **Box office** 11am-7pm Mon-Sat; 11am-6pm Sun. Closed Aug. **Tickets** 125F-205F; 100F student standby. **Credit** EC, MC, V.
High-quality comedies from light farce to satire are staged in this beautiful theatre, with an ornate eighteenth-century interior. Note that it's worth spending at least 100F to get a decent view.

Poche Montparnasse
75 boulevard du Montparnasse, 75006 (45.48.92.97). Métro Montparnasse-Bienvenüe. **Box office** 1-7.30pm Tue-Sat; noon-3pm Sun on performance days. **Tickets** 110F-176F. **Credit** V.
A small theatre known for its charming literary productions.
Wheelchair access.

Théâtre de la Huchette
23 rue de la Huchette, 75005 (43.26.38.99). Métro St-Michel. **Box office** 5-9.30pm Mon-Sat. Closed 1-15 Jan. **Tickets** 100F; 70F students (not Sat). **No credit cards.**
No surprises in the programme – this little Latin Quarter theatre has been performing Ionesco's *La Cantatrice Chauve* (*The Bald Prima Donna*) since 1957. High-school French will get you through. The company also stages a number of his other plays as double and triple features.

Théâtre de la Madeleine – Compagnie Valère-Desailly
19 rue de Surène, 75008 (42.65.07.09). Métro Madeleine. **Box office** 11am-7pm Mon-Sat; 11am-3.30pm Sun. **Tickets** 80F-240F; 165F over-60s; 85F students. **Credit** EC, MC, V.
A critic's favourite that deserves more attention, with a programme featuring a sprinkling of experimental works.
Wheelchair access, limited spaces.

Théâtre de Verdure du Jardin de Shakespeare
Pré Catelan, route de la Reine Marguerite, Bois de Boulogne, 75016 (42.71.46.03). Métro Porte Maillot, then bus 244, stop Bagatelle Pré-Catalan. **Box office** half hour before show, or by telephone. **Tickets** 80F-100F; 60F over-60s, students. **No credit cards.**
This theatre in a garden in the Bois de Boulogne – open May to October – presents French classics as well as Shakespeare.

The nearest Parisian equivalent to fringe theatres, the Café-Théâtres developed out of cabaret, and in the post-'68 era spawned such stars as Miou Miou and Gérard Depardieu. Shows run the range from pure cabaret and comedy to small-scale plays, and quality is just as variable. Venues are small, smoky, and don't necessarily include a café.

Au Bec Fin
6 rue Thérèse, 75001 (42.96.29.35).
Métro Palais-Royal or Pyramides. **Shows** 6.45pm, 8pm, 9.15pm, 10.30pm Mon-Sat; children's show 2.30pm Wed, Sat, daily during school holidays. **Restaurant open** 11am-3pm, 7.30pm-2am, Mon-Sat. **Tickets** 80F; 65F student; 45F under-10s. **Credit** MC, V.
An intimate 60-seater theatre above a restaurant. Expect to see short plays, comic sketches and *chansons paillardes* (bawdy songs), plus open auditions on Tuesday evenings.

Le Bataclan
50 boulevard Voltaire, 75011 (48.06.21.11). Métro Oberkampf. **Shows** 10.30am-7.30pm Mon-Sat. **Tickets** 110F. **No credit cards.**
One of the oldest musical halls of Paris hosts a heated Monday night stand-up improv competition called *Les Matchs d'Improvisation. See also chapters* **Nightlife** *and* **Music: Rock, Roots & Jazz.**

Blancs-Manteaux
15 rue des Blancs-Manteaux, 75004 (48.87.15.84).
Métro Hôtel-de-Ville or Rambuteau. **Shows** 8pm, 9.15pm, 10.30pm, Mon-Sat. **Bar open** 10am-midnight daily.
Tickets *single shows* 80F Mon; 70F Tue-Fri; *two shows* 110F Mon-Fri; 140F Sat. **No credit cards.**
Two 100-seat theatres staging lots of satires of *BCBG* life, and many one-person shows. One of the longest established café-théâtres.

Café de la Gare
41 rue du Temple, 75004 (42.78.52.51). Métro Hôtel-de-Ville. **Shows** 8pm, 10pm, Tue-Sat; 8.30pm Sun. **Tickets** 80F-100F. **Credit** V
A former stables of a Marais mansion that's been home to the same company for 20 years. Talents such as Coluche and Depardieu emerged here. Still one of the best for a fun evening.

Le Movies
15 rue Michel-le-Comte, 75003 (42.74.14.22). Métro Rambuteau. **Shows** 9pm, 10,30pm daily. **Restaurant open** noon-2.30pm, 7.30pm-midnight; Mon-Fri; 7.30pm-midnight Sat. **Tickets** 170F show plus meal; 80F show. **Credit** EC, MC, V.
Thursdays, Fridays and Saturdays, the bar area becomes a stage, mainly for stand-ups. Open-mike session every Sunday.

Petit Casino
17 rue Chapon, 75003 (42.78.36.50). Métro Arts-et-Métiers. **Shows** 9pm, 10.30pm, Tue-Sun. **Restaurant open** 9am-midnight daily. **Tickets** *one show* 70F; *meal and two shows* 220F Tue-Fri, Sun; 260F Sat, public holidays. **Credit** MC, V.
A trendy haunt that hosts one man/woman shows, double acts and short plays, with quite a good restaurant attached.

Point Virgule
7 rue Ste-Croix-de-la-Bretonnerie, 75004 (42.78.67.03). Métro Hôtel-de-Ville. **Shows** 8pm, 9.15pm, 10.30pm, daily. **Bar open** 3.30-11.30pm daily. **Tickets** 80F; 130F two shows; 65F unemployed, students. **No credit cards.**
A rather cramped stalwart of the circuit that has a reputation as a talent-spotter. Shows are mainly one-person affairs.

Théâtre Edgar
58 boulevard Edgar-Quinet, 75014 (42.79.97.97). Métro Edgar-Quinet. **Shows** 8.15pm, 9.30pm, 10.30pm, Mon-Sat. **Tickets** 80F-90F, 65F-70F students. **No credit cards.**
Good quality small plays in a suitably-sized venue. Some productions run for years, with an occasional change of cast.

English Language Theatre in Paris

Paris currently hosts a growing number of resident English-language theatre companies. The bilingual **Dear Conjunction** was founded in 1991 by Les Clack and Barbara Bray to perform new and established plays both in Paris and London, and they also read new plays regularly at the **Village Voice** bookshop (*see chapter* **Specialist Shops**).

The **Compagnie Robert Cordier** is a long-established international repertory company that performs in English, French or sometimes a slightly strange mixture of the two. They also have a drama school. Their Paris programmes mainly feature contemporary work, such as Shephard and Duras. Contemporary playwrights are also featured by the **On Stage Theatre Company** and the **Gare St-Lazare Company** of writer-director Bob Meyer.

A company that works mainly in education, but also occasionally performs for an English-speaking audience, is Ann and Andrew Wilson's **ACT**. Working at the **Main d'Or**, they mostly perform modern classics, and organise a month-long festival of theatre in English there each spring. All the theatres listed here regularly present productions in English.

Théâtre de la Main d'Or
15 passage de la Main d'Or, 75011 (48.05.67.89).
Métro Ledru-Rollin. **Box office** 10am-7pm. **Tickets** 140F; 80F over-60s, students. **No credit cards.** *Wheelchair access.*

Théâtre de Nesle
8 rue de Nesle, 75006 (46.34.61.04). Métro Odéon. **Box office** 2-7pm Tue-Sat. **Tickets** 70F, 100F. **No credit cards.** *Wheelchair access.*

Le Théâtre du Tourtour
20 rue Quincampoix, 75004 (48.87.82.48). Métro Rambuteau. **Box office** 2-8pm daily. **Tickets** 60F-100F. **No credit cards.**

In Focus

Business

Organisations and services that will help you get past first base in the Paris business world.

The 1990s have not been kind to corporate France. The economy is now pulling out of recession, but unemployment remains severe. France, however, has struggled to sustain an attractive environment for business, keeping inflation low and wages tight, and the country still has one of the highest rates of direct foreign investment in the world.

More than 8,000 foreign companies currently operate in the Ile-de-France region, and Paris hosts more international conventions than any other city in the world. Foreign investors own about one third of outstanding French stocks and bonds, and have taken good advantage of France's massive privatisation programme, begun in 1994.

As giant state-owned enterprises and Big Business are broken up, the hope is that small businesses will take their place. Self employment or starting a small business have been made easier and less expensive by the *loi Madelin*, which provides for a 30 per cent reduction in health-insurance payments in the first two years of business.

Foreigners who come to Paris to do business or start one will find a burgeoning community of English-speaking expat businesses open to new entrants. When dealing with the French business community, it's good to remember that, as in many countries, the French feel more comfortable working with someone they know – take every opportunity to cement business relationships over lunch.

Institutions & Information

Paris embassies are big, busy bureaucracies, and not always the best place to get information and advice. The French Embassy or consulate in your own country, your own government's trade office or professional associations may be more helpful. In Paris an excellent first stop for anyone initiating business in France is the **Bourse du Commerce**. A wide range of business information is also available on **Minitel** (*see chapter* **Survival**).

American Chamber of Commerce

21 avenue George V, 75008 (47.23.70.28). Métro George V or Alma Marceau. **Open** 9am-5.30pm Mon-Fri. Library open to non-members 10am-12.30pm Tue, Thur, 50F per day.
The American Chamber hosts two regular social events each month for its members, and has an active small-business committee. Its directory (available to non-members, 300F) lists US firms operating in France and Franco-American organizations in Paris.

Bourse du Commerce

2 rue de Viarmes, 75001 (45.08.37.06). Métro Châtelet-Les Halles. **Open** 9am-6pm Mon-Fri.
A branch of the **CCIP** (*see below*) housing a wide range of different services oriented towards new businesses. *L'Espace Création* (45.08.39.16) is a first stop for help and information when setting up in France. The *Centre de Formalités des Entreprises* (45.08.38.11) is a central office that will route your application to start a business to the myriad number of French authorities that have to be contacted as part of the process of company registration.

British Embassy Commercial Library

35 rue du Faubourg St-Honoré, 75008 (42.66.36.12/fax 42.66.95.90). Métro Concorde. **Open** 10am-1pm, 2.30-5pm, Mon-Fri, by appointment only.
The library has a wide range of information on the French market, and will also assist British companies who wish to develop their sales in France, set up a French subsidiary or find an agent to do so. An appointment is required.

Chambre de Commerce et d'Industrie Franco-Britannique

41 rue de Turenne, 75003 (44.59.25.20). Métro Chemin Vert or St-Paul. **Open** 2.15-5.30pm Mon-Thur; 2.15-4pm Fri.
The Chamber promotes contacts in the Franco-British business community through talks, social events, business briefings and seminars. Non-members can buy the annual trade directory and use the library, for a 50F per day fee.

Chambre de Commerce et d'Industrie de Paris (CCIP)

27 avenue de Friedland, 75008 (42.89.70.00). Métro George V. **Open** 9am-6pm Mon-Fri.
A huge organisation which provides an enormous range of services for businesses big and small. At the back of this building, at 16 rue Chateaubriand, is the best business library in the city, and one of the chamber's information centres. *Le Guide de Contacts* is a free guide to the Chamber's services, and *Foreigners: Starting Up Your Company in France*, one of the few publications in English, is 48F. The CCIP also provides trade, market and export information on Minitel 36.28.1992.

Créa Conseil

41, rue Saint-Augustin, 75002 (47.42.25.70). Métro Opéra. **Open** 9.30am-6pm Mon-Fri.
A non-profit-making association that offers tax, legal and regulatory advice to entrepreneurs starting up their own businesses. A consultation is 300F an hour, or 3,000F for setting up an *SARL* or limited liability company.

US Embassy Commercial Section

4 avenue Gabriel, 75008. (43.12.28.18, direct line to library). Métro Champs-Elysées-Clemenceau. **Open** 2-5pm Mon-Fri by appointment only.
A business library that also provides individual advice and assistance on contacts, research and information. The electronic information service, on Minitel 36.28.00.61, will respond to inquiries within 24 hours on weekdays.

Press & Publications

For business and financial news, the French dailies *La Tribune* and *Les Echos*, and the weekly *Investir* are the tried and trusted sources. German-owned *Capital*, its sister magazine *Management* and the weightier *L'Expansion* are worthwhile monthlies. *Défis* has tips and resources for the entrepreneur, while the new magazine *Initiatives* is for the self-employed. There's also the all-news business radio station *BFM 96.4*, and on the Minitel, 3615 CD offers real-time stock quotes.

The business directories *Kompass France* and *Kompass Régional* can be consulted on Minitel on 3617 KOMPASS, and, free of charge, in the **Centre Pompidou** library (*see chapters* **Sightseeing** *and* **Museums**), which also has detailed French market profiles. Standard English-language reference is *The French Company Handbook*, published by the *International Herald Tribune* (41.43.93.00). Almost every expat businessperson in Paris has a copy of *Paris-Anglophone* (120F), a listing of 4,000 English-speaking companies, professionals and organisations, published by **Association Frank** (*see below* **Internet Services**).

Banking and Finance

As well as the usual services, most major banks will refer you to lawyers, accountants and tax consultants at special discounted rates and fees, and several US and British banks provide other special services for expatriates. For everyday banking needs, *see chapter* **Essential Information**.

Samina Arnoult

26 boulevard de Clichy, 75018 (42.57.37.17/fax 42.59.58.19). Métro Pigalle. **Open** phone for appointment.
Financial advisers are a new and growing breed in France, and Ms Arnoult, bilingual and formerly of NatWest and Legal & General, is one of the best and the brightest.

Banque Transatlantique

17 boulevard Haussmann, 75009 (40.22.80.00). Métro Chausée d'Antin **Open** 9am to 6pm Mon-Fri.
This French bank is known for its expatriate services, and will even help you find an apartment. Ask for Laure Hebert or Eric Meunier in the private clientèle department.

Citibank

30 avenue des Champs-Elysées, 75008 (40.76.33.00) Métro Franklin D. Roosevelt. **Open** 9.30am-7pm Mon-Fri.
Banking by phone or Minitel, plus lunchtime and evening opening. To make an appointment with English-speaking staff, call Citiphone at 49.05.49.05, 24 hours daily.

Trade Fairs & Conferences

Paris has been the world's leading centre for international trade fairs for more than a decade, holding over 500 exhibitions a year, from the Paris Auto Show to the major fashion collections.

Fédération Française des Salons Spécialisés

22 avenue Franklin D Roosevelt, 75008 (42.25.05.80). Métro Franklin D Roosevelt. **Open** 9am-1pm, 2pm-6pm, Mon-Fri.
The free *Salons Nationaux et Internationaux en France* is a calendar of French trade shows. The information is also available on Minitel 3616 SALONS.

Major Exhibition Centres

CNIT

2 place de la Défense, BP 200, 92053 Paris La Défense (46.92.18.65). Métro Grande Arche de La Défense.

Palais des Congrès

2 place de la Porte Maillot, 75017 (40.68.22.22). Métro Porte Maillot.

Parc des Expositions de Paris

Porte de Versailles, 75015 (43.95.37.00). Métro Porte de Versailles.

Parc des Expositions Paris-Nord

Villepinte, BP 60004, Paris Nord 2, 95970 Roissy-Charles de Gaulle. (48.63.30.30). RER line B3 to Parc des Expositions.

Business Services

Accountants

France Audit Expertise

148 boulevard Malesherbes, 75017 (43.80.42.98). Métro Wagram. **Open** 9am-1pm, 2-7pm, Mon-Fri.
Handles companies of all sizes.

Maximilien Lambert

26 rue de la Pépinière, 75008. Métro St. Augustin (42.93.76.16/fax 42.93.76.09) **Open** 9am-6pm Mon-Fri.
This independent French-certified accountant and statutory auditor works with self-employed business people, offering reasonably priced services.

Copywriting

Ursula Gruber Communication Internationale

83 rue St-Honoré, 75001 (42.33.57.61). Métro Châtelet-Les Halles or Louvre. **Open** 9am-6pm Mon-Fri.
Specialists in multilingual adaptation of advertising copy. Some 200 professional copywriters work in 23 languages.

Text Appeal

133 rue des Pyrénées, 75020 (43.56.74.75). Métro Maraîchers. **Open** 8am-8pm Mon-Fri.
Elliot Polak's small international team can transform your ad for US, French, German, Spanish or Italian audiences.

Graphic Design

Design Principals

26 boulevard Raspail, 75007 (45.49.29.11). Métro Sèvres-Babylone. **Open** 9am-6pm Mon-Fri.
Editorial work such as book covers, art catalogues and annual reports for clients with multicultural and multilingual design problems are the speciality of this American team.

Rebus

18 rue Ste-Croix-de-la-Bretonnerie, 75004 (42.77.20.49). Métro Hôtel de Ville. **Open** 9am-7pm, Mon-Fri.

British design team that produce graphics for fashion houses, and also logos, books, video covers and top-quality brochures, promotional material and newsletters.

Lawyers

Claire Adenis-Lamarre
29 avenue Georges-Mandel, 75116. Métro Trocadéro (47.55.45.17/fax 47.55.17 03) **Open** 9.30am-1pm, 2-6.30pm, Mon-Fri.
Friendly French business lawyer, who speaks English and German, helps individuals start businesses and advises them on French commercial and employment law.

Levine & Okoshken
51 avenue Montaigne, 75008 (44.13.69.50/42.56.34.92/fax 45.63.24.96) .Métro Franklin D. Roosevelt. **Open** 9am-6pm Mon-Fri.
A specialist in tax and corporate law, with many English-speaking clients.

Shubert & Dusausoy
190 boulevard Haussmann, 75008 (40.76.01.43/fax 40.76.01.44) Métro Charles de Gaulle-Etoile. **Open** 9.30am-6.30pm Mon-Fri.
Specialises in helping English-speaking business people setting up in France.

Marketing Consultants

Business Development Network International
Paris office: 4 avenue des Jonchères, 78121 Crespières (30.54.94.66/fax 30.54.94.67). **Open** 9am-6pm Mon-Fri.
Elizabeth de Vulpillières knows hundreds of English-speaking business people in Paris, and offers regular opportunities to make new contacts at her frequent breakfast and 'Marketnet' meetings. Also one-to-one consulting services.

Saklad Consultants
10 rue du Docteur Roux, 75015. (45.66.76.48/fax 45.66.76.21). Métro Pasteur. **Open** 9am-6pm Mon-Fri.
A small, award-winning marketing firm run by Americans Michael Saklad and David Fischer that specialises in helping high-tech companies to get new customers worldwide.

Page Impact
6 rue Louis Georges, 92140 Clamart (40.95.70.37) **Open** 9am-7pm Mon-Fri; 9am-12.30pm Sat.
A bilingual French-English marketing team specialising in the design of customised newsletters for businesses to keep their clients informed about their products and services.

Translators & Interpreters

Certain documents, from birth certificates to loan applications, must be translated by certified legal translators, listed at the **CCIP** (*see above*). For standard French-English business translations, there are dozens of reliable independents. The Minitel offers a variety of translating services and aids. Check out 3615 MITRAD to find translators.

Association des Anciens Elèves de L'Esit
Centre Universitaire Dauphine, 75016. (44.05.41.46) **Open** *phone callers only* 9am-5pm Mon-Fri.
A translation and interpreting cooperative whose 1,000 members are graduates of one of France's top translating schools, **L'Ecole Supérieure d'Interprètes et de Traducteurs**, covering over 20 languages.

International Corporate Communication
3 rue des Batignolles, 75017 (43.87.29.29/fax 45.22.49.13). Métro Place de Clichy. **Open** 9am-1pm, 2-6pm, Mon-Fri.
Translators of financial and corporate documents: annual reports, prospectuses and shareholder communications.

Parvis Communications
15 rue Dubrunfaut, 75012, (53.17.08.78). Métro Dugommier. **Open** 9am-8pm Mon-Fri.
American Katherine Parvis specialises in French-to-English legal and business translations and consecutive interpreting. Rush jobs and house calls can be handled.

Couriers

For information on general postal services, *see chapter* **Survival**.

Chronopost
7 rue Hérold, 75001 (45.21.64.00/information freephone 05.43.21.00/pickups freephone 05.05.24.00). Métro Châtelet-Les Halles or Sentier. **Open** 8am-7.45pm Mon-Fri; 8am-1pm Sat. **No credit cards.**
A division of the post office, this is the most widely-used service in France for parcels of up to 30kg. There is also an international service.

DHL
59 avenue d'Iéna, 75016 (45.01.91.00). Métro Iéna. **Open** 9am-7.45pm Mon-Fri; 9am-4.45pm Sat. **No credit cards.**
One of the big names in international courier services.
Branch: 82 rue de Richelieu, 75002 (42.96.14.55).

Flash Services
32 rue des Blancs-Manteaux, 75004 (42.74.26.01). Métro Rambuteau. **Open** 9am-6.30pm Mon-Fri. **No credit cards.**
A local bike and van delivery company. Minimum charge for non-account customers for a delivery within Paris is 60F.

TNT Express Worldwide
For pickups call 48.19.48.19, or freephone 05.11.11.11. **Open** 8am-7pm daily (last delivery order 5pm; before 2pm for packages over 30kg). **No credit cards.**
Picks up packages but has no drop-off points in Paris.

Flash Services *flash to answer a call.*

Office Services

Computers & Office Equipment

FNAC Micro

71 boulevard St-Germain, 75005 (44.41.31.50).
Métro Cluny-La Sorbonne. **Open** 10am-8pm Mon-Sat.
Credit MC, V.
Computers, faxes, telephones, laser printers and accessories.
Other FNAC stores, particularly those at Montparnasse and
Les Halles, also have reasonable computer stocks, but fewer
accessories. *See also chapter* **Specialist Shops.**

KA

14 rue Magellan, 75008 (44.43.16.00). Métro George V.
Open *sales & rental* 9am-7pm Mon-Fri; *technical service*
9am-12.30pm, 2-6pm, Mon-Fri. **Credit** AmEx, V.
Sale and rental of IBM, Apple and Compaq computers.

Prorata Services

27 rue Linné 75005 (45.35.94.14). Métro Jussieu. **Open**
9am-7pm Mon-Fri; 10.30am-6pm Sat. **No credit cards.**
Stop in here to use top-of-the-line Macintoshes and PCs
decked out with CD-ROM, scanners and laser printers and
equipped with about every software program imaginable.
Prices are 1F a minute at the keyboard, but there are discounts if you take out a subscription or *carte d'abonnement.*
Prorata also has a computer-aided graphic design studio,
Studio PAO, close by at 15 rue Jussieu.

Internet Services

Association Frank

32 rue Edouard Vaillant, 93100 Montreuil
(48.59.66.58/fax 48.59.66.68/e-mail 100265.1435 at
Compuserve COM/web site http://www Paris-Anglo
COM). Métro Mairie de Montreuil. **Open** 9am-6pm Mon-
Fri.
List your English-speaking business free of charge in this
organisation's widely-used *Paris-Anglophone* directory, on
the Internet as well as in the next hard-copy edition. For a
fee they will also create a customised home page for you on
the World Wide Web.

Internet Way

204 boulevard Bineau, Neuilly-sur-Seine, 92200
(41.43.21.10/fax 41.43.21.11/e-mail: info@iway.fr/web
site http://www.iway.fr). Métro Pont de Neuilly. **Open**
9am-6pm Mon-Fri
Internet access for 490F a month, plus a 20F per hour online
fee. Also web-server development and hosting for those who
want to market via the Internet. Contact Corinne Aleman,
who speaks English.

Office Hire

CNIT

2 place de La Défense, BP 200, 92053 Paris La Défense
(46.92.18.65). Métro Grande Arche de La Défense. **Open**
6.30am-midnight daily.
The World Trade Centre, next to the Grande Arche in the
heart of La Défense, houses 800 firms and offers a permanent data-processing service, video-conference facilities and
offices and meeting rooms to rent. Social facilities include
the *Club Sari Affaires* business club, restaurants, a fitness
centre and a hotel.

Dernis Organisation

23 avenue de Wagram, 75017 (46.22.98.98). Métro
Charles de Gaulle-Etoile. **Open** 9am-7pm Mon-Fri.
Eight offices plus meeting rooms for hire, with multilingual
secretarial services, in a central location.

Générale Continentale Investissements

Les Collines de l'Arche, Immeuble Madeleine, Cedex 24,
92057 Paris La Défense (45.72.91.11/fax 45.72.91.12).
Métro Grande Arche de la Défense. **Open** 8am-8pm, by
appointment only.
Specialists offering high-tech offices mainly for medium- or
longer-term rental at La Défense and at Roissypole, the business district at Roissy airport.

Jones Lang Wootton

49 avenue Hoche, 75008 (40.55.15.15/fax 46.22.28.28).
Métro Charles de Gaulle-Etoile. **Open** 9am-6pm Mon-Fri.
Britain's leading office-rental firm also has branches at La
Défense, and in eastern Paris.

Removals & Relocation

The major companies Grospiron, Arthur Pierre,
Interdean, Desbordes and Transpaq International
are the big five of removals in France. Each of
them has several office around Paris, all listed
under *Déménagement* in the local yellow pages
(pages jaunes). There are in addition many relocation services in the city, which will also help with
such things as finding apartments and opening
bank accounts.

Cosmopolitan Services Unlimited

50 rue de l'Assomption, 75016 (45.27.84.30/fax
45.20.23.07). Métro Ranelagh. **Open** 9am-6pm Mon-
Thur; 9am-5pm Fri.
One of the bigger and better specialised relocation services.
Contact Joy Chevaud, who speaks English.

Grospiron

15 rue Danielle Casanova, 93300 Aubervilliers
(48.11.71.71/fax 48.11.71.70). Métro Fort
d'Aubervilliers. **Open** 9am-1pm, 2-6pm, Mon-Fri
Contact Nancy Ravenel for the English-speaking expat service.

Secretarial Services

Appeltel

215 rue Jean-Jacques Rousseau, 92136 Issy
(41.46.00.60/fax 41.46.00.90). Métro Mairie d'Issy
Open 8am-8pm Mon-Fri.
A small, bilingual French-English phone and fax-answering
service that caters particularly to small businesses, free-
lances and startups that can't afford their own full-time
receptionists or secretaries.

ECCO International

4 place de la Défense, Cedex 26, 92090 Paris La Défense
(49.01.94.94). Métro Grande Arche de La Défense. **Open**
8.30am-6.30pm Mon-Fri.
This branch of the large French employment agency group
specialises in bilingual secretaries and other office staff on
a permanent or temporary basis.

TM International

36-38 rue des Mathurins, 75008 (47.42.71.00). Métro
Auber. **Open** 9am-6pm Mon-Fri
Recruitment consultancy known for reasonable rates and
well-selected French-English bilingual secretarial staff.

Children

From funfairs to physics, Paris is full of attractions for kids.

Despite the rather stern Parisian view of childhood, which rushes three year olds into adult behaviour patterns and three course lunches, Paris is nevertheless a great place to explore with your offspring. Parks, squares and gardens are well-equipped with sandpits and play areas. And, should older children begin to pall at the glut of culture, you can always let them climb up something, to take in giant views or grotesque gargoyles (*see chapter* **Sightseeing: Viewpoints**).

Town halls (*mairies*) provide information on children's activities, and all *arrondissements* have public libraries with a children's corner, usually with some literature in English (for libraries, *see chapter* **Students**). The weeklies *Pariscope* or *L'Officiel des Spectacles* have sections *pour les jeunes*, listing activities. For shops for children, *see chapters* **Fashion** *and* **Specialist Shops**.

Help & Information

Inter-Service Parents
(44.93.44.93). **Open** 9.30am-12.30pm, 1.30-5pm, Mon, Tue, Fri; 9.30am-12.30pm Wed; 1.30-5pm Thur.
A free advisory service giving details of babysitting agencies, childminding associations and children's activities.

Message
c/o Susan Grossman, 48 boulevard St-Michel, 75006 (46.34.14.50); Moira Clark (34.80.05.88).
A 1,000-member network, geared toward English-speaking ex-pat expectant or recent mothers, as well as parents of older children new to Paris. Their quarterly pamphlet lists counsellors and want ads, plus a running schedule of events and playgroup meetings.

Babysitting/Child-Minding

Ababa
8 avenue du Maine, 75015 (45.49.46.46). **Open** 8am-8pm Mon-Fri; 11am-8pm Sat. **Rates** 30F per hour for two or fewer children, 35F for two or more; 60F booking fee (discounts for frequent use). Two hours' notice needed.
A competent, efficient team of 350 English-speaking babysitters, both male and female. Weekend sitting, day outings and tea parties also catered for.

A la Ribambelle
(46.78.90.90). **Rates** 700F 1½ hrs; 800F 3 hrs.
For parties: magicians, clowns and balloons supplied.

American Church
65 quai d'Orsay, 75007. Métro Invalides/RER Pont de l'Alma. **Open** 9am-10pm Mon-Sat; 9am-8pm Sun. **Rates** average 40F per hour; no booking fee.
English-speaking childminders offer baby-sitting services via a bulletin board at the church.

Contact B
10 rue Rodier, 75009 (45.26.81.34).
Open 9am-5pm Mon-Fri. **Rates** (negotiable) average 30F-35F per hour. One day's notice preferred.
Experienced, English-speaking day-time mother's help and babysitters (mainly British *au pairs* in need of pocket money). Write in advance if you need someone during a holiday.

Euro Baby
rue Jean-Pierre Timbaut, Levallois Perret 92000, (47.48.11.84). Ring after 7pm to make an appointment, preferably giving a few days' notice.
Rental of high chairs, playpens, cots, strollers and car seats for up to six months, covers and bedding included. Prices are roughly 35F a day, averaging 15F a day per month. There's a 10% discount for three or more items. Delivery within Paris costs 45F, and to the suburbs 65F.

Kid's Service
159 rue de Rome, 75017 (47.66.00.52).
Métro Rome. **Open** 8am-8pm Mon-Fri; 10am-8pm Sat; reduced hours Aug. **Rates** 30F per hour; 270F for 10 consecutive hours day or night; 58F booking fee.
One of the oldest baby-sitting agencies in Paris, with a young, dependable team. Qualified nannies or play supervisors at 30F an hour (48F for babies under three months).

Supervised Activities

Centre Pompidou – Atelier des Enfants
Centre Pompidou, rue Beaubourg, 75004 (afternoons only 44.78.12.33). Métro Châtelet-Les Halles or Rambuteau. **Sessions** July-Aug 2-3.15pm, 3.30-4.45pm, Mon-Sat; Sept-June 2-3.15pm, 3.30-4.45pm, Wed, Sat; reserve a place in person 30 minutes before session starts. **Admission** 30F.
A first come/first served workshop space for kids. Leave your child (aged six to 12) to such supervised artistic activities as constructing a 21st-century town out of polystyrene bricks. Includes visits to the modern art museum upstairs (*see chapter* **Museums**). Although activities are mainly manual and creative, a smattering of French is needed to get by.

Children's Academy on Tour
66 avenue des Champs-Elysées, 75008 (44.95.14.31). Métro George V. **Tours** Wed, Sat, Sun. **Tuition** 200-750F per outing.
Educational trips in English and French for teams of five children, ages six to 13, accompanied by a tutor. Tours include the opera, ballet, art galleries, museums, gardens, even rock concerts. The fee covers materials and refreshments. Mini-bus pickup in and around Paris.

Jardin des Enfants aux Halles
105 rue Rambuteau, 75001 (45.08.07.18).
Métro Châtelet-Les Halles. **Open** 10am-5pm Mon; 2-5pm Tue-Fri; 1-5pm Sun; times can vary, phone or consult notice at entrance. **Admission** 2.50F per hour.
An open-air children's activity garden for kids aged seven to 11, including underground tunnels, rope swings, secret dens and 'swimming pools' of coloured ping-pong balls. Well-supervised by a team of *animateurs*. Adults aren't

allowed, except from 10am to 1pm on Saturdays, when they can also bring younger children. Maximum stay one hour.

Musée du Louvre (Ateliers des Enfants)
(40.20.52.63/40.20.52.09). Métro Louvre.
Admission 28F; 95F for a four-session cycle.
There are art history workshops in English for children during summer holidays (and in French on Wednesdays and Saturdays throughout the year). The two-hour afternoon sessions are aimed at children aged between five and 16. Book at 9am by phone – first come, first served.

Parsons School of Design
14 rue Letellier, 75015 (45.77.39.66).
Métro Emile Zola. **Open** 1-5pm Wed, Sat. **Admission** about 75F an afternoon.
Student-organised informal groups in English for children aged seven to 14, covering fashion, design and architecture. Also some full-day classes during holidays. Ring Holly Warner, Student Services, for latest information. *See also* chapter **Students**.

Les Petits Dragons Playgroup
St George's Church, 7 rue Auguste-Vacquerie, 75016.
Métro Iéna. **Open** 9am-noon Mon, Wed, Fri. **Rates** from 400F monthly for three days a week to 2,150F monthly for 25 hours a week, depending on attendance.
Friendly places for children aged from 1½ (at the playgroup) to six. Unlike most *jardins d'enfants* which require formal registration, you can take your child in on an informal, long-or short-term, but regular, basis (book a week in advance).
Kindergarten 2 rue Jacquemont, 75017 (42.28.56.17). Métro La Fourche. **Open** 8.30am-7pm Mon-Fri.
Kindergarten Church of Scotland, 17 rue Bayard, 75008 (Grethe Gravesen, director, 49.52.01.03). Métro Franklin D Roosevelt or Alma Marceau. **Open** 9am-3pm Tue, Thur.

Summer Schools
If you are visiting Paris in the summer, you might consider putting your child into a programme that lasts a few weeks. For children aged between three and six, classes are usually in the morning, with afternoon recreational activity.
The Bilingual Montessori School of Paris
65 quai d'Orsay, 75007 (45.55.13.27); for ages 3-6. Field trips, art projects, music.
International School of Paris
96 bis rue de Ranelagh, 75016 (42.24.43.40 for ages 3½-11; 42.24.09.54 for ages 12-18).
The Lennen Bilingual School
65 quai d'Orsay, 75007 (47.05.66.55); for ages 2-8.
Rates 3,000F a month; 800F a week; 200F a day. Trips, arts and crafts, computers.

Green Areas

Parks are generally open dawn to dusk, daily. For the main Paris parks, *see chapter* **Sightseeing: Paris Parks**. The **Luxembourg** and the **Tuileries** both have sandpits, roundabouts, pony rides and ponds; similar attractions will be found in the city's other public parks. There is a boating lake and an artificial cave and waterfall at the **Buttes-Chaumont**, and there and at the **Parc Monceau** there are roller-skating rinks. Also a fun place for kids to explore is the **Parc de Belleville**, in the 20th. One of the nicest parks just outside town is the **Parc de St-Cloud**, métro Pont de St-Cloud, a rare Paris park where you can actually run on the grass, and very popular for picnics. In spring, the city's most popular funfair, the **Foire du Trône**, is held in the Bois de Vincennes (*see chapter* **Paris by Season**.)

Jardin d'Acclimatation
Bois de Boulogne, 75016 (40.67.90.80).
Metro Sablons, then short walk, or Métro Porte Maillot and Le Petit Train (5F, every ten minutes daily from behind L'Orée du Bois restaurant during holidays, and 1.30pm onwards Wed, Sat, Sun). **Open** 10am-6pm daily.
Admission 10F; free under-3s.
The classic funfair and amusement park, which has been welcoming Parisian families for 125 years. Some attractions cost about 10F extra: donkey rides, dodgems, remote-control speed boats or a trip down the 'enchanted river'. After the initial admission price, a lot is free: a hall of mirrors, the children's zoo, *guignol* theatre and an all wooden under-12s playground. *See also* **Musée en Herbe** *below*.

Le Parc Floral de Paris
route de la Pyramide, Bois de Vincennes, 75012 (43.43.92.95). *Métro Chateau de Vincennes, then 112 bus to Parc Floral or 15-minute walk.* **Open** *summer* 9.30am-8pm daily; *winter* 9.30am-6pm daily. **Admission** 10F adults; 5F 6-10s; free under-6s, over-65s.
On schooldays, this pleasant park has a slower pace than its western counterpart the **Jardin d'Acclimatation**. A large playground with the usual climbing frames and swings, ping-pong tables, pedal karts for 4-10 year-olds and a miniature train (5F per ride), all add to the experience. The Théâtre Astral presents children's shows (42.41.88.33 for details).

Parc de la Villette

Metro Porte de la Villette or Porte de Pantin.
As well as indoor thrills at **La Cité des Enfants** (*see* **Activity Museums** *below*), the Parc offers a surreal succession of eight themed gardens – all free. Best for children are the Monster Dragon slide, the Jardin des Voltiges obstacle course and the Jardin des Vents air mattresses, plus the touch and sound games; not to mention the scary noises of the Jardin des Frayeurs Enfantins and the mists and light effects of the Jardins du Brouillard and des Miroirs. Unusually for Paris, visitors are invited to picnic on 'green beaches' – the Prairie du Triangle and Prairie du Cercle lawns.

Museums

It's best to be ruthlessly selective when taking children to Paris' conventional museums. The **Musée d'Orsay**, though large, is absorbing, and has worksheets in English; the **Musée Carnavelet** and the **Musée de l'Homme** also have lots to interest older children. Giant places such as the **Louvre** and the **Musée de l'Armée** can be attempted so long as you plan which sections to see and don't try to do too much. Old favourites are the horrors of the **Musée Grevin** wax museum and the **Conciergerie**, and a new attraction is the **Musée des Art Forains** fairground museum (for the above, *see chapter* **Museums**). In a creepy vein, try the **Catacombes** and the **Egouts** (sewers) for underground excitement, and **Paristoric** gives the history of Paris in a lush slideshow (*see chapter* **Sightseeing**). Most museums have special programmes for children on Wednesday afternoons.

Activity Museums

La Cité des Enfants & Techno Cité

Cité des Sciences et de l'Industrie, 30 avenue Corentin Cariou, 75019 (36.68.29.30). Métro Porte de la Villette. **Open** 10am-6pm Tue-Sun (visits by session, normally 3-4 daily; phone for details or Minitel 3615 Villette).
Admission *day pass to Cité des Sciences* 45F adults; 35F under-16s; *Cité des Enfants only* 20F per session; *Techno Cité* 25F. **Credit** AmEx, MC, V.
Paris' most sophisticated modern attraction for kids. The science museum complex runs four or five 90-minute 'discovery' sessions a day with hands-on experiments for children. Three- to five-year olds learn how water flows by dabbling in waterfalls, or build a house in a mini-construction site with hard-hats, wheelbarrows and cranes. Children from five to 12 can see what a skeleton looks like when riding a bicycle, and observe how sound travels through tubes and telephones. Most activities are visually self-explanatory and the space is self-contained and well-managed. Parents are allowed to join in. Book at least three days in advance.
At brand-new **Techno-Cité**, children aged over 11 explore the mechanisms behind a gear-box, robot or helicopter, or how to programme computer software into a video game. Three more hi-tech sections (open from 31 October 1995) will let them loose on constructing prototype bikes and discovering the role of robotics in lifts and automatic parking. A visit to the **Cité des Enfants** or **Techno Cité** is best combined with a whole day out at the huge **Cité des Sciences et de l'Industrie** (*see chapter* **Museums**). Particularly good for children are the **Planetarium** and the **Argonaute** (a real submarine converted into a museum). Over-8s can play at being actor/producers at La Folie Video, or explore architecture at La Folie Arts Plastiques (open 2.30-5.30pm Sat, Sun; phone 40.03.75.15 to book).

Halle St-Pierre

2 rue Ronsard, 75018 (42.58.72.89). Métro Anvers or Abbesses. **Open** 10am-6pm Mon, Sun; 10am-10pm Tue-Fri; 2-10pm Sat. **Admission** *one exhibition* adults 25F, children 18F; *both exhibitions* adults 35F, children 28F. Formerly a branch of the **Musée en Herbe** (*see below*); shows temporary art and science exhibitions for children.

Musée de la Curiosité

Espace Magique du Marais, 11 rue St-Paul, 75004 (42.72.13.26). Métro St-Paul, Sully Morland. **Open** 2-7pm Wed, Sat. **Admission** 45F adults; 30F children.
Continuous conjuring shows, optical illusions, psychic phenomena and interactive curiosities in a vaulted cellar. Plus an exhibition of magic props including boxes for sawing ladies in two. English-speaking guides decline to reveal all the secrets. Children's courses in magic during school holidays.

Musée en Herbe du Jardin d'Acclimatation

Bois de Boulogne, 75016 (40.67.97.66).
Métro Pont de Neuilly. **Open** 10am-6pm daily.
Admission 16F adults; 13F children; free under-3s (plus 10F entry to Jardin d'Acclimatation).
An educational centre and art museum designed for children, frequently showing exhibitions to introduce them to the work of artists. During renovations (until about December 1995), it is temporarily rehoused in a huge tent.

Le Palais de la Découverte

avenue Franklin D Roosevelt, 75008 (40.74.80.00).
Metro Franklin D Roosevelt. **Open** 9.30am-6pm Tue-Sat; 10am-7pm Sun; closed public holidays. **Admission** 15F adults; 10F children; free under 7s.
Although it now looks tired alongside the **Cité des Enfants** (*see above*), this science museum still offers kids the chance to have a go at balancing balls on jets of hot air, or watching a commune of ants at work in a glass box.

It's not all learning at the **Cité des Enfants**.

Animals

Aquarium Tropical
*Musée National des Arts d'Afrique et d'Océanie,
293 avenue Daumesnil, 75012 (44.74.84.80). Métro
Porte Dorée.* **Open** 10am-5.30pm Mon, Wed-Fri; 10am-
6pm Sat, Sun. **Admission** 35F adults; 26F students; free
under-18s.
In the tropical aquarium downstairs, crocodiles and piranha
lie in wait, primed to gorge on whatever the keeper drops
into their tanks.

Centre de la Mer et des Eaux
*195 rue St-Jacques, 75005 (46.33.08.61).
RER Luxembourg.* **Open** 10am-12.30pm, 1.15-5.30pm,
Tue-Fri; 10am-5pm Sat, Sun. **Admission** 25F adults; 15F
students, under-12s; free under 4s.
Aquariums full of tropical fish, a giant diorama of undersea
life plus Jacques Cousteau films.

Une Journée au Cirque
(A Day at the Circus)
*parc des Chanteraines, 46 avenue Georges Pompidou,
92390 Villeneuve-La-Garenne (47.24.11.70). RER
Gennevilliers/ SNCF St-Denis.* **Sessions** 10am-5pm Wed,
Sun, public and school holidays; closed July-end Sept.
Tickets *show only* 70F-155F adults; 45F-95F under-12s;
day at circus and one meal 235F-295F adults; 195F-230F
under-12s; *menagerie only* 10F. **No credit cards.**
A circus aficionado from the age of 14, Francis Schoeller
throws a day-long extravaganza. Children can train with circus artists in clowning, conjuring, trapeze and tightrope.
There's lunch with the artists in the ring, followed by a two-
hour show of chimps, jugglers, magicians and all that raz-
zamatazz. Finally, Thierry le Pontier, who speaks English
(after a fashion), shows the children the big cats. Until
October 1995 Le Cirque de Paris is at *Le Cirque de Paris,
avenue de la Commune de Paris, 92000 Nanterre
(47.24.11.70). RER line A to Nanterre-Ville.*

Muséum National d'Histoire Naturelle
*57 rue Cuvier, in the Jardin des Plantes, 75005
(40.79.30.00). Métro Monge, Jussieu or Gare
d'Austerlitz/RER Austerlitz.* **Open** 10am-5pm Mon, Wed-
Fri; 11am-6pm Sat, Sun; *Grande Galérie de l'Evolution*
10am-6pm Mon, Wed, Fri-Sun; 10am-10pm Thur.
Admission 4F-25F.
The natural history museum is made up of several buildings,
including the *Galerie d'Anatomie Comparée et de Paléontologie*,
with skeletal remains of both prehistoric and contemporary
creatures. The impressive new *Grande Galerie de l'Evolution*,
complete with suspended whale, investigates the origins of life
up to man's own interventions in nature. Child-oriented films
and illustrated texts accompany exhibitions. In the *Espace
Découverte*, kids aged five to 12 have hands-on contact with
various specimens and experiments, using microscopes. Also
in the Jardin des Plantes is the **Ménagerie**, a small zoo. *See
also chapter* **Museums.**

Zoo de Vincennes
*53 avenue de St-Maurice, 75012 (44.75.20.10/00).
Métro Porte Dorée.* **Open** 9am-6pm daily; *Oct-Mar* 9am-
5.30pm daily; *Dec-Jan* 9am-5pm. **Admission** 40F adults;
20F 4-16s; free under-4s.
The zoo tries to replicate the habitats of animals so that lions,
tigers, elephants and rhinos wander in relative landscaped
freedom. Spacious paths make it easy to push prams. Check
at entrance for feeding times of seals and sea lions (4.30pm),
pelicans (2.15pm), penguins (4.30pm), the panda (9.30am,
5pm) and other beasts. Avoid weekends, and Wednesday
afternoons; in summer there's likely to be a queue at most
times. A miniature train tours the zoo and the park, and
there's a lake with boats for hire (from 40F-44F per hour).

Theatre & Guignol

Theatre
Many of Paris' fringe theatres (*café-théâtres*) pre-
sent children's shows on Wednesday, Saturday
and Sunday afternoons during school term times,
and more frequently during school holidays.
Tickets usually cost 40F-60F. *See also chapter*
Theatre.
ACT, the English Theatre
*Theatre de la Main d'Or, 15 Passage de la Main d'Or,
75011 (40.33.64.02). Métro Ledru Rollin.*
This resident English-language theatre presents a regular
Christmas season panto, and some other productions suit-
able for children during the year.
Au Bec Fin
*6 bis rue Therese, 75001 (42.96.29.35). Métro Palais
Royal.* **Kids'** shows Wed, Sat.
Cafe d'Edgar
*58 boulevard Edgar Quinet, 75014 (42.79.97.97). Métro
Edgar Quinet.* **Kids'** shows 2.30pm Wed, Sat.
Admission 40F.
Point Virgule
*7 rue Ste-Croix-de-la-Bretonnerie, 75004 (43.71.43.48).
Métro Hôtel de Ville.* **Kids'** shows 10am, 2.30pm Wed;
3pm Sat; 4pm Sun. **Admission** 60F adults; 45F kids.
Sentier des Halles
*50 rue Aboukir, 75002 (42.36.37.27). Métro
Sentier.* Times, prices variable; see local press for details

Guignol
Guignol puppet theatres first appeared in the last
century as a mouthpiece for striking weavers in
Lyon, and the have evolved into the French equivalent of Punch and Judy. There's no wife-batter-
ing, but the policeman comes in for a good deal of
flak, and there are loads of opportunities for audience participation.
Guignol du Parc de Choisy
*square de Choisy (opposite 149 avenue de Choisy), 75013
(43.66.72.39). Métro Place d'Italie.* **Shows** (weather
permitting) 3.30pm Wed, Sat, Sun; 3.30pm daily July,
Aug. **Tickets** 10F (group discounts).
Marionnettes des Champs-Elysées
*rond point des Champs-Elysées, 75008, corner avenues
Matignon/Gabriel (42.57.43.34). Métro Champs-Elysées-
Clemenceau.* **Shows** (weather permitting) 3pm, 4pm, 5pm
Wed, Sat, Sun; closed Aug. **Tickets** 12.50F.
Marionnettes du Luxembourg
*Jardin du Luxembourg, 75006 (43.26.46.47/
43.29.50.97). RER Luxembourg.* **Shows** (covered)
2.30pm, 3.30pm, 4.30pm Wed, Sat, Sun, public holidays;
closed in July, Aug. **Tickets** 22F.
In low season and when audiences are thin, performances
may be confined to 2.30pm.
Marionnettes de Montsouris
*Parc Montsouris, entrance avenue Reilles/rue Gazon,
75014 (46.65.45.95). Métro Cité Universitaire.* **Shows**
(covered) 3.30pm, 4.30pm Wed, Sat, Sun; 3.30pm, 4.30pm Sat;
closed July, Aug. **Tickets** 14F.
Théâtre Guignol-Anatole
*Parc des Buttes Chaumont, entrance opposite town hall,
75019 (43.98.10.95). Métro Laumière.* **Shows** (weather
permitting) 3pm, 4pm, Wed, Sat, Sun; 3pm, 4pm daily
during school holidays. **Tickets** 12F.
Théâtre de Polichinelle Parisien
Parc Georges-Brassens, 75015 (48.42.51.80). **Shows**
3pm, 4pm, 5pm Wed, Sat, Sun; 3pm, 4pm, 5pm daily
during school holidays. **Tickets** 14F.

Theme Parks outside Paris

For **Disneyland Paris**, *see chapter* **Trips out of Town**.

Château et Parc Zoologique de Thoiry

Thoiry en Yvelines, 78770 (34.87.52.25/info in English 34.87.45.90). **Transport** *By train* from Gare Montparnasse to Montfort l'Aumaury, then by taxi; phone Château for taxi details and book in advance. *By car* Autoroute A13 west, then A12, N12 and D11 (45km/28 miles). **Open** *winter* 10am-5pm, *summer* 10am-6pm, daily. **Admission** *park* 97F adults; 77F children; *château* 30F adults; 25F children. **Credit** AmEx, MC, V.
Half an hour from central Paris, this safari park offers the incongruous sight of 80 species of animal (lions, elephants, monkeys) roaming the grounds of a château. Less ferocious beasts can be viewed from a little train that tours parts of the gardens. Other incongruous specimens on show are the mainly-English cricket players most summer weekends. There's also a reptile house, a tearoom and a picnic area.

France Miniature

25 route du Mesnil, 78990 Elancourt (30.62.40.79).
Transport *By train* RER line C to St-Quentin-en-Yvelines, then bus 420 every hour at a quarter to the hour. *By car* A13 direction St Quentin-En-Yvelines/Dreux, then Elancourt Centre. **Open** *mid Mar to mid Nov* 10am-7pm daily; *summer holidays* 10am-11pm Sat. **Admission** 68F adults; 48F 3-13s; under 3s free; group discounts.
An outdoor museum of France with over 200 models of monuments and sites reduced to a 30th of the original size. Latest additions include the Moulin Rouge, Montmartre and Sacré Coeur, which join such landmarks as Notre Dame, the Eiffel Tower and the Port of St-Tropez.

La Mer de Sable

60950 Ermenonville (16.44.54.00.96 or 36.68.26.20).
Transport *By train* RER line B to Roissy-Charles de Gaulle, then shuttle (10am only) or taxi. *By car* A1 to exit 7 for Ermenonville. **Open** *Apr-8 Oct* 10am-6pm Mon-Fri; 10.30am-7pm Sat, Sun. **Admission** 75F; free under 3s; (group discounts).
Amid forests and a stretch of sand deposited millions of years ago by the sea, this Wild West theme park has the usual attractions, plus canoeing down rapids, animals, a village of puppets and afternoon shows which include a politically incorrect Indian attack and rodeo-style horse-riding stunts.

Parc Asterix

60128 Plailly (16-44.62.31.31/recorded English information 44.62.34.34). **Transport** *By train* RER line B to Roissy-Charles de Gaulle, then shuttle 9.30am-1.30pm, 4.30pm-closing time (30F return). *By car* Autoroute A1 towards Lille, exit Parc Asterix. **Open** *1 July-4 Sept* 10am-6pm Mon-Fri, public holidays; 10am-7pm Sat, Sun. **Admission** 150F adults; 105F 3-11s; free under-3s. **Credit** MC, V.
Just 35km (22 miles) from Paris, this theme park dedicated to plucky Gaul Asterix offers an enjoyable escape back to the days of gladiators, slave auctions and feasts of wild boar. There are rides, games, parades, music, puppeteers, roving actors and bilingual staff. Expect a half-hour wait for the more popular rides at weekends. Prices and opening times will be reviewed during summer 1995; phone to check.

Parc de Saint Vrain

91770 Saint Vrain (64.56.10.80). **Transport** *By train* RER line C to Bouray, then taxi. *By car* Autoroute A6, exit at Viry onto N445/D19 to Brétigny-sur-Orge. **Open** *Apr-Oct* 10.30am-6pm daily. **Admission** 79F adults; 69F 2-10s; free under-2s. **Credit** MC, V.

A safari park 45km (28 miles) from Paris, with free-roaming beasts and birds, and outdoor scenes featuring dinosaurs and prehistoric men. Take it in by riverboat or monorail.

Eating Out with Children

Unless trapped in a food wilderness around the great monuments, you should have no trouble finding places to fuel kids' energy. French restaurateurs regard children as customers like everyone else, and even without special under-12s menus there is something for every palate. **Chicago Meatpackers** and **Léon de Bruxelles** (*see chapter* **Restaurants**) offer children's menus and kids' shows or toys. Listed here are some places that make an extra effort to welcome children.

Bistro Romain

30 rue St-Denis, 75001 (40.26.82.80) and numerous other branches. Métro Châtelet-Les Halles. **Open** 11.30am-1am daily. **Credit** AmEx, DC, EC, V.
Asterix theme, and children's menu at 39.90F

Café de la Jatte

60 boulevard Vital-Bouhot, 92200 Neuilly (47.45.04.20). Métro Pont de Levallois (if on foot, cross to island via pedestrian footbridge; by car, take Pont de Courbevoie). **Open** noon to 3pm, 8pm-midnight, daily. **Credit** AmEx, DC, EC, JCB, V.
This upmarket restaurant, on the Ile de la Grande Jatte, offers a children's menu, Sunday lunch only, at 70F, with colouring sets and balloons. There's a life-size model dinosaur skeleton to gawp at, suspended above the galleried dining-room, and a courtyard below for stretching restless legs .

La Crêperie des Artistes

55-57 rue St-Denis, 75001 (tel 42.33.08.16).
Métro Châtelet-Les Halles. **Open** 11.30am-midnight daily. **Credit** AmEx, EC, MC, V.
Sympa pancake house with good play area for infants. Children's menu 35F.

Flunch

1 rue Caulaincourt, 75018 (45.22.39.52) and three other branches. Métro Place de Clichy. **Open** 11am-10pm daily. **Menu** 24F. **Credit** MC, V.
Cheap'n'cheerful self-service with under-12s 'menu Flunchy'.

Hippopotamus

29 rue Berger, 75001 (42.33.66.11/45.08.00.29). Métro Châtelet-Les Halles. **Open** 11am-1am Mon-Thur, Sun; 11am-1.30am Fri, Sat. **Credit** AmEx, EC, MC, V.
This steakhouse (there are 13 branches) has sheets of games, pictures to colour, crayons and balloons. Children's menu 47F.

Hôtel Meridien Montparnasse

19 rue du Commandant Mouchotte, 75015 (44.36.44.00). Métro Montparnasse-Bienvenüe or Gaîté. **Open** *Sept-June* noon-3.30pm Sun. **Average** 220F adults; 110F children under 12; free under-4s. **Credit** AmEx, DC, MC, V.
'Baby Brunch' is a veritable banquet of mini-pizzas, quiches, burgers, waffles and candyfloss, with games, drawing or singing competitions, facepainting, treasure hunts, leaving prezzies. Parents have their own buffet in peace next door.

La Patata

25 boulevard des Italiens, 75002 (42.68.16.66). Métro Opéra. **Open** 11.30am-midnight daily. **Credit** MC, V.
Baked spuds with various accompaniments. Under-12s dine for 38F with gifts and balloons.

Gay & Lesbian

Gay Paris is booming, and lesbians are finally claiming a higher profile.

Visitors eager to discover gay life in Paris should have an easy time of it. In the Marais, and along rue Keller, near the Bastille, and rue de la Ferronnerie in Les Halles clusters of cafés, bars and clubs allow you to flit from one to the next for a quick taste of a scene whose distractions make up in depth what they lack in breadth. **Banana Café**, **Le Bar** and **Bar Bi** are currently the places most in vogue. In these streets gays, or at least gay men, are more visible than ever, giving a carefree picture of gay life in Paris.

Historically, France has no tradition of legitimised discrimination through anti-gay laws (except for a brief time under the Vichy regime), and anti-gay violence is virtually non-existent. Moreover, the French remain indifferent to the sexual proclivities of others. As a result, many gays here have often felt no strong need for high-profile gay activism.

But in the last decade, with the spread of Aids (in French, *Sida*) – France has by some way the highest incidence of the epidemic in western Europe – the French gay community has mobilised to fight the disease, and to combat apathy and fear. A media campaign in 1994 has done much to improve Aids awareness, and red ribbons abound. Also, the new **Centre Gai & Lesbien** has already made itself a visible and audible presence in the scene. It may not be obvious at first glance, but Paris' gay community can be as serious as it is fun.

General Information

Centre Gai & Lesbien

3 rue Keller, 75011 (43.57.21.47). Métro Ledru-Rollin. **Open** 2pm-8pm Mon-Sat.
An active and friendly community centre near the Bastille, with up-to-date information on the gay/lesbian scene, as well as a variety of support groups that meet weekly. It publishes *3 Keller* (*see* **Media, Groups & Contacts**), and serves as an umbrella and meeting point for a wide range of gay associations.

Eating & Drinking

Bars & Cafés

Amnésia

42 rue Vieille-du-Temple, 75004 (42.72.16.94). Métro Hôtel de Ville. **Open** 10am-2am daily. **Credit** MC, V.
A great place to meet for a drink, if you can get a table at this pleasant, mixed café in the heart of the Marais scene. Light lunches are served until 4pm.

Banana Café

13 rue de la Ferronnerie, 75001 (42.33.35.31). Métro Châtelet-Les Halles. **Open** 4.30pm-dawn daily. **Credit** AmEx, MC, V.
Celebrity-sightings have been reported at this mixed and *very* trendy hangout, which pulls in the less famous but still fabulous by the droves, straight as well as gay. Weekends are teeming, especially when theme parties or go-go boys are on offer. Hope for a seat on the outdoor terrace to see the be-seens posing along the café-lined pedestrian street. Happy hour from 5pm-7pm.

Le Bar

5 rue de la Ferronnerie, 75001 (40.41.00.10). Métro Châtelet-Les Halles. **Open** 5.30pm-2am Mon-Tue; 5.30pm-3am Wed, Thur, Sun; 5.30pm-4am Fri, Sat. **Credit** MC, V.
Tight attire seems *de rigueur* for the slender young and not-so-young things who continue to cram into this place. There are four bars on three levels, the lowest with plenty of dark corners, which explains the predatory looks above.

Bar Bi

23 rue Ste-Croix de la Bretonnerie, 75004 (42.78.26.20). Métro Hôtel de Ville. **Open** 3pm-2am daily. **No credit cards.**
The latest addition to the Marais circuit is proof that you can't get enough of the same thing, as this very popular, up-beat bar has drawn crowds away from its neighbours. We don't quite get the name, as there seems nothing 'bi' about it. Happy hour daily from 6pm-8pm.

Le Central

33 rue Vieille-du-Temple, 75004 (48.87.99.33). Métro Hôtel de Ville. **Open** 2pm-1am Sun-Thur; 2pm-2am Fri, Sat. **Credit** AmEx, MC, V.
One of the oldest gay bars in the area. Young trendies are in the minority here, making the ambiance low-key and friendly rather than uptight and posey. Popular with tourists.

Le Keller

14 rue Keller, 75011 (47.00.05.39). Métro Bastille. **Open** 10pm-2am daily (men only). **No credit cards.**
A long-established leather bar. The clientèle look a bit rough and worn, but their bark is worse than their bite, slaps heard from beyond the pool table notwithstanding.

Yes, we have the **Banana Café**.

La Luna

28 rue Keller, 75011 (40.21.09.91). Métro Bastille.
Open 5.30pm-dawn daily. **Admission** free Mon-Thur;
50F (includes one free drink) Sat, Sun. **Credit** MC, V.
One visit to the basement maze explains how this cruise bar
made its successful comeback. Regular use of a gym is a plus
in this beefy crowd, which swells at weekends.

Mec Zone

27 rue Turgot, 75009 (40.82.94.18). Métro Anvers.
Open 8pm-2am daily (men only). **Credit** AmEx, MC, V.
A leather bar with videos, a harness, and plenty of people
willing to fill it. Certainly not for the squeamish.

Mic Man

24 rue Geoffroy l'Angevin, 75004 (42.74.39.80).
Métro Rambuteau. **Open** noon-2am Mon-Thur, Sun;
noon-4am Fri-Sat. **No credit cards.**
A bar of the old school: friendly with a basement with videos.
You can guess the rest.

Le Piano Zinc

49 rue des Blancs-Manteaux, 75004 (42.74.32.42).
Métro Hôtel de Ville. **Open** 6pm-2am Tue-Sun.
Admission free Sun-Thur; 45F (includes one free drink)
Fri, Sat. **Credit** AmEx, MC, V.
A Paris landmark. Three bars on three levels, and an old-
fashioned piano-bar cabaret that includes anyone who wants
to join in. Often extremely crowded, but very friendly.

Quetzal

10 rue de la Verrerie, 75004 (48.87.99.07).
Métro Hôtel de Ville. **Open** noon-2am Mon-Fri; 4pm-2am
Sat, Sun. **No credit cards.**
This bar can barely contain the muscled crowd it still
attracts. Especially packed at the weekend and during happy
hour (6-8pm Mon-Fri, 5-7pm Sat, Sun).

QG

12 rue Simon-Lefranc, 75004 (48.87.74.18). Métro
Rambuteau. **Open** 5pm-2am daily. **No credit cards.**
Another, but new, dark and steamy leather bar with an even
darker and steamier downstairs. Appropriate attire handy.

Subway

35 rue Ste-Croix-de-la-Bretonnerie, 75004
(42.77.41.10). Métro Hôtel de Ville. **Open** 2.30pm-2am
daily. **No credit cards.**
It may no longer be the star of the street, but the Subway
continues among the front rank of Marais bars. The crowd
is young, and the 6-8pm two-for-one beer blast is frenetic.

Le Trap

10 rue Jacob, 75006 (unlisted phone).
Métro St-Germain-des-Pres. **Open** 11pm-4am daily (men
only). **Admission** 50F Fri-Sat. **No credit cards.**
Ring the bell to be let in to this long-time Left Bank haunt,
where upstairs means 'back-room'. If the light flashes it's not
a raid, just someone else at the door. The Trap attracts all
types, which makes for an often friendly mix. It's always
packed at weekends.

Restaurants

The restaurants listed here mostly cater to a mixed clientèle,
but are run by gay people and/or are gay-friendly.

L'Amazonial

3 rue Ste-Opportune, 75001 (42.33.53.13). Métro
Châtelet-Les Halles. **Open** noon-3pm, 7pm-1.30am, daily.
Average 75F-160F. **Credit** AmEx, MC, V.
A lively 120-seat restaurant with a terrace and plenty of
exotic touches. The food is French, with a pinch of Brazilian
seasoning. Brunch every Sunday, noon-4pm.

Chez Tsou

16 rue des Archives, 75004 (42.78.11.47).
Métro Hôtel de Ville. **Open** noon-2pm, 7-11pm Mon-Sat;
7-11pm Sun. **Average** 90F. **Credit** MC, V.
The inexpensive but tasty fare here makes this Chinese
restaurant in the Marais a neighbourhood favourite. The
large pavement terrace, perfect for checking out the passers-
by, is another definite plus.

Le Corset

18 rue Greneta, 75002 (40.41.00.61).
Métro Etienne-Marcel. **Open** 8pm-12.30am daily.
Average 175F. **Credit** MC, V.
The cross-dressing 'waitresses' don't fool anyone, but they
do assure a saucy good time.

Fond de Cour

3 rue Ste-Croix-de-la-Bretonnerie, 75004 (42.74.71.52).
Métro Hôtel de Ville. **Open** noon-2pm, 7.30-11pm, Mon-
Thur; noon-2pm, 7.30-11.30pm Fri; 7.30-11.30pm Sat.
Average 250F. **Credit** AmEx, EC, MC, V.
Reasonable food in a charming courtyard setting. The
French menu changes about five times a year.

Foufounes

40 rue Vieille-du-Temple, 75004 (42.78.86.12). Métro
Hôtel de Ville. **Open** 7.30pm-midnight Tue-Fri; noon-
midnight, Sat, Sun. **Average** 150F. **Credit** MC, V.
A relatively inexpensive place, with unpretentious food and
very popular with locals, especially on Sunday afternoons.
Brunch is served on Saturdays and Sundays from noon to
5pm. Reservations accepted in the evening only.

Majestic Café

34 rue Vieille-du-Temple, 75004 (42.74.61.61).
Métro Hôtel de Ville. **Open** 9am-2am daily. **Average**
120F. **Menu** 79F. **Credit** AmEx, DC, MC, V.
One of the nicest hangouts in the Marais, the Majestic pulls
in an attractive, varied crowd. It serves a limited menu of
flans, salads and sandwiches.

Au Rendez-vous des Camionneurs

72 quai des Orfèvres, 75001 (43.54.88.74).
Métro Pont-Neuf. **Open** noon-2.30pm, 9-11.30pm, daily.
Average 160F. **Menu** 86F (lunch), 120F (dinner).
Credit AmEx, MC, V.
Traditional, quality French cuisine served in a small,
family-run restaurant. Reservations are advised.

Entertainment
Clubs & Discos

The nightclub scene in Paris is defined more by dance music
than sexual orientation, and many of the hottest *boîtes* attract
mixed crowds. Many clubs, such as **Folies Pigalle** and **Le
Bataclan**, have weekly gay nights (*see chapter* **Nightlife**).
Keep an eye out for one-nighters, which are heavily promoted
in the gay press. Admission usually includes one free drink.

Club 18

18 rue de Beaujolais, 75001 (42.97.52.13). Métro Palais
Royal. **Open** 11pm-dawn Wed-Sun. **Admission** free
Wed, Thur, Sun; 65F Fri, Sat. **Credit** MC, V.
This hangover from the seventies can be fun if you like it
camp, and at least they're friendly.

L'Ekivok

40 rue des Blancs-Manteaux, 75004 (42.71.03.29).
Métro Rambuteau. **Open** 11.30pm-dawn Tue-Sun.
Admission 50F Fri, Sat. **Credit** AmEx, MC, V.
This tiny cellar club pulls in a mainly gay crowd interested
in disco, ambient, techno and house among other types of
music. Popular theme parties.

L'Insolite

33 rue des Petits-Champs, 75001 (42.61.99.22).
Métro Bourse. **Open** 11pm-dawn daily. **Admission** 50F
Fri, Sat. **Credit** MC, V.
Another leftover from the seventies, when rue Ste-Anne was
the centre of gay nightlife and disco reigned supreme. The
disco beat carries on, but with plenty of room for easy listening, techno and popular MTV-style dance tunes. The not-
so-young crowd here is like the music – undaring,
unpretentious but fun for an evening.

Gay Tea Dance at Le Palace

8 rue du Faubourg-Montmartre, 75009 (42.46.10.87).
Métro Rue Montmartre. **Open** 5-11pm Sun.
Admission 60F. **Credit** MC, V.
The oldest and some would still say the best, even if Régine
has bought the building. The music is good and all that bare
muscle-toned flesh can be enticing. Men only.

Le Queen

102 avenue des Champs-Elysées, 75008 (42.89.31.32).
Metro George V. **Open** 11.30pm-dawn daily. **Admission**
free Mon-Thur, Sun; 80F Fri, Sat. **Credit** MC, V.
A big gay success story that attracts an exhibitionist crowd.
Seventies' Disco Queen on Mondays, house music most other
nights, and muscle and drag shows on Saturday when it's
invariably packed. Be on the look out for men-only *Les
Mousses* foam parties. Shame about the nasty door policy
and tyrannical bouncers who only grudgingly admit women.
See also chapter **Nightlife**.

Scorpion IV

25 boulevard Poissonnière, 75002 (40.26.01.50).
Métro Rue Montmartre. **Open** midnight-7am daily.
Admission free Mon-Thur, Sun; 70F Fri, Sat.
Credit MC, V.

One of the fauna at **Le Queen.**

The place where all the waiters and hairdressers seem to go
when they can't get into Queen, perhaps drawn by the
nightly drag shows at 4am. Monday is seventies night,
Tuesday house and garage, and Thursday techno.
Weekends draw masses in from the suburbs.

Men-Only Cinema Clubs

Docks

150 rue St-Maur, 75011 (43.57.33.82).
Métro Goncourt. **Open** 4pm-2am daily. **Admission** 45F.
No credit cards.

Banque Club

*23 rue de Penthièvre, 75008 (42.56.49.26). Métro
Miromesnil.* **Open** 4pm-2am Mon-Sat; 2pm-2am Sun.
Admission membership only, 45F. **No credit cards**.

Saunas

If you just want to work out, *see chapter* **Sport &
Fitness**. Saunas listed here are men-only.

IDM

4 rue du Faubourg-Montmartre, 75009 (45.23.10.03).
Métro Rue Montmartre. **Open** noon-1am Mon-Thur;
noon-2am Fri-Sun. **Admission** 95F (under 26, 60F). **No
credit cards**.
The nearest thing in Paris to what was a New York bath
house. Popular on Sundays, with a gym, sun beds, steam
room and lots of action upstairs.

Univers Gym

*22 rue des Bons-Enfants, 75001 (42.61.24.83). Métro
Palais Royal.* **Open** noon-1am Sun-Thur; noon-2am Fri,
Sat. **Admission** 90F; 60F under-26s. **No credit cards**.
New, clean and friendly with a small gym and bar upstairs,
and a sauna, steam room, and giant video screen downstairs.

The Great Outdoors

One of the best ways to cruise in Paris is to saunter down
the street. The **Champs de Mars**, close to the Ecole
Militaire, is a night-time favourite; another is **Square Sully
Morland**, at the tip of the Ile-St-Louis, although you'll have
to hop the fence – locals seem undeterred by the infrequent
police sweeps. On anything remotely approaching a warm
day, the picturesque **Tata Beach** (on the banks of the Seine
below the quai des Tuileries, 75001) becomes a veritable
Fellini movie of sun worshippers. Things get decidedly
raunchy after dark, when the bars close. In fine weather, it's
also worth visiting the **Terrasse du Bord de L'Eau**
(Jardin des Tuileries, 75001) just to see what some people will
do to find an excuse for coming here: jogging, walking the
dog or strolling the grandmother seem to be favourites.
Things heat up after they lock the gates in the evening (there
are no gates on the avenue de Général Lemonnier side). One
word of caution, though: avoid the hustlers that congregate
in the Bois de Boulogne.

Shopping
Books

Les Mots à la Bouche

6 rue Ste-Croix-de-la-Bretonnerie, 75004 (42.78.88.30).
Métro Hôtel de Ville. **Open** 11am-11pm Mon-Fri; 11am-
midnight Sat. **Credit** EC, MC, V.
Gay-interest literature from around the world, including a
good selection of guide books and foreign magazines and
other publications. There's also a wide range of art books in
the basement gallery space.

Clothes

Body Guard

11 rue de la Ferronerie, 75001 (442.33.50.31).
Métro Châtelet-Les Halles. **Open** 1.30pm-1am daily.
Credit AmEx, MC, V.
Up-to-the-minute but not a second longer, fashions that fit like a second skin.

La Boutique et les Hommes

88 rue des Dames, 75017 (42.93.10.21).
Métro Rome or Villiers. **Open** 11am-7.30pm Mon-Thur; 11am-8pm Fri, Sat. **Credit** AmEx, DC, MC, V.
'The emporium for the modern man': designer underwear, stylish desk accessories, chic shaving utensils and the like.

Boy'z Bazaar

5 rue Ste-Croix-de-la-Bretonnerie, 75004
(42.71.94.00). Métro Hôtel de Ville. **Open** noon-9pm
Mon-Thur; noon-midnight Fri, Sat; 2pm-9pm Sun.
Credit AmEx, DC, MC, V.
Newly opened one-stop shopping for any occasion, regardless of taste. Drag, uniforms, gym-cum-club wear and leather creations all under one roof.

Factory's

3 rue Ste-Croix-de-la-Bretonnerie, 75004
(48.87.29.10). Métro Hôtel de Ville. **Open** noon-8pm
Mon-Sat; 3-7pm Sun. **Credit** EC, MC, V.
More skimp for men who like to flaunt it. Everything from underwear to swimwear via the odd rubber perfecto. Young, fun, and very casual.

Homme Sweet Homme

43 rue Vieille-du-Temple, 75004 (48.04.94.99).
Métro Hôtel de Ville. **Open** 2-7pm Mon; 11am-7pm Tue-Sat. **Credit** MC, V.
Tart drag for disco boys destined for the ultra-violet dance floors of Rimini, Ibiza or Fire Island.

Sex Shops

IEM

208 rue St-Maur, 75010 (42.41.21.41). Métro Goncourt.
Open 10am-7.30pm Mon-Sat. **Credit** AmEx, EC, MC, V.
Billed as the 'largest sex shop in Paris', if you're unable to find what you're looking for here, maybe it's time to start questioning the wisdom of what you want to do.
Branches: 4 rue Bailleul, 75001 (42.96.05.74); 33 rue de Liège, 75008 (45.22.69.01).

French Art

64 rue de Rome, 75008 (45.22.57.35). Métro Europe.
Open 9.30am-7pm Mon-Sat. **Credit** EC, MC, V.
A large video outlet with a vast selection of French and US adult movies. Prices run from around 200F to 500F.

Gay Pride/La Marche Homosexuelle

Organising committee based at the Centre Gai & Lesbien,
3 rue Keller, 75011 (43.57.21.47). Métro Ledru-Rollin.
Like most European cities, Paris celebrates Gay Pride day in late June. The week-long festivities are smaller than in New York or London, but grow larger every year. The city has tried to marginalise the main parade by routing it away from the centre, but in 1995 the *défilé* returned from eastern Paris, winding its way from Montparnasse to the Bastille via the boulevard St-Germain. Several of the bars and clubs have floats, and everyone's free to join the fun. In the evening, there are several soireés about town. Events from debates to *bal musettes* are held in the week running up to the parade.

Bastille Day Ball

quai de la Tournelle, 75005. Métro Pont Marie. **Date** 13
July, 10pm to dawn. **Admission** free.
Organised by the gay community, but open to all, this huge open-air dance on the embankment is one of the largest events on Paris' social calendar. Note that in future years it may be held at a different venue, and even on a different date.

Groups

A selection of gay organisations that meet regularly in Paris.
ACGLSF *c/o Centre Gai & Lesbien, 3 rue Keller, 75011
(43.57.21.47). Métro Ledru-Rollin.* Information, meetings and activities for the hearing-impaired.
Beit Haverim *Postal address BP 375, 75526 Paris
cedex 11 (46.32.19.36).* An association for the Jewish gay community.
Boysline *c/o Centre Gai & Lesbien, 3 rue Keller, 75011
(43.57.21.47). Métro Ledru-Rollin.* Events and activities aimed at helping young gays overcome shyness and loneliness. Meetings every other Tuesday, 3pm-8pm.
CGPIF *Postal address BP 120, 75623 Paris cedex 13
(43.64.32.75).* Federation of gay amateur athletic groups. Organised sports include football, volleyball, basketball, karate, swimming and running. They also organise the French delegation to the Gay Games.
David & Jonathan *92 bis rue de Picpus, 75012
(43.42.09.49). Métro Michel Bizot.* **Open** 24-hour answerphone. Inter-denominational Christian group. Meets Fridays, 6-8pm.
Gay Cowboy Lesbian Cowgirl *(43.48.00.69).*
American-run country and western dancing and classes for the uninitiated. Meetings on Thursdays from 8.30-10.30pm at at the London, 33 rue des Lombards, 75004.
Gay Motor Club *Postal address BP 94, 75522 Paris
cedex 11 (42.23.99.90).* Part of the Gay and Lesbian Motorcycle Clubs of Europe. Regular get-togethers and a monthly take to the road.
Gai Retraités *(47.37.75.07).* **Open** 11am-4pm. An organisation for retired gay people.

Press & Media

Most publications listed here are available at any large newsstand, and **Les Mots à la Bouche** (*see above*), but you might find many for free in gay bars and shops. Look out, too, for gay free sheets, which are appearing all the time.
Action Act Up Paris' free monthly.
Double Face A free adjunct published by *Illico* (*below*) found in most bars and hangouts. Lists useful addresses and phone numbers with the odd 'lifestyle' feature.
Exit A bi-weekly newpaper which takes a journalistic approach to covering gay news.
FG 98.2 FM (40.13.88.00). Paris' gay radio has broad appeal with house and techno music. News and information coverage speaks to its core listeners, although its commitment to Aids education sometimes sits oddly with explicit lonely hearts phone-ins.
Illico The monthly *Illico* has reduced its free circulation and become more raunchy, with gossip, photo-features and lots of telephone and Minitel numbers.
3 Keller The **Centre Gai & Lesbien**'s monthly free magazine covering activities at the centre as well as a smattering of interesting current events.
Minitel Services Over the past few years, despite threatened crackdowns, the number of gay contact/cruise networks, often with dubious acronyms, carried on the Minitel has mushroomed (*see chapter Survival*). Don't forget that they're in French, and it's you who pay.
Tribus Last year's successful new media launch. This monthly sells out quickly as much for the events calendar and listings as for the arts and entertainment features.

Health

Even a dream vacation can end in tears, so if you pick up more than your knight in shining armour, here are some gay-friendly addresses to help. For full information on all health services, and Aids/HIV services, *see chapter* **Survival: Health**.

Ecoute Gai *(44.93.01.02)*. **Open** 6-10pm Mon-Fri. A help-line organised by the AMG (*see below*), specifically geared towards psychological problems.

Point Santé – Association des Médecins Gais (AMG) *(48.05.81.71)*. *Métro Voltaire*. **Open** 6-8pm Wed; 2-4pm Sat. A telephone queries service run by an association of gay doctors in conjunction with the Centre Gay & Lesbien.

Aids Organisations

Act Up Paris *45 rue Sedaine, 75011 (48.06.13.89, Minitel 3615 Act Up)*. *Métro Bréguet-Sabin*. The highly politicised Paris chapter of the world-wide anti-Aids organisation. Meetings are at 7.30pm every Tuesday at the **Ecole des Beaux Arts**.

Patchwork des Noms *7 rue de la Guadeloupe, 75018 (42.05.72.55)*. *Métro Marx-Dormoy*. **Open** 2-6pm daily. France's ever-growing patchwork-quilt memorial for victims of Aids.

Lesbian Paris

Compared to the male gay scene in Paris, lesbians have had a much lower profile. Over the last couple of years, though, there have been signs that this is changing. A new group **Les Lesbiennes Se Déchaînent** has been set up to make lesbians more visible, and has demanded a higher profile in the Gay Pride march (*see above*). There's also a popular lesbian film festival, **Quand les Lesbiennes Fond du Cinéma**, held each autumn at Créteil, with a wide range of films, plus debates and exhibitions. Lesbians now share with gay men the **Centre Gai & Lesbien** (*see above*); several militant groups are based at the **Maison des Femmes** (*see chapter* **Women's Paris**).

On a lighter note, lesbian chic has hit Paris, and the hit French movie of 1995 was *Gazon Maudit*, a comedy that featured a lesbian having an affair with the wife of a yuppie, and moving in with them. In general, the Parisian lesbian scene tends to lipstick and glamour far more than leather and Doc Marten's.

Information, Groups & Media

Les Archives, Recherches et Cultures Lesbiennes (ARCL)

Maison des Femmes, 8 Cité Prost, 75011 (answerphone, 43.56.11.49 outside opening hours). **Open** by appointment and 7-10pm Fri.
This organisation produces audio-visual documentation and feminist magazines, and also run an archive and library with a variety of lesbian and feminist documents, essays and novels. They publish a yearbook and information bulletins on lesbian and women's activities.

Lesbia

Not exactly flamboyant, but this monthly is the leading lesbian journal. Also organises occasional parties and discos.

Les Lesbiennes Se Déchaînent

c/o Centre Gai & Lesbien, 3 rue Keller, 75011 (43.57.21.47). *Métro Ledru-Rollin*.
An active group set up in 1994 to give lesbians a more visible presence in Paris, and which has already had a sizeable impact. Their timely agenda includes visibility, homophobia, health awareness and making a lesbian presence felt at **Gay Pride**. Their Tuesday night socials are at 8pm in the Café du Trésor (5/7 rue du Trésor, 75004), but it's down to business on Fridays at 8.30pm in the Centre Gai & Lesbien.

MIEL

Maison des Femmes, 8 Cité Prost, 75011 (answerphone 43.79.61.91). **Open** 7.30pm first and third Thursday of the month.
Created in 1981, this is a militant discussion group based at the Maison des Femmes. Their social evening – Caféteria Hydromel – is every Friday from 8pm.

Cafés, Bars, Restaurants & Clubs

La Champmeslé

4 rue Chabanais, 75002 (42.96.85.20).
Métro Bourse. **Open** 6pm-2am daily. Cabaret from 10pm Thur. **Credit** MC, V.
The pillar of the Paris lesbian bar community, mixed in front and women-only at the back. Quiet early on, but often picks up late on Thursdays and weekends. Cheap drinks for birthday girls on Zodiac nights – 15th of each month.

Chez Nini Peau de Chien

24 rue des Taillandiers 75011 (47.00.45.35). *Métro Bastille*. **Open** noon-2pm, 8-11pm, Tue-Sat. **Average** 120F. Menu 59F (lunch only) 89F, 119F. **Credit** MC, V.
Run by lesbians, this restaurant has a mixed clientèle at lunchtimes and on weekday evenings, but becomes much more lesbian-orientated at weekends.

L'Ego Club

50 rue de la Chaussée d'Antin, 75009 (42.85.20.38).
Métro Chaussée d'Antin. **Women's nights** 10pm-dawn Wed; 7pm-dawn Sun. **Admission** free. **Credit** MC, V.
Twice a week it's women's night at the club. A mix of fun-seekers gather on Sundays, especially for the karaoke (7-9pm). Wednesdays it's disco.

L'Entr'acte

25 boulevard Poissonnière, 75002 (40.26.01.93).
Métro Rue Montmartre. **Open** 10pm-dawn Mon-Fri, Sun; 11.30am-dawn Sat. **Admission** 50F Sat after 1am. **Credit** MC, V.
After years of seediness, L'Entr'acte has bounced back as the trendiest lesbian club after a change of management. The usual mixture of techno and house, plus the odd splash of Madonna keeps the coolest of chicks coming back for more.

El Scandalo

21 rue Keller, 75011 (47.00.24.59). *Métro Bastille*.
Open 8pm-2am daily. **No credit cards**.
The trendy lesbian bar of the moment, mainly for a young, lipstick crowd who come here not only for a good time, but to enjoy the various exhibitions that are put on here.

Le Privilège/Kit-Kat

3 cité Bergère, 75009 (42.46.50.98).
Métro Rue Montmartre. **Open** *Le Privilège* 11.30pm-dawn Tue-Sun; *Kit Kat* 6am-noon Sat, Sun. **Admission** *Le Privilège* 90F Sat; Kit Kat 60F; drinks 70F.
This mixed, flamboyant club next to Le Palace is the surviving offspring of the legendary Katmandou. Lesbian glamour on Friday and Saturday nights at Le Privilège; the after-hours Kit Kat next door is very popular with gay men. Selective door policy. *See also chapter* **Nightlife**.

Students

Paris is the place to study French, fashion or haute cuisine – and you don't need to starve in a garret in the process.

If you come to Paris expecting to find a militant student body reminiscent of May '68, you may be disappointed. In the last few years, students have organised over issues such as educational rights and unemployment, but a number of factors combine to make if difficult for the student movement of old to re-emerge – among them, the fact that most students live with their parents, and the fragmented, dispersed nature of French universities.

The university of Paris proper is split into 18 separate units spread around the city and suburbs, of which the renowned **Sorbonne** is just one. Competition for places grows ever fiercer, as any student who has completed secondary school can apply, and overcrowding and high drop-out rates are perennial problems. The situation is different in the prestigious, selective *Grandes Ecoles*, the specialist institutes, such as the *Ecole National d'Administration* (ENA) or the *Ecole Polytechnique*, which are unchallenged at the top of the French educational tree. A degree from one of these elitist institutions guarantees a wealth of job offers.

Students at French universities study either for a *License*, a three-year degree course, or a two-year *DEUG*. Many students now take vocational or business-oriented courses, and many do what is called a *stage*, a practical, in-service traineeship in a particular job, after their main degree. Students on such courses are called *stagiaires*.

STUDYING IN PARIS

Paris has something to offer every kind of student, of any age, whether they want to improve their French or make the most of Paris' cultural opportunities by studying photography, fashion or haute cuisine. Most foreign students study at private colleges, but students from other EU countries can enter the university system via the **Erasmus** scheme (*see below* **Courses & Classes**).

Despite the dispersal of the modern university, Paris' students still crowd out of the science campus at Jussieu and the Sorbonne to pack the Latin Quarter cafés between lectures. Foreign students tend to hang out in this area at night, but it's the cheaper bars of the Bastille and the outer *arrondissements* that are most popular with French students.

A wide range of students' services and discounts make budget living possible despite Paris' expensive reputation. To claim most discounts (around 10F off some cinema seats, up to 50 per cent off standby theatre tickets and museums, and 20 per cent in some hairdressers), you must have a French student card or an International Student Identity Card (ISIC). Be warned that ISIC cards are only valid in France if you are under 26.

Information

AJF (Acceil des Jeunes en France)
119 rue St-Martin, 75004 (42.77.87.80). Métro Rambuteau. **Open** 10am-12.30pm, 1.30pm-6pm, Mon-Fri. Opposite the Centre Pompidou, the AJF provides discount travel and event tickets, and help and information on temporary accommodation and many other matters, to anyone aged 18-30. They are always busy, so it's best to turn up rather than phone. It also has a same-day reservation service for bookings in youth hostels and some other budget accommodation, for a 10F fee (*see chapter* **Accommodation**). **Branches:** 139 boulevard St-Michel, 75005 (43.54.95.86); *June-Sept only* main hall of the Gare du Nord, 75010 (42.85.86.19).

CIDJ (Centre d'Information et de Documentation Jeunesse)
101 quai Branly, 75015 (44.49.12.00). Métro Bir-Hakeim/RER Champ de Mars. **Open** 10am-6pm Mon-Sat. As the name indicates the CIDJ is mainly a library, where many French students seek career advice, but it also houses the main youth bureau of the ANPE (*Agence Nationale Pour l'Emploi*), the state employment service (*see chapter* **Survival**). It is not, though, a good place to look for job offers, as queues are long, and many employers think that foreign students who use the CIDJ are desperate to do any kind of work. It also has information on work and study, as well as social life, hobbies and sports, and, while it does not have an accommodation service, the CIDJ can provide you with a list of cheap hotels and hostels for short-term stays.

CROUS (Centre Régional des Oeuvres Universitaires et Scolaires)
39 avenue Georges Bernanos, 75005 (40.51.36.00). RER Port-Royal. **Open** 9am-5pm Mon-Fri. The CROUS is best known for its student restaurants, the **Restos-U** (*see below* **Cheap Meals**), but is also the best place to book a bed in the **Foyers** or student residences (*see below* **Student Accommodation**). It also organises cheap trips, excursions and sports and cultural events, provides information on accommodation and jobs, and offers theatre and concert tickets with substantial discounts (15%-50%). The ISIC card is accepted. There is a Resto-U and sports facilities in the building.

UCRIF (Union des Centres de Rencontres Internationales de France)
72 rue Rambuteau, 75001 (40.26.57.64). Métro Châtelet-Les Halles. **Open** 9am-6pm Mon-Fri. Operates a language school and several cheap, short-stay hostels in France, including 14 in Paris. They also organise social events for those hostels, and there's no age limit.

Courses & Classes

Erasmus Programme

In Britain: *NARIC, The British Council, Medlock Street, Manchester, M15 4AA (0161-957 7065).*
In France: *Ministère de l'Enseignement Supérieur et de la Recherche, 61-65 rue Dutot, 75015 Paris (40.65.65.89).*
The Erasmus scheme enables European Union students with a reasonable standard of written and spoken French to spend a year of their degree in the French university system, following appropriate courses. The Erasmus offices listed above will be able to help with general enquiries, but applications must be made through the student's home university, which will have full information about the scheme.

Cours d'Adultes

Information: *Hôtel de Ville, Place de l'Hôtel de Ville, 75004 (42.76.40.40.) or on Minitel 3615 Paris.*
An enormous range of adult-education classes, from accountancy and computing to pottery and pâtisserie, are run by the City of Paris. Participants pay a minimal contribution towards fees for the classes, which take place in various local *mairies* and colleges around Paris. To enrol you must have a residency card, a *carte de séjour*. For information on the courses available enquire at the *mairie* of your *arrondissement*, or obtain a complete list from the address above.

Ecole du Louvre

34 Quai du Louvre, 75001 (40.20.56.31).
Within the Louvre complex, this prestigious school runs several courses on art history and archeology which are open to foreign students. Those not wanting to take a full degree can sign up as *auditeurs*, which allows you to attend lectures.

CIDD Découverte du Vin

30 rue de la Sablière, 75014 (45.45.32.20). Métro Mouton-Duvernet. **Open** 9am-7pm Mon-Fri. **Fees** *soirées* 200F-300F; 360F per class; 860F three classes; 1,280F five classes.
The best wine courses are in the French regions, but the CIDD offers a start, with both beginners and advanced classes, some in English. Courses include identifying wines and wine-tasting, plus open-house days with producers, *soirée gourmande* lectures and tastings with a grower-producer, and tours. Week-long summer courses cost 3,250F.

Cordon Bleu

8 rue Léon Delhomme, 75015 (48.56.06.06). Métro Vaugirard. **Open** 9am-7pm Mon-Fri. **Fees** 200F-4,950F.
Come here for three-hour sessions on classical and regional cuisine, market visits, one-day cookery workshops with chefs, and two- to five-day gourmet sessions on summer menus, bread baking, cheese tasting and other topics.

Ecole de Gastronomie Française Ritz-Escoffier

15 place Vendôme, 75001 (42.60.38.30). Métro Opéra. **Fees** *demonstration* from 230F; *one-week courses* 5,350F; *12-week diploma* 69,600F; phone for details.
A huge range of courses. Afternoon-long demonstrations, a choice of 14 week-long summer courses in such subjects as regional cookery, chocolate and cake making, and courses of up to 12 weeks that are more for professionals. Classes are great fun: smaller and more international than at the Cordon Bleu, and more hands on – plus, of course, it's at the Ritz.

INSEAD

Boulevard de Constance, 77251 Fontainebleau (admissions office 60.72.40.00).
This highly-regarded international business school, in a regal location near Napoleon's favourite château at Fontainebleau, offers a ten-month MBA programme, in English. The 450 students are drawn from all over the world.

Parsons School of Design

14 rue Letellier, 75015 (45.77.39.66). Métro Emile Zola.
Open 9am-5pm Mon-Fri. **Fees** 350F registration fee plus 1,850F per non-credit course or 2,472F per credit course.
This American art and design college, linked to its New York parent, offers courses in fine arts, fashion, interior design, illustration, photography and computing, in English. For children's courses, *see* chapter **Children**.

Spéos Paris Photographic Institute

8 rue Jules Vallès, 75011 (40.09.18.58). Métro Charonne.
Open 10am-1pm, 2-6pm, Mon-Fri. **Fees** *full-time (Jan-May, Oct-Jan)* 36,500F per semester; *14-week courses (six hours per week)* 4,500F per term; *weekly courses (up to four)* 3,000F per week.
The courses offered, all in English, include fashion, fine art, photography, photo-journalism, computer imaging, and intensive workshops. A deposit is required, and payment is accepted in US dollars or sterling as well as francs.

Free Lectures

The **Collège de France** at 11 place Marcelin Berthelot, 75005 (44.27.12.11) and the **British Institute** (*see below*) both offer a range of free lectures, in French and English respectively. The Collège de France attracts top intellectuals to hold forth on a variety of subjects, while the talks organised by the British Council focus on English literature, and include poetry readings and book signings. Call in or phone for lecture lists.

Language Courses

Alliance Française

101 boulevard Raspail, 75006 (45.44.38.28). Métro St-Placide. **Open** *reception* 9am-6pm Mon-Fri. **Fees** *enrolment fee* 250F *extensive* 1,350F per month; *intensive* 2 700F per month; *business French* 4,800F per month.
A highly-regarded, non-profitmaking French-language school. Teachers are highly trained, and courses run from complete beginners' to specialist (conversation, business, translation, literature). There's also a *médiathèque*, a film club, talks and lectures. Courses begin at the start of every month, with enrolment a few days before. Also a good place to look for small ads for accommodation or part-time work.

Berlitz France

38 avenue de l'Opéra, 75002 (44.94.50.00). Métro Opéra.
Open 9.30am-6.30pm Mon-Fri; 8am-12.30pm Sat. **Fees** *four week intensive* 8,765F; *individual 60 hrs* 29,735F.
Well known and effective, but expensive, and mainly used by businesses. There are several schools around Paris, offering day and evening classes on a group or individual basis.

British Institute

9 rue Constantine, 75007 (45.55.71.99). Métro Invalides.
Open phone for details. **Fees** 2,400F-4,000F per term.
The Institute's main role is to provide English teaching for Parisians, but it also offers courses at various levels (not beginner) in French, particularly in different specialities such as professional translation, commercial French and literature. Enrolment in the one-term courses is on the basis of a test. It is also possible to study at the Institute for a three-year degree in French from the University of London, and a post-graduate MA in translation. To obtain details in Britain, contact the University of London, Senate House, Malet Street, London WC1 (0171 636 8000, ext 3920). The Institute also provides lectures, a library, outings and visits. Fees are lower for EU citizens.

Eurocentres

13 passage Dauphine, 75006 (43.25.81.40). Métro Odéon. **Open** 8.30am-6pm Mon-Fri. **Fees** *four week intensive (30 hours per week)* 6,900F.

Intensive classes (lasting 2 to 24 weeks) are for a maximum of 15 students, with summer courses running from July to September. Courses emphasise communication rather than grammar, and include cultural activities and the use of an audio-visual *médiathèque*. Accommodation can be arranged.

Institut Catholique de Paris

21 rue d'Assas, 75006 (44.39.52.68). Métro Rennes. **Open** 10am-4pm Mon-Fri. **Fees** *enrolment fee* 300F; *15-week semester* 2,850F-3 150F.

A reputable school offering fairly traditional courses in French language and culture. The equivalent of a French *bac* is required, plus proof of residence. Students must be aged 18 or above, but don't have to be Catholic.

Université de Paris/la Sorbonne – Cours de Langues et Civilisation

47 rue des Ecoles, 75005 (40.46.22.11, ext 2664/75). Métro Cluny La Sorbonne or St-Michel/RER Luxembourg. **Open** 10am-noon, 2-4pm, Mon-Fri. **Fees** 3,100F-10,300F per half-year.

The classes for foreigners at the Sorbonne ride on the name of this eminent institution and make use of some of its facilities, but you are unlikely to brush elbows with French students. Courses are more grammar- than conversation-based, and traditionally structured. The main course includes lectures on politics, history and culture, as well as obligatory language-lab sessions. Language-only courses are also available. Courses are open to anyone over 18, and in great demand. Register several months in advance.

Libraries

The last of former President Mitterrand's celebrated *grand projets*, the **Bibliothèque Nationale de France**, is finally due to open in November 1996, if all goes to plan. Bringing together the vast collections of the **Bibliothèque Nationale** and the **Bibliothèque de France**, with ten million books and 350,000 periodicals, the library will be accessible to the general public as well as researchers for consultation or borrowing (*see also chapter* **Sightseeing**).

On a smaller scale, each part of the University of Paris has library facilities for enrolled students, while all Paris *arrondissements* have free public libraries. To obtain a library card you will need a *carte de séjour* or other ID and two other documents proving residency in the relevant district, such as a recent phone bill or tenancy agreement. Most local libraries have magazine, record and children's libraries. Book loan is free, but there are charges for record and video libraries. A full list of libraries is available from any municipal library.

American Library

10 rue Général Camou, 75007 (45.51.46.82/45.51.47.47). Métro Alma-Marceau or Ecole Militaire, then cross Pont de l'Alma. **Open** 10am-7pm Tue-Sat.

A 60F per day charge for non-members, and only members can take books on loan (525F per year; 735F family rate; 210F under-12s). There are monthly talks by authors, and a reading hour at 2.30pm Wednesdays for the age 3-5s, for free.

Bibliothèque Historique de la Ville de Paris

Hôtel Lamoignon, 24 rue Pavée, 75004 (44.59.29.40). Métro St-Paul. **Open** 9.30am-6pm Mon-Sat.

Reference books and documents on all aspects of Paris' history, housed in one of the classic mansions of the Marais. There is a particularly strong theatre section.

Bibliothèque Nationale

58 rue de Richelieu, 75002 (47.03.81.26). Métro Bourse. **Open** 10am-8pm Mon-Sat.

Until the new mega-library by the river (*see above*) finally opens, this grand nineteenth-century building will continue to house France's public-deposit library, and an immense collection of engravings and photographs. To obtain a reader's card you must be an accredited researcher. Other sections of the building are open to the public, and host a range of exhibitions (*see chapters* **Sightseeing** *and* **Museums**).

Bibliothèque Publique d'Information

Centre Pompidou, rue Beaubourg, 75004 (44.78.12.33). Métro Châtelet-Les Halles or Rambuteau. **Open** noon-10pm Mon, Wed-Fri; 10am-10pm Sat, Sun.

Paris' mega-public library, within the Pompidou Centre, receives an average of 11,000 visitors per day (the longest queues are at midday). It has a large English-language section, a large selection of newpapers, and language laboratories, which have to be booked well in advance.

British Council Library

9-11 rue Constantine, 75007 (49.55.73.00). Métro Invalides. **Open** 11am-6pm Mon-Fri.

A home away from home for British residents, and also a good place to meet French students of English. As well as books there are daily newspapers, and a language teaching centre. Annual membership is 230F, and for non-members there is a consultation fee of 25F per day. The British Institute also has its own café.

Discothèque des Halles

Forum des Halles, 8 Porte St-Eustache, 75001 (42.33.20.50). Métro Châtelet-Les Halles. **Open** noon-7pm Tue-Sat.

Records on vinyl, CD and cassette available on loan, plus sound archives, videos and musical and choreographic literature and documents open for consultation.

Documentation Française

31 quai Voltaire, 75007 (40.15.70.00). Métro Rue du Bac. **Open** 10am-6pm Mon-Wed, Fri; 10am-1pm Thur.

The official government archive and central reference library, with information in detail on just about any aspect of French life you may wish to research.

Student Accommodation

The best places to find budget accommodation for medium- to long stays are the **Foyers** or the **Cité Universitaire**. Foyers are student hostels, with beds in individual or shared rooms for rents of about 2,000F per month. Rooms generally have to be booked for at least a term. Further information and bookings are available through the **CROUS** and the **UCRIF** (*see above* **Information**). The Cité Universitaire is Paris' closest equivalent to a campus, and provides budget rooms for foreign students with the advantages of a whole range of facilities and student services on site. For more on budget hotels and hostels, *see chapter* **Accommodation**.

FLAT-HUNTING

Good places to find ads for flatshares and cheap flats are the free magazine *FUSAC* (*see chapter* **Media**), and the noticeboards at the British Institute, the Alliance Française and the American Church (*see chapter* **Survival**). If you're looking to rent a flat yourself, be prepared for this to require large amounts of cash. As students often cannot provide proof of income, a *porte-garant* (guarantor) is required. This role is usually filled by a parent, who must write a letter (in French) declaring that he/she guarantees payment of rent and bills. Bring this with you, or you'll waste time waiting for it to be sent. You will also probably have to pay over a large initial deposit, an agency fee and the first month's rent before you can move in. Short-term flat agencies (*see chapter* **Accommodation**) can simplify things, but are not cheap either. For more on all aspects of flat-finding in Paris, *see chapter* **Survival**.

Chambre contre travail

A common form of accommodation for students (more for women than men) is a *chambre contre travail*, free board in exchange for work or English lessons, on an au pair basis. You will normally have your own room; the amount of child-care or housework required varies. Ads offering rooms can be found at course accommodation offices, the British Institute or the centres listed *above under* **Information**.

Cité Universitaire

19 boulevard Jourdan, 75014 (45.89.68.52). RER Cité Universitaire. **Open** *administration* 9am-3pm Mon-Fri.
If you are enrolled on a university-style course (Sorbonne, British Institute or similar) or are a *stagiaire* and under 30, you can apply for a place at the Cité Universitaire – a huge campus of halls of residence, with architecture indicative of different countries, on the southern edge of Paris in the 14th *arrondissement*. There are excellent facilities (tennis courts,

a pool, theatres, music studios and a restaurant), and a friendly atmosphere to compensate for the rather basic rooms. Rooms must be booked for the entire academic year (October to June). Rents are about 1,900F per month for a single room, 1,500F per person for a double, and 2,050F-3,500F for *stagiaires*. Prices vary according to which *maison* you live in. All UK citizens must apply in first instance to the *Collège Franco-Britannique*, stating which hall they wish to live in. From 1 July-30 September rooms are available for rent to anybody with an ISIC card, for 90F-140F per night.

Cheap Meals

Cheapest Parisian supermarkets are the **Ed L'Epicier** chain, which are fine for basics, although it's advisable to check sell-by dates on their fresh produce. You can also get great bargains at street markets at the end of the day, when prices for fruit and greens are often slashed. Also, being on a low budget doesn't mean you'll never eat out again; you just have to be selective. Once you've settled in you're bound to find a favourite café with a 70F menu. *See also chapter* **Restaurants**.

Resto-U

10 rue Jean Calvin, 75005 (43.31.51.66). Métro Censier-Daubenton. **Open** 11.30am-1.45pm, 6.30-8pm, Mon-Fri; times vary Sat, Sun, phone for details.
3 rue Censier, 75005 (45.35.41.24.). Métro Censier-Daubenton. **Open** 11.15am-4pm Mon-Fri.
3 rue Mabillon, 75006 (43.25.66.23). Métro Mabillon. **Open** 11.30am-2pm, 6-8pm, Mon-Fri.
5 rue Mazet, 75006 (46.33.20.17.). Métro Odéon. **Open** 11.30am-3.45pm Mon-Fri. **No credit cards**.
CROUS (*see above* **Information**) runs a chain of Restos-U (university restaurants), of which only some are listed here. Food is not hugely appetising, but the three-course meals are very cheap. Buy a carnet of tickets at 12.70F per ticket. A full list of restaurants and times is available from the CROUS or the restaurants listed here. An ISIC card is required.

The student's standby for economy eating in Paris, the **Resto-U**.

Women's Paris

Parisiennes still seem to depend on charm to get their way, but 'feminisation' at the top may herald more direct clout.

Paris has always been allegorically represented as a woman. A typical turn-of-the-century cartoon shows her, resplendently dressed in crown and furs, throwing the contents of her chamber pot over a miserable old lady (labelled *banlieue* – the suburbs) in the street below. The cliché of the *Parisienne* as a haughty coquette has persisted too.

Most Parisian women create feminism on their own terms, using *la séduction* to their advantage in everyday life, while not losing sight of their own feminist agenda. It is perhaps such contradictions, along with an argumentative French academic tradition, that have led the French feminist movement into breaking up into squabbling, disunited factions, as it remains fundamentally ambivalent about its own image and status.

In recent times, perhaps the greatest display of women's solidarity came in 1975, as a bill legalising abortion was finally passed by Simone Veil, Minister for Health in the conservative government of Valéry Giscard d'Estaing. This was after fierce lobbying from such celebrities as Simone de Beauvoir, actresses Catherine Deneuve and Jeanne Moreau and novelist Françoise Sagan, who were among those who took to the streets and declared publicly that they had already broken the law by having abortions themselves.

Impressive, colourful women have featured strongly in the history of French feminism. Astute salon hostesses in the seventeenth and eighteenth centuries wielded political power behind the scenes, by hosting gatherings of influential men. In 1791, a year ahead of Mary Wollstonecraft's *A Vindication of the Rights of Woman*, the playwright and revolutionary Olympe de Gouges set out *The Declaration of the Rights of Woman*. But hopes that *égalité* would be extended to women were crushed by a reactionary backlash, and de Gouges was guillotined for "having forgotten the virtues of her sex".

Under the Napoleonic code of 1804 women were classed as legal incompetents alongside children and the insane. The French Left long feared that women were under the thumb of a reactionary church, and in 1888 Léon Richer, himself the head of the French League for Women's Rights, declared that giving women the vote would be dangerous, and would lead to the collapse of the Republic within six months. In fact, it wasn't until 1944 that General de Gaulle's France finally gave voting rights to *le sexe faible*, in part in recognition of the crucial role played by women in the Resistance to the German occupation.

Despite an initial flurry of enthusiasm in the late forties, female political figures have remained a scarce commodity. Newly-coined President Chirac, however, has made much of his appeal to women, and during his electoral campaign promised loudly to 'feminise' French government. He caused an immediate stir by including no fewer than 12 women in his first administration.

If France has remarkably few women in senior professional posts, those at the top in their fields, such as Anne Sinclair, Claire Chazal and Christine Ockrent in TV, or the writers Elisabeth Badinter, Héléne Cixous and Julia Kristeva, are all high-profile and exert a great deal of influence. Also, France's excellent maternity and health provisions have facilitated combining work and family life to such an extent that 82 per cent of women in the Ile-de-France region now work.

However, equality in the workplace is still some way off, with women's salaries on average 20 per cent lower than those of their male counterparts, in spite of the equality laws of 1972. At work, as in most other walks of life, the notion of politically correct behaviour is regarded with bemused derision, so it comes as no great surprise that sexual harassment cases are practically unheard of in France. Flirtatious advances are commonly put down to nothing more than harmless Latin bravado. French advertising, too, can raise the hackles of the mildest of anglophone feminists, with images of naked, pouting temptresses used to sell anything from yoghurt to bathroom fittings.

In 1983 Yvette Roudy, then Minister for Women's Rights, attempted to introduce a bill eliminating sexism from advertising, but was overpowered by the press and arts community. Since then French women have remained remarkably silent on the subject. Even the feminist writer Elisabeth Badinter has declared that such acceptance is natural, coming from centuries of exposure to the nude in French art, with figures such as *Marianne*, the symbolic bare-breasted leader of the Revolution, epitomising the delicate balance between strength and eroticism so sought after by the modern Parisienne.

For information on the lesbian scene and facilities in Paris, *see chapter* **Gay & Lesbian Paris**.

SEXUAL HARRASSMENT

Paris is unthreatening for a woman, although the usual precautions (not going out alone between 2am and 5am and avoiding ill-lit streets) apply as in any other large city. Violent crime tends to be concentrated in suburbs, but areas to avoid at night include the Bois de Boulogne and the Bois de Vincennes. Though not in the same league as Italians when it comes to bottom pinching, many French men are nevertheless ever-ready with the smouldering gaze or pick-up line. The best brush-off is the cold blank stare so beloved of Parisian women, but if you feel in need of self-defence/self-esteem classes, call *Terre des Sources* (40.59.86.52) for details of their courses, which run one weekend in the month for four months.

Information Centres

Maison des Femmes

8 cité Prost, 75011 (43.48.24.91). Métro Charonne or Faidherbe-Chaligny. **Open** 3-8pm Mon, Wed, Fri; *café open* 8pm-late Fri.

It is perhaps a reflection of the limited interest in feminism in Paris that the main centre for women's activities is still situated down a dingy alley (despite campaigning for new premises) and only manages to open for a few hours each week. Nevertheless, it is enthusiastically run and hosts a feminist library, a café and 13 women's groups in an environment that's strictly women-only (call for details). It also publishes the bulletin *Paris-Féministe*, which is a useful guide to what's going on. The volunteers at the *Maison* will be able to point you in the right direction, whether you are looking for legal or employment advice, a rape crisis centre or wish to become involved in one of their many (all fairly militant) discussion or support groups.

Bibliothèque Marguérite Durand

79 rue Nationale, 75013 (45.70.80.30). Métro Tolbiac. **Open** 2-6pm Tue-Sat.

A collection of 28,000 books, some in English, on the history of women and feminism, based on the books and papers assembled by feminist pioneer Durand, founder of the women's newspaper *La Fronde*, and which she donated to the state in 1931. Posters, postcards and photographs are also available for consultation.

Centre Nationale d'Information et de Documentation des Femmes et des Familles (CNIDFF)

7 rue du Jura, 75013 (43.31.12.34). Métro Gobelins. **Open** *phone calls* 9am-12.30pm Mon-Fri; *in person* 1.30-5.30pm Tue-Thur.

Legal, professional and health advice for women. You can consult its information services or order any of its useful publications on Minitel 3615 CNIDFF.

Service Droits des Femmes

31 rue Le Peletier, 75009 (47.70.41.58). Métro Le Peletier. **Open** *phone calls only* 9am-12.30pm, 3-5pm, Mon-Fri.

In 1981 President Mitterrand created the Ministry for Women's Rights, with a sizeable budget and feminist Yvetty Roudy at the helm. In 1986 it was abolished by the conservatives, and replaced by the far humbler *Secrétariat d'Etat aux Droits des Femmes et de la Vie Quotidienne*, the department which runs this service. They provide a variety of documents on employment, rape, the status of single women and other aspects of women's rights, all available on request.

WICE (Women's Institute for Continuing Education)

20 boulevard du Montparnasse, 75015 (45.66.75.50). Métro Duroc. **Open** 9am-5pm Mon-Fri. **Membership** 350F individual; 500F joint; 250F students.

An expatriate cultural/educational centre with a mainly American membership, which runs courses on art, history and literature, plus guided tours of museums and on different areas of the city and topics of interest. Membership benefits also include several shop and leisure facility discounts, as well as a library and resource centre providing information on such issues as citizenship, integration and apartment hunting. Social evenings include wine tasting and conversation groups.

Bookshops

See also chapters **Specialist Shops** *and* **Gay & Lesbian Paris**, *and the* **Maison des Femmes** (*above*) *for its library.*

La Brèche

9 rue de Tunis, 75011 (43.67.63.57). Métro Nation. **Open** noon-8pm Mon-Sat. **Credit** V.

Good if small selection of women's books, mostly in French.

La Fourmi Ailée

8 rue du Fouarre, 75005 (43.29.40.99). Métro Maubert-Mutualité. **Open** noon-7pm Mon, Wed-Sat. **Credit** AmEx, MC, V.

A bookshop specialising in feminism and works by women, conveniently attached to an excellent tea shop. Good selection of books on theatre, philosophy and art, with some English poetry collections.

The **Librairie des Femmes**. *See page 296.*

Librairie des Femmes

74 rue de Seine, 75006 (43.29.50.75). Métro Mabillon.
Open 10am-7pm Mon-Sat. **Credit** AmEx, MC, V.
Paris' main feminist bookshop is owned by Editions des Femmes, and run in association with Antoinette Fouque's political group *Alliance des Femmes pour la Democratie*. There's also a gallery area, and leaflets on cultural activities.

Media

Magazines

Paris Féministe is the bulletin of the **Maison des Femmes**, and the intriguingly named *Marie Pas Claire* is the publication of a new group of militant young *féministes*. The quarterly *Femmes Artistes* provides an insight on women's contribution to the arts world. *Madame Figaro*, on the other hand, which comes with the Saturday edition of *Le Figaro* newspaper, is a favourite of the well-heeled Parisian *BCBG* set.

Radio & Television

If you're interested in taking a look at the current popular heroines, you should watch news broadcasters Anne Sinclair and Claire Chazal in action, or Laure Adler, feminist writer and former cultural adviser to Mitterrand, leading a host of cultural debates in *Cercle de Minuit* (Mon-Thur around 12.30am on France 2). Mireille Dumas' weekly documentary *Bas les Masques* (Wed 10.35pm on France 2) is worth tuning into for perceptive coverage of a whole range of social issues. Or you can listen to the women-oriented slots on:

Paris Plurielle (106.3 MHz)

(48.13.00.99). **Time** 7pm Tue.

Radio Libértaire (89.4 MHz)

(42.62.90.51). **Time** 6.30pm Wed

Film

Festival de Films de Femmes

Maison des Arts, place Salvador Allende, 94000 Créteil (49.80.38.98). Métro Créteil. Minitel: 3615 1er Siècle.
Dates March. **Admission** 35F per film, 30F students; 10 film subscription cards for 200F.
A women's film festival, with an impressive selection of international films by female directors. Held every spring in Créteil, just outside Paris.

Accommodation

Union des Foyers des Jeunes Travailleurs (U.F.J.T)

12 avenue du Général de Gaulle, 94307, Vincennes (41.74.53.56). **Open** *office* 9am-5pm Mon-Fri. **Credit** MC, V.
An organisation running several hostels throughout Paris, many specifically for women. To be eligible you must be a non-resident of France aged between 18-25 and able to prove that you are either working, or unemployed but looking for work. Accommodation is in individual or double rooms, with breakfast and one other meal often included in the monthly charge. All hostels ask for a deposit of about 1,700F, plus an

initial fee of 130F, with prices varying from 1,475F per month for a shared room to 2,650F per month for a single with meals. Call for further details.

YWCA

22 rue de Naples, 75008 (45.22.23.49). Métro Villiers.
Open 9am-7pm daily. **Rates** *per night (minimum three nights)* 90F (shared room with 2 or 3 others), 110F (single); *per month* 2,035F-2,600F. **No credit cards.**
Individual and dormitory rooms (up to four beds) for women aged 18-24: mainly students and working women. Breakfast and an evening meal are included in the monthly price.

Relaxation

See also chapters **Sport & Fitness** for recreation *and* **Services** for skin care.

Hammam de la Mosquée

39 rue Geoffroy St Hilaire, 75005 (43.31.18.14). Métro Censier-Daubenton. **Open to women** 11am-8pm Mon, Wed, Sat; 11am-9pm Thur. **Admission** 65F; towel rental 20F; massage 50F. **No credit cards.**
Languish in marble steam rooms, take an invigorating massage, or lounge on comfortable mattresses in the Mosque's Arab bath, before nipping next door for mint tea and unbelievably sweet cakes. *See also chapter* **Cafés & Bars**.

Help & Health

To obtain the Pill, a diaphragm or the morning-after pill, you'll need a prescription (available, on appointment, from the first two places below or from a *généraliste* or gynaecologist). Spermicides and Condoms (*préservatifs*), are available from pharmacies, and there are now dispensing machines in the odd métro station, club lavatory or street corner. For reasonably-priced sanitary products, supermarkets rather than pharmacies are your best bet. For more information on all health services, *see chapter* **Survival**.

Centre de Planification et d'Education Familiale

27 rue Cunonsky, 75017 (48.88.07.28). Métro Porte de Champerret. **Open** 9am-5.30pm Mon-Fri.
Free consultation, in French, on family planning and abortion. Phone for an appointment.

MFPF

10 rue Vivienne, 75002 (42.60.93.20). Métro Bourse.
Open 9.30am-5pm Mon-Fri (appointment needed).
For contraception advice and prescriptions.

SOS Help

(47.23.80.80). **Open** 3-11pm Mon-Fri.
English-language helpline. Listeners can refer you to English-speaking lawyers, doctors and so on.

Violence Conjugale – Femmes Info Service

(40.02.02.33). **Open** 10am-8pm Mon-Fri, public holidays.
Telephone service to help battered women, directing them towards medical aid or shelters, if need be.

Viols Femmes Informations

4 square Ste-Irenée, 75011 (05.05.95.95/45.82.73.00). MétroSt Ambroise. **Open** 10am-6pm Mon-Fri.
A freephone, in French, for dealing with rape.

Trips Out of Town

Travelling Beyond Paris

Practical information on how and when to strike out beyond the city.

The French have had *congés payés* (paid holidays) since 1936, and traditionally take them in July and August. And since 20 per cent of the population live in the Paris region, when they leave for their holidays it looks a lot like the exodus of Moses and the Israelites for the Promised Land. Weekends to avoid travelling on at all costs are those at the beginning, middle and end of July, and again at the middle and end of August. The other favourite holiday time in France is from mid-February to mid-March, when holiday-makers don snowsuits and depart *en masse* for the ski slopes. If you are travelling in these peak periods, it's advisable to reserve accommodation in advance; at other times, it's often easy to find a hotel on the day of your arrival, and most local *Offices du Tourisme* provide some sort of same-day booking service.

Increasing numbers of French people now take their holidays outside of the main seasons. After all, sunny May mornings in the Dordogne or brisk November walks along the Normandy shore can be delightful. However, always check before you set off that the sights and hotels you've based your break around haven't closed for the season.

INFORMATION

The Paris tourist office on the Champs-Elysées and its branches in the main train stations (*see chapter* **Essential Information**) stock some leaflets on the French regions. There are also several regional tourist offices (addresses are available at the Paris tourist office). When you arrive in a town, local Tourist Offices are useful sources of city maps and information on local sites and events, and can usually help with accommodation.

Logis de France/Gîtes de France

Fédération Nationale des Logis de France *83 avenue d'Italie, 75013 (45.84.70.00/booking 45.84.83.84).* **Gîtes de France** *35 rue Godot de Mauroy, 75009 (49.70.75.75/Minitel 3615 Gîtes de France).* **Open** 10am-6.30pm Mon-Fri; 10am-1pm, 2-6.30pm, Sat.
Hotels that are members of the association **Logis de France** are often a good bet. Ratings (one to three chimneys) are judged on hospitality as well as facilities. Most are traditional, family-run hotels, often with a restaurant, and mainly in small towns and villages. An annual guide is available from bookshops or the national federation. Another option

is the ever expanding number of *Gîtes* or rural holiday cottages, which can be rented for anything from a weekend to several weeks. Details and regional lists are available from the umbrella organisation **Gîtes de France**, which also covers rural bed-and-breakfast places and farm campsites.

Travelling by Train

A comprehensive rail network is the main means of public transport for getting around France, for there are few long-distance bus services. Several attractions within the Paris suburbs, notably **Versailles** and **Disneyland Paris**, are served by stations on the **RER** suburban rail network (*see chapter* **Getting Around**). Most locations further from the city are served by French national railways, the **SNCF**, one of the most efficient networks in the world. It has certain drawbacks such as strikes, strange hours and slow internal exchange of information; nonetheless, trains almost always run on time.

Each Paris mainline station serves a different region. Leave from **Gare Montparnasse** for Brittany and southern Normandy; **Gare St-Lazare** for northern Normandy and the Dieppe area; **Gare du Nord** for north-east France, the most important Channel ports, Belgium, the Netherlands and points east; **Gare de l'Est** for Strasbourg, Champagne and southern Germany; **Gare de Lyon** for Burgundy, the Alps, Provence, the Riviera and Italy; and **Gare d'Austerlitz** for south-western France and western Spain. It will be clear from your ticket which station to leave from.

The SNCF's prestigious *TGV* (*Train de Grande Vitesse*, or high-speed train) has revolutionised journey times on trunk routes, and the high-speed network is gradually being extended to all the main regions. On the downside, travel by *TGV* requires a hefty additional supplement and obligatory reservation, and their introduction can also mean that there are fewer mainline trains to lesser towns. Night trains are no cheaper than daytime services, and much slower, but will save you precious day-time when travelling long distances. For an additional charge shared sleeper cabins (*couchettes*) and first-class only, private or semi-private *wagon-lit* compartments are also available.

Reservations & Tickets

An enormously complicated computer booking system, unwisely called *Socrate*, was introduced in 1993 for all SNCF trains. It initially went through massive teething problems, but most have now been ironed out, and it is now relatively workable, despite the maze of tariffs. There are different tariff bands (Red, White and Blue periods) to encourage passengers to travel outside peak hours, and a range of discount cards such as the *Carte Vermeil* for pensioners and *Carissimo* for people aged under 26. Tickets even carry itemised information to show how the final sum was reached.

Reservations for *TGV* and night trains can be obtained at SNCF stations or through a travel agent. You can make a preliminary reservation through the Minitel or by phone: you must then pick up and pay for the reservation within 48 hours. **Before you board any train, *always* stamp your ticket in the little orange *composteur* machines located by the platforms.** Inspectors on trains are authorised to charge for the full price of a ticket, plus a fine, if this is not done.

SNCF Central Information Service

(information 45.82.50.50/reservations 45.65.60.60).
Open *information* 7am-10pm daily; *reservations* 8am-8pm daily; *car transportation* 8.30am-7pm Mon-Fri; 9am-1pm Sat. **No credit cards**.
The central numbers deal with information and reservations for all services and stations. No payments can be made by phone – all payments must be made at stations.

Minitel Reservation

(Dial 3615 or 3616 and enter the code SNCF)
For more on Minitel services, *see chapter* **Survival**.

Travelling by Car

French roads are divided into *Autoroutes* (motorways, featuring an 'A' in front of the number), *Routes Nationales* (national roads, with an 'N' in front of the number) *Routes Départementales* (local, roads, with a 'D' in front of the number) and tiny, rural *Routes Communales* (with a 'C'). The *Autoroutes* are toll roads (*péages*), although some sections, including the area immediately around Paris, are free. It may cost several hundred francs

to get to the south of France, but motorways are impeccably well-maintained and have a speed limit of 130kph (80mph). On most *Routes Nationales* the official limit is 90kph (56mph). For information on car hire, *see chapter* **Services**; for more on driving in and around Paris, *see chapter* **Survival**.

Various *portes* (gates) of the Périphérique give access to the main roads out of Paris. To go **south** (Lyon, the Riviera) or **south-west** (Tours, Bordeaux) take the Porte d'Orléans or Porte d'Italie to the A6; to go **west** (Versailles, Normandy), take the Porte de Saint Cloud to the A13 or the N307; to go **east** (Nancy, Strasbourg), follow the Seine east towards the Porte de Bercy for the A4; and to go **north** (Lille, Chantilly), take the Porte de la Chapelle to the A1. All the other *portes* lead to smaller, slower highways.

Travelling by Plane

If you are travelling to anywhere some distance from Paris and are in a hurry, France has a well-developed internal flight network. Prices for internal flights are usually quite high, but recently-introduced competition may mean that prices on major routes, such as Paris-Marseilles or Paris-Toulouse, will come down. As on the trains, flights are divided into Red, White and Blue tariff periods, and there are various youth and student discount schemes.

Air France

119 avenue des Champs-Elysées, 75008 (44.08.24.24).
Métro Charles de Gaulle-Etoile or George V. **Open**
telephone reservations 8am-8pm Mon-Sat; *in person* 9am-6pm Mon-Sat. **Credit** AmEx, DC, EC, MC, V.

Air Inter

119 avenue des Champs-Elysées, 75008 (47.23.59.58).
Métro Charles de Gaulle-Etoile or George V. **Open**
telephone reservations 7am-9pm daily; *in person* 9am-midnight Mon-Sat; noon-midnight Sun. **Credit** AmEx, EC, MC, V.

Day Trips

Within a few miles of Paris you can find magnificent palaces, artists' retreats, and also Mickey Mouse.

Most of France is no more than five hours from Paris by *TGV*, but the places we've chosen can easily be visited in a weekend, or even in an afternoon. Until October 1996, calls outside the Paris area should have the prefix **16**; for more information, *see chapter* **Survival**.

Chartres

Rodin called **Chartres Cathedral** the 'French Acropolis'. Certainly, this twelfth-century Gothic structure, with its exquisitely mismatched towers, is one of the most striking sights in France. Most famous are its breathtaking stained-glass windows, the finest in the world, but the cathedral is so full of remarkable details that a full examination of it amounts to a virtual complete study of medieval culture. It is also a major religious shrine, as it was built to house the *Sacra Camisia* (said to be the garment worn by the Virgin Mary when she gave birth to Jesus) donated to the city in the ninth century by the Carolingian King Charles I, 'the Bald'. This relic is now displayed, only slightly frayed after nearly two millennia, in the Cathedral Treasury.

If you can, drive to Chartres. Even from the motorway the view of the cathedral, unobscured by high-rise blocks and hoardings as it slowly rises over the Beauce plains, is extraordinary. From the train, the first impression of the cathedral silhouette is less dramatic. Or you could walk to Chartres with the troops of student pilgrims who file through the Rambouillet Forest to the city every spring. This medieval rite of atonement was revived by the poet Charles Péguy (1873-1914).

The most famous cathedral tours in town are led in English by the remarkably learned and highly entertaining Malcolm Miller. He specialises in deciphering the medieval picture codes in order to 'read' the messages in the stained-glass windows. Mr Miller's tours are generally at noon and 2.45pm Mon-Sat (30F adults, 20F students). To organise a separate tour at different times, phone 37.28.15.58.

Other sights in Chartres include the Romanesque **Eglise St André** (twelfth century), the **Eglise St Pierre** (thirteenth century) and **St Aignan** (sixteenth century). A well-marked walking tour linking them takes you through medieval streets and river scenes. The Tourist Office has tours on tape of the Old City in different languages, which cost 35F for two (100F deposit on the cassette player).

Indoor sights in Chartres include the **Musée des Beaux-Arts** in the former Bishop's Palace next to the cathedral, and the **Centre International du Vitrail** (stained glass centre – beside the cathedral, closed Tue). The fascinating **Conservatoire de l'Agriculture** covers the evolution of agriculture. If you have a car, ask the tourist office for directions to the **Maison Picassiette** just outside the centre (22 rue de Repos; 37.34.10.78; closed Tue), a colourful naïve mosaic house constructed with bits of broken pottery by a former Chartres civil servant.

Getting There & Information

By car take the A11 direction Le Mans, exit Chartres (88km/55 miles). *By train* hourly from Gare Montparnasse (less than an hour).
Office du Tourisme *place de la Cathédrale, 28005 Chartres (37.21.50.00).* **Open** *Mar-May, Oct* 9.30am-6.30pm Mon-Fri; 10am-6pm Sat; 10.30am-1pm Sun; *June-Sept* 9.30am-6.45pm Mon-Fri; 9.30am-6pm Sat; 10.30am-12.30pm, 2.30-5.30pm, Sun; *Nov-Feb* 9.30am-6pm Mon-Fri; 10am-5pm Sat; 10.30am-1pm Sun.

Conservatoire de l'Agriculture

1 rue de la République, 28300 Chartres (37.36.11.30). **Open** 9am-12.30pm, 1.30-6pm, Tue-Fri; 10am-12.30pm, 1.30-7pm, Sat, Sun. **Admission** 25F adults, 10F children.

Where to eat

Its popularity with tourists means that Chartres is over-endowed with fast-food joints. Otherwise, a good choice for a sit-down dinner is **La Vieille Maison** *5 rue au Lait (37.34.10.67)* or the nearby **Buisson Ardent** *10 rue au Lait (37.34.04.66).* **Café Serpente** *2 Cloître Notre Dame (37.21.68.81)* has cheap meals and is near the cathedral.

Versailles

Versailles was a rural backwater when Louis XIII, attracted by the plentiful game in the neighbouring forests, decided to build a modest château on its swampy land. In 1661, Louis XIV ordered Louis Le Vau to renovate the château and in the following years, the original structure was encased by a grand building in stone. Le Nôtre also began to lay out the gardens, transforming the marshland into terraces, gardens and paths.

It was not, however, until the next decade that the real work on the transformation of Versailles began, after the Sun King decided that the Parisian palaces he already enjoyed were inadequate, and that as the greatest monarch in Europe he needed an altogether grander, and separate, stage all to himself, away from the grimy and sometimes

Versailles *at dusk.*

obstreperous city. His declared intention was to move the entire court to Versailles. In 1678 Jules Hardouin-Mansart took over as principal architect, and dedicated the last 30 years of his life to the construction of the building, enlarging it by five times its original size. The north and south wings were added, as was the Hall of Mirrors, the Wings of Ministers and the stables. Over 22,000 workers laboured for half a century on the project; the palace could house 20,000 people, including all the courtiers and royal ministers, who were reluctantly obliged to move there. Louis himself moved in in May 1682, even though the work was far from complete, and rarely set foot in Paris from then on.

Voltaire described Versailles as 'a masterpiece of bad taste and magnificence'. Like a stretch limo, it impresses more by size and sheer lavishness than anything else. Under the *ancien régime*, 'Versailles' was a tangible symbol of the remoteness of the monarchy from the rest of the country. After the royal family were forcibly removed to Paris in 1789 the palace was largely neglected until 1837, when Louis-Philippe made it a museum.

In the middle of the courtyard in front of the château is a statue of Louis XIV on a horse, erected by Louis-Philippe. To the right is the **Chapelle Royale**, dedicated to Saint Louis, begun by Hardouin-Mansart in 1699 and finished in 1710 after his death by his brother-in-law, Robert de Cotte. In the north and south wings is a **history museum**, with a collection of paintings from the seventeenth and eighteenth centuries.

The first floor of the main body of the château is the most impressive, with the **King's** and **Queen's Grand Apartments**, as well as the famed **Hall of Mirrors**. The painter Lebrun decorated all three, and Louis XIV died in the King's Bedroom in 1715. The **Apollo Salon** was an appropriate throne room for the Sun King, while the **Mercury Salon** was where the corpses of Louis XIV and Louis XV were displayed for eight days before being taken to St-Denis. In the Queen's apartments are the Queen's bedroom, where princes and princesses were born almost in public, before witnesses, and the Queen's antechamber, with one of Versailles' most famous

paintings, *Marie-Antoinette and her Children* by Elizabeth Vigée-Lebrun.

The Hall of Mirrors, the epitome of Louis's concept of grandeur, is 73 metres long, with 17 mirrors echoing the 17 windows looking onto the terrace. The ceiling was painted by Lebrun with scenes from the King's reign. It was here too that Bismarck maliciously decided to proclaim the unification of Germany in 1871, while Paris was under siege, and where the Treaty of Versailles was signed at the end of World War I.

Outside, the park stretches over 815 hectares, and is dominated by its grand perspectives, especially the view down the X-shaped Grand Canal. Magnificent statues are scattered throughout the formal gardens, and there's also a spectacular series of ponds and fountains, served by an ingenious hydraulic system designed by Le Nôtre. Near the château is Hardouin-Mansart's **Orangerie**, whose vaulted gallery could house over 2,000 orange trees; towards the Grand Canal is the picturesque **Colonnade** and **Le Potager du Roi** (the King's Vegetable Garden), currently being restored.

On the north side of the park is the **Trianon**, with its châteaux (the Grand and Petit Trianon) and outbuildings (the **Pavillon Français**, **Belvedère** and **Hameau de la Reine**). The main palace being a little unhomely even for *Le Grand Louis*, in 1687 he had Hardouin-Mansart build the Grand Trianon, a pretty, but still scarcely tiny, palace of stone and pink marble. It was a place of rest and entertainment, where Louis stayed with his last mistress, Madame de Maintenon. Napoleon, who made little use of Versailles, also stayed there a number of times with his second empress, Marie-Louise, and had it redecorated in Empire style. It was extensively restored in the 1960s.

The Petit Trianon is a perfect example of neo-Classicism, and was built for Louis XV's mistress Madame de Pompadour, although she died before its completion. Marie-Antoinette did, however, manage to take advantage of the *Hameau de la Reine* ('Queen's Hamlet'), 12 mock farm buildings are arranged around a lake, where the Queen of France could play at being a lowly milkmaid.

From May to October the great fountains in the gardens are set in motion, to music, each Sunday in the **Grandes Eaux Musicales**, and four times a year the **Grandes Fêtes de Nuit**, a *son-et-lumière* and fireworks display that seeks to capture something of the grandeur of the celebrations of the Sun King, are staged. For details, *see chapter* **Paris by Season**.

Getting there & Information

Versailles is 20km from Paris. *By car* the most scenic route is via the N185 from Porte de Saint Cloud. *By train* RER line C to Versailles-Rive Gauche (**don't** get off at Versailles-Chantiers, which leaves you far from the centre of town), or SNCF from Gare St-Lazare.
Office du Tourisme *7 rue des Réservoirs (39.50.36.22).* **Open** *May-Oct* 9am-7pm daily; *Nov-April*

A u b e r g e
DU CHEVAL
BLANC

☆ ☆ ☆

Situated in the heart of a village in the Ile-de-France, the Auberge du Cheval Blanc allows you to relive the good old days. In this former post house you will live under the magic spell of the finest French traditions.

22 elegant rooms, ornamental gardens, a shaded terrace. Gastronomic restaurant (seasonal and local specialities of the Brie region). Rooms and lounges for functions, business lunches and meetings.

Just 30 min. from Paris, 50 min. from Roissy-Charles de Gaulle, 40 min. from Orly and a mere 2km from the Disneyland Paris® theme park.

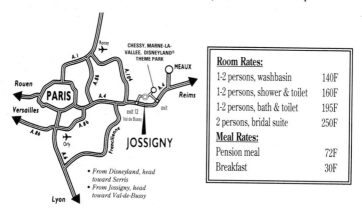

Room Rates:

1-2 persons, washbasin	140F
1-2 persons, shower & toilet	160F
1-2 persons, bath & toilet	195F
2 persons, bridal suite	250F

Meal Rates:

Pension meal	72F
Breakfast	30F

- *From Disneyland, head toward Serris*
- *From Jossigny, head toward Val-de-Bussy*

2, RUE DE LAGNY - 77600 JOSSIGNY
TEL: (1) 64.02.24.27 FAX: (1) 64.02.41.61

9am-12.30pm, 2-6.15pm, daily. Staff will also be able to supply details of the Grandes Fêtes.

Château de Versailles

(30.84.74.00). **Open** *Château* (May-Sept) 9am-6pm, (Oct-Apr) 9am-5pm, Tue-Sun. **Closed Mon** & holidays. *Grand Trianon* (May-Sept) 10am-6pm, (Oct-Apr) 10am-12.30pm, 2-5.30pm, Tue-Sun. **Closed Mon** & holidays. *Petit Trianon* (guided tours only) 9am-6pm Tue-Sun. **Closed Mon** & holidays. Gardens times vary, usually dawn-dusk Tue-Sun.

Admission *Château* 42F adults; 28F 18-25s, over-60s; free under-18s; *Grand Trianon* 23F adults; 15F 18-25, over-60s; *Petit Trianon* 13F adults; 9F 18-25s; *gardens* free (except on Sun for **Grandes Eaux**).

Centre de Musique Baroque

16 rue Ste Victoire, 78000 Versailles (39.02.30.00). **Tickets** 60F-300F.
The centre organises concerts of baroque music at Versailles from January to June.

Where to eat

The elegant **Trianon Palace** *1 boulevard Reine (39.50.34.12)* has a luxury restaurant (average 650F), a hotel and health club. Less extravagant but also recommended are the **Rôtisserie Ballester** *30 bis rue des Réservoirs (39.50.70.02)* and **Le Pot au Feu** *22 rue de Satory (39.50.57.43).*

Other Châteaux Near Paris

Chantilly

In the middle of a lake, cream-coloured Chantilly looks like the archetypal French Renaissance château, with its domes and turrets. In fact the over-the-top main wing is a largely nineteenth-century reconstruction, as much of the original was destroyed during the Revolution. Beside it the **Petit Château** – what remains of the original château built in the sixteenth century for Anne de Montmorency – seems much humbler. But Chantilly is notable for its artistic treasures – three paintings by Raphael, the tiny *Three Graces*, the *Virgin of the House of Orléans* and the *Virgin of Lorretto*; Filippino Lippi's *Esther and Assuarus*; several mythological scenes by Poussin; and the medieval miniatures from the *Très Riches Heures du Duc de Berry* (facsimiles only are usually on show), plus another fine Book of Hours, the *Heures d'Etienne Chevalier.*

In the eighteenth century the gardens, laid out by Le Nôtre, were famed for the extravagant banquets held there by Louis-Henri de Bourbon, Prince de Condé. Today, the park is rather dilapidated, but still contains an extensive canal system and an artificial 'hamlet' pre-dating that of Versailles. To one side is an 'English Garden' laid out in the nineteenth century in a supposedly English style.

To the south of the château is the extensive **Forêt de Chantilly**, which has numerous footpaths and is popular with picknickers in summer, especially around the Etangs de Commelles.

Chantilly's other claim to fame is as the home of French racing, for this is where the most impor-

tant French racing trainers have their stables, and the town has a major **racetrack** (*see chapter* **Sport & Fitness**). The eighteenth-century Great Stables once housed 240 horses, 500 dogs and almost 100 palfreys and hunting birds. Today they are open as a living museum of the horse and pony.

Senlis, 9km (5 miles) east of Chantilly, has been bypassed since its glory days as the royal town where Hugh Capet was elected king in 987. Its historical centre contains several old streets, a fine, predominantly Gothic cathedral, some chunks of old city wall and the remains of a Roman amphitheatre.

Getting There

Chantilly is 41km (25 miles) from Paris. *By car* take the A1, exit Chantilly and then the D924, or the N16 directly from Paris. *By train* frequent trains from Gare du Nord, then 30 minute walk or short taxi-ride to the château.

Château de Chantilly

(44.57.03.62/44.57.08.00). **Open** *Musée Condé* (1 Mar-31 Oct) 10am-6pm Mon, Wed-Sun; (1 Nov-28 Feb) 10.30am-12.45pm, 2-5pm, Mon, Wed-Sun. Closed **Tue**. **Admission** 37F adult, 32F under-18s; 10F aged 3-11; *park only* 17F adult, 10F under-18s.

Musée Vivant du Cheval et du Poney

Grandes Ecuries (44.57.13.13/44.57.40.40). **Open** *Apr-Oct* 10.30am-6.30pm daily (closed Tue in April and Sept); *Nov-Mar* 2-5.30pm Mon, Wed-Sat; 10.30am-6.30pm Sun. **Admission** 45F adult, 35F under-18s (50F/40F Sat, Sun). Dressage demonstrations at 11.30am, 3.30pm, 5.15pm, daily.

Abbaye de Royaumont

95270 Asnières-sur-Oise (30.35.88.90). **Open** *Mar-Oct* 10am-12.30pm, 2-6pm, daily; *Nov-Feb* 10am-12.45pm, 2-5.30pm, daily. **Admission** 20F adult; 14F 7-16 years, under-26s, over-60s; free under-7s.
About 5km (3 miles) south-west of Chantilly are the remains of a Cistercian monastery founded in 1228 by Saint Louis, King Louis IX. Only ruins of the early Gothic church remain, but the monastic buildings give some idea of its former wealth. It's a very pretty site, and is now used as a cultural centre hosting courses and concerts.

Fontainebleau

Fontainebleau seems a quiet town by the Seine, fairly typical of the environs of Paris. That is, until you see the sumptuous palace which dominates the town. In 1528, Francis I brought in Italian artists and craftsmen – including Primaticcio – to aid his architect Gilles le Breton in transforming it from a neglected royal mansion into the finest Italian Mannerist palace in France. This style, between the Renaissance and the Baroque, is noted for its extreme, often bizarre, details such as grotesque masks, contorted figures and crazy fireplaces, all of which gave sculptors an ideal chance to show off their virtuosity.

Unlike Versailles, however, Fontainebleau has a charm that comes from its very disunity of design. Successive monarchs felt so at home here that they added bits of their own. Henry IV added two courtyards and a tennis court, Louis's XIV and XV added further classical trimmings, and Louis XIII added the celebrated double-horseshoe staircase that dominates the principal courtyard. Napoleon, who loved the place, added several ornate rooms as well.

The gardens still have the weird grotto built for Francis I, and Le Nôtre inevitably got his hand in somewhere. However, they were largely relaid at the beginning of the nineteenth century in the less formal *style anglaise*, oddly enough for Napoleon.

The **Fontainebleau Forest** where Francis I liked to hunt is now used by Parisian weekenders for walking, cycling, riding and rock climbing. It covers 25,000 hectares (61,750 acres) and is a ten-minute stroll from town. A free map, available from the tourist office, marks all the paths. It's worth driving, or cycling, down the road from **Barbizon** (*see below* **Artists' Corners**) to the Gorges d'Apremont, the Gorge de Fronchard and the Seine valley.

Getting There
Fontainebleau is 65km (40 miles) from Paris. *By car* A6 to Fontainebleau exit, then N7. *By train* from Gare de Lyon to Fontainebleau-Avon (50 minutes), then bus marked Château.

Information, Cycling & Riding
Office du Tourisme *31 place Napoléon Bonaparte, 77302 Fontainebleau (64.22.25.68).* **Open** *June-Sept* 9.30am-6.30pm Mon-Sat; 10am-12.30pm Sun; *Oct-May* 9.30am-12.30pm, 1.45-6pm, Mon-Sat.
Cycle Hire: Georges Mullot *Gare de Fontainebleau (64.22.36.14).* **Open** 9am-7pm daily. **Rates** *mountain bike* 120F per day, 80F half-day; *touring bike* 100F per day, 60F half-day; *mini-bikes* 60F per day, 40 half-day. ID needed. **Credit** V.
Horse-riding: Société Hippique Nationale *avenue de Maintenon, 77302 Fontainebleau (60.72.22.40).* **Open** 7.30am-11.30am, 2-8pm, Mon-Sat.

Château de Fontainebleau
(60.71.50.70). **Open** 9.30am-5pm Mon, Wed-Sun. Closed Tue. **Admission** 31F adults; 20F 18-25s, OAPs; free under-18s; Sun 20F for all.

Where to eat
A prosperous commuter town, Fontainebleau has a great variety of reasonable restaurants. Alsatian dishes are the fare at **La Petite Alsace** *26 rue de Ferrare (64.23.45.45)* and imaginative French cooking at **Croquembouche** *43 rue de France (64.22.01.57).*

Rambouillet

Although not the most beautiful château in the Ile-de-France, Rambouillet is redeemed by its surrounding 20,000 hectare forest. There has been a château on the site since 1368, but all that remains of the original edifice is the tower, and much of the present structure dates from the eighteenth and nineteenth centuries. In 1699, it was bought by the financier Fleuriau d'Armenonville, who commissioned Le Nôtre to design the park and canals. Unfortunately for the banker, Louis XIV later ordered that the property be sold to him for one of his sons, the Count of Toulouse. This count's heir, the Duc de Penthièvre, had the English garden laid and created the **Chaumière aux Coquillages** for his daughter, the Princesse de Lamballe. In 1783, Rambouillet was

bought again, by Louis XVI, and the **Laiterie** (dairy) built for that incorrigible amateur milkmaid Marie-Antoinette. Most recently, it was from Rambouillet that de Gaulle ordered his troops to advance on Paris for the liberation in World War II.

You can only visit the interior of the château with one of the official guides. It's best known for its exquisite oak panelling, but you can also gawp at Marie-Antoinette's boudoir, Napoleon's decorative bathroom, and the **Salle de Marbre** with its grey and pink marble dating from 1556. Make sure to visit the splendid Chaumière aux Coquillages, a kind of summer house the inside walls of which are entirely covered with shells, including oyster shells carved in the shape of leaves. It took seven years to decorate, and also includes a hidden room, adorned in the style of Pompeii.

Château de Rambouillet
Rambouillet, 78120 (34.83.00.25). By car take the A13 west, then A12 south and N10. *By train* from Gare Montparnasse to Rambouillet, then one km walk or bus to château. **Open** *Apr-Sept* 10am-11.30am, 2-5.30pm, *Oct-Mar* 10am-11.30am, 2-4.30pm, Mon, Wed-Sun. Closed **Tue**; *laiterie and chaumière* closed **Mon, Tue**.
Admission 27F adults; 18F students under 26; 10F 12-17s; free under-12s. *For château, laiterie and chaumière aux coquillages* 30F.

Vaux-Le-Vicomte

Less well-known than Versailles or Fontainebleau, and certainly less crowded, this château has a story almost as interesting as the building itself.

Nicholas Fouquet (1615-1680), one of the wealthiest men in France, bought the site in 1641. He was the protégé of the ultra-powerful Cardinal Mazarin, who governed France until Louis XIV came of age. In 1653 Fouquet was named *Surintendant des Finances* (equivalent to finance minister), a position that brought him yet more wealth, and brought the nation closer to bankruptcy. Fouquet then set about building himself a humble abode, and assembled three of France's most talented men for the job: painter Charles Lebrun, architect Louis Le Vau and landscape gardener André Le Nôtre, all of whom later worked at Versailles.

In 1661, Fouquet held a huge soirée for the inauguration of his château and invited the King. They were entertained by jewel-encrusted elephants and spectacular imported Chinese fireworks. Lully wrote music for the occasion, and Molière a comedy. The King, who was 23 and ruling *de facto* for the first time, was outraged by this ostentatious show of wealth – above all by the way in which Fouquet's grandeur seemed to overshadow his own. Shortly afterwards Fouquet was arrested, and his embezzlement of state funds exposed in a show trial. His personal effects were taken by the crown and the court sentenced him to exile; Louis XIV promptly changed the sentence to solitary confinement.

Fouquet's wife sold Vaux-Le-Vicomte before it was even finished. The most telling symbol of the fallen magnate is the unfinished, domed ceiling in the vast, elliptical Grand Salon, where Lebrun only had time to paint the cloudy sky and one solitary eagle holding the chandelier in its beak. Fouquet's *grand projet* did live on in one way, however, for it is clear that Louis XIV was so impressed by the château that it inspired him to build Versailles, to the extent that he took away Fouquet's architect and workmen to do it.

When entering the grounds via the outbuildings, bypass the **Carriage Museum** unless you've time to spare. As you round the moat, the square, sober frontage doesn't prepare you for the Baroque rear aspect. Watch out for the fountains, which spout from 3pm to 6pm on the second and last Saturday of every month. The biggest draw however are the candlelit evenings, which transform the château into a palatial jack-o-lantern with hundreds of flickering candles illuminating both house and gardens.

Getting There
Vaux-Le-Vicomte is 60km (37 miles) from Paris. *By car* take the A6 to Fontainebleau exit; follow signs to Melun, then N36 and D215. *By train* from Gare de Lyon to Melun, (40 minutes) and then by taxi (80F-100F, there are no buses). Remember to arrange for a taxi to come back for you afterwards. *By tour coach* **Paris-Vision** run half-day and day trips from central Paris (*see chapter* **Sightseeing**).

Château Vaux-Le-Vicomte
77950 Maincy (64.14.41.90). **Open** Château and gardens *Apr-mid Oct* 11am-5pm daily. **Admission** 56F adults; 46F under-16s. *Candlelit visits to the château and gardens* 8.30-11pm Sat. **Price** 75F adults; 65F children. **Restaurant** 11am-6pm Mon-Fri, Sat; 7.30-11pm Sun.

Artists' Corners

Many artists have, at different times, sought rural peace away from Paris in the countryside of the Ile-de-France. They and the places where they stayed have become inseparable, and these villages offer great insights into the artists' work.

Van Gogh at Auvers-sur-Oise

Auvers-sur-Oise, 30 kilometres north of Paris, has become synonymous with the name of Van Gogh, even though the Dutch painter only spent 70 days in what was then a small agricultural village. However, during his time there, he executed over 60 paintings, drawings and sketches, including many since-famous works. He arrived on 20 May 1890, and rented a room at the Auberge Ravoux. On 27 July, he fired a bullet into his chest, and died two days later. His grave is in the cemetery, alongside that of his beloved brother, Theo.

Despite being so near to Paris and industrial Pontoise Auvers still retains a surprising degree of rustic charm. The cornfields, where Van Gogh painted his famous crow painting, the town hall, across the square from the inn, which he painted

on Bastille day, and the church, have barely changed. Van Gogh was not the only painter to set up his easel in the town. Cézanne stayed for 18 months between 1872 and 1874, not far from the house of Doctor Gachet, who was the subject of portraits by both him and Van Gogh; and the landscape painter Daubigny built his studio in the town in 1861. As well as visiting the various artistic sites, be sure to stroll through the charming stone-walled lanes near the tourist office.

Getting There & Information
Auvers-sur-Oise is 35km (22 miles) north of Paris. *By car* A15 and then at exit 7 take the N184 towards Chantilly, exit Méry-sur-Oise for Auvers. *By train* from Gare du Nord or Gare St-Lazare direction Pontoise, change at Persan-Beaumont or Creil for Auvers-sur-Oise, *or* RER line A to Cergy-Préfecture, then bus for Butry, stopping at Auvers-sur-Oise.
Office de Tourisme *Manoir des Colombières, rue de la Sansonne, 95430 Auvers-sur-Oise (30.36.10.06).* **Open** 9.30am-12.15pm, 1.30-5.45pm, daily.

L'Atelier de Daubigny
61 rue Daubigny, 95430 Auvers-sur-Oise (34.48.03.03). **Open** *Easter-31 Oct* 2-6.30pm Tue-Sun, bank holidays. **Admission** 20F adults, free under-14s.
Built in 1861, Daubigny's house is surrounded by a beautiful garden, and decorated with murals painted by himself, his son and daughter. There are landscapes as well as flower motifs, and tableaux from fairy tales. Most of the paintings are from 1864-1874. Fellow artists Corot and Daumier helped him in his work on the large view of Lake Como that stands in his lofty studio.

Château d'Auvers
rue de Léry, 95430 Auvers-sur-Oise (34.48.48.50). **Open** *May-Oct* 10am-6.30pm, *Nov-Apr* 10am-5pm, Tue-Sun. **Admission** 50F adults; 40F over-60s; 35F 6-25 years; free under-6s.
In 1994 the seventeenth-century Château de Léry opened up as an entirely new-model museum devoted to the Impressionists. This is not just a case of pictures on the wall; it's more like the 'Impressionist Experience'. There's a fabulous, 1½-hour headphone tour, which vividly describes the scorn poured on them by the artistic authorities, and the exhibits include a reconstruction of a *guinguette*, a beach, a café in which paintings of café life are projected, a waiting room, and a train, this time with projections of Impressionist landscapes. The tour also includes contemporary caricatures mocking the Impressionists' style, and even an animated version of Degas' *Women Ironing* (*Les Repasseuses*).

Musée de l'Absinthe
44 rue Callé, 95430 Auvers-sur-Oise (30.36.83.26). **Open** *June-Sept* 11am-6pm Wed-Sun; *Oct-May* 11am-6pm Sat, Sun. **Admission** 25F adults; 20F students, over-60s, 14-18s; free under-14s; *twin ticket for château & Musée* 65F.
Oscar Wilde claimed that there was nothing in the world more poetic than a glass of absinthe. Numerous painters, including Van Gogh, Picasso and Monet, depicted it in their works and this museum (opened in 1994), is dedicated to the drink. The collection includes posters and memorabilia.

Musée Daubigny
Manoir des Colombières, Rue de la Sansonne, 95430 Auvers-sur-Oise (30.36.80.20). **Open** *May-Oct* 2.30-6.30pm, *Nov-Apr* 2.30-6pm, Wed-Sun. **Admission** 20F.
A collection of paintings, drawings and engravings from the 19th and 20th centuries.

La Maison de Van Gogh

Auberge Ravoux, place de la Mairie, 95430 Auvers-sur-Oise (34.48.05.47). **Open** 10am-6pm (last tickets at 5.30pm) Tue-Sat. **Admission** 25F adults; free under-12s; 50F family ticket (2 adults, 2 children).

Not, in fact, Van Gogh's house, but the inn where he rented a room during his time in Auvers, for 3.50F a day. The tour of the house concentrates more on atmosphere than on great numbers of Van Gogh's paintings or possessions. After climbing some stairs, you reach his tiny room, the cheapest in the *Auberge*, which is completely bare except for a wicker chair. Next to it is the room of another artist, set out as it would have been at that time: a spring bed, a chair and a washstand with a basin and a jug. You then climb up to the attic there is a projection room with a video on Van Gogh's time in the village.

Monet at Giverny

In 1883, Claude Monet moved his large personal entourage (one mistress, eight children) to Giverny, a rural retreat 80km (50 miles) northwest of Paris. He died in 1926, having immortalised his flower garden, and the water-lilies beneath his Japanese bridge. In 1966, Michel Monet donated his father's property to the Académie des Beaux-Arts, who transformed the modest estate into the major tourist site it is today. Don't be put off by the tour buses in the car park or by the outrageously enormous gift shop – the natural charm of the pink-brick house, with its cornflower-blue and yellow kitchen, and the rare glory of the gardens survives intact. A little tunnel leads (under the road) between the flower-filled Clos Normand garden in front of the house to the second, Japanese, water garden with its pool, canals, little green bridges, willows and water lilies.

This is such an easy day trip that it can be concluded in Paris with a visit to the quiet **Musée Marmottan** (*see chapter* **Museums**), also a must for Monet enthusiasts. However, if you want to spend the night, **La Musardière** (32.21.03.18) is a moderately-priced little inn (with a crêperie) at the entrance to the **Musée Claude Monet**.

Getting There

By car take the A13 from Porte d'Auteuil to Bonnières, where you cross the Seine and follow D201 to Giverny. *By train* trains from Gare St-Lazare to nearby Vernon take 45 minutes; then a 5km (3 mile) taxi or bus ride (buses to Giverny stop in front of the station). You can rent bicycles by the day or half-day from Vernon station, or cross the river and go along the D5 to Giverny on foot.

Musée Claude Monet

Giverny, 27620 Giverny (32.51.28.21). **Open** *Apr-Oct* 10am-6pm Tue-Sun. **Admission** 35F adults; 25F students; 20F 7-12s; free under-7s.

Musée Américain Giverny

99 rue Claude Monet, 27620 Giverny (32.51.94.65). **Open** *Apr-Oct* 10am-6pm Tue-Sun. **Admission** 35F adults; 20F students; 15F 7-12s; free under-7s.
Just up the road from the Monet Museum, this museum opened in 1992 and is devoted to American artists who came to France, inspired by the Impressionists. Most of the works on show are pretty chocolate-boxy.

Monet's garden at **Giverny**.

Rousseau & Millet at Barbizon

A rural hamlet straggling along a single country lane into the forest of **Fontainebleau** (*see above*), Barbizon was an ideal sanctuary for pioneers Corot, Théodore Rousseau, Daubigny (*see above* **Auvers-sur-Oise**) and Millet. From the 1830s onwards, these artists, the Barbizon school, demonstrated a new concern in painting life and landscape as they really were, and paved the way for the Impressionists.

Hordes of other artists soon followed them to Barbizon. Many stayed at the **Auberge du Père Ganne** inn, painting on the walls and furniture of the long-suffering (or perhaps far-sighted) Ganne, in lieu of rent. The three main sights at Barbizon are all on this single road, and although it's enormously touristy, some of the atmosphere remains. Commemmorative plaques point out who lived where. Millet and Rousseau are both buried in the churchyard at nearby Chailly.

Not far from Barbizon, on the other side of Fontainebleau, the painter of horses Rosa Bonheur lived at **Thomery** on the banks of the Seine. From about 1865, another group of painters, among them Bazille, Monet, Sisley and Renoir, also began frequenting the area. Sisley settled in the historic town of **Moret-sur-Loing**. His house and atelier are not open to the public, but, as another part of the Impressionist Experience, the tourist board (60.70.41.66) now organises *Déjeuner sur l'Herbe* picnics in period dress on the banks of the Loing and boat trips during the summer.

Getting There & Information

By car A6 to Fontainebleau, then N7 and D64 to Barbizon. *By train* from Gare de Lyon to Melun, then taxi. **Office du Tourisme** *55 rue Grande, 77630 Barbizon (60.66.41.87).* **Open** 10am-12.30pm, 2-6pm Mon, Wed-Fri; 10am-6pm Sat, Sun.
The office is in the former home of artist Théodore Rousseau.

Atelier Rosa Bonheur

12 rue Rosa Bonheur, 77810 Thomery (60.70.06.19).
Open 2-5pm Wed, Sat. **Admission** 15F.
The well-known horse-painter's studio has been left in much
the state it was at her death: easels, paintings, clothes (including
a Sioux outfit given by her friend Buffalo Bill) and the
strange artefacts she accumulated.

Maison et Atelier Jean-François Millet

27 rue Grande, 77630 Barbizon (60.66.21.55).
Open 9.30am-12.30pm, 2-5.30pm, Mon, Wed-Sun.
Admission free.
The most influential of the Barbizon painters, Millet was
especially interested in depicting the realities of peasant life,
to which he ascribed an almost saintly value. Many of his
greatest works are in the **Musée D'Orsay** (*see chapter*
Museums). He moved here in 1849 to escape cholera in
Paris, and remained, living very simply, for the rest of his
life, painting the local people and their work in the fields.
The house has been rather altered, but contains memorabilia
of the artist, some of his prints, and drawings and paintings
by his followers.

Musée de l'Auberge du Père Ganne

92 rue Grande, 77630 Barbizon (60.66.22.27). **Open**
Apr-Oct 10am-12.30pm, 2-6pm, Mon, Wed-Sun; *Nov-Mar*
10am-12.30pm, 2-5pm, Wed-Sun. **Admission** 25F, free
under 12s.
Just reopened, but this artists' inn was already on the tourist
trail in the 1850s. Some rooms have now been reconstructed
as they were in the last century, including a near-legendary
sideboard painted by some of the artistic habituees. The inn
now contains the municipal collection of paintings, prints
and documents on the Barbizon school.

Disneyland Paris

Out to the east of Paris, near the new town of
Marne-la-Vallée, Mickey and pals continue their
struggle to win over the hearts and pockets of
the European public. And, despite continuing
financial problems, the restructuring of the parent group and a change of name (nobody's supposed to mention 'Eurodisney'), they appear to
be slowly succeeding. Some 8.8 million visitors
crossed the portals into Mickey's magic kingdom
in 1994, 3.5 million of them French and over a
million from the UK. You'll find yourself a long
way from French culture here, in a world of
transposed Americana where the staff (all bilingual) largely manage to keep up have-a-nice-day
grins all day long. But, it's undeniable – a trip
out here can be a great, fun day off from the city,
with the promise of total exhaustion at the end.

Visiting the Park

The theme park is divided into five parts, all
grouped around **Main Street USA**, with its cod
Victorian shops and vintage cars, but it's small
enough to skip from one part to another as you
wish rather than follow any set route.
Fantasyland is the part most suitable for young
children, with gentle rides and Alice's Curious
Labyrinth, an Alice in Wonderland maze up to the
top of Sleeping Beauty's castle. Beyond here,
Mickey characters take second place to film-set

adventure in tropical **Adventureland**, Wild West
Frontierland and futuristic **Discoveryland**.

Don't attempt to get round all the attractions in
one day. Aim instead to do as many as possible of
the spectacular big-thrill rides: **Big Thunder
Mountain** rollercoaster; the dank and dripping
Pirates of the Caribbean; Star Tours, a
bumpy intergalactic rocket ride with tongue-in-
cheek commentary by a rookie robot pilot; and
Indiana Jones et le Temple du Péril, a scary
loop-the-loop tour in a rickety ore truck. Note that
some rides can be scary for young children, and
some have minimum age and height requirements.
All rides can have queues often of around 40 minutes, but as the number of rides gradually increas-
es, the pressure should get less.

In its latest attractions, Disneyland Paris has
been attempting to prove its Gallic credentials by
paying tribute to Jules Verne. **Les Mystères de
Nautilus**, which opened in 1994, takes you into
Captain Nemo's submarine (all red velvet and
brass fittings), complete with attack by giant
squid. The big event of 1995 was the opening of
Discovery Mountain, the twenty-first century
big brother of the original Space Mountain at
Disneyland in California. It's inspired by Verne's
Voyage to the Moon, and intrepid voyagers will be
shot up a 20-metre long cannon into outer space.

Souvenir shops are everywhere, so even if all
the rides (except the shooting gallery) are free, be
prepared for your children to extract some
Mickey Mouse ears and a whole pile of junk out
of you. There are plenty of places at which to get
all-American burgers and barbeques, but if you
want to try the Disney take on French cuisine,
head for l'Auberge de Cendrillon in Fantasyland.

Festival Disney

Five minutes' walk from the gates and next to the RER station, the Festival Disney complex has bars and restaurants
decorated with American memorabilia, more souvenir
shops, a post office and (sharp intake of breath) a
tobacconist. There's country music at Billy Bob's Country
& Western Saloon, but don't bother with the pricey Wild
West show.

Hotels

Should you feel the urge to sleep-over with Mickey, there
are six hotels at the Disneyland complex providing over
5,000 rooms (*central booking number 60.30.60.30*). Prices
are based on bedrooms for four persons and vary according to season. Top of the range is the sugar-pink
Disneyland Hotel (1650F-1990F), but a 15-minute shuttle ride from the park is the **Davy Crockett Ranch**,
which has log cabins to rent (630F-770F) and some tent
and caravan pitches.

Essential Information

Marne-la-Vallée (64.74.30.00; from UK 0733-33-5567).
Open *Oct-23 June* 10am-6pm Mon-Fri, Sun; 10am-8pm
Sat; *24 June-Sept* 9am-11pm daily.
Admission *Apr-Sept* 195F adults; 150F 3-11s; prices
rising in Oct '95, but not confirmed at time of writing.
Credit AmEx, DC, EC, MC, V.
Getting there: *By car* (32km) A4 to exit 14, and follow
signs. *By train* RER line A to Marne-la-Valley-Chessy.

Further Afield

Leave the Parisian sprawl behind and head for the beaches and Champagne houses of the French hinterland.

If you have a little more time in Paris, and are able to explore a little further, then the French regions close to the city make ideal places to explore over a weekend stopover, or perhaps longer. The three below offer beaches, architectural glories, and the pleasures of the grape.

Until October 1996, all calls outside the Paris area should have the prefix **16**; for more information, *see chapter* **Survival**.

The Châteaux of the Loire

Seat of power of the Valois kings, the Loire valley became the wellspring of the French Renaissance. Francis I was the main instigator, bringing architects, artists and craftsmen from Italy to build his palaces, and musicians and poets to keep him amused. Royal courtiers followed suit with their own elaborate residences. The valley is now an easy weekend trip from Paris: we've concentrated on the area between Chambord in the east, and Azay-le-Rideau in the west.

The vast **Château de Chambord** (54.50.40.00) is Francis I's masterpiece, and was probably designed in part by Leonardo da Vinci. It's a magnificent, but also rather playful place, from the ingenious double staircase in the centre – it was possible to go up or down without crossing someone coming the other way, although you could glimpse them through the open fretwork – to the wealth of decoration and the 400 draughty rooms. Built in the local white stone, with decorative diamonds and other shapes applied in black slate, its extraordinary forest of turrets, domes and crazy chimneys are brilliantly seen from close up as you walk around the parapet.

In total contrast of scale is the charming **Château de Beauregard** (54.70.40.05) nearby at Cellettes. Its main feature is the unusual panelled portrait gallery, depicting in naive style 327 famous men and women. The precious character of the room is accentuated by its fragile, blue and white Dutch Delft tiled floor. The château also boasts the tiny panelled *Cabinet des Grelots* (bells).

From here the road to Amboise follows one of the most attractive parts of the Loire valley, under the looming towers of the **Château de Chaumont** (54.20.98.03) and past numerous roadside wine cellars dug into the tufa cliffs (with equally numerous opportunities to indulge).

The lively town of Amboise, not far from Tours, grew up at a strategic crossing point on the Loire. The **Château Royal d'Amboise** (47.57.00.98) was built within the walls of a medieval stronghold, although today only a (still considerable) fraction of Louis XI's and Charles VIII's complex remains. This is the château where Francis I grew up, but its interiors span several styles from vaulted Gothic hall to nineteenth-century Empire style. Across the gardens from the main remaining wing, the exquisite Gothic chapel has a richly carved portal, fine vaulted interior and, supposedly, the tomb of Leonardo da Vinci.

From the château, it's a short walk up the hill past several cave dwellings to the **Clos Luce** (47.57.62.88), the Renaissance manor house where Leonardo da Vinci lived at the invitation of François I for the three years before his death in 1519. There's an enduring myth of a – so far undiscovered – tunnel linking the two. The museum concentrates on Leonardo as Renaissance Man: artist, engineer and inventor. It's part furnished as a manor house of the period, part filled with large models derived from Leonardo's drawings of inventions, from a helicopter to a hydraulic drilling machine.

An oddity just outside the town is the pagoda of **Chanteloup**, an eccentric eighteenth-century pagoda built when chinoiserie was the rage, in the grounds of a now-demolished château. There's a panoramic view from the top.

South of Amboise, the sixteenth-century **Château of Chenonceau** (47.23.90.07) occupies a unique site on a bridge spanning the river Cher. Henry II gave the château to his beautiful mistress Diane de Poitiers, until she was forced to give it up to a jealous Catherine de Médici, who commissioned Philibert Delorme to add the two-storey long gallery that extends across the river. Chenonceau is packed with tourists in summer, but its watery charm, fine tapestries and paintings (including a portrait of Diane de Poitiers) are well worth seeing. Visits are fortunately unguided.

Seeming to rise directly out of the water, **Azay-le-Rideau** (47.45.42.04), built on an island in the river Indre west of Tours, must be everyone's idea

*The **Château de Chambord**, the greatest construction of Francis I.*

The amply-stocked cellars of **Champagne Taittinger***. See page 312.*

of a fairytale castle. Built between 1518 and 1527 by Gilles Berthelot, the king's treasurer, it combines the turrets of a medieval fortress with the new style of the Italian Renaissance.

At **Villandry** (47.50.02.09), it's not the château but the Renaissance gardens that are of interest. One part is a typical formal garden of geometrical shapes made with neatly cut hedges and flowers; much more unusual is the *jardin potager*, where the neat patterns are done not with flowers but with artichokes, cabbages and other vegetables in what has to be the ultimate kitchen garden.

Getting There

By car. The best way to get around the region. Take the A10 direct to Blois (182km), or leave at Mer for Chambord. An attractive route follows the banks of the Loire from Blois to Amboise and Tours, along the D761. *By train* A much less-desirable option: TGV from Gare Montparnasse to Blois or Tours, from where it's possible to visit some châteaux by coach. *By tour coach* several tour companies in Paris run trips to the Loire (for addresses, *see chapter* **Sightseeing**)

Where to Stay & Eat

The small town of Amboise is a pleasant, centrally placed stopping-off point with several hotels. Within the town, try the small, family-run **Hôtel Le Français** *1 place Chaptal (47.57.11.38). Double room 190F,* or the **Lion d'Or** *17 quai Charles-Guinot (47.57.00.23). Double 292F-312F.* For something a little grander, try the **Château de Pray** at Chargé, 3km outside the town *(47.57.23.67. Double 550F-720F).* It has gardens overlooking the Loire. Other possibilities and a greater choice of restaurants are to be found at Tours.

Normandy

In English the phrase 'Normandy beaches' may be inseparable from 1944, but for Parisians the area has long meant the seaside, and has been a favoured place for weekenders for over a century.

Rouen

The capital of Normandy is a cathedral town of contrasts. The centre retains lots of drunken half-timbered buildings and narrow streets, while the port areas by the Seine were almost totally destroyed by bombing during the war. Begun at the start of the thirteenth century, **Cathédrale Notre-Dame** spans the Gothic periods. Of the two towers, the north tower, Tour St Romain, dates from the early period while the more *Flamboyant* Tour de Beurre is from the late fifteenth century. Among the tombs inside is that of Richard the Lionheart. Nearby is the famous Gros-Horloge gateway, with its ornamental clock over the busy medieval rue du Gros Horloge.

The **Musée des Beaux Arts** (26 bis rue Thiers/35.71.28.40) has just been renovated. It contains one of France's best regional art collections, including works by Velázquez, Perugino and Caravaggio, some wonderful oil studies by Géricault (a native of Rouen) and a few Impressionist works by Monet and Sisley.

Getting There & Information

Rouen is 137km (85 miles) from Paris. *By car* A13 direct from Porte d'Auteuil. *By train* from Gare St-Lazare.
Office du Tourisme *25 place de la Cathédrale, 76000 Rouen (32.08.32.40).* **Open** *May-Sept* 9am-7pm Mon-Sat; 9.30am-12.30pm, 2.30-6pm, Sun; *Oct-Apr* 9am-12.30pm, 2-6.30pm, Mon-Sat; 10am-1pm Sun.

Dieppe & the Alabaster Coast

An important port since the Middle Ages, Dieppe is also the nearest seaside town to Paris. The area around the harbour along quai Henri IV is charming, packed full of little fish restaurants, and there's an interesting maze of old streets between here and the newer quarters fronting the promenade. Since July 1994, Ferries from Britain go to a new port, while the old port has become the Dieppe marina. The beach, mainly shingle, is overlooked by the gloomy Château de Dieppe. Leave town by the coast road for a twisting scenic drive along the cliff top. Just along the coast to the west is the celebrated churchyard of **Varengeville-sur-Mer**, where Cubist painter George Braque is buried, and further on towards Le Havre is the little seaside town of **Etretat**, famous for its cliffs, which are eroded into arches jutting out into the sea.

Getting There & Information

Dieppe is 171km (106 miles) from Paris. *By car* take the A13 to Rouen and then the N27. *By train* frequent trains from Gare St-Lazare (2-2½ hours).
Office du Tourisme de Dieppe *Pont Jehan Ango, 76200 Dieppe (35.84.11.77).* **Open** *May-Sept* 9am-1pm, 2-6pm, Mon-Sat; 10am-1pm, 3-6pm, Sun; *Oct-April* 9am-noon, 2-6pm, Mon-Sat.

Deauville & the Côte Fleurie

Deauville and its sister town **Trouville** were the height of fashion at the turn of the century when depicted by painters such as Matisse and Raoul Dufy, and they still retain a flashy seaside charm. Deauville, the smarter and more sophisticated of the two, likes to call itself the 21st *arrondissement* of Paris. It's full of bizarre half-timbered seaside villas, and has two great luxury hotels, the Hôtel Normandy, standing behind a ridiculous array of beams and turrets, and the Hôtel Royal. There's also a faded Casino, a large marina, fish restaurants and a wood-boarded prom along the long sandy beach. It's a good place for a touch of French-family seaside life, complete with sand surfing, trotting horses and cockle collectors.

High society returns for the polo and horse racing at the end of August and the American film festival in early September. **Trouville**, on the other side of an estuary and linked by a bridge, is more of a working fishing port, but with many good restaurants. On the port, **Les Vapeurs** (160 boulevard Fernand-Moureaux/31.88.15.24) is undoubtedly the most stylish.

Going west from Deauville is an almost continuous series of seaside resorts. Most celebrated for its literary associations is **Cabourg**, for in its Grand Hôtel Proust wrote part of *A la Recherche du Temps Perdu*, and his Balbec is based on Cabourg.

East of Deauville, across the Seine estuary from Le Havre, the old fishing village of **Honfleur** is tourist-filled but picturesque enough to make a visit worthwhile. The centre of town is the Vieux Bassin, the old inner port surrounded by tall, narrow, slate-hung houses. There are plenty of fish restaurants, and a network of narrow streets to explore. Among the more unusual buildings are the wooden tower of the Eglise Ste-Catherine, the massive stone structures of the Greniers de Sel (former salt warehouses) and France's oldest folk museum.

Getting There & Information

Deauville is 207km (129 miles) from Paris. *By car* take the A13 to junction 28A. Honfleur is 16km (10 miles) from Deauville. *By train* from Gare St-Lazare to Deauville takes about 2½ hours.
Office du Tourisme de Deauville *place de la Mairie, 14800 Deauville (31.88.21.43).* **Open** 9am-12.30pm, 2-6.30pm, Mon-Sat; 11am-4pm Sun.
Office du Tourisme de Honfleur *place Arthur-Boudin, 14602 Honfleur (31.89.23.30).* **Open** *May-Sept* 9am-noon, 2-6pm, Mon-Sat; *also 1 July-15 Sept* 10am-noon, 3-5pm, Sun; *Oct-Apr* 9am-noon, 2-5.30pm, Mon-Fri; 9am-noon, 2-6pm, Sat.

Bayeux

Although Normandy was the scene of bitter fighting in World War II, most people still link Bayeux with the Battle of Hastings. The conflict in 1066 is immortalised in the Bayeux Tapestries, on view at the **Centre Guillaume le Conquérant** (rue des Nesmond/31.92.05.48). In 58 scenes, they present a chronicle of the background and the actual fighting at Hastings. Sewn by Anglo-Saxon needlewomen, the tapestry is in remarkably good condition, and extraordinarily lively and vivid. Its borders are full of fantastic details, from mythical beasts and monsters to everyday scenes of hunting, ploughing and feasting, before the narrative gets embroiled in battle and the borders too begin to fill up with corpses.

Bayeux itself is worth a visit, both for its thirteenth-century cathedral, with a very elaborate belfry, and the attractive golden stone houses that line its narrow streets. It was was the first French city to be liberated in 1944 (on 7 June). Not far from Bayeux, in the village of **Arromanches**, is the most celebrated beach of the war.

Following the invasion the allies created an entire port here, the celebrated Mulberry Harbour, out of prefabricated cement blocks towed across the Channel. Today, you can see the remains of this extraordinary construction on the beach. The **Musée du Débarquement** (place du 6 Juin, Arromanches/31.22.34.31) tells the story of the landings. This area also contains some of the most unspoilt sandy beaches on the Normandy coast, although even today some are littered with ruined bunkers and concrete landing ramps.

Getting There & Information

By car take the A13 via Lisieux and Caen (268km/166 miles). *By train* from Gare St-Lazare (2 hours 25 minutes). **Office du Tourisme** *Pont St-Jean, 14403 Bayeux (31.92.16.26)*. **Open** *mid Sept-May* 9am-noon, 2-6pm, Mon-Sat; *June-mid Sept* 10am-noon, 3-6pm, daily.

Where to Stay & Eat

In Bayeux the old coaching inn **Lion d'Or** *71 rue St Jean (31.92.06.90)*, has simply decorated rooms looking out on a stone courtyard (double 400F) and a good restaurant serving regional specialities. **Hôtel Notre Dame** *44 rue des Cuisiniers (31.92.87.24; double 150F-260F)* is a pleasant hotel just by the Cathedral. **Gîtes** (*see chapter* **Travelling Beyond Paris**) and **Chambre d'Hôtes** (bed-and-breakfast) are very well developed in this area: tourist offices have details.

Champagne

The Champagne region has two celebrity cities, Reims and Epernay, but it's also possible to follow a signposted route through the countryside.

Champagne, the most strictly regulated of all alcohol, is produced in a double distillation process from the juice of Pinot Noir, Chardonnay and Pinot Meunier grapes grown on the chalky soil of France's 62,000 acres of champagne fields. The distillation process, perfected in the seventeenth century, is fully documented in Epernay's **Musée de Champagne**. However, it's more fun to tour the champagne cellars themselves, and almost all the houses offer tours.

Moët & Chandon, the region's largest producer, attracts over 160,000 visitors each year to its 28km (17 miles) of subterranean vaults in Epernay. Alternately, try the attractive cellars of **Champagne Pommery** in Reims, which occupy Gallo-Roman chalk mines and are decorated with art nouveau bas-reliefs and Emile Gallé sculptures. **Champagne Taittinger**, similarly, doesn't look much until you descend into the cellars: on the first level are the vaulted Gothic cellars of a former monastery; below are the strangely beautiful, Gallo-Roman chalk quarries. Wear your woollies: champagne vaults are cold and clammy.

The city of **Reims** is also worth a visit even from a teetotaller's point of view. The magnificent cathedral of **Notre Dame**, begun in the thirteenth century – with its winsome 'smiling angel' sculpture – is one of the most beautiful in France, despite heavy shelling in World War I. This, together with erosion, means that many of the carvings have been replaced by copies; the originals are on show next door in the **Palais de Tau**, the Bishop's palace.

Getting There & Information

By car take the A4 from Porte de Bercy to Reims (150km/95 miles); for Epernay exit at Château-Thierry and take the N3. *By train* from Gare de l'Est to Reims takes about 1½ hours, to Epernay about 1¼ hours. **Office du Tourisme d'Epernay** *7 avenue de Champagne, 51201 (26.55.33.00)*. **Open** *mid Oct-mid Apr* 9.30am-12.30pm, 1.30-5.30pm, Mon-Sat; *mid Apr-mid*

Dom Perignon remembered at **Epernay**.

Oct 9.30am-12.30pm, 1.30-7pm, Mon-Sat; 11am-4pm Sun, public holidays.
Office du Tourisme de Reims *2 rue Guillaume-de-Machault, 51100 Reims (26.78.45.25)*. **Open** 9am-7.30pm Mon-Fri; 9.30am-5.30pm Sun, public holidays.

Musée du Champagne

13 avenue de Champagne, 52100 Epernay (26.51.90.31). **Open** *Apr-Nov* 10am-noon, 2-6pm, Mon, Wed-Sun. **Admission** 10F adults; 5F under-12s.

Moët & Chandon

20 avenue de Champagne, 52100 Epernay (26.54.71.11). **Open** *Nov-March* 9.30am-12.30pm, 2-5.30pm, Mon-Fri; *April-Oct* 9.30am-12.30pm, 2-5.30pm, daily; last tour 1 hour before closing time, tours in English every 20 minutes. **Admission** 20F (incl glass champagne).

Champagne Pommery

5 place Général Gouraud, 51100 Reims (26.61.62.63). **Open** *Mar-Oct* 10am-7pm daily; tours in English 11.30am, 1pm, 2.30pm, 4.30pm, daily; *Nov-Feb* closed Sat, Sun. **Admission** free.

Other Champagne Houses

The following are all based in Reims. Ring in advance for visiting times.
Krug (26.84.44.20); **Mumm** (26.49.59.70); **Piper-Heidsieck** (26.84.43.44); **Louis Roederer** (26.40.42.11); **Taittinger** (26.85.45.35); **Veuve Clicquot** (26.85.00.68).

Where to eat

The haute cuisine mecca in Reims is Gérard Boyer's restaurant at **Château des Crayères** *64 boulevard Henri Vanier (26.82.80.80)*, located in an imposing Second Empire château on the south-east fringe of town. Within town there are numerous brasseries, restaurants and cafés, grouped around the place Drouet d'Erlon.

Survival

Survival

Life's little mysteries: where to find a house, park your car, get a job, fall ill and pray.

In an emergency phone:

Police	17
Fire	18
Ambulance	45.67.50.50

Living & Working in the City

Bureaucracy & Residency

Anyone from abroad coming to live in Paris should be prepared for the sheer weight of bureaucracy to which French officialdom is doggedly devoted. In general, expect loads of paperwork, whether it's for acquiring a *carte de séjour* or resident permit, opening a bank account, reclaiming medical expenses or getting married.

Among the documents you may find yourself having to produce regularly are a *Fiche d'Etat Civile* (essential details translated from your passport by the Embassy/Consulate) and a legally approved translation of your birth certificate (embassies will provide lists of approved legal translators; for general translators, *see chapter* **Business**). You are also meant to be able to prove your identity to the police at all times, so if you don't have a *carte de séjour*, keep your passport with you.

Cartes de Séjour

Your most important document will be your *carte de séjour*. Officially, all foreigners, both European Union citizens and non-Europeans, who stay in France for more than three months must apply for a permit. EU citizens can obtain them without great difficulty from the police station in avenue du Maine in Montparnasse (*see below*); citizens of the US and other non-European countries have to attend one of four different centres, according to the *arrondissement* in which they are staying. For details and directions, call 53.71.51.68. The basic *carte de séjour* is valid for one year, and once you have it you can open a bank account, use various municipal facilities and carry out other necessary tasks. People who have had a *carte de séjour* for at least three years, have been paying French income tax, can show proof of income and/or are married to a French national can apply for a *carte de résidence*, valid for ten years.

Commissariat du 14e *Arrondissement* (14th *Arrondissement* Police Station)

116 avenue du Maine, 75014 (42.60.33.22). Métro Gaîté or Montparnasse-Bienvenüe. **Open** 9am-5pm Mon-Fri. For information on residency and work permits for EC nationals. You will be directed to the appropriate service according to your nationality and status.

Working in Paris

All **EU nationals** are legally allowed to work in France, but they must apply for a French social security number and *carte de séjour*. Some job opportunities can be studied at the local branches of the *Agence National Pour l'Emploi* (ANPE), the French national employment bureau, although the juiciest jobs never make their way onto the ANPE notice boards. The ANPE is also the place to go to sign up as a *demandeur d'emploie* (employment seeker), to be placed on file as available for work and to qualify for French unemployment benefits, should you be entitled to them. Contact your local ANPE office for details. If you are coming from Britain, you can only claim unemployment benefit in France if you were already signed on before you left.

Non-EU nationals cannot legally work in France, unless they obtain a work permit, which is rarely authorised. Unless they possess French working papers, they are not entitled to use the ANPE network.

Help-wanted ads sometimes appear in the *International Herald Tribune*, although the 'sophisticated personal companion' sort make up the bulk of them. Offers for English-speakers are sometimes listed on notice boards at language schools and the various Anglo establishments around town, like the American Church and Cathedral (*see below* **Religion**); most are for baby-sitters and language tutors. Positions as waiters and barstaff are often available at the city's many international-style watering holes: non-papered individuals may be hired under the table, but UK nationals have a better chance, being legal. The free publication *FUSAC* carries some job ads for English-speakers, mostly of the odd-job variety (*see chapter* **Media**).

If you expect to be looking for any work of a more professional kind, have your CV (resumé) translated, including French equivalents for any qualifications. Most job applications require a photo and a handwritten letter; French employers are very attached to handwriting analysis when choosing candidates.

Working in France: The Ultimate Guide to Job Hunting and Career Success à la Française by American Carol Pineau is a very useful book. Would-be workers can find a copy at any of Paris' English-language bookshops (*see chapter* **Specialist Shops**). Although the book is tailored to Americans, it does contain information for EU nationals, and general advice on job-seeking in France.

Apartment Rentals

Despite the years of recession, the rental market in Paris still strongly favours the landlord, with studio and one-bedroom flats fetching the highest prices. Flats do often change hands, particularly from May to October, but the competition for them is extremely keen.

As a result, the best flats go by word of mouth. Those that are advertised in newspapers are generally handled by agents. When negotiating to obtain a flat, especially if you do so through an agency, you can expect to be required to provide a dossier with a variety of personal and financial information about yourself, and to have to make some substantial payments of money, on top of the basic rent, before you can move in. Agencies or individual landlords will probably require you to present pay-slips (*fiche de paie/bulletin de salaire*) for three to four times the amount of the monthly rental, and as a foreigner in particular you may also be obliged to furnish a financial guarantee – a signed certificate by another party saying they pledge to pay, should you default on your rent payments. However, foreigners also sometimes have an edge in flat-hunting because they are perceived by landlords as wealthy, temporary, and unaware of their substantial rights as tenants under French law.

Payments that must customarily be made when taking out a new rental agreement include the first months' rent, a security deposit (*une caution*) equivalent to two (or more) months' rent, and an agency fee, if applicable. It is, though, not legal for landlords to demand more than one month's rent in advance. The security deposit is against any material damage to the flat, and is reimbursed any time up to two months after the flat has been vacated and the landlord is satisfied as to its physical condition. It is also customary for an inspection of the premises (*état des lieux*) to be performed by a bailiff (*huissier*) at the beginning and end of the rental period, to assess the flat's condition. The cost of this inspection (around 1,000F) is shared by landlord and tenant.

Expect to pay roughly 100F per month for every square metre (3,500F a month for a 35m2 flat, and so on), but in chic neighbourhoods rental rates can be 50- to 100% more.

Rental laws

The legal minimum period for a rental lease (*bail de location*) on an unfurnished apartment is three years, and one year for a furnished flat. Both are renewable. During this period the landlord can only raise the rent by the official construction inflation index – usually around 5% per annum. At the end of the lease the rent can be adjusted, but tenants can object to any increase before a rent board if it seems exorbitant. Tenants can be evicted mid-lease for non-payment of rent, or if the landlord wishes to sell the property or use it as his own residence. It is nearly impossible to evict non-payers between October and March, as it is illegal to throw people into the streets in winter.

Landlords sometimes ask that tenants, especially foreign, pay rent in cash and do without a written lease. This can get you flats not otherwise available, but the renter may have difficulty in establishing his or her rights – which, in addition to avoiding tax, is why landlords do it.

Flat hunting

The largest lists of ads offering furnished (*meublé*) and unfurnished (*vide*) flats for rent are in Tuesdays' *Le Figaro*. Most are placed by agencies. Pricey flats offered to prosperous foreigners, and occasionally to students, are advertised in the daily *International Herald Tribune*, and accommodation ads also appear in the English-language bi-weekly *FUSAC* (*see chapter* **Media**), although, again, rents tend to be higher than you might find in the French press.

In ads, landlords often list a visiting time; prepare to meet hordes of other flat-seekers on the staircase and take your supporting documents and cheque-book with you, as it may be necessary to sign on the dotted line and pay something up-front immediately. Non-agency listings from the various publications are also available via **Minitel** services. *Particulier à Particulier*, a free weekly publication that's mostly for buyers/sellers, but has some rented accommodation, is also found on Minitel, 3615 Code PAP. It's published every Thursday. There's also a commercial Minitel flat rental service on 3615 LOCAT.

For more on flat-sharing and au-pair style accommodation, *see chapter* **Students**. Notice boards with flat ads are also maintained in the American Church and the American Cathedral (*see below* **Religion**), as well as in many language schools and other places frequented by foreigners. Local bakeries also often post up notices of flats for rent direct from the owner, and if you're looking in a particular neighbourhood or building it may be useful to knock on the doors of local *concierges*, but they're rarely co-operative.

Allô Logement

6 rue Agrippa D'Aubigné, 75004 (42.71.31.31).
Métro Sully-Morland. **Open** 9am-5pm Mon-Thur; 9am-4.30pm Fri.
Advice (in French) about renting or buying an apartment. Run by the Mairie de Paris.

BIPO (Bureau d'Informations et de Protection des Occupants)

6 rue Agrippa D'Aubigné, 75004 (42.71.31.31).
Métro Sully-Morland. **Open** 9am-5pm Mon-Thur; 9am-4.30pm Fri.
Free telephone advice and information service on housing benefits, rent legislation and related matters. Will also help and advise on tenants' rights in disputes with landlords.

SOS Locataire

42 bis rue Sedaine, 75011 (48.06.82.75). Métro Voltaire. **Open** 2.30-5pm Mon, Tue, Thur, Fri.
Legal advice on tenants' rights.

Electricity & Gas

Electricity in France runs on 220V. Visitors with British 240V appliances can simply change the plug or use a converter (*adaptateur*), available at most hardware shops. If you have US 110V appliances you will need to use a transformer (*transformateur*) available at the **FNAC**, Darty chains or in the basement household department of the **BHV** (*see chapter* **Specialist Shops**).

Gas and electricity are supplied by the state-owned **EDF-GDF** (*Electricité de France-Gaz de France*). They are the ones to contact for queries concerning supply, bills, or in case of power failures, gas leaks and so on. Call the office in your *arrondissement* (check your bill or in the *Pages Blanches*). However, they are of no assistance if you have an immediate problem in your flat, in which case you'll have to phone a plumber or electrician (*see* **Emergency Repairs**). During the day it's best to phone a local repair service, which you'll find in the *Pages Jaunes* under *Plombiers* or *Electricité*.

Emergency Repairs

There are many 24-hour emergency repair services dealing with plumbing, electricity, heating, locks, car repairs, carpentry and much more. They usually charge a minimum of 120F call-out charge and 160F per hour's labour, plus parts. Below we list the most reputable:
Allô Assistance Dépannage *(05.07.24.24/42.50.91.91).*
Numéro Un Dépannage *(5th arr. 43.31.51.51/8th arr. 47.20.90.10).*
SOS Dépannage (47.07.99.99): double the price, but claim to be twice as reliable.

Locksmiths

For a local locksmith, look in the *Pages Jaunes* under *Serruriers*. If you're locked out in the middle of the night, *see above* **Emergency Repairs**.

Communications

Postal Services

If you're simply mailing a letter or postcard, it is much quicker to buy stamps at a tobacconist (*tabac*) than at a post office. Post offices (*bureaux de poste*) are open from 8am to 7pm Monday to Friday; 9am to noon Saturday. All are listed in the phone book: under '*Administration des PTT*' in the *Pages Jaunes*; under '*Poste*' in the *Pages*

Blanches. For general information phone 42.80.67.89. To facilitate matters, seek out the automatic envelope-weighing machines that now grace most post offices – they instruct you in English, print out the postage and give you back change.

Main post office
52 rue du Louvre, 75001 (40.28.20.00). Métro Châtelet-Les Halles or Louvre. **Open** 24 hours daily for *Poste Restante*, telephones and telegrams.
This around-the-clock, full-service post office is also the best place to get your mail sent to if you haven't got a fixed address in Paris. Mail should be addressed to you in block capitals, followed by *Poste Restante*, then the post office's address. There is a charge for each letter received.

Late-opening post office
71 avenue des Champs-Elysées, 75008 (44.13.66.00). Métro Franklin D Roosevelt. **Open** 8am-10pm Mon-Sat; 10am-noon, 2-8pm, Sun.
There is a basic postal service only after 7pm.

Postcodes
Letters will arrive sooner if they feature the correct five-digit postcode. **Within Paris**: postcodes always begin with '75'; if your address is in the 1st *arrondissement*, the postcode is 75001; in the 15th the code is 75015. The 16th *arrondissement* is subdivided into two sectors, 75016 and 75116. Some business addresses now have a more detailed postcode, followed by Cedex number which indicates the *arrondissement*. For postcode information throughout France, phone 42.80.67.89.

Telephones

The great majority of public phones in Paris now use phonecards (*télécartes*). They can be bought at *tabacs* (tobacconists), post offices, airports and train and métro stations. Cards cost 40F for 50 units and 96F for 120 units. *Télécartes* are decorated with pictures and ads, and there has been a craze for collecting them, but in the last few years this particular mania has died off a little. Most *télécarte* phones also accept major credit cards.

The minimum fee for a call in a coin-operated call box within Paris is generally 1F (it can be 1.50F or 2F, so it's advisable to carry a fistful of change), which allows you a three-minute call. The blinking signal indicates it's time to insert another coin. Most cafés have coin phones, but these may be

Most pay phones are now télécarte-*only.*

reserved for customers. A few old-fashioned cafés have meters to monitor your call – you tell the *patron* you want to phone, he turns on the phone set in the booth and when you've finished your call you pay about 1F-2F for each unit you've used.

Post offices usually have both coin and card phones, and a few still have *cabines* operated by window attendants.

Using a *Télécarte* phone
In a phone box, the initial instructions on the digital display screen should read *décrochez* ('pick up'). Pick up the phone and insert your card into the slot when the instruction *introduire votre carte* appears. The screen should read *patientez SVP*. When *numérotez* appears, this is your signal to dial. The number of units left on your card is displayed on-screen. If you have any trouble, replace the handset, remove the card and start from scratch. *Crédit épuisé* means that you have no more units on your card. Finally, hang up (*raccrochez*), and don't forget your card.

If you are using a credit card, insert the card, key in your PIN number and then *patientez SVP* should appear. You then continue as above.

Dialling within Paris
Until October 1996 (*see* **Phone number changes**), all Paris phone numbers have eight digits; central Paris numbers begin with a 4, and increasingly with a 53; suburban numbers might begin with a 3 or a 6. Freephone *numéros verts* all begin 05, while numbers beginning with 36 (like the *météo* or weather, games and dating services) operate on a more expensive premium rate.

Out of town
Until October 1996 (*see* **Phone Number Changes**) If you're dialling **from Paris to another part of France**, dial 16, wait for the low-pitched steady tone, then dial the eight-digit number, which begins with the area code.
• If you're dialling **from the provinces to Paris**, dial 16, wait for the tone, then dial 1, and then the eight-digit Paris number.
• If you're dialling **from province to province**, simply dial your correspondent's eight-digit number.

International calls
Until October 1996, dial 19, wait for the low-pitched, steady tone, then dial the country code, followed by the area code (omitting the 0 for UK codes), and finally your correspondent's number.

International dialling codes:
Australia 61; **Canada** 1; **Irish Republic** 353; **New Zealand** 64; **United Kingdom** 44; **USA** 1

Phone Number Changes

From October 1996 all French telephone numbers will have ten digits. Numbers in Paris and the Ile-de-France will start with **01**, the rest of France will be divided into five zones (**02-06**). The old system of dialling 16 to the provinces will be abolished. International dialling codes will begin with **00**.

If you don't have the correct country code or area code, or if you have any problems getting your call through, contact the operator (*see below* **Telephone Services**).

Charges

Charges depend on the distance and duration of the call. Calls within Paris cost 73 centimes for about three minutes, standard rate. Within Metropolitan France, calls outside a 100km (60 mile) radius are charged at the same long-distance rate regardless of distance.

Calls to the UK cost 3.65F per minute peak rate; calls to the US cost 6.69F per minute peak.

Reduced rates

Reduced rates on calls within France apply from 10.30pm to 8am during the week, and from 2pm Saturday to 8am Monday. Calls are as much as 50% cheaper.
Reduced rates to the UK and Northern Ireland from 9.30pm to 8am Monday to Friday; from 2pm Saturday and all day Sunday and public holidays. Cost: 3.04F per minute.
Reduced rates to the US and Canada: the cheapest rates apply from 2am to noon Monday to Friday; the cost is 4.98F per minute. Another cheap rate (5.72F per minute) applies from noon to 2pm, as well as from 8pm to 2am, Monday to Saturday, and also from noon to 2am Sunday and public holidays.

Telephone Services

Operator assistance, French directory enquiries (24 hours daily) dial 12.
International directory enquiries (24 hours daily) dial 19.33.12; followed by the country code (if you haven't got the country code, ask the operator on 12).
Alarm calls (24 hours daily) dial *55*, then the time at which you wish to be called. The system uses a 24-hour clock, so you dial four digits. For example, to be called at 8.30am dial *55*0830 followed by #; to be woken at 2.45pm dial *55*1445#.
Engineers (24 hours daily) if your phone is out of order, dial 13.
News international news (French recorded message, 24 hours daily) dial 36.65.44.55.
Telegram (24 hours daily) all languages, dial 05.33.44.11.
Time (24 hours daily) dial 36.99.
Traffic news (24 hours daily) dial 48.99.33.33.
Weather for specific enquiries on weather around the world and throughout France dial 45.56.71.71 (24 hours daily); for a recorded weather announcement for Paris and region, dial 36.65.02.75 (24 hours daily).
English language small ads phone 36.68.92.68 (366 U-WANT) for the 'speaking small ads'. Touch-dial your way around the menu to hear ads for anything from household goods to French lessons and studios to rent. Most ads are in English, some are in French. *See also* **Minitel**.

Phone books

Phone books are found in all post offices and in most cafés (ask if you don't see them by the phone). The White Pages (*Pages Blanches*, two volumes) lists names of people and businesses alphabetically. The *Pages Jaunes* (Yellow Pages) lists businesses and services under category headings.

Fax & telex

Faxing facilities are available at the main post office (*see above* **Postal Services**), at most modern hotels and in telex agencies (listed in the *Pages Jaunes* under 'Telex'). *See also* chapter **Services**.

Le Bi-Bop

The trendy accessory in France is a lightweight pocket-book mobile phone. Put out by France Telecom at 990F plus a 54.50F per month subscription charge, they're generally cheaper than car phones. Minimum six-month subscription.

Disabled Travellers

Disabled visitors to Paris are strongly advised to buy the specialised guide *Access in Paris*. The tourist office (*see chapter* **Essential Information**) also produces a free pamphlet, *Touristes Quand Même*, giving details of facilities for the disabled at major tourist attractions. For details of minibus hire companies that specialise in disabled transport and public transport facilities, *see chapter* **Getting Around**.

Access in Paris

An excellent English-language guide for the disabled by Gordon Couch and Ben Roberts, published by Quiller Press, London (price £7). Can be ordered from RADAR, 25 Mortimer Street, W1N 8AB (0171 250 3222).

Association des Paralysés de France

22 rue du Père-Guérain, 75013 (44.16.83.83). Métro Place d'Italie. **Open** 9am-12.30pm, 2-6pm, Mon-Fri. This association publishes a guide, *Où ferons-nous étape?* (where will we stop off?), listing hotels and motels around France with facilities for the disabled (80F by mail).

Minitel

Le Minitel is an interactive information service pioneered by France Telecom, the state-owned phone company, and available to any telephone subscriber. Users are issued a small videotex screen and keyboard, connected to the telephone line, which allows access to hundreds of services – hotel and ticket reservations, airline and train timetable information, weather forecasts, a constantly-updated phone directory and so on.

As well as all kinds of business information you can find on the Minitel dozens of recreational lines that include 'dating' hook-ups, many of them highly raunchy and with enticing names like *Cum* (cost: 60F per hour). There's a particular boom in gay minitel lines. There are also horoscope, film credit or pop quiz connections, all of which can make astronomical inroads into your phone bill, as will any 3615, 3616 or 3617 prefixed numbers (3614 are less expensive).

Minitel rates

Basic Minitel directory use is free for the first three minutes, then costs 36 centimes per minute. Hotels are often Minitel-equipped and most post offices offer free use of the terminals for basic telephone enquiries.
Minitel directory in English dial 3614 on the phone, wait for the beep, press *Connection* on the Minitel keyboard, then type *ED* and press *Envoi*.
Telephone Directory Information for all of France: dial 11 on the phone, wait for the beep and press *Connection*, then type in the name and city of the person or business whose number and/or address you're looking for, and press *Envoi*.

Fill up alongside Baroque splendours.

Driving in Paris

If you drive in France with your own car you will need to take the car registration and insurance documents (an insurance green card, available from insurance companies and the AA and RAC in Britain, is no longer compulsory but you are strongly advised to take one). It is also very advisable to carry with you spare light-bulbs, a first-aid kit and a red warning triangle, although, again, these items are no longer obligatory.

As you come into Paris you will inevitably meet the *Périphérique*, the giant ringroad around central Paris which carries all the heavy traffic in, out and around the city. Map out your route carefully as you approach Paris, or you may end up going round the Périphérique several times. Its intersections – which lead onto other main roads – are called *portes* (gates). Driving on the Périphérique is not as hair-raising as you might expect, even though it's often congested. However, morning and evening rush hours (especially Friday evenings) and the beginning and end of the peak local holiday times (July-August) are times to be avoided like the plague.

Traffic condition information for the Ile de France can be had by phoning 48.99.33.33. There is also an organisation called *Bison Futé* which hands out brochures on regional traffic conditions at the *péages* (toll stations) on motorways, suggesting routes that are likely to be less crowded. For more information on driving outside Paris, *see* chapter **Travelling Beyond Paris**.

There are also some points to be born in mind wherever you drive in France:
• France now uses white headlights like the rest of Europe, but if you're driving a British right-hand drive vehicle the lights must be screened or adjusted for left-hand drive.
• It is obligatory for drivers and front- and back-seat passengers to wear seat belts at all times.
• Children under ten are not allowed to travel in the front of a car, except in a special seat facing backwards.
• You are not allowed to stop on an open road unless the car is driven off the road.
• At intersections when no signposts indicate the right of way, the car coming from the right has priority. Many roundabouts now give priority to those on the roundabout, but if this is not indicated (by road markings or *vous n'avez pas la priorité*), priority will still be on the right. This applies to some of the most hair-raising turns in Paris – the Arc de Triomphe and place de la Concorde – where you will discover sneaky drivers try to have continual priority by zipping round on the right.
• When oncoming drivers flash their lights at you this means that they will *not* slow down (contrary to British practice) and are warning you to keep out of the way.
• In Paris, try not to be put off by honking, screeching brakes and general aggression from other drivers. It happens all the time, so it's best to get used to it.
• Do not leave anything of value in your car, and do not leave bags or coats in view on the seats.
• Carry some loose change while driving, as it's quicker to head for the exact-change line on toll bridges or *péage* motorways. Cashiers can, however, give change and many *péages* accept credit cards.

Breakdown Services

Motoring organisations such as the AA or RAC in Britain do not have reciprocal arrangements with an equivalent organisation in France as they do in most European countries, so for members and non-members it is equally advisable to take out additional breakdown insurance cover.

These breakdown services offer 24-hour assistance (the smaller the organisation, the cheaper):

Aleveque Daniel

212 rue de la Croix Nivert, 75015 (48.28.12.00/42.50.48.49). **No credit cards**.

Aligre Dépannage

14 rue Alsace-Lorraine, 75019 (49.78.87.50). **No credit cards**.

Allô Bernard Dépannage

92 rue Cartier Bresson, 93500 Pantin (48.34.24.34). **No credit cards**.

Assist-Auto

22 rue Abbé Groult, 75015 (45.31.00.00). **No credit cards**.
Cash in any currency accepted.

Parking

There are still a few free on-street parking areas left in Paris, but they're usually full when you find them. If you park illegally, you risk getting your car clamped or towed away (*see below*). In central zones parking meters have been replaced by *Horodateurs*, pay-and-display machines, usually one for each block. To avoid having to use large amounts of change you can buy special cards to use in them from *tabacs*.

In the last few years several underground car parks have been built in central Paris (notably on the Champs-Elysées and in place Vendôme), but they are expensive (10F-15F per hour). Michelin maps show the underground car parks in the city, indicated by the 'P' sign. You can also get information on street parking by phoning 43.46.98.30 (9am-5pm Mon-Fri).

24-hour parking

The following car parks, listed in order of *arrondissement*, are all open 24 hours daily:
Parking Pont-Neuf *place Dauphine, 74001 (46.33.97.48).* 12F per hour; 90F 24 hours.
Parking des Pyramides *opposite 15 rue des Pyramides, 75001 (42.60.53.21).* 12F per hour; 80F 24 hours.
Berri Washington *5 rue de Berri, 75008 (near the Champs-Elysées) (45.62.72.09).* 13F per hour; 80F 24 hours.
Chauchat-Drouot *12 rue Chauchat, 75009 (42.46.03.17).* 13F per hour; 111F 24 hours.
Ask at the entrance for the special 70F *forfait*.
Paris-Gare de Lyon *193 rue de Bercy, 75012 (40.04.61.26).* 12F per hour; 127F 24 hours.
Tour Montparnasse *17 rue de l'Arrivée/10 rue du Départ, 75015 (45.38.68.00).* 12F per hour; 100F 24 hours.
Place de Clichy/Montmartre *12 rue Forest, 75018 (43.87.64.50).* 12F per hour; 70F 24 hours.

Parking near the Périphérique

If you've come to Paris by car, it's a good idea to park in the outskirts of the city and then use public transport (*see chapter* **Getting Around**). The car parks listed here are by the various main entrances into Paris, and near Métro stations.

North:
Porte de St Ouen *17 avenue de la Porte de St-Ouen, 75017 (42.29.31.96).* **Open** 8am-10pm daily. **Rate** 20F per hour or day.
Porte de Clignancourt *30 avenue de la Porte de Clignancourt, 75018 (42.64.03.82).* **Open** 7am-10pm Tue-Fri; 7am-11pm Sat, Sun. **Rate** 45F per 24 hours Tue-Fri; 100F per 24 hours Sat, Sun.
East
Porte de Bagnolet *rue Jean Jaurès (in front of Hotel Ibis), Bagnolet (43.63.19.99).* **Open** 5am-1am daily. **Rate** 300F per 24 hours.
South
Porte d'Italie *8 avenue de la Porte d'Italie, 75013 (45.89.09.77).* **Open** 7am-8pm Mon-Sat. **Rate** 40F per 24 hours.
West
Porte Maillot *place de la Porte Maillot, 75017 (40.68.00.11).* **Open** 24 hours daily. **Rate** 100F per 24 hours.

Clamps & Car Pounds

If you've had the misfortune to have your car clamped, contact the local police station. There are eight car pounds (*fourrières*) in Paris, most of them covering several *arrondissements*. You'll have to pay a 471F removal fee plus 21F storage charge per day; add to that a parking fine ranging from 230F to 900F (for parking in a bus lane).
1st, 2nd, 3rd, 4th: *Parking St Eustache, Forum des Halles, place Carrée entrance, level-5, 75001 (42.21.44.63).* Métro Les Halles. **Open** 8am-8pm Mon-Sat.
5th, 12th, 13th: *18 boulevard Poniatowsky, 75012 (43.46.69.38).* Métro Porte de Charenton. **Open** 24 hours daily.
6th, 7th, 14th: *33 rue du Commandant Mouchotte, 75014 (43.20.65.24).* Métro Montparnasse-Bienvenüe. **Open** 8am-8pm Mon-Sat.
8th, 16th: *Parking Etoile Foch, 8 avenue Foch, underground parking level-2, 75016 (45.01.80.13).* Métro Charles de Gaulle-Etoile. **Open** 8am-8pm Mon-Sat.
9th: *43 bis boulevard des Batignolles, 75008 (42.93.51.30).* **Open** 24 hours daily.
10th, 11th, 19th, 20th: *15 rue de la Marseillaise, 75019 (44.52.52.10).* Métro Porte de Pantin. **Open** 8am-8pm Mon-Sat.
15th: *51 boulevard Général Martial-Valin 75015 (4.54.20.31).* **Open** 8am-8pm Mon-Sat.
17th, 18th: *8 boulevard Bois Leprêtre, 75017 (42.63.37.58).* Métro Porte de St Ouen. **Open** 7am-8pm Mon-Sat.

24-Hour Petrol Stations

1st 336 rue St-Honoré
2nd place de la Bourse
3rd 42 rue Beaubourg
5th 36 rue des Fossés St-Bernard
7th 6 boulevard Raspail
8th corner of avenue des Champs-Elysées and avenue George V; place de la Madeleine
10th 1 boulevard de la Chapelle; 2 rue Louis-Blanc; 166 rue du Faubourg St-Martin; 152 rue Lafayette; 1 boulevard de la Chapelle
12th 55 quai de la Rapée
13th 2 place du Docteur Yersin
14th avenue de la Porte de Châtillon
15th 95 boulevard Lefebvre
16th 24 avenue Paul Doumer
17th 6 avenue de la Porte de Clichy
18th 30 avenue Porte de Clignancourt
20th 217 boulevard Davout
Périphérique Porte de Vincennes

When going to an embassy or consulate, it's advisable to phone and check opening hours, and you may also need to make an appointment. Outside of office hours consulates generally have answerphones which will give you an emergency contact number. For a full list of embassies and consulates in Paris, look in the phone book under *Ambassades et Consulats*. For general inquiries or problems with passports or visas, it is generally the consulate you need. For specialised business services provided by the US and British Consulates, *see chapter* **Business**.

Australian Embassy

4 rue Jean Rey, 75015 (40.59.33.00). Métro Bir-Hakeim. **Open** 9am-5.30pm Mon-Fri. **Visa section** *(40.59.33.06).* Open 9.15am-12.15pm Mon-Fri.

British Embassy

35 rue du Faubourg St-Honoré, 75008 (42.66.91.42). Métro Concorde. **Open** 9.30am-12.30pm, 2.30-5pm, Mon-Fri. **Consulate** *9 avenue Hoche, 75008 (42.66.38.10). Métro Charles de Gaulle-Etoile.* **Open** 9.30am-12.30pm, 2.30-5pm, Mon-Fri. **Visa information** *16 rue Anjou, 75008 (42.66.06.68). Métro Concorde, Madeleine.* **Open** 9am-noon Mon-Fri to fill in applications; 2.30-4.30pm to collect passports.

Canadian Embassy

35 avenue Montaigne, 75008 (44.43.29.00). Métro Franklin D Roosevelt. **Open** 8.30-11am, 2-5pm, Mon-Fri. **Visa section** *(44.43.29.16).* Open 8.30-11.30am Mon-Fri.

Irish Embassy

12 avenue Foche, 75016. Consulate 4 rue Rude, 75016 (45.00.20.87). Métro Charles de Gaulle-Etoile. **Open** for visits 9.15am-noon Mon-Fri; **by phone** 9.30am-1pm, 2.30-5.45pm, Mon-Fri.

New Zealand Embassy

7 ter rue Léonard-de-Vinci, 75016 (45.00.24.11). Métro Victor-Hugo. **Open** 9am-1pm, 2-5.30pm, Mon-Fri.

South African Embassy

59 quai d'Orsay, 75007 (45.55.92.37). Métro Invalides. **Open** 9am-5pm Mon-Fri.

US Embassy

2 avenue Gabriel, 75008 (43.12.22.22). Métro Champs Elysées-Clemenceau. **Open** 9am-6pm Mon-Fri. **Consulate and visa section** *2 rue St-Florentin, 75001 (43.12.22.22). Métro Concorde.* **Open** 8.45-11am Mon-Fri.

All EU nationals staying in France are entitled to take advantage of the French Social Security system, which refunds up to 70 per cent of medical expenses. British nationals should obtain form E111 before leaving the UK (or form E112 for those already in treatment), as this is a prerequisite for obtaining a refund in France. Nationals of non-European countries should make sure they take out insurance before leaving home. Consultations and medicine have to be paid for in full at the time of purchase, and are reimbursed, in part, on receipt of a completed *fiche*.

The French Social Security system is complex and involves tedious bureaucratic procedures. If you do get ill while in France the doctor will give you a prescription and a *feuille de soins* (statement of treatment). At the pharmacy, the medication will carry *vignettes* (little stickers) which you must stick onto your *feuille de soins*. Send this, along with your prescription and form E111, to your local *Caisse Primaire*

d'Assurance Maladie (listed in the phone book under *Sécurité Sociale*). Refunds can take a month or two to come through. Be sure to make a photocopy of all forms and receipts, just in case.

Emergencies

The following services are open 24 hours daily.
Ambulance (SAMU) (45.67.50.50).
Fire department (Sapeurs-Pompiers) (18).
If there is a real medical emergency, these are the people to call rather than the ambulance. The fire brigade will arrive much more quickly and are trained paramedics. They are also specialists in letting people whose keys have gone missing back into their flats.
Medical Emergency Line (15).
A 24-hour helpline for reaching doctors (most of whom speak some English) or a private ambulance for urgent cases. Also for vital information on medical emergencies, nearest hospitals or pharmacies, and so on.
Nurses (SOS Infirmiers) *(43.57.01.26/36.60.50.50).*
House calls only. Charges are 1,025F for a 12-hour shift, 1,315F per day at weekends.
SOS Médecins (47.07.77.77/43.37.77.77)
If you don't know of any doctors or are too ill to leave your bed, this service specialises in dispatching doctors for house calls. Anything will be taken on board, from emergency action to treating and prescribing medication for a cold. A normal home visit in Paris or its suburbs costs about 300F before 7pm, 450F thereafter.
Urgences Dentaires de Paris *59 avenue Kléber, 75016 (47.07.44.44). Métro St-Marcel.*
Will offer advice by phone or refer you to nearby dentists. No house calls, except for the disabled and the elderly.

Hospitals

For a complete list of hospitals in and around Paris, consult the *Pages Blanches* (White Pages) under *Hôpital Assistance Publique*, or ring their headquarters, *40.27.30.00*. All hospitals have an emergency ward open 24 hours daily. The following is a list of hospitals specialising in particular fields:

Burns

Hôpital St Antoine *184 rue du Faubourg St-Antoine, 75012 (49.28.20.00). Métro Faidherbe-Chaligny.*

Children

Hôpital Necker *149 rue de Sèvres, 75015 (44.49.40.94). Métro Duroc.*

Dog Bites

Institut Pasteur *209 rue de Vaugirard, 75015 (40.61.38.00). Métro Pasteur.* **Service Anti-rabique open** 9am-noon Mon-Fri; 9-11.30am Sat.

Drugs

Hôpital Marmottan *19 rue d'Armaillé, 75017 (45.74.71.99/45.74.00.04). Métro Argentine.*

Poisons

Hôpital Fernand Widal *200 rue du Faubourg St-Denis, 75010 (40.05.45.45). Métro Gare du Nord.*

American Hospital in Paris

63 boulevard Victor Hugo, 92202 Neuilly (46.41.25.25). Métro Porte Maillot, then bus 82 to the terminus opposite the hospital. **Open** 24 hours daily.
A private hospital. French Social Security will refund only a small percentage of treatment costs, although the hospital has an agreement with Blue Cross insurance in the US whereby hospitalisation costs are covered by policy holders (but not consultation fees). All personnel speak English, although most are not native speakers.

Hertford British Hospital (Hôpital Franco-Britannique)

3 rue Barbès, 92300 Levallois-Perret (46.39.22.22).
Métro Anatole-France. **Open** 24 hours daily.
A private hospital. Most doctors are English-speaking.
Linked to BUPA.

General Clinics

Centre Figuier, *2 rue du Figuier, 75004 (42.78.55.53).*
Métro St-Paul. **Open** 9am-7pm Mon-Fri; 9-11am Sat.
Centre Médico-Social, *3 rue Ridder, 75014*
(45.43.83.78). Métro Plaisance. **Open** noon-6.30pm Mon-Fri; 9.30am-noon Sat.
These centres are smaller and less bureaucratic than regular hospitals, and often more convenient for minor problems.
They also carry out HIV tests (*dépistages*).

Pharmacies

Pharmacies can be spotted from afar by a green neon cross.
They have a monopoly on issuing medication, and even on the sale of certain brands of deodorant, shampoo and skin-care lotion. Many other everyday items such as toothbrushes, razors and sanitary products are usually much cheaper in supermarkets.

Most pharmacies are open from 9am or 10am to 7pm or 8pm, sometimes with a break for lunch. Staff can provide basic medical attention like disinfecting and bandaging wounds (for a small fee) and will indicate the nearest doctor on duty. French pharmacists are highly trained and you can sometimes avoid having to make a visit to the doctor by describing your symptoms to them and seeing what they suggest.

Paris has a rotating system of *Pharmacies de Garde* – pharmacies that open at night and on Sunday on a duty rota basis. Any local pharmacy, when closed, places a sign in its window indicating the nearest open pharmacy for the particular day or hour. Below we list late-opening pharmacies, in order of *arrondissement*.

Allô Pharma

(40.54.01.02). **Open** 24 hours daily. **Delivery charge**
150F urgent; 60F non-urgent. **No credit cards**.
This service transports your prescription medication when pharmacies are closed (non-prescription exceptions can be made). Manned primarily by medical students who speak some English, they work in association with **Dérhy**.

Cariglioli/Pharmacie des Halles

10 boulevard de Sébastopol, 75004 (42.72.03.23). Métro Châtelet-Les Halles. **Open** 9am-midnight Mon-Sat; noon-midnight Sun.

Dérhy/Pharmacie des Champs

84 avenue des Champs-Elysées, 75008 (45.62.02.41).
Métro George V. **Open** 24 hours daily.

Matignon

2 rue Jean Mermoz, 75008 (43.59.86.55). Métro Franklin D Roosevelt. **Open** 8.30am-2am Mon-Sat; 10am-2am Sun.

Altobelli

6 boulevard des Capucines, 75009 (42.65.88.29). Métro Opéra. **Open** 8am-12.30am Mon-Sat; 3pm-midnight Sun.

La Nation

13 place Nation, 75011 (43.73.24.03). Métro Nation.
Open noon-midnight Mon; 8am-midnight Tue-Sat; 8pm-midnight Sun.

Pharmacie d'Italie

61 avenue d'Italie, 75013 (44.24.19.72). Métro Tolbiac.
Open 8am-midnight daily.

Doctors & Dentists

A complete list of practitioners is in the *Pages Jaunes* under *Médecins Qualifiés*. In order to get a Social Security refund, make sure you choose a doctor or dentist registered with the state system; look for *Médecin Conventionné* after the name.
Consultations cost around 100F with a generalist and 130F with a specialist.

Centre Médical Europe

44 rue d'Amsterdam, 75009 (42.81.93.33/dentists 42.81.80.00). Métro Liège. **Open** 8am-7pm Mon-Fri; 8am-6pm Sat.
Practitioners in all fields under one roof, charging minimal consultation fees (110F for foreigners). Appointments advisable.

Complementary Medicine

Contact the organisations below for information on acupuncture and homeopathy. Most pharmacies also sell homeopathic medicines.

Académie d'Homéopathie et de Médecines Douces

2 rue d'Isly, 75008 (43.87.60.33). Métro St-Lazare.
Open 9am-11.30pm, 2.30-5.30pm, Mon-Fri.

Association Française d'Acuponcture

3 rue de l'Arrivé, 75015 (43.20.26.26). Métro Brochart.
Open 9.15-11.30am, 2.15-5.30pm, Mon, Tue, Thur, Fri; 1.30-6.30pm Wed.

Centre d'Homéopathie de Paris

48 avenue Gabriel, 75008 (45.55.12.15).
Métro Champs Elysées-Clemenceau. **Open** 8am-6pm Mon-Fri; 9am-1pm Sat.

AIDS, HIV & Sexually Transmitted Diseases

See also chapter **Gay & Lesbian**.

AIDES

247 rue de Belleville, 75020 (44.52.00.00). Métro Télégraphe. **Open** 9am-8pm Mon-Fri.
Volunteers providing a range of services for Aids-sufferers.

AJCS (Association des jeunes contre le Sida)

36 rue Geoffroy L'Asnier, 75004 (44.78.00.00). Métro St-Paul. **Open** 10am-7pm Mon-Fri; 2-8pm Sat.
An anti-Aids youth association.

Dispensaire de la Croix Rouge

43 rue de Valois, 75001 (42.61.30.04).
Métro Palais Royal.
A medical centre specialising in sexually related problems.
Also offers HIV tests (*dépistages*). Phone for opening hours, which vary.

FACTS (Free Aids Counselling-Treatment-Support)

190 boulevard de Charonne, 75020 (44.93.16.32). Métro Alexandre-Dumas. **Open** phone for details.
Provides ongoing English-speaking support groups and other assistance for people with or affected by HIV/Aids.
They can also be contacted through the American Church (*see below* **Religion**).

Institut Vernes

36 rue d'Assas, 75006 (44.39.53.00). Métro Rennes.
Open 8.15-11am, 1-3.30pm, Mon-Thur; 8.15-11am Fri.
Free consultations for all venereal diseases except HIV/Aids.
Appointments not taken, but be prepared to queue.

Positifs

1 rue Labat, 75018 (46.06.00.04).
Telephone counselling and advice for HIV positive people.
The hours of operation vary, but a recorded message gives
a contact number.

SIDA Info Service

(05.36.66.36). **Open** 24 hours daily.
Free AIDS hotline for information and advice.

Help & Advice

Administrative

CIRA (Centre Interministeriel de Renseignements Administratifs)

(40.01.11.01). **Open** 9am-12.30pm, 2-5.30pm, Mon-Fri.
Answers all enquiries concerning French administrative procedures, or directs you to the competent authorities.

Fiscal Problems

Town Halls: If you need help understanding tax legislation, the *mairies* of each *arrondissement* run a weekly fiscal
information and advice service. Sessions, run on a first come,
first served basis, are from 2-4pm on Tuesday for the 1st to
the 10th *arrondissements*; from 2-4pm on Friday for the 11th
to the 20th *arrondissements*. A full list of *mairies* can be
found in the phone book.

Legal

Town Halls also answer legal enquiries (free service). Phone
for details and times; ask for *consultations juridiques.*

Avocat Assistance et Recours du Consommateur

*8 quai du Marché Neuf, 75001 (43.54.32.04). Métro St-
Michel.* **Open** 2-6pm Mon-Fri.
Lawyers here deal with consumer-related cases. The fee is
200F for a consultation.

Direction Départmentale de la Concurrence, de la Consommation, et la Répression des Fraudes

*8 rue Froissart, 75003 (40.27.16.00). Métro Sébastien-
Froissart.* **Open** 9-11.30am, 2-5.30pm, Mon-Fri; 24-hour
helpline.
Write to or phone this subdivision of the Ministry of Finance
with consumer complaints. They will investigate, put pressure on the seller to satisfy you and/or instigate litigation.
Be sure to include an explanation of the problem, copies of
your receipt and any correspondence with the seller in your
letter to the agency.

Palais de Justice

*Galerie de Harlay, Escalier S, 4 boulevard du Palais,
75004 (44.32.48.48). Métro Cité.*
Open 9.30am-noon Mon-Fri.
Free legal consultation. Arrive early and pick up a numbered
ticket. For phone advice, *see* **SOS Avocats** *below.*

Help Lines

Alcoholics Anonymous in English

(46.34.59.65).
The 24-hour recorded message gives schedules of the AA
meetings at the American Church (*see below* **Religion**) and
some members' phone numbers for additional information.

SOS Avocats

(43.29.33.00). **Open** 7-11.30pm Mon-Fri.
Free legal advice over the telephone.

The automatic toilet, a French invention.

SOS Dépression

(44.08.78.78). **Open** 24 hours daily.
People listen and/or give advice, and can send a counsellor
or psychiatrist to your home in case of crisis.

SOS Help

(47.23.80.80). **Open** 3-11pm daily.
English-language crisis hotline. A team of listeners have all
gone through a few-months' training period. If they can't
help, they will refer you to doctors, lawyers, etc. who can.

SOS Racisme

1 rue Cail, 75010 (42.05.44.44).
Métro La Chapelle. **Open** 3-6pm Mon-Fri.
A non profit-making association defending the rights of eth-
nic minorities.

Police & Security

If you are robbed or attacked you should report the
incident as soon as possible. Officers at the central
police headquarters on the Ile de la Cité will assist
any foreigners who have been victims of crime. To
report a crime officially, though, you will need to
make a statement at the *commissariat* in the
arrondissement in which it was committed. To find
the appropriate *commissariat*, phone the
Préfecture number day or night, or look in the
phone book. You will be asked to make a statement, which will be typed out for you. It is unlikely that stolen goods will be recovered, but you will
need the police statement for insurance purposes.

Préfecture de Police Centrale

9 boulevard de Palais, 75004 (53.71.53.71). Métro Cité.
Open 24 hours daily.

Public Toilets

Paris overflows with clean public conveniences, if you're willing to pay. Free public loos are usually disgusting. The city is dotted with 24-hour, coin-operated, automatic toilets, oval booths topped with a glowing *toilettes* sign. Insert a 2F piece then push the curved door inwards to enjoy up to 15 minutes' privacy in a heated compartment that's scrubbed and disinfected after each use. (Rumour has it that hookers and impetuous couples use them as makeshift bedrooms, so comfortable and convenient are they) They are a far cry from the legendary Parisian *pissoirs* (traditionalists can visit the city's sole remaining *pissoir* on the boulevard Arago, just in front of La Santé prison complex).

Conventional pay-on-entry public conveniences are located in the entries of some métro stations, indicated by a blue and white sign at street level marked *toilettes-WC* (2F to use a stall and 1F to use men's urinals). These facilities are only open in the daytime. Café toilets are reserved for customers' use, but you can often sneak down the staircase to use them without being called to order by the *patron*. Sanitation is iffy, and you may well find *toilettes à la Turque*. Department stores and well-heeled cafés tend to have a *Dame Pipi*, an attendant who'll expect you to drop 2F into her saucer before using the facilities, which she makes sure are clean.

Religion

Churches and religious centres are listed in the phone book (*Pages Jaunes*) under *Eglises* and *Culte*. Paris has several English-speaking churches and other religious communities. The *International Herald Tribune*'s Saturday edition lists Sunday's church services in English.

The Anglo-French Jewish community has 'roving' services as they do not have their own synagogue. For further details contact MBE – 204 Kheilat Gesher, 208 rue de la Convention, 75015 (30.15.08.80).
American Cathedral *23 avenue George V, 75008 (47.20.17.92). Métro George V.*
American Church in Paris *65 quai d'Orsay, 75007 (47.05.07.99). Métro Invalides.*
Church of Scotland *17 rue Bayard, 75008 (48.78.47.94). Métro Franklin D Roosevelt.*
St George's English Church *7 rue Auguste Vacquerie, 75016 (47.20.22.51). Métro Charles de Gaulle Etoile.*
St Joseph's Church *50 avenue Hoche, 75008 (42.27.28.56).* Roman Catholic services.
St Michael's Church of England *5 rue d'Aguesseau, 75008 (47.42.70.88). Métro Madeleine, Concorde.*

Vets/Animals

Dispensaire Populaire de Soins pour Animaux
8 rue Maitre-Albert, 75005 (46.33.94.37). Métro Maubert Mutualité. **Open** 9.30am-6pm Mon-Fri; 9am-11am Sat.
No vaccinations against rabies, but very small fees for check-ups and castrations. Phone for an appointment.

Size conversion chart for clothes

Women's clothes									
British	8	10	12	14	16	18	•	•	•
American	6	8	10	12	14	16	•	•	•
French	36	38	40	42	44	46	•	•	•
Women's shoes									
British	3	4	5	6	7	8	•	•	•
American	5	6	7	8	9	10	•	•	•
French	36	37	38	39	40	41	•	•	•
Men's suits/overcoats									
British	38	40	42	44	46	•	•	•	•
American	38	40	42	44	46	•	•	•	•
French	48	50/52	54	56	58/60	•	•	•	•
Men's shirts									
British	14	14.5	15	15.5	16	16.5	17	•	•
American	14	14.5	15	15.5	16	16.5	17	•	•
French	35	36/37	38	39/40	41	42/43	44	•	•
Men's shoes									
British	8	9	10	11	12	•	•	•	•
American	9	10	11	12	13	•	•	•	•
French	42	43	44	45	46	•	•	•	•
Children's shoes									
British	7	8	9	10	11	12	13	1	2
American	7.5	8.5	9.5	10.5	11.5	12.5	13.5	1.5	2.5
French	24	25.5	27	28	29	30	32	33	34

Children's clothes
In all countries, size descriptions vary from make to make, but are usually based on age or height.

Further Reading

History, Art & Culture

Beevor, Antony, & Cooper, Artemis: *Paris After the Liberation*
A great account of life in the city in the years of rationing, liberation, political instability and existentialism on the Left Bank.
Christiansen, Rupert: *Tales of the New Babylon*
The Paris of Napoleon III, from sleaze, the spread of department stores and prostitution and Haussmann's bulldozer to the bloody events of the Commune.
Cole, Robert: *A Traveller's History of Paris*
A useful general introduction.
Cronin, Vincent: *Napoleon.*
A fine biography of the great megalomaniac who left France wondering what-might-have-been for ever.
Fitch, Noel Riley: *Literary Cafés of Paris*
Who drank where and when.
Littlewood, Ian: *Paris: Architecture, History, Art*
A good general survey intertwining the city's history with every era of its treasures in stone, paint and glass.
Marnham, Patrick: *Crime and the Académie Française*
Fascinating, wry accounts of the quirks and scandals of Mitterrand-era Paris.
Martin, Hervé: *Guide to Modern Architecture in Paris*
An accessible, bilingual illustrated guide to significant buildings in Paris since 1900, arranged by area.
Mitford, Nancy: *The Sun King* and *Madame de Pompadour*
Nancy Mitford's biographies, although now some years old, are still the classic and most lively accounts of the glitter and indulgence of the courts of the *ancien régime*.
Johnson, Douglas, & Johnson, Madeleine: *Age of Illusion: Art & Politics in France 1918-1940*
Every aspect of the culture of France in an era when Paris was more than ever at the forefront of modernity.
Rudorff, Raymond: *Belle Epoque: Paris in the Nineties*
The great Exhibitions, the *fin de siècle*, the birth of modernism and of modern cabaret: Paris in its most glamorous and best-remembered era.
Salvadori, Renzo: *Architect's Guide to Paris*
Plans, illustrations and a guide to Paris' growth, of interest to the general reader as well as to architects.
Schama, Simon: *Citizens*
Giant but wonderfully readable account of the Revolution, in every one of its myriad aspects
Zeldin, Theodore: *The French*
Idiosyncratic and enormously entertaining survey of modern France.

Literature

Abaelardus, Petrus (Peter Abelard) & Heloise: *Letters*, and, by Abelard alone, *The Story of Abelard's Adversities*
The full details of Paris first great drama.
Aragon, Louis: *Paris Peasant*
A great surrealist view of the city.
Balzac, Honoré de: *Père Goriot*
All of Balzac's 'Human Comedy' deals with Paris, but the story of old Goriot is one of the most acute of his novels.
Céline, Louis-Ferdinand: *Mort à Crédit (Death by Credit)*
Remarkably vivid, largely autobiographical account of an impoverished Paris childhood.

Hemingway, Ernest: *A Moveable Feast*
He may be irritating, but this is still the classic portrait of twenties' ex-pat Paris.
Hugo, Victor: *Notre Dame de Paris* and *Les Misérables*
Quasimodo and the romantic vision of medieval Paris; in *Les Mis*, Hugo (pictured) takes up all the social torments and giant passions of the romantic era, at great length.
Littlewood, Ian: *Paris: A Literary Companion*
Great selection of pieces by all kinds of writers on Paris.
Miller, Henry: *Tropic of Cancer* and *Tropic of Capricorn*
Low-life and lust in Montparnasse.
Orwell, George: *Down and Out in Paris and London*
Unbeatable portrait of the bars, back streets and hotel kitchens of Paris in the 1920s.
Perec, Georges: *Life, A User's Manual*
Classically Parisian, intellectual take on modern life.
Restif de la Bretonne, Nicolas: *Les Nuits de Paris*
The sexual underworld of the Paris of Louis XV, by one of France's most famous defrocked priests.
Queneau, Raymond: *Zazie in the Metro*
Paris in the 1950s: bright and very *nouvelle vague*.
Sartre, Jean-Paul: *Roads to Freedom*
Existential angst as the German army takes over Paris.
Simenon, Georges: The *Maigret* series.
All of Simenon's books on his laconic detective provide a great picture of Paris and its underworld.
Stein, Gertrude: *The Autobiography of Alice B. Toklas*
Ex-pat Paris, from start to finish.
Suskind, Patrick: *Perfume, or the Story of a Murderer*
Murder in Paris on the eve of the Revolution.
Vian, Boris: *Froth on the Daydream*
Wonderfully funny surrealist satire, superbly translated: Paris in the golden era of St Germain, with Sartre appearing to give a lecture on the back of an elephant, amid his adoring fans.
Zola, Emile: *Nana* or *L'Assomoir*
As with Balzac, any number of Zola's novels give a superb vision of Paris; these are perhaps his most vivid accounts of the underside of life in the Second Empire.

Food & Drink

Larousse Gastronomique
For those who want to know every detail about French food.
Toklas, Alice B: *The Alice B. Toklas Cookbook*
Literary and artistic life again, with instructions on how to cook fish for Picasso.
Wilson, Robin: *The French Food & Wine Dictionary*
A handy small glossary.

Index

buses 13
  night buses 13
business 276-279
business schools 291
Butte aux Cailles 131

c

cabaret 179-181
cabs 13-14
Café de Flore 120
Café Marly 165
cafés 164-168
  gay 285-286
  lesbian 289
café-théâtres 274
Caisse natinale des Monuments
  Historiques 49
camping 30
canals 113
Canal St-Martin 114
canal trips 60
car hire 210
Carrousel du Louvre 43, 103, 195
carte de séjour 314
cash machines 5
Catacombes, Les 57
Cathédrale de Notre Dame de
  Paris 39, 91, 100
Catherine de Medici, tomb of 57
cemeteries 59
cemetery tours 58
Centre Pompidou 47, 95, 105, 222,
  247, 280
Chagall 45
Champagne 312
Champs-Elysées, see Avenue
  des Champs-Elysées
Channel tunnel 14
Chantilly 303
Chapelle des Girondins 43
Chapelle du Martyre 118
Charles V 67
Charles X 75
Chartres 300
Château de Malmaison 57
Château de Vincennes 48
Châteaux of the Loire 308-310
cheese 205
childminders 280
children 280-284
Chinatown 131
Chirac, Jacques 36, 86, 87, 119
chocolate 204
Chopin 59 (tomb)
Christian Lacroix 186
churches for concerts 257
Cimetière de Montmartre 59
Cimetière de Montparnasse
  59, 130
Cimetière du Père Lachaise
  59, 114
cinemas 249-252
  men-only 287
circus 283
  alternative 271
Cité des Enfants 56
Cité de la Musique 56, 256
climbing 265
clubs 174-181
  gay 286-287
  lesbian 289
coach tours 57
Colette 59 (tomb)
Colonne de Juillet 43

Comédie Française 69, 271
Comme des Garçons 186
communards 79
communications 315-317
complementary medicine 321
concert halls 255
Conciergerie, La 43, 91, 99
confectionery 204
conferences 277
consulates 320
contraception 296
cookery courses 291
copywriting 277
costume hire 211
Cour Carrée 43
couriers 278
Couvent des Dames
  Auxiliatrices 118
Crazy Horse Saloon179
credit cards 5
crime 6
Curie, Marie 52 (tomb)
Curie, Pierre 52 (tomb)
customs 3
cycling 265, 268; *see also* **Tour de
  France**

d

dance 247-248
Dalí, Salvador 223
Danton 43, 49, 73
Daubigny 305
Deauville 311
de Beauvoir, Simone 59 (tomb)
Défense, La 133
Dégas 59 (tomb)
De Gaulle, Charles 84-85
Delacroix 59 (tomb), 224
delicatessens 206
dentists 321
Descartes 51
détaxe 184
Dieppe 311
diving 265
Deux Magots, Les 120, 167
disabled travellers 14, 317
Disneyland Paris 307
doctors 321
Dreyfus, Alfred 81
driving in Paris 318
dry cleaners 211

e

Ecole des Beaux-Arts 51
Ecole Militaire 128
education 291
  for women 295
Eglise du Dôme 55, 128
Eglise-St-Louis 55, 128
Egouts de Paris, Les 57
Eiffel Tower 39, 81, 94, 128
Eiffel, Gustave 41
electricity 315
Elysée Palace 116
embassies 320
emergencies 314
employment 290, 314
  for women 295
English Gardens 36
Etoile, *see* Place Charles de
  Gaulle
Eurostar 14
exhibitions

Exhibition Universelle 41, 50, 55, 79
exhibition centres 234, 277
existentialism 85

f

fashion 184-193
feminism 294
festivals 31-35
  film 252
  gay 288
  music 33, 257
FIAC 237
film 249-253
  film museums 252
  festivals 252
  festival for women 296
fire service 314
fireworks 31-35
Fitzgerald, Scott 122
florists 211
Folies Bergère 179
Fontainebleau 303
Fontaine des Innocents 110
Fontaine de l'Observatoire 121
food & drink 203-209
  delivery 211
football 269
foreign exchange 5
formal wear rental 211
Forum des Halles 49, 110
Francis I 67, 91, 303, 308
French Open 32, 270
funicular 50, 60
funfairs 31-35

g

galeries 109
Galeries Lafayette 194
Garnier, Charles 45
gas 315
Gaultier, Jean-Paul 186
gay Paris 285-289
Gîtes de France 298
Giverny 306
golf 265, 269
gourmet food 206-209
Goutte d'Or, La 119
Grande Arche de la Défense 41
Grande Halle de la Villette 56
Grand Palais 50
graphic design 277
guignol 283
guillotine 74
guingettes 178-180

h

hairdressers 213
Hardouin-Mansart, Jules 47, 55,
  92, 301
hats 191-193
Haussmann, Baron 36, 77, 93, 99
haute couture 185
haute cuisine 139-142
health 320-322
  for women 295-296
health clubs 265-266, 296
helicopter tours 60
Héloise 59 (tomb), 100
helplines 322
Hemingway, Ernest 104, 122
Henri II, tomb of 57
Henri IV 44, 67, 99
history 63-86

St-Paul-St-Louis 107
St-Pierre-de-Montmartre 91, 118
St-Roch 104
St-Séverin 52, 91, 125
St-Sulpice 51, 120
Salle des Gens d'Armes 43
salons 71, 237
   beauty 212
salons de thé 172-173
Sartre, Jean-Paul 59 (tomb)
saunas (men-only) 287
science and technology
   museums 232
secretarial services 279
security 323
Seine 44
   boat trips 60
Sentier 112
services 210-214
   business 276-279
sexually transmitted diseases
   321
sewers 57
Sévigné, Mme de 43, 69
shoes 193
shopping 184-209
   antiques 195
   bookshops 197
   bookshops for children 197
   bookshops for women 295
   bookshops for gays 287
   CDs 201
   children's clothing 193
   department stores 194
   designer boutiques 185-188
   florists 199
   food & drink 203-209
   food markets 209
   furniture 198
   gay 288
   jeans, sports & casual wear
      188-189
   jewellery 191-193
   hats 191-193
   late-opening 208, 316
   lingerie 189
   markets 201
   perfume 196
   records 201
   sales 184
   scarves 191-193

sex shops 288
shoes 193
shop opening hours 6
tax refunds 184
toys 197
vintage & discount clothing
   190-191
smoking 6
SNCF 298-299
snooker 267
Sorbon, Robert de 52
Sorbonne, La 52, 66, 124, 290, 292
sport 264-270
Stein, Gertrude 122
students 290-293
summer schools 281
swimming pools 267-268

tattooists 213
taxis 13
télécartes 316
telephones 316-317
television 245
tennis 268, 270; *see also* **French
   Open**
theatre 271-274
   for children 283
   English-language 274
theme parks 283-284, 307
ticket agencies 214, 271, 290
time 6
Time Out Paris 246
tipping 6
Toklas, Alice B 122
Tomb of the Unknown Solidier
   36
Toulouse Lautrec, Henri 117
Tour de Clovis 52, 126
Tour de France 33, 36
Tour Eiffel, *see* **Eiffel Tower**
Tour de l'Horloge 43, 99
tourist information 5
Tour Montparnasse 58, 129
Tour St-Jacques 49
tours of Paris 57-60
trains 10
train tickets 11, 298
traiteurs 206
translators 278
travel agencies 214

travel, discount 290
travel passes 11
*Très Riches Heures du Duc de
   Berry* 303
trips out of Paris 298-312
Trocadéro 50, 116
Trouville 311

UNESCO 128

Val-de-Grâce 52, 92, 126
Van Gogh 305
Vaux-Le-Vicomte 304
Venus de Milo 43
vegetarian restaurants 163
Vercingétorix 63
Versailles 69, 300-303
vets 323
video rental 214
Vidéothèque de Paris 49
viewpoints 58
Villette, La 56, 232, 281
Viollet-Le-Duc, Eugene 39, 93
visas 3
vocabulary 6, 136
Voltaire 52 (tomb)

walking tours 58
wall, fortified 47, 66, 107, 126
weather 6
Wilde, Oscar 59 (tomb), 122
windmills 118
wine bars 171-172
wine buying 207
wine courses 291
wine museum 234
women 294-296
World War I 81
World War II 82
writers in Paris 122-123, 229

youth hostels 30

Zola, Emile 52 (tomb)
zoos 283

Paris Guide
Advertisers Index
Please refer to the relevant sections for addresses/telephone numbers

Maps

Street Index

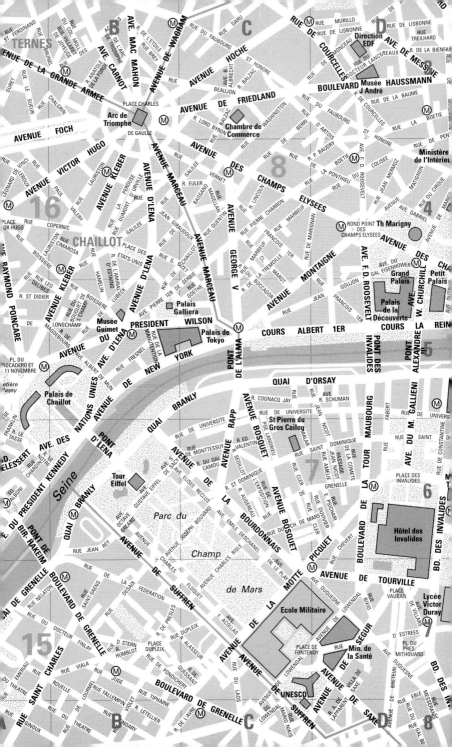

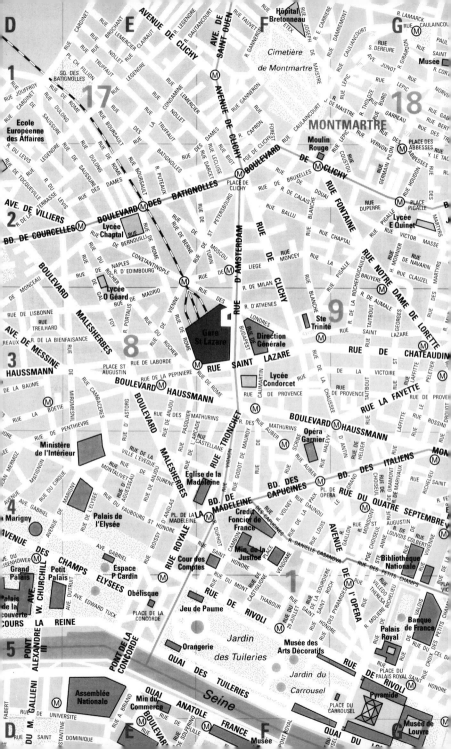

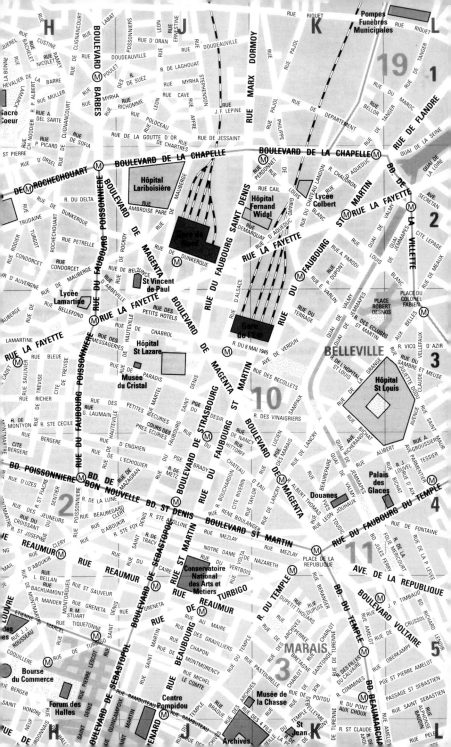

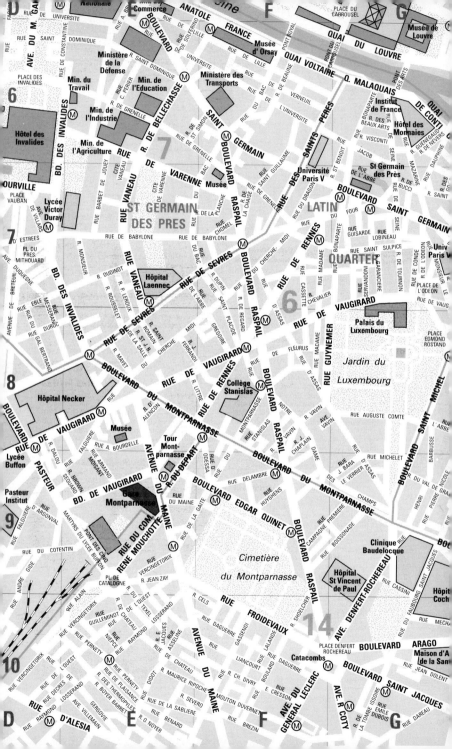

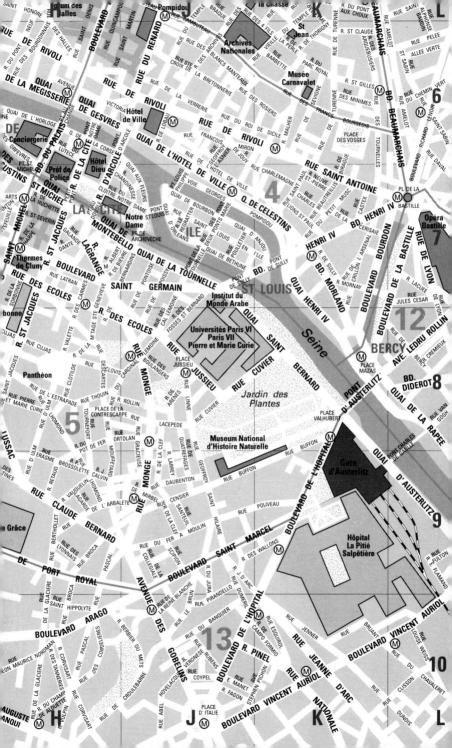

Paris by Arrondissement

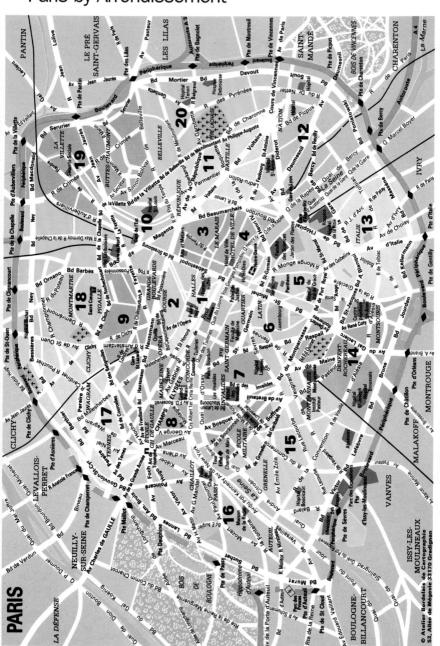

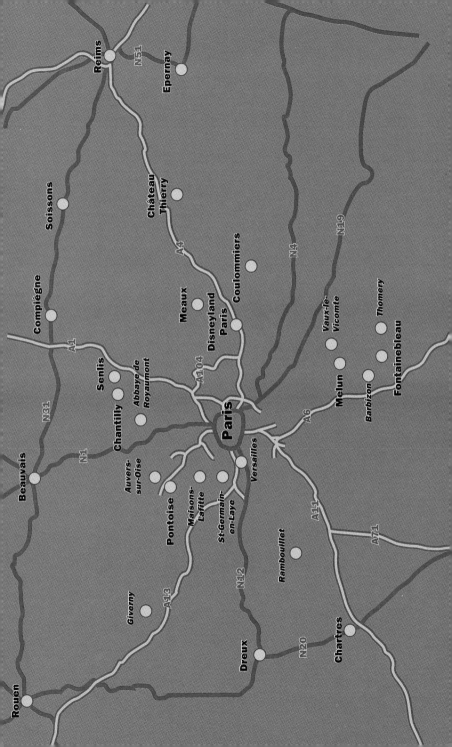

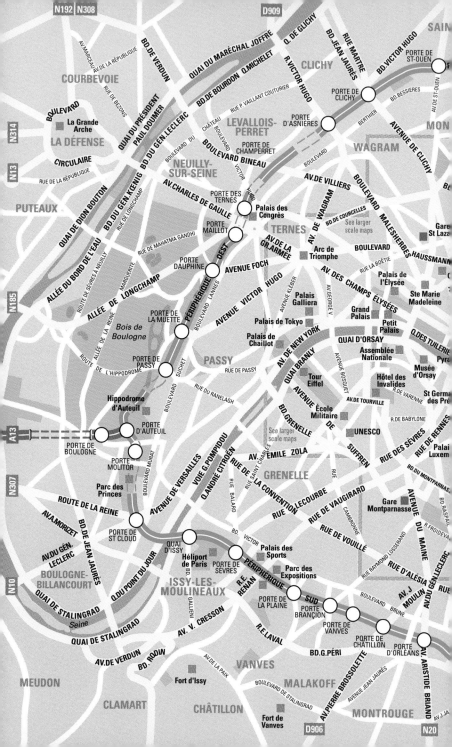

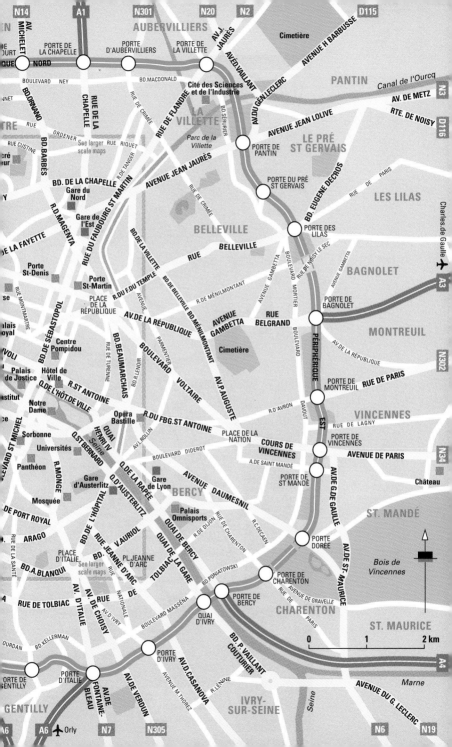

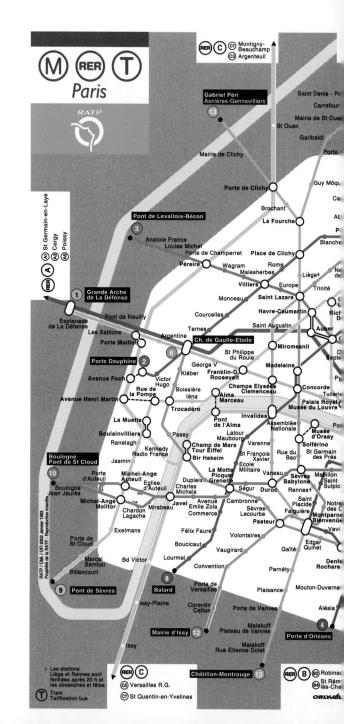

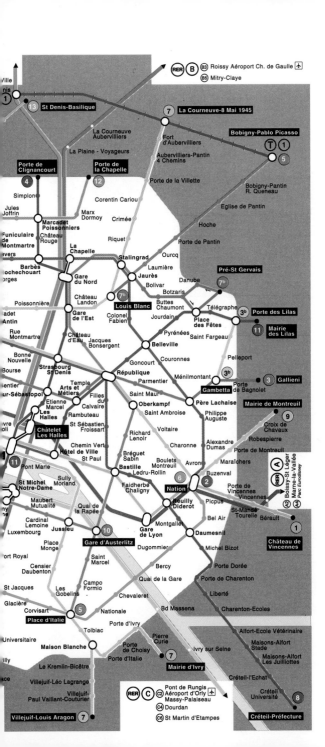

Paris: RER

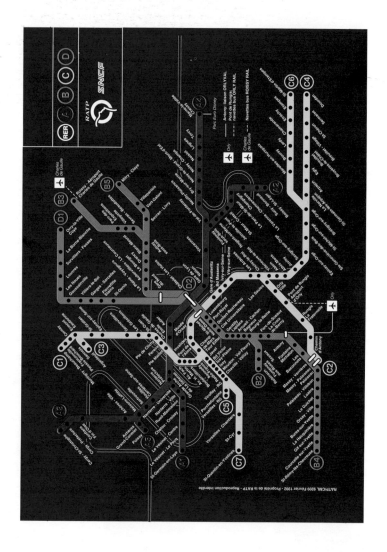